Islam's Predicament with Mo

Islam's Predicament with Modernity presents an in-depth cultural and political analysis of the issue of how Islam has become a potential source of tensions and conflicts in post-bipolar world politics, and how this might be peacefully resolved.

Looking at the issue of modernity from an Islamic point of view, the author examines the role of culture and religion in Muslim societies under conditions of globalization, and analyses issues such as law, knowledge and human rights. He engages a number of significant studies on cultural modernity and Islam and draws on detailed case studies, rejecting the approaches of both Orientalists and apologists, and calling instead for a genuine Islamic pluralism that accepts the equality of others. Situating modernity as a universal project, he argues that a separation of religion and politics is required, thus presenting a challenge to the Islamic worldview.

This critical analysis of value conflicts, tensions and change in Islamic civilization will be of interest to scholars and advanced students of international relations, social theory, political science, religion, Islamic studies and Middle Eastern studies.

Bassam Tibi is Professor of International Relations at the University of Göttingen and A.D. White Professor-at-Large at Cornell University. He taught and lectured at thirty university across the world in all the five continents.
In 2009–09 Tibi is Senior Research Fellow at Yale Univesity. Between 1982 and 2000 he was at Harvard University in a variety of affiliations, the latest of which as the Harvard Bosch Foundation Fellow 1998–2000. Tibi is a prolific author and published in the past thirty years monographs in English, the first of which was *Arab Nationalism. Between Islam and the Nation-State* (3rd expanded edition 1997) and the last is his Routledge book: *Political Islam, World Politics and Europe* (2008).

Islam's Predicament with Modernity

Religious reform and cultural change

Bassam Tibi

Routledge
Taylor & Francis Group

LONDON AND NEW YORK

First published 2009
by Routledge
2 Park Square, Milton Park, Abingdon, Oxon OX14 4RN

Simultaneously published in the USA and Canada
by Routledge
270 Madison Avenue, New York, NY 10016

Routledge is an imprint of the Taylor & Francis Group, an informa business

© 2009 Bassam Tibi

Typeset in Baskerville by
Taylor & Francis Books
Printed and bound in Great Britain by
CPI Antony Rowe, Chippenham, Wiltshire

British Library Cataloguing in Publication Data
A catalogue record for this book is available from the British Library

Library of Congress Cataloging in Publication Data

Tibi, Bassam.
Islam's predicament with modernity : religious reform and cultural change /
Bassam Tibi.
    p. cm.
Includes bibliographical references and index.
    1. Islam–21st century. 2. Islamic renewal–Islamic countries. 3. Globalization–
Religious aspects–Islam. 4. Religious awakening–Islam. 5. Culture conflict–
Islamic countries. I. Title.
    BP161.3.T53 2009
    297.2'7–dc22

                                        2008037898

ISBN: 978-0-415-48471-8 (hbk)
ISBN: 978-0-415-48472-5 (pbk)
ISBN: 978-0-203-88155-2 (ebk)

Contents

Acknowledgments

This book has grown from a variety of cross-cultural and international research projects, listed in the last part of the Introduction and in the first note of each chapter. The work related to it was embedded in those projects and draws on their findings. This book can also be viewed as a sequel to my Routledge monograph *Political Islam, World Politics and Europe*, completed between 2003 and 2006 but first published in 2008. The present study claims to be the summation of my life's work. I have pursued research on the subject matter since the early 1990s. Unlike the 2008 book, this one does not focus on political Islam; rather, it deals with Islam in general, its core argument being that Islam has a predicament with cultural modernity. This argument is combined with the idea that the predicament has become a source of tensions and conflicts. The case is made for religious reforms and innovative cultural change, with the view that both could provide options for a peaceful resolution of conflict. Peace is therefore a major concern of the book. The 2008 book ends its chapter 7 with a debate on democracy and democratization, presented as the solution for the political crisis. This would be the proper response to existing political challenges. The present book analyzes a cultural predicament and proposes reform and change as the needed solution. This is a different focus, given the fact that the predicament is a civilizational one, as are the related implications. The presented insights are combined with thinking about the future prospect of the Islamic world, as conceptualized in terms of Ibn Khaldun's "*ilm al-umram/*philosophy of civilization." In this thinking I have not been alone, but was lucky enough to have been a participant in global networks, which I acknowledge below, all of them located outside the German academia – in which I am not only a loner but also silenced. This is sad, but true.

The present book owes much to the impetus provided by research into the place of Islam and culture in international relations. At the head of the list is the Culture Matters Research Project/CMRP pursued at the Fletcher School, Tufts University, and the first person I should mention is Professor Lawrence Harrison of the Fletcher School, who chaired the CMRP. Repeated visits to the Fletcher School in order to write two contributions to Lawrence Harrison's *Developing Cultures* were both memorably pleasant and productive. In the final stages of writing this book, in spring 2008, I was based in Washington and traveled to

Tufts to present my ideas to Larry's highly intelligent postgraduate students in his class at the Fletcher School. The final draft was completed at my home university of Göttingen, Germany.

Throughout, the book follows the pattern of Chapter 1, the research background of the text and all the references to the publications that emerged from it being noted in the first note to each chapter. I shall not repeat the references here, but ask the reader to consult what I have written there and to view it as the detailed acknowledgment. Nonetheless, one other project should be added to Professor Harrison's CMRP as a source of inspiration for the present book. This is the Cultures and Globalization Project of Y. Raj Isar and Helmut Anheier. Its findings are reflected in Chapter 5. And so I single out my colleagues Larry Harrison, Helmut Anheier, and Y. Raj Isar, who gave particular support to the publication of this book, jointly with other scholars. Among them is Professor John Kelsay, to whom I am grateful for his support. German professors are conspicuously absent from the list – I will not comment on this, but leave readers to draw their own conclusions.

Two other persons, not members of the scholarly community, were unhesitating in their support for the completion of this book. One is my editor, Joe Whiting, who has again been most supportive; he helped to breathe life into the project and to make it a reality. The other is my staff assistant, Elisabeth Luft. As a scholar who combines computer illiteracy with the stubbornness that each chapter must be rewritten – at least ten times – I am unable to write without technical assistance. In these circumstances, during the past decade Elisabeth Luft has been the major figure in my scholarly life in terms of book writing. Elisabeth Luft not only word-processed most carefully all of the drafts of the chapters that follow, but also drew my attention to my shortcomings. I also need to mention my research assistant Nicole Klitzsch, who was most important in the 2008 book; she provided research assistance for the first five chapters on this book before departing for Belfast, Northern Ireland, with a PhD grant. Following Nicole's departure, Thorsten Hasche took over and provided welcome research assistance. Thorsten's contribution was most helpful. I am grateful to Paola Celli, my production editor, for her continued cooperation in this second Routledge book, and to Judith Oppenheimer for her superb copy-editing and straightening of my English.

Despite all the global networks, there are only two universities, of which I am a faculty member, that I have to thank for their support: the German Georg-August-University of Göttingen, where I have had tenure as Professor for International Relations since 1973, and Cornell University, where I have had the honor to be A.D. White Professor-at-Large since 2004. I note with sadness that my German home university has decided to abolish International Studies upon my retirement in 2009, and to close the center that I built up over a period of thirty years and which gained an international reputation. My chair for International Relations/Islamology will be changed to a chair for educational "didactics." It is sad that, in an age of globalization, the oldest university in northern Germany can afford to abolish International Relations and Islamology – as presented in this book. Despite my sadness – and, admittedly, some indignation on my part – I acknowledge my gratitude to the University of Göttingen, which has been my home from 1973 to 2009. This is also an acknowledgment for the background of this book, which could not have been accomplished without the infrastructure provided by the University of Göttingen, as well as numerous generous periods of leave which made it possible to travel around the world and undertake research on all continents.

Bassam Tibi
Center for International Studies
The University of Göttingen/Germany
June 2008

Preface

This book deals with the burning issue of "Islam's predicament with modernity" and assumes that this issue generates related problems that can be identified as one of the major sources of tensions and conflicts. A Muslim myself, I can claim to have experienced this predicament throughout my life and maintain that this *conditio humana* also applies to all other Muslims. The difference between me and many Muslim co-religionists is that I take the liberty of candidly acknowledging the issue, while others are evasive and place the blame for it solely on the West. I was born into a Muslim "*ashraf*/noble" Damascene family where, until the age of eighteen, I was socialized in Islamic values and thinking. Despite my later education in critical thinking in Europe, this Islamic socialization continues to shape my life and work. In short, the fact that I – along with few exeptions – was socialized in Damascus and schooled there in the cultural system of Islam is a determining factor in my thinking. Nevertheless, the scholarly value of detachment that I learned in the West has led me to view Islam as a subject for study, setting my beliefs on the side. In this sense, my inquiry is detached from my religious beliefs. Some co-religionists and postmodernists may dislike this, but I maintain that scholarly knowledge has no religion. I find it amusing that some Western "unbelievers" who claim to embrace my culture in criticizing Orientalism accuse me of "self-Orientalization." I decline to make any comment on this Orientalism in reverse. Life is too short to waste in dealing with nonsense.

In earlier books I have repeatedly alluded to the predicament that is analyzed in the present study, but I have never dealt with it as a separate subject in itself, because in each of the earlier cases the subject matter was different. At the beginning of the 1990s I coined, not only in advance of Huntington, but also with *a totally different meaning*, the idea of inter- and intra-civilizational conflict. In this book I make an in-depth analysis of the assumption of Islam's predicament with cultural modernity and relate it, from this perspective, to the study of conflict. This is a combination of cultural studies and the approach of international relations to conflict studies.

Following the Introduction and Chapter 1, the first part of the book – Chapters 2 to 4 – singles out three issue areas: knowledge, law, human rights, and pinpoints sources of conflict within Islamic civilization, as well as in its extended relations to non-Muslim others. I begin by assuming that cultural tensions emerge from the predicament and I trace how they then develop into conflict. The first level is an inner-Islamic conflict. Under the conditions of globalization this conflict within Islam then broadens into an international one, and its effects spill over.

The analysis argues for the existence of tensions on an international, inter-civilizational level, which are articulated in international action. The inner-Islamic and international levels mingle with each other. Hereby, politics is becoming religionized and religion is subjected to politicization. Underlying the tensions are conflicting images of the self and of the other. Of course, there are socio-economic and political constraints underlying the conflict, and I do not overlook these. However, it matters to the analysis that political, social, and economic concerns are articulated in religious–cultural terms. This is not merely a cover, nor does it happen instrumentally, as some Westerners contend. The religionization of conflict gives it a new form. Conflict becomes intractable, because beliefs are not negotiable. It is wrong to argue that these Islamist Muslims are virtually secular because they are using or abusing religion for non-religious ends. No, they are acting as believers, and this is the way I have always encountered them, as people acting in "good faith," never as cynics. Profane Westerners fail to understand the place of culture and religion in politics, and this is the real Orientalism, often presented as Orientalism in reverse. These Westerners believe that they understand the issue better than Muslims. They also behave as if they know what Muslims think and want. This is a kind of Western patriarchy, which I view as a neo-colonial mindset.

I started writing this book incrementally in the early 1990s, when my thinking about cultural change in Islam included the issue areas of knowledge, law, human rights, and secularization. The manuscript of the present study was already complete in a preliminary draft when, at Cornell in September/October 2007, I first came across a book on political theory written by the American Professor John Brenkman which supports some of my views. At Stanford a month later I happened to read a special issue of *The Economist* on religion. These two publications are not the work of experts on Islam, but it is sad to have to acknowledge that the authors of both seem to understand the issue better than many scholars of established Islamic studies, who are mostly not political scientists. Deplorably enough, these scholars seem to be more preoccupied with accusing one another of Orientalism and with the practice of political correctness than with actually studying burning issues in the field. It is a fact that most of these scholars are reluctant to admit into their work any thinking about cultural tensions related to Islam. I see these tensions every time I travel to the world of Islam and talk in Arabic with my co-religionists. The study of conflict has to be introduced into Islamic studies. Self-censorship and politicization are highly detrimental to the academic culture of scholarship.

John Brenkman, the above-mentioned author of the book *The Cultural Contradictions of Democracy*, is a political scientist from the field of political theory. As stated, he is not a student of Islam, but he rightly recognizes that, since 9/11, political theory can no longer be pursued without reference to what he terms "Islam's civil war," which has become "geopolitical." In fact, this is exactly the trajectory of the present study. In his book Brenkman devotes only a few pages (pp. 165–70) to Islam and he does not venture into the substance of his argument because he is not a student of Islam. His views, however, deserve close attention. The other publication is *The Economist* issue on "The New Wars of Religion" (November 3–9, 2007). Its cover announces that it includes an "18 pages special report on faith and politics." The report covers all religions, but the central place given to Islam in this story is acknowledged. The editorial states:

> Most Western politicians and intellectuals assumed religion was becoming marginal to public life ... as an irrelevance to foreign policy ... Once again, one of the world great religions has a bloody divide ... The religion that invades the public square most overtly is Islam ... teaching that the primary unit of society is the umma, the international brotherhood of believers ... it forces people to follow shari'a laws ... religious conflicts ... have a religious component much harder to solve ... The new wars of religion may prove as intractable.

In accordance with *The Economist*'s policy, neither the editorial nor any of the short articles included in the 18-page report is identified by an author's name. But it becomes clear, through a careful reading, that none of the writers involved has an expert knowledge of Islam. Nevertheless, the phenomenon is well identified as one that occurs in all religions, even though it is neither analyzed nor well understood. However, as *The Economist* rightly acknowledges, Islam lies at the very center of the "new wars of religion." In my earlier Routledge book on political Islam (2008) I have explained the centrality of Islam to post-bipolar world politics. That study includes a political analysis of the transformation of Islamic universalism – in the course of a process of politicization – into a politics that leads to a religion-based internationalism with the claim of a new world order based on Islamic tenets. In this book I inquire into the cultural–religious roots of the phenomenon addressed and suggest that they are to be found in Islam's predicament with cultural modernity. This predicament is thus the subject matter of this new book. The authors of *The Economist*'s special issue state the right phenomenon, but their thinking is characterized by a confusion that is exacerbated by a lack of professional knowledge about Islam. These journalists fail to provide any viable explanation because they are superficial. In contrast, the present book aims to present an explanation for "Islam's geo-civil war" as the most significant variety of "the new wars of religion," and to seek and to recommend a remedy for it.

The present inquiry is an international relations study that deals with Islam through a cultural approach. Some will consider it problematic to analyze cultural tensions and argue that they develop domestically, regionally, and internationally into political conflict. I argue that the source of this tension and conflict should be sought in Islam's problems with cultural modernity. The generated tensions occur not only among Muslims, but also in their relations to the "non-Muslim other" in an international environment of crisis. I hasten to add that I am not only a Muslim, but also a scholar involved in peace studies and in mediation. I therefore study conflict from the point of view of peace and conflict resolution. Clearly, this commitment means that I dismiss the damaging rhetoric of a *Clash of Civilizations*. Among my credentials is having co-authored in 1999 with Roman Herzog – by then President of the Federal Republic of Germany – the book *Preventing the Clash of Civilizations*, in which an argument against Huntington is presented. I also pride myself on having been awarded the highest German medal of state, the "Bundesverdienstkreuz" (First Class) by President Roman Herzog in 1995, in recognition of my "mediation between the civilizations through establishing better knowledge about Islam in Europe." The Spanish government elected in 2004 repeatedly invited me to participate in its events on "Alliance between Civilizations," above all that of 2006 commemorating the six-hundredth anniversary of the death of the great Muslim philosopher Ibn Khaldun in Granada in 1406. Ibn Khaldun – whose work is not known to Huntington – was the founder of "*ilm al-umran*/science of civilizations." To study conflict in pursuit of a resolution is not to engage in a "clash," because a conflict is not a clash. A conflict can be peacefully resolved in a process of negotiation that can assume the shape of a dialogue between civilizations, whereas a clash is based on an essentializing view and on fault lines. When it comes to violence, I view it with disdain and am disposed to counter it, without abandoning my rejection of the rhetoric of "war on terror." Thus, I was among the scholars invited by the Club of Madrid to co-author the study *Democratic Responses to Terrorism* (edited by Leonard Weinberg, Routledge 2008). In short, I maintain my contention that culture can be a source of tensions and place value conflicts at the center of my inquiry. It is shortsighted, even vulgar, to reduce these value conflicts to a "clash of interests" (F. Gerges) or – worse – to deny them altogether.

And now, I return to my reading at Cornell University of John Brenkman's book *The Cultural Contradictions of Democracy* (Princeton University Press). Brenkman states "Islam ... is ... engaged in a civil war ... it is embroiled rather in a geopolitical civil war" (p. 21). Brenkman boldly asserts the "uncomfortable truth that ... most of the dangers are coming from the Muslim world" (p. 165). Some would accuse him of Orientalism, but his concern is a valid one, namely, that "the United States and Europe must learn how to deal with ... conflicts generated within and between ... radical Muslims and the West" (ibid.). This is definitely not the concern of my book. That is a different one, namely, how Muslims themselves deal with this "nature of the crisis," which I relate to Islam's predicament with modernity. Still, the cultural blind spots in Western policies contribute to the exacerbation of this predicament. If only the politicians of the West were willing to learn properly from the cultural analysis of political conflict, some de-escalation could be achieved.

Brenkman acknowledges the rift within Islam as one between "radical Islam, competing for the hearts and minds of Muslims" (p. 158) and "so-called moderate Islam ... in a precarious position between authoritarian regimes on the one hand and the radicals ... on the other" (ibid). I position myself and this book in this "so-called moderate Islam" striving for change and reform, not only for accommodation, but also to ensure a better future for Muslim people. If the options presented in this book are not feasible, then there is *no* hope of a light at the end of the tunnel of intra- and inter-civilizational conflicts. The future will be dark, like it or not!

Brenkman's relation of *The Cultural Contradictions of Democracy* to the repercussions of "Islam's Geo-Civil War" is located in his deliberations on "Political Thought in the Fog of War." In his discussion he draws on the philosophical ideas of authors ranging from Hobbes and Kant to Hannah Arendt and Jürgen Habermas, in the context of political topicalities. What matters to the present book is Brenkman's acknowledgment of the pertinence of the "world democracies' response to Islam's geo-civil war" (p. 17). To date, none of these responses has been proper or adequate, because the significance of Islam is not well understood, whether in political thought, by US politicians, or by scholars. Brenkman states the issue in this manner: "American arrogance was matched by American ignorance." I could not agree more! Thus, I have pointed above to the cultural blind spots in Western policies vis-à-vis Islam in which arrogance and ignorance reinforce one another.

Today, there is no united West. Europe and the USA are Western, but also different. In contrast to the USA, contemporary Europe tends to be modest, but its politicians and public are even more ignorant than those residing in Washington, DC. I live as a Muslim in Europe and know what I am talking about. This book claims to be a contribution to improving the situation on both sides of the Atlantic. However, it is written basically for Muslims who are willing to engage in reform and change. I have chosen to write in English because it is not only the *lingua franca* of the modern world, but it is also used by Muslims. In my life as an author I have written twenty-seven books in German, published between 1969 and 2007, and another seven in English. My German experience has been more than depressing. The German "Kulturnation" knows nothing about contemporary Islam. In claiming modesty, Germans replace their arrogance with a mentality of self-defeatism. In Germany, liberal Muslims are sidelined in favor of Islamists, to whom German politicians and magazines prefer to talk. After living in Germany for forty-six years I have given up the German case as lost, and I have therefore chosen to write this book in English. After all, to write German is a form of concealment, and this is not my choice.

I will conclude this preface by turning to the potential for contestation and rejection of the cultural international relations approach that is followed in this book, and try to dispel it by reassuring the reader: I focus on the cultural roots of conflict, but am wary of falling into the trap of culturalism. I refer to Brenkman's "Islam's geo-civil war" to suggest that Islam's predicament with modernity is the source that generates tensions, conflict, and even a new kind of war called global jihad. In Brenkman's view "the democratic world will be engaged for several years" – I correct that to "several decades" – with this geo-political but culturally determined situation. It is not purely cultural – to argue so would be wrong. It is embedded into an overall, multifaceted context.

The remedy consists in religious reform and cultural change. These avenues provide hope for a better future and this book aims to contribute to that end. Civil Islam is proposed as the proper alternative to an Islam at "geo-civil war." I hope it is not a wishful thinking to believe that civil Islam is viable; it may prove capable of accommodating cultural modernity in authentic Islamic terms. The Introduction that follows is guided by this view and aims to help the reader to become acquainted with the major themes and with the structure of the present book. To guide the process of reading the eleven chapters I recommend starting with the Introduction. Finally, I repeat: I have chosen to write this book, as a summation of my life's work, in English after the devastating experience of forty years of writing books in German – with almost zero impact. The German magazine *Der Spiegel* published a special issue on Islam in Europe under the dreadful title *"Allah im Abendland/*Allah in Christendom," in which my contribution to understanding Islam in Germany and Europe published between 1970 and 2007 has been treated as completely non-existent. No one can deny me my feelings: I was reminded of the legacy of the annihilation of the Jews in Germany in regard to my work published in German. This is a devastating record of my life in Germany, expressed here in strong words – words that reflect how alien a Muslim feels in the country that I once loved. Even those Muslims in Europe, who strongly disagree with my reform Islam, agree with me completely when I contest the way in which we are treated by Europeans in the Old World.

Bassam Tibi
Washington, DC

Introduction
Cultural tensions, modernity, globalization, and conflict

In a way, the present academic study of Islam's predicament with cultural modernity can be introduced by stating that it deals with the new and changed place of religion and culture in the present age. The focus is on Islam in the context of overwhelming globalization and post-bipolarity. In this overall context, one encounters a return of the sacred, associated with political claims. True, in the case in point, the Islamic civilization, the challenge is much older; it emanates from its exposure to modernity. However, under the conditions of post-bipolarity the context of the predicament assumes a new shape. There are cultural tensions that lead to international conflict. This is the major theme of the book. Some readers who are new to my work may single out one feature of the book to contest self-referentiality every time I refer to my own cross-cultural experience and relate it to the issues addressed. Readers who know me well are familiar with this aspect of my work and understand it. I therefore ask new readers for their understanding and beg their indulgence. I believe these references to be neither superfluous nor merely personal; they matter to the subject of the book as a current study of Islam that claims to be an academic inquiry – one that is underpinned, however, by the life experience of a Muslim on five continents during the past four decades. During this experience I have lived through all of the problems addressed. I therefore hope that this book will fulfill my intention of presenting a mature intellectual work to mark my retirement from a global academic career. I view this book as the summation of my work over the past four decades, and in this sense the few autobiographical asides form part of the undertaking.

For many reasons, I have chosen to start the introduction in this way and to begin with a personal note, which needs some justification. The inclusion of lived events in an academic inquiry is the result of relating them to the subject matter of the following eleven chapters, and this legitimates the autobiographical asides. During review of my manuscript some readers reacted positively to this, one noting that "these add a good bit of interest to the scholarly narrative." I feel well understood, and this judgment makes me happy. However, I know from the reviews of my earlier books that there are others who do not like this style of writing. In the preface to my Routledge book published in 2008 I engaged in scholarly justification of my personal style with references to Thomas Kuhn and René Descartes. I would appreciate readers consulting those pages, and assure them that I have done my best to restrict the autobiographical asides to underpinning the arguments that I present.

A personal note

This book represents the conclusion of my institutional academic career. Parallel to its publication I am supposed to become a professor emeritus. My life as a writer began forty years ago, when my first book was published in Frankfurt in 1969 (*Die arabische Linke*, reviewed by the late Hisham Sharabi in the *Middle East Journal*, 1970), while I was still a PhD student. Since then I have written twenty-seven books in German and a further seven monographs in English. My publications in Arabic were restricted to numerous articles published between 1968 and 1971. By that time, I was an active member of the Arab left. These articles were followed by some chapters in Arabic, the last of which was my contribution to *"Azmat al-Demoqratiyya fi al-watan al-Arabi*/Crisis of Democracy in the Arab world" (1983). My work has been translated into sixteen languages. I have engaged in writing as both: a Muslim and a scholar. Not only by birth but also by faith and by primary socialization I am a Muslim, born into an *ashraf* (noble) family. I grew up in a Muslim environment and had a Muslim schooling in Damascus. By chance, I became a German–European citizen. I confess that I am not sure about this, because this citizenship is more of a legal issue than a matter of identity. Therefore, I sincerely concede my ambiguity with regard to belonging to Germany.

The Damascus story was followed by a journey to Europe. The part of this story that occurred in European academia began with an education in Frankfurt, where I was lucky enough to study under great scholars of the caliber of Max Horkheimer, Theodor Adorno, Jürgen Habermas, and Iring Fetcher, as well as Alexander Mitscherlich and Carlo Schmidt. Today, all these scholars rank as historical figures and great personalities. In addition to the combination of an Arab Islamic and a European upbringing under the influence of great thinkers, a third segment has been added to my life. This began in the US, in the context of numerous affiliations and fellowships, the most important of which was at Harvard University during the rich years 1982–2000. This Harvard affiliation was interrupted by Princeton 1986/87, Ann Arbor/Michigan 1988, and Berkeley 1994. The US segment in my life, which is the richest part of my academic career, has been continued at Cornell University (2004 to date). All this has been in addition to my German position as Professor of International Relations at the oldest academic institution of northern Germany: the Georg-August-Universität of Göttingen. Of course, there have been numerous leaves and sabbaticals; my German university was generous enough to let me go whenever I wanted to. I am most appreciative of this, despite all the injustice and discrimination that I suffered at Göttingen – and about which, out of decency – I prefer to remain silent. In the cross-cultural life that I have outlined I had to accommodate a variety of different cultures and to bridge between fundamentally divergent worlds. Thus, this personal note matters to the theme of the book, as well to the manner of its writing.

The cultural diversity that exists within Islamic civilization is enhanced on a global level. In the 1980s I lived and taught in West Africa (Cameroon, Senegal, Nigeria, etc.). From 1995 onwards I added a Southeast Asian connection to my life, starting with Indonesia and continuing in Singapore. This experience helped me to overcome the Arabo-centrism that I had internalized in Damascus. Despite this cross-cultural journey, which encompasses most parts of the world, I have to confess that I have never succeeded in finding a real home anywhere in the world since leaving Damascus on October 26, 1962. Thus, I understand the yearning for authenticity, identity politics, and ethnicity, but I reject them all in favor of cultural modernity. Why do I mention this personal story that started with my journey to Europe, and continued from there to the rest of the world? This book is not an autobiography, and this personal note is, rather, a prelude to an academic book. Well, I am making in this autobiographical aside to pass on the following message.

Today, the Islamic civilization is no longer a world of Islam, or an Islamicate for itself. Under the conditions of globalization it is incorporated – against its will – into a combination of an international society and an international system. Both are determined by cultural and institutional modernity. In addition to this incorporation, people of the Islamic world not only travel, but also migrate for good to non-Islamic parts of the world. Migration and exposure to modernity are great challenges to deal with, and at a very high price: the feeling of being uprooted and identity problems. Except in scholarship, I have had – ever since leaving Damascus in 1962 – no home. I will finish with this story now and pick it up later on in relation to the subject matter and arguments of the book. The remainder of the introduction focuses on presenting the substance of this academic inquiry. At issue are assumptions, a methodology, and an inquiry into the major themes of Islam's predicament with cultural modernity. These issues are seen in the light of a journey from the Arab part of the Islamic civilization to the West (Europe and the US), and then from the West to the non-Arab part of this civilization (West Africa and Southeast Asia). This personal account is only a complementary section, on the fringe of the present undertaking, and these autobiographical asides serve to present the matter at issue, as illustrated in a life "Between four worlds" later on in this Introduction. I will now move on to the major assumption of the book, followed by a presentation of its substance, structure, and individual chapters.

What is "Islam's Predicament with Modernity" all about? And why do religious reform and cultural change matter to the study of value conflicts?

In my work, I share with multiculturalists a positive view of diversity, but I am wary of the pitfalls of the romanticization of difference. Throughout this book I operate on the assumption that cultural differences may also generate tensions that can develop into political conflict. This subject is new in this field, and therefore may not be welcomed. Every addition to scholarship in the academic study of Islam, because of its novelty, faces some rejection by the establishment. In the US and in Europe, Islamic studies are mostly dominated by disciplines other than the social sciences, not to mention international relations, the discipline of this book, which is almost absent from Islamic studies. This new book has been completed independently of my earlier contributions to the study of Islam. It is presented as a monograph on Islam's predicament with modernity, viewed as a major source of tensions and conflicts. This predicament has been mentioned repeatedly in my earlier work, but has not been examined as a subject in itself in an in-depth analysis. In my 2008 book *Political Islam, World Politics and Europe*, the focus was on politics, not on religion and culture. This sequel ventures into the predicament and locates it in the study of the cultural constraints of conflict. Only in this limited sense is the present inquiry a continuation of the research documented in my earlier book.

At first, the predicament with modernity is viewed as a cultural one, but it is then placed into the overall structural context – not, however, in a reductionist manner; it is then related to conflict studies. Thereafter the analysis also views the potential for an Islamic contribution to a peaceful conflict resolution. The actualization of this potential depends on the willingness of the people concerned to engage seriously in efforts to come to terms with the predicament. Basically, the book views religion as a cultural system and infers that cultural change in the Islamic civilization has to be underpinned by religious reform. This combination of cultural change and religious reform would provide the underpinnings of a peaceful resolution of conflict. Of course, this has to be combined with politics for material development – but that is not the subject matter of this study. Rather, it focuses on the idea that the place of culture and religion in society has been changing under the conditions of post-bipolar globalization. The analysis of culture and religion is embedded in the study of change in the international environment.

It is well known that Islam – next to Christianity – is one of the only two world religions with universal claims. Unlike Christianity, however, which underwent processes of reformation and secularization, Islam faces a predicament with cultural modernity. The basic problems are not yet solved. The need for separation of religion and politics creates a challenge to the Islamic worldview. Given the fact that the Islamic people are present all over the world, it follows, then, that this predicament matters to all of humanity. Muslims constitute the majority in fifty-seven countries, assembled as states in the Organization of the Islamic Conference (OIC). This is the only international organization in the world that is determined by belonging to a religion. In terms of minorities, one finds Muslims all over the world, whether in the capacity of a religious community, as in India, or in their capacity as immigrants in a diaspora culture within Western Europe. In this century of global migration, the migratory diaspora of Islam, particularly in the West, is added to Islam in Asia and Africa.

Thus, the conflicts resulting from Islam's predicament affect other people of the West and of the rest of the world, whether through Islam as a significant factor in the international system, or as a migratory diaspora existing in the West but alien to it because of a failure to integrate.

In an academic world in which scholarship is deteriorating because of increasing politicization, many tend to base their judgments on ideological bias and sound bites, not on balanced research. Therefore, the approach of this book needs to be protected from the possibility of discrediting. I assure my readers that this association of a cultural predicament with tensions and international conflict views neither religion (understood as a faith) nor culture as sources for the production of meaning, as sources of conflict. This book is not based on such an argument. However, it is a fact that under conditions of globalization tensions do emerge that are articulated in religious and cultural terms. To reiterate: this does not happen in an instrumental manner. To state it differently: political, social, and economic problems are shaped by a cultural language of religion. This is a religionization of these problems, and that is exactly what "Islamic politics" is all about. This happens on local, regional, and international levels. My work on these issues has been influenced by my participation in an international research project on Culture and Globalization. In Chapter 5 I try to make this influence clear. The argument is that unresolved and unsettled issues are embedded in Islam's predicament with modernity. Tensions and conflicts emerge.

There is another issue area that also compels me to dissociate this book from the well-known and disputed thinking of Orientalism and Orientalism in reverse. My dealing with Islam's predicament with modernity is based in the discipline of international relations, and is therefore located methodologically in the study of conflict. However, the present undertaking is an interdisciplinary analysis. It is pursued by a liberal Muslim scholar who has no interest whatsoever in engaging in a "clash of civilizations," nor in turning the table around, for instance, from Orientalism to Orientalism in reverse. The preceding personal note should make my concern clear. Unlike Orientalists, I relate the study of Islam to social reality. I engage in the study of conflict because I am interested in peaceful conflict resolution. I claim to have founded – along the lines of earlier Sovietology – the discipline of Islamology. This Islamological study of real Islam is located in the study of international conflict within international relations and is combined, in an interdisciplinary manner, with the sociology of religion, as well as with cultural and development studies. I should make clear that I not only dissociate my work equally from Western Orientalism and from the response to it that is defined as an Orientalism in reverse, but also from the rhetoric of a "clash of civilizations." I maintain that a conflict is not a clash, the difference being that the first can be resolved, while a "clash," by contrast, is an essentialization of tensions.

In the main, I argue that culture and religion provide a means for articulation. When contestation in a situation of conflict is articulated in religious terms it inflames existing tensions and intensifies the crisis. In Islamic culture, religion is believed to stand above reality. Nevertheless, when culture and religion undergo a politicization they become an undercurrent for igniting tensions that lead to conflict. This is no contradiction. Within this set-up, social, political, and economic concerns are intermingled with culture and they take on a religionized form. I reiterate: culture and religion are not, by nature, a source of conflict; only in their embedment in crisis-laden situations do they become a part of a religionized conflict. If articulated in religious terms, a conflict is not only exacerbated, it also becomes intractable. No true believer would ever accept to abandon claims based on faith, or lay them on the table for negotiation.

In short, religious and religionized claims are not negotiable. If Islam's unresolved predicament with cultural modernity under conditions of globalization is religionized, then it becomes the underlying constraint of a kind of a new local, regional, and international conflict. Cultural change and religious reform are required to defuse tensions, to prevent the religionization of the conflict, and to smooth the way to its resolution through negotiation and dialogue.

After a clear delineation of the subject matter of the present book I continue by asking "What is modernity?" In the search for an answer, I subdivide modernity into two interrelated segments: cultural and institutional. For a proper understanding of this issue, I draw on the work of Jürgen Habermas and Anthony Giddens to establish clarity regarding the different meanings of modernity. The reference is to two different but interrelated segments of modernity. Jürgen Habermas discusses the philosophical discourse of modernity as a culture, based on norms, values, and a rational-secular view of the world. Giddens focuses on the institutional dimension, which means power underpinned by the tools that emerged from modern science and technology. In the course of European expansion, people of the Islamic civilization have encountered these two different but interrelated dimensions of modernity. However, they were exposed largely to a single aspect, namely to modernity as a European power project of expansion. It was the gunpowder of Napoleon's army in Egypt in 1798 that Muslims faced, together with his announcement that he was bringing them the ideas of the French Revolution. The world of Islam was exposed to a European expansion that mapped it into new global structures. There are further implications and painful results. I know this, and I here refrain from writing another book on Islam and the West, because literature on the issue exists in abundance. Instead, I aim to present a book that is unique in its approach to the study of Islam, with a focus on the cultural sources of tensions that lead to conflict, being a part of the story of Islam and modernity as embedded in the mentioned European expansion.

While writing a book that is committed to a rational discourse of cultural modernity, I acknowledge my awareness of the postmodern argument of multiple modernities. Despite my deep commitment to pluralism, articulated in Chapter 7, I dismiss this argument and prefer to join Habermas, who asks in his book on cultural modernity whether postmodernism was not really a means of legitimizing a "revolt against modernity," bringing back pre-modernity as a "counter-Enlightenment in the garb of post-Enlightenment."[1] Cultural modernity is a project based on the recognition of the primacy of reason. According to this understanding of rationality there exists only one modernity, shared by the whole of humanity. This rationalism was once included in the classical heritage of the Islamic civilization, during its better days. To argue otherwise would imply a kind of a racism that reserves rationality to Europeans and Westerners. This book is committed to an earlier tradition in Islam, based on the human rationalism that Muslims then shared with the rest of humanity. To put it differently: the cultural roots of modernity existed in Islamic thought. For this reason, I join the Muslim philosopher Mohammed al-Jabri in arguing that cultural modernity is consonant with the heritage of Islamic rationalism, which was undermined by the *fiqh*-orthodoxy of Islam. As al-Jabri states, "the Averroist spirit is adaptable to our era, because it agrees with it on more than one point: rationalism, realism, axiomatic method approach." In short, the rationality of cultural modernity is not alien to Islam. It was, however, alien to Salafist *fiqh*-orthodoxy in the Islamic past, just as it is to totalitarian Islamism at present.

Islamology as a study of Islam and conflict in post-bipolar politics

The inquiry into Islam's predicament with cultural modernity, which builds up the background of conflict, requires three analyses. The first needs to be focused on the predicament itself, the second on the conflict that it generates, and the third is expected to provide options for a resolution of conflict. This book is poised to upgrade the study of religion and culture in society and in world affairs. It is not the concern of this study to deal with Islam as a faith, since it looks at religion as a "*fait social*/social fact" in political and social realities and not as a divine phenomenon. Along these lines, Islam is conceptualized as a cultural system that is always in flux, and is therefore placed in a historical and social context. It is therefore by no means essentialized. Commitment to religious reform in the study of Islamic civilization is a normative concern related to cultural change and is motivated by a search for peaceful conflict resolution. It is guided by an analysis of the real, existing Islam and of the emerging conflict, while seeking conflict resolution.

Since the late 1960s, and in particular since the late 1970s, two sources of thinking have affected my reasoning about Islam: first, training in the history of ideas in political philosophy, and second, the ensuing study of conflict in international relations. In this context, and based on the study of Islamic thought since my years as a young student in Frankfurt, I published my first book, *The Arab Left*, in 1969, as mentioned above. At the time I was still a PhD student. That book was reviewed most graciously by the late Hisham Sharabi in the *Middle East Journal* in 1970 and drew the attention of Sharabi's close friend, Edward Said, at that time not yet so well known. In 1972 Said invited me to the US to speak on the "Arab Left," in which I was an activist, at the Annual Convention of the Arab American University Graduates/AAUG, held in that year in Boston. That paper was my very first publication in English and was included in the volume edited by Edward Said, *The Arabs of Today. Perspectives for Tomorrow* (1973). During the same decade I was exposed to the pain that my ideas were and continue to be unwelcome to the al-Azhar orthodoxy. In 1979, I presented my paper "Islam and Secularization" at the first Islamic Congress on Philosophy of Islam and Civilization (see Chapter 6, note 1) and was rebuffed. Ever since, I have been developing an awareness of the connection between cultural-political thought and conflict.

Prior to the foundation of the new approach that I prefer to identify as Isla-mology, I touched on Islam – not yet, however, as a new force – in earlier books that focused on secular subjects, such as my *Arab Nationalism*, and *Militär und Sozialismus in der Dritten Welt*. The story of Islamology started in my very first book focused on Islam, namely *The Crisis of Modern Islam* (1980 in German, US edition 1988). In that book I paid my farewell to Marxism, which I had adopted as a frame of reference during the years of my education in the "Frankfurt School" of Max Horkheimer and Theodor Adorno. From the late 1970s onwards, I started to look at religion and culture not only beyond the confines of economic reduc-tionism, but also beyond mere political analysis. This was the beginning of my thinking about the place of religion as a cultural system in the processes of social change and about the related conflicts, later to become a foundation for Isla-mology. Five years later, in my book on *Islam and the Cultural Accommodation of Social Change* (1985 in German, US edition 1990), this process was laid out. As already stated, my concern was not only to avoid Western Orientalism, rightly criticized by Edward Said – with whom I was once a friend – but also the Isla-mic Orientalism in reverse unveiled by S. J. al-Azm. In my view, both Orient-alism and Orientalism in reverse, though at odds, essentialize religion and culture in one way or another. In my study of Islam I had to learn that Muslims have problems not only with the West but also with themselves. I recognized that for a proper understanding of the issues not only a kind of new research, but also a considerable degree of detachment is required.

Anthony Giddens wrote a book *Beyond Left and Right*. Applied to the study of Islam, the phrase would sound, in modified form, like this: "Beyond Orientalist demonizing and beyond defending Islam in an Orientalism in reverse." What is needed today is to understand Islam as a social and political reality that is both determined by the structural environment and also determinative of it in an interplay between culture and society. This is the approach adopted in the pre-sent book. It is most deplorable that many scholars have lost sight of it during the course of the heated polemics between Orientalists and Orientalists in reverse. At times, when I read books by members of the US Islamic studies establishment, I ask myself: are these folks talking about Islam, or are they obsessed with the polemics flaring between them?

The social-scientific study of Islam and its civilization, presented as the new discipline of Islamology, proposes a new approach. And it also strives to put aside the polemics of Orientalism and Orientalism in reverse. The methodology of Islamology is not that employed by the traditional Western courses in Islamic studies run by philologists, historians, and cultural anthropologists. As Maxime Rodinson once noted in his *La Fascination de l'Islam*, traditional Orientalism is not only a mindset that reflects a combination of prejudice and supremacy, but also one that expresses the hegemony of philology in Islamic studies in Europe. When it comes to the US, one needs to add to this source of hegemony the disciplines of cultural-relativist anthropology and of narrative history. Both are under the influence of Edward Said. Again and again, I dissociate my work from both, i.e. from Orientalism and from an Orientalism in reverse that not only turns the tables and continues to essentialize, but also utterly fails to introduce new perspectives. In contrast, the social sciences, in particular international relations, need to be introduced into the study of Islam. In this sense, and in view of Islam's predicament with modernity, the methodology of the new discipline of Islamology is based on the study of international conflict and the underlying cultural tensions in post-bipolar politics. The culture-based conflict is nourished by the perceptions underlying the polarization between "them" and "us" as an imagery of Islam under siege. In this process the ethnicization of a transnational *umma* occurs under conditions of globalization. Basically, the problems and the conflicts are inner-Islamic. However, the context of globalization gives the conflict an international character that is shaped by transnational religion.

The term used to conceptualize the issues outlined is "religionized politics." In the analysis of Islam's predicament with cultural modernity, a promising avenue is to engage in the study of three issue areas singled out for this analysis: knowledge, law, and human rights, because they are most pertinent. Discord generates tensions that lead to conflict; this book therefore devotes a chapter to each, in the context of the study of religionized politics and conflict.

The overall context of the return of the sacred and the related objective of desecularization is post-bipolar politics. It is argued that post-bipolar conflicts first emerge from tensions on local ground, i.e. in our case within the world of Islam itself. The prevailing cultural worldview, combined with the outcome of disruptive social change, is among the constraints that generate the tensions often articulated in the context of identity politics. The related issues are embedded in a disordered international environment. This issue, which arises in the guise of identity politics, is analyzed in Chapter 5. Next to the local are the regional and international levels. It is clear that people of the Islamic civilization do not live in a so-called "world of Islam" as a world in itself, but are, rather, incorporated into an increasingly globalizing world. Uncritical Muslims view globalization as a threat, which they perceive within a framework that is based on an imagery of Islam under siege. This perception is among the sources of cultural tensions.

As discussed in my 2008 book, *Islam, World Politics and Europe*, the twenty-first century does not indicate the proclaimed "end of history," but rather an age of conflicts and uncertainty. Islamology is the study of conflict in the religionized politics of civilizations. The conflict is also related to the revived idea of "*Siyadat al-Islam*/Islamic dominance," which is not only contradicted by facts on the ground, but also runs counter to the requirements of a political culture of pluralism for world peace in the twenty-first century (see Chapter 7). In its study of conflict and of the potential for conflict resolution, this book bids farewell to the Islamic doctrine that demands submission and subjection to an abstract Islamic authority. It engages not only in a rethinking of the prevailing Islamic universalism, but also in a questioning of it. Chapter 3 contributes to this end through a criticism of the reinvented shari'a in the contemporary shari'atized Islamist internationalism. At issue is not only the ideology of a "global jihad," but also a transnational movement based on a politicization and shari'atization of Islam. On the basis of the cultural ideology outlined, the Islamist movement incites tensions that lead to conflict.

The Islamological approach proposed for the study of Islam could be rejected in some circles. There are reasons to reiterate this misgiving. In this book I dismiss not only Western Orientalism, in line with the original intention of Edward Said, but also the opposing Islamist and Saidist mindset of Orientalism in reverse. The latter thinking is, deplorably, shared even by some postmodernists, who contribute to the distortion of the critique of Said in the name of Saidism. To be sure, the once-legitimate critique of Said is not the Saidism of Orientalism in reverse. This is a formula invented by Sadik J. al-Azm. In fact, the currently prevailing postmodern worldview of some Western scholars, dubbed as Saidists, is based on a preconception that implies a variety of Orientalism, even if reversed. It has to be stated, from the point of view of a liberal Muslim scholar, that there are some Western scholars who even behave like neo-colonialists when they impose their nihilist postmodernism on non-Europeans, and then call them names when they refuse to abide by their Western views.

Based on experience, I anticipate such a contestation. I stand by the idea of an Islamic predicament with cultural modernity and by the proposed approach of Islamology, with its focus on the study of conflict. Some may dismiss it as an "Islamophobia," but it is not. In this context, one can state a resemblance between Muslims, on the one hand, who accuse other Muslims of "*kufr*/heresy," and Western scholars, on the other, who proceed in the same manner in their discrediting of dissent with the accusation of Orientalism. Critical Muslims are accused of "*kufr*/heresy" by Salafists and Islamists and, in a similar vein, of self-Orientalization by Christian and atheist Western postmodernists. Among the unpleasant observations in the current debate is the suppression of free speech in research and in politics, both by scholars and by believers.

Unlike Western concepts for the study of Islam pursued by cultural relativists, this book departs from an assumed universality of rational knowledge, discussed at length in Chapter 2. In addition, the book is quite balanced in many ways. The epistemology used revives the authority of the medieval Muslim philosopher Averroes, who – as Mohammed al-Jabri puts it – set out to define "the universality and historicity of knowledge." In short, the method of this book is to combine the rationalism of medieval Islamic *falsafa* with modern social science methodology in order to study culture and religion in the context of conflict. The focus on the study of conflict in the presented Islamology is based on rational knowledge of post-bipolar politics in the twenty-first century. The statement of the need for religious reform and innovative cultural change is the option for peaceful conflict resolution for which this book opts.

The research background of the book

The research for this book, with its major theme of Islam's predicament with modernity, has been guided by the insight that religion can be reformed and culture can change. If Islam is not essentialized, then it can be reformed and culturally renewed. If all kinds of essentialism are dismissed, and reference to the Qur'an itself is done in a historicizing manner, then it is possible to legitimate change in the direction of modernity. One is reminded of the Qur'anic verse "Allah does not change people, unless they change themselves" (sura 13, verse 11). This is an authentic Islamic idea that authoritatively allows Muslims to engage in changing themselves and in making their culture consonant with modernity. I am a Muslim social scientist and these thoughts determine my thinking.

The research background of this book is the study of the reality of the contemporary politicization of Islam into an Islamism. It is acknowledged that people of Islamic civilization are exposed to existential choices. Islamists reduce the major ills of Islamic societies to the exposure of Muslims to Western globalization and then cultivate a sense of self-victimization, related to the already mentioned perception of an Islam under the siege. All the chapters in the present book argue against these blame games without overlooking – even for a moment – the fact of the dominance of the West. It is real and it creates a problem. However, if one respects Muslims as acting individuals/subjects and does not view them in an Orientalist manner as "people without history," being an object of realities created by others, i.e. by the West, then it can be assumed that these acting subjects have an active part in the process of determining existing realities. They also share responsibility for their fate, and are not simply victims of action taken by others. Surprisingly, this view can also be found in the work of the foremost Muslim revivalist, al-Afghani. He argues that Muslims are not only capable of shaping their own destiny, but are also partly responsible for their present miserable state of affairs. Thus, al-Afghani places the blame on Muslims and accuses them of "*jahl*/ignorance." Exposure to European expansion is the context, but not the source of their ills. Departing from this understanding, which I share with the true revivalist al-Afghani, it is recognized that the prevailing pattern of defensive-cultural responses to an external exposure leads nowhere.

In contrast to a defensive culture, a Muslim acceptance of the potential for religious reform and for cultural change in Islamic civilization is a promising avenue. Such efforts could help Muslims to take responsibility for their ills and – on these grounds – to engage in action for a better future. This idea of cultural innovation is therefore – next to the diagnosis of a predicament – the core thought of the entire present book; it determines its structure and predominates in all of its eleven chapters. It is made clear that willingness to engage in religious reform is the *conditio sine qua non* for the accomplishment of the needed cultural change in Islamic civilization. There can be no overcoming of Islam's predicament with cultural modernity without these reforms. Again, the litany of complaints, of blame games, and of self-victimization ends in an impasse, and this is a bleak prospect for the world of Islam. Only Muslims can provide better options for their own future.

All the ideas included in the present book are related to new findings reached in multiple research that was accomplished in many international projects. This book grew and greatly benefited from these various international research projects, which are associated with decades-long thinking on the subject. This reference to the long research history of the book, and also to its global links, is not self-referential. My allusion to the projects in which my work has been embedded is no self-congratulatory boast – it merely legitimates the singling out of five core issue areas addressed in the related chapters.

First: the failure of modernization. Earlier, it was supposed that the decolonization process is bound to modernization, as well as to secularization. The falsification – not only in scholarship, but also in reality – of the evolutionist assumptions of the theory of modernization was related to a crisis of development. It has also been – in the sense of Thomas Kuhn – a scientific crisis in this field of study. One of the promising avenues for getting out of this impasse has been the Culture Matters Research Project/CMRP chaired by Professor Lawrence Harrison at Fletcher School, Tufts University. I was a member of the research team and contributed to its two volumes, published under the title *Developing Cultures* (see Chapter 1, note 1). This may provoke an objection, because the project applies the assumption of economic, social, and political change in "developing countries" to culture also. Change is supposed to promote development and is therefore accepted. But why should this idea not also apply to religion and culture? Why are they both exempted? To be sure, the notion of "developing cultures," which was put forward against all the odds, had no bad connotations. In arguing that cultural change and religious reform are needed to bolster social, economic, and political development one is on the right path. This is a major insight, which will be discussed in more detail in Chapter 1, and it determines all the following thinking. The significant lesson to learn from failed modernization is that there can be no successful modernization without the inclusion of culture and religion. Both need to be subjected to thoughtful change and to innovative reform that will help Muslims to understand their real world and the international environment of their lives.

In addition to participation in the Culture Matters Research Project/CMRP, it may be asked, what other kind of research was done in pursuit of writing this book? Of course, there are the preceding three decades of research that underpin my thinking on the subject. I apologize for the self-referential remark that my work has also been supported by rich, cross-cultural experience on the ground. In this context, I learned the validity of the wisdom that "thinking is research," articulated by the late Oxford scholar of international relations Hedley Bull. This inspiration shapes the understanding of research practiced in this book, which does not use any quantitative data or related methods. I claim, however, to present fully-fledged, solid research and robust analysis. The countless informal interviews that I have conducted during the past three decades in about twenty Islamic countries refer to meaning and to a worldview, and are not a subject for quantitative methods. Here also, the notion applies that "thinking is research" (H. Bull).

Second: the return of the sacred and the choice between shari'atization and religious reform. This issue is a general one and its relevance is not restricted to Islam. Europe has been described as an "empty white space in the map of religious fundamentalism" (Martin Marty), as Europeans themselves tend to view the self in post-Christian terms. Thus, they are addressed as an a-religious people. In spite of this a-religiosity, however, the old world seems to become the location for the greatest challenge of the return of the sacred. The Muslim newcomers make strong reference to their religion and articulate all of their problems in religious terms. The presence of an Islamic diaspora in the modern societies of Europe is the presence of people with strong religious identity. The Islamic contestation of secularization, of secularity, and of secularism occurs not only at home (see Chapter 6), but also in the diaspora. It indicates the return of the sacred to Europe also. This happens with a Muslim mindset that precludes religious reform and essentializes Islam. Again, it is not the task of the present book to deal with Muslim immigrants living in Europe, because I have done this extensively in my book *Political Islam, World Politics and Europe*. Nevertheless, the idea of religious reform is related generally to the interaction between Europe and Islam, and therefore has also to be addressed here.

There are some pundits who naively believe that a transformation of Islam will occur in Europe. As is analyzed in Chapter 6, secularization and de-secularization have become a European concern. Instead the transformation of Islam in Europe that was forecast, immigrants are calling for the establishment of shari'a in Europe and insisting on their separateness. My thinking on these issues has been integrated into the Cornell project on *Religion in an Expanding Europe* (Cambridge University Press, 2006), of which I was a member, and this is also reflected in the present book. To be sure, I do not share the view of the chairpersons regarding the argument of multiple modernities, and I am also in disagreement on basic matters with some of the authors of that project. My agreement is restricted to acknowledging the new role of religion and its impact in world politics and in Europe. The world of Islam is the major theater.

No doubt, the possible Europeanization of Islam in its European diaspora could have an impact, through ripple effects, on the world of Islam itself. I admit that this is not the reality, but rather my wishful thinking. Nevertheless, I do engage with the related thinking, but without the naivety that Islam in Europe will change the world of Islam itself. Therefore, the focus of this book is the Islamic world, not

Europe. The fact is that the world of Islam comes to Europe via its diaspora. To date, Europe has failed to shape this diaspora along a European identity.

Third: culture, conflict, and globalization. These three interrelated notions were the subject of a project chaired by Professor Helmut Anheier of UCLA and Professor Y. Raj Isar of the American University of Paris, in which I worked on Islamic identity politics. Identity politics generate cultural tensions that develop into conflict. The concept of conflict is central to the discipline of international relations, and to this book also. In the project mentioned, the scholars involved studied cultural tensions to find out how they could lead to conflict. I was given the assignment of examining this assumption in the case of Islam and in the related identity politics, as situated in a context of world politics. The result of the research verifies the assumption that cultural currents undergird conflict (see Chapter 5, note 1). However, this insight is reached and stated without falling into the traps of culturalism or essentialism. The findings related to this research are reflected in Chapter 5 of this book.

Fourth: Orientalism, and who studies change? The question of who can study Islam better and more properly – Muslims or Westerners – is a contentious area. I reiterate my stance, that the earlier debate on this concern was a legitimate one, as a critique of the Orientalism of Westerners. However, the debate was dramatically derailed – as already stated – into an Orientalism in reverse. The answer to the question whether Western scholars can make a contribution to the study of Islam is affirmative, but I hasten to add that dealing with the issue by Muslims themselves is not only most relevant, but should also be welcomed. There is a need to overcome Western patriarchy in scholarship, be it in the old colonial or the new, postmodern shape. The alternative kind of research pursued by Muslims was conducted in a project at the Emirates Center for Study and Research/ECSR. I was lucky enough to be involved in pondering about the Gulf beyond the age of oil. In this fourth project in the present listing I presented the views on cultural change that are included in this book. I was most pleased to see positive responses from co-religionists to my plea for reform and change, as expressed at the ECSR project. The related research findings are covered in Chapter 10, which includes the second case study. The first case study – on Egypt – is included in Chapter 9 and grew from the Culture Matters Research Project/CMPR at Fletcher School, mentioned above as the first project.

Fifth: religious-cultural pluralism, trialogue, and cultural modernity. The thinking on religions in the context of pluralism that is included in Chapter 7 is related to a project conducted by Professors John Roth and Leonard Grob in cooperation with the Center for Advanced Holocaust Studies/CAHS at the US Holocaust Memorial Museum – supported by the Center's associate Victoria Barnett in 2007. It was designed as a trialogue. There, I continued my decade-long thinking on pluralism between cultures and religions. Another highlight of this process was the research on this subject at the Asian Research Institute of the National University of Singapore/NUS. In 2005 I had tenure as a senior research fellow at the Asia Research Center/ARI of that university. ARI's director, Anthony Reid, engaged a group of visiting faculty in a research project on *Islam in Plural Southeast Asia*. This is the title of the book based on the hypothesis that pluralism is the best platform for peace between religious-cultural communities. A third source of inspiration for Chapter 7 was Cornell's cross-regional symposium organized by Professor Davydd Greenwood. The venture brought together scholars working on three regions: Southeast Asia, South Asia, and Europe. With this threefold experience I thought about how Jews, Christians, and Muslims – and, of course, people who do not want to believe – could share in the cultural modernity of pluralism.

The five issue areas outlined and the related research projects have had a great impact on the structure of the present book, which claims to be the first comprehensive study of Islam's predicament with modernity as viewed from a professional international relations perspective. The book situates the analysis of the predicament within the study of conflict and proposes that thinking on religious reform and cultural change can smooth the way for peaceful conflict resolution.

At this point a line needs to be drawn between the present book and my earlier book, *Political Islam, World Politics and Europe*, published at the beginning of 2008. It was completed in the years 2003–6. In that book I argue in the final chapter that political Islam (Islamism) is neither an alternative nor the expression of a solution, as its exponents contend. Islamists say: "*al-Islam huwa al-hall*/Islam is the solution." In contrast, I state that the solution is the culture of democracy. In this book the focus is on culture and conflict, and here I argue that Islamism is not "another modernity," as some believe. In an earlier period (1989–93) of my scholarly life, my work in the Fundamentalism Project at the American Academy of Arts and Sciences was a source for learning from the related research. There, I learned that Islamism is a political religion and not a strategy for development. I have not added this research, as a sixth issue area, to the five identified above, because it was published elsewhere. In addition to co-authoring one of the five volumes (Volume 2) of the Fundamentalism Project, I wrote in that connection my own monograph, *The Challenge of Fundamentalism* (University of California Press, 1998, updated 2002). In the present book, the related findings are inherently present in the thinking of all eleven chapters.

Between four worlds

Following this content-based and issue-oriented outlining of the major themes, in this section I return to and continue the personal story begun above as a "Personal Note." To avoid any misunderstanding of the many personal references that follow, it is necessary to underline and reiterate that the autobiographical asides should not distract from the fact that this book is, on all levels, an academic study and a scholarly contribution, not a personal record. However, the present story is related to a Muslim scholar who has spent his academic life working and teaching around the globe. During a life that has included activities in more than thirty universities located in all continents I have experienced all of the cultural tensions analyzed in this book. Between 1962 and 2008 I lived between Melbourne, Australia and Berkeley, California and, in between, in South Asia, in the Middle East, Africa (North, West, and East), and – of course – much of Europe. In all of these places I studied religion, culture, and conflict in my own way. In the course of a cross-cultural life I encountered the need for reform and change under the conditions of globalization. Critics who disagree with my views should not use this fact as a pretext for disregarding the scholarly findings and the book altogether. That would be unfair, to say the least, but I would not be surprised if it happened. The environment of scholarship has changed in the direction of greater politicization at the expense of academic civility, and to the detriment of scholarly knowledge. I regret to say this, but I have been exposed as much to this biased scholarship as to the intercultural tensions caused by living in conflicting cultures. Scholarly values and the culture of detachment demand that a scholar be impartial to and tolerant of dissent. This is the model, but not the reality, of Western scholarship.

It is not an exaggeration to state that – in the twenty-first century – Islam is the foremost case in point for the study of religion and culture in the context of tensions and conflicts. That has already been made clear by some allusions in the Preface. This statement also rests on my personal experience during a life in the trans-cultural context of globalization. However, it is not a personal story, because the new place of Islam in today's world touches the life of every Muslim. To be caught between divergent cultures is not a negative experience, because it enriches through cross-cultural fertilization. However, it can be very painful. I came to realize that feeling uprooted from the local culture of one's own upbringing, together with exposure to cultural tensions, could become a source of conflict. Based on my own experience, I reiterate that reference to this background should not distract from the fact that the present book is, in all its aspects, an academic study of Islam's predicament with modernity. At issue is an inquiry into cultural diversity and on its potential to develop, in a politicized shape, into a source of cultural fragmentation. It explains how identity politics in Islamic civilization uses diversity in its response to globalization and how, in this context, it contributes to igniting tensions and conflicts. In tune with the cultural turn of our age (i.e. culture moves to the fore) – associated with a return of the sacred – the traditional wisdom that change is restricted to economy and to social and political structures is challenged. In this book the place of religion and culture in the processes of societal transformation in the post-bipolar politics of international relations is discussed. My knowledge on this subject matter of *Developing Cultures* (Lawrence Harrison) developed in the context of four worlds.

The *first* world in my life, between 1944 and 1962 was – as a Muslim born and schooled in Damascus – the Arab part of the Middle East. The *second* has been Europe, where I moved in 1962, at the age of 18, to study in Frankfurt and later to become an immigrant – not by choice, but as a kind of fate. The encounter with the Frankfurt School of Max Horkheimer and Theodor Adorno, and also with Jürgen Habermas's discourse of cultural modernity became one of the intellectual sources of inspiration in my thinking. As will be demonstrated in

Chapter 6, the discourse of cultural modernity is based on secular standards that stand in conflict with the inherited values of pre-industrial cultures that are believed to be divine, but that are an expression of pre-modernity. The question arises, whether it is appropriate to use this European standard in the study of Islam under conditions of globalization. The question leads us back to the equally very unproductive and unpleasant debate on Orientalism and its reversal. One is exposed to some biased scholars who would indiscriminately qualify the approach used here as an Orientalism. In response to this reproach, I refer not only to my Muslim background, but also to the fact that the present book is based on a cross-cultural biography. The authentic Islamic upbringing and socialization that I received in an Islamic environment in Damascus protects me from such a stupidity. The question comes to my mind: are we Muslims not like other humans? If so, then rational knowledge and its claim to universality applies to us too. The ethnicization of knowledge, dismissed in Chapter 2, not only inflicts damage on scholarship, but also closes all avenues for the intercultural communication that is needed in pursuit of conflict resolution under conditions of globalization. Therefore, the final chapter of the book ends in a defense of the universality of cultural modernity. There is an Islamic illusion of semi-modernity, which is based on the adoption of technical tools, combined with rejection of the related values. The dismissal of this illusion is among the conclusions in Chapter 11.

With few exceptions, I lived almost exclusively in Europe during the years 1962 to 1982, torn on a local level between Damascene Islam and the ethnic German part of Europe. I left Damascus to study in Germany and was lucky to do so under great academic teachers – fortunately, in the Frankfurt School. After learning the German language and a supplementary school attendance, I spent the years 1964 to 1970 physically and in person studying with the great Max Horkheimer, Theodor Adorno, and Jürgen Habermas, as well as with the political philosopher Iring Fetscher. The latter was the supervisor of my first PhD in Frankfurt (the second – Dr. habil. – was obtained from Hamburg University). During my life in Europe I have experienced not only "cultural modernity," but also the "*Dialektik der Aufklärung/*Dialectics of Enlightenment." I can assure my readers that the ugly face of Europe is well known to me – I am not a naive modernizer.

From 1982 to date I have moved beyond Europe and extended my life into North America, to include a *third* component in the four, interconnected worlds. The US is Western, but it is a world of its own and very different from ethnic Europe. The Middle East and Asia/Africa are non-Western and partly Islamic, but they are different, too. However, all Muslims are exposed not only to cultural modernity, but also to the deplorable and consequential racialization of Muslim peoples in the developments post 9/11. When I enter the US – as a Muslim who is highly positive about America – I am obliged, because I present a German passport with the information "born in Damascus," to go to what is named the "second inspection." Every time this happens to me I feel deeply racialized and – against my will – located negatively in the imagery of an "Islamic *umma* collectivity" in which people are viewed as "suspects." This treatment in the US often leads to the feeling of being traumatized by this new racialization. It also implies an essentialization of Islam and its people. Sadly, Muslims also essentialize themselves in a defensive-cultural manner in response to this politics. Despite this criticism, I need to give the United States credit. Unlike the ethnic-exclusive Europe, which is the second world of my life, America is inclusive; it offers home and identity as well. No one at Harvard or Cornell ever treated me as an alien in the way that this happens in the German academic environment, which is supposed to be my home. I reiterate: this is not a personal story, rather it is a European case of exclusion that all Muslims living in Europe suffer. I am fearful of the consequences for the future, and at Cornell and Stanford Universities 2007/08 I developed the scenario of an "ethnicity of fear" for Europe in the twenty-first century. From the point of view of an immigrant, the most off-putting thing about Europe is the self-congratulating response to any criticism. For some Germans, there is no discrimination, no othering, and no social exclusion – period! A Germanic professor celebrated as an expert on immigration decried the critique by Muslim immigrants such as the Turkish-German feminist Neçla Kelek and me as "a lamentation" – and did so while speaking to top politicians.

The positive aspect of Europe that is most significant for my German life – and has a great impact on my thinking – was the encounter with Holocaust survivors Max Horkheimer and Theodor Adorno. These great Jewish scholars were my academic teachers in Frankfurt. I also need to mention the Jewish philosopher Ernst Bloch. All of these scholarly giants shaped my life anew. Horkheimer and Adorno fled Nazi Germany to the US, but they returned to Europe out of love for its civilization, despite all of its evils. From Horkheimer and Adorno I learned critical thinking. Following this line of thought – and also in the tradition of the Islamic rationalism of Averroism – the present book views knowledge as universal and therefore refers to European social science and defends it against postmodernism. I argue that Western theories (e.g. Max Weber's) could provide appropriate tools for the study of Islam's predicament with cultural modernity. I combine this approach with the tradition of Islamic rationalism that views human reason as universal. Based on these assumptions, I dismiss the fashion of cultural relativism.

In this book I reject the divide that has been established between Islam and the West by cultural relativism. I also do this practically in my journey. There is a *fourth* world which greatly affected my knowledge of Islam. After the Arab Middle East, Europe, and the US, I made a further journey into the non-Arab parts of the world of Islam, first in sub-Saharan, primarily West, Africa and thereafter in Southeast Asia. There I discovered Islamic civilization beyond its Middle East-Arab boundaries and confines. In the 1980s this journey included a dozen sub-Saharan countries, where I encountered Afro-Islam. In addition, and after 1995, I traveled to many parts of Southeast Asia, lived in Indonesia and discovered there a civil Islam. In these parts of the world I encountered non-Arab Islam, with great benefit. All of these varieties of Islam can be studied with the help of universal knowledge beyond the confines of cultural relativism.

In Singapore, I studied religious pluralism, but was dismayed and disappointed to see, in neighboring Malaysia, a kind of an ethnic-religious exclusivism that the Muslim Malay portion of the population practices. The Southeast Asian experience, together with my work in Africa, became the source of the *fourth* world of my life. It helped to overcome the Arabo-centric view of Islam that I internalized during my upbringing in Damascus. Again, these references are neither a distraction nor a digression; they are embedded in the cross-cultural scope of the present inquiry. At issue also is reference to the expression of a cross-cultural awareness that helps to underpin the scholarly insights of this book.

In my earlier book, *Political Islam, World Politics and Europe*, I referred in the preface to the great philosophers of cultural modernity – such as Descartes and Kant – to underline that humans think as subjects in their search for knowledge about the objective world. Consequently, in their efforts to look for objectivity, scholars, like all other humans, never abandon their subjectivity (note: this notion should not be confused with subjectivism). Even though I confess to not being a postmodernist, I acknowledge that in any analysis there is always a dimension of narrative, i.e. of subjectivity; however, clearly in the above-mentioned Cartesian sense of subjectivity, not of subjectivism. To deconstruct a narrative is not to negate the facts that underpin it and then end up in rubble as the result of an epistemological nihilism, which I dismiss. Certainly, every narrative has a core of objectivity, and this applies equally to the knowledge included in the presented book. This statement is most pertinent also to the narrative of Islam's predicament with modernity and to its peoples' perception of being under siege. This perception is based on a narrative, and there is some truth to it. The racialization of Muslim people that I complain of above is only one modest evidence of this perception and of what underpins it. One should beware of sound bites and not read into this statement that I share the view of an Islam under siege. I do not. The contention of a predicament is a different issue.

Cultural modernity, ethnicity, and Islam

On the side, I add one more project to the five research projects introduced above in the section on the research background of this book, even though the topic is not central to this book. It is the Stanford project on Ethnicity in Europe Today (2007/8). I believe, however, that ethnicity matters for the study of Islam and globalization. Globalization is often positively viewed as a source of cosmopolitanism. In fact, however, the shrinking of the world has contributed more to divisive ethnicity than to uniting cosmopolitan attitudes. Earlier, it was believed that cultural modernity contributes to overcoming ethnicity and leads to a cosmopolitan lifestyle in all cultures, but it did not do so. Just as much as there is a return of the sacred, there is also a return of ethnicity.

In the life between four worlds outlined above, I realized to what extent ethnicity persists. After eighteen years in Damascus I spent most of my life in the West, where I learned in my daily life that the assumed cosmopolitanism is no more than a rhetorical liberal pronouncement, even a stunt. Muslim immigrants to Europe are ethnically and socially excluded and they are denied a sense of belonging. Therefore they resort to their ethnic migrant identity. My very close attachment to German culture and deep love for its language are documented in the twenty-seven books that I have written in German, but this has not sufficed to facilitate a crossing of the ethnic-exclusive German threshold. There are European politicians and academics – above all, Germans – who indulge, in a self-congratulatory manner, in endless talk about the integration of Muslims, but they barely deliver what they promise. My search for refuge in other places in five continents worsened the issue. Ethnicity prevails not only in Europe. Living, lecturing, teaching, and doing research in numerous cultures across the world resulted in my becoming even more uprooted than ever before, and also in more pain. Given my privileged status as a professor, who, despite a deep knowledge on all these issues, fails to manage, it has to be asked how all other ordinary Muslims deal with their exposure to uprootedness in a disruptive world of uncertainty. The result is ethnicization, coupled with religionized identity politics. No wonder there are tensions and conflicts. This is reality, not a constructed polarization.

In the Stanford project mentioned above I confronted my peers with the outlined and shocking reality of Europe, where ethnicization is occurring under the conditions of globalization. This process is happening elsewhere (e.g. Iraq, Pakistan, Afghanistan) too. In all of these cases, the encountering of the ethnic other does not always happen in an enriching or receptive manner. An encounter with the stranger can be combined with a sense of fascination, but also with pain and tensions, not to mention cruelty. The response of Muslim immigrants in the West to an ethnic-exclusivist othering by the Europeans is the Islamist identity politics that they pursue. I am aware of how much this process worsens Islam's predicament with modernity, and that is why the issue is addressed here, because it contributes to the imagery of an Islam under siege that blocks any possibility of change.

The racialization of Muslim immigrants in Western societies undermines an accommodation and any bridging under conditions of globalization. It also affects the world of Islam itself. Instead of integration, a self-ethnicization of the Muslim *umma* is taking place. In its religious meaning, *umma* is not an ethnic concept at all, since it refers, rather, to a universal community of believers. However, the reality of the *umma* in Europe is definitely ethnic. A similar process could occur on a global basis if the imagery of Islam under siege were to result in an alleged clash of civilizations that became a self-fulfilling prophecy: the *umma* as a global ethnic group confronting the infidels.

Why do I address this issue here, given that the research plan for the book deals neither with Europe nor with global migration and diversity? Why this "digression"? There is a reason for the repeated reference to ethnicity in Europe. It is the fact that the ethnicization of Islam in the European diaspora worsens Islam's predicament with modernity, and also – as shown – that it could become a global source for related conflicts. While Muslims are challenged to engage in religious reform and cultural change, the European civilization, the homeland of cultural modernity, needs to fulfill what its model promises, but fails to deliver. The conclusion of this short section is that it is a fallacy to believe that Islam's predicament with modernity could be solved on European soil. Based on my experience as a Muslim immigrant in Europe, I challenge the view that the diaspora of Islam will be, as some US pundits believe, the location for a change that could affect Islam at home. It is true, Europe is a battlefield of Islamism, but it is most unlikely to be the model of change for Islam. Europeans themselves do not know much about this issue, even though, in a self-congratulatory manner, they accuse Americans of ignorance about Islam. The fact is that they too are ignorant. So, how could the Europeans be a model? Many experts turn a blind eye to ethnicity in Europe. Again, the view that Europe could be the place where Islam's predicament will be solved, or where Islam and democracy meet, is wrong. The potential is nil.

In the Stanford project on Ethnicity in Europe Today I maintained that there are two mutually reinforcing ethnicization processes, one among Muslim immigrants and the other among Europeans. I came to the conclusion that, under conditions of the new globalization, cultural and religious diversity not only tends to become a source of cultural fragmentation, but also contributes to promoting tensions and conflicts. The assumed standardization in culture has proven to be a fallacy based on mere wishful thinking. In Europe, the socially marginalized Muslims have no chance of engaging in an accommodation with a cultural modernity. In contrast, they resist integration in society, in the name of cultural diversity. The outcomes are ethnic enclaves, known as parallel societies. In this conflict-ridden situation, religion viewed as a cultural system becomes a framework for identity politics. I reiterate: Europe has become a battlefield of Islamism, but not a model for Islam to cope with its predicament with cultural modernity.

I conclude this section by stating that ethnicity runs counter to the idea and reality of pluralism of religions. The process of self-ethnicization of Muslims undermines the establishment of a cultural and religious pluralism in which diversity is attached to shared, core cultural values. This pluralism could never emerge and thrive in such an ethnic environment. As will be argued in Chapter 7, acceptance of religious pluralism is needed as the basis of a reform, but it is not in place. Ethnicity and pluralism are incompatible, and therefore "ethnic pluralism" is a contradiction in terms. The ethnicization of Islam in Europe is a very bad model. This is another reason why Europe will not become a theater for reform and change in Islam. The outcomes, rather, are tensions and conflicts.

Again: Islamology and the study of conflict

Let us now return to Islamology's social-scientific approach, introduced earlier, for the study of the interrelation of Islam and conflict in post-bipolar politics. The cross-cultural background of the present study, based on experience in global research networks, underpins the hypothesis that reform and cultural change in religion-based societies contribute not only to a positive transformation of society, but also to conflict resolution. Islamology is therefore not only a discipline for the study of cultural sources of conflict, but also for its resolution on different levels. One of these is related to cultural change and religious reform in a post-bipolar world-political context. The other is related to dialogue with the non-Muslim other. This dialogue can only be successful in a pluralistic set-up.

The study of conflict has never been the concern of traditional Islamic studies. The new discipline of Islamology deals with local and international conflicts that are underpinned by tensions related to religion and culture. In a perceptual rivalry between "them" and "us" as images of the other and the self, imagined communities emerge. The context for this process is the earlier outlined condition of racialization and self-ethnicization in which the Islamic notion of the *umma* assumes a different meaning in concrete situations: here it is ethnic, there it is a transnational *umma*. The related conflicts are not merely ideological, in that they emerge from a discrepancy between cultural change and social change. These issues are embedded in an international environment of polarization pursued through identity politics. It is intriguing, even most disturbing, to see that scholars who point out this conflict are accused of polarization. After I presented my paper to the Stanford project Ethnicity in Europe Today, some participants accused me of polarization. In reality, the ethnic parties involved are those who engage in ethnic polarization. I did not invent it. I was merely studying a situation on the ground. Of course, polarization is constructed by the parties involved, but in a conflict-ridden situation this kind of construction becomes a social reality in itself.

My thinking as a Muslim scholar living and commuting between four worlds and torn between the worldviews of different civilizations has found an intellectual shelter in the work of Max Weber. His notion of value-free knowledge, viewed as an expression of objectivity, may not apply fully, but it can be modified through reference to Habermas, who relates knowledge to *"Erkenntnisinteresse/ human interest."* With this in mind, in my research I maintained an awareness of the interest underlying the search for objective knowledge. Stated in epistemological terms, scholars are advised to develop an awareness of the interest driving their research in a situation of conflict. This is no contestation of objectivity. In following this recommendation I state my interest in the Islamological study of conflict: it is the search for accommodation and for a better place for Muslims in the twenty-first-century world. The Islamological analysis of conflict is thus free of any polarization. On the contrary, the plea for religious reforms and for cross-cultural fertilization in an age of religionized politics is driven by an intention to defuse existing tensions between civilizations. The problem is stated, the competing options are presented, and solutions are discussed. It is argued that Muslims need to engage in cultural change and religious reforms so as to ensure that Islam becomes a part of "democratic world peace" under conditions of religious and cultural pluralism that are based on rules to be shared by all. This makes diversity more sustainable and is therefore the preferred option. Muslims need to do their homework by rethinking the inherited Islamic concepts.

In anticipation of the findings in Chapter 7, I argue here that a culture of pluralism that combines diversity with universally accepted values and rules would be the best avenue for reducing cultural tensions and for preventing their development into conflict. Islamology deals not only with conflict, but also with ways of resolving it. In this sense it is divorced from the Cold War mindset of the earlier Sovietology, even though it shares with it the study of a global conflict.

In contemporary Islamic civilization there are two sources of conflict that seem to stand in contradiction to one another. On the one hand, you have the worldview that reinvents Islamic universalism by giving it the shape of an Islamist internationalism aimed at a remaking of the world order. On the other, you have ethnicity and ethnic conflict, which are fully related to local constraints. However, the global and the local affect one another in an interplay. Also, ethnic conflicts are embedded in transnational networks.

In my outlining of this Islamological study of conflict I am aware of the fact that there are Salafist and Islamist Muslims who dispute not only this inquiry, but also all kinds of related scholarly and rational thinking about Islam. Accusation of Islamophobia for relating Islam to conflict is on their agenda. For them, there exists only one immutable Islam and only those who submit to it are considered true Muslims. That submission is expected to be unquestioning, and those Muslims who so submit are considered to be "true believers." It is impossible to win the minds and hearts of those people who think in this way. Of course, there are other contenders, namely those Western essentialists who see in every Muslim a *homo Islamicus*. The most recent variety of this Western thinking in the racialization of all Muslims is the so-called "war on terror." Some Muslims respond to these Westerners with generalizations about conspiring "Jews and crusaders" – and also, of course, about their alleged Muslim allies – also ranked as "infidels" because they are accused of deviation from faith. In a project conducted with two Muslim colleagues in Melbourne, Shahram Akbarzadeh and Fathi Mansouri, I expressed my misgivings about the one-sided critique of the demonization of the other. One should not restrict the criticism solely to disapproving of the ways in which Islam is viewed in the West. One needs also to acknowledge candidly that Muslims engage in demonizing the "other" in their Westphobia. It follows that Western Islamophobia and Islamic Westphobia are two sides of the same coin; they reinforce one another. The development from tensions to conflict and its underlying constraints are the object of the study of the new discipline of Islamology. The approach focuses neither on faith nor on scripture. Instead, Islamology deals with reality and the related conflicts. However, unlike Sovietology, it is balanced. Islamology points indiscriminately to all evils, be they based in Islamophobia or in Westphobia. Sovietology was charged with anticommunism. Islamology not only is poised to be free of Islamophobia, but also claims to provide patterns for conflict resolution in a bridging process between the civilizations.

A part of the conflict to be illuminated by this Islamological study relates to modernity and the war of ideas. This notion of the "war of ideas" is believed to be a recent Western one denoting the competition of rival concepts such as jihadism and democratic peace. It is, however, much older and one can find it in the early literature of political Islam. It exists in the writings of Sayyid Qutb. The Islamists Ali Jarisha and Mohammed Zaibaq have revived it and maintain that "Jews and crusaders" are waging a war of ideas against Islam. Today, it is a risky venture to do impartial research in a world divided into Orientalist "right-wingers" who demonize Islam, and left-wing scholars who – as Orientalists in reverse – share a romanticization of the other in the benign colonial tradition of admiring and hating the "*bon sauvage*." The real right-wing Islamists are viewed, in this dichotomic distortion of a world turned upside down, as proponents of a liberation theology that contests Western globalization. Some Westerners overlook that political Islam's war of ideas includes not only incitement, but also Jew-hatred as a clear indication of a new antisemitism (e.g. Qutb, Jarisha and Zaibaq). One encounters not only Islamists, but also Western scholars who, in a war of ideas, use the propaganda of "invading crusaders." The formula *The New Crusaders* is used as the title of a book published by an Ivy League university press in the US. In such a world, rationality goes out of the window.

There is no doubt that globalization generates social inequality. In this process, Muslims are active subjects, and they are also responsible for determining their own destiny. They are not the subject of a "crusader conspiracy," as insinuated in the war of ideas. The defensive-cultural response to external exposure – be it globalization or the "war on terror" – is neither innovative nor creative. In contrast, cultural change can help to engage in promising activities for a better future. One cannot be a serious scholar and at the same time indict Western policies in the world of Islam – as flawed as these are – with an outrageous book title such as *The New Crusaders*. This formula resembles the propaganda language of Islamism that scholars are supposed to avoid.

Of course, one should side in the conflict against any totalitarianism. People of the Islamic civilization are part of humanity at large. Any related tensions and conflicts should be analyzed in order to suggest and promote a peaceful resolution. This is a better option than to join in the war of ideas that Qutb called for.

In the remainder of this introduction I shall discuss the structure of the book in more detail and introduce its eleven chapters, showing how they are linked to one another. This will be done in four steps that reflect the process followed in writing the book.

The structure and the substance of the book and its first step: the predicament and the related issue areas

In its first step the book introduces the major themes in Chapter 1, followed by an analysis of the three issue areas related to it in Chapters 2 to 4. In Chapter 1 I formulate the book's major assumption: Islam has to change in light of its predicament with modernity, and this is a feasible project. This assumption sounds like a self-evident statement, but it runs counter to the established view of an essential Islam, whether in the West, in the traditional orthodox-Salafist Islam, or in Islamism. The believed immutability of Islam is shared not only by contemporary Islamist and by Orientalist Western essentialism, but also by most common believers. The view of a *homo Islamicus* is for the one a belief, and for the other a prejudice. Belief in an immutable Islam is based on the authority of the revealed text and on the Islamic doctrine that the Qur'an is based on verbal inspiration. The Muslim *ulema* believe that it provides a point of finality for humanity. It is true that the revealed text does not change, but its understanding by human beings is always subject to time and space. Therefore, reform Islam places the text that is perceived to be divine into a historical context and permits thinking about it. To avoid ambiguity, it is emphasized that religious reform is much more than just the provision of another interpretation of the text of the Qur'an. In an effort at a historicization of an Islam understood to be always in flux, Chapter 1 aims first to shatter the Islamic belief of immutability.

The point of departure of Chapter 1 is that Islamic civilization has problems with modernity under conditions of globalization. These problems are viewed as a novel predicament. The assumption based on this argument is that the predicament of Islam with modernity gives rise to cultural tensions and to conflict. The chapter then presents the concepts of religious reform and cultural change as an avenue for peaceful conflict resolution. Religious reform relates to the concept of change and to its cultural accommodation. To reach this end, an awareness on the part of the Islamic people of the realities on the ground beyond the divine text is a basic requirement. This awareness should replace the inherited scriptural references.

Further, Chapter 1 draws on the findings of the UNDP report of 2002 completed for the United Nations by Arab experts. This report suggests that the Arab world – being the core of the Islamic civilization – is, on a variety of counts, an underachiever. It not only lags behind all international standards of development, but is also not competitive with rising non-Western parts of the world (e.g. India or China). Then a major question is asked: why is this so? The chapter joins with the authors of this UN report and also of the CMRP team (see Chapter 1, note 1) in arguing that the cultural factor matters. It also adds religion, viewed as a cultural system, to argue for religious reform. In contrast to medieval Islam, which was, in its time, a leading civilization, the contemporary world of Islam – of course within inner diversity, and thus to varying degrees – is, comparatively speaking, among the least developed and the least democratized parts of the entire world. Islam yesterday and Islam today are therefore not based on the same culture. This first chapter suggests that a combination of cultural change and religious reform is needed to overcome the malaise and to provide the societies of contemporary Islam with better future prospects. The contemporary predicament with cultural modernity gives rise to questions, themes, and the related basic assumptions all dealt with here. The conceptual frame of reference of the present study is also outlined in Chapter 1.

The predicament analyzed in general in Chapter 1 is determined to exist in three basic issue areas: knowledge, law, and human rights. These are the themes of Chapters 2 to 4, in which these three areas of Islam's predicament with modernity are singled out and subjected to an in-depth analysis. Chapter 2 starts with the interplay of culture and knowledge under the conditions of exposure to modernity. It views contemporary Islamic civilization as torn between reason and Islamization. In a contestation of postmodern cultural relativism a universal knowledge is argued for. In view of the fact that the knowledge prevailing in a society informs best of the performance of its people, this subject has been chosen as the central theme in the study of an exposure to cultural modernity. In international relations knowledge is – as argued with E. Haas in Chapter 2 – power. Students of Islam are familiar with a debate among educated Muslims on the instruction of the Prophet to borrow knowledge "even from China." In contrast to this open-minded Islam, at present Islamists call for an Islamization, i.e. for a purification, of knowledge. It is conceded that every culture is related to a pattern of knowledge, but without, however, sharing the ridiculous conclusion of a cultural anthropology of knowledge. Cultural diversity does not stand in contradiction to the idea that rational knowledge can be shared by people of different cultures and religions. In contrast to postmodernism, rational knowledge is viewed as universal. What is black and what is white is never a matter of dispute among rational people. Borrowing from others is also an essential part of human history, and is also most prominent in Islam. It is argued first that cultural modernity also includes an agenda for reason-based knowledge. Even though this rationalism is not alien to medieval Islam, it creates a predicament for contemporary Muslims. Why? Have they forgotten their own classical heritage? It is one of the tasks of Chapter 2 to provide solid answers to these questions. There is a connection between Chapter 2, on knowledge and Chapter 8, on authenticity. For Islamists today, authenticity means "purification" of Islam from the influence of all alien knowledge. In the better days of Islam, Muslims learned from other cultures. This cross-cultural learning did not harm their authenticity; they were free from this spirit of purification, and in this mindset Muslim rationalists enriched Islamic civilization through cultural borrowing from the non-Muslim other.

Three arguments stand at the core of Chapter 2. *First*, rational knowledge is reason based and is therefore decoupled from faith and from the sacred. According to this understanding, knowledge about society and its polity has to be secular. On this basis, only rational and secular knowledge could claim universal validity. *Second*, cultural knowledge could impede or promote the transformation of society. If it admits a related thinking that is subject to change and denies immutable knowledge, then it opens the door to a better future. *Third*, cultural diversity between and within the various civilizations can be combined with shared cultural knowledge. Thus, the chapter rejects the assumptions of cultural relativism applied to knowledge in anthropological studies through the formula of "anthropoligization of knowledge." From the point of view of universal rationality this approach is a non-starter. In anticipation of the discussion in Chapter 8, on the Islamic classical heritage of the Hellenization of medieval Islam based on universal rationalism, a reference is made to Islamic thought in that epoch. The reference contradicts both the political program of an Islamization and Western cultural relativism. The agenda of an Islamization of knowledge ends up in the preaching of a kind of flat-earthism. In the end, it hampers not only progress in Muslim societies, but also intercultural communication between Muslims and the non-Muslim other. The de-Westernization drive of the Islamists does not end in the search for an "Islamic science" based on an exclusive divine knowledge, but it is also extended into a holistic program. This defensive culture exacerbates Islam's predicament with modernity, instead of resolving it.

The next issue area in Islam's predicament with cultural modernity is law in relation to state, and society. In this context, contemporary Muslims engage in a reinvention of the shari'a in a pursuit named in this book the "shari'atization of Islam vs. legislative constitutionalism." This invention occurs in opposition to accommodation of secular and legislative law, which is an essential part of cultural modernity. In the West, legal and other scholars confuse globalization and universalization; thereby they overlook the fact that each civilization has its own legal tradition. In Islam, law is still shari'a. During the course of European expansion and at an earlier stage of globalization Muslims succumbed to the Western concept of universal law. Today, and in the context of an Islamic revival, the contestation is expressed within the framework of the return of the sacred. It is associated with the claim for a shari'atization of politics and society. This is the agenda of an Islamization that legitimizes an alternative Islamist model pursued in a spirit of purification.

The universalism of Islam serves to underpin the claims made for a remaking of the world in line with the tenets of a constructed shari'a as divine law. Islamists turn the tables round: they switch their predicament with modernity into one of others and contend a decline of secular law. In this context, the post-bipolar *New Cold War* (Mark Juergensmeyer) between the religious and the secular is extended into a legal contest. Chapter 3 therefore locates the claims associated with the return of the sacred in legal politics. Contemporary Islamic and Islamist legal politics is committed to an agenda of shari'atization of Islam. It begins with the construction of a constitutional law for what is contended to be an Islamic polity. Islamists develop this idea further to claim an Islamic state. This concept heralds a conflict related to Islam's predicament, and is not the solution, as it is pronounced to be. Then, the shari'atization agenda is extended into a claim for an Islamic shari'a-based world order. The claim is coupled with an envisioned de-secularization that is attached to a "purification" of law along the understanding already outlined. In this thinking, Islam is expanded into a global civilizational project based on Islamic authenticity. The Islamist Anwar al-Jundi is the ideologue of a purification project presented in the garb of "authenticity." It is intriguing to see some postmodernists – without knowing these details – approve what is named "authenticity."

A further part of the analysis of Islam's predicament is provided in Chapter 4. Here, the third issue area singled out is individual human rights. The analysis begins with "the principle of subjectivity" (Habermas) viewed as an embodiment of modernity. It is also the substance of the concept of individual human rights. There are Muslims and non-Muslims who deny the place of culture as a dimension of the lack of human rights and simply reduce the related violations to political authoritarianism. These people overlook the cultural predicament at issue.

Today, some Salafists and Islamists emulate Christians in their assertion that individual human rights are rooted in one's own religion. In contrast to these beliefs, Chapter 4 argues that individual human rights, understood in the specific meaning of the entitlement of the individual vis-à-vis state and society, are a novelty based in cultural modernity; they are secular and therefore not rooted in any religion. The fact that the "principle of subjectivity," on which the concept of individual human rights rests, is secular contradicts all religious claims. Individual human rights expose all religions to a predicament with cultural modernity. Starting with this insight, Chapter 4 assumes a related conflict and attempts to explain it. According to the doctrine of "*faraid*/duties," a Muslim has obligations to the *umma*, but no rights as entitlements. Submission to God's rules and to the *umma* is the substance. Islam's exposure to modernity in the context of the introduction of a concept of rights puts this cultural system into a predicament and generates conflicts. Also in this domain, religious reform and cultural change are needed, but are ignored by authoritative Muslim human rights authors (Ghazali, Imara). In a similar vein, "The Islamic Declaration of Human Rights" simply ignores all of the current challenges. Instead of providing an Islamic cultural foundation for individual human rights, these people distort the true meaning of these rights to engage in defensive-cultural apologetics based on the self-congratulating assurance that Islam is not only the source of all knowledge and of law, but also of all human rights. The results are tensions that Muslim people face in their knowledge of the world, as well as in their understanding of law. Globally, the Islamic world heads the violators of human rights. Add to this the fact that most Islamic countries are underachievers in the post-bipolar process of global democratization.

The second step: from tensions to conflict

The discord over values creates tensions that lead to conflict. The assumption is that value conflict matters. This is not a cover for what is viewed as a "clash of interests." The assumption of a value conflict is formulated in Chapter 5, in which an analysis of cultural-religious tensions is provided, with a focus on the related identity politics. These are the two major themes in Chapter 5, which are central to the entire structure of the present study. The significance of this chapter resembles that of the stage-setting Chapter 1, in which the major assumptions and themes of the entire inquiry are presented.

Chapter 5 translates the analysis of the preceding first step into the language of international relations and its study of conflict. Islam's predicament with cultural modernity is viewed as a pertinent issue for the study of conflict in the twenty-first century. This cannot be well understood without dealing seriously with the construction of fault lines, as expressed in Islamic identity politics guided by a perception of Islam under siege. One encounters, in this context, two major issue areas relevant to the creation of tensions and fault lines, namely the jihadization of jihad and the shari'atization of shari'a, to be analyzed at length. In the search for solutions, Chapter 5 concludes with a debate on a civil Islam and on its potential to provide light at the end of the tunnel, i.e. peaceful conflict resolution. The plea for a civil Islam compels reiteration of the repeatedly emphasized need for religious reform and cultural change that provide a way out of the predicament. Civil Islam is in conflict with Salafism and also with Islamism. Instead of engaging in a polarization, as both of these do, civil Islam aims to bridge between civilizations. However, a civil Islam is unthinkable without a religious reform and cultural change that is based on an acknowledgment of the predicament that leads to tensions and conflicts. This insight leads to the third step in this undertaking, in which highly topical themes are addressed.

The third step: secularization and pluralism between reform and authenticity

In order to come to terms with Islam's predicament with modernity, an Islamic embracing of secularization and of pluralism is an option that may not be a popular choice but that is urgently needed, even though it is denied authenticity. Chapters 6 to 8 engage in this third step. To begin with, secularization is viewed as a social process of inner differentiation in society. It is often confused with the ideology of secularism, incriminated by Islamists as a "*kufr*/heresy," or more, as a *mu'amarah*, a Jewish conspiracy against Islam. One finds this antisemitic propaganda put forward unambiguously in the literature of political Islam, for instance by Faruq Abdul-Salam. In putting this aside, one has to acknowledge that the challenge Islam faces in its predicament with cultural modernity is related to the secularization process in society and in its international environment.

As noted, confusion between secularism and secularity prevails among Muslims. The distinction is that the first is an ideology, while the second is a state of affairs in society and polity. From the late nineteenth century until 1967 secularism prevailed as an ideology among Western-educated Muslim elites, but it has declined in developments since 1967. These secular outlooks corresponded neither with secular structures in society, nor with a change in the prevailing worldview. Along with the return of the sacred performed by political Islam, a process of de-secularization has been launched. Chapter 6 covers the Islamic debate on secularization and de-secularization and analyzes Islam's predicament with the disenchantment of the world that forms the substance of cultural modernity. It is argued that cultural modernity is by definition secular, and therefore it is inferred that the formula "Islamic modernity" is a contradiction in terms. It is intriguing to see that "Islamic modernism" has different meanings, one of them denoting an ideology of conformism. Comparatively speaking, no one claims a Jewish or a Christian modernity, so why then an Islamic modernity?

The view articulated throughout the book is that the claim for a unique and peculiar Islamic modernity only serves as a legitimation for the pervasive evasion of Islam's predicament. This is made even more clear in Chapter 7, on pluralism. This is a concept that has its origin in political science. It is based on the combination of political diversity and a consensus on core values and rules in a system of parliamentary democracy. In past years I was involved in the implementation and application of this concept to religion and culture. When it comes to Islam, one faces great obstacles. Basic among them is the Islamic view of the history of humankind as one of divine revelations. Islam is believed to be the final one among them and therefore it claims to be the only true and complete monotheism. There are many Muslims who infer from this belief the *"siyadat al-Islam*/supremacy of Islam" and who advance it to a claim. Now, pluralism acknowledges diversity, but also presupposes the equality of all actors. The application of this concept to religions as religious pluralism requires that Muslims accept the equality of all the religions of the non-Muslim others. This requirement can only be fulfilled by a reform Islam. This is a highly difficult and equally unpopular task, often silenced by a reference to "Islamic sensibilities," while altogether ignoring the sensibility of the non-Muslim other.

The combination of the two themes of secularity and pluralism in the bundle of issue areas is enhanced in Chapter 8 by the inclusion of authenticity in the basket. This theme is related to Islam's predicament with cultural modernity, since the authenticity of borrowings from cultural modernity is questioned. Here, diversity and cultural revival are put on the table. Further in Chapter 8, the idea of a revival of the classical heritage of Islamic rationalism is referred to. The background to this reference is that some contemporary Muslim opinion leaders flatly reject secularity and pluralism, using the argument that they are alien to Islam. Instead of cultural borrowing, they reclaim authenticity. The foremost Islamist ideologue of authenticity, Anwar al-Jundi, defines the source of cultural modernity, enlightenment, as a "Jewish masterplan" and discards it in the name of *"asalah*/authenticity." A close reading clearly reveals what authenticity means for him: cultural purification. In contrast to this, the student of Islam encounters the inherited conflict between *"falsafa*/rational philosophy" and *"fiqh*-orthodoxy" in Islam. Chapter 8 reminds us of this inner-Islamic conflict, because it is pertinent to the contemporary debate on authenticity. In their resistance to the project of modernity, Islamists and Salafists speak of an authentic revival of a suppressed tradition. Most Muslims resort to tradition when they face exposure to modernity. This is also a search for authenticity that mostly takes place in pre-modern cultures. Clearly, culture is hereby often not only constructed, but also reinvented and imbued with a new meaning, although presented in the garb of authenticity. Chapter 8 turns the table on the Salafists and Islamists and argues that medieval Islamic rationalism (e.g. Averroism) was then more authentic than is the political Islam of today.

Social deprivation and cultural alienation predate post-bipolarity, but it is only since the end of the East–West conflict that the search for authenticity in culture and politics has moved to center stage. However, it is guided by an ideology of purification and ends up by othering all that is considered to be alien to the self. This alienates Muslims from the rest of humanity, because they reject everything alien to them as "un-Islamic." Chapter 8 therefore challenges the established meaning of the notion of authenticity as a search for foundations that excludes borrowing from others. As said, I turn the table on Islamists and state that this is not an Islamic tradition. In this way I expose authenticity as a concept for promoting an Islamist agenda of cultural purification. In contrast to this Islamist mindset and its related efforts, I put forward the argument that the heritage of medieval Islamic rationalism is authentic, even though it was based on learning and cultural borrowing from others. Hellenism was the major source of inspiration for Islamic rationalism. Its heritage provides the real, authentic sources for those among today's Muslims who are willing to solve Islam's pre-dicament with cultural modernity on Islamic grounds. The chapter joins the contemporary Muslim philosopher Mohammed al-Jabri in arguing that a better future for Islam "can only be Averroist." Ibn Rushd/Averroes was the leading rationalist of the medieval Islamic heritage. The onus is on open-minded Muslims to revive this legacy, as Chapter 8 proposes.

The reference to the example of Hellenization in medieval Islamic civilization serves not only as a model to draw on for the present, but also because it underpins the fact that Islam is in a position to engage in cross-cultural fertilization. In its capacity as an open Islam, it was capable of thriving as a leading civilization. The argument that the provision of an Islamic cultural underpinning is a requirement for promoting the process of rationalization/secularization is combined with a reference to authentic sources. A comparison is made between two Islamic experiments: Hellenization and Westernization. The first was successful because it was authentic, the second failed, not only because of the different unfavorable conditions, but also because it lacked authenticity and therefore could not strike roots. I definitely use the term "authenticity" in this book with a different meaning.

The fourth step: case studies

Based on the hard work achieved in the outlined three steps of the first eight chapters, the book moves on, in this fourth step, its final part, to case studies. Egypt and the Arab Gulf are selected. For good or for ill, Egypt has been the model for all developments that have occurred in the Islamic world. This assertion is supported by the case study in Chapter 9, which demonstrates that all of the themes in this book are best exemplified by the case of Egypt. The predicament itself and all tensions and conflicts can be observed in that country, whether secularization and de-secularization, or the search for authenticity. Egypt has been the central stage for the encounter of Islam with cultural modernity. This process began in 1798, when Napoleon came to that Islamic country.

All developments in the world of Islam, stretching from early Islamic reform and modernism in the nineteenth century, across the interval of secular nationalism of the twentieth century, up to the present rise of political Islam, started in Egypt. For this reason Egypt has been chosen for the case study in Chapter 9. As already stated, with the invasion of Egypt by Napoleon, who came there as a conqueror, the ideas and the spirit of the French Revolution entered, by "a cunning of reason" (Hegel), the world of Islam. Egypt, when confronted with Europe, displays the two basic dimensions of modernity already discussed in Chapter 1: first, the institutional dimension of power that begins with Napoleon in Egypt in 1798 and continues with the British colonization; second, the cultural modernity that contributed to the rise of Western-educated Egyptian elites with their modern, reformist, and secular outlooks. These developments and directions are all analyzed in this case study. The failure of modernization in Egypt is related to the fact that all of these elites evaded openly addressing Islam's predicament. This failure led to the rise of political Islam. The first movement of Islamism, the Society of the Muslim Brothers, was established in Egypt in 1928 and remains located there as a center of political Islam that has become a transnational movement, operating around the globe. From Egypt the Muslim Brothers spread to all parts of the Islamic civilization, including its diaspora in Europe and even the US. The analysis of all of these mentioned stages underpins and demonstrates the great significance of Egypt to the study of Islam and modernity. The choice of this country as a characteristic case is justified by the facts. The case study allows for some far-reaching generalizations.

The second case study, in Chapter 10, deals with the Arab-Persian Gulf. The choice could be contested by the fact that the small but wealthy five Gulf states (Kuwait, Bahrain, Qatar, Oman, and the United Arab Emirates/UAE) are, on most counts – foremost, culturally and religiously – not so significant as Egypt. This is true. However, the oil wealth and the geo-strategic significance of these states place them, despite all odds, at center stage. Therefore, it is argued that development in the Gulf matters not only to the West, but also to the Islamic world, as well as to the world at large. In a research project conducted in Abu Dhabi at the Emirates Center for Political and Strategic Studies a team of experts (of which I was a member) engaged in thinking about the future of the Gulf beyond oil. The chapter is based on the research done in this context and draws on the related findings. It proposes reforms and changes for the accommodation of a culture of progress that could contribute to better transformation of the Gulf societies in a future beyond oil. The reforms proposed and discussed in the chapter touch on the overall subject matter of this book and are of great relevance to the outlooks it presents. It is highly pertinent to note that the proposition of reform and change found in that Arab Muslim country open ears and, even more, that the results were published in Arabic and English (see Chapter 10, note 1) in Abu-Dhabi.

And what are the preliminary conclusions?

At the end of the journey, comprising eight theme-focused chapters and two case studies, the book ends in Chapter 11 with conclusions drawn from the work accomplished. The conclusions are embedded in a general debate on cultural modernity and the Islamic illusion of splitting it so as to allow an Islamic dream of semi-modernity. The notion of cultural schizophrenia was once introduced by the Iranian Muslim scholar Daryush Shayegan in his analysis of Islamic civilization, *Confronting the West*, concerning the two opposing options of "Westernization and Islamization" (chapter 2 in his book). No doubt there is something in the notion of cultural schizophrenia, but I dismiss the choice that he presents. In contrast to Shayegan, I argue that the choice is much broader and I also have a different take. Above all, Muslims have the more promising choice of cultural change and religious reforms, of avoiding not only the polarization between "Westernization and Islamization" but also the pitfalls of cultural schizophrenia. An authentic Islamic embrace of cultural modernity should not be dismissed as Westernization. It is feasible to pursue innovative cultural change and far-reaching religious reforms in creative and rational Islamic terms.

The reader is reminded of the two dimensions of modernity, the one institutional and the other cultural. Shayegan's notion of "Islamic societies confronting the West" dilutes highly important distinctions. There are Islamic and Islamist responses to modernity, with the illusion that the revival of tradition will do. This revival is, however, by no means the expression of a re-traditionalization of politics, as some suggest. The reference to tradition as a response is embedded in the project addressed as semi-modernity. Islamists recognize that they cannot prevail without adopting basic items of modernity, and thus they are poised to embrace instrumentally modern science and technology. At the same time they dismiss the human-based worldview and the secular values that underpin the instrumental modernity they are willing to adopt. Their splitting of modernity into techno-scientific instruments and culture is coupled with an inclination to adopt the one and simultaneously to dismiss the other. It is embarrassing, but I have to mention it for the sake of integrity: the Nazis were instrumentally highly modern, but they flatly dismissed cultural modernity. That was also semi-modernity, and it provides a historical lesson. Muslims and Islamists today seem not to have learned this lesson. Their mindset of instrumental semi-modernity is analyzed and identified in Chapter 11, with the conclusion that this semi-modernity evades all the aspects of Islam's predicament with modernity that are analyzed in the present book. It provides no way out. Islamic and Islamist "half-modernists" fail, in consequence, to provide any light at the end of a very dark tunnel. The predicament will persist so long as Muslims reject addressing the issues and the related challenges. This missing homework Muslim needs to be addressed, in all openness.

The book relates this "semi-modernity" to its core idea, namely to the assumption that cultural tensions emanate from Islam's predicament and lead to international conflict. There is a perception of an Islam under siege which is, in this context of conflict, most perilous. The adoption of the instruments of modernity in "Islam's geo-civil war" (John Brenkman) serves to fight against those who are perceived as the enemies of Islam putting it "under siege." This mindset does not help to come to terms with modernity, but rather is a threatening reality of terror. The use of modern science and technology in the pursuit of parochial ends in religionized conflicts is a real threat, and this is not a myth. At issue is not only what is named E-jihad and cyber-jihad, but also nuclear proliferation. Iran is a case in point. When conflicts are religionized they become intractable – see Hamas in Palestine and Hezbollah in Lebanon. The perils matter to Muslims and to non-Muslims alike. Those who do not admit the study of cultural tensions viewed as a source of international conflict turn a blind eye to a major dimension of post-bipolar world politics, as well as to the new role of Islam in religionized conflicts. In contrast, the present book is a modest contribution aimed at enlightening the reader on these issues. The religionization of conflict by Islamism is definitely not a passing fog. At issue is a phenomenon that seemingly will prevail throughout the new century. There are many scholars who are not receptive to this analytical forecast. Knowing the obstacles in the way of this thinking, I not only hope that this book will see light, but also for readers who will be willing to listen to the argument before contesting it. The deplorable culture of sound bites that dominates today has taken the place of careful reading. This is obvious in the debate on Islam and on its place in the twenty-first century. The issues addressed are serious, and they deserve a serious debate. It would be a minimum of civility and impartial scholarship to expect admission of the debate that this book claims to open.

The predicament: the exposure to cultural modernity, and the need for an accommodation

Religious reform and cultural change in Islamic civilization

Continuing the themes of the Introduction, where the course was outlined, in this chapter I address the major subject matter of the book. The chapter acquaints the reader with Islam's predicament, applying the approach of "developing cultures," adopted from the Culture Matters Research Project/ CMRP.[1] The starting point is the historical reality of the Islamic civilization's exposure to cultural modernity in the context of European expansion and the globalization that this has triggered. In fact, modern science and technology provided the tools that enabled this expansion to occur successfully. Since then, Islam has been not only in crisis, but also in conflict with itself. In pondering the European expansion, which was facilitated by the achievements of modernity, Hegel in his *Rechtsphilosophie*/Philosophy of Law noted that civil society in Europe is driven, by its own dynamic, to expand beyond its boundaries and reach out to the entire world.[2]

The process at issue is general in its coverage of the entire globe, triggered by European expansion. This process has affected all other civilizations, above all that of Islam. This last fact is true for the simple reason that Islamic civilization also has a claim to universality. The Islamic project of globalization long predates the Western one. The global rise of the West since the sixteenth century, particularly within the framework of a "military revolution"[3] during the years 1500–1800, is perceived to have occurred at the expense of Islam. Add to that, that European expansion also succeeded in encompassing the Islamic world. The Muslims, who were conquerors, now became the conquered. For them, this is hard to swallow. Earlier, from the seventh century through the seventeenth century, Islamic civilization had prevailed and dominated in important areas of the world. However, it failed to stretch its model of globalization[4] to cover the entire world, as did European civilization later on. Due to its techno-scientific accomplishments, based on the Industrial Revolution, Western civilization was able to conquer the entire world and to envelop it in its civilizational project. This process has created lasting pain for people of the Islamic civilization. The politicization of the related cultural-religious tensions has led to conflict which is articulated today as a defensive-cultural response that legitimates political and violent action.

These givens are the starting point for dealing with the change in contemporary Islamic societies in the context of post-bipolar politics, and this is what underlies the phenomenon of Islam's predicament with modernity, which predates post-bipolarity. Today, the Islamic people contest the outcome of this development and are staking a claim to reverse it. However, in this contest Islamic civilization lacks the tools needed to deliver what it claims. The result is an international conflict arising from the tensions related to Islam's predicament with modernity.

That having been said, there is nothing more remote from my mind, as a scholar of Muslim faith, than to engage in Huntington's "clash" rhetoric. When I identify a conflict and deal with it, I determine first that it is a conflict and not a clash, and look for peaceful solutions. In this undertaking I neither essentialize nor polarize. Unlike a clash, conflict can be solved. In the search for a way out, this book proposes religious reform and cultural change in the Islamic world. This is viewed as the solution to the crisis and is the frame of reference determining all the thinking of the present book.

Introduction

The focus of this chapter is the exposure of the civilization of Islam to cultural modernity and the predicament emerging therefrom – not on modernity itself. Nevertheless, the reference to modernity needs to be spelled out so as to make the issue clear. Here I will confine myself to distinguishing between two dimensions of the same modernity, the one cultural and the other institutional. In his *Philosophical Discourse of Modernity*, Jürgen Habermas outlines what cultural modernity is, namely the "principle of subjectivity/*Subjektivitätsprinzip*," as based on the major European historical events of the Renaissance, the Reformation, the Enlightenment, and the French Revolution.[5] The other dimension of modernity is related to power and it is this institutional modernity, analyzed by Anthony Giddens,[6] that Muslims know best. However, the two dimensions are related to one another, similarly to the *Dialectic of Enlightenment*, which includes not only enlightenment, but also a dark side that it has.[7]

Non-Westerners, whom Europeans deny to have any history,[8] have been the victims of a European expansion[9] facilitated by institutional modernity. Napoleon pronounced the principles of the French Revolution to the Muslim people on his conquest of Cairo in 1798, but they felt only the power of his army's guns. Later, Muslim rulers thought that importing a European army would adjust the imbalance of power.[10] This real history is the background to the Muslims' confusion and their equation of cultural modernity with institutional modernity, as addressed in the Introduction. This will be discussed in more detail in this chapter. The conflict based on the exposure of the Islamic people to Europe and to Western civilization is anything but a "clash of civilizations."[11] Institutional modernity is also a modernity of power and of hegemony. However, exposure to cultural modernity is a different issue. It was exposure to a worldview that helped Europe to advance – a worldview that is human centered and no longer God centered. To state this is not to deny religion, but just to restrict it to faith. Secularization[12] should not be equated with atheism, as is done today by most Islamists and Salafists. In contrast, I refer to it with the Weberian meaning that is also employed by Habermas. It simply means the "*Entzauberung*/disenchantment" of the world. This rationality was not alien to Islam when it had a highly developed civilization, as this book will argue. One of the pillars of European cultural modernity is the Renaissance. Those who study history without a Eurocentric bias are aware of the fact that Western civilization's Renaissance owes a great deal, culturally, to Islam. The Renaissance – and earlier the Hellenization of Islam – were bridges in the civilizational encounters between Islam and Europe. So why cannot cultural modernity be such a bridge in the twenty-first century?

In the first part of this book I will set all postmodern talk about "multiple modernities" on one side and focus instead on three issue areas of modernity that greatly affect Islam. After this introductory chapter I deal, in separate chapters, first with reason-based knowledge, second with law and legislative constitutionalism, and third with individual human rights. I am aware that this selection is not exhaustive. However, these are major issue areas of modernity. The predicament of Islam with cultural modernity predates the post-bipolar politics of civilizational conflict as well as the culture-based tensions that it generates and that lead to conflict. Nonetheless, post-bipolarity is the new context that gives the conflict a new shape. This chapter argues that religious reform and cultural change would open an avenue for a peaceful resolution of the conflict. Before reaching this level of analysis, one needs first to deal with the predicament itself, which is the task of this chapter

The starting point is the historical fact of the Islamic civilization's exposure to European expansion. This process has been related to a structural change in society, economy, and politics. This change in the Islamic world was determined by external powers and by the global standards that they established. Since decolonization, schools of thought based on Eurocentric evolutionism and the similarly minded modernization theory[13] have suggested that change in values and attitudes in the Islamic world will automatically follow the path of social and economic change. In reality, however, religion and Islamic values, norms, and worldviews persisted and did not change in the way that modernization theorists anticipated. In this chapter the idea of cultural change is connected with changes in religion itself, addressed in terms of religious reform. Without denying the existence of "essentialism" in Western scholarship (and among Muslims themselves), it can be said that this very notion, which implies that culture is essential and not changeable, has been degraded into an invective. The notion of essentialism is often employed in a meaningless manner to discredit those who do not subscribe to postmodern cultural relativism. Similarly to Edward Said's originally legitimate critique of Orientalism, which was then derailed to an Orientalism in reverse,[14] the cultural-anthropological criticism of Western essentialism has become stranded in a self-made impasse. Setting these unfruitful debates on one side, this book presents the idea that, alongside economically and politically developing societies, there are also developing cultures. Islam's predicament with cultural modernity expresses either a reluctance to change or an inappropriate pattern of change, such as the movement from shari'a to shari'atization. This change is detrimental to the people of Islamic civilization.

Why recourse to this topic as an opening? It is, of course, because in European thinking on Islam one finds the stereotype of a *homo Islamicus*, based on an essentialized preconception of people of the Islamic civilization. They are viewed as humans who act in accord with cultural patterns that do not change. Against this essentializing European prejudice, it can be argued that Islam has always been in flux. However, religious reform based on rethinking Islam is a different issue, more than a mere change. Not only are there the stereotypes of Western Orientalism, but there are also Muslims who essentialize Islam by putting it above time and space and thus dismiss any notion of change, not to mention reform. In contrast to both, this book argues for change. It seems to me, as a scholar of Muslim background, to be more promising to focus on the ways in which Muslims themselves respond to and view processes of change – understood with the meaning outlined above – rather than to spend time in Western debates on Orientalism and essentialism. I prefer not to respond to the discrediting of my work by those who accuse me of "self-Orientalization" and of "essentializing Islam." Attentive readers will easily discover that such reproaches do not apply and that they can never hold water.

In fact, the claim of "one unchangeable Islam above time and space" comes also from the Muslim Salafists, who conceive of a primordial Islam in these terms. A balanced Muslim critical reasoning must deal not only with the distortions of Orientalism, but also with the Islamic obstacle to change that is so detrimental to the people of the Islamic civilization. This is a much more promising endeavor than the boring debates of European or American students of Islam obsessed with their "Orientalism"[15] or an "Orientalism in reverse" (see note 14). One expects analysis, but instead gets biased opinion pieces. This straight talk is necessary in order to outline the agenda of this book, and also to defend it and its ideas against the possibility of being discredited.

Stated in plain language, Islam is – just as much as the people who adhere to the faith and its cultural system – always in flux, and thus subject to change. There are many Muslims who do not accept this idea. Some prudent Muslims concede that believers may change, but they continue to believe that Islam itself is above change because it is – as a final revelation – supposed to be perfect. This essentialized religion of Islam is precluded from change, and also from reform. In contrast to this view, the present book relates the concept of cultural change to religion and infers the need for religious reform that will allow Muslims to rethink existing concepts that they consider sacred. This is necessary for the cultural accommodation of social and political change. Muslims need to engage in a religious reform that goes far beyond the admitted reinterpretation of the holy texts in order to come to terms with the current issues. In a situation of crisis there is no escape from a rethinking of Islam that seriously addresses its predicament with cultural modernity. To engage in such an undertaking is neither heresy nor Orientalism; rather, it is an effort at cultural innovation for the benefit of Muslims and their civilization. To take up a position in the tradition of "defenders of reason" in Islam is a great service to this civilization.

As noted earlier, participation in the Culture Matters Research Project/ CMRP at the Fletcher School of Law and Diplomacy (see note 1) facilitated new insights into cultural change, which were applied to the study of Islamic civilization. It was recognized that value change is imperative in order to overcome a state of underdevelopment. Included here is religious reform, itself a key issue in the social transformation of society, as a means to smoothing the way to cultural change. The adoption of this approach in the present book reflects neither "culturalism" nor susceptibility to "Orientalism." In arguing that in no other civilization does "culture matter" for social change to the extent that it does in the Islamic world, I present an argument against essentialism – regardless of its source – as well as against all kinds of Orientalist bias.

One cannot repeat enough: courageous Muslims who dare to engage in a rethinking of their culture and of religion and to put their worldview in line with existing realities are neither involving themselves in cultural treason nor committing heresy – not mention the ridiculous accusation of "self-Orientalization." This insight runs counter to established wisdom. To question the religious claim to immutability is nothing less than to contribute to facilitating a process of change and to overcoming Salafist essentialism. Their inherited worldview prevents Muslims from accepting cultural and value change – which is occurring anyway and despite any beliefs to the contrary. Muslims socialized in this Islamic worldview[16] are confronted throughout their life with ongoing political and social change in Islamic societies. Those among them who recognize the need for cultural change and religious reform are familiar with the cultural obstacles standing in the way of development, as well as with the sanctions against thinking Muslims that are imposed by Salafists and Islamists.

The contemporary experience of democratization teaches that political change cannot successfully be introduced from outside while ignoring the insight that culture matters and that it can only be changed by the people concerned. In stating this, I am not ignoring the fact that the needed change matters as much to non-Muslims as it does to Muslims and their societies. As will be shown in Chapter 5, the Western as well as the non-Western environments of the Islamic world (e.g. Asia) alike are affected by conflicts ignited by political Islam. Democratization is a precondition for accepting pluralism and the vision of democratic peace proposed for all on a global basis. This perspective is challenged by the shari'atization of Islam and by the pressure of Islamists for an Islamic state, presented as "al-hall/ the solution" for the entire world of Islam. As will be shown in Chapter 3, this Islamist vision not only puts Muslims into conflict with constitutionalism in their own countries, it also prevents them from entering into democratic peace. It follows that cultural change in Islamic civilization matters to Muslims and non-Muslims alike, as it provides peaceful solutions to international conflict.

The preliminary assumption of this chapter, and which underpins most of the arguments in the present book, is that cultural value change is the avenue to a better future for Muslims and that it can be established by them alone, through religious reforms. The first requirement for embracing the idea of cultural value change is to overcome Islamic essentialism. This implies a willingness to rethink the belief in the immutability of Islamic thought. Of course, the Qur'an is directly revealed by Allah, but a historicization of Islam is possible, as well as an abandoning of all the burdens created by man in the name of God. The bottom line is this: real Islam has always been a product of history and humans are involved in creating it. Real Islam is the product of Muslims themselves. The reality is neither a reflection of divine scripture nor a deviation from what they think is right. It follows that Islam is always that which Muslims make of it and that historical, man-made Islam is not divine, despite all the efforts of the *ulema* to invoke God in it. In short, Islam changes with the course of development, in spite of whatever Muslim believers may think to the contrary. This reality of change stands in conflict with the a-historical Muslim Salafist worldview. After years of research in Morocco and Egypt, John Waterbury coined the term "behavioral lag" in order to describe the tensions arising from the inconsistency between what Muslims really do and what they think they are doing.[17] Cultural change and religious reform could help to overcome this behavioral lag, make Muslims accept human creativity and put their behavior and attitudes in line with each other. The values that underpin the inherited worldview of Muslim believers have to be reshaped in the course of cultural change and religious reform so as to establish the missing consonance with existing realities.

These introductory remarks on Islam and cultural change must also deal with the perception of "Islam under siege"[18] that determines contemporary Islamic public opinion and leads to an obsession with the West and "crusaders" in order to establish the imagery of an enemy. The European expansion addressed above was certainly real, and it is the source of the contemporary crisis of the Muslim world (see note 9). The contemporary ideology of neo-jihad or jihadism, which claims to be the struggle of the "oppressed people" of the Islamic civilization against the West,[19] is the basis of the debate on the questions: is the West to be blamed exclusively for the development deficits in the Islamic world? What is the Muslim share of responsibility for the present state of affairs? Is the prevailing culture a part of these deficits? Is it better to raise such questions candidly and to engage in a serious scholarly inquiry, or to join the Islamists in the blame game of "crusaders," as some US Middle East experts have chosen to do? Even after September 11, these people find university presses to publish their questionable work in which they accuse the so-called "new crusaders." Certainly, to say the least, this is borrowing the language of political Islam, not a scholarly vocabulary. US Islamic studies sideline themselves in this venture, to the extent of becoming insignificant.

In this chapter I admit such topical matters as the dreadful Iraq War. However, the focus is on culture and religion. I acknowledge that structural under-development and poverty matter, and I do not overlook the continual Western policy mistakes since the time of the 1917 Balfour Declaration. Nevertheless, the globalism of the West cannot be identified as the major source of all the problems that the Islamic world is suffering. Of course there are "structural roots," but the kind of analysis that carries this name, that ends in accusations, and that is combined with a cultural attitude of self-victimization will lead nowhere. The Iranian scholars Daryush Shayegan and Mehrzad Baroujerdi, who analyzed the attitudes of Muslim intellectuals "confronting and 'othering' the West" have coined the term "cultural schizophrenia."[20] This is a Muslim disease that distracts from dealing with the real, pressing issues, at the head of which is Islam's predicament with cultural modernity.

In earlier contributions I developed a concept of "defensive culture" to explain Muslim responses and attitudes towards cultural modernity in the crisis of modern Islam.[21] This defensive culture emanates from the exposure of the mostly pre-industrial countries of Islamic civilization to the industrialized West.[22] The current challenges compel cultural innovation. In fact, Japan could serve as a model, but contemporary Islamic thinkers have chosen their obsession with Europe. Their responses either are articulated in defensive-cultural rhetoric or assume the shape of conformism, i.e. instrumental adaptation without cultural value change based on religious reform. The attitudes related to the mindset of a defensive culture promote the explanation of things within the framework of a culture of self-victimization. In this context, one repeatedly encounters the polemical reproach of "*al-Gharb al-Salibi*/the West of crusaders." Islamist propagandists believe that the "crusaders" are at times instigated by the "*Yahud*/Jews" to invade the abode of Islam. One example for this is the popular conspiracy theory that views "the Jews" as "instigators of the Iraq war against Islam." It prevails to a disturbing degree and is the expression of "a new antisemitism."[23] The use of "the Jews" as a scapegoat serves further to distract from the real problems, which are, however, homemade. The attitude depicted here is itself part of the problem.

It is not simply the uncompromising Islamic way of approaching the issue that has impeded, and continues to impede, the necessary thinking. The inquiry is also hampered by the well-known, old cultural-relativist manner that now prevails in the West, primarily in cultural anthropology and Islamic studies. Scholars who deal with culture as a dimension of development are accused of having been tripped up by Orientalism. Cultural impediments to development are denied or ignored by the respective community of Western scholars, who impose a self-censorship that results in their overlooking the cultural constraints of underdevelopment. Under these conditions it is not easy to ask questions such as: are there any links between prevailing cultural values/attitudes, worldviews, and these social-structural realities? Is the Islamic world underdeveloped in comparison to the standards of the West? Worded differently: is a cultural pattern in Islamic societies responsible for the state of stagnation? What are the reasons underlying these constraints and is a comparison justified? These questions lead to the major hypothesis of the present book, namely a predicament of Islam with cultural modernity. This assumption guides all the thinking of the following chapters. In this chapter I continue the discussion with which the Introduction started. In so doing, in the following section I will examine anew a question that was asked during the last century by a very prominent Muslim, the revivalist Shakib Arslan.

"Why are Muslims backward, while others have progressed?"

The question that forms the heading of this section was asked in an earlier serious Islamic debate on these issues during the course of the early twentieth century and played an important role in it. The question touches on the place of culture in "*al-takhalfuf*/the backwardness" as stated by the Muslim revivalist Arslan in the title of one of his major works on contemporary Islamic civilization. In that debate no blame games were involved; rather, a serious – even if somewhat inadequate – reasoning was at work.

The debate is related to a story that goes back to the background of a series of articles written by the revivalist Shakib Arslan (1869–1945), who was titled Emir. Rashid Rida, the editor of the Islamic revivalist journal *al-Manar*, was asked by an Indonesian cleric back in 1929: "Why are Muslims backward, while others have progressed/*Limatha ta'akhar al-Muslimun wa taqaddama ghairahum?*" The question was forwarded to Arslan, who took it very seriously. Unlike contemporary Muslims, who are obsessed with global conspiracies, the revivalist Arslan acknowledged that "culture matters." However, he was not free from resorting to primordial cultural beliefs that smack of essentialism. He argued that religion and culture are based on essential values that come from God, and he drew the conclusion that no one is ever entitled to revise religious doctrines. Arslan believed that the cultural problem of Muslims lies basically in their deviation from these revealed Islamic values. By this explanation, on the one hand he admitted that "culture matters," but on the other hand he conceived culture in an essentialist manner. The outcome was, first, the mentioned series of articles published in *al-Manar*. A few years later Arslan collected these articles into a book for which he used the cited question as a title and which was published in Cairo in 1930.[24] This authoritative source of Islamic revival was also published twice in English, in Pakistan. Its wide distribution justifies reference to the question "Why are contemporary Muslims backward?" as a beginning for the analysis provided in this chapter.

According to the primordial mindset of Arslan, Muslims have deviated culturally from the cultural values of "true Islam." The lack of these essential values (primordiality) is the explanation that he presents for their state of "*al-ta'akhur/* backwardness." This is the reason why they have not progressed since the decay of their once highly developed civilization. One should note that Arslan refers in his book to the Western concept of progress, expressed by the neo-Arabic term of "*taqadum*/progress."[25] This Arabic term – as well as the Turkish *tarakki* – is a recent addition to the language of Islam. The term does not exist in traditional Islamic thought, nor in classical Islamic vocabulary. In Turkey, Kemal Atatürk linked this concept of progress to his views on Westernization.[26] In returning to Arslan, it is useful to quote his revivalist Islamic conception of "progress" as articulated in the following words:

> Sheykh al-Basyni – as others who ask the same question – may have assumed that the answer would be: the key to progress is to adopt the thoughts of Einstein … Pasteur … Thomas Edison … etc. … No, they are mistaken, if they assume this well, these scientific advancements are by-products, not origins in themselves. The jihad is the highest ranking science from which all other sciences are derived … If the Muslims followed their book (i.e. the Qur'an) then they would be in a position to reach the progress of the Europeans, Americans and Japanese in science and prosperity, while simultaneously keeping their Islam.[27]

The revivalism of Arslan seems not to have been an expression of religious reform, but rather a reinvigoration of the inherited Islamic worldview, even though in a modernist form. In Islamic studies this new revivalism, with its standard Islamic cultural explanation of present underdevelopment as expressed in Arslan's statement of 1929/30, is not only wrongly viewed as "Islamic modernism," but also misinterpreted as "Islamic nationalism."[28] The Islamic concept of the *umma* refers in a variety of ways to a universal community, but not to an "Islamic nation." In Islam there is no such thing. Even though Arslan was not really a modernist, his references to culture as being pertinent to progress in society are intelligent and continue to be worth mentioning. In this context I will refrain from further debate on modernization. However, his belief that deviation from divine values that are viewed as essential results in the "backwardness" of Islamic culture is misleading. In contrast, it is argued that only cultural change could contribute to establishing the values of progress that Muslims need. The mindset of religious reform is lacking in this "Islamic modernism." No wonder that this new direction failed to modernize Islam, and then waned.

If the flaws were as clear as is suggested, then why this recourse to Arslan? He was a scriptural believer who did not endeavor to question a single Islamic value. The reference serves to demonstrate that the inherited Islamic values subscribed to are considered a theocentric, not a man-centered view of the world, and thus to illustrate the view that they stand above change. This is indicative of fatalism rather than a contribution to accommodating cultural modernity. This pattern of revivalism is by no means cultural modernism. A further justification for the reference to Arslan is that it demonstrates the predicament of inherited Islamic cultural patterns with the values of modernity.

In terms of time, early Islamic revivalism was separated from contemporary political Islam by an interval of a few decades of secular nationalism.[29] Both, however, are characterized by similar inconsistencies that continue to prevail and that are becoming exacerbated. Nevertheless, there is an important distinction: contemporary Islamists place the blame on the West and acquit Muslims of any responsibility for the present ills in the Islamic world. In contrast, early revivalists, from Afghani on, never absolved Muslims from their share of responsibility. The tale that the West has invaded the abode of Islam in a bid to Westernize/Christianize it as a means to dominating it, determines the Islamic narrative. The related attitudes underpin the perception of "*al-ghazu al-fikri/* intellectual invasion" aimed at a "*taghrib/*Westernization"[30] of the Islamic world. The revivalist Afghani did not buy into such a conspiracy in order to explain the misery of Islamic societies and he made the point crystal clear, that if Muslims were not "ignorant" – as he phrased it – and therefore weak, then the West would never have been in a position to invade their abode and subject it to its rule. These themes dominate the culturalistic Islamic discourse and provide the standard explanation as to why Muslims in the modern age have been the losers in the competition with the West. The early Muslim revivalists, Abduh and Afghani, rightly argued that the West would never have succeeded in conquering the Muslims had they not been in a state of weakness. For this reason these true revivalists focused on the causes of the state of affairs, rather than engaging in blame games. However, they failed and were replaced by the secular nationalist modernizers such as Kemal Atatürk in Turkey and Sati al-Husri in the Arab world.

In contrast to Kemal Atatürk, early revivalists and contemporary Islamists do not share the view that the way to "*tarakki/*progress" is Westernization. They aim to modernize, but in their own way. This is not the approach of this book. Nevertheless, I acquit Atatürk of any blame of being involved in a "Jewish crusader civilizational conspiracy," as today's Islamists contend. This formula[31] reflects the antisemitic language of political Islam. The issue is the debate on civilization. One of the major pamphlets of Sayyid Qutb bears the title: *Islam and the Predicament of Civilization.*[32] Qutb spoke of a "clash" long before Huntington ever did. The accomplishment of Huntington is not the approach itself, but doing it from the opposite end of the polarized fault lines leading to the assumed "clash."

Understanding the predicament and its underlying constraints

In going beyond the conspiracy-driven thoughts of Islamism, as well as beyond Huntington's rhetoric of a "clash of civilizations," one needs to be serious and ask: why do people of the Islamic civilization lag behind global standards of democratization and development? The suggested answer is to be found by reference to the lack of religious reform, which underpins an inability to come to terms with Islam's predicament with cultural modernity. In the past and in the present, Islamic civilization is placed in this context. The focus of this book on Sunni Arab sources is not an expression of Arabo-centrism. It is a fact that the

Arab world, for a variety of reasons, continues to be the hub of Islamic civilization. The Arab origins of Islam determine the fact that Arab culture is the core
source of this civilization. A case study by von der Mehden on the interaction
between Muslims in Southeast Asia and the Arab world demonstrates that the
impact is only "one way," i.e. from the Arab world to Asia and not vice versa.[33]

The Arab region[34] is highly underdeveloped. This statement is supported by
the authoritative *Arab Human Development Report 2002* of the United Nations, a
very significant document. It was completed on behalf of the United Nations by
serious Arab experts and scholars – so Western postmodernists cannot use the
reproach of Orientalism.

The report presents a sober and enlightening analysis of the existing misery,
related to the fact that "the wave of democracy ... has barely reached the Arab
States."[35] In general, the report clearly states: "Compared with similar regions,
the Arabs suffer from a freedom deficit" (ibid.), and then points to the "lack of
genuine representative democracy and [to] restrictions on liberties" (ibid.). In
short, contemporary Arab governance lacks the political culture and practice of
democracy as well as individual human rights. This UN report lists three areas
of concern: 1) lack of freedom, 2) poor participation of women – due to the lack
of gender equality (of particular concern is the high proportion of female illiteracy), and 3) poverty related to very low gross national product (GNP). The basic
conclusion of the UNDP report is that the prevailing political culture is prone
neither to promoting democracy or gender equality, nor to accomplishment-
oriented behavior. The hard facts indicate that the prevailing cultural patterns of
Islamic civilization are not supportive of the promotion either of democracy or
of individual human rights. It follows that in a neo-oligarchical culture[36] cultural
change is an imperative. In a global comparison, Muslim societies are proven to
be underachievers almost in all fields. Given this fact, the uncensored explanation of the sad state of affairs in the Islamic world points also to domestic constraints. This kind of analysis runs counter to the prevailing obsession with
globalization and evil crusaders which put the blame onto others. It is more
promising to study cultural patterns than to engage in the cult of accusations.
One is compelled to ask "Why are Arab Muslim people silent about the existing
poor conditions of their miserable life and why do they not engage in resistance?" In place of upheaval, one encounters a revolt based on the quasi-religious
beliefs of political Islamism, favorable neither to cultural change nor to religious
reforms. To present political Islam as "other modernity" – as some postmodernists do – is a mere distortion, not to say a false representation of a warring
phenomenon. Political Islam and its jihadism are in fact the most recent variety
of totalitarianism.[37]

There are enlightened Muslims, such as Abdullahi An-Na'im, who earlier
acknowledged the tensions between shari'a-based values and international individual human rights standards and who – ahead of a setback – approved an
Islamic reformation.[38] Islamist Muslims disagree and insist on their own values
in the area of human rights. They infer that they are not against human rights in

general, but only against the Western concept. As will be discussed in Chapter 4 on Islam's predicament with individual rights, the rejection of cultural change and religious reform contributes to alienating the contemporary Muslim *umma* from the rest of humanity, due to the related lag of Muslim societies behind international standards.

As a Muslim, I ask myself why most of my co-religionists fail to acknowledge this predicament in order to find solutions. The answer that comes to mind was given to me when I was at school in Damascus. At the age of ten I dared to ask: "Why are the conditions we live under not in line with verse 3/110 in the Qu'ran: You are the best *'umma*-community' that has ever been raised up for mankind." The question was supported by reference to media coverage by a young Muslim boy who had discerned that the Europeans and Americans were more advanced than his own community. "So, why this, if Allah says we are superior to all non-Muslim parts of mankind?" My teacher replied without any hesitation: "We are in *'mihna/*crisis' and Allah is examining us." To me, as a ten-year-old, this answer was neither satisfactory nor convincing. I moved to the West at the age of eighteen for my academic training. That story has never left my mind. It has been the background of my desire, throughout my years of study in the West and the ensuing decades of academic research in the Islamic world itself, to get a better answer. The related thinking dominates the present book. I felt compelled to look for a more satisfactory explanation than I received in Damascus. A Muslim is better qualified than are Western postmodernists to address these issues. I state this without any Saidian bias.

Prudent Muslims of medieval Islam were in a position to accommodate Hellenism, through their mindset of being open to learning from others. Why cannot non-Islamist Muslims of the present age do the same? In the 1960s I was privileged to study with Max Horkheimer and Theodor W. Adorno of the Frankfurt School in Germany and to grow up in the environment of the new left and later on the 1968 movement. I came to the conclusion that the revived theories of Western imperialism and dependency were just as unconvincing an explanation of the deficient state of Islamic societies as had been my teacher of religion in Damascus. Then, during my undergraduate years in Frankfurt I came across the work of the fourteenth-century philosopher Ibn Khaldun on the rise and fall of civilizations. I read the *"Muqadimma/*Prolegomena" of Ibn Khaldun at first in 1965 and was deeply impressed by his reference to values and culture, i.e. to *asabiyya*, for explaining the state of people. Ever since, I have continued to read this *magnum opus* and to be inspired by it to look closely at the cultural discourse of Muslim communities and their values. After all, Ibn Khaldun was not only the greatest philosopher of history in Islam situated in the tradition of Hellenization, but also the founder of the *"ilm al-umran/*science of civilizations." It is a shame that Huntington's book on "civilizations" lacks any information about Ibn Khaldun and that his name is never mentioned. How can anyone speak with authority about the Islamic world who has such poor knowledge about contemporary Muslims and their *asabiyya*?

In order to understand the contemporary predicament one needs to distinguish between Western hegemony and the ills it has caused, on the one hand, and Western universal values of cultural modernity in a progress-oriented culture on the other. This chapter began with this distinction. The values of individualism, human rights, secularity, civil society, pluralism, and democracy should not be confused with Western hegemony. To apply the notion of cultural imperialism to Cartesianism in order to then speak of "epistemological imperialism" (Sardar) is to reject rationality. Analytical explanations need to replace the mindset of blaming others. One has to refrain from moralizing accusations that lead nowhere. In four decades of learning during a cross-cultural journey, I have been at pains to understand cultural modernity in relation to my religion and the cultural system of Islam within which I have been socialized. It is most dismaying to observe Western cultural anthropologists speaking of and despising, in a neo-colonial manner, the so-called "cosmopolitan travel plans"[39] of non-Western intellectuals who do not share their postmodern thinking. Westerners never cease to teach these enlightened Africans and Asians in the old, oligarchic style about what they consider to be best for them, thus denying them the ability to choose for themselves. However, this old, Western, colonial arrogance is presented in the new garb of a cultural-anthropological relativism. Let us put these polemics aside and be serious. One needs to address the issues themselves through free speech, unconstrained by censorship or scholarly pretensions. This book engages in such a manner, and may not be popular in its pursuit of uncensored questions that touch the heart of the core issue.

The background: from the glory of the Islamicate to "Islamic civilization under siege"

In the course of my decades-long pondering of Islam's contemporary predicament with cultural modernity and of the related state of affairs, I have never forgotten for a moment that medieval Islam was for many centuries the world's leading civilization. The positive "classical heritage" of that history[40] includes not only a tradition of learning from other cultures, but also an Islamic ability to accommodate most challenges. By contrast, contemporary Muslims lag behind the earlier accomplishments of their ancestors. The repeated wisdom of cultural diversity and differentiation needs to be applied to their own history[41] when Muslims talk about Islam. Advanced medieval Islam was the *falsafa*-Islam of rationalism, not the *fiqh*-Islam of orthodoxy. In this connection one is reminded of the historical fact that medieval Islam had a flourishing civilization based on rationalism. Among the great accomplishments of medieval "high Islam" was a tradition of rationalism as well as of science that has had an impact on modern times.[42] These conditions changed during the modern age, through the rise of the West during the period 1500–1800. This change was related also to a successful *Military Revolution*.[43] It ended the expansion of the "Islamicate" that had thrived during the jihad conquests, from the seventh to the seventeenth centuries.

The decline of Islamic civilization is a great historical wound to Muslims. For a whole millennium their civilization had dominated most parts of the world. During that time, Islamic civilization was the entity that – due to its high degree of development – "was the most expansive" throughout the world, as we learn from the great historian of Islam Marshall Hodgson, who adds that, in those earlier times,

> a visitor from Mars might have supposed that the human world was on the verge of becoming Muslim. He would have based this judgment partly on the strategic and political advantages of the Muslims, but partly on the vitality of their general culture.[44]

When did this vitality cease and why did this by then highly developed culture decline? Why did capitalism grow from the *"Geist des Protestantismus/*mindset of Protestantism," as Max Weber rightly states,[45] and not from an Islamic mindset? These questions need to be admitted into a free, scholarly debate – a debate that should also be free of defamation and accusations of Orientalism. If we discuss the issue rationally and answer questions in an uncensored atmosphere, as did the great French scholar of Islam Maxime Rodinson in his *Islam et Capitalisme*,[46] we can find all kinds of explanations. Islam as a faith does not create – as the myth of prejudiced Western Orientalists suggests – a *homo Islamicus*. The concept of "Orientalism," originally used by Edward Said to identify and to criticize this biased approach, was, to begin with, timely, and was justified as a concern with a real point to be made. However, contemporary US anthropologists – the Saidists – have derailed the debate and have also distorted the issue by moving from one extreme to the other. I share Rodinson's intention, but neither his preoccupation with economic constraints nor his Marxist underestimation of culture. In fairness, I concede that Rodinson does respect culture in part, but he fails to determine the role that it played in the historical process of the rise and decline of Islamic civilization. The second German edition of the cited work by Rodinson includes my introduction on the place of culture in Islam's development. Further, at a symposium on Weber and Islam, Rodinson was forced to back down and to admit some cultural role for Islam in social evolution.[47] It is on these grounds that I endeavor to diagnose the constraints underlying the development that led to the contemporary lag of Islamic civilization behind global standards of progress. The point at issue is the understanding of Islam as a "cultural system,"[48] i.e. a source of worldview and values, and not as a religious faith. Readers are reminded that the present study is a social-scientific contribution, not a theological inquiry into Islam.

It is certainly not an expression of essentialism to state that Muslims – despite all their cultural diversity – share a common worldview based on Islamic core values. Of course, these values are – as is culture itself – subject to change. However, the belief system, according to which these values originate in the Qur'an – viewed as the ultimate knowledge of God passed by Him to humanity via His *"rasul*/messenger" Mohammed – makes a difference. The Qur'an[49] is believed to be verbal inspiration that can be interpreted, but that never changes in substance. This cultural-religious belief that no knowledge can stand above that provided by the Qur'an (being the ultimate and absolute truth) rests on this understanding of the Qur'an. At this point begins the predicament of the people of Islamic civilization with change, on all levels. The Qur'an is believed to be the source of knowledge per se and no separation between belief and knowledge is permissible (see Chapter 2). It follows that all values are to be derived from this holy book. In the better days of Islam, Muslims were involved in controversial debates on knowledge and on the meaning of the Qur'an. They not only arrived at different interpretations (*tafsir* or more radical *ta'wil*), but also made a distinction between divine knowledge and philosophical knowledge (Averroes: double truth). However, no Muslim would ever be entitled to make a critical reading of the text of the Qur'an, as Christians read the Bible. In the light of the Reformation and the Enlightenment, understanding and the role of religion have changed. By contrast, in Islam questioning of the text is considered to be an act of *"kufr*/heresy" and is thus subject to incrimination. In other words, *"sultat al-nas*/the unquestioned authority of the text"[50] is an essential element of the Islamic worldview as based on scripturally fixed beliefs. Again, this worldview prevents Muslims from accommodating their view to a changing world. As a reform Muslim I do not share this Islamic essentialism and take the liberty of referring to it and thinking critically about it.

In Islam, there is a tension between belief in immutability and ever-changing reality. The related attitudes have been passed on, through child-rearing practices and education in faith schools, from one generation to the next, throughout the centuries of Islamic history. Muslim children go to the Qur'an school, as did I myself in Damascus, and learn how to read and write using the text of the Qur'an. They are too young to grasp its complex meaning, but nonetheless are compelled to memorize the text even though they often do not understand its content. This rote learning of the Qur'an is transmitted to other realms of knowledge. I recall how my generation at school in Damascus applied the pattern of rote learning to the study of science. We learned modern theories and notions by heart, answered questions in exams by speaking out or writing down what we had memorized, but without properly understanding. Everything was forgotten after the exam period. Under the influence of political Islam, contemporary institutions of learning are becoming politicized to the detriment of Islamic civilization. Now young Muslims learn that their civilization's only problems lie in their victimization by the West and through the siege of Islam.

In my research in a range of Islamic countries I recall young boys (there were no girls among them) walking along the promenades holding textbooks that they memorized for their exams. Beyond my own experience as a schoolboy in Damascus, I also observed this during my fieldwork in North and West Africa. Since my time in Damascus this learning process has not changed. However, exposure to modernity triggers a *Crisis in Muslim Education*[51] and this system of learning is incapable of dealing with it. In considering the fact that any knowledge transmitted through rote learning is devoid of thinking and questioning, one might argue that this education pattern will support neither religious reform nor cultural change. No accommodation to the culture of modernity can be promoted through such patterns of child-rearing and a related style of learning in educational institutions. It contributes not to a release of creativity, but instead to a strengthening of dependency and orthodoxy in Islam. This can only be changed through cultural innovation and religious reform. Without such an endeavor there is no way out of the crisis in the developmental process.[52] Instead of engaging in this endeavor, political Islam is exacerbating the situation by using education for the radicalization of Muslim youth.

There is a connection between rote learning of the Qur'an text, uncompromising dogmatic scripturalism, and the worldview that emerges from this unquestioning belief in the authority of the text as applied to reality. In this context, the belief system precludes any change to values and to the culture underpinning them. In medieval Islam this pattern was challenged by Islamic rationalists who introduced a different pattern of learning that went beyond the prevailing traditional Islamic education. The *ulema*-orthodoxy prohibited this reflexive learning, and this is a statement in itself. Despite these cultural obstacles, Islamic civilization was in a position to reach the highest level, due to the good fortune of the Hellenization of Islam.[53] This process occurred between the ninth and twelfth centuries on the basis of Muslim knowledge of and further development of Greek philosophy and science. This Hellenization facilitated a cultural change that smoothed the way for an Islamic acceptance of the primacy of human reason, and thus for the rise of an Islamic variety of rationalism.[54] A closer look at Islamic history during the medieval period helps to reveal not only cultural innovation, but also an intellectual and institutional battle that occurred at that time. On the one front were the Islamic rationalists and on the other the Islamic *fiqh*-scripturalists, i.e. orthodoxy. The fault lines were determined in the following manner by the medieval Salafist al-Mawardi as: "*bi al-aql aw bi al-wahi/* judging by reason or on the grounds of revelation."[55] In other words, a judgment based on human reason was to be condemned as heretical. According to this mindset the only true authority is the divine text, to be accepted as an authentic, Islamic source of compliance. Under the influence of this mindset, the *fiqh*-orthodoxy succeeded in establishing that the revealed text and its interpretations took the place of free reasoning in Islamic institutions of learning. This orthodoxy prevented the entry of Islamic rationalism into the education curriculum.[56] Knowledge transmitted in this way was the learning of the approved, essential Islamic pattern. Conflict erupted in medieval Islam, and its outcome was consequential in determining the compass of Islamic civilization. The *fiqh* won the battle; rationalism in Islam declined, and with it the civilization of Islam also. There is little knowledge, even among educated Muslims, of this history. Instead, one encounters an obsession with crusaders in order to explain the decline of Islamic civilization. Today, the history of the crusades has been reinvented. Islamists now see an alliance between the US and Israel that replaces the traditional European enemy: the US and the Americans are viewed as the *New Crusaders*,[57] acting in a "Jewish-Christian crusade against Islam." This perception is a distraction from all of the current issues. In fairness, one has to point out other, positive examples, in particular late nineteenth and the twentieth centuries, when efforts were made by enlightened Muslims to revive Islamic rationalism – but these, deplorably, waned.[58] A contemporary Islamic philosopher in this tradition, Mohammed Abed al-Jabri, unequivocally states that Muslims of the present face a choice: either to become involved in a revival of Averroist rationalism or to continue to decline.[59]

Institutionally, the conflict between rationalism and religious scripturalism in medieval Islam – and also today – revolves around the place of Islamic scriptural sciences (the study of the texts of the Qur'an and of the Hadith of the prophet, i.e. the Sunna tradition) in Islamic education. These disciplines were set in opposition to the Hellenized rational disciplines of philosophy and science. Back then, the Islamic orthodoxy was in full control of the institutions of learning, and thus in a position to prevent the inclusion of rational sciences in the curriculum of Islamic learning. Thus, it impeded the institutionalization and spread of rational sciences in Islam. One learns from Robert Wuthnow that, unless cultural innovations are institutionalized, they do not endure and cannot be successful.[60] This explanation helps in understanding why Islamic rationalism was short lived, and thus provides the background to the decline of the Islamic civilization. At present, the needed cultural change has to be combined with a civilizational revival of the suppressed classical heritage of Islam. Instead, political Islam claims to provide the solution to the present crisis. Conspicuously, Islamists never refer to the Islamic heritage of rationalism. Therefore, in my assertions, I argue that political Islam is an impediment, not the solution for Islam's predicament with modernity. The solution should be democracy,[61] not "Allah's rule," for God is not a ruler!

Certainly, the heritage of Islam is its rationalism, which introduced a separation between the religious and the worldly in Islamic thought. This philosophy failed to affect the Islamic worldview and to give it lasting shape. Islamic rationalism was doomed to decline. In other words, the impact of rationalism and the unfolding of Islamic civilization were limited. The Egyptian philosopher Mourad Wahba coined the formula "the paradoxon of Averroes"[62] to state that this great philosopher, during the course of the Renaissance, had a great impact on Europe and enjoyed European fame. At the same time, his work was dismissed in his own Islamic civilization, to the extent that his books were burned by the Salafist orthodoxy. This marked the end of Averroism in Islamic civilization, and the related civilizational decay.

Islamic civilization thrived not on the basis of shari'a, but rather on that of science and philosophy. This fact is often overlooked by those who claim to revive civilizational glory in Islam. Contemporary Islamic revival is based on the shari'a, not on the accomplishments of Islamic rationalists. However, the Islamic orthodoxy is replaced by lay Islamists who claim to be the true voice of Islam.

The medieval conflict between Islamic rationalism and shari'a orthodoxy continues to be highly relevant in our time. The Moroccan Mohammed al-Jabri addresses this "struggle for reason and rationality" in Islamic history as embedded in "the rise and fall of reason." In their polemics against the West, defensive-cultural Islamic writers underline their commitment to tradition. However, their tradition is not that which al-Jabri and similarly enlightened Muslims have in mind. In his "contemporary Arabic thought" al-Jabri complains that inherited thought "has never been able to go beyond this problematic (of tradition), because it has always ill-posed the problems that are associated with it."[63] Muslims continue to evade open-minded dealing with the question "what there would be to take it or to leave," as al-Jabri continues. In his words, the answer would be: "The survival of our philosophical tradition … can only be Averroist … The Averroist spirit is adaptable to our era, because it agrees with it on more than one point: rationalism, realism, axiomatic method and critical approach."[64]

In concluding this section and the attempt made here to understand the predicament of Islam and its constraints, one needs not only to refer selectively to enlightened Muslims such as al-Jabri, but also to reflect on the prevailing public choices. It is a fact that obsession with a looming conspiracy, combined with a mindset replete with accusations, has taken the place of an urgently needed critical view of the self. After the Arab defeat in the Six Day War of 1967, the Damascene philosopher Sadik Jalal al-Azm realized this need and proposed "*naqd thati*/self criticism" in order to explain the defeat, rather than blaming others for it. The Arab Islamic lack of a critical view of the self results in business as usual,[65] based on self-victimization and blaming of others for one's own shortcomings. To overcome this cultural deficit, new journals were established in the late 1960s (like *Mawqif* in Beirut, by Adonis), and many cultural efforts were undertaken by some critical Arab intellectuals. These people were honestly willing to deal with the cultural repercussions of the defeat. However, their efforts had no lasting effect.[66] In contrast, the competing "*hall Islami*/Islamic solution" (see note 61) was more appealing and was therefore successful. In the course of post-1967 developments, the Islamist mindset has become the source that has shaped contemporary Islamic thought, whether in the Middle East or in the Islamic world beyond. Cultural nostalgia, combined with Islamist activism, replaced the abortive post-1967 Arab Islamic enlightenment. I feel inclined to compare this twentieth-century Arab enlightenment with the earlier one of medieval Islam. Among the things both historical experiences share is the fact that they failed (see note 66). They were not able to strike roots in order to shape the prevailing worldview.

Cultural nostalgia vs. cultural change

Collective memories can be constructed, although they are presented as pure cultural revival. This is neither a new phenomenon, nor is it restricted to the Islamic world. However, today one encounters post-bipolar conflicts that are often imbued and burdened with identity politics based on collective memories in order to draw cultural fault lines. This is a new pattern of conflict, bolstered by a cultural nostalgia based on collective memories that underpin identity politics and which are associated with historical claims. Only a few seem to understand this novelty as a phenomenon in Islamic form. Among these scholars one finds John Kelsay, who makes it crystal clear that:

> it would be wrong ... to understand the contemporary call for revival among Muslims as simple nostalgia ... writers and activists ... have argued that the ascension of European and North American civilization in world affairs has been based on a failure of leadership in the Islamic world ... The mood of such writers *is not nostalgia, but outrage ... The call for renewal, then, relates to Islam and its mission.*[67]

Examples of this nostalgic mindset can be found in the writings of precursors of militant Islam, such as Sayyid Qutb or Abu al-A'la al-Mawdudi in the past and al-Qaradawi today. It is a fact that Islamic civilization was in the lead for almost a millennium – from the seventh through the seventeenth centuries – but then declined. Ever since, there has been a development-related gap between the civilizations of Islam and the West. In the nineteenth century Muslims wanted to match the West in a commitment to innovation and students were sent to Europe to learn. At issue was a limited innovation, restricted to the adoption of modern science and technology.[68] The first Islamic imam to be sent to Europe in modern times to take care of students was Rifa'a R. al-Tahtawi. However, he went beyond his assignment to accompany and religiously supervise the Muslim students. After himself becoming fascinated by European accomplishments, he sought permission to study. On his return from France Tahtawi became the first prominent Muslim student of Europe. In his Paris diary Tahtawi acknowledges the Islamic need to adopt Western accomplishments, stating "that Europeans, though Christians, are superior to Muslims in the sciences."[69] He was amazed to see that French students of religion (in Arabic: *ulema*) were not honored as scientists (also *ulema* in the language of Islam), for Europeans distinguish between scientific knowledge and religious belief, i.e. between scholars and preachers. However, Tahtawi shied away from religious reform. One misses in Tahtawi's thought a differentiation between the power of techno-scientific institutional modernity and the enlightenment of a cultural modernity, and the line is blurred.

In his Paris diary al-Tahtawi documents historically how a traditional Muslim responds to exposure to modernity and unconsciously displays Islam's predicament with that modernity. At first, Tahtawi urged his fellow Muslims to learn from Europe, but in a futher step he makes it clear that adoptions from the West have to be limited by what cosmic shari'a law permits and forbids. In consequence, even the modernist Tahtawi closed the door for cultural change and religious reform. In his view, Muslims are only entitled "to adopt what does not conflict with the shari'a," as clearly stated in his Paris diary. Here we have a clear example of the will to adopt selected items of modernity without, however, becoming fully modern.[70] To be able to handle a computer while at the same time being committed to a medieval worldview is definitely not an expression of openness to change in order to unfold a modern, progress-oriented culture. In my work I defined this attitude as an expression of "semi-modernity"[71] in which items of modernity are instrumentally adopted, but are separated from their underlying cultural implications, such as the worldview and its related values. The modernist Tahtawi proceeds in exactly this manner. He also refers to the Islamic tradition of learning, but presents as a source of legitimation a reference to Islamic glory, in the nostalgic sense outlined earlier. For the Muslim Tahtawi, adoptions are "repossessions." This argument states that Muslims were the first to unfold modern science and that their civilization declined while the West adopted major accomplishments from them. Now, Muslims are reclaiming these things and their adoptions from the West are nothing other than acts of repossession or retrieval. This cultural attitude demonstrates that Muslims claim superiority through their possession of ultimate knowledge revealed by Allah, even while they are in a state of underdevelopment. Thus, Muslims learn from others through a sentiment of nostalgia. Tahtawi's acknowledgment of the scientific superiority of the West is downplayed through the claim that European knowledge is traced back to Islamic sources. Again, the contention is that Europe adopted from Islam what Muslims are now retrieving. The fact is, however, that science and technology in modern times are different issues, as they are part and parcel of modernity. Lewis phrases the issue in this manner: "The older sciences lingered on for a while in the remoter lands of Islam, but from this time onwards science means modern Western science."[72]

As shown in the case of Tahtawi, the sentiment of nostalgia does not provide a real avenue for dealing with Islam's predicament with modernity; rather, it undermines such an undertaking. It promotes a sense of superiority, combined with an attitude of essentialization. It clearly burdens even liberal Muslims, as was the case in the thinking of a modern revivalist such as Tahtawi. When it comes to dealing with science and technology in the context of Islamic exposure to modernity, the nostalgia of Muslim glory that comes to the fore even in the Paris diary of Tahtawi resembles, in many ways, contemporary Islamic fundamentalist writings. Like Tahtawi, Islamists split modernity into "culture" (values) and "instruments" (science and technology). They adopt the latter while vehemently rejecting their related values. They never question their belief in the moral superiority of Muslims vis-à-vis non-Muslims and therefore they open their minds neither to cultural change nor to religious reform. In consequence, the Islamic dream of semi-modernity, i.e. shared by revivalist liberal Muslims of yesterday and the opposing Islamists of today, avoids tackling Islam's predicament.

In contemporary Islamic civilization there are four different streams, very uneven in their impact. First, there is political Islam – also named Islamism – which is the Islamic variety of religious fundamentalism. It seems to provide the most powerful contemporary response to modernity.[73] The message it conveys is clear: take the instruments of modernity and leave aside the worldview and related values. This attitude determined the response of the Arab press to the UNDP report. Within Islamism there are peaceful and jihadist directions. The jihadists of September 11 are the best illustration of this mindset. Their worldview was medieval, but they were able to handle the complexity of modern technology, including the complex computer systems of airborne navigation and of E-jihad.[74]

Then we have the second, the Wahhabi variety of Salafism, which is an orthodoxy that rejects any "*bid'a*/creative innovation." In Islamic belief *bid'a* means deviation from the right path. The Wahhabism of Saudi Arabia is a case in point.[75] However, there has been a change, related to the fact that factions of Wahhabism are moving in the direction of political Islam and its semi-modernism. Bin Laden has created links between political and Wahhabi Islam in his al-Qaeda,[76] which in this manner is building a bridge between Wahhabi orthodoxy and Islamism. However, the two remain different directions in Islamic thought and practice in the twenty-first century.

Third, there is the popular spiritual Islam or Sufism[77] of the religious *Tariqa* orders. This is a flexible Islam because it is based on oral traditions, not on scripturalism. The spread of popular Sufi Islam is mostly among illiterate rural people; educated Muslims, by contrast, express a scriptural shari'a Islam and its monolithic mindset, an Islam that stands against popular folk Islam. Sufi Islam is rather tolerant and open to pluralism, as the term "*tariqa*/path" (there are different paths to God) indicates. However, superstition is essential to Sufism and it is therefore not in line with a rational view of the world, nor is its pluralism comparable with the modern understanding of this notion.

The fourth stream is reform Islam, a position that is embraced in this book. In view of the need for cultural change it is the most important stream, even though it is the weakest variant in contemporary Islam. The first effort at a reform Islam can be traced back to Muhammad Abduh[78] in the late nineteenth century. Abduh's thinking sought an accommodation with modern culture so as to embrace its science and technology. Its earlier varieties failed, however, to manifest in a value change, which concerns the most important area in cultural change. This was not a concern of early Islamic reform. Abduh sought accommodation without a basic cultural change, and therefore his early Islamic reformism failed to deliver its promise. Today this variety of Islamic shari'a reform is history.[79] Contemporary thinkers of Islamic reform, like Arkoun, al-Jabri and Shahrur, are more daring, but they have little influence.

In general, the contemporary attitude of Islamic nostalgia correlates with the supremacist belief in an alleged Islamic moral superiority. Since this mentality does not match the realities of the world, it generates outrage. Professedly, the related sentiments run counter to modern pluralism. The popular public choices in today's Islamic civilization are not favorable to embracing the culture of modernity. The implication of this statement is that the perspective of a religious reform and cultural change to innovations is unlikely to materialize in the foreseeable future. Nonetheless, *Rethinking Islam*[80] is inevitable. Sadly, the Muslim who states this need, Arkoun, not only fails to deliver, but also loses sight of this issue in his francophone rhetoric.

Despite all the focus of cultural change, there is no doubt that the interplay between cultural and social change is decisive. To state it differently: there are also social requirements for cultural change. Still, religious reform is essential and the distractions of contemporary cultural nostalgia in the Islamic world exacerbate the existing predicament. Also, the Islamic dream of semi-modernity, which is not a culture of modernization is – as are the attitudes of Islamic nostalgia – an impediment, and not an Islamic renaissance with the outlook of a real cultural revival, it is also not one variety of the assumed multiple modernities.

The intrinsic connectedness of religious reform and cultural change

What Muslims really need to do in order to come to terms with their predicament with cultural modernity is to follow what the contemporary Islamic rationalist Arkoun recommends, namely *Rethinking Islam* (see note 80). Another Muslim philosopher, Mohammed A. al-Jabri, author of *Takwin al-aql al-Arab*/The Creation of the Arab Mind,[81] thinks that cultural change can only be promoted by a revival of the tradition of Islamic rationalism. Today, Muslims are under pressure to open their minds and free themselves from the nostalgic mindset, as well as from unthinking scripturalism and, equally, from obsession with a conspiracy designed against them. Of course, it is easier said than done, that religious reform and cultural change are required. The Egyptian scholar Hamid Abu-Zaid jeopardized his material existence simply by venturing in this direction in his book *Naqd al-Khitab al-dini*/Critique of Religious Discourse.[82] This is a telling story. Abu-Zaid was accused of heresy and sentenced as a *"murtad*/apostate," with the consequence that he was divorced from his Muslim wife against both their wills. This happened as a result of a court decision in Egypt and not through a *fetwa* issued by an underground Islamist imam. In the aftermath of this verdict, which is reminiscent of a Stone-Age so-called legal system, Abu-Zaid and his wife fled from Egypt to Europe, where he found a safe haven. More than two decades earlier, the Syrian philosopher Sadik J. al-Azm had a similar experience when he – back in 1969 – published his book *Naqd al-fikr al-dini*/Critique of Religious Thought.[83] Why this vehement Islamic rejection of critical thinking? The Islamic apologists believe that Islam needs no reform. In this mindset, critical reasoning is incriminated and leads to the risk of unpleasant consequences. The apologetic Muslim writer Muslehuddin articulates the related mindset in this manner:

> Divine law is to be preserved in its ideal form as commanded by God … The view … that the law should be determined by social needs [is mistaken] … God alone knows what is really good for mankind … Islamic society is the product of [shari'a] law and has ideally to conform to its dictates. The law … does not change.[84]

In the chapter on *shari'a*/Islamic law we will learn more about this Islamic orthodox worldview that inhibits material pursuits. Its extreme theocentrism nurtures irrationality and determines a fatalism according to which humans have no influence on their destiny. Wealth and true knowledge emanate only from God. In medieval Islam the Mu'tazilites acted as "defenders of reason" and argued, in their Islamic theology, that believers also have "*al-Ikhtiyar*/choice" and thus are responsible for their actions. The Mu'tazilites rejected fatalism, and lost. Today they still have some followers in Southeast Asia.[85] In contrast to the superseded Mu'tazalite tradition, today Islamic Salafist orthodoxy, with its fatalist worldview of uncompromising theocentrism, prevails. Contemporary Islamism, though modern, adopts the Arabic vocabulary replete with religious rituals of fatalism.[86] Religious language signifies the belief that man has little control over human destiny. The most popular formula is "*insh'a Allah (Inshallah)*/if Allah is willing." When a Muslim is asked whether a job will be done, he or she responds with "*Inshallah*" and thus denies the will of the self. If a traditional Muslim faces a challenge or is required to accomplish a task, the formula traditionally used is "*takwakal 'ala Allah*/rely on God." This mindset of fatalism needs to be changed through religious reform. The rationalist philosophers in Islam (al-Farabi, Avicenna, Averroes, etc.) and the theologian defenders of reason (*al-Mu'tazilites*), as well as contemporary radical-reform Muslim thinkers from Arkoun to al-Jabri, believe that this change is possible. However, this is not the prevailing public view. Rather, the dominant view is reflected in the following statement: "Those who think of reforming Islam are misguided ... Why should it be modernized when it is already perfect and pure, universal for all time?"[87] This understanding of Islam is expressed by the Salafist Mohammad Muslehuddin, who articulates a cultural attitude that is an obstacle to any kind of progress, since it rejects and precludes change. It is peculiar that the Arabic name *Muslehuddin* means the opposite of his mindset: "reformer of religion"!

The idea that dominates this book is that, without religious reform, there can be no real cultural change in the Islamic world. The concern of this idea is the belief of Muslims that there is only one revealed scriptural truth, based on the Qur'anic revelation which provides all rules to abide by. Any deviation from this system of "*faraid*/duties" can be condemned as "*kufr*/heresy," subjected to sanctions and in consequence entailing the "*takfir*/accusation of heresy."[88] This excommunication from the Islamic *umma* also carries the risk of being killed as an "unbeliever" or "apostate," which is the ultimate punishment. However, students of Islam are familiar with the fact that most Muslims do not, in practice, abide by the very tough religious rules of the shari'a. It is simply not feasible. Earlier in this chapter I referred to the fieldwork in Morocco of John Waterbury, who learned not to take at face value what people in that Islamic country say/believe, but instead to look at what they do. Their actual behavior does not match their proclaimed piety. In order to conceptualize the difference between what people say (pronounced religious conviction) and what they do (real behavior) Waterbury has coined the term "behavioral lag" (see note 17). It follows that cultural values are proclaimed, but do not determine the often pragmatic behavior. Is this what the Iranian D. Shayegan sees as an indication of "cultural schizophrenia"? I prefer to leave the question open, but maintain that the major problems of contemporary Muslim civilization are related to the eclipse of rational discourse since the decline of the Islamic rationalism of the medieval age. In this context, I reiterate the call of al-Jabri for a return to rationality as the ultimate way out of this unsatisfactory situation. This Moroccan philosopher courageously addressed the decline of "*al-aql*/reason" in Islamic history in his formula of "the rise and fall of reason" in Islam in order to support his appeal: "the future can only be Averroeist" (see note 59). Let it be stated candidly: this is not the mindset of today, and thus the great reluctance to engage in reform and change is interrelated.

Those Western students of Islam who, making reference to Edward Said, outlaw the critiques of the prevailing worldview in contemporary Islamic civilization and of the defensive culture of nostalgic Salafism as expressions of "Orientalism," are mistaken. I was a friend of Edward Said and I know that during his life he never represented some of the views that are attributed to him. My very last encounter with Said was in Chicago in March 2000. During this last encounter he denied the cultural relativism attributed to him. Nevertheless, I refer to the distinguished Damascene Muslim philosopher, Sadik Jalal al-Azm, who made the point that Said had been pursuing an "Orientalism in reverse" (see note 14). Unfortunately, Said never seriously responded to this authentic, liberal Islamic critique. To be sure, both Said and al-Azm were friends and all three of us became involved four decades ago in early reasoning on the *Arabs of Today. Perspectives for Tomorrow*.[89] In that book the three of us were forthright in our conviction that Arab Muslims need to reform and to change. None of us placed any blame on others. However, the great distraction of "Orientalism" divided us.

As stated by the Arab Muslim Bu Ali-Yassin, a Syrian social scientist educated in Europe, the real issue is a triangle of taboos that determines Islamic culture and its mindset. This triangle is rooted in three basic issue areas: religion, politics, and gender.[90] At present, it is not permissible to engage publicly in any thinking that touches on these issue areas. Those who dare to deviate from the prevailing views expose themselves in the Islamic world to sanctions, including the respective punishments, and in the postmodernist West to the accusation of Orientalism. Islamic societies can be reformed if they can be democratized and gender relations be remade in the polity. To think in the manner of Yassin is to commit oneself to an Islamic Enlightenment.

For a better understanding of the inner-connectedness of religious reform and cultural change it is more promising to enter into the thinking of Reinhard Bendix, who coined the term "spiritual mobilization" as a cultural requirement for social change. In his studies Bendix clearly distinguished between the adoption of modern items and of modernity itself. Bendix draws our attention to the phenomenon that "modernization in some sphere of life *may* occur without resulting in 'modernity'."[91] In applying the notion of the adoption of the instruments of modern science and technology to contemporary Muslims who do this without any accommodation of their cultural value-system to change, one can share the following description of Reinhard Bendix: "The gap created between advanced and follower societies and the efforts to close it by a more or less *ad hoc* adoption of items of modernity produce obstacles standing in the way of successful modernization."[92]

At this point, we are again faced with the two dimensions of modernity referred to at the beginning of this chapter. If Muslims only adopt items of modernity ad hoc, without religious reform and cultural change, semi-modernity will be the outcome. This is the theme of the concluding chapter of this book. At this stage it suffices to state that semi-modernity is an adoption of modern instruments, combined with a firm rejection of the man-centered values of cultural modernity. This concept of semi-modernity[93] enables us to understand the contradiction that Muslims adopt Western items of modernity – e.g. computer technology – and are able to handle them without, however, becoming modern in their thinking and behavior. The reason for this is that the related cultural values are dissociated from the adopted items (e.g. technical instruments) of modernity. This is the deep meaning of the predicament of contemporary Muslims with modernity. They permit neither change in cultural values and worldviews nor a religious reform.

To put it into plain language, the basic problem of Islamic civilization is neither the West, which perceptually revives the imagery of "the crusaders," nor the allegedly "conspiring Jews." The real problem is the prevailing politics based on a worldview that undermines reform and change and, in consequence, any real solution to Islam's predicament with cultural modernity. The mindset of semi-modernity is the outcome of a mind committed to pre-modern values and orientations and simultaneously willing to adopt selected items of modernity (technology). This mindset leaves no room for thinking about the predicament with cultural modernity. Contemporary Muslims need to learn that smoothing the way to the introduction of cultural and religious reforms is not against Islam, but rather is a resumption and revival of the Islamic mindset of rationalism. This endeavor is more promising than the "*al-hall al-Islami*/Islamic solution" pronounced by contemporary Islamists. The cure is a time-demanding one, despite the fact that time is running out for the Islamic people, who are marginalizing themselves in an age where overall globalization is changing all aspects of life. Muslims live in this world but create the imagined ghetto of a transnational *umma* under siege. This mindset rejects the cultural views shared by most of humanity.

Conclusions: whither the civilization of Islam?

The preceding analysis addresses a problem; it also seeks an explanation for the fact that most Islamic countries are underachievers and thus lag behind the international standards of the present world. The analysis makes clear that without religious reforms and cultural change there can be no promising prospect for a better life in the Islamic world. In arguing for cultural change, I am aware of the potential for being accused of "culturalism," but I believe that this would be meaningless. No prudent scholar would question the fact that cultural values determine the thinking of people as well as their worldviews and, consequently, their behavior. Of course, the dynamics of society and economics are crucial, though cultural attitudes could impede change. If one fails to understand the relevance of cultural change to the transformation of society, then the complexity of the problem, as well as a significant link in the chain, will not be understood at all.

Cultural anthropologists study change, but are mostly hostile to the potential of a universal cultural modernity. In this regard, the work of one unforgettable and exceptional cultural anthropologist, the late Ernest Gellner, is unique and extraordinarily excellent. He takes issue with the prevailing mindset of his colleagues. Rejection of the universal values of the West, parallel to an inherent admission of the absolutism of pre-modern cultures in the name of cultural relativism as prevailing in Western cultural anthropology, was not Gellner's choice. He points to a peculiarity: Islamic fundamentalists are definitely not in line with cultural relativism. However,

> logically, the religious fundamentalists of course are also in conflict with the relativists ... In practice, this confrontation is not so very much in evidence. ... The relativists direct their attack only at those they castigate as ... non-relativists within their own enlightened tradition, but play down the disagreement which logically separates them from religious fundamentalism. Their attitude is roughly that absolutism is to be tolerated only if it is sufficiently alien culturally. It is only at home that they do not put up with it.[94]

This statement provides a rational explanation of a Western postmodern mindset that tolerates Islamism, which is an Islamic variety of religious fundamentalism, not of a multiple modernity. For instrumental reasons, these postmodernists are greatly welcomed by the intelligent and well-informed among these fundamentalists; they "notice relativism pervasive in Western society" and also make use "of it for their own ends, even though they despise it and do not take much interest in its rationale."[95] The Western cultural relativists overlook the totalitarian face of Islamism, and Islamists hide their contempt for these "unbelievers." An alliance of strange bedfellows emerges.

Why do I refer to the cited controversy in the conclusion of this chapter? It is because of my conviction that the legacy of Ernest Gellner matters if one is set to go beyond the prevailing extremes of essentialism and cultural relativism. This is a necessity for understanding the value change that underpins cultural change. Under the conditions of current international standards it is necessary to understand that cultural innovations matter, but are impeded by the prevailing cultural patterns. In Cairo I once addressed this issue in a debate on the future prospects for development, and pleasantly encountered a receptive audience for the view that the *Future of Islamic Civilization*[96] primarily depends on cultural innovations. They continue to be absent. In short, the problem in the Islamic world is homemade and is not exclusively an outcome of globalization, even though it is embedded in its processes.

In this chapter I have made clear that among the impediments to change in the Islamic world is a reluctance to open one's mind to discerning one's own shortcomings in order to acknowledge what the above-quoted study of the UNDP states as being the problem. This UN report was polemically rejected in an article by Riyad Tabbarah, published in the influential *al-Hayat* newspaper, in which he argues:

> A closer look at and reading of the report reveals the distortions it includes as well as the great scholarly gaps it entails. This compels us to deal with it in great caution. This applies in particular to the major conclusions for the recommendation how to push forward Arab development.[97]

Underlying this stubborn rejection is the stated belief that "only a scientific standing that looks for ways for adopting modern technology without importing the related Western ills would be useful" (ibid.). By "ills" the quoted author obviously means the values of cultural modernity. A Muslim myself, I acknowledge that Christian Arab thinkers are free of such a mentality. It is a fact that some Christian Arab authors have addressed the issue of cultural change, but understandably they have shied away from relating the debate to religious reform. Most prominent among these Christian Arabs are Salamah Musah, Nadrah al-Yaziji, and George Hanna.[98] Today, the influence of these intellectuals from religious minorities is declining in face of the prevalence of political Islam. One should recall, in this context, that the introduction of the new cultural concept of the nation, which led to pan-Arab nationalism, can be traced back to the work of Christian Arabs.[99] However, this is history and cannot be repeated with other concepts. Even with regard to the concept of the nation, the work of the Christian Arabs is disputed today, with the inclination to link Arabism to Islamism and thus to de-secularize it. Today, we find no courageous thinkers such as the Christian Egyptian Salamah Musah, who asked for cultural change and made the radical criticism that traditional Arab culture is an obstacle to change. Also, we no longer find Syrian Lebanese Christians who shape major intellectual debates.

There is a decline in the contribution of Christian Arabs, who today have mostly escaped discrimination by the Islamists by migrating to the West. This is coupled with a notable decline in the quantity of translations from Western languages into Arabic. Western books are rarely translated into Arabic and they are replaced by a growing body of literature classified as "political Islam." Add to this deficit the problem of a vanishing mindset of reform in contemporary Islam. Luckily, one can still find a few important reform Muslims, such the Egyptian Mohammed S. Ashmawi, who is still active in the region but who lives under protection and every day faces the threat of being killed, as happened to Faraj Fuda in Cairo. Others, like Hamid Abu-Zaid, leave, but change in the diaspora, regrettably not for the better. Among the bright Muslims who are active at home is the Moroccan Mohammed Abed al-Jabri. He continues to teach in Rabat and to be critical. In general, most Muslim reformers escape and live in cultural asylum in Western Europe and North America. Under the influence of the diasporic environment some of them have become "defensive-cultural." I am among the reform Muslims who have found shelter in the West and hope that the ugly European othering will not compel me to change my critical attitude and to join forces with those so-called reformists (e.g. An-Na'im) whom I criticize here. As a Muslim I say, "God forbid."

The critique of Islam from the standpoint of cultural modernity is combined with a strong inclination to warn Europeans against self-congratulation. They, too, have their homework to do. One of the current tasks for today's West is to reconsider the culture of political taboos in a mind of cultural relativism. Free debate on current problems is undermined. The prevailing environment impedes uncensored addressing of current issues even by Muslims. I contend that Europe is also affected by the developments analyzed in this chapter. The identity of European civilization, which was once the source of universal standards of progress and development, is challenged: today Europe is host to about 32 million Muslims (20 million in the EU and 12 million in the Balkans) and is affected by what happens in the Islamic world. Europeans believe in accommodating political Islam – in whatever shape – through multiculturalism and appeasement. The overall problem is addressed by David Gress, who tells us:

> Although multiculturalism might seem to contradict universalism, the two were compatible; indeed, multiculturalism was simply universalism applied to cultural politics … universalism … never solved its fundamental dilemma of being both a Western idea – the idea that Westernization was global and irresistible – and an anti-Western idea – the idea that Western identity had fortunately come to an end … The dilemma of universalism derived from the ambiguities of the New West itself: … was it the fruit of a historic identity? … The dilemma posed the question of Western identity for the third millennium."[100]

This book deals with the universal claims of cultural modernity, and not with multiculturalism. However, this reference is made and is not a digression. Global migration, also from the Islamic world to the West, brings all of the problems of the Islamic world to Europe, while Europeans prefer to close their eyes. The drive towards shari'atization that is analyzed in Chapter 3 affects Europe also. Here, I just make this note, as I have tackled the Islamic migration in Western Europe and North America, together with the diasporic politicization of Islam to an Islamism and all of the related problems, at length in an earlier book.[101] In contrast to that earlier book, *Political Islam, World Politics and Europe*, this one focuses on developments in the Islamic world itself. From the viewpoint of the assumed predicament with cultural modernity, conflicts occur first within Islamic societies and then spill over. The related Muslim attitudes promote an international conflict that has other constraints. The underlying issue is the self-assertive rejection of cultural modernity, in the illusory belief of a de-Westernization of the world with the aim of Islamizing it. I am against the rhetoric of a clash of civilizations and therefore propose religious reforms and cultural change as a way out of Islam's predicament with modernity. Such a strategy could contribute to defusing the tensions and thus to bridging between the civilizations.

I summarize my conclusions based on this chapter as follows.

First, the impediments to a willingness to learn from others in today's world of Islam undermine the needed value change, which can only occur if accompanied by attitudinal change. Muslims need to give up their claim of moral superiority vs. non-Muslims in order to pave the way to establishing a cultural willingness to learn from others. Unlike early Arabic thought in the liberal age, contemporary Islamic thought is closed minded and *not* open to learning from other cultures. This impediment heads the list of major obstacles.

Second, the Islamic religious-cultural rejection of the notion of innovation is indicated by the very fact of its translation by the Arabic term *"bid'a/*creative innovation." In orthodox Islam (e.g. Wahhabism) *bid'a* is associated with heresy. The result is to preclude any cultural change because it touches on the believed purity of religion. The scriptural mind of Islam is the Islamic variety of essentialism that obstructs any cultural change and undermines the unfolding of an open mind.

Third, the political explanation that relates to an Islamic "Revolt against the West" refers not only to an upheaval directed against Western hegemony, but also to a rejection of Western values as such. As Hedley Bull puts it, it is considered to be "cultural liberation" to engage oneself in "cultural re-assertion ... of indigenous culture as exemplified in Islamic fundamentalism."[102] This attitude gives rise to the question whether this "Revolt against Western dominance ... is not a revolt against Western values as such" (ibid.). An Islamic resolution of the conflicts emerging from Islam's predicament with modernity would settle this issue. The Islamic rejection of cultural modernity reminds one of Habermas's question regarding another rejection, namely that advanced by the postmodernists. In his book *The Philosophical Discourse of Modernity* Habermas asks whether postmodern views on cultural modernity in fact reflect a pre-modern mindset and a counter-enlightenment.

Fourth, and last, I want to point to *the simultaneity of globalization and cultural fragmentation.* This is a formula coined in my earlier work[103] and means that the processes of globalization change worldwide structures in economy and politics, resulting in the emergence of a world economy and an international system of states, but that culture does not become universal. Culture is always related to production of meaning. Therefore, it is always local.[104] People of different cultures may use the same technological means (e.g. computers and the internet), however, without sharing the same values. I address this reality as an indication of cultural fragmentation, which stands in the way of universalizing the values of cultural modernity. A cross-cultural acceptance of cultural modernity promises a way out. I despise all "isms," including universalism and relativism. It is not a contradiction to support cross-cultural universality and to be against universalism. These are two different issues; one refers to a state of affairs, the other refers to an ideology.

In summary, it is safe to argue first, that there is a gap of structural development between the civilizations of Islam and the West; second, that it is embedded in a simultaneously increasing closeness in the interaction of both. This closeness has never been as intense as it is in the twenty-first century. This is the background of a conflict that assumes a civilizational shape. Some Americans inappropriately address this issue as *Jihad versus McWorld*. This is a misunderstanding of the conflict at issue. The necessary process of religious reform and cultural change in order to come to terms with cultural modernity is not an adjustment to McWorld. The currently anti-Western worldview prevailing in the Islamic world is self-defeating and ends in an impasse. At issue is a resistance to cultural change that is wrongly presented as a "protest against globalization," or as a jihad against it. The report of the prominent Muslim scholar Akbar Ahmed, who in a tour with young Americans in nine Islamic countries stretching from Indonesia to Turkey faced a disturbing situation, is alarming. Ahmed told the *International Herald Tribune* after his return from that tour: "The situation is very grave … No one knows what might happen … also no one knows whether moderate, modernist strains of Islam now so widely in retreat, can recover."[105] In addition to this bleak perspective, Akbar Ahmed admitted: "The trip left me taken aback by the almost collapse of the modernist model in which I grew up" (ibid.).

The quoted report of an enlightened Muslim involved in Islamic–Western inter-civilizational dialogue is not only alarming, but should also serve as a reminder to the West that it can only deal with those Muslims – like Akbar Ahmed – who are open to rationality. Akbar Ahmed was shocked – as the *International Herald Tribune* describes – when he witnessed a "delicate point of Islamic world history, with anti-Americanism near all time highs" (ibid.). One needs to correct the term "anti-Americanism," because a general anti-Westernism is at work here that also involves Europe. The cited report makes clear how much it matters for the world at large that Muslim people come to terms with cultural modernity through reform and change. This insight and the related recommendations govern all of the reasoning in the following chapters, in particular Chapter 5 in which the cultural sources of tensions that lead to conflict are addressed and analyzed in a candid and uncensored manner. Today, the civil war that is occurring within the Islamic civilization is being escalated into a geo-political war that not only does harm to the Islamic people, but also makes them a burden to the rest of humanity. Therefore, Muslims need to come to their senses and engage in a serious effort at accommodation to cultural modernity. The time for blame games, accusations, and self-victimization seems to be over, even though the inflammatory "war of ideas" continues unabated.

Chapter 2

Issue areas of the predicament I: modernity and knowledge

Torn between reason and Islamization

Knowledge is a basic issue area related to cultural modernity.[1] René Descartes established modern knowledge on the grounds of conjecture and doubt, guided by the principle *"cogito ergo sum/*I think, therefore I am." In contrast to what is described as an authentic "Islamic knowledge" based on faith, this modern Cartesian epistemology dismisses any claim of knowledge to be absolute, regardless of whether it is based on belief or on ideology. The basic pillar of modern knowledge is its recognition of the primacy of reason and the related subjection of all matters, including religion, to critical reflection. Jürgen Habermas restates Kant's views on this issue in the course of his introduction of "the principle of subjectivity" (on which the logic of cultural modernity rests) in this manner: "Kant carried out this approach of the philosophy of reflection in his three 'critiques' ...; he installed reason in the supreme seat of judgment before which anything that made a claim to validity had to be justified."[2] To determine the current problem, let it be stated at the outset that at issue are not only epistemology and knowledge, but also development and power. If the Islamic world fails to engage in *Building a Knowledge Society* (this is the title of the second UNDP report of 2003) in order to come to terms with modern knowledge in the sense outlined, then it will never be able to move forward.

Introduction

This chapter claims to rest on the philosophical assumptions of modern Cartesian epistemology, and therefore the polemics of "Cartesian imperialism" are strongly dismissed. The chapter also reflects an intellectual training of a Muslim in the Frankfurt School. I am, however, trained not only in philosophy but also in international relations. This book links the two disciplines and thus can be viewed as a philosophical contribution to the understanding of the cultural roots of international conflict. It is in this sense an international relations inquiry that argues by means of a philosophical discourse. Accordingly, the international relations perspective determines the major arguments. The inquiry draws on the book of Ernst Haas, *When Knowledge is Power*, in which it is argued that decision makers in world politics cannot be successful if they are not in possession of "changing knowledge about nature and human affairs."[3] It is self-evident that this "changing knowledge" has to be secular; it can never be immutable, as drawn from holy, revealed sources. In the case of what is viewed to be "Islamic knowledge" based on the Qur'an, knowledge is neither changing nor subject to revision and rethinking. Rational knowledge is, in contrast, about the real world, in that it is "knowledge available about the problem at issue; [it] influences the way decision makers define the interest at stake in the solution to the problem" (ibid., p. 9). It is not only the secular, reflexive, and "changing" character of knowledge that matters; the requirement of "being critical about one's knowledge" (ibid.) also has to be fulfilled. According to Haas, this implies "a readiness to consider the finality of what one knows and thereafter to be willing to redefine the problem" (ibid.). The present book argues for change and reform in Islamic civilization. In this context, knowledge is highly pertinent. Haas tells us that "change ... is caused mostly by the way knowledge about nature and about society is married to political interests and objectives" (p. 11). With this understanding in mind, this chapter inquires into the prevailing patterns of knowledge in the Islamic world and asks whether they promote change. The assumption is that they do not. The underlying argument is that Muslim societies are in a state of underdevelopment, because they lack the rational knowledge for a proper understanding of the world in which they live.

Based on the outlined understanding, I begin by stating that a rational view of the world existed in Islamic "*falsafa*/rationalism" (see Chapter 8). At that time Islamic civilization was highly developed. In Islam rationalism has always been in conflict with a religious knowledge that claims to embody the absolute. In classical Islam the rationalists lost the battle. Today, the prevailing epistemology in Islam is a major issue area in the predicament of Islamic civilization with cultural modernity. Therefore, this chapter puts forward some assumptions to guide an analysis of the issue and its related problems. In their objective of an "Islamization of sciences"[4] contemporary Islamists evade the burning issues altogether. They believe in solving all the problems in question through their agenda of Islamization. Despite the will to change in nineteenth-century Islamic reformism, one encounters there a similar evasion. The predicament is not addressed at all, as is more than obvious. It is for this reason that in this book I question the qualification of this thinking as "*islah*/religious reform." It did not reform anything.

Long before Descartes[5] and Kant, Islamic medieval philosophers engaged in a reason-based undertaking to grasp basic issues and they arrived at rational conclusions regarding their knowledge of the world. Averroes found a solution for the tension between reason and revelation in the concept of "*al-haqiqa al-muzdawaja*/double truth." This concept separates religious from rational knowledge while acknowledging the validity of both. The last great philosopher in Islamic history, Ibn Khaldun (died 1406), continued this line of reasoning, drawing in his *al-Muqaddima*/Prolegomena a clear distinction between one system of knowledge based on reason, and another based on revelation. For tactical reasons, Ibn

Khaldun pointed out the pitfalls of rational knowledge – related to its weakening of absolute belief – but he nonetheless presented the foremost philosophy of history as a *"ilm al-umran/* science of civilization" based on reason.[6]

Rationalism and universality are not the peculiar products of a Eurocentric mind. They are well known in the classical heritage of Islam. In medieval Islam rational philosophers not only established reason-based knowledge, but also acknowledged the universality of the related rational thought. Of course, there also exists in each case a culture-based knowledge, i.e. different and specific patterns of knowledge characterized by diversity. Given that cultures are local and never universal, cultural systems based on religion have their own cultural knowledge, as is the case in Islam. The argument established in the preceding chapter regarding the changeable character of any culture – as opposed to essentializations, no matter where a culture comes from – touches also on religious knowledge, which is also supposed to be subject to change. Thus, the admitted notion of religious reform is related to cultural change. This subject matter complicates the links between religion, culture, and knowledge discussed here in the light of modernity. The underlying assumption is that the admission of change allows a rethinking of religious precepts in order to accommodate them. This is exactly the authentic meaning of religious reform that seems not to be acceptable to devout Muslims. In a nutshell, the subject matter of this chapter is reason-based knowledge in conflict with absolute knowledge. The predicament of Islam with cultural modernity revolves around this conflict.

As has been made clear, cultural change in a civilization[7] is also related to knowledge. In Islam it is believed that the Qur'an alone is the major source of knowledge, as it is revealed by God. However, the Prophet asked the believers of his community to strive for knowledge *"wa law fi al-sin/* even in China."[8] In Islam, the worst possible blame is to accuse a person of *"jahl/*ignorance," as contrasted to the virtue of *"knowledge/ilm."* Now, it is necessary to determine exactly what knowledge is, and then to ask why this issue leads to the assumed conflict. In a simplistic manner, the conflict is addressed by some in terms of the dichotomous Huntingtonian clash of Islam and the West, i.e. of knowledge leading to a *global jihad* based on Islamization versus knowledge based on modern Western rationalism in the Weberian sense. I do not share this view and I dismiss the notion of a "clash." I have already made reference to rationalism in Islamic civilization, a tradition that is often overlooked. The assumed clash between Islam and rationalism is based on *jahl,* i.e. on ignorance, and not on knowledge of facts on the ground.

Basically, knowledge – viewed here as a source of political thought – matters to those commitments that are related to it. In Islam, the conflict is related to the competition between systems of scriptural-religious and reason-based knowledge. Thus, it refers to a classical conflict between *fiqh* as sacral jurisprudence, viewed to be "knowledge par excellence," and *falsafa* as reason-based Islamic philosophy.[9] This issue and the related tensions in Islam predate the rise of the West and its rationalism. At the time, Muslims were far ahead of Europe. However, the conflict between two rival worldviews within Islamic civilization itself was decided to the detriment of rationalism. This conflict assumes currency in its relevance to the contemporary predicament of Islam with modernity. The old conflict recurs in a new form as one between Islamism/Salafism and cultural modernity. Add to this new form the fact that, under conditions of globalization, the conflict assumes an international dimension that is very relevant to the study of international conflict, as this book suggests.

Why does knowledge matter to the study of religious reform and cultural change?

To answer the question raised in the heading of this section one needs first to ask "What is knowledge in Islam?" followed by "What are the sources?" As stated, in Islam knowledge is divine, as prescribed to Muslims by the Qur'an and the Hadith,[10] the two primary sources. In this regard, there is a difference between Islamic godly, and human knowledge. The classical dispute in Islam between *fiqh* and *falsafa* is most pertinent to the understanding of the predicament of Islam with cultural modernity. Islamist efforts to restore the divine, inspired by Sayyid Qutb and Hasan al-Banna, revive the old conflict over the sources of knowledge ("*wahi*/revelation" vs. "*aql*/reason"). These efforts are driven by an objective of Islamization of knowledge that is situated in an overall agenda for the Islamization of the world at large. The intellectual sources of this project are the writings of Qutb and al-Banna.[11] Both were obsessed with preaching jihad in the meaning of the use of force in what Qutb termed "Islamic World Revolution." In their thinking, epistemology was at the fringe. However, their jihad for Islamization is based on a knowledge essential to their universal project of a political Islam giving the world new perspectives.

In dealing with knowledge, and consequentially with the Islamist epistemological agenda placed in a political and social context, this chapter addresses additional questions to that posed in the heading. These questions are: do Muslims derive their knowledge exclusively from the revelation based on interpretation of the Qur'an? Is any reasoning beyond the scripture to be admitted? Is Islamic knowledge simply scriptural? Are Muslims entitled to admit "reason" as a source of knowledge without committing "*kufr*/heresy"? And last, but not least, the question above all: what needs to be done to legitimate cultural change and thus religious reform? If the only source of knowledge for Muslims were the Qur'an, then how could they communicate with other humans who did not share their beliefs? These non-Muslims make up the majority of humanity. It is an illusion to believe that these people could become Muslims through "*da'wa*/ proselytization" or be coerced into doing so. If pluralism is to be accepted, then this *da'wa* is a non-starter and Muslims are challenged to abandon their supremacist views, as will be discussed in more detail in Chapter 7 on pluralism. This supremacism matters here as it is relevant to knowledge. Muslims believe in the supremacy of their revealed knowledge, basing on it the supremacist worldview from which they derive their related claims. Thereby, they create a problem for themselves, which becomes a problem for others, too.

To start with a more promising option, I refer to the Qur'an, which, in the verse "we created you in peoples and tribes to get to know one another" (*al-hujrat*), acknowledges the diversity of humanity. The fact that there are non-Muslims should be perceived as an essential part of this diversity. To engage in "*da'wa*/proselytization" in intercultural communication is not acceptable by the standards of modernity. In order to base knowledge on reason, acceptance of the idea of cultural change as a change of values, worldview, attitudes, and thus of behavior is a basic requirement. It is for this reason that knowledge matters to an inquiry into religious reform and cultural change that aims to make Muslim people embrace, in their own cultural – albeit reformed – terms the values of cultural modernity, above all, those of religious and cultural pluralism.

The present inquiry begins with an attempt to determine whether the frame of human knowledge is universal or local. Knowledge has certainly always been both, and this is at one and the same time a source of the division within humanity and an intercultural bridge. It is true that each civilization has its own concept of knowledge, but it is equally true that throughout the history of mankind there have been all kinds of cultural borrowings of knowledge in the process of cross-cultural fertilization. The result of a shared, inter-civilizational knowledge in history is not only a fact, but also the essence of the intellectual heritage of the whole of humanity. It is only knowledge based on reason that can be shared by all humanity. Knowledge cannot be shared by others if it is exclusively based on a particular religion – unless people convert to the respective religion and thus share the same belief. In short, there exists no single religion designed to be shared by the whole of humanity, even though universalist religions do cultivate such a claim. The Islamic belief based on "*da'wa*/proselytization" is an example of this universalist monotheism. Humanity is expected to be united in one Islamic *umma* in order to establish world peace based on Islamic tenets. Even though the Qur'an, in sura *al-hujrat*, acknowledges diversity, pluralism of people of different faiths and cultures on an equal footing is alien to Islamic history, and the lack of it is part of the predicament.[12]

The subject of this chapter is rational knowledge, which has to be separated from particular beliefs in that it is based on human reason. This rationality can be shared by all. Of course, this assertion is based on a definite rejection of any racial or ethnic determination in this field. Much as I reject Weber's "occidental rationalism," my thoughts are also opposed to postmodern fashions that not only dismiss the universality of rational knowledge but also question any related objectivity, which is downgraded to a narrative. This is the underlying argument for the view that universal cultural modernity could unite a culturally and religiously diverse humanity by ranking human reason as the impartial "supreme court" (Immanuel Kant) for determining what is right and what is wrong in our knowledge. If one dismisses this rationality, then there can be no common ground for people to live together under the conditions of diversity and globalization. What from a religious point of view is right for a Muslim could be viewed as utterly wrong by a Hindu or by a Jew from their own particular perspective. Given that human reason has no religion or race, rationality can be regarded as human, i.e. as universal, and thus goes beyond divisive views and beliefs.

This understanding of knowledge matters in determining what is cultural change and what is religious reform. Rational knowledge that underpins change and reform is human and therefore it can be universal. This insight is the basis of the analysis that follows, which stands in contrast to postmodern views and their related beliefs. In the twenty-first century Islam faces cultural modernity. The Islamic variety of religious fundamentalism is not a rational response to this challenge;[13] it is a variety of neo-absolutism, not an alternative modernity, as some postmodernists would like to believe.

Humanity is determined by the diversity of cultures and civilizations, which today are linked to one another through globalization. There is a need to share knowledge and the rational view of the world so as to maintain diversity on the basis of mutual respect and tolerance and give peace a chance. This concept of cultural and religious pluralism based on rationality guarantees the combination of diversity and concurrence on basic values, such as equality of religions. One learns from history that Muslim–Christian encounters comprised jihad and crusades, i.e. war – waged in the name of peace – as well as cross-cultural fertilizations.[14] Nonetheless, there was no pluralism, but a consistent dismissal of common values by both parties. All religious civilizations are mostly self-righteous in their attitudes, and thus prone to imposing their own views on others. Their absolutist mindset stands in contrast to pluralism. The assumption of intercultural rational knowledge, which is secular and based on reason, challenges the recent project of the Islamization of knowledge (see note 4) as promoted by Salafists and Islamists even in their diaspora in the West. This concept presents an obstacle to Muslims not only in joining a democratic peace based on pluralism in the aforementioned sense, but also in engaging in cultural change and religious reforms. The revived vision of *"siyadat al-Islam/*Islamic supremacy" is not acceptable to non-Muslims and is based on knowledge that is contested by the standards of a rational knowledge that rests on cultural modernity.

Is it possible to establish universally valid knowledge about modernity and to relate to it cultural change and religious reform? The student of Islam William Montgomery Watt tells us in his thinking about Islam and knowledge in the age of modernity that there is a basic difference between people of Islamic and of Western civilization in their ways of determining what knowledge is. Watt argues:

> When Muslims think of knowledge, they think of what may be called "knowledge for living," whereas when a Westerner thinks of knowledge, it is mainly of "knowledge for power," that is, such knowledge enables one to control natural and material objects and human individuals and societies. It

is in respect of knowledge for living, consisting of religious and moral values, that Islam claims finality and self-sufficiency ... Muslims show surprisingly little interest in other forms of knowledge, even those which would be useful to them for practical purposes.[15]

It is true that for an ordinary Muslim believer "living" is perceived to occur under the rules of Islam, which are believed to be universal and thus to apply also to non-Muslims. This forceful and at times aggressive universalism was pursued in history through violent Islamic proselytization by means of jihad wars. Therefore, Muslims include the dimension of power based on jihad, in the knowledge that is embedded in this context of "living." The reference to jihad wars fought by Muslims for mapping the world into a *"Dar al-Islam*/house of Islam"* belies Watt's contention. Power is a historical fact in conquests that were pursued in addition to trade and commerce as a means for the expansion of Islam. The Islamic project of globalization lasted from the seventh to the seventeenth centuries. This Islamic project of mapping the world into a *Dar al-Islam* preceded the Western globalization process. The revival of Islamic collective memories of and knowledge about this first world project of globalization lead to conflict, as will be shown in Chapter 5 on cultural tensions.

The modern global structure that encompasses the entire world grew from European, not Islamic expansion. The reader is reminded of the fact that the rise of the West was facilitated by the success and the universal scope of the "Military Revolution,"[16] which underpinned European expansion. Muslims started to develop a curiosity about the source of the success of this new, European invading power; they believed they could undo the evolving asymmetry through a military borrowing from the enemy. Their "import of the European army"[17] failed to establish a balance with modern European military power. Muslim rulers also failed to understand that the European success was related to the secular knowledge on which modern science and technology are based.[18] Without seriously addressing the culturally determinable basic differences between the secular Western and Muslim religious understandings of knowledge, the early Muslim reformists[19] of the nineteenth century engaged in arguments favorable to adopting modern sciences into Islam. Based on the evasion mentioned, they believed that their project could be promoted by establishing harmony between modern knowledge and what they viewed as Islamic culture. My contention is that these early Muslim reformists failed because of their reluctance to permit a real change in values. They were reluctant to rethink the Islamic worldview in the context of real religious reform so as to accommodate religious belief to the new environment of a changed world. In fact, Muslim reformers evaded these issues altogether; their evasion resulted in an overall failure. This seems to be a recurring problem for Muslim reformers that continues to date. The most recent example of this phenomenon is the sea-change in the work of Abdullahi An-Na'im, discussed in Chapter 6. It is a change from a criticism of shari'a-based knowledge to an embrace of the shari'a itself.

In short, the issue is that Islamic reform in the nineteenth century was basically directed by the pragmatic need to overcome the power gap between Muslim and European knowledge – without, however, taking the liberty of revising the inherited religious doctrine. To date, this predicament with modernity remains not only current and unresolved, but also not discussed. With hindsight one can state that the tradition labeled "Islamic reform" failed to deliver anything. Islamic reformists were not willing to accept drawing a line between reason-based and revealed, divine knowledge. As stated in Chapter 1, I question the label "Islamic reform." At present there are some reformers, such as Mohammed Arkoun and to a less degree An-Na'im, who act from the diaspora in the West and thus have virtually no influence on what happens in the Islamic world itself. These reformers have their problems, too. Arkoun believes that the qualification of his work as "*islah/reform*" is a downgrading, since he believes that he is doing much more, that is, "subverting." Despite this presumptuous claim, the pronounced revolution is not in place. The "subversion" consists purely of rhetorics. The other reformer entangles his thinking in logical and sociological contradictions: An-Na'im wants "a secular state," but "no secularization." This is almost laughable.[20]

Not only the so-called reformers, but also the self-pronounced secularists who took over after the decline of Islamic liberalism had no agenda for establishing the cultural and religious knowledge that could underpin change and reform. Then came the watershed of 1967. Among the repercussions of the comprehensive Arab defeat in the Six Day War[21] is the decline of secular pan-Arab nationalism in favor of the rise of political Islam.[22] This happened first in the Arab world and then spilled over into other Islamic countries. There exists also a Shi'ite variety of political Islam, which came to the fore after the Islamic revolution of 1979. Contemporary history proved, however, that the Sunni Arab world – not the Shi'i Islam of Iran – continues to be the cultural core of Islamic civilization and to determine its worldview.[23] This applies also to the field of religion and knowledge.

Unlike Islamic reform and secular nationalism, political Islam has a civilizational project named "Islamization of knowledge." It grew from the process described and relates to the shari'atization of politics, to be introduced in the following chapters. The Islamist strategy combines the "Islamization of knowledge" with the shari'atization of law in its fundamentalist project of a de-Westernization of the Islamic world and of the world at large.

The civilizational conflict between cultural modernity and pre-modern cultures assumes, in the vocabulary of political Islam, a cultural-religious shape along the following lines stated by Sayyid Qutb:

> The battle is between believers and their enemies … it is neither political nor economic in its nature … at the hub of the conflict is the involved belief being the issue. The related options are: either unbelief/*kufr* or belief/*iman* is to prevail. This means either to accept *jahilliyya* [Islamic term for ignorance in the pre-Islamic age, B.T.] or Islam.[24]

The quoted words are basic and highly influential. Today, they determine the worldview of jihadist Islamism. One encounters this meaning with a slightly different wording in the repeated declaration of jihad by Osama Bin Laden. The application of the "battle" pronounced by Qutb to the Islamization of knowledge is relevant in the context of this chapter. Global jihad is, then, understood as a purification of the Islamic world from all non-Islamic knowledge. The call for jihad replaces the need for cultural change and for religious reform. Here we see how knowledge is intertwined with the study of cultural change and religious reform in the Islamic world.

For contemporary Muslims the fight against Western knowledge is essential in the "jihad against *kufr*/unbelief." In terms of the sociology of knowledge this is a kind of reassertion of the local versus the global and the particular versus the universal. This fight for "local Islam" against what globalization presents as "universal" becomes a pattern of identity politics. This ideology of identity can be faulted on two counts: *first*, it is not really local, for Islamism claims universality for itself and *second*, Islamists overlook the fact that reason-based knowledge existed in Hellenized Islam long before the West emerged as a new civilization from the sixteenth century onwards. Even though the Islamist agenda in the field of knowledge questions neither the idea of universal knowledge nor that of globalization, it rebuffs the pattern of universality of cultural modernity, which is identified with the "*gharb*/West." It is located in the tradition of the crusades. The alternative of Islamic knowledge is presented as being instead a forthright universal knowledge. It is argued that only the revival of the Islamic project of globalization could save "humanity from the abyss,"[25] as Qutb tells us in his agenda for the Islamization of the world.

What matters here is the potential of cultural change and religious reform for coming to terms with Islam's predicament with cultural modernity. Qutb's trajectory keeps the Muslims imprisoned in their impasse. In contrast, it is argued that secular knowledge is a requirement and a *sine qua non* for a way out of the present malaise. This position brings this book into conflict with postmodernists, who do not understand the "Revolt against the West" and end up, as Ernest Gellner rightly notes, in a mindset of rapprochement with political Islam. For their part, religious fundamentalists abuse relativists, who have clearly different approaches. As the late Gellner states of these strange bedfellows:

> Logically, the religious fundamentalists are of course also in conflict with the relativists ... In practice this confrontation (is) not so very much in evidence. The fundamentalists notice and despise ... relativism ... the relativists ... direct their attack only at those ... non-relativists within their own enlightened tradition, but play down disagreement [with] religious fundamentalism.[26]

Based on this insight, it is safe to state that some cultural relativists and postmodernists are more critical of the West than of religious fundamentalism. They fail to grasp that Islamism is the most powerful variety of a neo-absolutism that can be interpreted as the "new totalitarianism"[27] with regard to knowledge, polity, and society. Instead of a balanced view that acknowledges the two evils of Islamophobia and anti-Westernism, one encounters single-minded relativists who see only one of these evils and turn a blind eye to the other. Practically, cultural-relativist postmodernists share the Islamist propaganda of addressing the West as "crusaders." A rational debate is no longer possible, either with political Islam or with some similarly anti-Western minded cultural-relativist postmodernists. Both share the dismissal of cultural modernity. Unlike the postmodernists, the rejection of modernity by the Islamists is based on a dreadful antisemitism, for which the work of Anwar al-Jundi is only one of the major sources.[28] In addition, the rebuff is restricted to rejecting Western values in parallel to espousing modern science and technology. The result is semi-modernity, combined with an equating of rational knowledge with the ridiculous accusation of "epistemological imperialism" of the West.

Global jihad for an Islamization of knowledge, instead of religious reform

In the preceding section, the relevance of the acceptance or dismissal of rational knowledge to the pursuit of religious reform was established. It is argued that rationalism is not a "Western epistemology." Modern knowledge was used instrumentally to establish Western dominance, but it should not be equated with Western hegemony. Cultural modernity is based on universal knowledge. In Chapter 1 I referred to the Islamic illusion of semi-modernity and discussed it in some detail. Some Islamic revivalists prefer to use a different terminology for this semi-modernity. Those among them who claim to be scholars prefer to present themselves as "post-colonial" rather than "postmodern." However, in the cultural battle against the knowledge of cultural modernity they stand on the same front. The British-Pakistani professor Ziauddin Sadar, known as a representative of "post-colonial studies," ignores the medieval Islamic tradition of rationalism[29] and qualifies Cartesianism, in a sweeping generalization, as cultural and "epistemological imperialism."[30] To say the least, this formula is based on a laughable allegation about the rational mindset of Cartesianism. Much more intelligent is the study by the liberal Akbar Ahmed, in which an Islamic claim to postmodernity is put forward, with, however, full awareness of the fact that postmodernity – like modernity – is, in its origins, a Western concept. In the view of Akbar Ahmed, "the Muslim modernist phase was engendered by European colonialism,"[31] and he adds that Muslims submit to modernity "as a drive to acquire Western education, technology and industry. Ideas of democracy ... were discussed ... with reservation" (ibid). This statement tacitly supports those Muslim attitudes favorable to cultural modernity. However, the confusion of institutional and cultural modernity makes Muslims of this mindset shy away from embracing religious reform and cultural change. This should be the implication and the consequence of the willingness to accommodate modernity, but it is missing.

In awareness of its two dimensions, I make clear that modernity is a mixed bag. There is thus a need to draw distinctions within it. In reality, basically the institutional dimension (structures) has been *globalized*, and this is – as stated by Ahmed – what Muslims have experienced. In contrast, cultural modernity (values and rational worldview) has never been successfully *universalized*. One can dismiss with great justification the power dimension of institutional modernity related to instrumental reason, but at the same time it is no contradiction to defend the values of cultural modernity. The contemporary religious revival and its defensive-cultural reassertion underpin the rise of religious fundamentalism. In the Fundamentalism Project of the American Academy of Arts and Sciences it has been established that religious fundamentalism is a response to modernity, without, however, honoring the distinctions alluded to.[32] In some varieties of transnational religion one encounters a cultural reassertion that is articulated in the rejection of rational knowledge. It amounts to a wholesale rejection of the values of cultural modernity. As shown in the work done within the framework of the Fundamentalism Project, Islamic fundamentalists are, however, neither traditionalists nor postmodernists. They are modern in that they approve the adoption of alien instruments of science and technology in order to fight the West with its own weapons, but they rebuke the related cultural value system, defined here as cultural modernity. The result is an "Islamic dream of semi-modernity" based on a rejection of rational knowledge while the adoption of techno-scientific accomplishments is approved. This is an indication of splitting of modernity into two components believed to be unrelated to one another. I shall discuss this issue at length in the concluding chapter.

Let it be noted here that some Western writers fail to grasp the ambiguity of Islamic attitudes towards modernity when they put forward the misconception of multiple modernities. A lack of familiarity with the related Islamist writings underpins this misconception. The already quoted liberal Muslim writer Akbar Ahmed rightly comments: "Islamic and Western postmodernisms may have little … in common," even though both reject "the West's global civilization."[33] Akbar Ahmed shares the view of an "intellectual conquest of the Islamic world"[34] by the West, an allegation also put forward by Islamists in their propaganda. This similarity reveals how sensitive is the issue of knowledge for cultural change and how blurred the lines are, even between liberal and Islamist Muslims. It is noteworthy that the same liberal Muslim who in 1992 argued like the Islamists against the alleged "intellectual conquest of the world of Islam" was shocked when, in 2007, he left the Western diaspora to tour in Islamic countries and found, to his surprise, that "Frankly, the trip left me taken aback by the almost-collapse of the modernist model in which I grew up."[35] Liberal Muslims like the quoted Akbar Ahmed unwittingly had a part in creating this story. Through their inconsistencies, they have contributed to this collapse of the modernist project in the Islamic world.

Ahead of quoting the ridiculous notion of "epistemological imperialism" I noted the ignorance of Islamists about medieval Islamic philosophers who, on the grounds of rational thought, never contended an incompatibility between Islamic and non-Islamic cultural conceptions of knowledge. In contrast, the rejection of the knowledge of cultural modernity by the Islamists, combined with the view of the superiority of Muslim knowledge, creates a great predicament for contemporary Islamic civilization. The Islamist formula "*al-Islam ya'lu wa la yu'la alayhi*/Islam is superior, and nothing can be superior to it" is alleged to be authentic and is also related to the belief in the superiority of "Islamic knowledge."

Not only Islamists, but also orthodox Salafist Muslims believe that valid knowledge is exclusively identical with the Qur'anic revelation. For them it is the absolute knowledge, in that it constitutes the very finality for the whole of humanity. Therefore, the claim of validity is made not only for Muslims, but applies also to non-Muslims. In fact, this is religious-epistemological imperialism. Political Islam raises this claim, in its combination of religious universalism and political-cultural internationalism, to a pinnacle.

Unlike the Islamists of today, early liberal Muslims, like Rifa'a al-Tahtawi in the early nineteenth century, were thrilled by European accomplishments. Tahtawi expressed this fascination in his Paris diary.[36] Also, the revivalist al-Afghani explained the weakness of Islam by the stagnation of Islamic knowledge and did not shy away from acknowledging European progress based on knowledge.[37] Throughout the history of Islam, when Islam had a highly developed civilization – even prior to the rise of the West – rational knowledge always ranked highly and was viewed as universal. The encounter with Western imperialism that involved the abode of Islam established a new context. Despite the dreadful dimension of power related to the modernity that Muslims faced, they aimed for knowledge and education by European standards. The recent drive of de-Westernization to re-establish what is believed to be the true Islamic knowledge – within the framework of a "*hall al-Islami*/Islamic solution" – did not itself create the predicament with cultural modernity. The issue dates farther back, in that it already existed in Islamic reformism and modernism in the nineteenth century. However, the Islamization of knowledge that underpins the Islamist civilizational project of *global jihad* is a recent phenomenon. It is a misleading avenue and takes Islamic civilization nowhere, if not into an age of flat-earthism. The so-called "Islamic solution" results from a "distorted change," and it leads to another variety of "neo-oligarchy."[38]

The knowledge of cultural modernity is incorporated into globalization. As noted earlier, at issue is a structural globalization that is to be distinguished from a universalization of values and norms. In pointing to these issue areas as different realms, even though both touch on knowledge, one may ask: are there culturally sustainable and distinct non-Western ways of thinking which can be distinguished from what is viewed as the Cartesian discourse that underpins the rational modern view of the world? Again, is the contemporary Islamist rejection of Western rationality an expression of multiple modernity or is it rather a neo-patriarchal, anti-science mindset? Is a process of re-traditionalization at work, or is it a revolt against universal rationality?

The controversial character of this debate over culture and globalization is determined by taboos attached to it within the rules of political correctness. Ahead of the search for answers to the questions raised no one would dispute the fact that modern science and technology promoted the rise and the prevalence of Western civilization and originated in Europe. The other fact, of a contribution by Islamic rationalism to this process,[39] contradicts the project of an "Islamization of knowledge."[40] What is specifically Islamic? Using the example of "Muslim social science" I shall deal with the politics of the Islamization of knowledge that proclaims a specifically Islamic social science. It stands in opposition to the concepts of Western social science based on "*Entzauberung der Welt*/disenchantment of the world" (Max Weber). I consider this project as a setback for Islamic civilization, in which it falls not only behind universal knowledge, but also behind the standards accomplished in medieval Islam by Islamic rationalism.

The contestation of universal knowledge by contemporary Islamists results in anti-science. The introduction of the modern Western social sciences into Islamic institutions of learning has been part of the accommodation of modern science. Islamic fundamentalists assert their claim to simultaneously de-Westernize knowledge and Islamize scientific thought in the name of authenticity.[41] There are Islamists who combine this agenda with their *global jihad*, which is extended to knowledge of cultural modernity and is no longer restricted to Western hegemony. Western social science concepts based on universal rationality are despised and accused of Orientalism, not only by those who go far for an Islamization program in an Islamic dismissal of the European project of modernity and its "principle of subjectivity" (Jürgen Habermas), but also by the bulk of postmodernists. Some American and British cultural anthropologists share with Muslim fundamentalists their contestation of universal knowledge. The project of an Islamic sociology is combined with the indigenization of knowledge. Some scholars look at this as a "primarily Third World response" to the claim for universality of Western knowledge. It is also viewed as an

> explicit opposition to the importation of ... models of social science and especially to terminology and methods developed in and for the First World ... an emphasis on the distinctive ... cultural tradition, and the possibilities of finding inspiration there for new directions.[42]

No doubt, the concern is legitimate in order to counter Eurocentrism.[43] However, the unanswered question remains: where do we go from here? – and it continues to be pertinent. One can take issue with Max Weber, who was neither a historian of science nor an expert on Islam. It is appropriate to correct his view that science "in its state of development which we acknowledge as the valid standard" exists exclusively in the West,[44] and also to challenge his knowledge about Islam. Nevertheless, to accuse him of Orientalism is not satisfactory. Despite his flaws, Weber is right about objective knowledge, which he sought to establish on an interpretative level. However, this scientific tradition can be shared by both Muslim social scientists and Weberians, because the idea of objectivity in the sciences also has roots in Islamic rationalism. The Weberian concept of "Occidental rationality" rests at first on the modern understanding of science as it was developed in Europe from the seventeenth century onwards. However, the attribution of an occidental character of rationality is to be contested for the reasons mentioned. Weber's notion of "*Entzauberung der Welt*/disenchantment of the world" can also be applied to the contribution of Islamic rationalism. It is therefore a fallacy to dismiss Weber's idea as Orientalism. Edward Said disregards the Weberian rational thought in these words: "I think that Max Weber's studies ... blew him into the very territory charted and claimed by the Orientalists ... Although he never throroughly studied Islam, Weber nevertheless influenced the field considerably."[45]

Let it be stated in passing that, like Weber, Said never studied Islam professionally: he was an expert on English comparative literature. Said was not familiar with Islamic medieval tradition as a pattern of rationality based on the Hellenization of Islam. In this precedent for cultural borrowing from others, Muslim philosophers advanced a view of the rationalization of the world. They did this ahead of Weber, who did not know about this history. Along the lines of this Islamic heritage it is also possible for a Muslim to borrow the secular rational knowledge of Weberian sociology and to put it in line with Islamic rationalism. The implication of this assumption is that objectivity can be shared by Muslims and Westerners alike. Thus, the alleged occidental–oriental fault lines believed to exist between Western and Islamic civilization suggest that Muslims have their own knowledge. Those who promote the notion of a "clash of civilizations" essentialize and overlook the concepts of cultural change and religious reform addressed in this book. In the service of bridging between the civilizations of Islam and the West, change could help establish convergence. This is the substance of the claims of rational knowledge to universality, to be shared by Muslims and non-Muslims alike in an epistemological convergence. As I shall argue in Chapter 8, the Hellenization of Islam contributed to this convergence.

Rational knowledge, cultural change, and Islamic thought

The argument of this book refers repeatedly to the open-mindedness of medieval Muslim rationalists inspired by Hellenism, drawing a contrast between them and Islamists. Openness to other cultures requires a rational worldview, which is currently absent from the public choices in the Islamic civilization. The related predicament is expressed in the contemporary Islamization agenda as a contestation of the modern, reason-based, secular concept of knowledge.

Based on an inquiry conducted as a part of fieldwork in Egypt on *Islamic Fundamentalism, Modern Science and Technology* within the framework of the Fundamentalism Project, I have developed, in the Weberian sense, a typology of five ideal types of political Islam in order to study the response of Islamists to the challenge of modernity (see note 32). Here I restrict myself to addressing the related issue of worldview, but without going in any detail into that typology, in which I classify the rejections of cultural, not instrumental modernity, that are shared by all fundamentalists. There are great inner differentiations within these responses and we must speak of fundamentalisms, i.e. in the plural, when dealing with this subject matter.

In the Fundamentalism Project and in other studies it is acknowledged that responses to the challenge of cultural modernity are an issue that is not restricted to Islamic revivalism. At issue is a general phenomenon addressed by some distinguished Western scholars such as Daniel Bell, who predicted "the return of the sacred."[46] Religion returns in a political guise to reverse the "*Entzauberung/ disenchantment*" through a "remaking of the world."[47] This is neither an indication of an emerging "postsecular society" in the aftermath of the jihadist 9/11 assaults – as is wrongly contended by Habermas[48] – nor is it a postmodern phenomenon, as cultural relativism suggests. In contrast, we are dealing with neo-absolutism. In the contemporary simultaneity of Western relativism and Islamist absolutism, the Weberian concept of rationality and its concomitant quest for scientific objectivity come under fire. If this continues, then the result for Muslims will be deprivation not only from a scientific methodology with universal validity for the study of society and polity, but also from a rational view of the world. As the second UNDP Report of 2003 suggests, Arab Muslims are challenged to establish a "knowledge society." To date, they have been underachievers.

The agenda for an Islamization of the sciences and knowledge is an obstacle to a "knowledge society." The project that this agenda pursues contests the common basis for reason-based, i.e. secular, knowledge that can be shared by the whole of humanity. The assumptions of this rational, universal knowledge are based on a rational worldview. In "post-colonial studies" that engage in denouncing the prevailing scholarly standards of knowledge as an "epistemological imperialism of the West" (see note 30), rationality is reserved for Europeans. This is racism in reverse. The objective of abolishing the separation between belief and knowledge, which claims an Islamic epistemology based on divine Islamic revelation, is a new pattern of irrationalism. The term "Islamic" was traditionally reserved for theological disciplines. In the course of de-Westernization of the Islamic world, contemporary Islamists are leading Muslim people back into the Stone Age in the name of an "Islamic epistemology." The contemporary revolt of mostly semi-modernized Muslim intellectuals against the modern secular age is carried out by counter-elites who view themselves as *Defenders of God*.[49] This is also a new variety of jihad fought against rationality. It is a kind of jihad that is not helpful in opposing political coercion, economic deprivation, and social uprooting. The opposition needs to be directed against the authoritarianism that exists in the Islamic world and the culture that legitimates it. Parochial jihad does not promote cultural change.

The worldview of Islamism can never be properly explained by reference to economy and politics. At issue is a cultural-religious phenomenon that expresses a crisis of meaning which results in a politicization of religion. The pattern of knowledge that underpins the related worldview favors neither cultural change nor the needed religious reform. The justification for dismissing a rational view of the world by means of an authenticity-based Islamic particularism is a setback. The claim for authentic "Islamic knowledge," and more specifically for an Islamic social science, reflects a fundamentalist totalitarian ideology. What is on offer is not the knowledge that Muslims need in order to cope with their predicament with cultural modernity. Instead of analyzing and comprehending the crisis of Islamic societies on the grounds of rational knowledge, the Islamists engage in a preference for *global jihad* in order to remake the world. The result is a conflict with the international community. In contrast, shared rational knowledge would help people of the Islamic civilization to understand their place in the world of the twenty-first century and to engage in a change that would be in their interest.

While criticizing the notion of Islamic social science, it is necessary to make clear that I am not an unconditional believer in Western social sciences. I am aware of their prevailing normative character, even at times when they are statistically quantified to the bone. Nevertheless, it is nothing less than propaganda to flatly accuse Western scholarship of being "*qasira/*inadequate" and in general "*mu'adiya/*inimical" to Islam, as the late Egyptian fundamentalist 'Adel Husain contends in his work.[50] On his agenda one finds a call for these social sciences to be replaced by Islamic disciplines that are believed to be authentic only because they are based on the "*'aqida Islamiyya/*Islamic doctrine." This effort is viewed as a de-Westernization of knowledge. It can also be related to the doctrine of *global jihad* as formulated by Sayyid Qutb and applied here in a new form to the de-Westernization of knowledge. Islamic thought needs to relate authenticity to rationality, not to the Islamist civilizational, shari'a-oriented project. In facing their predicament with modernity Muslims need to understand that a so-called "post-colonial" relating of rational knowledge to the colonial European hegemony is nothing but a counterproductive, defensive-cultural response, articulated in a self-assertive manner. This is not the correct approach for a proper response to the challenge of the Islamic world's exposure to Western rule of the world. The formula "crisis of Islam"[51] addresses the cultural aspect of this phenomenon and suggests finding in it a crisis of the cultural system. Cultural change is needed in order to deal with the current socio-historical challenges. Islamized knowledge is not the right means for dealing with the challenge. The re-assertive and defensive-cultural response expresses, rather, a yearning for the Islamic glory of the past. This nostalgia is not a proper response. Cultural change combined with religious reform would be more promising.

At the core of the cultural change needed to establish rational knowledge in Islamic thought is an understanding of cultural modernity based on a man-centered, secular view of the world. In this respect, an awareness is required for which the historian of Hellenism Christian Meier coined the term *Könnensbewusstsein*.[52] This refers to man's awareness of his capability of developing knowledge to facilitate change in the social and natural environments. Based on knowledge, man is in a position to master his own life, regardless of supernatural forces such as God's will. The concept of *Könnensbewusstsein* has Greek origins and is based on secular knowledge. According to this determination, a human-centered view of the world runs counter to the orthodox Islamic belief in which God is the *"al-khaliq/* omnipotent creator"* and man is only an inactive *"makhluq/*creature," completely submissive to Allah's will. In the view of this Islamic belief humans are directed by Allah and deprived of a decisive will. This is nothing other than fatalism. In medieval Islam, Islamic rationalists went beyond such a worldview. The Mu'tazilites were among the theologian-defenders of reason in Islam. They maintained that man, although created by God, is responsible for human action. They were – in contrast to the *fiqh*-orthodoxy – predictors of the combination of "secular reason and religious faith."[53] These historical references make clear that contemporary Islamic civilization lags behind the accomplishments of medieval Islam. For Muslims themselves, this is a setback. Contemporary Islamists do not see it this way, because, for them, the human-centered, rational view of the world is – as expressed by the mind of Sayyid Qutb – an expression of *neo-jahiliyya*. In Arabic *jahiliyya* means, literally, ignorance associated with the pre-Islamic knowledge of the unbelievers. Qutb views cultural modernity as a heresy that results from "the suspension of Allah's sovereignty on earth ... in attributing the political rule to humans who in this way substitute God."[54] In fact, this is the best description of the cited notion of *Könnensbewusstsein* accomplished by Hellenism and adopted by Islamic rationalists. The conclusion is clear: cultural modernity is a heretical belief, because it assigns to man the capability of determining his own destiny, and thus results in unbelief; it is viewed as replacing belief, in God, and therefore it cannot be adopted by Muslims, who are asked to reject the knowledge of the cultural project of modernity based on the rational worldview of a *Könnensbewusstsein*. The Islamist and Salafist alternative is the theocentric worldview presented as the civilizational project of political Islam. The real alternative is, however, a cultural change combined with religious reform in order to come terms with the predicament with modernity.

Secular and religious knowledge: the civilizational project of reversing the "disenchantment of the world" and its implications

This book subscribes wholeheartedly to cultural diversity and is also strongly opposed to all forms of Euro-arrogance and Eurocentrism – and thus, also, of Orientalism. It is by no means a contradiction to adopt at the same time the well-known Weberian notion of "disenchantment of the world"! Modern, rational epistemology rests basically on the effort to establish objectivity in our knowledge of nature and society as a universal venture acceptable to humanity. Rational knowledge replaces the religious view of the world with a reason-based one. In Jürgen Habermas's interpretation, this occidental rationalism has "led in Europe to a disintegration of religious worldviews that issued in a secular culture" and this, as he continues, has also smoothed the way for a "reflective treatment of traditions that have lost their quasi-natural status."[55] This process occurred in the West and some elements of it existed in medieval Islamic rationalism. In the contemporary world of Islam, secularity came from outside, introduced as the ideology of secularism, but this is not identical to secularization, as will be shown in Chapter 6. However, rationalization of the cosmos on the basis of the intellect is not uniquely Western – as Weber wrongly assumes. In Islamic medieval rationalism one finds an Islamic variety of this rational view of the world. In Chapter 8 it will be shown that rationality was not alien to Muslims in the past, at the height of their civilization, but it does obviously seem to be a problem for today's Islamists.

In a nutshell, it can be argued that modern knowledge is based on a secular view of the world that is defined by man's consciousness that humans can determine all aspects of their life. This modern, rational knowledge is secular, never divine. The term "secular" should not to be equated with "areligious," or essentialized as a *"religion civile"* as is done by the French. Islamists use a wrong meaning of secularity to delegitimize secularization in the contemporary world of Islam. In their polemics against secularism, Islamists accuse secularists of atheism. Even Descartes acknowledged that man is created by God and had no problem with the insight that man is able to create knowledge for himself, by his own means, i.e. through reason. But Muslim intellectuals and spiritual authorities do not share this view. For them, knowledge emanates only from God. Even post-colonial studies, disturbingly, involve the evil of colonial rule in this debate in order to discard cultural modernity as "epistemological imperialism." Why do some Muslims invoke belief in Allah in such a way, so to disregard man's ability? The answer is given by the Muslim rationalist Mohammed Abed al-Jabri, who rightly states that "contemporary Arab thought … has never been able to go beyond this problematic, because it has always ill-posed the problems that are associated with it."[56]

This ill-positioning of the problems is documented in the civilizational project of Islamization pursued by contemporary Islamists, who are religious fundamentalists. Their mere ignorance of Islamic rationalism is amazing. They dismiss the ability of humans to *Könnensbewusstsein*, i.e. the ability to shape and determine their own destiny. Man's knowledge, as perceived by Descartes, stems from doubt and conjecture. On this basis emerges human knowledge of the objective world. The principle of *cogito ergo sum*, i.e. self-consciousness, enters upon doubt and helps to establish certainty on the grounds of abstract subjectivity. This is the epistemological basis for cultural modernity, which in itself has nothing to do with imperialism. The accusation is based on a ridiculous argument that is also shared by European postmodernists, who contest modernity, although for reasons other than those of some Islamist writers. Even though liberal, and not an Islamist, Akbar Ahmed outlines his understanding of Muslim thought in the following, most essentialist manner: "Faith versus skepticism, tradition versus iconoclasm, purity versus eclecticism – it is difficult to relate Islamic postmodernism to Western postmodernism in any coherent or direct manner, or even to establish a causal relationship between the two."[57]

Despite all disagreement, Ahmed must be praised and credited for his honesty, as well as for his integrity in setting the matter straight. Other Muslims use cultural relativism – despite their contempt for it – to advance their own anti-modern and irrational views in a disguised manner. Now, Ahmed aims to seek his own inspiration in order to establish an Islamic and very different, i.e. not cultural-relativist, postmodernism in bypassing modernity altogether. Even though Ahmed is at times tempted to ignore the facts – for instance when he earlier overlooked Islamic fundamentalism as a movement – he is able to comprehend correctly that "fundamentalism is the attempt to resolve how to live in a world of radical doubt" (ibid.). In other words, it can be acknowledged that there is a civilizational project. It rests on the search for knowledge based on the absolute, in response to the uncertainties of Cartesianism: the comfort of belief versus the discomfort of doubt. Ahmed – as also some Western postmodernists – views Islamic fundamentalism as an Islamic variety of postmodernism. This is truly a peculiar understanding of postmodernism, since Islamism is not a cultural relativism but rather an ideology based on neo-absolutism.[58] Political Islam is also the most recent variety of this type of totalitarianism. As mentioned earlier, Ahmed left his Western diaspora to tour in nine Islamic countries and was shocked by the creeping shari'atization. He was – as he states – "taken aback" by what he saw on the ground.[59] The belief that knowledge is based on a fundamental and absolutist "Allah's will" is essential to this breakdown. In contrast, Cartesianism helps man to realize an awareness of himself as *res cogitans*. In epistemological terms, this is the "principle of subjectivity" (Habermas) which establishes a foundation for the shift from the religious worldview to the modern worldview. Political religions dismiss this worldview and, in consequence, result in irrationalism. This is the case with the intolerable views of all religious fundamentalisms, revealing the limits of pluralism with regard not only to society and polity but also to knowledge and epistemology.

In an age of uncertainty religion provides certainty, which is not the business of knowledge based on reason. Under the different conditions of our "world-time" Salafists and Islamists view rational knowledge as a threat to their religious certainty. In a defensive-cultural, self-assertive manner, in their civilizational project they advance their religion-based view of the world and dismiss the notion of cultural change. Muslim writers like the late Syed M. N. al-Attas acknowledge their perception of threat quite frankly in these words: "Today's challenge posed by Western civilization ... is the challenge of knowledge ... which is productive of ... skepticism, which has elevated doubt and conjecture to the 'scientific' rank in methodology."[60]

For al-Attas and similar-minded Muslims, this modern knowledge, as based on assumption and doubt, is not simply a threat but altogether unacceptable. The Cartesian methodological principle of doubt and conjecture threatens religious believers with deprivation of certainty, just as change in society does. Medieval

Islamic rationalists solved the problem through their concept of "*al-haqiqa al-mujdawaja*/double truth." In their view, there is one domain for religious truth and another one, based on reason, for philosophical knowledge of the world. Averroes laid down the foundations of secular knowledge without infringing on religious certainty. Today, the Islamists seek the de-Westernization of knowledge in the sense of de-secularization and a reversal of the "disenchantment of the world." They upgrade their rejection of the West to a civilizational project that is presented as an alternative based on Islam. It is the model of the shari'atization of polity and society on the grounds of an Islamization of knowledge. This civilizational project seems to enjoy great popularity and is spreading through education. The Islamic theocentric worldview dominates de-Westernized, i.e. de-secularized education. Transmission of knowledge is no longer based on reason.

The implication of an "Islamic epistemology," presented in the Islamist civilizational project as the alternative, for Muslim people, to Cartesianism, is its support of irrational views. If it were to determine the future, then there would be no prospect either of cultural change or of religious reform. Instead, there would be a *global jihad* for the Islamization of knowledge with the aim of reversing the "disenchantment of the world." In denying doubt and conjecture as methodological scientific rules, people of Islamic civilization dismiss not only the achievements of cultural modernity, but also the rationalization of the world. This rationality can be summed up in this manner:

> ... in establishing the principle of subjectivity ... religious faith became reflective; the world of the divine was changed in the solitude of subjectivity into something posited by ourselves ... In modernity, therefore religious life, state, and society, as well as science, morality and art are transformed into just so many embodiments of the principle of subjectivity.[61]

The ideologues of political Islam reject this rationality. In the name of "*asalah*/authenticity" and of the so-called "Islamic awakening" they embark on the de-Westernization of knowledge in general and of the Islamic world in particular so to promote their own civilizational project, which is by no means a return to pure Islam and to tradition as they contend. Their "authenticity" can be demystified as an "invention of tradition" (Eric Hobsbawm). In its pursuit, they are at pains to implement modernity as a tool while emphatically rejecting its logic, that is, the "principle of subjectivity" (Habermas) as based on human reason and on the recognition of the "intelligible" capabilities of man. This is a conflict between two incompatible views of the world: the one of cosmic Islamism based on the theocentric Islamic worldview (*tawhid*), and the other of "*Könnensbewusstsein*" as a view of the world based on cultural modernity. This is a conflict between modern, reason-based, i.e. secular, knowledge and specifically Islamic pre-modern religious knowledge.

Medieval Islamic rationalists solved this conflict through their philosophy of "double truth," separating rational from religious knowledge, while acknowledging the valid domain of each. Along this line, the late Sheykh of al-Azhar in Cairo Jadul-haq Ali Jadulhaq, in a four-hour-long interview with me in his office (September 1989), confided in me his misgiving about the way in which Islamists look at the Qur'an and view it as the ultimate source of all knowledge, including science. This mindset is expressed by al-Attas, in his refutation of secular knowledge, with the argument: "The holy Qur'an is the complete and final revelation ... and there is no other knowledge – except based upon and pointing to it – that can guide and save man."[62]

In contrast, Jadul-haq was of the view that this thinking is dangerous to religion. In Cairo he told me: "Scientific knowledge can be falsified and we cannot admit this falsification procedure to the study of Qur'an which is a '*kitab hidaya/* book of ethical guidance,' not a source of science." This is the view of a Sheykh of al-Azhar. Another Muslim, Husain Sadr, believes that knowledge in Islam is utterly opposed to any Western, rationality-based concept, as he argues:

> The pursuit of knowledge in Islam is not an end in itself; it is only a means of acquiring an understanding of God and solving the problems of the Muslim community ... Reason and the pursuit of knowledge has a very important place in Islamic society but it is subservient to Qur'anic values and ethics. In this framework reason and revelation go hand in hand. Modern science, on the other hand, considers reason to be supreme.[63]

This muddling through does not work in a conflict between an attempt to reverse the "disenchantment of the world" and a rationality of human reason. In the twenty-first century people of Islamic civilization need to treat religious traditions reflectively and they also need to embrace the principle of abstract subjectivity, i.e. the view that man is able to establish human knowledge of the objective world and to use his discoveries to satisfy human needs. In order to achieve this epistemologically grounded goal, Muslim thinkers are challenged to engage in religious reform, not in the misleading project of an Islamization of the sciences.

The idea of religious reform was dismissed by the late fundamentalist Ismail al-Faruqi, who was killed by radical Muslims in February 1987. Faruqi believed that "the problem of the progress of science in Islamic society is not how far can society liberate itself from clutches of its religion, but how more truly Islamic can it make its educational program."[64] The contest within Islam over the correct civilizational project also revolves around contemporary Islamic education. Young Muslims learn to reject as heretical the view that modern knowledge is, in principle, revisable, and to be disturbed when Islamic knowledge is questioned by subjecting it to human reasoning. The idea that the shari'a is absolute stands in antithesis to the idea of the project of modernity, according to which all knowledge is revisable.

In short, the tensions between secular and religious knowledge are situated in the contest between two competing civilizational projects: one is based on disenchantment and the other is set to reverse the disenchantment of the world. Today, this conflict is reflected in the reality of Islamic madrassas spreading around the world – among other things, with Saudi funding.[65] Students learn in these faith schools that Muslims are victims living under siege and are threatened by the disenchantment of the world, because it deprives them of the certainty that Islamic belief grants them. This is not the sort of knowledge needed to embark on cultural change, not to speak of religious reform.

The claim for Islamic social sciences: the case of Islamization of sociological knowledge

In any society, knowledge and education are of central significance for development, because they determine culture and the ways that people think. The general approach of the Islamization of knowledge affects society and politics equally and is therefore most relevant to the future of Islam. In this regard, the discipline of sociology is highly important. The inquiry in this chapter into the Islamist dismissal of Western social sciences examines the argument that Western sciences are "*qasira*/insufficient" and, moreover, "*mu'adiya*/inimical" to Islam. They are also viewed as an aggressive ideology that is characterized by a Western Islamophobia and a neo-Orientalism. These arguments can be found in the work of the late and most influential Egyptian fundamentalist writer 'Adel Husain. He believed that this Islamophobia compels Muslims to go their own way and therefore to engage in an unfolding of what is labeled "Islamic sociology." A social-scientific Islamic knowledge should replace Western sociology. 'Adel Husain presented this approach at an important pan-Arab sociological congress and later published his ideas in a widely circulated collection of essays.[66] The criticism presented is of equal methodological and political relevance. Conceptually, Husain argues that Western sociology is a flawed tool for the analysis of Arab Muslim societies. In addition, he believes that Western sociology is politically replete with inimical sentiments towards Muslims and Islam. This biased Western knowledge compels Arab Muslims to seek their own scholarship and no longer to learn from others. To put it more precisely, Muslims need an Islamized social science based on the concept of the de-Westernization of knowledge. This de-Westernization is equated with de-secularization. These arguments resemble, in a way, the Saidian approach of accusing Western scholarship on Islam of Orientalism. The contribution of 'Adel Husain is both significant and representative. In this section I shall examine this jihad for the Islamization of sciences as a contribution towards establishing – along the path of Islamic awakening – an Islamic knowledge. During his lifetime, Husain was also the influential editor of the fundamentalist weekly *al-Sha'b*, when it was still published in Cairo by the Islamists. In the course of my fieldwork I was in a position to meet him frequently in Cairo and to witness personally the dissemination of his thoughts, with their related impact throughout the Arab world and even in the diaspora. In Washington I once took part in a panel with

Husain. It was organized by diaspora intellectuals of the Arab American University Graduates (AAUG). Husain made flatly wrong statements about Max Weber, as did Edward Said (note 45). This happened to such an extent that I was compelled to intervene and ask Husain, in public, whether he had ever actually read the work of this great Western sociologist whom he was accusing of Islamophobia. Some years later Edward Said accused Weber of Orientalism on similar grounds. I cannot refrain from observing that to deal with great thinkers in this way, in total ignorance of their work, is disgraceful.

Despite Husain's ignorance of Max Weber, this moderate Islamist was educated enough to know that the secular concept of knowledge on which modern sociology rests is based on the modern worldview. This Cartesian-based rationale is one of the sources of the modern science that evolved in modern Europe. Knowing this induced Husain to argue for the subordination of secular knowledge to the religious "*aqida*/doctrine." His agenda was to decouple the social sciences from cultural modernity. Any science that cannot be subjected to religious belief is – as phrased in Husain's angrily worded statement – "condemned, we have no need for it/*mal'un wa la hajata lana bihi*."[67] In such strong language is modern universal knowledge dismissed in favor of Islamic knowledge. There is a fashionable scholarly approach, named anthropology of knowledge, which supports what 'Adel Husain was doing. In this discipline, the Western understanding of science is viewed as a Western belief. In a similar vein, Husain dismisses the claim of Western science to universality and reduces it to a Western belief that competes with authentically Islamic science. Following this mindset, it is argued that Western science "rests on the knowledge of the people of the West as related to their own societies ... We note this to deprive Western social sciences of their claim to universal validity" (ibid., pp. 17–18). This statement by 'Adel Husain requires us to make a brief reference to the cultural-relativist approach of anthropology of knowledge just mentioned.

The distinction between "science" and "belief" goes back to Robert Merton. Adherents of the anthropology of knowledge consider Merton's distinction to be "no longer valid," as a well-known German cultural relativist baselessly contends. This fashion-prone German sociologist, Wolf Lepenies, states blatantly: "One might, quite on the contrary, define it as one of the aims of the anthropology of knowledge to analyze scientific knowledge as a specific kind of belief which is only part of the larger belief-system of a given culture."[68] This pure nonsense is expressed with the authority of Western scholarship. The implications of this relativism strike me as fatal. Earlier in this chapter I quoted Ernest Gellner at length (see note 26), displaying how cultural relativists play down their logical conflict with the religious fundamentalists and their related disagreement because they agree on discrediting Western culture. Muslim neo-absolutists and Western cultural relativists are strange bedfellows, but are united in their anti-Western attitudes.

The analogy drawn by Lepenies between sociology of knowledge (Karl Mannheim) and his intellectually poor anthropology of knowledge not only is unconvincing, but also cannot be simply downplayed as a nonsense. In fact, this mindset is highly damaging and has consequences for global intercultural relations. Among the consequences of this cultural relativism is to deprive the project of modernity (as based on the "principle of subjectivity," Habermas) and its claim to provide a universal platform for rational discourse between people of diverse cultures so as to establish shared knowledge. The result of Lepenies' thinking would be not only to abolish objective knowledge, but also to cement cultural fragmentation in a world that is increasingly globalizing and becoming more interconnected.[69] If this dismissal of universal knowledge, based on rampant cultural relativism, were to become the general principle, then it would become difficult for people of different cultures to communicate with each other. Knowledge and scholarly findings would be downgraded to "cultural beliefs" in the primitive manner presented. The consequence would be that local cultures would remain imprisoned in their own restricted confines and never go beyond their own particularism.

In this chapter and throughout this book I refer to culture, recognizing that it is always based on "local cultural meaning."[70] However, when it comes to establishing cross-cultural standards to be shared by the whole of humanity, it is imperative that people of different cultures engage in establishing a universal discourse so as to be able to communicate with one another. To ignore this need leads to denying people of different cultures the possibility of global, intercultural communication. This idea reminds me of an observation that I made in fall 2003, when I was teaching at the Hidayatullah Islamic State University of Jakarta. On campus there is a faculty named "Communication and *Da'wa*." In Islam *da'wa* means proselytization. The implication of the combination of the two terms is clear: intercultural communication is expected to be put at the service of "*da'wa*/proselytization." According to this peculiar understanding, our world eventually seems to have varieties of Islamic, Hindu, or Buddhist knowledge, but not any generally shared global discourse for communication among culturally divergent scholars and communities. If an overall human knowledge were beyond reach, then every community would be tempted to impose its views on others in the name of cultural communication and dialogue. This is the pivotal meaning of the concept of Islamization of knowledge, in which knowledge is based on belief.

In short, the claim of an Islamized sociology is part of the contemporary Muslim revolt against European modernity and is to be seen as a variety of the already mentioned "Revolt against the West." The related cultural revival is expressed here in terms of an Islamization of knowledge. The need for cultural change and religious reform is not on the agenda of this revival, which puts obstacles in the way of mutual understanding between Muslims and non-Muslims and also impedes options for a better future. In my view, contemporary Islam's predicament with reason-based modern knowledge is one of the major sources for undermining cultural innovation. The views of 'Adel Husain on an exclusively Islamic sociology do not promise to be helpful in the Muslims' search for future alternatives.

Islam's predicament and the two dimensions of modernity: culture and power

Heading to the end of this chapter, I resume the theme of the two dimensions of modernity discussed in the Introduction and in Chapter 1. I start with Mahatma Gandhi, who was once asked what he thought of Western civilization. His succinct response was "a good idea." I am inclined to apply this statement to cultural modernity also. It is a good idea; may be no more, no less. In reality, the unfolding of modernity has been a process that encompasses cultural and institutional realms equally. As already stated, the globalization of modernity has been basically restricted to its institutional and structural dimension. This is the power aspect that facilitates Western hegemony over the world, and this is the way in which European expansion led to the establishment of Western rule. Non-Western peoples did not enjoy an opening to see the positive aspects or the beautiful face of modernity.

In considering the reality of modernity that the common Muslim people experienced in a colonial context, one can understand Muslim attitudes. The Islamic perception of European modernity and of its pattern of knowledge has been related to it as a project of power, so why, then, should the Islamic civilization adopt it? Husain arguably states:

> It is understandable when people of the West praise their historical accomplishments related to the Renaissance and to Enlightenment. For them, these periods were in fact a progress in their own history. But why should we act in a similar manner? And why should we accept these achievements as an indication of a global Renaissance and of an international Enlightenment? Given that our people have been very much the victims of European expansion, then why should we appreciate Europe?[71]

A careful reading of this text reveals how cultural modernity (Renaissance and Enlightenment) is confused, in the Islamic perception, with European expansion, i.e. with the power aspect of modernity. This great confusion continues to prevail in contemporary Islamic thought. It is therefore necessary to clarify a basic historical and conceptual distinction between two already addressed different, but intrinsically interrelated, phenomena: the idea of a cultural project of modernity and the realities of the institutional dimension embedded in the globalization triggered by European expansion. Despite all legitimate criticism, one should beware of confusing knowledge for power with knowledge for an emancipation of humankind. These are the two dimensions of modernity, repeatedly distinguished from one another.

In Western political theory modernity is dealt with in a typically Eurocentric manner, restricted to the European cultural meaning of this phenomenon. Unfortunately, the revered Habermas is a case in point. Unlike Habermas, Anthony Giddens does not restrict his analysis of modernity to culture. In looking at globalization in its institutional dimension he realizes the power aspect. Giddens does not overlook the cultural aspect and concedes "that a coherent epistemology is possible – and that a generalizable knowledge about social life and patterns of social development can be achieved. But I want to take a different tack."[72] Both scholars, Habermas and Giddens, single out only one aspect, whether the cultural or the institutional dimension of modernity. Neither of them relates these dimensions to one another, as they exist in reality. Unlike Habermas and Giddens, the late Arab Islamist Husain was able to refer to both – however, with the confusion outlined earlier of the cultural and the institutional dimensions of modernity. The two dimensions are identified with one another and on these grounds rejected altogether.

It is a fact that cultural modernity has been an emancipatory project which – through disenchantment – has led to the liberation of man from oppressive traditions and from the quasi-natural religious status attributed to them. On the other hand, however, globalized institutional modernity has itself been oppressive towards others; as an instrument of power it helped to establish Western dominance over the rest of the world. As already stated, Muslims encountered modernity as a colonial rule that not only degraded them to sub-humans, but also denied them the glorious history they once had. Muslim peoples were added to the *People without History*.[73] Until today, German academic departments of history make no place in their discipline for the study of Islamic history. The German student of Islam and current Harvard professor Baber Johanson candidly acknowledges:

> World history has since the Middle Age been the field of Germanic and the Romance people. All other people are objects of their actions ... [This] organization of the study of history ... is still dominant [in Germany]. Even today the students of history study only Germanic and Romance peoples including the United States ... Efforts to change these structures have been of no avail during the last twenty years.[74]

Those Germans who continue to define themselves in the inherited image of the self as "*Kulturnation*/nation of culture" suggest in consequence that others, including Muslims (and, of course, Americans), have no culture. The statement by the German scholar Baber Johanson which discloses how Germans believe that they and the "*Abendland*/Christendom" are the only people with a history has to be placed in this context. This is the way world history is taught in history departments of German universities. Ever since the quoted statement, published in 1990, there has been no change. Even at the most prestigious University of Göttingen, where I teach Islamology within international relations (the only place with this focus at any German university), my chair will be abolished upon my retirement in 2009. Again, there is not a single chair of Islamic history in any German university history department. No wonder that this downgrading and discrimination leads Muslims to perceive Europeans as occupiers, oppressors, or even worse, as "*salibiyun*/crusaders." However, this defensive-cultural response is not helpful. I think that an agenda of cultural change would be more promising of a better future than is a sense of self-victimization. The way in which the University of Göttingen deals with my teaching and research in Islamology saddens me, but it does not drive me to believe in a conspiracy against Islam. I do not engage in self-victimization and blame games and I refuse to see "Jews and crusaders" looming behind a deplorable situation. Europeans also lag behind change, and they barely understand how Islam is changing Europe. However, this is not the subject of this book. The concern is here to make the distinction between the capacity for liberation in cultural modernity and the ugly face of Europe and the Europeans also. Despite my very negative attitude, based on forty-six years' living as a foreigner in Germany, I refuse to share the Islamic allegation that Western social sciences are "a plan to establish Western dominance over the world system." To me this seems to be simply a distortion of the truth. "All schools of thought in Western social sciences are a belief which serves as a tool for legitimizing Western imperialism and for establishing its rule."[75] Husain's view that the Western social sciences are based on beliefs resembles the cultural-relativist anthropology of knowledge of the German Lepenies. Both identify Western sociology as a cultural belief. This denial of objective knowledge degrades Western scholarship into a system for establishing Western hegemony:

> Current Western sociological theories are not only ignorant about our environment and about its historical background. They are, moreover, inimically minded theories which, in the best cases, look down to us. The worst we can do, is to adopt them, which would be tantamount to subjecting ourselves to the disdain these theories treat us with.[76]

Without doubt, with a few exceptions (e.g. the work of Maxime Rodinson), Western scholarship on Islam is overly Euro-arrogant. Therefore, I agree with Edward Said in his criticism of the tradition of Eurocentrism vis-à-vis Islamic civilization as Orientalism. However, the argument of the Islamist Husain demonstrates the critique of Orientalism and Western social sciences that results, in the work of the Saidists, in sheer absurdities. To criticize the West is a legitimate endeavor, but it has been derailed. On the one hand, one encounters a Western cultural relativism that conceals instead revealing, and on the other hand, the neo-absolutist mindset of contemporary Islamism. The outcome of both is similar, namely the call for the de-Westernization of knowledge. This happens despite the different objectives. Islamists like 'Adel Husain draw on Western theories – for instance that of self-reliance – to present Western theoretical approaches as a tool applied to cultural and development studies. It is a doubtful undertaking, to rebuff modern theories in Western social science on the basis of their being alien, with the help of European approaches. Husain contends that Arab Muslims need their own sociology so as to enable themselves to deal properly with the problems of dependency and autonomy. "Modern social sciences are nothing else than the export of intellectual dependency to us in the guise of Western social theories."[77] Husain engages in identity politics in order to present an alternative. His identity politics-driven option is "to establish autonomous sociological schools of thought, which precisely means Arab Islamic ones."[78] One finds this argument of authenticity in the bulk of the writings presented by contemporary Islamic fundamentalists, who subscribe to the identity politics approach that is so highly praised by fashionable, cultural-relativist postmodernism.

Identity politics emerges in the contemporary context of globalization[79] as a claim for "*al-asala*/authenticity" in order to free Muslims from "*al-taba'iyya*/dependency" in all realms, whether of education, language, or law. However, the result is not cultural liberation, but rather an Islamist variety of "anti-science".[80] At issue is a state of mind that promotes the continuation of backwardness. In the name of authenticity, Qur'anic instructions are called upon to replace all scholarly methodology. Even efforts at reforming the Islamic shari'a, to be dealt with in the next chapter, are dismissed as "*taghrib*/Westernization," to be countered by an overall and sweeping de-Westernization. This effort results in a cultural self-isolation of the Islamic world under the conditions of globalization. Consequently, this is also a closing of the way to an "open Islam" that embraces universal rationality and helps Muslim people to participate with humanity in the twenty-first century. This is the predicament.

The predicament is expressed, among other things, by an inability to deal with the accomplishments of cultural modernity: for instance, the subjection of religion and of tradition to critical reflection. To make reference to the power aspect of modernity in order to disqualify the standards of human reasoning achieved by the cultural project of modernity is more than a setback. The call for "Islamic social science" resembles – as anti-science – the call for a "German physics" under Nazi rule. This expression of "anti-science" not only hampers any effort by Muslims to come to terms with the Islamic predicament with modernity, but also alienates them from the rest of humanity. In short, the Islamization of knowledge in the name of authenticity and overcoming European modernity is a dangerous project of purification (see Chapter 8 on authenticity). It definitely does not provide the Islamic people with a solution to the crisis of their civilization. It hinders them from obtaining a "changing knowledge about nature and human affairs" (Ernst Haas), and thus not only harms them but also deprives them of power, given the fact stated by Haas that "knowledge is also power."

Conclusions

The Islamic encounter with cultural modernity has created a predicament for Muslims. In the twenty-first century Islamic civilization is moving, after a period of adjustment, towards a de-Westernization of knowledge. This is not only an expression of a defensive-cultural, re-assertive mindset in the Islamic world, but also a heading in a direction of anti-science. The politicization of this sentiment has also resulted in the rejection of culturally alien knowledge, including the political culture of democracy proposed for Muslim societies. The envisioned Islamization of knowledge leads not only to the rejection of learning from others, but also to rejecting the foremost heritage of Islam, namely Hellenization. To Islamize knowledge resembles the claim to Islamize democracy. The Islamists' drive to establish "*Hakimiyyat Allah*/God's rule" is by no means democracy. Islamization as a claim to de-secularization of knowledge is pursued by Islamists in their response to the challenges of modernity. My earlier analysis of *The Crisis of Modern Islam* (see note 51) ends in a characterization of the situation in terms of threat perceptions. There I proposed the term "defensive culture" to depict the responses to it. These Islamic responses to the challenge of modernity are at issue. Two decades after the publication of that book, today I am witnessing a religious-cultural aim to Islamize knowledge through a mindset of purification. This kind of effort indicates the preoccupation with defensive culture, not an attitude of cultural innovation.

In the glorious past of Islam at its civilizational height, Muslim philosophers embraced the thinking of Aristotle and accepted knowledge in its Aristotelian tradition as knowledge about the polity. The Aristotelian politics, in which the link between knowledge and action lies at the center of thought,[81] determined Islamic rationalism. The contemporary efforts at Islamizing knowledge are a setback. Instead of developing an agenda for dealing with modernity, contemporary Islamists resort, for instance, to an "Islamized political science"[82] that lacks all of the indispensable traits of Aristotelian *politeia* as the rationale needed for establishing human knowledge of the polity.

The conclusions drawn from the analysis presented in this chapter are in agreement with John Waterbury of Princeton, who later, and until his retirement, acted as President of the American University of Beirut/AUB. John Waterbury, who is extremely well acquainted with Islam and speaks Arabic like a native, argues that the Islamization of knowledge would end in "a new era of flat-earthism." He continues by stating that this era "may emerge in the Middle East in which the epistemology underlying social science inquiry may well be rejected as a culturally alien importation, a tool of the devil, or at the very least, a tool of the adversaries of Arabs and Islam."[83] The outcome of such a flat-earthist era, which is, in fact, already in place, would be that "certain questions will not be asked, not merely because they are politically sensitive but because they are potentially blasphemous" (ibid.). The second report of the UNDP (2003) on knowledge in the Arab world documents the intellectual closing of this world region and the lack of a "knowledge society." Access to knowledge from outside the Arab world is limited, if not forbidden. This bleak reality at the core of the Islamic civilization affects the rest of the Islamic world. To be sure, there are similar developments in the West itself. Westerners have no reason for self-congratulation. Western scholarship may not be characterized by "flat-earthism," but in the US, as well as in European academia, some beliefs – such as post-modernism – seem today to replace scholarship. It is no longer possible to ask "certain questions" and remain unscathed. The sanctions against the spirit of free inquiry are not only tough, but at times also highly primitive. In some cases this happens to such a degree that one is inclined to question the great Norbert Elias in his assumption that the "civilizing process" in Europe – and the West – has transformed primitive views and manners in the direction of more civility.[84] Based on my life in the West, I tend to doubt this assumption.

In summing up, it can be stated that the conflict between reason-based and divinely revealed knowledge lies at the core of Islam's predicament with cultural modernity. An agenda for an Islamization of the sciences and de-Westernization of knowledge is not the way out. This program aims at decoupling scientific knowledge from modern, reason-based and secular knowledge, and thus from its foundations. In doing thus, Islamists contribute to the departure of their civilization from global standards, falling back into an era of "flat-earthism." The politics of the Islamization of knowledge is not a signal of a cultural awakening. It is rather a great obstacle that precludes the overcoming of Islam's predicament with modernity. The proper response to the challenge would be to place the sciences, as an expression of modern secular knowledge, on an agenda of religious reform and cultural change, instead of engaging in a global confrontation between secular cultural modernity and religious culture. Contemporary ideologies of Islamic fundamentalism and jihadism nurture the illusions of a *global jihad* to map humanity into an envisioned Islamic order. These illusions lead twenty-first century Muslims nowhere. Muslim people deserve better knowledge that will help to smooth the way to cultural change and religious reform. This would be their best avenue to a better future. The subject is surrounded by taboos and there should be no escape from dealing with them. The ancestors of contemporary Muslims were more developed because they recognized the primacy of reason as the only road to rational knowledge. Medieval Muslim rationalists were open minded and willing to learn from other cultures. In contrast, contemporary Muslims close their minds in the name of authenticity. In consequence, they are lagging behind global standards. Today, Muslims are challenged to emulate medieval Islamic rationalism; they are a long way behind it.

Chapter 3

Issue areas of the predicament II: cultural modernity and law

The contemporary reinvention of shari'a for the shari'atization of Islam

In modernity there is an interconnection between the structural level of societal transformation and the normative level of value change. The latter touches on cultural change and religious reform. The related processes also include the development of law. In view of the existing civilizational diversity there exists no universal law, so what "law" are we talking about? In Europe, and generally in the West, secular legislative law made by man, with its Roman roots, is often equated with law in general. The implication is an assumed universality.[1] Therefrom grows the notion of universal law which, however, is challenged in our post-bipolar age. Currently, people of different cultures are developing an awareness of the self that occurs under conditions of cultural diversity. This process is often paired with reference to one's own legal tradition. In fact, each civilization has its own legal traditions. The cultural turn also implies the revival of these traditions. In this context of diversity and identity politics, the concept of a universal law comes under fire. In considering the fact that law is always a cultural concept, one may consent to questioning the notion of universal law, since there exists no analogous world culture. Does it make any sense to speak of Islam's predicament with modernity if the notion of law cannot claim universality?

Another question needs to be added to this one, and is based on the argument of diversity. Does this argument apply equally to the secular and the religious? The "return of the sacred"[2] creates at present a challenge to the assumptions of Max Weber regarding secularization as a rationalization that is expected to occur in the shape of a "disenchantment of the world."[3] In the course of the twenty-first century the reversal of secularization to a de-secularization[4] gives rise to a question that challenges Weber's assumption. There is a reference to multiple modernities. Is modernity no longer based on the universalization of secularity? The contemporary de-secularization is promoted by Islamism which is a strong variety of religious fundamentalism (see Chapter 6). The agenda of the religious fundamentalists in question is a remaking of the world. They are set to replace the secular order with a religious one. So what are the implications? The concept of law matters in this context. There is a competition between *lex divina* and a secular understanding of law as legislated law.

Later on, in Chapter 6, I operate on the assumption that there is a conflict related to a contest between the secular and the divine. In the present chapter I confine the analysis of this rivaltry to questions of law and argue that shari'a and democratic constitutionalism are in a conflict that is embedded in the process of the emergence of competing legal-civilizational claims. The issue is obscured if this conflict is reduced either to so-called "multiple modernities" or to a so-called "cultural misunderstanding." In so doing, one overlooks the real conflict related to Islam's predicament. It is a fact that the Islamic revival is taking the form of political Islam, in which the divine legal claim of a shari'a is articulated as top priority. The major question asked in this chapter concerns the place of law in the cultural change that the Islamic world needs. It is argued that the contemporary reinvention of the shari'a in the shape of an alternative civilizational project is not the appropriate pattern for Muslim people in the twenty-first century. The shari'atization of Islam not only ends in an impasse, but it is also coupled with conflicts on all levels.

The process of a shari'atization[5] of Islam that is addressed here refers to an ideological linking of law to religion. This undertaking is then extended to the domain of constitutional law. In view of the assumption that legal change is also a cultural change that requires religious reforms, one needs to ask whether this new constitutional understanding of shari'a is helpful or detrimental for Muslims. Muslims are challenged to adapt to the conditions of globalization. The call for implementation of shari'a is exactly the defensive-cultural reverse agenda. It is an impediment to any accommodation. In the view of Joseph Schacht, in general, Islam is, for Muslims, "law." This interpretation supports the inquiry pursued in this chapter that relates law to culture. I therefore operate on the assumption that cultural change can never be successful if a change in the understanding of law, via religious reforms, continues to be lacking. In short, the use of shari'a in the Islamist concept of an overall shari'atization is not the pattern of change that Muslims need in the twenty-first century; rather, it adds new obstacles to the already existing ones. The following analysis examines this assumption within the framework of an overview of what is perceived to be Islamic law and cultural modernity.

Introduction

When the Muslim Abdullahi An-Na'im was still a reformist, he was among the very few legal scholars in Islam who unequivocally and succinctly acknowledged that "the Qur'an does not mention constitutionalism."[6] It follows that those who construct shari'a as an Islamic constitutional law, in an effort at de-secularization, are constructing a post-Qu'ranic legal body, i.e. they are creating their own product, but claim that it is divine.[7] The subject matter of this chapter is how shari'a develops into a civilizational project[8] that is used to articulate a contestation. This project not only alienates Muslims from all non-Muslims, but also contributes to igniting tensions within Islam, as it does with others also. Democratic Muslims do not share in this project. Some Islamic reformers, as An-Na'im was, are ambiguous and in this way lose their credibility. There are Westerners who lack intimate knowledge and an understanding of this phenomenon and project into it their ideology of multiple modernities. The real issue, however, are Muslims themselves; their problems with cultural modernity do not indicate an emerging other modernity. The construction of a civilizational project of their own under conditions of globalization is a questionable undertaking. One can argue with the 1990 Muslim reformer An-Na'im that the analysis "has clearly shown that this [democratic, B.T.] conception of constitutionalism is unattainable under shari'a,"[9] to add the future perspectives that An-Na'im then outlined, namely, that "only two options would be open to modern Muslims: either abandon the public law of shari'a or disregard constitutionalism" (ibid.). Only eighteen years later, the same reformer revives shari'a and now believes in combining it with a "secular state" without "secularization," i.e. without divorcing the divine from politics. This will be discussed at length later on, in Chapter 6 and so I will limit my criticism here to pointing out the inconsistencies and ambiguity in the thinking of this Islamic ex-reformer. In fact, this is part of the predicament.

Shari'a and democracy are incompatible. So how could another modernity emerge from the shari'atization project? What kind of modernity does this shari'atization imply, if any? The thinking of An-Na'im in 2008 is neither logical nor consistent; it reflects the problems of Muslims with modernity. The prevailing worldview in contemporary Islamic civilization that determines Islamic revival is one that is taking the shape of political Islam (Islamism). One cannot talk about shari'a and evade Islamism under the pretext of being a lawyer, as An-Na'im does in arguing that this is the business of political scientists. Given the fact that the worldview of the Islamists is more favorable to the shari'atization project than to democracy, no liberal Muslim can have it both ways, that is, to approve the shari'a and still go for the secular state. This is an illusion of the earlier, reforming An-Na'im in his recent work, which is full of contradictions.

At issue is clearly a revival of the shari'a through an invention of legal traditions that stands in contrast to democratic constitutionalism. This invention is falsely presented by some "pundits" as a cultural innovation, but it is clearly articulated in scriptural terms as a claim to a return to primordial Islam. Combined with the politicization of religion, this shari'atization results in a new totalitarianism.

The preceding remarks touch on Islam's predicament with modernity and address the reluctance to accept change. This attitude is contrasted with the need for cultural innovation under the conditions of globalization. The return of the sacred as a shari'a-based civilizational project leads, however, to a dichotomy between the universality of law and the invention of constructed legal shari'a traditions in Islam, addressed as shari'atization. Against this project, the argument for cultural change and religious reform is continued, and in this chapter is extended to the realm of law. It would certainly be not only a mere misunderstanding, but above all a violation of my thinking, if some readers were to infer from my arguments that I am proposing that Muslims should succumb to Western universalism – a position viewed by some as Orientalism. On the contrary, this book subscribes to cultural diversity – without, however, falling into the trap of cultural relativism. The framework of the thinking pursued here is cultural modernity in which pluralism is combined with diversity. A sharing of core values on a cross-cultural basis can be extended to basic legal values, and this does not violate diversity.

Among the concerns of this chapter is to understand the international conflict that is emerging and resulting in a *New Cold War*[10] between the religious and the secular. Religious revivalism seems to determine post-bipolar politics and the rise of political religions. Among these, political Islam is the most pertinent, due to its universalism. This statement is made while overlooking the polemics that Islam is the constructed "new enemy" of the West. This accusation resembles the defamation of those who criticized the human rights violations of communism. Yesterday the accusation was of anti-communism; it now continues in a very similar manner with the notion of Islamophobia. In both instances, an accusation of sin is at issue, and behind it one finds an intention to discredit critics instead of dealing with their arguments. It is imperative to put aside these ideological games and to focus on the real issue, which is the decline of secular ideologies, followed by the return of the sacred. This process, which determines realities in the Islamic world, challenges the views of Weber on Islam and its civilization.[11] At work is a re-enchantment of the world through a revival of the religious view of the world in a post-Weberian context. The core issue today is no longer the earlier, anti-colonial defensive-cultural ideology (jihad as a response to the imperialism of the West[12]), but rather the offensive claim of a remaking of the world in accordance with divine precepts based on Islamic law.

The shari'atization project can be traced back to the call for a revival of shari'a by Sayyid Qutb in the late 1950s and early 1960s. Back then, no one took the call seriously. In contrast, shari'a is today a public choice that no one can afford to ignore. In his *Signposts along the Road* Qutb contends that he sees humanity on the "*hafat al-hawiya*/brink," revealing "a crisis of the West and bankruptcy of its democracy."[13] On the very next page of this book one reads the proposition that "only Islam is eligible to lead humanity after the pending breakdown of Western civilization" (ibid.). This thinking is continued in a further step, articulated in a major book on *World Peace and Islam* (see note 13) in which Qutb argues that only Islamic dominance can guarantee world peace, based on a universal shari'a. According to this understanding, Islamic governance under "*Hakimiyyat Allah*/God's rule" is a universal legal rule, i.e. for the entire humanity. The cosmic worldview of the shari'a serves as a framework to advance the claim of a remaking of the world. It is put forward in a confrontational style that belies the accusation that the West is searching for a new enemy. In fact, the Islamists themselves are those who declare the non-Muslim other as an enemy. Thus, the declaration of war comes from political Islam. It envisions replacing the present secular international law with an invented shari'a that claims to be not only a constitutional law, but also an international law.[14] This is the meaning of the Islamist agenda of a "remaking of the world"[15] based on the shari'atization of world politics.

In a world shaped as a global village, the environment of change is also global. In the earlier epoch of polarity there existed an artificial division of humanity into blocks, as compared to the division of today, which is related to a real heterogeneity of civilizations. The earlier neglect of this civilizational fault line was not shared by political Islam. Its supporters underscored these divides, in line with their mastermind Qutb, who laid the foundations. Political Islam translates Islamic religious universalism into a political internationalism based on an imagined, transnational *umma*. It replaces the Marxist proletariat in the new "Islamic world revolution," declared by Sayyid Qutb as "global jihad."

The shari'atization of law and politics in the Islamic world that indicates the return of the sacred relates to a failed introduction of modernity, heralded by a crisis of the nation-state and unsuccessful secularization. At issue also is a development crisis. Earlier strategies are now not only questioned, but also reversed. For instance, there is a shift from acculturation to de-acculturation, from modernization to re-traditionalization, from Westernization to de-Westernization, and, above all, from secularization to de-secularization. The shari'atization of Islam is a project of global de-secularization; it is not consonant with the "secular state." An-Na'im's reasoning of 2008 on this issue is therefore highly inconsistent and flawed; it also reflects a change in his thinking that is detrimental to reform and cultural change. Given the ongoing shari'atization, coupled with de-secularization, one might ask: was Max Weber wrong? And if so, then why? Why has the return of the shari'a as an invented legal tradition been not only possible, but also successful as the opposite path to the disenchantment of the world? Are we heading towards a "post-secular society"? These are the pertinent questions underpinning the reasoning in this chapter, which focuses on shari'a versus universal secular law in the context of the predicament of the Islamic people with modernity. Religious reforms as a basis for cultural change in the realm of law are presented as way out of this crisis-ridden situation.

This introductory outline provides an orientation to locate the subject matter at issue within the general debate pursued in the book as a whole. The revival of shari'a in a politicized form in Islamic civilization is analyzed, and the claim that it is also a constitutional law is related to the return of the sacred. This return does not indicate a religious renaissance, but rather a claim to be replacing the secular world order with a divine one. This issue was addressed long before 9/11 by a well-informed student of Islam, John Kelsay, who asked in a free and scholarly, but – to some – politically incorrect manner the following pertinent questions, hitherto ignored in Western scholarship:

> Who will provide the primary definition to world order? Will it be the West ... or will it be Islam? ... The question for those who envision world order, then, is: who determines the shape of order in the new international context? The question suggests a competition between cultural traditions with distinctive notions of peace, order and justice.[16]

The questions lead to the necessity of acknowledging a conflict that is ignited by the ongoing competition between shari'a and democratic constitutionalism, i.e. between legal concepts related to the return of the sacred and secular legislative law. This conflict gives expression to Islam's predicament with modernity. Its resolution requires a Muslim engagement in cultural change and, consequently, in related religious reform. Is this wishful thinking? Why are some Muslims evasive, to the extent of distortion? Isn't it intellectually inconsistent to argue that a secular state is possible not only without secularization, but also under the shari'a?

Democratization without cultural change? Secular state without a secularization: the reinvention of tradition and its shari'a as a constitutional law

In his masterpiece on the origins of the shari'a Mohammed S. al-Ashmawi refers to the fact that the term "shari'a" occurs only once in the Qur'an. Based on his evidence, I add to Ashmawi that this notion has no legal meaning in the Qur'an.[17] In fact, the development of a legal system known as shari'a[18] is related to post-Qur'anic efforts undertaken by human beings, i.e. by the *ulema*, who established the *madhahib* as law schools in Sunni Islam. These "*faqihs*/legal scribes," however, restricted their thinking to civil law and to a "*hudud*/penal code." It was not until the work of Ibn Taimiyyah (1263–1328) that shari'a was associated with "*siyyasa*/state administration," thus becoming an order of the state.[19] This addition undertaken by the medieval *faqih* Ibn Taimiyya explains his appeal and the great influence of his work on contemporary "radical Islam." This reference is used to present the most powerful variety of the return of the sacred in a combination of *Medieval Theology and Modern Politics*.[20] One is reminded of Schacht's remark that in Islam religious thought is law.

Can Muslims continue unabated with this burdening legacy, together with their claim for a de-Westernization of law and their questioning of the universality of secular law? Is modern law culturally limited to the West? In arguing for the universality of law and against shari'atization, I draw on the heritage of rationalism in medieval Islam, ignored by both Islamists and Western Orientalists in reverse (see Chapter 8). This reference serves to underpin the view that not only rationalism, but also secular thought is not exclusively European. In medieval Islam there existed an Islamic variety of rationalism that was based on the Hellenization of Islam. It flourished and led to the acceptance of the primacy of reason.[21] In this Islamic heritage one encounters a virtual separation of religion and politics. To prove this, I refer to the thinking of al-Farabi and the school of Averroism, identified as Islamic rationalism. It is true, they failed to strike roots in Islamic civilization, as did the view of Weber which became a part of European culture. Nonetheless, the separation of knowledge and faith remains alive in the tradition of Islamic rationalism that belies the authenticity claimed by political Islam. It tries to Islamize knowledge[22] and law at the expense of a better future for Islam.

In this chapter I follow Max Weber's typology of political rule, according to which democracy is identified with legal rule[23] (*legale Herrschaft*). Westernization as related to Western expansion established also a universalization of law,[24] but did not contribute to democratization forming the basis of legal rule. The present religionization of politics and politicization of religion lead to conflict[25] and provide no solutions. Muslims are pressed to change, both at home and in the diaspora.[26] The process of shari'atization versus constitutionalism runs counter to accommodation both at home and in the diaspora, as well. These problems have reached Europe through its expansion.[27]

So how can democratization in the pursuit of "legal rule" be accomplished by Muslims? Law is very important here. It is a notion rooted in culture – as is religion, viewed as a cultural system. Religion evolves beyond faith, into a political and social matter. The result is religious fundamentalism that preach selected tenets of the sacred so as to apply them to all realms of life, including law.[28] The invention of shari'a, presented as Islamic revival, should be located in this Islamic variety of the return of the sacred.

It is tragic to see Iraq under a US rule that is presented as a model for the democratization of the Islamic world. The toppling of a secular dictatorship resulted in bringing to power people who claim that divine law is comprehensive and even that it is a source for constitutional law in a democracy in the Islamic world. Neither religious reform nor cultural change has even been mentioned in Iraq. Ahead of issuing the new Iraqi constitution, the major Arab newspaper *al-Hayat* reported from Baghdad in its Saturday, May 7, 2005 edition that the Committee of Islamic Ulema had issued a pronouncement according to which that institution requested that the final and permanent constitution for a democracy in Iraq should be based on Islamic shari'a law. The speaker of the committee, the Islamic scribe Adbulsalam al-Kubaisi, worded the claim – according to *al-Hayat* – as follows:

> We are about writing the major and general principles on which the constitution has to be based. We do not care for a referendum, but insist that Islamic law should be the major source/*al-masdar al-asasi* of the constitution.

What is the background of this development? Under the dictatorship of Saddam Hussein in Iraq, which was a *Republic of Fear*, there was no law. According to a common understanding shared by Sunni and Shi'i democratic Muslims, there was a need for change, but certainly no need for a constitutional legal system based on shari'a. The outcome of the process of so-called democratization was the imposition of a constitution that succumbed to the US demand: no mention of the term shari'a. But reference to shari'a was established under a different name: "Islamic rules." Sunni and Shi'i Iraqis have different understandings of what shari'a is, not to mention what Islamic constitutional law means.

The Third International Congress for Comparative Constitutional Law, held in Tokyo in September 2005, considered the reference to religion with the new understanding of a relationship between state and religious community as a constitutional law. In applying this understanding to political transformation in the broader Middle East, one can state that no democratic constitutionalism could be established in the context of the return of religion in a political shape. The transformation in Iraq was characterized first by ruthlessness and lawlessness and later on by the Islamization of law through the tacit introduction of the shari'a. The present post-Saddam Iraqi constitution provides that Islam is "a fundamental source of legislation"; it further stipulates that "no law" can be legislated that "contradicts the rules of Islam." What are these? Who determines them? As stated, no reference to the shari'a was allowed by the US, but such is the very meaning of these phrases. The rivalry between Sunnis and Shi'is was not over this understanding of law as shari'a being the "*lex divina/*sacral law" of Islam, but over what kind of shari'a should be introduced and what is meant by "Islamic rules." At issue were divergent understandings of democracy and of the rule of law, and these existed not only between the US and the new Shi'i leadership in Iraq, but also among Muslims themselves.

While quoting Ashmawi, I mentioned earlier that only one verse in the Qur'an (sura *al-Jathiya*, verse 45/18) mentions "shari'a" – with the meaning, however, of morality, not of law. In the century following the Islamic revelation of AD 610–32 the four legal schools (*madhahib*) of Islamic law were established on the basis of diverse interpretations of the Qur'an revealed by God. This fact makes clear the post-Qur'anic character of the shari'a. In addition, this Islamic law was never codified. During the course of Islamic history, shari'a as an interpretative law developed into a civil law and also into a penal code. By contrast, today in the Islamic world the call for shari'a reflects the constructed concept of an Islamic state with no roots in traditional shari'a. This shari'a project, propagated throughout the Islamic world in the context of the politicization of this religion and the Islamization of law, hampers any project of introducing constitutional law as a foundation for democracy and legal rule. The necessary cultural change and religious reform have not been mentioned at all.

There can be no democracy without a constitutional foundation. The lack of real constitutional law in countries of Islamic civilization corresponds with the existence of two different understandings of democracy and the rule of law. It is a fact that the related values are in conflict with one another: the Western secular and the Islamic shari'a-based understandings of constitutional law. It is a historical fact that a legal code named shari'a never existed in early Islam. Islamic law is – as has already been mentioned – an interpretation of the Qur'an and therefore it has never been codified. It follows that there is no common understanding among Muslims of shari'a as a basis for legal rule. Apart from this great diversity within Islam, any shari'a contradicts the rules of legal pluralism, which combines diversity with basic commonalities, and at the head of which is also democratic constitutionalism. There can be no democratic, shari'a-based rule of law. The early statement by An-Na'im applies: abandon shari'a or disregard constitutionalism. Unfortunately this former Muslim reformer changed his view. Today, he views shari'a as a "source of liberation" – as stated on page 290 of his 2008 book (see note 9).

Again, the diversity of cultures needs to be combined with a common concept of law. One may recognize the religious legal traditions revived as an invention of tradition. In this case, Islamic shari'a law hampers a cross-cultural democratic peace based on the recognition of commonalities grounded in constitutional law. In its present form Islamic shari'a is neither eligible to be a model for constitutional law nor is it compatible with universal legal standards. Therefore, the cultural change in the envisioned process of democratization of the Islamic civilization first requires religious reforms that include a rethinking of those Islamic values and norms which contradict human rights-based constitutionalism. In other words, the claim of the shari'a to offer a viable option for providing constitutional law is highly questionable, whether for the Islamic world, for the world at large, or for the Islamic diaspora in Europe. In short, the conflict is not between Islam and the West, but rather between shari'a law and democratic constitutionalism. It cannot be resolved without a cultural change that is comprised of religious reforms to legitimate a secularization process.

In order to determine the subject matter of this chapter, namely the overshadowing of constitutional law by the return of the sacred, further clarification of three issue areas is needed.

First, law is in Islam shari'a, but – as stated – there is no common understanding among Muslims of precisely what is meant by the notion of shari'a. This dispute is equally a scholarly, religious, and – in our time – even a political one that includes sectarian violence. In short, shari'a is divisive; it separates Muslims from non-Muslims and it also creates fault lines between Muslims themselves.

Second, the term "*dustur*/constitution" and the derived new meaning of shari'a as constitutional law are in fact recent additions to Islamic thought and its tradition. One cannot find the neo-Arabic term "*dustur*/constitution" in the terminology of classical shari'a but, despite this invention, Islamists and Salafists essentialize Islamic law in their shari'atization project.

Third, individual human rights, of which freedom of faith is part and parcel, are – despite all claims to the contrary – a novelty for contemporary Islam. The issue has generated much dispute among Muslims and it will be discussed at length in the next chapter, in rejection of the claims of the Islamists.[29]

Shari'a and freedom of faith

Among basic human rights is freedom of faith. The shari'a law exacerbates problems and, instead of engaging in reform, it puts obstacles in the way of provision of this right. Human rights is the topic of the next chapter. Nevertheless, freedom of faith under Islam is singled out here as a core question. Also, in making a distinction between scriptural and historical Islam it is most relevant to deal further with the subject as a source of conflict between shari'a and democratic constitutionalism. Here, I propose the following three levels for an analysis of the conflict, highlighted by the core question of freedom of faith:

- *First*, the level of the classification of non-Muslim monotheists (Jews and Christians) in terms of *dhimmitude*,[30] i.e. as people who enjoy Muslim toleration in being allowed to retain their religious beliefs – however, under the restrictions of Islamic rule and of not being considered equal to Muslims. On this level one can state that there is a lack of religious pluralism in Islam, which claims superiority for itself.
- *Second*, the level of non-monotheist religions (all others beside Judaism, Christianity and Islam), which are considered an expression of *"kufr/*unbelief" and to be fought against, in accordance with Qur'anic provisions against infidels.
- *Third*, the level of Muslims who either leave the Islamic faith through conversion or choose not to believe (atheists, or agnostics). Such Muslims are considered to commit either *"riddah/*apostasy" or *"shurk/*heresy" and therefore are to be punished as unbelievers. The *riddah* doctrine clearly indicates lack of freedom of faith in Islam, because it forbids conversion, under penalty.

These levels indicate the existence of three "categories" in relation to freedom of faith. The two elements in Islamic constitutional understanding of interpretative shari'a law support the validity of the hypothesis that shari'atization of the law contradicts democratic constitutionalism and all human rights. Some agree with the fact that shari'a has never been codified, making it a highly flexible legal system. This may apply to the classical shari'a, but not to its understanding in the new shari'a references of political Islam, which is understood in a highly dogmatic and selective manner. For instance, all of the above-mentioned three levels are confused by Islamists, who classify all those who disagree with their view as *"kafirun/*infidels."[31] Their call for *"tatbiq al-shari'a/*implementation of shari'a" is also directed against all those classified as *kafirun*. One finds people of Muslim belief who are presented under this label. Thus, the denial of freedom of faith, as part of the Islamist violation of human rights, touches Muslims and non-Muslims equally. The politicization of shari'a (civil law) and its advancement to the status of a constitutional law (*dustur*) results in a totalitarian state.[32]

In the Islamic understanding of law there is an urgent need for a change that first will allow Muslims themselves to enjoy freedom of faith. The two elements in Islamic shari'a-related doctrines, i.e. the already mentioned *"riddah/*apostasy" and the admission of *takfir* (declaration of a Muslim to be an unbeliever) in old and new Islamic legal thought are clear violations of freedom of faith. The status of *dhimmitude*, i.e. viewing monotheist believers as inferior to Muslims, is today an expression of discrimination rather than of tolerance. The normative contention that a change in this situation, to the extent of establishing freedom of faith in Islam, requires an Islamic religious reform is based on a commitment to cultural pluralism in Islam. This is a basic issue area of Islam's predicament with modernity.

Traditional Muslim *"ulema/*scribes" view the shari'a as "holy given." Therefore they do not allow the provisions of shari'a to be subjected to any scrutiny.[33] There are only a few Muslim scholars who go beyond these limits, as did Najib Armanazi in his 1930 book on international law in Islam[34] and, in our time,

Mohammed Said al-Ashmawi.[35] At present, Islamic writings on this subject can be classified in two categories: first, classical shari'a is upheld, albeit in a new guise as in the authoritative books of al-Azhar and some muftis, like the murdered Subhi al-Salih of Lebanon.[36] Second, shari'a is reinvented in contemporary Islamism, as is shown in this section. It is stated candidly that in the Western study of shari'a one encounters quite poor scholarship. Since the two major books on shari'a – truly unprecedented to date in their high standard – the one by Joseph Schacht and the other by Coulson, there have been no such ground-breaking studies on the subject. Most Western publications deal with very limited areas of Islamic law, of interest to only a few very specialized legal scholars, but not to the general reader. Among the few Western students worth mentioning who deal with Islamic law are Eric Vogel of Harvard University, Elisabeth Meyer of the University of Philadelphia, and David S. Powers of Cornell University. In comparison, most Muslim writings on shari'a do not meet scholarly standards and should be classified in the two categories listed above. The Islamist call for the implementation of shari'a prevails and it undermines both cultural change and religious reform. Under the dominance of this public choice, Islam's predicament with modernity continues among the ills of Islamic civilization in the twenty-first century.

Islamic shari'a law in past and present: what change?

The contemporary revival of the shari'a in an invented form is bound up with the return of the sacred and indicates a lack of religious reform. In Islam, religion is identified with shari'a, and it follows that a deep grasp of this issue is basic to an analysis. Well-informed Muslim reform-oriented legal scholars such as the former Supreme Court judge Mohammed Said al-Ashmawi rightly question the understanding of shari'a as a divine law that underpins a legal system. In arguing that *"usul al shari'a/*the roots of the shari'a*"* are based on human interpretation, Ashmawi deprives the reinvented shari'a of its claim to be a divine law of any and all foundation. The contention of a shari'a constructed by humans is therefore not really based on God's revelation. So when does the perception of shari'a as God's commandment prevail? To provide an adequate answer a historical overview will be useful.

Throughout the history of Islam the Muslim legal scribes (the *ulema*) who constructed the *"madhahib"* as the four schools of Sunni Islamic law have divided the shari'a into *"mu'amalat/*worldly civil law*"* and *"ibadat/*cult*"* regulating divine matters. The shari'a segment of *mu'amalat* was a kind of civil law restricted to the regulation of marriage, divorce, inheritance etc., but it also includes a *"hudud/* penal code."* Law making in both realms has been based on the interpretation of the divine sources. This is the revealed text. However, these interpretations are viewed as sacral, not as human thinking.

The substance of the traditional Islamic shari'a law lies in its interpretative character. At no point of the early history of Islam was there ever any reference to constitutional law. The four legal schools, the Hanafi, Shafi'i, Maliki, and Hanbali, determined in Sunni Islam what the shari'a is.[37] All of these four *madhahib*-schools are in agreement on the basics. For instance, no Muslim has the right to leave the *"umma*/Islamic community," whether through conversion to another religion or through renouncing "*iman*/belief" in Islam altogether. This will cost a Muslim his life. In this realm there exists a consensus among the *ulema* that such an action is to be persecuted as "*kufr*/heresy." Physical punishment, as fixed by the *hudud* law, is the sentence in shari'a for abandoning the Islamic faith, which is viewed as "*riddah*/apostasy." It is a death sentence.

Even though it does not guarantee freedom of faith, traditional shari'a is not totalitarian as is the shari'atized law of today. In tradition, it is the responsibility of the *umma*, not of the state, to execute a sentence pronounced by a *kadi*/judge. The Islamic scribes, being the legal scholars, never dealt with the realm that we address today as constitutional law under state jurisdiction, and only some of them ever pondered the matter of the state. In general, Islamic *fiqh* is not a state law, given that the "*dawla*/ state" was beyond the deliberations of the *faqihs*, i.e. legal scholars in Islam. There is one exception in medieval Islam. This is Ibn Taimiyya, who coined the term "*al-siyasa al-shar'iyya*/shari'a law politics" (see note 19). Until the revival of this thinking in recent developments related to political Islam, Ibn Taimiyya was almost the sole exception in Islamic legal history. It makes a great difference that the new trend in Islam – as expressed in the course of the return of the sacred – is based on reviving the thinking of the medieval *faqih* Ibn Taimiyya. This reference occurs at the beginning of the twenty-first century. One encounters in the Islamist call for "*tatbiq al-shari'a*/implementation of the shari'a" a combination of Ibn Taimiyya and a modern understanding of constitutional law. The new constitution of Iraq, which was framed in the name of democratization, is a case in point. It provides a basis for the question: are democratization and the establishment of the rule of law in Islamic civilization consonant with a shari'a based on an invention of tradition, with clear totalitarian implications? The invention of an Islamic state does not reflect any change in the meaning of a cultural foundation for the introduction of democratic rule. In principle, a reference to reinterpreted traditions could help. Can Islamic shari'a law be reformed to bring it into line with the need for change and democratization?

In the study of shari'a one encounters great diversity, related to the absence of codification of the law. Therefore, one is inclined to ask those who call for shari'a: "Which shari'a?" The above-mentioned fact that there is no common understanding of the shari'a in Islam supports this urgent question. The agenda of a shari'atization of law as a guideline for politics opens the door to the arbitrary politics often practiced by humans in the name of divine law and identified earlier as having totalitarian implications. As a traditional interpretative law, shari'a was always subject to both individual and "*madhahib*/legal school"-related interpretation of the Qur'an and the Hadith. The traditional interpreters of shari'a practiced a kind of tolerance within the Islamic community. They never incriminated disagreement and difference as "*kufr*/heresy," as is often done today

by Islamists. Shari'a's involvement in politics was restricted in the past to providing the caliphs *post eventum* with legitimacy on religious grounds. This political
shari'a was more or less a mere justification of the political deeds of the ruling
IMAM so as to legitimate his politics as being in line with divine provisions.[38]
The early *faqihs* were never independent in their rulings and also had no reason
to venture into laying out a constitutional law as a domain of the shari'a. Again
asking the question of our present century: "Which shari'a?" one encounters
different understandings of Islamic law. Among them three are pertinent.

First, the scriptural understanding of the Quran'ic verse in sura *al-Jathiya*,
which reads: "We have ordained for you a shari'a to live in line with it/*wa
thumma ja'alnaka minha shari'atun bi al-amr fa attabi'uha*" (sura 45, verse 18). The
traditional understanding of this shari'a is morality, not law. The Qur'an text contains the provision "to enjoin the good and forbid the evil/*al-amr bi al-ma'ruf
wa al-nahi an al-munkar*." In short, according to this understanding shari'a is a
morality of conduct for *summum bonum*. Thus, it is clearly not yet a legal system.
The restriction of shari'a to a morality is acceptable to a reform Islam free of the
rigid legal rules that are claimed to be divine under the present ideology of
shari'atization. There is a need to revive the original Qur'anic understanding
of morality, following a two-track strategy: first, to refute in Islamic terms the
popular call for the shari'atization of law, and second, to contain any arbitrary use
of the shari'a in violation of human rights. The legal reference to God is constructed by humans and assumes a sacral character. The legal corpus of the
shari'a itself is human, since shari'a is definitely a post-Qur'anic construction.

Second, in the course of the eighth century four Muslim scribes, Abu Hanifa,
Ibn Hanbal, al-Shafi'i, and Ibn Malik, established the four legal schools in Sunni
Islam that carry their names. Traditionally they were – and continue to be –
restricted to civil law, but they also cover the sacral matters of faith as *ibadat*. At
issue is whether freedom of faith can be related to these schools. In fact, in
Islamic law monotheists alone (Jews and Christians) enjoy a fairly restricted
freedom of faith within the framework of *dhimmitude* (see note 30). Under this law
Christians and Jews are expected to live under Islamic rule/domination. Believers
of other, non-monotheist religions are denied this limited freedom altogether.

Third, at present and since the flourishing of political Islam, shari'a has
attained a political dimension, often reinvented along the well-known understanding of the reinvention of tradition.[39] Any reinvented tradition is never the
same as the old one, since it includes a reintroduction based on a new reading.

The present reinvention of the shari'a in the shari'atization politics covers new
and broad areas. The result is a totalizing shari'a that clearly legitimates totalitarian rule in the name of religion. With reference to the authoritative theorist of
totalitarianism Hannah Arendt, who dealt with the separation of the private and
the public that goes back to the Greek polis as the *vita activa* of a functioning
polity, I view any abolition of this separation as a totalitarian set-up.[40] The
totalitarianisms of communism and fascism were earlier cases in point. With
reference to the work of Hannah Arendt, I suggest viewing the political order

envisioned by Islamism (to be sure, not Islam) as a variety of a new totalitarianism. This shari'a-based order of *"Hakimiyyat Allah/*God's rule" reflects a totalitarian rule. It is legitimated by a totalizing shari'a that cannot be in line with any form of constitutionalism as a legal rule.

The difference outlined between shari'a in the past and shari'a in the present related not only to differences in the understanding of law. At issue also is the community of the *umma*. Earlier, it was a trans-tribal, highly cohesive *umma*. At present, it is transformed by the new totalitarianism into an imagined *umma* with a transnational basis and ignores all inner differentiations in the Islamic world. This imagined *umma* negates a pluralist democracy and diversity within Islam.[41] Some students of Islam suggest that political Islam is committed to democratization. The new Iraqi constitution is supposed to be the most democratic constitution in the entire Middle East, but the practices related to it do not support this contention. Elsewhere, as in the case of Egypt, Islamists are not in yet power, but are organized in an anti-regime bloc, voicing in their protest the grand formula "No to Mubarak, yes to the shari'a."[42] Under the rule of President Anwar Sadat the Egyptian constitution was changed so as to lay down that the shari'a is the source of legislation. The earlier wording was "one of the sources." But this seems not to be what the Muslim Brotherhood envisions. It wants more:[43] a totalizing shari'a underpinning a shari'atized totalitarian state. This is not *Islam without Fear*.[44] Islamism provides neither the cultural change needed nor the religious reform required, not to speak of democratization.[45] In short, Islamism is not the way out of Islam's predicament with modernity. It is mentioned in passing that, despite his appeasement politics, Sadat was assassinated.

It is sad to state that throughout the Islamic world the current choice seems not to be between dictatorship and democracy, but rather between secular dictatorship with lip-service to shari'a and the totalitarian, shari'a-based *"Hakimiyyat Allah/*God's rule" envisioned by political Islam. The choice is thus between autocracy and theocracy. Egypt is a case in point. If there were to be regime change there, then it would be a transition from the authoritarian Mubarak regime not to democracy, but rather to a shari'atized Islamic state. As happened in Iraq, a secular dictatorship has been replaced by a religionized order. The growing political Islam and its call for a totalizing shari'a seem at present to be the foremost popular choice. In contrasting this with the parallel call for democracy, one faces a very complex issue. In an *International Herald Tribune* report on the situation in Iraq in 2005 the overall context was addressed in such a way that the report is worth quoting at length:

> What role will Islam have in the constitution? ... [at issue is to] try to strike a middle ground between Islamists, who want to stone adulterers to death, and secularists who want a pure separation of law and religion ... it would be politically impossible to adopt a purely secular constitution because Islam is central to the culture ... the argument for Islam's cultural influence is strong, and experts expect to see a reference to Islam's influence in the new

constitution ... A compromise would be to declare Islam as a source of Iraq's law but not the only source ... Declaring Islam the principal inspiration for Iraq's laws could be dangerous: Islam undefined. ... (under these circumstances shari'a) would be then the constitution behind the constitution.[46]

In fact, this is exactly what happened in Iraq under the label of democratization. The cited report addresses the topicality of the shari'a for constitutional law, which leads to questions about freedom, including freedom of faith. The pertinence of the issue goes beyond the Iraqi case. The general issue is, again and again, Islam's predicament with cultural modernity. In the light of the crisis of modernity, a return of the sacred is occurring in the context of the demand for implementation of shari'a. Religious reform has no place in this agenda.

In conclusion, it can be stated that there is a contest between "secular" and "political-religious" concepts of order – wrongly interpreted by some in terms of a "clash of civilizations," but more rightly by others as grounds for a *New Cold War*,[47] i.e. a war of ideas. This contest heralds the emergence of a real conflict based on the return of the sacred. As stated earlier, one can admit shari'a in the sense of a morality and also as an ethical guide to orient the constitutions of Islamic countries, but no more than that. Shari'a in itself is not a constitution, as is claimed in the case of Wahhabi Saudi Arabia, nor is it a source of legislation. The text of the Qur'an is abused when it becomes a constitution to legitimate despotism and a basis for arbitrary politics in religious garb. Here, the difference between Saudi Wahhabi orthodox Salafism[48] and Islamism is the difference between traditional despotism and modern totalitarianism. One must have cultural sensibility when dealing with the conflict at issue in order not to offend Muslims, but at the same time unequivocally counter any totalitarianism in the name of politicized religion. It is not an offence to religious sensitivities to counter the religionization of politics.

Is the universality of law possible under conditions of a cultural diversity based on civilizational identity politics?

Cultural change and religious reform under the conditions of a return of the sacred in a political guise need to be acceptable to Muslims. Truly, in this situation the shari'a is a pendulum swinging between ethics and politicization. Ethically, the Qur'an does include some – if limited – opening for freedom of faith. In a selective manner one can refer to the provision "*la ikrala fi al-Din/*no compulsion in religion" (sura 2, verse 256), supported by some other verses in which the Qur'an teaches the believers not to coerce, i.e. not to "compel others to believe" (sura 10, verse 99). But there are other verses with a different meaning. What matters in this chapter on law is that shari'a Islam regulates all issues through the prescriptions of a constructed divine law. Unlike other religions, where religious scholars are basically theologians, in Islam we find, in contrast, learned men of religion, "*ulema/*scribes," acting as sacral "*faqihs/*jurists" (in Arabic: *fuqaha*), not as "*mutakallimun/*theologians." In medieval Islam a religious tradition of "*kalam*/theology" was unfolded. True, there were those Mu'tazilite theologians who acted as *Defenders of Reason*, but their thoughts never succeeded in determining the mainstream in Islamic civilization, in contrast to the *fiqh*-Islam (Islamic sacral jurisprudence) that had and continues to have a monopoly over the interpretation of religious affairs in Islam. For these jurists the idea of cultural change and of the related religious reform is unthinkable. For instance, a reform that supports the recognition of freedom of faith is dismissed. Instead, deviation is viewed as an apostasy that is subject to the penal code of *hudud*. This mindset is completely incompatible with pluralism, freedom, and cultural change.

In order to dissociate the critique of shari'a (in particular the vision of it represented by Islamism) from Islamophobia, it is very pertinent to reiterate that in the text of the Qur'an the term "shari'a" occurs only once, as already stated above (sura 45, verse 18). It is argued that in the Qur'anic meaning shari'a is an ethical, not a juridical concern. From this insight one can infer that shari'a, in the meaning of a legal system, is a post-Qur'anic construction performed by humans. Dismissal of shari'a in Islamic history and of shari'a as a part of every-day Muslim culture is dismissal of a tradition in which a cultural system is rhetorically imbued with legal provisions, but shaped pragmatically by reality. A better tradition in Islam is that of rationalism, or the other tradition guided by Sufi mysticism. Neither Muslim philosophers nor Sufi Muslims were positive about the *ulema*, who continue to have the legal power of interpreting what is in line with the shari'a and what is considered to be a deviation, subject to punishment. Contemporary Islamists do not have the authority of the *ulema*, but refer to the doctrines of shari'a as a divine law in order to legitimate their action. In Islam as a religion-based civilization the distinct legal shari'a tradition overlooks the diversity of a great number of local cultures within Islam. Cultural diversity within a civilizational unity in Islam is exposed to a global system with an international law, which is based on one legal tradition that claims universality for itself and, therefore, general acceptance. International law is based in Western legal tradition. The contemporary revival of non-Western cultural traditions, as expressed by the return of the sacred, revives legal traditions also. People perceive international law as legal "alien instructions." In this regard, two universalisms clash. Islamic and Western civilization both claim universality with regard to their respective law. The denial for each other's claim to universality leads to inter-civilizational conflict, at present suppressed in the West in the name of political correctness.

Throughout the part of my life that relates to living as a Muslim immigrant in Western Europe I have seldom encountered a European legal scholar who has been willing to question the universal character of European law. When the term "law" is used it always, and in all law schools, refers to the tradition that has evolved within Europe based on Roman law. The other extreme is represented by cultural relativists, who are mostly cultural anthropologists. Most of these scholars seldom have any professional knowledge of law, but they have no inhibitions about contesting the universality of law. In terms of facts on the ground, one can refer to the global system and its inherent international structures to argue for the need of a universally accepted notion of law in order to establish common rules. Article 1 of the United Nations Charter rules the settlement of international disputes by peaceful, that is legal, means, supposedly valid for all people and states. However, this article ignores the fact that in reality there exists no shared understanding of law. The UN is an international organization of all peoples, but international law, whether it is in its origin or in its cultural roots, is basically a European one. Therefore, the claim to universal validity of this law is not underpinned by general acceptance by non-Western peoples.

In our post-bipolar age one needs to acknowledge that although there is only one international law, a diversity of legal traditions and systems exists, parallel to the diversity of cultures and civilizations. When it comes to placing constitutional law in this context we see Salafi Muslims and Islamists applying the Western notion of "*dustur*/constitution" to the Qur'an so as to view this revelation as an Islamic constitution with validity for the whole of humanity, in line with Islamic universalism. To understand this situation a reference to the Oxford jurist H. L. A. Hart is worthwhile. Hart shows how European-structured law becomes international law, binding for new states.

> It has never been doubted that when a new, independent state emerges into existence … it is bound by the general obligations of international law … Here the attempt to rest the new state's international obligations on a "tacit" or "inferred" consent seems wholly threadbare.[49]

The previously addressed return of the sacred indicates a change in world-time. This is a cultural turn. Thereby, religion, which by its nature is a "cultural system" that determines the worldview of people in religion-based civilizations and also their cultural attitudes and legal traditions, comes to the fore as a political issue. Diverse cultures and civilizations are exposed to a global set-up and thus also to an international law; they are involuntarily subsumed into it. On the surface, this reality conceals the conflict between modern European positive law and the traditional concept of sacred law. They exist alongside one another in the same world-time. There is a global environment in which all non-European civilizations, predominantly Islam, are embedded. The return of the sacred in the shape of a defensive culture is paired, in this context, with a "*lex divina*/divine law"; it is perceived to be God-given, even though constructed by humans through their interpretation of a holy scripture. The result is a man-made law. In modern democracies, in contrast, the law makers are professedly the elected parliamentarians, who act as legislative institutions. In Islam, the non-elected *ulema* act similarly as humans, but claim, in their capacity as interpreters of the scripture, not only to be legal scholars, but also to determine what God's sacral, divine law is. In this contrast one faces two competing legal traditions: legislative democratic vs. interpretative authoritarian law. This is an essential part of Islam's predicament with modernity, which leads to the question: how can cultural change be promoted under these conditions? The answer is: through religious reform that smooths the way to cultural change. Islam is changeable, not essentialist!

The basic requirement of legal religious reform is to admit that the notion of law can be subjected to free reasoning. This can be described as a philosophy of law. In every legal tradition there exists a distinction between legal philosophy and legal practice. This is pertinent to the present inquiry. At the level of legal practice one encounters many similarities between the sacral shari'a law and some dogmatic traditions of Western secular law, since both, in their practice, handle law in a similar manner. In both cases the text is not questioned, but is interpreted and applied simply, whether the legal source be the Qur'an or the code of positive law. The difference, however, is that the shari'a has neither been codified nor been endowed with any legal institution independent of the ruler on the basis of a division of power. Shari'a thus allows great room for arbitrary law making in the guise of an interpretation of God's revelation. Another basic distinction between shari'a and positive law is this: a secular legal rule can be altered by any parliament in a legislative act, but sacral law cannot be changed. This leaves room only for interpretation, whatever one may associate with this, in the name of God.

In view of the situation analyzed and in the light of legal-cultural diversity among humanity, Muslim jurists need an "Islamic Reformation"[50] not only so as to provide favorable answers to current challenges, but also as a means to come to terms with cultural modernity. Conversely, a shari'atization of law in order to legitimize de-Westernization through an Islamization of the law seems not to be an appropriate Islamic response. The call for "*tatbiq al-shari'a/*implementation of shari'a" is not only imbued with anti-democratic implications, it also alienates Muslims from the rest of humanity. The future of a world of Islam over-shadowed by a return of the sacred voiced by political-totalitarian movements will remain bleak if a reinvented shari'a continues to prevail. Shari'a is not in consonance with international standards of law and it contradicts democratic constitutionalism in substance. The conflict is not only with other civilizations (not only of the West), but also within Islamic civilization itself. There is a democratic Islamic opposition to the shari'atization of culture and politics. Also, in Asia non-Muslim people have great problems with the shari'atization process, whether in Malaysia or in Indonesia. In short, it is not only the West. Here, one can state that Islam's predicament with pluralism,[51] as it applies to the domain of law, is pertinent to Muslims and non-Muslims alike.

Is shari'a without shari'atization of the state thinkable?

The right of cultural diversity is used to legitimate the claims of minorities to cultural rights. In fact, Muslim minorities in Europe enjoy these rights, but deny them to others in the name of shari'a. It is dismaying that Muslims in places where they constitute the majority, as in Nigeria or even in Malaysia, disregard minorities and impose their views on them. Does the right of cultural diversity apply to the claim for a shari'a? It contradicts the principles of open society, to say the least. No ruler of an Islamic state could ever afford to be critical of the shari'a in public. Some rulers criticize some aspects of the shari'a in private, but uphold it when they speak in public. Given the taboos, are there any grounds for moderation? Can shari'a be reformed, or perhaps be reduced to a legal ethics, rather than abandon it altogether in an age of globalization? This is not only a most delicate issue, but also most relevant in view of the fact that the return of the sacred is very powerful. It is an expression of a cultural revival in non-Western civilizations, combined with reviving legal traditions, even though in an invented shape. This is the overall context in which the rise of political Islam extends its claims into the legal sphere. At issue is also a conflict within Islam, and Turkey is a case in point: there, religious fundamentalists and secular modernists clash with one another.[52] This conflict also includes a polarization between shari'a and international law. One way of dealing with this situation is through an effort to establish a cross-cultural international ethics that would serve as a cultural underpinning for a universal constitutional law that would also be acceptable to Muslims. This effort can be viewed as a strategy for averting inter-civilizational conflict.[53] In the Islamic world itself, there is a need for an Islamic endeavor to rethink shari'a. This is another phrasing of the plea for religious reform. It is foolishness to ignore legal-civilizational differences; it is imperative that they are properly grasped. This section sets out by giving recognition to cultural diversity – however, only if combined with a search for commonalities. The same concept is needed for world peace and a universal law that underpins it. Also needed is a shared legal terminology. In this reasoning I refer to the work of the German philosopher of law Theodor Viehweg and include it in my thoughts on the possibility of a reform Islam. Cultural borrowing is alien not to Islam, but to Islamists, who seek a purification of Islam in a politicized return of the sacred. The latter results in a politics of Islamization, which contributes to alienation of Muslims from the rest of humanity. In contrast, this section engages in a reform of shari'a situated in the context of establishing an understanding of law that is shared by the whole of humanity.

I refer to Viehweg's approach in order to examine how useful it could be for the pursuit of a shari'a reform. In Viehweg's words, the tradition of European legal terminology can be summarized with the formula "Legal terminology prefers the assertive to the instructive form of expression for constructing a legal reality of its own."[54] In contrast, Islamic legal terminology constantly uses the instructive form. Thus the distinction is made between *halal* and *haram*, i.e. between what is permitted and what is forbidden. It is a central component of Islamic law that basically consists in providing instructions. Can this determination be changed? As already argued, Islamic shari'a law is also interpretative and – as repeatedly stated – has never known a tradition of legal codification. The interpretations of the Qur'an, being the substantial source of Islamic law, explicitly set forth what is *halal* and what is *haram* in an instructive style; this cultural product of legal terminology has been handed down from the seventh century and continues to pervade contemporary Islamic legal thought. Despite the difference in structure of the legal terminology in these two diverse traditions, however, similarities can be found in the method of handling the legal text in European law and in the shari'a. These similarities matter for basing the idea of an international society on cross-cultural norms and values that ensure legitimacy for a commonly accepted international law.

The predicament in our age of the return of the sacred is the simultaneity of the need for commonalities and the reality of civilizations drifting apart from one another because of the revival of divergent legal traditions. The civilizational diversity corresponds with the great legal differences existing between these traditions. In the context of the current revival of these traditions in a reinvented form, Islamic values come into conflict with established legal standards. This process has intensified during the course of post-bipolar developments. The formally still existing international consensus on legal norms, and hence on international law itself, has entered on the one hand into a state of crisis within the West itself (Europe and the US) and on the other into a conflict with non-Western civilizations. The claim to a de-Westernization of law[55] in Islam is an indication of this crisis in the global system. An international society without a legal basis, however, would not only be a social entity without a consensus on peace, it would also be characterized as an "anarchical society" (H. Bull) in the sense of lacking a working order. Since the ending of bipolarity, political Islam has contributed to a kind of a "new world disorder."[56]

In this context, the idea of a democratic peace based on common constitutional standards offers a platform for the cultural establishment of a pluralist international order, but legally it presupposes a consensus between rival civilizations. Such platforms would constitute a material substantiation for the principles contained in the UN Charter, which are, in a certain regard, postulative, not the reality itself. Such a consensus would be free of the premature, purely formal inclusion of new states into an international legal order in the formation of which they had no part and which came into existence without them. Hart addresses these issues in his book referred to earlier in this chapter. For my part, I elaborate on the concept of intercultural international morality (see note 53) and dissociate it from the premises and implications of Westernization. Western values should not be imposed, in the guise of universality, on non-Western cultures. There is a need for values with a universal meaning, while at the same time respecting cultural diversity – however, not without limitations. In this mindset the question needs to be asked: how can we establish legal and constitutional universal values in Islamic terms? In my view, a rethinking of Islam through religious reform is an option. At issue is the creation of a local-cultural underpinning for legal universal values so as to smooth the way for their acceptance. If shari'a can be reformed and restricted to an ethics, it could fit, as a normative orientation, into a plurality amid diversity combined with a cross-cultural consensus. The cultures communicating and interacting with one another need to acknowledge and respect each other, including their related beliefs – however, on the grounds of a consensus that is rejected by the traditional shari'a and even more so by the Islamist understanding of shari'a. Cultural diversity can only thrive on the basis of the true acceptance of cultural and religious pluralism as a common ground. In Chapter 7 on pluralism this problem will be addressed as an aspect of Islam's predicament.

The inherited and never authoritatively revised Islamic dichotomy[57] of "we" and "they," i.e. between the spheres of "*dar al-Islam*/house of Islam" (literally, of peace) and the world of unbelievers identified as "*dar al-harb*/house of war" or "*dar al-kuffar*/abode of unbelievers," contradicts all norms and values of religious and cultural pluralism. It is, in addition, totally incongruent with existing realities. This statement of fact should not be silenced for the sake of political correctness. The reluctance to reform reflects an Islamic resistance to change. This is an Islamic essentialism, not an imputed one, and again it is part and parcel of the predicament.

At present one encounters Islamic and Islamist criticisms of international law that are associated with the rejection of the prevailing conditions of a world dominated by the West. The revival of the notion of Islamic law is related to the cited classical dichotomy of a world reborn under conditions of post-bipolarity. This thinking collides head on with the concept of world peace based on democracy and cultural pluralism. In order to abandon this dichotomy (house of Islam versus house of war) religious reform is needed, but it is nowhere in sight. Efforts at a renewal of Islamic law will be bound to fail if they are not disentangled from the inherited dichotomist thinking that is read into the present. Muslims need to understand that social change requires also a cultural change, and this has to go hand in hand with religious reform.

The idea that there is a potential for reform in the shari'a runs counter to the agenda of shari'atization that essentializes Islam. In view of the popularity of shari'a as a public choice, one needs to argue for legal reform. This project presupposes a cultural accommodation of social change that is not yet in sight. One is reminded that law is a part of any cultural system. It follows that a legal-reformist reasoning on the interpretation of law that is compatible with a general concept of law is an undertaking in cultural change. To read the Qur'an as an "open texture" in the understanding of H. L. A. Hart could be most promising, as much as an Islamic embracing of the juristic hermeneutics by Viehweg. Both approaches could be, for Muslims, a helpful cultural borrowing. Muslims live in this difficult age of the return of the sacred without this potential for reform within Islamic law. The idea that Islamic thought could be freed from shari'atization inspires the following legal-philosophical reasoning. At issue is a model *for* the reality, but not yet *of* it. Ahead of this venture it seems imperative to continue making the effort to understand the origin of the shari'a in Islamic history, while relating this issue area to the universality of international and constitutional law.[58] This debate is occurring in the context of cultural change and religious reform.

The place of shari'a law and its unfolding of Islamic civilization

Islamic civilization unfolded in Arabia (the Arabian peninsula), where Arabs were organized in nomadic, segmented tribes and were thus stateless. The birth of Islam in Arabia occurred in a Bedouin environment. The foundation of Islam in Arabia resembled a radical revolution that changed all aspects of Arab life. Arab nomads made their living by means of the "camel economy" as well as through robbery, making raids on merchant caravans (*ghazu* actions). Mecca and its trading tribe, the Quraisch, were the exception. In this materially under-developed culture there was no fixed legal system beyond inherited customary law. In this milieu thinking revolved around the daily needs of life. The Arab Bedouin was "a realist, and the tough life in the desert has not prepared him particularly well for reflection on the infinite" – in this manner Maxime Rodinson describes the nomadic social organization of Arab tribes as the background for the emergence of Islam as a civilization.[59] There were, though, two relatively developed urban centers of trade and agriculture: Mecca and Medina. This is the background of Islam, which is viewed as an urban culture directed against tribal life and that contributed to establishing a tradition of written law and the unfolding of a new civilization.

In pre-Islamic Arabia the two urban centers of Mecca and Medina regulated their social life by developing forms of customary law. Islam changed Arab culture in that it provided a cultural system for a new civilization that included a tradition of law. Since the eighth century this tradition has been shari'a, a post-Qur'anic construction. I continue to argue that in the Qur'an "shari'a" means morality, not law. When Islam was established in the seventh century there was no concept of shari'a as a legal system; it was developed a century later. That legal system was definitely not a constitutional law by that time. What is named "the constitution of Medina" is nothing other than a modern reading of the Islamic past. The new legal tradition, known as the classical shari'a, was the work of religious *fiqh*-scholars. Thus, the holy scripture was viewed as God's revelation, but the divine law is a purely human interpretation of the Qur'an. Any shari'a reform is pressed to acknowledge this fact as a point of departure.

Analogous to the confusion of divine revelation and human reasoning there exists in the history of Islamic law another confusion of *fiqh* (sacred jurisprudence), made by human beings, and shari'a, viewed to be God's commandment. In Islamic history the *faqihs* were established as the guardians of the shari'a. However, they were never an independent institution in Islam. They were closer to political power than to God and to date continue to be subject to the rulers. In Sunni Islam the *ulema* acted as legitimators of the rulers, issuing *post eventum* their *fetwas* in support of whatever the ruler did as action done in the name of Allah and in line with his shari'a.

In the view of the foremost student of law in Islam, Joseph Schacht, to understand Islam is to understand Islamic law, whether in the past or in the present. Schacht also points out, equally correctly, that *kalam* (Islamic theology) scholars have never been able to achieve the same status as *fiqh* (Islamic jurisprudence) scholars in Islamic history. Semantically, *fiqh* means knowledge, but juridical science as *fiqh* is considered in Islam to be knowledge par excellence, above time and space. The term *alim* (plural *ulema*) means scholar in Arabic. In Islamic history, the *ulema* have always been the guardians of legal Islam, which has been in a state of permanent antagonism with the very spiritually oriented Sufi Tariqa Islam (Islamic mysticism), but has nevertheless always managed to keep the upper hand. This background explains why in Islam shari'a and *fiqh* were not only confused, but also put on an equal footing by these scribes, who produced human knowledge disguised as sacral knowledge. These clerics continue to be interchangeably addressed either as *faqihs* or as *ulema*. Keep this in mind: in Islamic civilization *fiqh* is knowledge par excellence.

In pre-Islamic times, the Arabs were – as already stated – organized in primitive tribes. Pre-Islamic Arab culture was nevertheless a literate one, due to the high standard of the written Arab language, with a very rich tradition in poetry. There existed, however, no written law. Nevertheless, under the third caliph, Othman, the first great written document in Arabic, the Qur'an, was produced and became the foundation of the worldview of the Islamic civilization for the centuries that followed. The legal tradition that emerged later on has to be placed in this context. It is a fact and not an expression of Arabo-centrism that, because Arabia was the birthplace and the Qur'an is in Arabic, the Arab world became the core of Islamic civilization. The Qur'an,[60] revealed between AD 610 and 632, constitutes the first primary source of Islamic law. The second primary source is the *sunna*, based on the *hadith* tradition, which consists of the law-making proclamations handed down by the Prophet. There are two further components of Islamic law, considered to be complementary secondary sources: *ijma'* (*consensus doctorum*) and *qiyas* (conclusion by analogy), performed by the *faqihs*.

One may speak of the twenty-first century as an age of competition between secular and divine law. Unlike secular law, the shari'a-related legal concepts are greatly imbued with religious meaning. In this tradition, revealed Qur'anic truth is considered to provide the absolute standard. Based on the belief in the verbal inspiration of the Qur'an by Allah, shari'a is viewed as both eternal and immutable, i.e. a-historical, above time and space. The jurisdiction of shari'a is unlimited. One should beware, however, of confusing this absolutism with the totalizing shari'a of the present. Absolutism in traditional Islam was related to despotism; shari'atization as a pattern of the present is a variety of contemporary totalitarianism. Those Western scholars who use the terms "Orientalism" and "essentialism" in this context fail to understand that this is the understanding of shari'a in an authentic tradition of Islamic law by Muslim *faqihs* in the past and Islamists in the present. That Western scholars should call Muslims Orientalists is ridiculous!

Despite the placing of shari'a by Muslim *faqihs* above history, it is a fact that Islamic law was subject to a historical record. This history may be divided, according to Coulson's research, into three phases:[61] the *first* phase, comprising the post-Qur'anic development up to the ninth century, may be described as the formative phase, during which an Islamic legal system was developed; the *second* phase is much longer, as it stretches from the tenth to the twentieth centuries and documents the rigidity of this law. This rigidity is reflected by the view of the *faqihs* that reality is to be determined by law, and not the other way around. The scribes established that shari'a is valid as divine truth for all time and they precluded its modification by history. In medieval Islam, the school of *falsafa* rationalism did not succumb to this worldview.

In the twentieth century, after the introduction of the European institution of the secular nation-state into the Islamic world,[62] a *third* phase began in the historical development of Islamic law. This phase refers to the emergence of new states. Since they have been unable to cope with the challenge of development and to accommodate modernization, the related regimes have failed to come to terms with an international environment that is based on a universal understanding of modern law. In modern times, classical Islamic law and its legal doctrines were exposed to new conditions that made clear to what an extent they were being phased out. In all instances of this third phase, European law was introduced from the outside, but it lacked local cultural foundations. Nevertheless, it replaced the shari'a law. At times it coexisted with unchanged Islamic law in terms of a simultaneity of the unsimultaneous. The unsuccessful modernization resulted in the call for a shari'atization that, it was believed, would provide a way out of the crisis. This return of the sacred in the shape of a shari'a-based political Islam has in fact been going on since the 1980s. One can view this process as the new, fourth phase, not included in Coulson's scheme: it relates to the de-Westernization of law, parallel to a revival of shari'a. This process clearly shows Islam's predicament with modernity, which continues to be relevant and is reflected in the need for cultural change and religious reform. The shari'atization politics does not mend this crisis-ridden situation, on the contrary, it exacerbates it.

The contemporary invention of an Islamic law, with its notions of sacral jurisprudence, engages in a confusion of *fiqh* and shari'a that continues to prevail and to have consequences for establishing the unity of religion and law[63] in Islam, which differs from Christianity. There exists no church system, for Islam is organic rather than an ecclesiastical religious system,[64] and worldliness is pronounced in Islam. This explains why "*fiqh*/sacral jurisprudence" is more central to Islam than "*kalam*/theology" has ever been. This legal system of *fiqh* is viewed – despite the fact of its emergence piecemeal during the history of Islam – as an absolute entity in its capacity as a divine law revealed by God, even though *fiqh* as law making is performed by human beings, i.e. by the *faqihs*, and therefore definitely not revealed by God.

"*Hijal*/deception" and self-deception served in Islamic legal history as a means to ignore history and overlook change. This tradition continues to prevail in a world of sovereign states. The *faqih* and *ulema* claim that the shari'a offers no less than the fundamental as well as universal valid basis for an international law in an age of nation-states. As Tu'aima blatantly puts it:

What is fundamental about Islam is that it is a religion for the whole of humanity. Muslims hence have an obligation to proselytization for Islam in order to bring all those whose hearts are open to Islam into its fold. As long as Muslims proclaim their religion in order to disseminate it, Islam is in a state of either peace or war [*dar-salam* or *dar-harb*]. Circumstances falling between these two are regulated by means of international treaties.[65]

This self-congratulatory statement of 1979 documents that the inherited dichotomic divide of the globe of the seventh century into "house of peace/ Islam" vs. "house of war/non-Muslims" – though utterly outdated – continues to prevail in contemporary Muslim thought. The enlightened Muslim legal scholar Najib Armanazi admits the embarrassing fact that this centuries-old dichotomy has never been subjected to any revision or updating. The ultimate incongruence of this worldview with the realities in which Muslims live is a part of Islam's predicament, which applies in general to Islamic legal tradition. The claim to shari'atization of Islamic politics resulting from the politicization of religion does not provide any light at the end of the tunnel. The above-described Islamic dichotomy results – long before Huntington – in the understanding of a clash of civilizations, i.e. in a polarization: Islam vs. non-Islam on a global scale. This is the worldview set down and vigorously articulated in the writings of Sayyid Qutb, who continues to be the major voice of political Islam. The novelty he introduced was only the idea of an Islamic world revolution, interpreted as contemporary "global jihad." Qutb's legal thinking is not yet the shari'atization agenda of today. It is restricted to providing a guideline (*ma'alim*) to this project, as one major book by Qutb suggests.

Thinking about reform in Islamic law as a cultural change: a plea to admit a "rethinking of Islam"

Undertaking any step from the inherited scriptural Islamic thought towards free reasoning as determined by the topical discourse borrowed from Viehweg – as presented above – requires an admission of free reasoning. The Muslim reformist Mohammed Arkoun describes this approach as *Rethinking Islam*.[66] A reform of Islamic law can hold promise only if it goes beyond the restrictions of an exegesis of handed-down law and fulfills the requirements set out by Arkoun. Only such an endeavor could be culturally innovative and help in adjusting to an international law beyond imposition. The defensive-cultural claim of shari'a for the entire world stands in blatant contradiction to the principles of a worldwide cultural pluralism. The cited reference by Tu'aima highlights the urgency of reforming Islamic law. These remarks give rise to the question of law and international morality. A cross-cultural bridging in the age of the return of the sacred requires Islam to accommodate to cultural modernity. This modernization has to be placed in the overall context of the need for a new legal reasoning, namely in cultural change and religious reforms by Muslims themselves. Do we find acceptance for this thinking? The answer is both yes and no. Human rights[67] is a field for this ambiguity and the subject is covered in Chapter 4.

One of the bright, contemporary Muslim minds, Mohammed al-Jabri,[68] says "yes" to this thinking and calls for a revival of Islamic rational philosophy. Awareness of ancient Greek philosophy in classical Islamic thought is highly relevant to the present. That period was known as the "Hellenization of Islam."[69] If this could be accomplished, then Muslims would be in a position to emulate cultural modernity. In this instance, rationalism and secularization in Islam would be accepted. If these requirements were approved, then cultural change would be within reach. At this point I draw on the sociology of religion developed by Niklas Luhmann and use it as a frame of reference[70] to grasp the function of differentiation related to social change. Knowing Islamic sensitivities, I emphasize that any functional differentiation in society affects the religious system by reducing religion to a partial system. This would be by no means an elimination of religion, as many Muslims fear when, in a war of ideas, they polemically equate secularization with the abolition of religion.[71]

Instead of saying "yes" to the needed rethinking of Islam, at present we are witnessing the drive of Islamism for a politicized shari'a, i.e. a wholesale de-secularization so as to reverse what has been occurring in the Islamic world since the late eighteenth century. This shari'atization is certainly no religious renaissance, but rather a return of the sacred with an invented legal tradition. In this context, shari'a is not reformed; rather, it is invoked as a totalizing shari'a, giving it the shape of a divine law revealed by God, not subject to historical developments. One is reminded of the post-Qur'anic legal system constructed by Islamic *fiqh* scholars, who are human, but claim that their human thinking be viewed as "God's law."

In the study of the history of law in Islam one can see how legal practice has been adjusted to the changed reality – always, however, while maintaining legal norms themselves basically untouched. The inconsistency that emerges from the tensions between the inherited norm and the corresponding reality has been described as "behavioral lag." This term was coined by John Waterbury to conceptualize the observed incongruence between what Muslims think and what they actually do.[72] Can a legal philosophy emerge in Islam that allows human reasoning on law to counter the shari'atization that is currently pursued by Islamism to the detriment of Islam? Also, Islamists refer to the norms of the shari'a, but they do something else, namely, invent tradition. The inherited "cultural schizophrenia" (Shayegan) is a spirit also continued by Islamism.

From a formal point of view, the virtual deviation from the norm in practice is often the starting point of every process of jurisdiction undertaken by a modern European jurist. This is also the case in Islamic law. Here, too, the principle applies: "The legal norm has an existence independent of social reality within its fundamental sphere of validity,"[73] even though it is conceived of as applied by people and is not a divine revelation like the shari'a. In this respect, with regard to the introduction of innovations the Islamic jurist could learn a great deal from the European jurist and from his way of dealing with legal norms. Both the theory of topical discourse and juristic hermeneutics could be integrated into a reformed Islamic legal system, as well as allow a concept of rights underpinning freedom of faith. With this aim, and at this juncture, the concern is not with theological argumentation, but rather with the process of independent legal reasoning as a cultural discourse based on legal philosophy. In leaving aside the question of the origin of law (whether legislation or divine revelation) I interpret law along the lines of H. L. A. Hart's thinking, as an "open texture." This is a term coined by Hart to describe a fixed written structure of norms, open to an interpretation that also allows a rethinking of the non-legal norm itself. This seems to be acceptable to Muslims because it combines "*tafsir*/exegesis" with "*ijtihad*/free reasoning." Hart points out that all legal systems, whether traditionally handed down or legislative in character, represent a compromise between two legal requirements, "the need for certain rules" and "the need to leave open." He adds that "in every legal system a large and important field is left open for the exercise of discretion by courts,"[74] and reminds us that recourse to the same handed-down law can have different content at different times and in different systems. If this view could be accepted in Islam, then a de-essentialization of the shari'a could be managed and the Islamic people would be able to join the world community on the basis of a substantive legal reform. Even though it provides a promising perspective, at present this endeavor seems not to find acceptance. The contemporary ideological premises, characterized by a rejection of cultural borrowing from others, promote the attitudes of the exponents of political Islam in their drive towards shari'atization in an age of the return of the sacred.[75]

Authenticity of reform is highly relevant and it has to be related to the potential for "flexibilization" of the Islamic notion of law in Islamic terms. "Flexibilization" is a technical term employed in the German juridical debate. It refers to the non-rigid handling of legal norms for dealing with tensions between reality and dogma. This is not tantamount to bending of the law at the interpreter's discretion; rather, "flexibilization" conveys the notion of a certain pliancy in the process of law making and jurisdiction. In the present crisis situation and at this juncture I view "flexibilization" of Islamic law as being the better alternative to the politicization of Islam, which results in a totalizing shari'a based on the Salafist and dogmatic Islamic belief in immutability. The truth is that change – even in legal reasoning – has always occurred in Islamic history, although it is dismissed. The agenda of shari'atization and the related practices indicate, in a way, a pattern of change; however, it is not the one that people of Islam need in order to come to terms with the predicament addressed in this book.

In following a legal reasoning committed to reform so as to underpin the proposition of opening the Islamic cultural system to "change," one is confronted with the essentializing cultural view that shari'a, interpreted as God's revelation, is essential, and therefore no human is authorized to change it. This is not an Orientalism by Westerners, but rather a prevailing Islamic orthodoxy. Nevertheless, it stands in contradiction to the practice of shari'a in Islam. It has always been adjusted to change, despite the belief in the immutability of the divine legal norms. Hence, the tensions addressed as a behavioral lag between what Muslims really do and what they believe they are doing characterized the behavior and attitudes of pious Muslims. It follows that there is a simultaneity of cultural persistence and of behavioral conformism. A legal philosophy that could subject such simultaneity and its inconsistency to reasoning has not only been lacking, but has also been rejected by Islamic *fiqh*-orthodoxy. The conformist adjustment was merely pragmatic in nature, while avoiding any rethinking of values and norms. The "flexibilization" aimed for here would, unlike the former Islamic *hiyal*-legal tradition (*"hiyal*/legal tricks"*) have to incorporate a full cultural awareness of social and cultural change. An Islamic embracing of the theory of law as an "open texture" in Hart's sense, in addition to the topics theory of Viehweg, to be presented in this section as a juristic hermeneutics, would provide some tools that would be of great help on the path to modernization of Islamic law. The aim is to establish an Islamic discourse of legal reasoning that runs – in the norm and in legal practice alike – from actual social givens to textual under-standing, not vice versa, as the *ulema* and the *faqihs* have done in their centuries-old essentialism. For these scribes the text is the point of departure. The result is pure or selective scripturalism, believed to be essential though subject to change. The present shari'atization does not provide a viable alternative; rather, it continues the old predicament unabated in a new form of shari'a.

In an Islamic-enlightened tradition of learning from others, I draw on three German scholars, first on Ralf Dreier's critical evaluation. Second is Josef Esser, to whose work I refer for "disclosing topical forms of thinking as an indis-pensable element in the channeling of meta-dogmatic assessment criteria and in ensuring accuracy."[76] It is only in this sense that I make recourse to Viehweg's hermeneutical approach of topical discourse. It not only addresses the dogmatic system as such, but is designed to argue against the preconceived idea of a system that claims to be perfect and definitive. Advocating the adoption of this topical reasoning in Islamic law could contribute to an openness in the legal system that would smooth the way to religious reform. It is stated in passing that this approach is the middle ground between a legal reasoning based on secular-ization, on the one hand, and religious scripturalism, on the other. Pains are taken on this middle ground to mediate between reason and religious belief.[77]

In better times of Islamic history, open-mindedness existed in parallel to an intellectual plurality that was admitted even in religious debates. The tradition of Hellenized Muslim philosophers, as well as the early debates from which the legal internal differentiation of Islam arose (the emergence of the four legal schools, the *madhahib*), not to forget the Mu'tazilite *Defenders of Reason*,[78] deserve to be mentioned as a proof in this context. Innovative Muslim thinkers went beyond the *taqlid*, i.e. the submission to the authority of predecessors as tradi-tionally practiced by *fiqh* scholars, and engaged in *ijtihad* for creative law making. *Ijtihad* is individual, independent legal reasoning. Nevertheless, all Muslims were bound to operate on the basis of the shari'a. Islamic modernism, which first came into existence in Egypt during the second half of the nineteenth century,[79] never dared to question this tradition and never truly engaged in gearing up for a reform of Islamic law in the twentieth century. Reform never meant more than lip-service to a revival of the *ijtihad* tradition in Islam. The contemporary return of the sacred in the form of political Islam aims at the revival of scriptural shari'a in an envisioned shari'atization of the state that is combined neither with reform nor with cultural innovation based on a rethinking of Islam. The claim to return to a primordial Islam is in reality an invention of tradition. There is change, not a revival of what was inherited. It is, however, a change that is devoid of reflective reasoning.

To counter this shari'atization it is proposed to revive the *ijtihad* tradition in an enhanced way that also includes an effort to advance and promote free reasoning in Islamic legal ethics. This effort would facilitate a pathway for the introduction of topical thinking into Islam, as pursued in the following deliberations. If leading Muslim thinkers were receptive to this approach, then the introduction of a concept of rights that allows freedom of faith and thinking could become feasible. As I shall argue in Chapter 4, Islamic doctrine is based on "*faraid*/duties," not on rights. Therefore, in classical shari'a there is no concept of rights. An Islamic reform has to be guided by an effort at enlightenment in order to promote cultural change and religious reform. This is a requirement for the introduction of the concept of individual human rights. Muslims need to beware of stranding themselves in familiar apologetics by claiming that Islam includes all concepts of human rights and is in no need of borrowings from other cultures. In fact, this is the prevailing mindset in Islamic human rights writings that negate the substance of these rights.

The "topics" approach refers to "that technique of thought which focuses on problems."[80] Drawing on Viehweg, I add his words, that "the issue is: thinking in terms of problems."[81] One needs to address Islamic ethics in a thoroughly systematic way, and the realities in Muslim societies through a developmental process. The Islamic ethical system should be freed from lapsing into the fossilized tracks of scholastic *fiqh* doctrine. Viehweg advocates bearing in mind a dovetailing between system and problem,[82] emphasizing that "topics" cannot be understood without subsuming the integrity of the problem within some kind of order. In putting "problems" to the fore, the reading of the legal text – secular or divine – is no longer scriptural-dogmatic. Thinking in terms of problems certainly helps to embrace the system as a whole while viewing its components, as well as the concepts and statutes of jurisprudence. This philosophy of law is needed in reasoning on Islamic law to facilitate the adoption of this method, which entails looking at the real social problems of Islamic societies, and not primarily from the point of view of the texts. Those reform-committed Muslims are challenged to introduce such a topical discourse into Islam. This includes grasping the idea that the function of topical themes lies in "serving the discussion of problems ... The topical themes, which intervene in an assisting capacity, derive their respective meanings from the problem itself."[83] If this task is accomplished, then the fixation on "*sultat an-nas*/authority of the text" that hampers innovations could be overcome. While remaining loyal to the viewpoint of opposing imposition, and instead favoring cultural change from within, I am fully aware that topical thinking – universal as it may be – cannot be introduced into Islamic law by starting from scratch. There are disavowing traditions that have been upheld for centuries and we cannot simply dismiss or ignore them by wishful thinking. One can start, however, from a stance of interpretation, itself an art that has always been admitted into the domain of Islamic *fiqh* scholars. Therefore, it could be accepted even by those Muslims committed to tradition if they were willing not only to think independently of the text but also to be open minded to rational arguments coming from other cultures, such as those emanating from cultural modernity.

With a focus on the "topics" approach, it is argued that Muslims could read the revealed text of the Qur'an as an "open texture" (Hart) within the framework of "*tafsir*/interpretation." If this were to be combined with *ijtihad*, i.e. free reasoning, then the door could be opened for reform. Viehweg highlights interpretation as an element of "topics" in arguing that this involves forging new possibilities for deriving meaning without damaging the old meanings. I refer to this insight while acknowledging that fixed designations can shift into new angles. The procedure offers an opportunity to give new applications to old precepts. These aspects of topical thinking presumably render Viehweg's theoretical framework more acceptable to Muslim jurists, who fear the loss of their heritage but accept "*tafsir*/exegesis" as part of Islamic law, which is based on the interpretation of divine scripture. Of course, there are limits to interpretation. According to Viehweg, not every interpretation fulfills the requirements of topical thinking. To return to the definition cited above, Viehweg stresses: "Not every interpretation (explanation, exegesis, hermeneutics) does this, but every one is capable of doing it. It is part of topics."[84] At issue is the combination of interpretation with reasoning, while avoiding scripturalism. Muslim reformers failed to fulfill this requirement. Therefore, Islamic reform failed to achieve any progress. The writings of Islamic modernists since Afghani are characterized by the fact that they utterly fail to rethink the inherited religious dogma.[85] In other words, one can assume a lack of willingness on the part of Islamic scribes to engage in topical reasoning. In Islamic history they were never committed to real cultural change through religious reform. The *ulema* would never come to terms with the Islamic predicament with modernity, because their minds are closed.

There was one exception, and this is a very important piece of Islamic writing, dating from 1925, whose author, Ali 'Abdelraziq, was a *fiqh* scholar at the Muslim al-Azhar University and also, by then, a Supreme Court judge. It contains an interpretation of Islam that may be construed as topical in the sense defined by Viehweg. The book was published in Cairo in 1925 under the title "*al-Islam wa usul al-hukm*/Islam and Patterns of Government"[86] and engaged in a reasoning that leads to the conclusion that Islam is only a religion for the spiritual sphere, and not a system of government based on shari'a. In Islamic civilization this view counts as a revolutionary interpretation. However, his argument cost the author his livelihood at that time. 'Abdelraziq was impeached from all of his positions, including his office as a judge, and was also deprived of his professorship at al-Azhar. Despite the price that he paid, his work continues to be one of the most important milestones for Islamic reform. The contestations of Muslims opposed to cultural change and to religious reform in the Islamic discourse of shari'a law are only a cultural countering that prevents Muslims from joining the modern world.

The way in which Islamic *fiqh*-orthodoxy responded to the religious reform of Ali 'Abdelraziq, by ruining him personally and depriving him of his means of existence, displays the intolerant manner in which the *ulema* establishment deals with all reformers. Today it is even worse. 'Abdelraziq would have been killed by Islamists, not merely dismissed and sidelined, as happened to him in 1925. Islamists invoke the weapons of *takfir* (pronouncement as an unbeliever and excommunication of a Muslim from the *umma*) to give religious legitimacy to the execution of culturally innovative Muslims. The notion of *takfir* is used against bright, reformist Muslims who do not share the views of religious orthodoxy and of the Islamists. Some, like Faraj Fuda, have been killed by radical Islamist groups. There is in Arabic the better notion of *tafkir*. It can be translated as topical thinking in Islamic law. Today, it is equated with *takfir* (excommunication from the *umma* on a charge of unbelief). This happened to Hamid Abu Zaid, who fled to the Netherlands in order to save his life after he was subjected to a *takfir* sentence following the publication of a book in which he engaged in free Islamic thinking.[87] Faraj Fuda, who remained in Cairo, did not survive.[88]

In concluding this section, it is reasonable to end with a reference to the Pakistani fundamentalist Muhammad Muslehuddin to illustrate the current issue. This person is an Islamist with a Western education, being a graduate of London University. Muslehuddin discredits all those who engage in legal reform.[89] Using his case one can show how criticism of Western Orientalism derails to wrong conclusions. Among the victims of his Islamist defamation is Malcolm Kerr.[90] During his life he was a highly respected political scientist at the University of California, Los Angeles. He completed basic research on legal and religious reform in modern Islam. Kerr was murdered by Shi'i Muslim fanatics in Beirut in January 1984 while he was acting as the President of the American University of Beirut/AUB. Muslehuddin discredits all reform attempts in the apodictic statement: "Those who think of reforming or modernizing Islam are misguided, and their efforts are bound to fail. ... Why should it be modernized, when it is already perfect and pure, universal, and for all time?"[91] In his view, therefore, the task of Muslim jurists is restricted to interpreting the shari'a in order "to comprehend and discover the law and not to establish or create it."[92] Such a rigid definition of the work of jurists, who in this case cannot be scholars in the Weberian sense, clearly leaves no room either for topical thinking or for topically oriented interpretations that allow an introduction of religious pluralism and freedom of faith. The critique of *dhimmitude*-doctrine is not an

Orientalism. I recommend the abandonment of this label, as it has become not only an obstacle to research but also – in the hands of some postmodernists – an "Orientalism in reverse."[93]

It is quite ironic that the Arabic name Muslehuddin means "the reformer of religion." This anti-reformer uses the accusation of Orientalism, which lacks any logic, to refute Kerr's rational, scientific method, which attempts to comprehend Islamic law in rational terms. Muslehuddin argues that any critique of a divine law is bound to fail:

> Divine law is to be preserved in its ideal form as commanded by God, or else it will be devoid of its capability to control society which is its chief purpose. The mistaken view of the Orientalists is due mainly to the fact that the real good may be rationally known and that the law should be determined by social needs, while all such needs are provided for in divine law and God alone knows what is really good for mankind.[94]

This view is quoted in full, because it reflects the prevailing contemporary Islamic thinking in the age of the return of the sacred. These thoughts make full use of shari'a law to provide a directive for the establishment of a God-given order. In contrast to this shari'atization of politics, the process of jurisdiction is expected to comprise the formulation of a question, and its answer calls for an evaluation in accordance with norms. This evaluation needs to be derived from the appropriate legal text in which those norms are laid down – in this case, the Qur'an. Those Muslims who read the Qur'an in an open-minded manner, as an "open texture," would be in a position to open a pathway to cultural change beyond the essentialization of the text of the Qur'an. Religious reform promises a way out of this impasse. Muslims like Muslehuddin close the gate of the Muslim ghetto of a perceived "Islam under siege" and thus prevent Muslims from joining the rest of humanity.

Conclusions

In a third step in the endeavor to deal with Islam's predicament with cultural modernity, this chapter has focused on law. In this step an attempt has been made to provide a historical and problem-oriented analysis of the development of the classical shari'a into a shari'atization of Islam under conditions of the return of the sacred. New problems are at stake, but they are carried over in the framework of classical shari'a, giving it a new form in "that a specific current issue is carried over into the text … and a preconception of the problem is brought out of the text that does not coincide with the historical preconception."[95] This description of the procedure that projects a new meaning into the text of the Qur'an is borrowed from the German legal scholar Esser, who is not writing here about Islam. Nevertheless, his formulation is a superb description of how a highly complex issue is being handled by simple-minded Islamists, who may fail to grasp it. Nonetheless, that is exactly what they are doing, much as does a European judge who refers to a legal text to tackle a problem independent thereof.

Despite the references to the hermeneutic cognitive method that could contribute to an enormous enrichment of Islamic law, the chapter is basically about the search for an opening to cultural innovation in order to come to terms with Islam's predicament with modernity. The obstacles to this reasoning in an age of the return of the sacred – as expressed by political Islam – are tremendous. They are mostly political, but are articulated with a religious-cultural legitimation. This is what the shari'atization of Islam is all about.

Among the findings of this chapter is knowledge of the contemporary shari'a as a pattern based on a tradition invented by political Islam. It stands in contrast to the potential of a civil Islam and contradicts democratic constitutionalism. Further, it is not open to religious reform. Therefore, it is not receptive to the appeal for an integration of topical discourse into Islamic legal philosophy. Based on these findings, it is inferred that the mindset of *fiqh*-orthodoxy, as well as that of political Islam, have been in the past and currently are obstacles to a reform Islam in Islamic thought. It is acknowledged that Islamist and, equally, Salafist positions are more popular at present than are those of a civil Islam. The contemporary form of Islamic civilization indicates all the characteristics of the return of the sacred. It is emphasized by the constitutional claims of political Islam. Those are an obstacle to true democratization in the Islamic civilization.[96] It follows that any rethinking of Islam in pursuit of a cultural change to transform Islamic legal thinking into a system of legally enforceable "rights and duties"[97] faces tremendous impediments. Islamists reverse the order of the secular agenda and argue that society ought to be "the product of sacred law and to be seen in an ideal way in harmony with its ordinances."[98] This drive is boosted by the Islamist and Salafist perception of Islamic law as an immutable body at the core of Islam in general.

To sum up, the call for *"tatbiq al shari'a*/implementation of Islamic law" is the agenda of contemporary Islamist movements that today constitute the core opposition throughout the Islamic world. At issue is not another modernity, but rather a totalitarian project of a shari'atization of politics and of society. This is by no means, as some US pundits suggest, a "Liberal Islam."[99] On the surface, Islamism seems to be a movement that is directed against the rule of authoritarian regimes in Islamic civilization. From the point of view of a democratization limited to an electoral procedure, a project of regime change may result in bringing Islamists to power. This would be a move from authoritarianism to totalitarianism, not towards democratization. In this context, an accusation of essentialism and of Orientalism would be not only misplaced but also a distraction – if not a distortion – by Western scholars. This leads away from the real issue. Westerners who do this suffer neither despotism nor totalitarianism; instead they live in the luxury of freedom, but allow themselves to stand in judgment on people of other cultures for which they lack sensitivity and whose plight they mostly have not experienced from within.

To avoid any misunderstanding by readers who may be skimming through this book, I cannot conclude this chapter without emphasizing that the deliberations presented here are not against the shari'a altogether. In the text of the Qur'an shari'a is a morality. Historically, this concept was developed by Islamic scribes into a kind of divine civil law, but it was never a constitutional or state law as it is now promoted by the Islamists in the context of a shari'atization of Islam. Qur'anic shari'a should not be an ideological tool in the service of politics, whether in the past or in the present of Islamic civilization. Again, in the Qur'an shari'a is a morality. The present return of the sacred as a project of the Islamization of law is not only *not* about this morality, it also incriminates any rational reasoning as a heresy. All in all, the shari'atization of Islam stands in stark contradiction to the need for a cultural change and religious reform in Islam. At present, there is a challenge to rethink shari'a in all of the following issue areas:

1. The placing of non-Muslim monotheists (Jews and Christians) as *dhimmis*, i.e. protected minorities. This is not legal equality. Muslims need instead a religious pluralism that places the non-Muslim other on an equal footing.
2. The place of all other non-Muslims and non-Monotheists (Hindus, Buddhists, etc.) as "*kafirun*/unbelievers" in Islamic thought.
3. The placing of Shi'is by Sunnis as heretics and vice versa.
4. The discrimination of Sunnis by Shi'is (e.g. "liberal" Iraq).
5. The doctrine of *takfir* targeting thinking Muslims (violent persecution and even execution of reformists and intellectuals) and excluding them from the *umma*.
6. The discrimination of all religious minorities within Islam (Baha'i, the Ahmadiyya, etc.) by the Sunni orthodoxy.
7. The gender issue and discrimination against women.

All in all, political Islam does not herald any kind of a religious renaissance, as some uninformed Western observers suggest. Its project of shari'atization exacerbates existing problems, is evasive, and does not present a legal system that is capable of tackling the seven listed issue areas. In fact, political Islam reflects Islam's predicament with cultural modernity. A reading of the Qur'an as "open texture" could start with the verse "there is no compulsion in religion" (Qur'an, sura 2, verse 256) combined with another verse "you have your religion and I have mine" to open the way to the establishment of a spirit of religious pluralism (see Chapter 7). Freedom for religious reform in contemporary Islamic civilization is in line with this Qur'anic ethics. Nevertheless, it has to be stated candidly that the legal reform that is hoped for in Islam is not yet in sight. Instead, the contemporary shari'atization of Islam prevails and determines the major hallmark of the return of the sacred, which occurs in the form of a political Islam. To keep my thoughts in an Islamic framework I remind my fellow Muslims of the Qur'anic commandment: "Allah does not change people, unless they change themselves" (sura 13, verse 11). The reluctance to cultural change and religious reform that continues in post-bipolar Islam is bad news for the twenty-first century. The good news is that there are still some Muslims who engage in *Rethinking Islam* in order to resolve the conflicts related to the contemporary predicament. These Muslims are a tiny minority within the *umma* and are often subjected to *takfir* in the above-mentioned meaning (see number 5 in the list). They nevertheless are a source of hope.

Issue areas of the predicament III: Islam, the principle of subjectivity, and individual human rights

The third issue area singled out in the present inquiry on Islam's predicament with cultural modernity relates to individual human rights. These are understood as law that provides legal entitlements. This understanding is based on a concept of rights that attributes to individuals entitlements that they claim vis-à-vis state and society. This is a core issue of cultural modernity. The chapter first argues generally that individual human rights[1] expose all religions to a radical challenge. Islam is no exception, despite all Islamic claims to the contrary. It is not only Christian theologians who claim that the roots of these rights are in their own religion; Muslim revivalists similarly believe that the origins of human rights are found in the teachings and doctrines of Islam.[2] Both are mistaken. Individual human rights are intrinsically modern, and also secular; they are based on the principle of subjectivity, of the identity of the self. This principle is an embodiment of cultural modernity.

In short, individual human rights – in the meaning of secular entitlements – do not exist in any religion. Period. Given these facts, the question is: what reform do religions need to undergo and in what kind of change do cultures have to engage in order to accommodate the concept of individual rights as an entitlement? These questions pinpoint one of the sources of Islam's predicament with cultural modernity, hence this third step focuses on this aspect of the predicament. The centrality of the issue of individual human rights is the reason for its selection – after knowledge and law – as the subject of this chapter.

Introduction

In the study of individual rights and modernity Jürgen Habermas's *The Philosophical Discourse of Modernity* is a most valuable resource. It helps to determine clearly what "cultural modernity" means in substance. The book is viewed as one of the most authoritative studies on cultural modernity as based on "the principle of subjectivity," as Habermas states in these words:

> The principle of subjectivity determines the focus of modern culture … it liberates the knowing subject … The moral concepts of modern times follow

from the recognition of the subjective freedom of individuals ... founded upon the rights of the individuals.[3]

This principle of subjectivity materialized in the first legal concept of individual human rights, namely – as Habermas states – "the declaration of the rights of man ... [which] validated the principle of freedom of will against historically preexisting law" (ibid.).

No unreformed, theocentric religion would ever share this understanding of human rights as individual entitlements vis-à-vis state and society. The meaning of individual human rights is intrinsically modern, as well as secular. It contradicts all forms of "historically preexisting law" (Habermas), primarily divine law, and hence also the Islamic shari'a law. It follows that individual human rights are among the issue areas of Islam's predicament with cultural modernity. The principle of subjectivity can also be termed "self-identity," as in the work of Anthony Giddens (see note 3), but here I follow Habermas. The outlined substance of individual human rights is, again, an accomplishment of cultural modernity, which creates a civilizational challenge to others. The Sunni Arab Middle East is the cultural core of Islamic civilization and it is affected by this challenge. The focus of this statement is not an indication of Arabo-centrism. Looking more closely at Islamic history, and given the fact that the Qur'an was revealed in Arabic, one is compelled to acknowledge the Arab place as the cultural core of Islamic civilization.[4]

The seminal report of the UNDP[5] on the Arab Middle East refers to home-made problems and deals with the lack of validity of individual human rights in the Islamic world. The report basically accepts the relevance of cultural explanations. Top of the shortcomings listed in the UNDP report is the lack of democratic freedom and the poor state of individual human rights. Some authors explain despotic rule and authoritarianism in the Islamic world by reference to the colonial legacy, thus placing the blame for the current state of affairs on others. It is a fact that contemporary Islamic civilization is, by international standards, an under-achiever in the domain of human rights. It is also a fact that people in the Islamic world are denied freedom and individual human rights. I maintain that this is a home-made problem, not a colonial legacy. If this evaluation is wrong, why is India, despite its colonial legacy, a functioning democracy that guarantees human rights to its citizens, including minorities, in their capacity as individuals? By contrast, one might ask why Wahhabi Saudi Arabia, a medievalist, absolute monarchy, has never been subjected to colonial rule and yet lacks all such rights? These examples contradict the obsession with a colonial legacy. The comparison between India and Saudi Arabia is not an idle one; it shows up the error of the monocausal reference to colonialism as an explanation not only for the lack of individual human rights, but also for the problems of new states. There are other reasons, and an honest inquiry must consider the reality of exposure to cultural modernity and its related predicament. Of course, there is a colonial and post-colonial context, and I do not ignore it. However, single-minded reference to this aspect is insufficient for an in-depth analysis of the current issue. It is a great mistake, and also Eurocentric, to view non-Western cultures solely in the European context of colonial and post-colonial constraints.

In relation to this discussion one is compelled to ask: what is the real issue? In Asia and Africa there are other people besides the Western *"tiers-mondistes*/third worldists."[6] The nativist approach that some third-world anthropologists elevate so as to place the blame on others is flawed thinking. However, there are other non-Westerners who, as rationalists, admit reasonable arguments and do not simply throw them out of the window. The seventy Arab opinion leaders who convened in November 1982 in Limassol, Cyprus (not in an Arab city) to discuss *"Azmat al-Democratiyya*/the crisis of democracy" (see note 1) in the Arab world provided an example of such rationalism in their refusal to engage in blame games. It is remarkable that these Arabs were denied the possibility of meeting in an Arab city and therefore went to Cyprus. I had the privilege of joining this group, from which the Arab Organization for the Defense of Human Rights emerged. In our discussions in Limassol we were aware of the fact that "individual human rights" are a European concept based in cultural modernity. We also acknowledged that these rights are a recent addition to the political ethics of Islam. At the same time we were conscious of another fact, namely that those rights can be established only on a local and authentic basis in the Islamic world. In other words, individual human rights can be introduced successfully and thrive only if they are supported by a cultural underpinning that ensures that they will strike local-cultural and civilizational roots. Of course, I do not overlook the institutional dimension, but I put it aside here in order to maintain the focus. The idea of the need for a cultural underpinning of individual human rights[7] relates the matter to two issues. First, the compatibility of shari'a and individual human rights. In this context I continue to argue for law reform, as already discussed in the preceding chapter on shari'a. The second issue relates to the challenge of individuals empowered with rights, an issue that is embedded in the debate on Islam's predicament with cultural modernity. The question of authenticity matters also, and it will be discussed later on, in Chapter 7. This issue also touches generally on the universality of rights and on cultural relativism, as well as on the implied particularism and authenticity.

Having made the argument clear in the foregoing remarks, I will now add the dimension of international conflicts. These emerge from Islam's predicament with modernity, as can be demonstrated by the example of human rights. The analysis of this dimension will be pursued in Chapter 5. It is noted here that this conflict is not a matter only for Muslims. The reason for this is the circumstance that today neither the upholding nor the violation of individual human rights is any longer the concern of a local culture or a specific civilization in a discrete country. No intelligent person will doubt the need for a morality shared across cultures that is based on a common set of norms and values. This concern also encompasses an inter-civilizationally based political culture, to be accepted by the entire international community. Underlying this need is the place of human rights in international relations.[8]

In the absence of a cross-cultural international morality and of an inner-Islamic underpinning for individual human rights one is compelled to connect the issues to each other. In the Arab core of Islamic civilization one faces a situation that was described by S. E. Ibrahim, at an international meeting of the Club of Madrid that took place in March 2005, in these words: "We freedom and human rights loving Muslims are twisted between the autocracy of our despotic rulers and the theocracy of the Islamists opposing their rule." This is the issue, and it makes it clear that Islamism is not the light at the end of the tunnel, as some Westerners believe.

Truly, neither the West nor sentiments of Islamophobia can be blamed for the severe violation of human rights in the Islamic world, in particular at its Arab core. Those cultural relativists who dismiss the universality of human rights by emphasizing the specific character of local cultures unwittingly end up by distracting attention from pressing issues. During the UN congress on human rights in Vienna in 1993, the then Saudi Minister of Foreign Affairs pretended to speak for other Muslim colleagues who were present. In this capacity, he argued that, for Muslims, human rights are based on and derived only from the Islamic shari'a. This is a non-starter. As shown in the preceding chapter, shari'a is one of the issue areas of Islam's predicament with modernity. The hypothesis in this chapter is that shari'a is an obstacle to individual human rights, understood as entitlements. On all counts, shari'a is in conflict with these individual rights.

The requirement to place Islam within a universal pluralism of cultures and religions presupposes the establishment, with Islamic participation, of a cross-cultural understanding of human rights as individual entitlements. The problem is that the concept does not exist in Islam. It evolved from modern European thinking on natural law, and further, there is nothing Christian about it. For a number of reasons, I keep reiterating that Western civilization is secular and it has elevated these rights within its societies to the status of secular-legal institutional standards. Similarly, the Universal Declaration of Human Rights (UDHR) established by the United Nations in 1948 is secular, just as are the covenants of 1966 which went into effect in 1976. Today these rights enjoy the status of international law. Can one in this context talk about a universally accepted legal rule, whether on domestic or on international grounds? The answer is intricate, and it is yes and no. There is no real consensus over law and human rights. The repeated reference to the secular character of both individual human rights and democracy dissociates these rights from religious claims in order to de-legitimate the Islamist contention of authenticity related to law and rights as entitlements. These are neither Christian nor Islamic.

Many states of the Organization of the Islamic Conference/OIC (fifty-seven states) formally endorse the notion of international law, as well as democratic legal rule. However, this is mostly lip-service. In practice, these states are reluctant to accept a consensus on the substance of these legal notions. The rejection of the substance of international law, combined with recourse to shari'a, alienates assertive Muslims not only from the West but also from the international community as such. Contemporary modern Islamists, and also the traditional *ulema* of Islamic *fiqh*-orthodoxy, believe that the Islamic shari'a is divine law, not just a methodology or an ethics[9] for law making. The result is that the Weberian notion of legal rule,[10] being an element of cultural modernity, is not accepted. Recognition of rights as entitlements is meaningless if there are no legal rules within these rights which are institutionalized and protected by society.

Let it be said candidly: the shari'a – believed to be superior and pure, according to the worldview of Salafists and Islamists – establishes fault lines – like those of Huntington's *Clash of Civilizations*. Individual human rights have no legitimacy whatsoever in the shari'a. In mobilizing against the civilization of the West, contemporary Islamists reject the legislation of any rights by humans. To them, this is pure heresy. In their view this would result in dismantling the sovereignty of Allah, the one and only law maker. In this kind of thinking the "principle of subjectivity" outlined at the outset has no place.

For Islamists only a *"nizam al-Islami/*Islamic system of government"[11] based on the shari'a can be admitted as the correct order. The American Sudanese legal scholar Abdullahi An-Na'im (when he was still a reformer) and the Egyptian judge Muhammed S. al-Ashmawi argue against the revival of the shari'a which is – as shown in Chapter 3 – a reinvented set-up.[12] If Qutb's[13] views that shari'a is the only model for Islamic civilization prevail, then totalitarian regimes like those already existing in Iran and Sudan could refer to shari'a to legitimate their rule. As An-Na'im puts it, shari'a is "not the appropriate vehicle for Islamic self-determination in the present context. Shari'a was in fact constructed by Muslim jurists … although derived from the Qur'an and sunna, shari'a is not divine because it is the product of *human interpretation* of those sources."[14] Where are the fault lines of a conflict between the shari'a and the universality of human rights located?

That individual human rights have validity as international law on a formal level is great progress. However, this should not distract attention from the reality that – despite the present world of nation-states – there are civilizations with their own concept of law. Civilizations interact with one another through global communication across borders, with no world government or central authority in place. The UN provides a framework for human rights, but it has no means of enforcing this international law.[15] No other institution is capable of enforcing legal norms worldwide. Civilizations and cultures do not share common norms, values, and outlooks in parallel to a prevailing and overwhelming globalization. There is no worldview shared by all. This fact also applies fundamentally to individual human rights. Thus, the notion of establishing cross-cultural foundations for a universal morality that is shared by all civilizations founders on the rock of shari'a. The lack of law enforcement in the system of international relations corresponds to the lacking of a cultural legitimacy in cultures and religions because of the absence of a consensus on core values.

Under the conditions of a Western hegemony, the plea for shared values to connect civilizations to one another is sunk by the fact that human rights are a cultural concept based on values that originated in Europe.[16] While this concept is related to cultural modernity, it has not been successfully universalized so as to give it validity for the whole of humanity. Islam's predicament with modernity[17] is embedded in this context. In world affairs there is an international system of interaction, but there is not yet an international society based on shared values.[18] It follows that individual human rights are not yet materially valid on an international basis. In many Islamic countries there are ministries for human rights, but the reality does not correspond to what they proclaim.

Shari'a, cultural diversity, and human rights

There is an urgent need to join things up in the domain of human rights. Without cultural change and religious reform no progress can be made in the promotion of individual human rights. It has to be acknowledged that the concept grew from the notion of natural law. So how could it, as a secular concept, obtain legitimacy through the assistance of a culture based on religion? Would reform help to make this happen? Is there a morality of law?[19] Is a far-reaching reform in Islam conceivable?

Underlying the realities of individual human rights as established in Western societies are real cultural and social processes of individuation that have occurred in the wake of modernity. With the adoption of its basic tenets in the Universal Declaration of Human Rights in 1948, this concept became an international one sponsored by the foremost international institution, the United Nations (see note 15). To repeat the core problem: human rights do not only originate from a European context; they are also abused by US foreign policy. Nevertheless, they are a cultural concept that has developed into an international law, parallel to the fact that there is neither a world culture as a common ground for sharing, nor a world government to enforce this law. The US abuse of human rights not only does damage to the international morality of these rights, it also, under conditions of a "Revolt against the West," hampers international efforts to make the rule of law binding.[20]

Under these conditions, individual human rights are not only contradicted by the shari'a, which promotes a real clash between civilizations, but also undermined in international society. The Islamic world is supposed to participate in the international community, but it does not do so. The outcome is a culture- and religion-based conflict which revolves around the secular and the religious.[21] The overall historical background of the emergence of a system and society in world affairs is the Peace of Westphalia of 1648. The community of states that emerged from this process was exclusively European, but was named an international society. With World War II and the overall processes of decolonization, the system was expanded to comprise the whole world; it not only assumed diversity, but also became a source of conflict. Despite this diversity, the system of law that had regulated the earlier European system of states has, during the course of globalization, has become a system of international law. In the previous chapter, the late Oxford law scholar H. L. A. Hart was quoted as criticizing the assumption that when a new, independent state comes into existence "it is bound by the general obligations of international law."[22] Hart did not share the assumed basing of the new state's international obligations on a consensus that evidently does not exist. This very notion applies to the universal acceptance of the United Nations' Universal Declaration of Human Rights. The assumed consent has, in reality, no corresponding acceptance in the Islamic world, as well as in other non-Western states.

The historical background referred to above may explain some of the traits of the contemporary "Revolt against the West" (see note 20) and civilizational conflict. The fact of the lack of a cultural underpinning for the universalization of consent helps to explain the conflict over human rights in non-Western cultures. Instead of such a confrontation, one should engage in establishing cross-cultural foundations for human rights as an appropriate basis for crossing the fault lines that the shari'a establishes between Muslims and non-Muslims. The issue is that human rights are situated in a globalized, yet culturally fragmented world. To understand this, I remind the reader not only to recall the distinction between the international system and international society, but also to understand the simultaneity of cultural fragmentation and structural globalization in the world of the twenty-first century.[23]

The argument for universal validity of individual human rights in a world of rival civilizations does not ignore diversity. The problem is, as the late Hedley Bull states, that the distinctions between the international system of states as a system of interaction among units organized as sovereign states and international society are becoming consequential. To be sure, an international society is not what politicians mean when they refer to it in their window-dressing speeches. International society only

> exists when a group of states, conscious of certain common interests and common values, form a society in the sense that they conceive themselves to be bound by a common set of rules in their relations with one another ... An international society in this sense presupposes an international system, but an international system may exist that is not an international society.[24]

A universalization of individual human rights could underpin such an international society on a global scale. But this is wishful thinking, not a reality. There are no shared values. Does the lack of "a common set of rules" related to the acceptance of universal human rights mean that there exists no international society at all? Does the Islamic world, heading towards a shari'atization that is unfavorable to human rights, stand on its own, outside the international community? Do Muslims reject the prevailing common values and rules in current international society, to which the Universal Declaration of Human Rights (UDHR) and the covenants of 1966 belong, only because they are European in origin?

The current surge of culturally self-assertive movements in non-Western countries is characterized by the hallmark of a "Revolt against the West." Islamic fundamentalism[25] was viewed by Hedley Bull as the most prolific variety of this phenomenon. In the area of international law, one can observe great resentment towards the West, despite the fact that most non-Western countries, earlier grouped as the "Third World," comply, even if not wholeheartedly, with international law. In his introduction to international law, Michael Akehurst rightly notes: "Third World states often feel that international law sacrifices their interests to the interests of Western states."[26] Hence, the drive towards a de-Westernization emerges as a means to liberation. Would this also include individual human rights? What is the Islamic position in this regard?

What complicates a proper response to the questions is the former abuse of human rights law by the US "for Cold War propaganda purposes."[27] *Raison d'état*-based policies are silent about human rights violations (e.g. in Saudi Arabia), when they suit those policies. However, this criticism of Western policies should not be confused with the substance of the concept of human rights. Its claim to universality stands on the establishment of a cross-cultural basis for its validity as a foundation for international morality. Therefore, these universal rights should be defended against an alleged Islamic authenticity.

The core issue in the debate on Islam and the universal validity of individual human rights should be addressed in the context of exposure to modernity and the related predicament, not as a polemics of Western policies against instances of violation of human rights. After the Vienna human rights conference of June 1993, the foreign ministers of the Association of South East Asian Nations/ ASEAN convened in Singapore in July to turn the tables on the European states by denouncing the European Community's policy of tolerating human rights viola-tions on its own continent.[28] This was happening at the time in Bosnia. It was highly deplorable, but the convening ministers willingly missed the point. It is assumed that human rights, as an international law, are shared by all, despite diversity. In the domain of human rights, the cultural relativism that contests the universality of these rights seems to prevail as an unexamined assumption.

No doubt, the universal validity of human rights cannot be promoted on the basis of a Western ideology of universalism. The establishment of cross-cultural foundations is necessary so as to make norms and values such as human rights universally acceptable. The distinction between universalism and cross-cultural foundations is often not well understood. People of culturally different outlooks cannot interact with one another on the basis of imposed norms and values. Without supporting universal values by means of a local-cultural underpinning, no cultural bridging is possible within the context of diversity. While arguing the place of human rights as universal rights, I not only reject cultural relativism, but also criticize universalism. In plain language: cultural relativism results in deny-ing human rights to non-Westerners. This is a crime.[29] However, a sweeping Western universalism is not the solution.

The earlier reference to human rights standards at an international level[30] should not be undermined by reference to cultural diversity. When Abdullahi Ahmed An-Na'im was a critic of the shari'a, he argued in favor of adherence to international human rights standards. In highlighting the interplay between the specifics of the civilization of Islam and the universalization of human rights standards in our present world, An-Na'im acknowledged the European origins of the modern concept of individual human rights, as well as the conflict. Today, the same Muslim adopts the implementation of the Islamic shari'a and abandons universally accepted standards. In his early work An-Na'im was receptive to "a drastic reform of Islamic law."[31] Today, he no longer condemns the violations of human rights in the Muslim world as he did in the past, when he was of the view that "humanity can no longer disclaim responsibility for the fate of human beings in any part of the world."[32] The An-Na'im of the US diaspora supports shari'a and forgets that Sudan is among those Islamic countries that violate human rights in the name of shari'a. In Chapter 6 I shall take the issue with this changed An-Na'im.

Islam and human rights. Torn between cultural fragmentation and universalization: acceptance, rejection, or abuse

As will be argued in the following chapter on cultural tensions, different understandings of values could lead to conflict.[33] The repeated violations of human rights in the Islamic world are one of the sources of tensions and conflict. The globalization of structures does not apply to the cultural terrain. There is no world culture and no standardization of norms, values, and worldviews. The globalization of structures does not create a world civilization. The reference to normative standardization makes it imperative not to confuse two different levels of analysis. It has become common sense to argue that shared legal frameworks are required in order to establish a stable legal foundation for a world order based on shared, common ground. Yet legal frameworks are based on specific cultural norms and values. This was made clear in the preceding chapter on the subject of shari'a and its values. I repeat the reference to the idea of a simultaneity of structural globalization and cultural fragmentation. The acceptance, rejection, and abuse addressed here are embedded in this framework.

The argument for the foundation of a universal morality is not presented in opposition to the existing cultural diversity. This cultural diversity is not only accepted, it is also combined with the search for commonalities in the legal domain of human rights. In this mindset, efforts are made to unfold a concept that can be legally established on a cross-cultural foundation. This could pave the way to Muslim acceptance of human rights, rather than mere lip-service to them. It is unfortunate to acknowledge that this lip-service, combined with a merely rhetorical condemnation of the violation of human rights, forms part of the abuse. One has also observed that references to these violations are often discarded as Islamophobia, while no one talks about Westphobia in the West, or anti-Westernism in the Islamic world. In fact, no discussion of human rights concerns in the countries of the former Third World can take place without putting this question in the forefront. Human rights concerns become a delicate issue when acknowledgment of their secular and ethical-universal claims is related to the example of the foremost non-Western civilization, i.e. to Islam and its legal concepts and frameworks, described as shari'a. Only those liberal Muslims who are willing to admit religious reform[34] and who do not prevaricate would be in a position to achieve this task.

Among the world's 1.6 billion Muslims there is a tiny minority of liberal reform Muslims who accept individual human rights in full. Deplorably, this minority is shrinking. An example is the retreat of the earlier reformer An-Na'im, who once wanted an Islamic Reformation and was critical of those who applied the shari'a to an agenda for an "Islamic human rights"[35] scheme. This ideological framework stands in opposition to any reform in Islam.[36] Today, An-Na'im argues for shari'a. This is a tragic example for the practice of authenticity, which is the theme of Chapter 7.

Some Western authors avoid any critique of contemporary Islam so as to escape the fashionable blame associated with the invective "Orientalism." A prominent Muslim scholar, S. J. al-Azm, identified this approach as "Orientalism in reverse."[37] For the sake of an enlightened Islam, one must acknowledge that the debate conceals serious disparities between the establishment of Islamic human rights schemes and international human rights. The superficial difference between those Muslims who flatly reject human rights legal norms as Western and those who seek to establish specifically and exclusively Islamic human rights schemes is not significant. At issue is not a party hostile to these rights and in opposition another one that embraces them, but rather two parties who are in practice not favorable to the substance of individual human rights. The hostility of political Islam towards substantive human rights indicates the politicization of the cultural fragmentation of humanity. In her book on *Islam and Human Rights* Ann E. Mayer states that those Islamic authors who are at pains to establish specific Islamic human rights schemes "are reluctant to state openly that following Islamic criteria entails departures from the norms of international law."[38] One cannot consent to the shari'a, as An-Na'im does, and at the same time follow universal standards of law.

The cliché of "Orientalism" is used today to attack the critics of Islamism and I therefore discard it. In my reasoning and throughout this book I make a commitment to cultural modernity, which is by no means an Orientalism, as is contended by the "Orientalists in reverse." My criticism of the global political and economic dominance of the West is clear. It is possible to engage in this criticism and yet to avoid detrimental, anti-Western attitudes. Earlier, I coined the term "defensive-cultural attitudes"[39] so as to properly understand the overall sentiments existing in non-Western societies, foremost among them the Islamic ones. This culture determines the attitude of Muslims in relation to international law, including legal human rights concepts. These also are cultural concepts. The link between international relations and the claim for universality, in the sense of a cross-cultural validity of international human rights law standards, is based on the principles of cosmopolitan justice. As Terry Nardin puts it, these principles "have tended to be expressed in terms of the idea of internationally protected human rights. The Idea of human rights follows directly from the ideal of a universal human community."[40] In order to take into account this most important insight, we need to go beyond the rigid concepts established in scholarship.

In post-bipolar international relations Islam has become a political reality that can no longer be studied properly without basing the issues on a concept of culture and civilization.[41] This domain has hitherto been neglected in international studies; today it is pivotal in unraveling the existing simultaneity of structural globalization and cultural fragmentation. There is a cultural contestation of legal norms and values that claim to be universalized in line with processes of globalization. The contemporary "Revolt against the West" (note 20) hampers intercultural communication[42] and intensifies cultural fragmentation. This revolt creates obstacles and contributes to the politicization of existing value-related conflicts between civilizations.

In concluding this section on cultural fragmentation, it can be stated that the reference to cultural differences may explain the Muslim hostility to individual human rights. However, there are other factors. At this point, it is important to state, from the observations made, what is required of Muslims if they are willing to embrace the valid standards of international human rights law.

Muslims are basically required to distinguish between the dominance of the West and the universality of international individual human rights law standards. It is possible to criticize one aspect (hegemonic rule) while accepting the other (the achievements of cultural modernity). If both aspects are confused, then no progress can be made, particularly in the area of human rights. In such a case, unresolved cultural conflicts will, in future, be ignited.

Individual and collective human rights – a conflict?

Islam is not only a religious faith, but also a distinct cultural system. In this system collective, not individual, rights shape the worldview. The concept of human rights, as Mayer rightfully stresses, is "individualistic" in the sense "that it generally expresses claims of a part against the whole."[43] The "part" identified by Mayer is the individual who lives in civil society and is entitled to rights. The "whole" is society and state in an overall political structure. Islam is not familiar with such distinctions. In Islamic doctrine the individual is viewed as a limb of a collectivity, which is the "umma/community of believers." Further, rights are entitlements and are thus different from duties. In Islam, Muslims, as believers, have "fara'id/duties" vis-à-vis the collectivity of the "umma-community," but no individual rights in the sense of entitlements. A monolithic umma-collectivity is invented in the twenty-first century, an imagined community in world politics. This is the legitimacy of Islamist internationalism[44] and also of Islamic identity politics.

A balance is needed between the individual and the collectivity. The principle of subjectivity is based on cultural modernity, of which the concept of individual human rights is a basic component. It is the concept of this subjectivity that determines humans as free individuals. This concept underpins the processes of individuation in the development of modern civil society. I began this chapter with a reference to Habermas in order to outline the notion of the "principle of subjectivity" (see note 3) and I retain this reference as an orientation throughout the chapter. Is there a conflict involved?

Based on this, I contest the Islamization programs supported by self-professed and alleged exponents of specifically Islamic human rights schemes. These programs lead to a conflict with the standards of international human rights law. The legal scholar Ann Mayer provides an analysis of these programs and concludes that "[t]he Islamic schemes do not offer protection for what international law deems fundamental rights."[45] Mayer also finds that Muslim authorities on human rights "have no sure grasp of what the concerns of human rights are."[46] This conclusion is supported by substantial analysis of basic Islamic documents on human rights. In fact, Islamic proclamations do not embrace universal human rights standards.

The discussion up to this point makes clear that there is a basic conflict between cultural modernity and pre-modern doctrines. It is therefore assumed that a civilizational conflict[47] is at work. This relates to the incompatibility of restrictions on the individual in Islam with the notion of individual freedom in cultural modernity. Islamic apologetic authors refuse to see this conflict between individual rights and the Islamic situating of the individual, viewed as a limb in an organic *umma*-collectivity.

In Islam not only believers but also non-Muslims are viewed as a collectivity. In the shari'a there are restrictions not only on the rights and freedom of women, but also on non-Muslim monotheists, viewed as the collective religious minorities of the *dhimmis*. This collectivity has a second-class status.[48] Islamic human rights schemes are "evasive on the question of protections for freedom of religion [t]hey also evince a general lack of sympathy for the idea of freedom of religion."[49]

In short, there is a conflict between pre-modern doctrines of obligation and universal concepts of rights as entitlements based on cultural modernity's principle of subjectivity. The conflict is between obligations (*fara'id*) and rights. There is a challenge to Muslims to develop schemes that are not ambivalent about human rights. Instead of doing this work, apologetic Muslim writers claim that Islam was the very first to establish human rights. Behind this claim one sees a contestation of the Western concept of individual human rights. The substance of a situation in which Islam and human rights are in conflict over values and worldview is denied.

This chapter addresses human rights in line with the contributions made by major scholars in the field (Vincent, Donelly, etc.), who are based in international relations. It is argued that the predicament of Islam with cultural modernity is one of the sources of Islam's inner civil war, which is carried on in the form of a conflict over international human rights. This conflict between Islam and an international society framed by the West is by no means a clash of civilizations. I have repeatedly made clear that I do not share Huntington's views, but I do acknowledge his contribution of bringing culture into international studies. I therefore refrain from joining the club of those who discredit

Huntington without ever having read his work. There is a clear distinction between criticism and defamation. My concern is not to defend Huntington, but rather the right to address the issues.

As an aside, I note that my contribution to the volume of the former German President Herzog engages in the project of *Preventing the Clash of Civilizations*. I do so without ignoring the conflict that exists between a local-cultural worldview and an international standard related to cross-civilizational morality. The substantive issue is the globalized civilization process.[50] In post-bipolar politics civilizations matter. The civilization of Islam unites a variety of local cultures spread throughout Asia, Africa, and parts of Europe (12 million Muslims in the Balkans plus 20 million in the EU diaspora). Europe was not alone in its conquests; Islam also conquered during its period of expansion (seventh to seventeenth centuries), which was halted by the European expansion of modern times.[51] This reference to history makes clear that the contemporary conflict has roots.

In the past there were not only conflicts, but also bridges. The Greek legacy adopted by the Muslims provided such a bridge. At present, cultural modernity and its tradition of individual human rights, understood as entitlements of the individual, could establish such a bridge. These human rights are universal; there can be no specific Islamic human rights in the name of authenticity.

This book engages with such a proposition, but also acknowledges the constraints and obstacles to Muslims' accommodation of cultural modernity and its principle of subjectivity. It has become a received wisdom to view human rights violations almost exclusively as the result of oppressive regimes, i.e. as being primarily political in nature. In a politically correct manner, all cultural constraints are either overlooked or not given due importance. Above all, the conflict between the "collective" and the "individual" in the concept of rights is ignored.

Given that democracy has classical Greek roots, but evolved as a political culture in the West, one can state that there are bridges. Hellenism was shared by the Islamic rationalism of medieval Islam. Muslims of today need to emulate their own tradition of rationalism to which the contemporary rationalist Mohammed al-Jabri[52] points an orientation. This debate will be continued at length in Chapter 7. Here it suffices to point out that Hellenized Islam is relevant to the search for a cultural foundation for human rights in contemporary Islam.

In a project run in better time under the leadership of An-Na'im at the Wilson Center in Washington,[53] we asked how civilizational standards of human rights could be respected in non-Western societies in which democratic values are not established, and also what should be done to make Muslims speak the language of human rights in their own tongue. If this cultural foundation could be accomplished, then the conflict could be resolved. The remedy for dealing with Islam's predicament with the standards of international individual human rights law is for Muslim states that are members of the international system to join international society. This can be done by embracing the universal morality that stems from global civilizational standards. There are barriers to the global establishment of human rights. It has to be stated candidly and in plain language that these barriers are also related to the values of local cultures. Based on the work of Norbert Elias, one can make reference to his notion of *The Civilizing Process* (see note 50) in order to advance the argument that humanity could share common standards. Human rights should be part and parcel of these standards, to be established inter-civilizationally. However, this vision requires cultural change and religious reform. In her clear analysis of the failure to meet inter-national standards of human rights in the Islamic world, Ann Mayer fails, how-ever, to properly grasp this issue when she mistakenly argues that "the stakes in the battle over human rights standards are ultimately political."[54] Against this misleading argument I maintain that there are definitely cultural obstacles to the establishment of human rights standards in Muslim countries. These obstacles underpin the conflict addressed in this section. I am aware that it is unpopular to argue that there is a relationship between globalization, culture, and conflict. In a research project on culture and globalization, in which post-bipolar politics was among the issue areas, a team of scholars argued that cultural tensions are one of the sources of conflict. The findings of that research project, of which I was a member, will guide the reasoning of Chapter 5.

A basic requirement for establishing acceptable universal standards of mor-ality and law in Islam – as in any other civilization – is the acceptance of indi-vidual human rights. Muslims are challenged to learn how to come to terms with the principle of subjectivity. Scholars who are preoccupied with cultural diversity and constrained by rules of political correctness in their study of the Islamic world end up by falling into the trap of "Orientalism in reverse." I repeat: in the beginning, Said had a point, but today his thinking has become an obscure concept that is not worth the expenditure of any time. Most damaging is the fact that the concept of Orientalism does not allow any criticism, whether of despotic regimes ruling the Middle East, of fundamentalism, or of the Islamic pre-modern view of the world. All these ills go undisputed, in the name of respect and recognition for other cultures.

The Western debate on Orientalism did not exclude the field of human rights. In fact, those who are supposed to subscribe to or who are susceptible to Orientalism claim that the "Orient" is different from the West. Difference becomes sacral. Ann Mayer makes the point that the critique of Orientalism in the domain of human rights runs into the same scheme, i.e. of accepting "the quintessentially Orientalist notion that the concepts and categories employed in the West to understand societies and cultures are irrelevant and inapplicable in the East."[55] Apologetic Muslims join in, condemn critical comparisons, and believe that they see in them "sinister political objectives" of "Jews and crusa-ders."[56] I am a Muslim and I ask: is it legitimate that I can be tortured, in vio-lation of my individual human rights, in the name of diversity? I leave the reader to answer that question.

While viewing Islam on a global scale in cultural terms, I do not ignore the diversity of local cultures within Islamic civilization. I also avoid making sweeping generalizations. Despite a great inner-cultural diversity within this civilization, all local Islamic cultures share the common standards of their civilization. Related to it, they also have a worldview in common. Scholars who exclusively stress the diversity of Islam often ignore that Muslims, be they in the Middle East, South Asia, or sub-Saharan Africa, share a common and virtually consistent worldview and speak of themselves as a civilizational entity. In this manner they view the self as an *umma*-collectivity. Of course, this is an imaginary collectivity, but there is something to it, otherwise no one would take notice of it in international politics. Islamic civilization is a real, not a constructed entity. It matters to world politics and to the study of international conflict with the aim of world peace based on peaceful conflict resolution.

The notion of common civilizational standards of human rights is in conflict with contemporary Islamism. The violations of human rights are related not only to the practices of undemocratic regimes, but also to the Islamization programs of the opposition. The issue is not that simple. In a recent article an Egyptian author states plainly: "While Arab elites at least pay lip service to democracy, democratic ideals seem to be of far less concern to the broader public ... [D]emocracy is not at present a major concern of the Arab masses."[57] While the undemocratic regimes in the Middle East use the concept of *"fara'id/ duties,"* they did not invent it. It is an Islamic cultural concept, as old as Islam itself. In the Islamic worldview of the majority of Muslims there is no concept of rights. Exposure to the individualistic concept of human rights and its values leads to conflict. Individual human rights are not accepted by the Islamist opposition to undemocratic regimes. Both rulers and their opponents use Islam for legitimatory purposes. Both define a religious-cultural collectivity against individual rights. With regard to individual human rights as entitlements, one is reminded of the statement of S. E. Ibrahim, quoted in the introductory section of this chapter: "liberal Muslims are twisted between authoritarian rulers and totalitarian Islamists."

To conclude, and in short, rights have to be established on a cross-cultural basis in a local cultural setting and also to be protected institutionally. The absence of a cultural concept to underpin these rights in some local cultures forces their absence in the societies of those cultures. Reference to oppressive regimes and their undemocratic programs, as well as to the Islamization of the opposition, cannot convincingly explain the problems at issue. Again, the issue is cultural modernity and the predicament of some pre-modern cultures in coming to terms with it. Cultural change in developing cultures and religious reform are the roads to establishing individual human rights in the Islamic civilization. The bottom line is that rights are universal and so there are no specifically "Islamic human rights."

Conclusions

The argument of this chapter has been supported by two sources. One is normative. It is Habermas's reference to the "principle of subjectivity" as the backbone of cultural modernity from which individual human rights emanate. The other is both descriptive and analytical. It is the UNDP report of 2002 in which it is acknowledged that the lack of a culture and related institutional practice of human rights is a home-made phenomenon in the Islamic countries of the Middle East. The report describes and analyzes the sad state of affairs in the Middle East. Both sources explain the ills of the contemporary Islamic Middle East and are most pertinent to the analysis provided in this chapter, which focuses on the predicament of Islam with individual human rights as a predicament with cultural modernity. The inference is the need for changes in the cultural system of Islam. The obstacles in the way of establishing Islamic human rights standards are related to prevailing cultural patterns and to the related worldview.[58]

The conclusion of this chapter is that there is an interrelation between Islam and culturally based resistance to human rights. In the context of structural globalization and cultural fragmentation one can dismiss the ideology of universalism. This is justified, but still it is an escape. In contrast, I argue in favor of the establishment of cross-cultural foundations for the norms and values of human rights on legally and politically universal grounds. I am not playing with words when I opt for universality of values and at the same time criticize the ideology of universalism. Muslims could embrace universal values and engage in a cultural change that would alter their worldview and the cultural patterns and attitudes related to it. The conflict stated in this chapter, between Islamic human rights schemes and international human rights standards, could be resolved if Muslims were to admit change and reform. However, if they fail, then tensions will continue to prevail and could then assume the shape of an inter-civilizational conflict. This can be averted. The often-advanced accusation of "essentialism" with reference to culturally based resistance to individual human rights in Islam is pure defamation, and has no basis. It results from unwillingness to understand the conflict at issue and to deal with its roots.

Existing Islamic human rights schemes do not contribute to resolution of the conflict that has been identified. They conceal rather than reveal the conflict emanating from a predicament with modernity. These schemes obscure the incompatibility between individual and collectivity-oriented concepts and the related conflict that is analyzed in this chapter. Further, they blur the boundaries between duties and rights. Again, to understand this issue properly one has to deal with the deep-seated dominant, cosmological worldview among most Muslims. I contend that the prevailing Islamic view of the world is the crucial source of the Islamic predicament with cultural modernity, and thus with individual human rights that claim universality. The present conflict within Islam, to which Ann Mayer briefly refers, is not a new one. Nevertheless, Islamic human rights authors "uphold the primacy of Revelation over reason and none endorse reason as a source of law,"[59] as Mayer rightly states. This is the major source of the conflict, which is one between a human-/reason-centered and a cosmological-theocentric view of the world. A similar conflict existed in medieval Islam, when Hellenized Islamic rationalists were accused of heresy by the Islamic *fiqh*-orthodoxy because they admitted human reason in obtaining a proper knowledge of the world. This reference reinforces the meaning of the "principle of subjectivity," i.e. the human-centered view of the world, for any legal underpinning that determines human beings as individuals entitled to freedom. Individual human rights are therefore individual entitlements. This is part and parcel of cultural modernity based on the "principle of subjectivity." For an Islamic adoption of this concept Muslims need to engage in a "reform of Islamic law." No individual human rights can be achieved in the Islamic world without relating this issue to the very basic normative and structural requirements of cultural modernity and to the worldview emanating from it. Cultural borrowing is not alien to the positive "heritage of Islam," as will be argued in Chapter 7.

It is distressing to see a Muslim who formerly stated an "incompatibility of *shari'a* and modern standards of International Relations and human rights"[60] and today seeks shelter in the shari'a. The stated incompatibility is a fact. It creates tensions, among other things, between a cosmological-theocentric and a human-centered view of the world. The resulting cultural fragmentation in the structurally globalized system of international relations leads to conflict. The best conflict resolution would be for Muslims to embrace human rights as entitlements, which presupposes a serious dealing with the predicament with cultural modernity. Muslims need to go beyond relating man to "*fara'id*/obligations," not rights. This requirement is not fulfilled by the current politicization of Islam into a religious fundamentalism. The issues addressed in this chapter are, first, a concern for Muslims, but since the conflict is not restricted to the Islamic civilization the issue is also pertinent to world politics. The universal morality of human rights is necessary for a peaceful resolution of conflicts between Islam and international society. This would be a contribution to establishing commonalities in order to bridge between the conflicting civilizations. What could be more appropriate in this pursuit than an international acceptance of human rights in world politics,[61] also accepted by Muslims? However, only on the basis that they do their homework.

Today, under the conditions of post-bipolar politics, we live in a changed world. Islam is increasingly significant to world politics, together with the expanding presence of Muslims in Europe and in North America. This leads to a more intense interaction between civilizations. This factor stresses the need for a "common discourse about ethics."[62] This chapter articulates a conflict between shari'a claims and secular individual human rights that affects post-bipolar world politics. The needed ethics have to be based in cultural modernity. In contrast to this need, the contemporary Islamist shari'a reasoning is based on a supremacist worldview that claims moral superiority over others. It is articulated in the formula "*al-Islam ya'lu*/Islam is superior." This mindset hampers cultural change and religious reform and intensifies Islam's predicament. The lack of individual human rights in the Islamic world[63] prevents Muslims from joining in with the age of globalization, and no claim to authenticity can support this negative state of affairs.

Chapter 5

Islam's predicament as a source of conflict

Cultural-religious tensions and identity politics

With this chapter[1] the reader arrives at the core of the current inquiry and is then exposed to the major idea and the assumption of this study, namely, that cultural tensions lead to conflict. In the course of outlining the subject matter at issue in the Introduction, a line was drawn between Islam's predicament with modernity – as analyzed in Chapters 1 to 4 – and the place of Islam in the post-bipolar world politics of conflict, which will be addressed here. Reference to this line is essential to determining both the substance of this chapter and the new discipline of Islamology pursued in this book. It is presented in this book as a study of post-bipolar international conflict, with a social-scientific focus on religion and culture.

The kind of study pursued in this chapter and throughout the book can only be accomplished in an interdisciplinary manner, even though it is heavily embedded in international relations. Despite the focus on culture, the reader can rest assured that under no circumstances do I overlook the political and economic constraints generated by globalization. However, I will maintain the focus on my subject matter. I am well aware of the reference to structural underpinning. The Islamological approach seeks – without any reductionist or culturalist bias – to illuminate the new place of religion and of culture in post-bipolar international conflict. In this context, Islam's predicament with modernity, as the core issue analyzed in Chapter 1, has been demonstrated in Chapters 2 to 4 in relation to three basic issue areas. Here, I go a step further and relate this predicament to the new pattern of conflict that has emerged and prevails in post-bipolar politics.

Introduction

Given the sensitivity of the issue, and the potential for accusations that can be expected, ranging from culturalism and Orientalism to Islamophobia, my present analysis begins with an awareness of the risk that I am navigating in stormy waters. Therefore, I start the chapter by making some clear distinctions. When Islam is addressed and incorporated into the study of conflict I never touch on religion as a faith. Islam is first looked at as a cultural system that underpins a worldview, and in terms of the values on which it rests and which determine the behavior of persons socialized in this pattern. It is assumed that rapid social change triggered by ever-intensifying globalization exposes people of the Islamic civilization to great challenges. Underlying the predicament at issue is the blocking of cultural innovations by the religious-Salafist orthodoxy that dominates the educational establishment – with great consequences. In order to come to terms with the current challenges Muslims need the cultural innovations that they are denied. This denial is often carried out by Muslim leaders in the name of faith and authenticity. Cultural change is a basic necessity for accommodation to a changed international environment. If this does not happen, tensions occur and conflict is the outcome. To forbid these issues to be addressed is tantamount to undermining a proper understanding of the place of Islam in post-bipolar politics. Islamology seeks to provide this understanding.

In the course of my participation in the research for the World Cultures research project on Culture, Conflict and Globalization (see note 1) I learned to see how religion and culture could develop in a crisis-ridden situation, in the context of a politicization process, into a source of tensions. This is the overall context of international conflict in post-bipolar politics. In contrast to the response to this challenge that is articulated through a politicization of religion, we could have a willingness to engage in religious reform as a means to an accommodation. This accommodation would provide the basis for peaceful solutions contributing to a de-escalation of conflict. Defensive-cultural identity politics does not contribute to this end; rather, seems to replace innovative cultural change. Defensive-cultural self-assertion impedes the search for peaceful conflict resolution. This pattern of identity politics, as currently spreading, is based on an Islamic perception of the self as an imagined community under attack. It is the transnational *umma* of Islam perceived to be under siege. This Islamic identity politics leads to conflict in the name of fighting a jihad against the imaginary enemies of Islam: the crusaders, the Jews, and their Muslim allies.

Existing realities belie the sweeping generalization by which globalization is viewed as an overall process that implicitly leads to a kind of cultural standardization. The opposite is true. Identity politics is a means for cultural self-assertion against the effects of globalization, and it ends in fragmentation. Cultural divisions are established in the name of promoting the search for authenticity. This issue will be analyzed in Chapter 8. Thus, the argument here is limited, to the extent that globalization does not mean standardization. Rather, globalization leads to cultural fragmentation. This development generates tensions and conflict. Islamic civilization is presented in this study as the most significant case in point. The perception of an Islam under siege – already mentioned – strengthens identity politics in its quest for a polarization between "we" (*umma*) and "them" (the West or, even worse, "the alliance of Jews and crusaders"). I hear and read about this not only in the world of Islam, but also in the culture of diaspora mosques in Europe. This incitement is often tolerated in the name of religious freedom.

In the context outlined, identity politics becomes a power in itself to ignite polarization and generate conflict. For a proper understanding of the issue one has to ask under what conditions religion, culture, and civilization contribute to conflict in post-bipolar world politics. Unfortunately, general agreement is conspicuously absent, not to mention consensus among scholars regarding accepted definitions of religion, culture, and civilization. The failure of scholarship to establish a common terminology in this field results in related issues being *un*settled, a situation that leads to much disorientation and confusion. This chapter therefore first proposes a working definition of culture, to be related to the understanding of conflict; then an attempt is made to discover how this definition can be applied to Islam and Islamism in post-bipolar politics.

The statement of the existence of cultural diversity under conditions of globalization is guided by the norm of mutual respect and acknowledgment of the equality of the other. In other words, diversity can only be admitted within the framework of cultural and religious pluralism. The lack of acceptance of the cultural legitimacy of pluralism in some cultures leads to cultural-religious tensions. The issue of pluralism is addressed here in passing only, as it is the subject of Chapter 7. As in the case of the definition of culture, the meaning of pluralism is among the unsettled issues and therefore it, too, is a recurrent one.

The study of culture-based conflict comprises a search for solutions not only in the search for an exit strategy, but also as a contribution to peace. I do not see this orientation in the fashionable debate on cultural hybridity.[2] There seems to be no light at the end of the tunnel, because this debate simply overlooks the conflict situation and so fails to provide a way out of the existing impasse. Prudent scholars who acknowledge the place of culture in the study of conflict and globalization refer critically to the fact that the established debate on culture is "expressed along remarkably mechanical lines,"[3] as Roland Robertson states. This legitimate critique dismisses the practice in which culture is either reduced by some to a determined factor, or seen as determinative by others. This criticism is referred to in order to renew the previously articulated argument of an interplay between social and cultural change;[4] they cannot and should not be reduced the one to the other in the mechanical manner criticized by Robertson.

In relating these debates to Islam and to its predicament with modernity one first has to acknowledge the great cultural diversity within this civilization. This fact runs counter to the Muslim orthodox view that there is one culture named Islam, and also to the view of an Islam perceived in monolithic terms by some Orientalists. There exists neither such an Islamic entity, nor the so-called one *Islam mondialisé*, as Olivier Roy wrongly and indiscriminately contends in his sensational book title. However, it is true that the view of a coherent *umma* is based on the Islamist belief in an imagined community. This is supported by the fact that all diverse Islamic local cultures share a kind of family resemblance, and on this basis they are grouped perceptually into one entity, which I propose to name an "*umma*-civilization." I repeat: this entity is a culturally diverse grouping, and no monolith. Muslims' awareness of the self as an *umma* allows them to speak of one "Islamic civilization."[5] This understanding has been already established in Chapter 1, without engaging in any essentialization. It would be ridiculous to vilify the approach as Orientalism. A benign, neo-colonial mindset is at work when some Westerners forbid Muslims to see in their community an Islamic *umma*-civilization. In fact, this self-awareness as a civilization united against a perceptual or imagined enemy (the West) is an essential element of the Islamic worldview.

For the sake of distinction and clarity, the terms "culture" and "civilization" are not used interchangeably. Throughout this book different meanings are established for the two notions. For a proper understanding of Islam in post-bipolar politics and of its place in the related conflicts, whether on a local, regional, or global level, it is imperative to acknowledge the combination of cultural diversity and civilizational unity that exists in Islamic politics.[6] This is a part of the underpinning of the tensions and conflicts that will be illuminated in this chapter. There are pre-modern ethnic and religious cultures[7] in which the collective self is not only asserted in a self-glorifying manner, but also put to use in establishing fault lines vis-à-vis the other. The "other" is culturally perceived as a threat to one's own, often constructed identity; thus, identity politics is always based on fault lines. In this context, there is a search for a so-called cultural authenticity, as will be discussed in detail in Chapter 8. The related mechanism of drawing boundaries and making delineations between groups on the basis of collective identities of imagined communities results in mobilization against the cultural other. The outcome of this mobilizatory identity politics are tensions that escalate into a conflict which at times includes bloodletting. The late twentieth-century politics of Islamic identity is continued in the new millennium and provides a clear example in support of this contention. The preoccupation with "*asalah*/authenticity," as promoted by the aim of de-Westernization, is used as a means for purification, certainly not for hybridity. Also, tensions are not only restricted to identity politics on the general level of the relations between one civilization and others; at the same time they assume the shape of a local identity politics in conflict within the civilizational community itself. One can refer to examples such as ethnic or sectarian strife (e.g. shi'a vs. sunna, Arabs vs. Kurds, etc.) and the conflict between Islamists and secular Kemalists in Turkey. The killing within the community (e.g. Iraq, Afghanistan and Somalia, among others) is one of the salient features of this "purification"-based identity politics. The enemy can also be within.

On a global level one can see that the actors are driven by rival images of the self and the other. These images are related to either a real or a perceived Islamophobia and result in a cultural anti-Westernism. The issue is not only a cultural one related to perceptions. It becomes political when cultural tensions lead to a real conflict. It is the actors involved, and not this book, that engage in a culturalization of the issues in a conflict situation. This contributes to an attitude of exclusivism and to zero-sum-thinking that prevents peaceful conflict resolution, because negotiations for a mutually acceptable settlement are not admitted. In short, compromise and rational negotiation are seldom within reach in culturally or civilizationally rooted conflicts. When politics is religionized the door is closed. The PLO and Israel were able to talk and establish the Oslo Peace Accords, but Hamas and the Jews do not, and cannot. In 2007/08 there were global efforts to find a resolution of conflict that would be acceptable to both parties. The Fatah-based Palestinian President Mahmud Abbas (Abu Mazen) was willing to compromise and therefore participated; Hamas, which rules in the Gaza Strip – on the basis of an election the results of which were not recognized by the US and the European Union – condemned those efforts in religious-cultural language and accused Abu Mazen of treason.

Defensive-cultural identity politics and tensions

The notion of cultural and religionized tensions that lead to conflict is based on a specific understanding of values and worldviews.[8] Islam is viewed as a cross-regional civilization characterized by great inner diversity, related equally to local cultures and to religious sectarianism. Despite all this diversity, Muslims nonetheless share a universal worldview combined with local meaning and outlook. The existing interconnectedness between ethnicity, religion, culture, society, and economy points to issue areas that are yet to be defined in relation to one another. This should not be done along mechanical lines. Culture is both determined by and determinative of globalization. One of the basic arguments of this chapter is that the political culturalization of the place of Islam in world politics in the twenty-first century is pursued by the actors themselves, and not by outsiders. This pursuit assumes the shape of defensive-cultural identity politics, which leads to tensions and conflicts, and is combined with a claim to authentic legitimacy that is put forward in an Islamic guise.

The existing asymmetries in the global political environment affect society, the economy, and politics and promote cultural tensions. The structural gap supports cultural perceptions or misperceptions of the other. Among these one encounters the imagery of an "Islam under siege," surrounded by perceived enemies. This is the basis of a defensive culture. To reiterate: the related tensions lead to international conflicts. The major assumption on which all chapters of this book rest is the predicament of Islam with cultural modernity: it is embedded in this local–global context and is also central to it. This is the meaning of the overall context of the "Revolt against the West" (see note 25) on the part of non-Western cultures shaped by religion. With the exception of the very few highly secular societies of the West (e.g. France and its *laïcité*), culture in the rest of the world is mostly associated with religion – even in the secular United States. However, in our post-bipolar age secularity is challenged in general, and especially by political Islam and its claims. It is intriguing to see the radical, secular republic of France – with a 10 percent segment of its population comprised of mostly socially marginalized Muslims – face this challenge and to observe how it responds to it.[9] However, awareness of this new phenomenon of "religion in international relations" is growing fairly slowly.[10]

Identity politics based on religion as a cultural system also nurtures a corresponding political ideology that grows from the politicization of religion. This
ideology emerges in a cultural-political set-up that heralds a return of the sacred which
is occurring under conditions of globalization. Under these conditions the
defensive-cultural rebellion assumes religious legitimacy. Cultural-religious tensions
are ignited and lead to conflict. In the case of Islam, the pivotal argument rests
on the fact that social reality, not a belief system, is the determinant. Of course, it is
also a social reality that perceptions imbued with faith affect cultural behavior and
action. One is reminded of the example of jihadist activism. The reader is reminded
generally of the understanding of religion as a *fait social*. All features of the following
trinity can be found in the Islam of the twenty-first century: "religionization of
politics," the "politicization of religion," and "culturalization of conflict." The tensions that emerge in this context and lead to conflict on local, regional, and
international levels are related to a predicament with cultural modernity.

In Geertzian anthropology the notion of culture indicates a locally determined
social production of meaning. This meaning is adopted in the present work,
with, however, a reference to religion as a *fait social* in the Durkheimian tradition.
This is the understanding that shapes the thinking in this chapter. I do not look
at culture "as if it were an isolated island," as the late Geertz once self-critically
described his approach at a dinner at my house in Princeton. By then, in 1986/87,
I was a visiting member of faculty. Geertz gave me permission to quote his phrase
in public, on the condition of adding that he was reconsidering his earlier understanding by looking at the international environment of a cultural community.
However, he shied away not only from recognizing the collective reference to
religion shared by all Islamic local cultures, but also – as most cultural-relativist
anthropologists do – from acknowledging the place of conflict. Today, religion
serves equally as an identity reference related to the perception of belonging to an
umma-community under siege, and as a source of conflict. To be sure, it is a civilization, not a local culture, that embodies this imagined *umma* community. This
reference to belonging to a civilization is cross-cultural. The civilizational community
of Islam reflects a combination of cultural similarities and political ideology that
is based on the perception of an imagined community.[11] Today, any reference to
"civilization" has the potential to be charged and associated by the uninformed
public with the rhetoric of Huntington's "clash." Those scholars familiar with
the research background of this issue know, however, how ridiculous this suspi-
cion would be. They also know that Muslims themselves understand their own
entity as a civilization. In the past, serious scholars like Norbert Elias and Fernand
Braudel employed the concept of civilization. This concept is also used by influential Islamist ideologues, like Sayyid Qutb, who look at the *umma*-community as
a civilization intrinsically shaped by a civilizational universalism. The constructed civilizational identity of the Islamic collective *umma* politicizes the dogmatic claim of "one Islam" and becomes a source for the rise of tensions among
Muslims, and also in their relations with non-Muslim others. This worldview is
not favorable to religious and cultural pluralism; it not only negates the existing

general diversity, i.e. of numerous local-cultural systems, but also diversity within Islam. As Qutb once worded it, in a way also adopted by Bin Laden: the fault line is between "*iman alami*/global belief" and "*kufr alami*/global unbelief." The relation between both constructed entities is defined in terms of a cosmic war of jihad. This misleading jihad is also a challenge to enlightened Muslims who are set to establish alternatives, but with an Islamic legitimation.

The notion of an Islamic collective identity is based on the fact that Islam is a universal faith that has generated a cross-cultural civilization. It is not a mere construction. However, its use in contemporary tensions leads to culture-related conflicts. The Qutb/Bin Laden fault line constructed as a front by Muslim believers fighting the "*kafirun*/unbelievers" revives collective memories of an earlier globalization project that dominated for a thousand years: from the seventh through the seventeenth centuries. This is the collective memory of a glorious Islamic history. The Islamic *futuhat* (Islamic conquests) fought in that age aimed to map the entire globe into "*Dar al-Islam*/the Islamicate." The rise of the West overtook this Islamic globalization. The reality of history is this: from the seventh to the seventeenth century Muslims (first the Arabs, then the Ottoman Turks) fought jihad in pursuit of Islamic globalization. Today the related collective memories are constructed on the basis of the historical revival of the classical Islamic conquests, which were real[12] and – as stated – which lasted for ten centuries.[13] Today there are historians who interpret this Islamic expansion, legitimated by religion, as a variety of imperialism.[14] For their part, contemporary Islamists revive this history so as to construct cultural memories in order to nurture the perceptual cosmic war of civilizations in which they engage. The ideology that legitimates this cosmic war is called jihadism. The process begins by igniting tensions that lead to conflict. These conflicts can only be resolved in pursuit of democratic world peace (see note 6) if Muslims really engage in an appropriate Islamic engagement with their predicament with cultural modernity. As argued throughout this chapter, defensive-cultural patterns and the related identity politics contribute neither to a coming to terms with the current challenges, nor to a peaceful conflict resolution.

In short, Islamic identity politics is based on the perception of a cultural threat that is connected to fault lines between the self and others who are viewed as incompatible collectivities. The current debate over Islam, globalization, modernity, and postmodernity persists on the surface, evades the issues, and results in overlooking what really matters.[15] The revival and construction of collective memories refers to the Islamic glory of the imperial past. These collective memories underpin a war of ideas that is not restricted to a simple nostalgia. As John Kelsay states, at issue is a disagreement over the order of the world. This issue is phrased in cultural terms of tensions, conflict, and perceived threat:

> We would be wrong to understand the contemporary call for revival among Muslims as simple nostalgia. ... The mood is not nostalgia but outrage over the state of the world.[16]

In a defensive-cultural response[17] to the perceived threat ("Islam under siege"), cultural attitudes unfold in a triangle of globalization–culture–conflict. Underlying this are three issue areas: 1) Islam's predicament with cultural modernity, 2) the tensions within an Islam that is torn between its past glory and its present civilizational decay, and 3) compensation of this through a cultural revival of collective memories in the face of real or constructed enemies in a defensive-cultural identity politics.

To protect the idea that cultural tensions lead to conflict and to dissociate it from the notion of a "clash of civilizations," I emphasize my disagreement with the way in which Huntington addresses Western–Islamic tensions. The political analytical study of conflict that emerges from cultural tensions has nothing to do with the rhetoric of a clash, which serves as an essentializing pattern. A conflict can be peacefully resolved by negotiations. In a clash there is a constructed dichotomy between culturalized/religionized collectivities of the self and the other. Thus, Huntington's thinking resembles that of Islamism. In the political realities of Chechnya, Xinjiang, Kashmir, Thailand, Indonesia, the Philippines, in addition to the core conflict in the area of the greater Middle East, there are tensions between the collectivities of the self and of the "other," not a clash. It is not always the West, but also Russia and other non-Western actors with partly Islamic populations, like China, India, Israel etc., that are involved in a situation that is defined as conflict with the world of Islam. The involved parties could go to the negotiation table, address the issue, defuse the tensions, and solve the conflict. However, when a perception of threat prevails and is combined with an Islamic preoccupation with the "enemies of Islam," then a cultural discourse of self-victimization takes the place of accommodation. The outcome is polarization. Again, and despite acknowledging this, I maintain my refusal to embrace the notion of a "clash."

The rise of Western civilization – not to be confused, as is so often done, with Western Christendom – begins culturally with the Renaissance.[18] Politically and economically, this occurred within the framework of European expansion. It was supplemented by the modern technology of *A Military Revolution*.[19] It created the greatest challenge ever to Islamic civilization, as is illuminated in the work of Bernard Lewis.[20] Certainly, the idea of the West[21] is strongly related to the cultural claim of universal Westernization. The new globalization project came into conflict with that other universalism that is based on the idea of *Dar al-Islam*. Both universalisms want to cover the entire globe. In reality, the colonial conquests were not only a very real threat, but also very humiliating to Muslims, who believe that "*al-Islam ya'lu wa la yu'la alayhu*/Islam is superior, and nothing can be superior to it and to its claims." This image of the Muslim self is contrasted with the reality that emerged from the European expansion. The image expressed the earlier reality, in which the world was subjected to the rule of a universal *Dar al-Islam*. Western globalization took over and replaced Islamic dominance with its own domination. The revival of cultural memories of this history – both real and constructed ones – has become a source of tensions and conflict in a "return," not an "End of History." Since the demise of bipolarity, this issue has become one of the basic features of world politics in its new shape. Islam is a challenger, but it is itself also challenged by the new environment. To be sure, the two determinations, i.e. to be challenged and to challenge, are often confused with one another by the actors involved, and by scholars too.

Instead of a serious Islamic reasoning on the sources of the Islamic predicament also related to the history outlined above, Sayyid Qutb engaged in a project of Islamic revival that aimed at a reversal. He acknowledged that the West continued to prevail in terms of power, whether economically, politically, or militarily. However, Qutb maintained that only Islam has the moral authority and superiority to lead. This idea becomes a mobilizing device in post-bipolar politics, and it troubles Muslims and non-Muslims alike. This was the theme of my study that preceded this book,[22] *Political Islam and World Politics*. In this new study the focus is on the cultural sources of the conflict that results from Islam's predicament with cultural modernity. Here I view Islam from the inside, and see a predicament of civilization. As stated in the Introduction, this predicament affects the life of every Muslim – and this author is no exception.

Unlike the Islamists of today, the early nineteenth-century Muslims were willing to look at the problems and to deal with some of the real issues in order to accommodate to changed conditions. Their efforts may not have been satisfactory, but they have to be acknowledged and respected. One of these was a conformism that was limited to adjusting to the changed world that was now dominated by Europe.[23] However, this happened without any significant efforts in the direction of cultural change and religious reform. In pursuit of this conformism, Islam was separated from politics, particularly after the abolition of the caliphate in 1924, but there was no substantive process of secularization in society. In contrast, the contemporary Muslim and Arab revival[24] heralds the return of the sacred to politics. The target is not only Western hegemony but also all the cultural impacts related to the European expansion. Today, "cultural globalization" is contested in a "Revolt against the West"[25] that is aimed at undoing what was accomplished as a cultural Westernization of the world. The failed project of Westernization has led to a crisis of modernization in which a project is proclaimed of global cultural Islamization based on de-Westernization. This is expressed in the formula: "*al-hall huwa al-Islam*/Islam is the solution." The project envisages a purification of the world of Islam in knowledge, law, and human rights. These issues were analyzed in the earlier chapters.

Unlike the ideologies of decolonization and the related anti-colonialism, the present cultural anti-Westernism is not restricted to opposing the hegemony of the West. Earlier, secular, anti-colonial nationalism was poised to modernize, and it embraced such Western concepts as the sovereignty of the nation-state.[26] There was a change of course at the turn to the twenty-first century. It was a change from the prevailing mindset to a new one based on the combination of religionization and culturalization of politics. The process began somewhat earlier and contributes to emerging tensions and, in consequence, to conflict, in a more radical way. Again, secular nationalism (e.g. pan-Arabism) was based on a cultural borrowing from Europe, i.e. through the adoption of the modern and very European idea of the nation. This ideology also restricted its political scope to ambitions of a territorial nature. All other national movements of decolonization did the same, even those that were inspired by jihad. That anti-colonial jihad was restricted to the claims of pan-Islamism (Islamic unity); it was not a global jihad, as is the recent one, which is directed by an Islamist internationalism. There is a significant distinction between pan-Islamic jihad, as a response restricted to contesting Western colonial rule,[27] and jihadist internationalism. Unlike the earlier anti-colonial jihad, contemporary global jihadism, rooted in political Islam, extends its scope to encompass the entire globe. This is the global jihad based on a political internationalism that is set to remake the world order, in contrast to anti-colonial jihad, which was a quasi-national, pan-Islamic movement.

The reader is reminded of the nineteenth century's Islamic revivalist al-Afghani, who borrowed the "pan-ideology" of the West and applied it to Islam in order to develop it into a concept for the promotion of pan-Islamism. To reiterate the most important distinction: the present political Islam goes much further and constructs an Islamist internationalism[28] based on the politicization of classical Islamic universalism. There are many "experts on Islam," like James Piscatori and others, who not only fail to understand the difference between the territorial and the nation-state, but also completely ignore the great and highly significant distinction between pan-Islamism and Islamist internationalism.[29] Those who confuse scholarly concepts and fail to understand Islamic politics[30] compel me to reiterate: the basic issue is not so much the flaws in question, but the inability to understand how "culture matters" to the study of social, political, and economic conflicts. Defensive-cultural identity politics ignites tensions and gives the conflict a religious-cultural guise.

Links between Islam's predicament with modernity and cultural tensions leading to conflict

Based on my earlier and repeated unpleasant experience, I feel that repetition is imperative in order to ensure a proper understanding of the major argument of this chapter. It is most important to make clear the distinction between clash and conflict as applied to the notion of "civilization." To avoid the deplorable polemics of the Huntingtonized debate, I refer to the source of my thinking on this subject: the great fourteenth-century philosopher of Islam Ibn Khaldun. Huntington is not familiar with this thinker and his *Prolegomena*, and so any reference to his work is completely absent from Huntington's "clash" book. Ibn Khaldun was the first thinker in the history of ideas to establish the "*ilm al-umran*/science of civilization."[31] He was the very last great philosopher of high caliber that the Islamic civilization produced before it began to decline. Here I draw on his reasoning on the subdivision of humanity into civilizations and enrich this reference to his approach with two additions.

First, a distinction between culture and civilization. The reader is reminded of the understanding of the two terms used: *culture* is based on a local production of meaning; a *civilization* encompasses more, in a cross-cultural sense.

Second, unlike the study of civilizations by Ibn Khaldun and the study of culture some six centuries later by Clifford Geertz, I am looking at the international environment of cultures and civilizations and not viewing them as entities in themselves. The study of international conflict is located in this context of the global interaction between cultures and civilizations. Thus, the framework of my analysis is the study of conflict related to Islam's exposure to cultural modernity in the overall context of globalization.

To update the study of civilizations and in continuation of the very high standard set by Ibn Khaldun's work, it can be said that the two volumes published by Norbert Elias are today the foremost contribution to the study and to the theory of civilization. They were published under the title *The Civilizing Process*.[32] This magnificent work matters to the present study of Islam as a civilization, and also in the context of international conflict.

The work of Norbert Elias is relevant to the present analysis because it includes many inspiring and pertinent insights. Unlike Ibn Khaldun and Clifford Geertz, Elias does not restrict his thinking on culture and civilizations to a study of their inner structure; he also addresses their environment. In the first volume of his magnum opus, *The Civilizing Process*, Elias inquires into the unfolding of European civilization that occurred first among the higher ranks of society, changing their manners and behavior. He then looks at the top-down standardization of civilizational change in society. In the second volume he addresses the link between European expansion and the mapping of the world to the standardization of the civilizing process. Unfortunately, Elias does not go far beyond identifying the issue, and he fails to provide an in-depth analysis of the assumed globalization of the civilizing process. Certainly, the birth of Islam was also related to a civilizing process, during the course of which the Arab Bedouin developed from uncivilized nomads to become people of the foremost civilization in medieval history. I am aware of some Eurocentric connotations in Elias's theory, but I overlook them in order to maintain the focus on the study of Islam and cultural modernity in the context of the assumed globalization of civilizational standards. Elias's work is very valuable for this study. Nonetheless, I do not share his view of civilizational standardization. Instead, I maintain the view of a fragmentation that contributes to the culturalization of politics, and thus to conflict. I do so, however, without overlooking the existence of civilizational standards, established on a global level through the process that Elias analyzes. However, the civilizing process should not be equated with a process of global standardization. Without a doubt, prevailing global structures and their related standards do affect the world of Islam, although it retains its inner configuration. Certainly, the abolition of the Islamic caliphate in 1924 by Kemal Atatürk, founder of modern Turkey, was paralleled by the introduction of the European institution of the nation-state into the world of Islam. It is true that, ever since, all parts of the world – including the countries of Islamic civilization – have been mapped into the European Westphalian system.[33] However, there are tensions related to the simultaneity of the construction of a uniting, modern nation-state and and the fragmentation of ethnic, tribal, and sectarian communities. The tensions are concealed by national flags and symbols, but these do not create a nation out of a tribe.[34] The conclusion is that modern states (e.g. Iraq) emerged as the result of a transplantation without a process of nation building. The post-Iraq War developments made abundantly clear that there is no Iraqi nation; rather, there are sectarian communities fighting one another in an ethnicity of fear. This remark points to the major theme of this book and leads to the conclusion that the world of Islam has been mapped into the global structures of the modern world – without, however, a real introduction and embracing of cultural modernity. The institution of the nation-state that today exists nominally in the world of Islam lacks all the elements of the related political culture. Iraq and Afghanistan – next to Somalia – are only a few cases in point.

In short, the entry of the world of Islam into the international system, and its situation within global structures, conceals the conflict between the local-cultural, i.e. subordinate, identities of individual Muslims and the superordinate, civilizational-related identity that is imposed on them. This conflict is not completely new, because the *umma* identity provided by the ideal of a universal Islam that is supposed to subdue all local identities also generates conflicts. I will set aside the history of inner-Islamic wars (the Ridda war 632–34, Fitna war 658, etc.) and focus instead on the conflict between the imported notion of "the nation" – translated into Islamic languages by the term "*umma*" – and other competing identities. At present, the rise of political Islam is reviving some Islamic patterns in an invention of tradition. In this context, the cross-cultural identity pattern of a universal Islamic *umma* is envisioned as comprising not only all Muslims, but also the world at large, in a project of a global Islamization. Political Islam not only articulates the links between Islam and conflict, but also furthers the underlying tensions. It spreads the antisemitic prejudice that the nation-states in the world of Islam grew from the dissolution of the universal Islamic order on the basis of a "Jewish-crusader conspiracy."

This quoted Islamist resentment nurtures the rejection of the modern nation-state in the world of Islam. The institution is a novelty, and it imposes on its population[35] a citizenship based on a constructed, superordinate national identity that is alien to them. The existing nation-states lack institutional and structural substance and are thus nominal state entities. For this reason they have barely succeeded in the objective of forming a nation based on shared identity. The lack of substance beyond formal sovereignty explains the sectarian and ethnic strife (e.g. in post-Saddam Iraq[36]) in these failed states. This is the local and regional level of conflict. Then there is the international level, related to a new configuration of the world of Islam, subdivided into nation-states, which reflects Islam's predicament with cultural modernity as one of the sources of conflict.

In a context of post-bipolar politics, the intensifying structural globalization, combined with cultural fragmentation, indirectly supports movements of contestation. These ethnic-cultural and religion-based movements promote collective identity politics. The overall problems are mixed with a revival of local-cultural ethnicity, as well as with collective memories of a universal Islamic civilization. As was shown earlier, the resulting tensions grow from the perception of a cultural threat (e.g. "Islam under siege"). In this context, a distinction is made between political-social conflicts on the one hand, and their cultural perception on the other. It matters that the articulation of conflict occurs in religious terms. In the academic debate, the issue is often blurred by some scholars who view culturalization and religionization as a cover that conceals other sources of conflict. This view not only overlooks the mix of culture, religion, society, economy, and politics that is occurring, but also ignores the links between Islam's predicament and the structure of conflict.

This book challenges reductionist thinking that simplistically reduces cultural articulation to economic constraints. The most imperative variety of this thinking is to view the struggle for oil in Iraq as the major source of the entire tragedy that has been taking place there since the wars of the 1980s, the 1990s, and 2003 onwards. This is indicative of a simplification of a popularized Marxist understanding that regularly reduces conflicts to their social and economic roots. This is a vulgar Marxism that overlooks the fact that culture is neither determined nor determinative. Again, it is part of an interplay. As a former Marxist educated in the Frankfurt School, I have learned to view such interpretations as an expression of vulgar Marxism. Now, I study Islam's predicament with cultural modernity not as a superstructure (Marx: *Überbau*) on an economic foundation. It is by no means an essentialization to relate the issue to cultural values and the prevailing worldview. For instance, neither *The Dream Palace of the Arabs*,[37] nor *Moroccan Authoritarianism*,[38] nor *Arab Neopatriarchy*[39] are economic issues; they are related to culture. These issues are referred to by quotation of authors who are all Middle Easterners. It would be ridiculous to dismiss the reasoning of these quoted Muslim scholars with the invective of Orientalism or of "self-Orientalization."

The effort to link Islam's predicament with cultural modernity to tensions located within the triangle of "globalization–culture (local)/civilization (cross-cultural)–conflict" must include cultural perceptions in its analysis. If cultural perceptions are politicized, then not only does disagreement occur, but also hostility is ignited between groups that are defined in terms of collective cultural identity. In this understanding "culture" contributes to tensions and conflicts in Islamic politics. If this were not the case, then one could put Islam aside and focus instead on economic globalization and power struggle, and on those grounds ignore all of the cultural undercurrents of the conflict. This procedure would be highly consequential for an analysis of polity and society in the world of Islam. In contrast to this, the approach of Islamology is proposed as an international relations discipline based on the study of post-bipolar conflicts. Islamology dismisses any reduction of tensions to a socio-economic set-up or to power struggle. One cannot ignore the views of those who engage in a culturization of politics. Here let me state pre-emptively that I study the interplay of culture and economics, but that I beware of drawing reductionist conclusions.

There are three major flaws in this field of study. *First*, economic reductionism. *Second*, the opposing flaw of culturalism. *Third*, the view that all conflicts are about the struggle for power. In contrast, I maintain that there is an interplay between culture, society, and economics, and place them on an equal footing (see note 4). It is unfortunate to see that the flaws identified here prevail in the literature on this subject. On the one hand, there is a generation of cultural anthropologists who view local cultures as discrete islands (e.g. Geertz), and on the other hand there are those who ignore culture altogether, articulating a sweeping economic or political globalization. All other aspects of people's lives are ignored. This book argues against the mainstream on the one hand maintains that cultures and civilizations matter to the study of conflicts in the world of Islam and in world politics, and on the other dismisses the view that conflicts articulated in cultural-civilizational terms are merely a reflection of a "clash of interests."[40] One encounters this simplistic view in superficial studies, which should be ignored. It is foolish to argue in this manner. Huntington is wrong – but some of his critics are wrong also!

While culture is acknowledged as a significant source of meaning, it is also used to articulate tensions and conflict. That said, one should warn against the over-simplification of an "essential Islamic culture." This distortion can be found in the works of Huntington and those who follow him. Again, at issue is the interplay between socio-economic, political, and cultural constraints, as they are all embedded in globalizing structures (note 4). None of these cultural or structural constraints can be separated from one another, nor can any of them be reduced to the other (e.g. reducing culture to economy or vice versa) if they are to be properly understood. In Islam, culture is related to a distinct and intrinsic process of production of meaning and is virtually always in flux. Therefore, there exists no immutable culture based on Islamic rulings. Despite the resistance of Islamic orthodox Salafism to change, one can establish the argument of change and refer to the fact of cultural production being embedded in a global environment shaped by both of the dimensions of modernity outlined in the Introduction and in Chapter 1. To reiterate: there are not only Western students of Islam who essentialize in an Orientalist manner. In the past, Salafism, and today, the ideology of political Islam, both engage in exactly the same thinking, even in a reversed manner. This essentialization, be it Western or Islamic, should be dismissed as Orientalism or Islamist "Orientalism in reverse."[41] Both reflect the two interrelated mindsets that are dismissed in the present analysis.

Based on the preceding framework and its assumptions, it is argued that globalization on the one hand reflects a shrinking of the world that brings people of different cultures closer to each other and thus exposes Muslims to non-Muslims, but on the other hand creates a situation of conflict. This exposure of people of different cultures to one another does not automatically lead to the emergence of common outlooks, but rather to the generation of political-cultural tensions. The ideology that emerges in this context articulates not only disagreement, but also a perception of threat. The results are fragmentation and culturally based hostilities. In a defensive-cultural response to the current challenges an opportunity to deal properly with the predicament of cultural modernity is wasted. These processes make it abundantly clear that there are links between Islam's predicament with modernity and the complex of cultural tensions and conflicts in politics.

The links at issue are documented in a politicization of religion and a corresponding religionization of politics. Admittedly, a related culturalization of conflict is constructed in the context of identity politics, but every construction is a part of the reality. Thus, these constructions become a major source of the tensions that create fault lines on the basis of reviving cultural collective memories. The interrelated wars of ideas and of collective memories are most pertinent to the study of the cultural undercurrents of conflict.

To wrap up, the findings of this section can be summarized by stating that Islamic beliefs assume a contemporary political-cultural form in a crisis situation. This new form is embedded in globalization and all of its ills. However, these cultural attitudes are not a simple reflection of economic structures. The culturally articulated contestation that emerges from a perception of threat is, for the people concerned, inherently and intrinsically Islamic in its nature. The conclusion is that no instrumental use of religion is involved when a conflict is culturalized. Beliefs are deeply involved; the religious-cultural articulation of political and socio-economic issues is made as an expression of faith. Muslim people involved in conflicts believe that they act "*fi sabil Allah*/in the path of God," i.e. as "true believers" and not as a party to the economic-political conflict of a "clash of interests." Qutb made it clear that "*iman*/belief," not an interest, is the issue. In a duality of reshaped cultural-religious beliefs and political-economical ills, selective memories are revived and placed in the time-space context of globalization. Nevertheless, they are not fully determined by this process and so they stand partly on their own terms. Needless to say, this statement reflects neither an Orientalism, nor an essentialism. I repeat what I learned as a young student in the class of Theodor W. Adorno: the interpretation of culture as *Überbau*, i.e. as a reflection of the economy, is nothing but an indication of a vulgar Marxism. Today, it is intriguing to see this vulgar-Marxist mindset spreading, among people classed as liberals, even among conservatives. Clearly, the Marxist idea, whether in its sophisticated origin or in its vulgarization by some elements of the left, is not helpful in understanding the place of religion in today's world politics.

The blocked resolution in Islam's predicament with modernity

Today, the world of Islam and its extension as a diaspora in the West are under pressure to deal with great problems in a crisis situation. The issues are related to a failure in modernization and development in the world of Islam and to poor integration of the diaspora into European societies. In order to deal with the resulting crisis Islamists propose that "Islam is the solution." We saw young Muslims in the Parisian suburbs during the uprising of 2005 shouting *"Allahu Akbar"* in order to legitimate their action as jihad. This was definitely more an invention of tradition than a jihad itself. The issue was social marginalization. However, in this, as in other cases, the conflict was articulated in cultural and religious terms. This reference to religion and culture should be taken seriously and not viewed as a "cover" or pretext for something else. Hostilities ignited by cultural tensions lead to conflict that cannot be solved if "culture" is kept out of the issue. What is it all about?

At issue behind the revival of Islam is the return of the sacred, which in Islam assumes the shape of a cultural resurgence. The related articulations reveal a variety of defensive culture[42] that could, in the course of its development, assume an offensive character. A case in point is the so-called jihad, first for an Islamic state and then for an Islamic world order.[43] It is true that contestation of the present world order is the driving force. However, it is based on cultural-religious foundations, which means that more than an indication of anti-globalization is at issue: the issue is the order of the world.[44] To put it differently, we are dealing not only with a contestation, but also with the quest for an alternative world order, with the objective of a remaking of the world.

Islam's claim for global power addresses a mix of religion, culture, and politics, all imbued with nostalgia. In this one sees again the simultaneity of structural globalization and of cultural fragmentation. By the notion of fragmentation I refer to the religionization of politics and politicization of religion, bringing to the fore a cultural articulation of conflict. Here, dissent is articulated as cultural fragmentation. At issue is a discord over norms, rules, and values that accompanies the contestation of structural globalization. In a nutshell, there is no cultural globalization.

On the basis of the framework outlined here, the study of Islam in the late twentieth and early twenty-first centuries is compelled to consider five issue areas of discord. They can be identified in the context of the overall concern with simultaneity of structural globalization and cultural fragmentation. These issue areas are *first*: identity politics; *second*: an imagined community; *third*: invention of tradition; *fourth*: the selective drawing on historical events in the revival of cultural heritage; and *fifth*: the construction of collective historical memories, next to selective sentiments and choices. In all these issue areas the cultural self is defined in opposition to the cultural other, resulting in the creation of tensions and fault lines. The cultural ideology of political Islam covers all of the five issue areas and it arises – as this chapter contends – from the unresolved predicament of Islam with cultural modernity.

The perception of the Muslim self as a collective entity named the "Islamic *umma*" is also viewed in terms of a civilization victimized by the West under conditions of globalization. This is the perception of Islam "under siege." It is defined by creating a fault line against the cultural other, primarily the rival West, who is the cause of the suffering. This basis for conflict is determined in cultural terms. Only those who lack the capability to read Islamic sources, primarily the Arab ones – of course, including Huntington himself – are prone to take the view that the idea "clash of civilizations" is the product of a Harvard professor. The idea can be found from the 1930s on, in the early writings of political Islam. In a way, Huntington is unwittingly in line with political Islam's polarization between Islam and the West, but he is certainly not the inventor of this tradition. In contrast to Huntington, this chapter identifies the constructed tensions without making any essentialization, as they are articulated in a cultural ideology. Next to the explanatory attempt made here, this chapter seeks peaceful conflict resolution. At issue is a policy for averting the fault lines, be they real or constructed.

The predicament originated in the nineteenth century, but intensified during the course of the twentieth century. In the twenty-first century it has become a determining factor in world politics. The related historical facts begin with the Islamic military defeats that led to the abolition of the caliphate in 1924. This decisive date was followed by the birth of political Islam in 1928, when the Muslim Brotherhood was founded.[45] Those who refer to the creation of Israel, to the injustice done to the Palestinians, and to the Arab–Israeli conflict in order to identify the major source of the conflict are mistaken. Even worse, some refer to the Iraq War of 2003 either to belittle or to justify the anti-Western and anti-Jewish sentiments of political Islam. These "experts" overlook the fact that political Islam and the conflict predate the birth of Israel (1948). Real experts know that there was no US engagement in the Middle East prior to the Suez War of 1956. At issue are not the topicalities of contemporary politics, but rather the consequences of the challenge of cultural modernity and the Islamic predicament that has emerged from this process. The story can be traced back to the seventeenth century, when Europe – with the help of the *Military Revolution* – first halted Islamic jihad expansion, and then rolled back the Islamic presence in Europe.

The civilizational Western–Islamic rivalry is both constructed and real, being rooted in history. At present, it can be related to the revival of the idea of Islam as a civilization, attached to its claims to become a universal power. This claim is articulated in the writings of Sayyid Qutb.[46] This is the context of the constructed Islamic identity politics, the chief issue in the checklist of discord presented above. As noted earlier, in a material sense, there is today no Islamic civilization as an imperial entity; since the decline of the last Islamic empire, Muslims have been dispersed. However, the self-image of Muslims as an *umma* shows that Islam continues to provide the basis for awareness as a civilization, despite the abolition of its order. The outcome of relating the numerous local Islamic cultures to one another through their shared values and a common worldview is the self-perception of an imagined community.[47] This is the second issue area, linked to the first one of identity politics in the checklist above.

The previously addressed fragmentation that parallels the intensification of globalization indicates that the shrinking of the world creates neither common outlooks nor shared identities; rather, it contributes to the emergence of fault lines. Under these conditions of globalization the mobilizatory idea of an *umma*-community is revived in imagined civilizational terms that give it a new form of legitimacy. The related concepts have been invented in a process that can be observed and identified through the revival of two Islamic cultural traditions that are connected with a new meaning: shari'a and jihad. The invention of tradition in these two cases assumes the forms of shari'atization and jihadization of Islam. This becomes a source of conflict when contesting what is perceived to be an alien imposition, via Westernization, on Muslims. The Westphalian order of sovereign states is among the targets of the Islamist contestation.

Islamic revival in its current Islamist form places de-Westernization at the head of its agenda. In the search for an authenticity of the self, a selective revival of Islamic heritage is undertaken. Not only is it selective, it is also guided by a spirit of purification (see Chapter 8). Nevertheless, the real authenticity of tradition is not in line with these revived and constructed collective memories. The war of memories that is waged focuses on two competing models of globalization: the Islamic and the Western. This reading of history ignores the actual heritage of Islam, in which rationalists of medieval Islam engaged in learning from others, not in constructing exclusiveness and fault lines, as contemporary political Islam does.[48]

The realities of the outlined five issue areas do not indicate an end of history, but rather the cultural use of history in the promotion of a conflict that grows from the creation of cultural tensions. This is, rather, a constructed "Return of History." It is inferred that a culture of tension and conflict is pursued by political Islam, as demonstrated by the five issue areas. The identity politics of the Islamists, as based on their belief in an imagined, exclusive *umma*-community, contributes to a dissociation of Muslims from the rest of humanity and, consequently, to their alienation. In the European diaspora of Islam this is of even greater consequence, because the spirit of this venture results in the cultural separation of enclaves of Muslim immigrants from the polity in which they live. This perception of the self as an Islamic civilization in contrast to the other, in the scheme "we versus they," is the basis of cultural fault lines. Politically, a cultural space is claimed for Islam; it is connected to four concepts of political Islam that promote tension and conflict. These concepts are:

First, the neo-Islamist concept of *"nizam*/system,"* presented as *"hakimiyyat Allah*/rule of God." In this concept one encounters a political-cultural redefinition and a reinvention of Islam. The *"nizam Islami*/Islamic order" is designed to establish the Islamic state in the world of Islam, to be followed by a new order envisioned for the world in general. This Islamic system is not to be confused with the traditional caliphate, as misleading comments of some "pundits" contend. A *nizam Islami* is based on *"hakimiyyat Allah*/God's rule" and it stands in contrast to the popular sovereignty of the secular nation-state. This is not the traditional caliphate. Those who describe political Islam as a scenario for establishing a "new caliphate" are not well informed and are not knowledgeable about the literature produced by the Islamists themselves. There are a few Islamists (e.g. those of *Hizb al-Tahrir*[49]) who talk of re-establishing the caliphate, but this view does not reflect the mainstream in political Islam (see note 6), which subscribes to the *nizam Islami* in the sense just explained.

Second: the concept of Islamic constitutional law based on the reinvention of the Islamic shari'a as a divine Islamic state law. The term "shari'a" occurs only once in the Qur'an (sura *al-Jathiya* 45, verse18). In the eighth century, following the revelation of the Qur'an in the seventh century, Muslim scribes developed shari'a into a system of civil law (*mu'amalat*), without, however, any effort at codifying it.[50] Thus, shari'a as a legal system is post-Qur'anic. There is a systematic explanation for the basic feature of shari'a as non-codified law. In contrast to legislated law, shari'a is interpretive in character and therefore cannot be codified. Dogmatization or rigidization of the shari'a should not be confused with codification. At present in political Islam, shari'a has acquired the meaning of a state law for an Islamic order for the world of Islam itself and for the world in general. The tensions ignited by this call for "*tatbiq al-shari'a/*implementation of shari'a"[51] can be illustrated by the topical case of Iraq, where a constitution was issued by the Islamic parties after the toppling of Saddam Hussein. This constitution prescribes that no legislation can contradict "Islamic rulings." This is shari'a by another name. The attempted but failed democratization of Iraq shows how the fault lines related to ethnic and sectarian tensions have been constitutionally established in the name of freedom. On this basis it is argued that there is a conflict between shari'a and democracy, ignited by the project of the shari'atization of Islam.

Third: the rebirth of jihad, reinterpreted into a concept of jihadism. In facing Western-dominated globalization and under exposure to cultural modernity, the Islamic revivalist al-Afghani called for jihad in an anti-colonial spirit, as a response to imperialism. However, the more recent revival of jihad, in the form of jihadism, by political Islam, represented by the Muslim Brotherhood in Egypt, is a new *irregular war*, a concept explained in my earlier book on *Political Islam, World Politics and Europe* (see note 6). Hasan al-Banna is the source for the transformation of jihad into jihadism. He engaged in this reinterpretation of jihad in his capacity as founder of the Muslim Brotherhood, a movement that has resulted in new realities and is today one of a few major transnational Islamic movements, with awesome global links. It is thus tampering with history to draw a line between al-Afghani and al-Banna, as is done apologetically by Tariq Ramadan, the disputed grandson of al-Banna. The alleged line between the two has no basis at all in modern Islamic history.

Fourth: the concept of the Islamization of knowledge. This effort is related to problems analyzed in Chapter 2. This concept implicitly questions the view of humanity as an entity based on the concept of the person not only entitled to universal human rights, but also related to other humans as equals despite all cultural diversity. To be sure, the color- and religion-blind concept of the person is a departure from the assumed ability of a human to attain knowledge, via human reason, to be shared by the entire humanity. This is the meaning of cross-cultural fertilization. At its height, Islamic civilization was capable of attaining high standards in scientific accomplishment because great medieval Muslim rationalists (Farabi, Ibn Sina, Ibn Rushd, etc.) embraced the Hellenist legacy and shared the concept of a common, human reason-based knowledge. Science in Islam was closely linked to an open mindedness that allowed this cultural borrowing. Since the last third of the twentieth century, the sentiment of an open-minded Islam is no longer shared by revivalists and Islamists. Instead, they establish fault lines through their agenda of an "Islamization of knowledge." In so doing, they are not only taking a backward step for Islamic civilization, but also igniting tensions and conflicts between Muslims and others in the pursuit of a purification agenda. Just as there can be no Western or Islamic physics, there can be no rational religion-based knowledge, in contrast to that produced by human reason. As shown in Chapter 2, the pursuit of an Islamization of knowledge is guided by an attitude of a neo-absolutism that is based on the Islamist political-cultural program of de-Westernization of the cosmos, which results in a new flat-earthism.

Cultural tensions and fault lines

The unresolved predicament of Islam with cultural modernity under conditions of globalization generates cultural tensions that contribute to the creation of fault lines. The outcome is a conflict. In the world of Islam the project of modernization and secularization that was pursued after the abolition of the caliphate has failed. No real secular measures were wholeheartedly undertaken, not to mention cultural secularization. Today, it can be safely said that the modernization project is despised by Muslims in general, and in particular by the representatives of political Islam. Some disparage it even as an "inner colonization." Some Islamists speak of an "Orientalism from within" so as to discredit Muslim modernizers, thus sharing a view of postmodernity even though they reject its mindset, because they are, in truth, neo-absolutists, not cultural relativists. This is reflected in the thinking of Islamists in Turkey in their contestation of Kemalism, also shared by some modernists. Islamists draw a constructed, utterly false historical line from the first crusade in 1096 to the colonial incursion of Europe that began in the late eighteenth century with Napoleon in Egypt (1798). Then they extend this line to the present (US troops in Iraq) and believe that they see in this historical development a continuity of "Western globalization," viewed as a conspiracy carried out by the "new crusaders" in the world of Islam. "World Jewry" is also invoked in this conspiracy-driven view of history. In reality, this is an invented history. The real history is this: the Jews of Jerusalem stood by the Muslims in their defense of the city against the invading crusaders.[52] In an act of retaliation the crusaders burned the Jews alive in their Jerusalem synagogue. The Jews fled to the great synagogue where they were – in an anticipation of the Holocaust – exterminated. These hard facts contradict the invented history of the Islamists, who ignite wars of constructed memories, together with a war of ideas, in order to create fault lines. This return of history is reduced to nostalgia over the Islamic "*futuhat*/expansion" aimed at mapping the globe into *Dar al-Islam*. In the Islamist view, Islamic globalization was undermined in the past by the crusaders in alliance with the Jews, and in the present by Western globalization. The revival of the Islamic project is opposed to the so-called "Jewish-Christian conspiracy"[53] of Western globalization. The return of history and nostalgia revolve around the question of which model of globalization will be victorious in shaping the future order of the world. The perceived conspiracy of Westernization is seen as a *"ghazu/*conquest"[54] of *Dar al-Islam* pursued by "Jews and crusaders." The call to fight a jihad against this *"mu'amarah/*conspiracy" aims at an all-encompassing de-Westernization of the world as an act of purification.

In the quest for an overall Islamic identity in the battle of identity politics the self is constructed in civilizational terms so as to mobilize the *umma* against the West and defeat its "Jewish-Christian conspiracy" that is targeted at Muslims worldwide. Therefore, there is a clear link between identity politics and the mobilization of tensions cultivated by political Islam. While accusing the West of Islamophobia, Islamists have no inhibition about engaging in unfolding a West-phobia. A Muslim writer qualifies this sentiment as *Cultural Schizophrenia.*[55]

There are three levels on which this polarization is occurring in the form of a war of ideas. Ironically, one is inclined to assume that this polarization is pursued by the Islamists as a contribution towards making the Huntingtonian "clash of civilizations" a kind of a self-fulfilling prophecy. The three levels of an Islamist politics of fault lines are located in the approach of inter-civilizational tensions and conflicts. They are:

First, the global level of polarization, i.e. the tensions between the world of Islam and the rest, primarily the West.[56] To be sure, there are also other constructed enemies, such as the Russians in Chechnya, the Hindus in Kashmir, and foremost, Israel and the so-called "world Jewry," believed to be the instigators of a global conspiracy against Islam. Some Islamists think that Jews have incited the Bush administration to go to war in Iraq in pursuit of this conspiracy.

Second, the inner-civilizational level of polarization within the world of Islam itself. The jihad of political Islam is also directed against secular Islamic elites that are suspected of being infected by "the virus of Westernization," such as the Kemalists in Turkey, the Francophones in Algeria, and all other Muslim secularists. For Islamists, the "virus of secularization of Islam" can only be extinguished by the envisioned jihadist purification of Islam from all foreign influences.

Third, the diasporic level of polarization in Europe. Islamists agitate against integration. Thus, they fight for an Islamic space in Europe, as a kind of state-free communitarianism (e.g. *banlieues de l'Islam* in Paris, as well as in parts of Berlin that are viewed as parallel societies). This goal is pursued in the name of preserving Islamic identity. The mosques are attached to non-religious places such as bazaars, residential areas, study centers, etc. in order to create an autonomous Islamic space to make full segregation possible. This is done in the name of religious freedom and identity politics so as to ethnicize Islam in Europe. This politics becomes a source of ethnic conflict and polarization. Thus, Europe has been described as a battlefield of Islamism. This was the subject of my earlier, 2008 book.

All in all, a superimposed Islamic ethnic identity is constructed to supersede real, i.e. subordinate local Islamic identities (Turks in Germany, Maghrebis in France) and construct a diasporic unity of Islam in Europe. On all of the aforementioned three levels the politics of polarization contributes to the creation of fault lines between Muslims and non-Muslims. In Europe, Islamist behavior resembles that of European right-wing extremists in othering aliens. The arsons of Maghrebi and West African gangs, committed as an Islamic uprising in Paris in winter 2005 (continued in 2007), provide an illustration of dangerous scenarios for polarization within Europe itself. This fact is officially denied. This is a perilous twenty-first century perspective and is not restricted to European societies – it also happens within Muslim societies.

On all three levels mentioned, not only is violence committed, but also wars of collective memories and of ideas are waged. The issue is the world order and the aim is to remake it in the twenty-first century. In this context, tragedies – such as Bosnia – provide material for agitation. History is degraded into a source of propaganda to support the allegation of a "Judeo-Christian genocide" targeting Muslims as a "race" in an alleged new Holocaust. In fact, there is no such thing as an Islamic "race," for the *umma* in Islam is a multiracial community. It is exclusively based on shared faith. Everybody can join in. It is intriguing to see how, on the surface, this phenomenon assumes the form of anti-globalism, a spirit that then unites the forces of political Islam with even the European left. It is most disturbing to see this Islamist ideology of an extreme political right embraced by a European left that knows little, if anything, about its strange new bedfellow. There is no doubt that some gravely mistaken Western policies (e.g. Bosnia, Palestine, Iraq) are added to Western silence over crimes (Chechnya, Kashmir) and help to strengthen the Islamists in their war of ideas and collective memories and in their perception of an "Islam under siege." Islamists are not only victorious in this domain, they also feel morally superior to a West that does not defend its own values. Generally, the culturally defined non-Muslim other is targeted as an enemy. In these wars, waged without regular armies, a line is drawn globally that stretches from Jerusalem/Cairo/Baghdad to the Islamic periphery in Asia and also encompasses the diaspora of Islam in Europe. Europeans do not like to discern this message. According to these perceptions, the world has become a battlefield in a cosmic fight between Muslim believers and all others, demonized as "*kafirun*/unbelievers."[57] This is the dichotomist language of Qutb adopted by Bin Laden. The constituency susceptible to it is great. The appeal contributes to the most dangerous variety of tensions and fault lines, articulated in cultural-religious terms. Thus, the new invention of a religionization of politics and conflicts is not merely an academic undertaking, it also reflects a world political reality.

From fault lines to conflict: jihad and jihadism

The tensions ignited by the politicization of religion are based on the fault lines analyzed here. In the case of Islam, the concept of jihad in its new form of jihadism informs us of the basic nature of contemporary Islamist revivalism. Within the framework of an invention of tradition, jihadism pursued in the context of identity politics acquires new meaning, quite different from the classical jihad in Islam.[58] In its new definition jihad contributes to the fervor of the war of collective memories that supports a claimed return of history of civilizations. This venture promotes a sense of self-victimization, in which Muslims view themselves as the victims of a Judeo-Christian Western conspiracy; its hidden hand acts behind the cloak of globalization. This imagery has been cultivated to underpin the call for jihad, perceived as an act of self-defense in a situation of "Islam under siege." The jihadists who engage in a cosmic war to counter real, perceived, or constructed powers that are considered to be the enemy, believe that they speak and act on behalf of the cross-cultural *umma*-community. The near enemy is comprised of the secular Muslim elites. The far enemy consists of the "crusaders and world Jewry." Through the construction of fault lines in this sense Islamists envision uniting diverse Muslim communities in an internationalism.

To understand this better, it has to be explained what the cultural tradition of jihad is and how it has developed today into jihadism. In fact, they are two different concepts. Despite the differences, jihadist terror is viewed by its perpetrators as a revival of jihad. In truth, not every Islamist is a jihadist, but jihadism is rooted in Islamism. Therefore, every jihadist is an Islamist. For the sake of honesty one has to acknowledge the unfortunate fact that jihadism is at work as a powerful force within political Islam in the twenty-first century. Its appeal, as a deadly idea emerging from the cultural ideology of Islamism, is tremendous. Jihadists are non-state actors who fight with a cultural orientation and legitimate their waging of an irregular war by reference to reinvented religious-political doctrines. In their pursuit of a purification of the Islamic *umma*, Islamists create fault lines, not only between "true believers" and the "*kafirun*/unbelievers," i.e. all non-Muslims, but also within Islam. Those Muslims who are despised as deviators are excommunicated from the *umma* through *takfir*. Who are the jihadists? Are they only one segment of political Islam? We are definitely not dealing with individual fanatics, nor with extremists who could be classified as "criminals," nor are we dealing with people who have no relation to the cultural concepts of Islam. The new jihadist mindset is a major source of tension and conflict within the Islamic civilization and it rests on an interpretation of Islam. Jihadism is also a globally networked movement. This movement contributes greatly to muddying the waters of Muslim–Western cultural and political relations. Jihadism is a movement based on transnational religion, not a "crazed gang" (E. Said) of criminals.

To explain the distinctive character of traditional jihad some "pundits" speak of non-violence and argue that jihad is based purely on self-exertion. This allegation is belied by the Qur'an, in that its text allows Muslims to resort to "*qital*/physical fighting" for the expansion of Islam. Even though this violence is an expression of war, it is clearly not terrorism. In Islamic history, the fighting of jihad wars as *qital* was subject to strict rules that are listed in the Qur'an. In contrast, terrorism is, by definition, a war without rules, thus the term "irregular war" that is applied to it. In the new Islamist interpretation of jihad with an "ism" added to it, the meaning has changed. Unlike restricted traditional jihad, the new *jihadiyya* is an expression of unrestricted, irregular war, which is a variety of modern terrorism. What matters here is the cultural-religious justification of violence by the jihadists, who view themselves as "true Islamic believers"; other Muslims are despised as deviators from the right path of Islam. In many mosques, including those of the Islamic diaspora in Europe, young Muslims are taught and socialized in the mindset of jihadism. The outcome is a poisoned mindset of tension and conflict. Clearly, jihadism gives expression to the already addressed contemporary "Revolt against the West."[59] As a public choice, jihadism enjoys enormous popularity. In order to successfully counter this "deadly idea," Muslim cultural alternatives are needed. Among these is a cultural education in democracy and an enlightening revival of Islamic rationalism. The underlying aspect of all of these issues, namely Islam's cultural predicament, has to be the centerpiece of the Islamic homework in the quest for a civil Islam.

Here, in this chapter, is not the place to deal with the cultural-political roots of jihadism. Suffice it to say that it can be traced back to the work of Hasan al-Banna and Sayyid Qutb in terms of the history of ideas, and historically to the movement of the Muslim Brotherhood. These are the foundations of Islamism as a political and military interpretation of Islam, represented by transnational religion since the twentieth century. Even though it is a novelty, jihadism is presented as a simple revival of the cultural heritage. This cultural virus is spreading through the assistance of an Islamist education that is pursued by the teaching activities of some mosques and used as an instrument of indoctrination. The madrassas and those Islamic faith schools, whether in the diaspora or in the world of Islam itself, are the institutions of learning that are abused by Islamists in their promotion of the fault lines between believers (Muslims) and the "*kafirun/* unbelievers" (non-Muslims). The cultural tensions and fault lines then develop into a conflict that is intensified by the business of purification from non-Muslim cultural influence.

The Islamist agenda is pursued in a confrontational manner; it also creates divides within Islam. Sayyid Qutb (executed in Cairo in 1966) made the message crystal clear: jihad is a "permanent Islamic world revolution"[60] for de-centering the West in order to replace its order with "*Hakimiyyat Allah/*God's rule," first in the world of Islam and then on a global basis. In their practice of cultural purification, early pre-al-Qaeda Islamists have always honored Qutb's differentiation between the two steps, the local and the global. In the first step, jihadist strategy aims to topple secular regimes at home. Only after accomplishing this task does it prescribe moving – in a second step – to global jihad. This is the distinction between the near and the far enemy; it has been confused by al-Qaeda, which engages in global jihad ahead of remaking the world of Islam itself.

The reference to jihadism is made in this chapter because it is relevant to the present analysis, due to its promotion of cultural fault lines. This mindset can be combated by a strategy for *Preventing the Clash of Civilizations* (Herzog) in the ongoing "war of ideas." It is neither a war between Islam and the West, nor a war between believers and unbelievers. The real issue is a contest between "global jihad" and "democratic peace." These cultural concepts compete to shape the twenty-first century. The Islamic requirement for pro-democracy Muslims is *Rethinking Islam* (Mohammed Arkoun). On this basis they can join democratic peace after a religious reform that absolves Muslims from the duty of engaging in culturally legitimated jihad as a fight pursued for *"Hakimiyyat Allah*/God's rule." Thus, the next step in addressing the fault lines is to present the shari'atization of politics and society that is believed to underpin "God's rule." The civilizational project of Islamism not only reflects the inability to come to terms with cultural modernity, but also documents a reluctance to address current issues that burden Islamic civilization.

Cultural shari'atization as a source of conflict

Chapter 3 of this book paves the way to understanding the culturally based tensions in a war of ideas over the order of the world in the twenty-first century. In this context, shari'a is advanced as a claim for a divine order at all levels of state and society. The mindset of this shari'a is contrary to pluralism and is thus opposed to democratic peace. There is a cultural concept of shari'a in Islam.[61] However, the shari'atization of Islam is based on an invention of tradition that creates an obstacle to achieving democracy in the world of Islam. The related tensions can be observed locally and globally. The call for shari'a contributes within nation-states to all kinds of divides, especially in multi-ethnic and multi-religious societies. In spring 2005 a range of civil society-based religious communities from all major segments of multi-ethnic Malaysia launched an initiative for an inter-religious dialogue among these communities in order to establish a consensus over the values and rules that can ensure inner, peaceful coexistence. The only religious community to reject this bid and refuse to join in was that of the Muslims. Their justification was based on the argument of their leaders that Muslims base their conduct on the shari'a and non-Muslims have no right to co-determine Muslim conduct. On the basis of shari'a, non-Muslims are expected to subject themselves, as protected minorities (*dhimmi*),[62] to a Muslim majority. When Muslims themselves constitute a minority they claim the application of shari'a (e.g. India) as a human right, but when they rule they deny similar rights to non-Muslims. This hypocrisy underpins a culture-based divide and is a double standard that stands in complete contrast to religious-cultural pluralism, as will be shown in Chapter 7.

As stated, the contemporary understanding of shari'a is based on a cultural invention of tradition aimed at a shari'atization of state and society in the name of Islam. This issue was discussed at the Third International Congress for Comparative Constitutional Law in Tokyo (September 2005, see Chapter 3, note 1). On that occasion it was argued that international terrorism is menacing international society. It was then asked whether religion as a faith and a cultural view of the world could be dissociated from this menace so as to contribute to peace among rival religious communities, rather than tensions.[63] The previously discussed return of the sacred in a political form also touches on religion as a source of law and legislation. To relate religion to law is to point to its cultural meaning. In this context, one encounters different cultural understandings of the rule of law. The Islamization of law through the introduction of a political shari'a does not bridge, but in contrast creates tensions and fault lines between peoples characterized by diversity.

Due to the character of the shari'a as a constructed divine law based on the interpretation of the Qur'an, it is against any form of human legislation. As outlined earlier in this chapter, Islamic law has always been interpretative in character. This explains why it was never codified. Again, it is not a legislative law. In addition, it was mostly restricted to cult and to civil law. By contrast, the present call for shari'a is virtually a call for the political order of a constructed Islamic state. The new idea of a shari'a state has no foundation in Islamic tradition. This statement applies also to the allegation that shari'a is a constitutional law. These issues were discussed at length in Chapter 3. The repeated reference is restricted to the character of shari'a, as a constructed law, becoming a source of tensions and conflicts not only within Islamic civilization, but also in its relations to the "cultural other," i.e. to non-Muslims. At issue is a cultural concept that is today a source of fault lines. Shari'a is also, in the understanding of an Islamization agenda, not consonant with democracy, and it contradicts inner peace in a pluralist society. The selective reference to Islamic heritage includes a so-called revival of Islamic shari'a law in countries of Islamic civilization. The examples of the so-called liberated Iraq and another prominent case, namely post-tsunami Aceh in Indonesia, present the respective shari'atization of culture as a process in which different and rival understandings of democracy and rule of law are under issue: the Western secular versus the Islamic shari'a-based understanding of constitutional law. Due to the historical fact that there is no law book named shari'a –because Islamic law, as stated, is based on the interpretation of the Qur'an – the understanding of what shari'a is can be quite arbitrary. It follows that the call for shari'a not only alienates Muslims from non-Muslim others, but also creates rifts within the Muslim *umma*-community itself. In short, and to reiterate: the call for shari'a is a source of tension and can even lead to war, as has been the case in the Sudan.[64] The non-Muslim Sudanese people do not accept being subjected to a shari'a order and therefore rebel against its imposition. The tensions develop into conflict and thus into a bloody war. Underlying this process is Islam's predicament with modernity.

To establish an inter-cultural peace it is necessary for Muslims to learn to view non-Muslims as equals, and no longer to classify them as *dhimmi*. The diversity of cultures needs to be related to the establishment of commonalities, one of which is to insist on cultural and religious pluralism. This debate will be carried out in Chapter 7. The current process in the Islamic civilization of an invention of shari'a is often mistakenly perceived as an Islamic revival. It is not. In fact, it contradicts the needed pluralism of religions and cultures on all counts.

Future prospects: civil Islam and reform versus Islamism

The present book suggests that there is a predicament and it proposes religious reform as a means to coming to terms with it, and that Muslims should engage in an innovative cultural change within the framework of conflict resolution. With this in mind, the present chapter provides an analysis of the tensions and conflicts arising from processes of globalization that exacerbate Islam's predicament with modernity. Among other things, the analysis has shown that Islamic civilization is in a crisis that generates tensions and fault lines in world politics. This predicament is advanced to the subject matter of the new discipline of Islamology, which claims to deal professionally with the potential of international conflicts to emanate from the inner problems of Islamic civilization and the failed secularization process.[65]

In its crisis, Islamic civilization faces a variety of choices. It is acknowledged that the prevailing public choices are articulated in the world of Islam today in cultural terms, and unfortunately they are expressed by Islamists. In view of this reality, better perspectives for dealing with Islam's predicament with cultural modernity are needed; however, these are undermined in power relations. The West is a part of the problem and I do not overlook the conflict between the world of Islam and Western hegemony, while arguing for *Preventing the Clash of Civilizations*.[66] To propose a cross-cultural morality as a bridge –in place of fault lines – between civilizations is not to overlook conflicts. The suggested acceptance of cultural modernity, based on a rational worldview to be shared between Muslims and non-Muslims, is an essential part of the needed conflict resolution. Yet, such an achievement is not in sight and to hope for it is not merely wishful thinking. Despite the bleak outlook, one is compelled to ask: what can be done to bring it about? What is feasible? For a better future, Muslims need a civil Islam that admits religious reform and cultural change and helps people of the Islamic civilization to accommodate to their international environments. Muslims are not alone in the world and therefore they need to abandon not only their Islamo-centrism, but also their related supremacist attitudes.

The complex reality of a simultaneity of structural globalization and cultural fragmentation compels one to admit that there is no such thing as cultural globalization leading to the alleged McWorld.[67] There is, rather, dissent over basic cultural matters. Drinking Coca Cola, wearing jeans, and using computers does not automatically affect or change the views, values, and cultural attitudes of the people who engage in this consumerist behavior. The assumed cultural fragmentation is related to value divides, not to a culture of consumerism. If these divides are politicized, then they become a source of real tensions and fault lines and lead to conflict. For instance, the politics of a cultural Islamization is embedded in the reality of competing worldviews that lead to a fight over the concept of an order for the world in the twenty-first century. The reader is reminded of Sayyid Qutb, the foremost source of political Islam, and of his articulation of those beliefs that lead to tensions. Today his views are highly popular and therefore commonly shared among many Muslims who are prone to Islamism. It has to be emphasized that it is Qutb and not Huntington who first identified civilizational fault lines between Islam and the West. Qutb based his contention on a divisive worldview, coupled with a vision of a new order for the world. This is the cultural source of the ideological Islamization of regional conflicts. According to this understanding, there are historical stages in the development of a conflict of this kind. Islamism promotes this conflict, whereas a civil reform Islam could contribute to conflict resolution. The historical stages mentioned are:

- The first stage, in the past, relates to collective memories of the intrusion of an expanding Europe into the abode of Islam. Since the late eighteenth century the Muslim people are no longer conquerors, but rather conquered people. In Europe, they are today an ethnic underclass. Therefore, Muslims are compelled to ask themselves: "How could this happen to us given the Qur'an's attributing to us the status of 'khair umma/the foremost community?" This question was asked by the first Muslim to go to Europe in order to study in Paris. In the nineteenth century the imam Rifa'a R. Tahtawi, who became a student, provided some interesting answers to this question in his *Paris Diary*. This thinking was repeated in the early twentieth century by the revivalist Shakib Arslan, in the title of his book *Why are Muslims backward while others have progressed?*[68]
- The second stage relates to the present, as characterized by a failed modernization. The secular nationalism that provided legitimacy to the nation-state has been challenged in the world of Islam by the unfolding of a new variety of *"sahwa Islamiyya/*Islamic awakening"[69] that envisions a different order for the state. This challenge assumes the form of a political Islam. There are different responses to the "European expansion." What complicates the cultural accommodation of ongoing structural globalization is a reluctance to admit change and reform.
- After reviewing the two stages of the past and the present, one is inclined to ask: what are the future prospects? Will the future continue to be determined by the public choices that political Islam provides through its radical call for a cultural de-Westernization? This is an articulation of the Islamic variety of the "Revolt against the West" (Bull), certainly not a dealing with the predicament at issue. This revolt is set to establish a new world order for the twenty-first century. This envisioned "remaking" along Islamist lines leads Muslims nowhere. Certainly, it leads to conflict and disorder. The capabilities needed in order to realize its vision are certainly not in place. Islamism pronounces order, but it delivers disorder. The related identity politics fosters mobilization and supports disarray in a crisis-ridden conflict situation.

The outlined interrelation of the past (collective memories) and an awareness of the present are combined with some future prospects. One has to place Islamic civilization in an overall context to make the centrality of the issue abundantly clear. Muslims are torn between a civil Islam that takes them in the direction of rationality, and Islamism. Even though unpopular today, Max Weber's "*Entzauberung der Welt*/disenchantment of the world" continues to be an option that is relevant to the world of Islam in the twenty-first century. This option is consonant with medieval Islamic rationalism and its concept of a "*madina fadila/* perfect state" (Farabi), which is a secular concept. This tradition was suppressed by the Muslim *fiqh*-orthodoxy. The repeatedly quoted Moroccan philosopher Mohammed al-Jabri is among those Muslims who plead for a revival of Islamic medieval rationalism (Averroism) that could present a solution for the inter- and intra-civilizational conflicts that result from cultural tensions. In his view, "the survival of a philosophical tradition to contribute to our time can only be Averroist."[70]

The contemporary madrassas and other faith schools in today's world of Islam not only promote tensions, they also foster the conflict. In this manner, these institutions contribute to the politicization of Islam on a global level, and not to the needed cultural change, not to mention religious reform. Among the policies needed are those related to promoting a civil Islam that allows innovations, in particular in institutions of education. Also, an inter-civilizational dialogue – in the understanding of conflict resolution – is required in order to deal with burning issues. In contrast, Islamism closes the door to a better future for Muslims and puts them into conflict with themselves as well as with the rest of humanity.

Conclusions

The debate pursued in this chapter on Islam and its predicament with cultural modernity, viewed as the source of the tensions and conflicts in post-bipolar politics, has not shied away from a search for solutions. Given the fact that the Islamic civilization is characterized by great diversity and that it is composed of a great number of local Islamic cultures related to one another by a family resemblance, the needed solutions have also to be diverse; they could be quite numerous. The reader is reminded of the repeatedly presented differentiation between the terms "culture" and "civilization." Culture is local, civilization is cross-cultural. The terms should not be used interchangeably. It follows that the study of tensions and conflict has to be related to local cultures and cross-cultural civilizations on different levels. The overall framework for the analysis of these issues is determined by the conditions of contemporary globalization.

Tensions begin with an identity politics that revives Islamic collective memories. These revolve around the history of jihad and crusade (e.g. the stage of the past), and turn then to the present in a defensive-cultural sense of self-victimization. In this context the West is viewed to be guilty of ending the Islamic *futuhat*-expansion that lasted from the seventh to seventeenth centuries. Viewed from this background, Western globalization replaced Islamic dominance. Along this line, the present state of the misery of the *umma* is viewed as an outcome of the situation of an Islam under siege. In contrast to this worldview, it is argued that the decline of Islamic civilization was related to an inner development, a part of which was the decline of science and technology. The rise of Europe and its expansion, which succeeded in replacing the Islamic globalization with a European one, was intrinsically related to science and technology.

The collective memories addressed here revive, in a constructed manner, a historical contest between two models of globalization, both related to civilizations. Unfortunately this is happening on the basis of blame games. This contributes to tensions and fault lines. From a historical point of view, the needed conflict resolution has to respect a situation in which globalization is combined with cultural and religious diversity. It is argued that cultural modernity can be shared and accommodated, while any preservation of diversity has to occur in terms of cultural and religious pluralism. A prerequisite for establishing this pluralism as a promising avenue for Muslims, in their relations with others, is a Muslim acceptance of religious reform. This is another area of policy for Muslims themselves, to be dealt with in Chapter 7. The contribution of the West to this end would be to promote more justice, and not to interfere in the affairs of the Muslim world (e.g. the Iraq War) in pursuit of Western hegemony. The West needs to learn that the well-being of Muslims matters to its security. What happens in the world of Islam spills over into the West. The problems are not only defensive-cultural Muslims, but also the West's cultural blind spot in its interactions with and policies towards the world of Islam.

This chapter on cultural and religious tensions cannot be concluded without again asking the question: are the described tensions between Islam and the West a reflection of a structural conflict (with regional varieties), i.e. are they a "culturalization of interests" in a conflict situation? Or are they based on a "misunderstanding"? Throughout this book I see an interplay at work between structure and action and warn of evasions. The interplay in question is analyzed without overlooking the weight of the structural constraints that underlie the current defensive-cultural attitudes. The predicament of Islam with cultural modernity touches equally on culture and religion, which are, of course, always in flux. Culture and religion cannot be reduced to economy and politics. The issue is related to real tensions, not to a misunderstanding. Politicians and scholars who contend this engage in an escape. They shy away from acknowledging the embedment of culture and religion in conflict, and thus evade all of the issues at stake.

In a nutshell, it can be stated that the currently constructed Islamic cultural views of the self and of the other are a part of the conflict itself. The constructed jihad and shari'a, believed to be in a revival, are cultural notions that ignite tensions. The development of jihad into jihadism and of shari'a into an agenda of shari'atization are inspired by a politics of Islamization that is presented as identity politics. The cultural revival in the world of Islam is, in itself, a more complicated issue than Islamist ideologies are willing to acknowledge. Thinking in a mindset of fault lines – as political Islam promotes – leads to a deepening of the already existing cultural divides.

Finally, in talking of conflict, one has to acknowledge – next to the global level – two other pertinent levels: that of the world of Islam and that of its diaspora in Europe. Poverty in the world of Islam boosts migration to Europe. The marginalization of Muslims in Europe and the failure of the model of Europeanization in the world of Islam (e.g. the *Revolution from Above*[71] by Kemalism in Turkey) are most detrimental and consequential phenomena. The failure of modernization promoted the rise of political Islam in state and society, both at home and in the diaspora. The flawed policies of the West (e.g. the Iraq War) are among the constraints, but they are not the primary cause of tensions and conflicts. Those who suggest this explanation are mistaken. Without any essentialization, it is stated that culture – on both sides – is involved. Culture is not determined, it is not a simple reflection of material realities. Therefore, culture is part of a complicated interplay.

Stated in the language of the present book: reference to cultural constraints in the study of conflict while pointing to Islam's predicament with cultural modernity is an approach that places religion and culture in an overall context. This approach makes clear that conflicts cannot be solved simply by politics. What is needed is religious reform and cultural change, to be tackled by Muslims themselves. Those who close their minds to an understanding of this dimension of culture-based tensions and conflicts deny themselves the possibility of grasping the addressed developments altogether, whether in scholarship, in politics, or in press and media. The present book, in particular this chapter, hopes to generate a debate on the change that is needed on the levels mentioned above. This includes the hope of not being silenced in presenting the new approach, but rather of being listened to. Isn't this the *conditio sine qua non* of true scholarship: to listen to arguments and to debate, not to flatly reject and then silence all disagreement?

Cultural change and religious reform I: the challenge of secularization in the shadow of de-secularization

Secularism and secularization are among the major themes embedded in heated debates not only in contemporary Islamic civilization[1] but also in Western social sciences. This book relates these debates to its major theme, i.e. Islam and cultural modernity, which is, in substance, a secular project. Earlier, it was assumed that the modernization of society and politics leads to secularization. Today, the return of the sacred is a social fact[2] and it implies the challenge of de-secularization. I stand by Max Weber's "*Entzauberung der Welt*/disenchantment of the world" against postmodernism, notwithstanding the acknowledgment of a crisis of cultural modernity and also of secularity. This statement is consistent in itself, but it is inconsistent to argue that there can be a secular state that is not based on the secularization of society, as is contended by some Muslims who want to eat their cake and have it.

Introduction

Among the many contemporary fashions (e.g. postmodernism) that make full use of the return of the sacred is one that constructs a post-secularity. The reader knows from the Introduction and the earlier chapters how much I admire Habermas's discourse of cultural modernity, but I am distressed to see how my academic teacher has retreated in the aftermath of 9/11 and abandoned earlier positions. Habermas embraces the argument of post-secular society. Earlier, he was as a staunch critic of postmodernity and tough on Derrida. I value Habermas as my academic teacher and as the foremost theorist of the discourse of cultural modernity. But his present work engages in a contestation of the West itself. Habermas joined forces with Derrida in making anti-American pronouncements, visited Iran and made apologetic judgments. Thereafter, he invented the notion of post-secularity. Against Habermas[3] I argue that the return of the sacred is not a religious renaissance; rather, it is a backward move. It is the expression of a "new totalitarianism" presented by a political religion. Habermas ignores all of these facts. The debate on post-secularity (see note 3) is not a major concern of this chapter, even though it touches on its major assumption, that religious-cultural tensions lead to a political conflict that is articulated in religionized claims. It follows that de-secularization, now being given the name "post-secular society," is perilous. Nevertheless, the concern here is with secularization itself, which I continue to propose as a strategy for Islam in the context of cultural change and reform. Postmodern, so-called post-secularity is not my concern, and it is a non-theme in the Islamic world. There, the options are different: either the "*Hakimiyyat Allah*/rule of God" or secular democracy. The envisioned *Hakimiyyat*-order is definitely not postmodern; rather, it is a totalitarian rule.

It is necessary to remind the reader of the chain of argumentation followed in this book so as to locate the current issue within the overall predicament of Islam with cultural modernity. The subject matter was first presented in general terms and then illustrated in three issue areas. In a second step, Chapter 5 engaged in the study of conflicts that arise from this predicament. In a further step undertaken in this and in the following chapter it is argued that cultural change and religious reform are avenues for peaceful conflict resolution. The chosen themes are "secularization" in this chapter, and "pluralism" in Chapter 7. In thinking about a means of diffusing tensions and conflicts and in seeking for solutions, I envisage an Islamic embrace of the separation between religion and politics and a pluralism of religions as the better option for a promising future. How can this be accomplished?

First of all, it is necessary to reform and rethink the shari'a by reducing it to morality, so as to counter the shari'atization of politics that results in the call for an Islamic state – identified as a totalitarian, religionized order. This was debated in Chapter 3. There, I quoted and endorsed Abdullahi An-Na'im, who was a liberal Muslim, in his venture for an Islamic reformation back in 1990. I have been waiting for almost two decades to see how An-Na'im will fulfill this promise of a reformation. Of course, there is no way, other than societal, cultural, and institutional secularization. An-Na'im, who knows from his home country of Sudan the meaning of political persecution in a state that claims to apply shari'a, remains critical of such an order and therefore argues in his long-awaited 2008 book for a secular state. So far, so good, but a closer reading leads to the discovery of a shocking inconsistency, coupled with a U-turn from a wholesale rejection of shari'a to an embracing of it. An-Na'im states his agenda at the outset, in illogical terms: "I am calling for the state to be secular, *not* for secularizing society."[4] An-Na'im promises in his preface to present a new book that is "the culmination of my life's work." The book that he presents is, however, a highly confused and equally confusing contribution. Notice these words: "The secular state I am calling for is ... for *promoting* the role of Islam in public life." Two pages further on he establishes what this phrase means: "Shari'a should be ... a source of liberation and self-realization." What, then, is a secular state? It is appalling to lose a Muslim ally, who I believed was participating in the project of a search for an Islamic solution to the predicament with modernity. I can hardly understand how a professor can argue for a secular state and at the same time be against a secularization of society. In a personal communication An-Na'im defended his stance with the argument that he is a legal scholar, not a social scientist. This is even worse, to the extent of being laughable, to say the very least.

Let us set aside An-Na'im, the former promiser of "reformation," and focus on scholarly knowledge on the current issue. I sincerely hold to Max Weber's view that cultural change in society is a prerequisite for an "*Entzauberung*/disenchantment" of the world that will underpin secularization. This notion remains valid and leads to the concept of rationalization as secularization. The "secular state" that An-Na'im wants lacks all of these requirements and thus finishes up as a shari'a state, not a secular order. At issue is universal knowledge, not a particular statement from a professor of law. The validity of this knowledge is not limited to societies of Western civilization. The secular solution to the predicament discussed earlier could contribute to conflict resolution, but not in the evasive manner of some Muslims who lay aside all major issues and pronounce what can only be described as wishful thinking.

Secularization is often contradicted by the search for authenticity and by cultural relativism. I will put this issue on one side for now, but will not evade it, because it will be discussed at length in Chapter 8. The focus is here on the resumed Weberian debate on secularization, which is challenged by the resurgence of religion in a new process of de-secularization. At first, one is compelled to acknowledge a conflict. To gain a proper understanding, two divergent systems of knowledge have to be distinguished from one another: one is secular and the other is cosmic-religious. This concern was made clear in the earlier debate in Chapter 2. There, the findings support the argument that a universally valid social-scientific thinking on the subject matter is not only generally possible and welcome, but also feasible in Islamic terms. The classical legacy of Islam includes significant precedents. The Weberian thinking on politics in a process of secularization is based on rational universal knowledge. As stated, there was in Islam a variety of this tradition that admitted secular-rational knowledge. To this point I add the view that real social and political processes of secularization should be distinguished from the European ideology of secularism. This distinction between an ideology of secularism and a social-cultural process of secularization is most pertinent in relating the core issue under discussion to Islam (see note 1). However, acknowledging that an a-religious secularist ideology may not be compatible with Islam should never mean introducing shari'a through the backdoor, as An-Na'im does. The processes of secularization can and do occur in societies in which people draw on Islam for their faith and ethics. However, this is not a "negotiating the future of shari'a" that the book title announces. A secular state with no secularization, as imagined by An-Na'im, is beyond any logical comprehension. This is not a matter of academic distinction between social science and law. Such reference serves only to justify evasion of the issue, and it is nothing other than self-deception to believe that it is not the business of a lawyer to deal with the secularization of society.

To avoid the confusions and flaws that determine An-Na'im's book *Islam and the Secular State*, I prefer, by way of introduction, to begin this chapter by distinguishing between three terms: secularization, secularity, and secularism. In the Islamic debate these terms are often confused and An-Na'im is not the first

Muslim to do so. Some do this on purpose, so as to support the spread of an anti-secular mindset among Muslims. Others do it for other reasons. In the course of his research in Indonesia, Robert Hefner witnessed there the unfortunate trend that "for Muslim conservatives secularization meant secularism pure and simple ... [it] implied the relegation of Islam to political impotence."[5] In this popular understanding, secularization is viewed both adversely as a purely European phenomenon, and thus not applicable to Islam, and also to mean a supposed vanishing of religion. One finds similar questionable arguments in Western postmodern thinking. The late Ernest Gellner pointed out this striking similarity between Islamic absolutism and Western relativism. He took issue with this kind of thinking, of which he was highly critical.

The concern here is the potential of an Islamic reform to support the idea that secularization is compatible with Islam, using substantial arguments. I acknowledge that it can be culturally underpinned by a rational Islamic discourse to deal with Islam's predicament with modernity. It is most unfortunate that postmodernists shy away from dealing with the issue openly. In talking about the religious and the secular in Islam there is need of an unending effort to distinguish between what is divine and what is merely constructed by humans. Many of the inherited burdens of Islam were constructed by man, in a powerful tradition that was established in the name of religion. Human views are presented as allegedly "divine" in order to safeguard their provisions beyond rational questioning.

Now, to the distinctions. It has to be made clear that secularization in society is a requirement for a *secular state*. In contrast, dogmatic *secularism* is an ideology of some Westerners. The distinction between these terms implies an argument for *secularity*, as a state of affairs that underpins a *secular order*. This does not mean abolition of religion. In any process of structural and institutional secularization the necessary decoupling of religion from politics and from other realms of non-religious knowledge can be supported by religious reform. Are there precedents for this thinking in Islamic tradition? The answer is yes, and it can be supported by reference to medieval Islamic rationalism. Separation between the worldly and the religious existed in an authentic form, as I shall argue in Chapter 8 on authenticity. The philosophical thinking of Islamic rationalism was adopted in Europe on the eve of the Renaissance (see note 11). In Chapter 8 I argue for a revival of this authentic Islamic tradition, which could contribute to the establishment of a cultural foundation for secularization. This revival could help to counter the invention of tradition in the name of a constructed, not a real, authenticity.

The reality of an age shaped by political Islam is not only dismaying, but runs counter to the real needs of Islamic civilization. At present, use of the term "*al-ilmani/*secular" is associated not only with the ideology of "*ilmaniyya/*secularism," but also with fears related to an accusation of "*kufr/*heresy." The killing of the Egyptian writer Faraj Fuda in June 1992 is a supporting case in point. The authoritative *fetwa* that ensued, issued by the late Salafi-orthodox Sheykh Muhammad al-Ghazali, legitimized the killing as a shari'a-based execution and argued that the secularist intellectual had been rightly slain.[6] Muslims who engaged in secular thinking were warned that they would face the accusation of heresy and share the fate of Faraj Fuda if they failed to comply. In 1979 it was still possible to present a paper on "Islam and Secularization" at 'Ain Shams University in Cairo and to leave the country unscathed (see note 1), despite fierce attacks in the press. Today, this would be unthinkable, it would be suicidal. It was reported to me that a German diplomat was interrupted during his lecture at al-Azhar simply for quoting me, even though he did so most carefully. The result was a disturbance that was only ended by an intervention on the part of the dean, who was called upon to calm the heated audience. I hope that a liberal Muslim living in Europe would be spared this, and also be allowed freedom of speech on the idea of secular Islam. Some Muslims who share my thoughts prefer to be evasive so as to avoid any calamities. This is a lack of courage in the face of totalitarian attitudes. In talking without discrimination about diversity and tolerance, or respect for other cultures, one should never forget the need to protect open society from its enemies!

The problem in the Islamic world is that rapid social change is often not accompanied by a supporting cultural change and religious reform. This constitutes a development lag. To determine the interrelationship between the two patterns of change I created the formula, in the title of one of my earlier books, of *The Cultural Accommodation of Social Change* (1990). As a result, I was accused by non-Muslims (e.g. Charles Kurzman) of "Orientalism." Of course, it is not "Orientalism" to think about religion and to reduce it to a part-system in society in a process of secularization and rationalization. Secularity is a state of affairs in a modern society where religion no longer determines all aspects of life in a quasi-organic manner, but is not abolished. There is a correspondence between religious, cultural, and social constraints. This changes in the course of secularization. Among the consequences is an awareness that knowledge of religion, as a faith, and knowledge of society, as a reality, are different issue areas. One can only relate the one to the other if one is aware of this distinction.

In contemporary Islam, orthodox Muslims and Islamists fail to understand the place of religion in the functional differentiation of the social system.[7] One can add to this flaw their deliberate confusion of secularity, secularism, and secularization. To reiterate: *secularity* is a state of affairs in society; *secularization* is a social process; and finally, *secularism* is an ideology. The substance of secularity is no more and no less than a separation between religion and politics. This is a social reality that results from the development of society; it is not a "Jewish conspiracy"[8] designed against Islam, as the Islamists contend in their antisemitic jargon. On the basis of thoroughly confusing the terms and their different meanings, Islamists polemically contend that secularization in society is a project hostile to Islam. Probably this is the reason why An-Na'im takes a stand against secularization.

The Islamists contend that there is a "Jewish conspiracy" underlying secularism that is set to impose on Muslims a project of separation between state and religion. Islamists believe that this conspiracy has the objective of "weakening a unitary

Islamic *umma*" for the benefit of crusaderism and Zionism. In this atmosphere, no rational debate on the issue is possible. The term "war of ideas," used in the West for the contest between democracy and jihadism, is, in its origin, an Islamist expression: "*harb al-afkar*." Islamists incite cultural tensions under polarized conditions in order to lead to a political conflict in a *New Cold War*, waged as a war of ideas between the secular and the religious.[9] The Salafist and Islamist contribution to this war is immense. The vast Salafist and Islamist literature in which secularity and secularism are confused is indicative of this war of ideas.[10]

This introduction to the current issue can be closed by reiterating the reference to the public execution of Faraj Fuda, in order to emphasize that in the present state of affairs it is a great risk for a Muslim to subscribe publicly to secularity. It is therefore most disturbing to see a debate on this issue being blocked in Western scholarship and free speech being undermined. One cannot repeat enough not only how important it is for open society, in particular in the Islamic diaspora and in Western scholarship, to support secular, reform-minded Muslims rather than sidelining them, but also that one cannot have it both ways – the "secular state" and "shari'a" (see note 4) – as some Muslims believe. This is no longer secular reasoning, not to mention a reform of Islam.

Secular and reform Islam draw on the precious tradition of Islamic rationalism to refute the invented traditions of the Islamists, which are imbued with new meanings. Evasion, on the other hand, is not the solution that Muslims need. With reference to the medieval Islamic political philosophy of al-Farabi,[11] I argue for the separation of religion and politics without shari'a; this is not a reference to the history of ideas, but rather to issues related to secularization and de-secularization. I repeat: in order to establish, in a general sense, Islamic legitimacy for cultural change and religious reform, reference to medieval Islamic rationalism contributes to dealing with the predicament of contemporary Islam with modernity. Those Muslims who dismiss secularization as a rationalization of the world unwittingly side with political Islam, which rejects any "secular state." In contrast to those Muslims, I see in a cultural secularization an avenue to peaceful conflict resolution. Shari'a should be reduced to a morality; it is not a divine law.

Secularity and Islamic history: between the age of reason and the setback of darkness

Recourse to the intellectual history of Islam would help to underpin secularization in Islamic terms, in order to set the stage for a debate on secularity and modernity beyond the propaganda of a "war of ideas." De-secularization in the contemporary world in general, and in the Islamic world in particular, should not be seen as a positive sign. This develpment is highly consequential. In the intellectual history of medieval Islam, Hellenization contributed to the emergence of a rational Islamic philosophy. Islamic rationalism was a rival to the tradition of "*fiqh*/ sacral jurisprudence." Hellenized Islamic rationalism provided the foundation for a marked stimulus to the development of rationalization, which became part of the history of the emergence of scientific thought in Europe. In the Islamic world itself, this impulse of rationalization, and hence to a rational view of the world,[12] was suppressed. This is part of the story not only of the decay of Islamic civilization, but also of an undermining of secularization. The Egyptian philosopher Mourad Wahba once addressed this simultaneity as *The Paradoxon of Averroes*[13] in order to depict the conflict between reason and revelation, i.e. the secular and the religious within Islamic civilization in medieval times. The paradox is that Europe appreciated Averroes, while Islamic civilization dismissed his work; the Salafist orthodoxy even outlawed it. Today, the books of Averroes are either ignored, or – even worse – burned in public.

Muslim philosophers agreed with the concept of reason-based and therefore secular knowledge, as well as with its claim to universality. However, they restricted its validity to worldly matters. Islamic rationalists[14] maintained their respect for religion. By contrast, *fiqh*-scholars of the Islamic orthodoxy insisted on the view that the immutable revelation is the sole and unrestricted source of truth as valid knowledge of the world (*sola scriptura*). According to this understanding, the divine and the merely human were confused. "*Fiqh*/sacral jurisprudence" is merely human knowledge; it was and continues to be presented as "divine." Thus it enjoys unquestioned validity in all spheres. The victory of *fiqh* over rational philosophy in Islam marked a setback, a return to darkness, and it marked the end of the civilizational height of Islam.

Every reference to the high accomplishments of medieval Islamic civilization must be connected to the notification of a tragedy, namely that the legacy of rationalism in Islamic civilization did not endure. Islamic philosophers lost the battle to those who upheld the *fiqh*-orthodoxy.[15] Unlike the European Enlightenment philosophers, Islamic rationalists were not daring. They evaded a conflict with *fiqh*-orthodoxy and restricted their rational efforts to distinguishing between divine and worldly truth. For Muslim philosophers, the source of truth continues to be the Qur'an. Nevertheless, in their philosophy they based worldly truth on reason. The "*fuqaha*/sacral jurists" were neither appreciative nor conciliatory; they polarized and established the fault line in clear terms: "*bi al-wahi aw bi al-'aql/* either revelation or reason."[16] This is a formula invented by the medieval *faqih* al-Mawardi. In his reversal of the high rank attributed to rational knowledge by the medieval Islamic philosophers, al-Mawardi advanced the view that revelation is the foremost source of knowledge. This is the view of Islamic *fiqh*. *Fiqh* means "the foremost knowledge." In religious terms, it is a human interpretation of the scripture and thus cannot claim to be divine, but – as stated – in the past, as in the present, *fiqh* is confused with shari'a and even identified with it so as to present it as divine, in contrast to reason-based knowledge.

The contention of a separation of religion and politics is not only based on a reference to Islamic rationalism in general, but is also supported specifically by a reading of *al-Madina al-fadila* by al-Farabi (note 11).

In his work on the perfect state, Farabi argues that only a philosopher is capable of running a virtuous order. Unlike *fiqh*, Islamic philosophy was reason based, and its decline and its failure to determine the prevailing worldview and the course of Islamic civilization has great consequences. The inherited burdens still prevail in the twenty-first century. Today, one finds the work of the late medieval *faqih* Ibn Taimiyya,[17] but not the writings of rational philosophers such as al-Farabi, on the reading lists of the Islamists. The model for the future of Islamic civilization is presented by these people in a Salafist reference to the Islamic state of Medina (622–32). Here is an Islamist reading of history, not the history itself. In order to question this reference I refer to the intellectual history of Islam in an earlier age of reason, so as to show that rationalism did exist, even though it was short lived. Contemporary Arab Muslim rationalists are set to revive this tradition.[18]

The short interval of secular nationalism and Islamic liberalism

The modern idea of a secular polity entered the Islamic world in the context of its exposure to modernity. The historical background of secular thought in modern Islam was the crisis of Islamic order in the nineteenth century. After the abolition of the caliphate in 1924, Turkey was at the center of the rise of secularism in the Islamic world.[19] The story of the secularization in the Islamic world started with Muslim military defeats, beginning with their failure to capture Vienna in 1683. This was followed by further humiliations. Thus, Islamic rulers found themselves compelled to send Muslims to study at European universities in order to discover the mystery of "European military superiority." Their solution was the project of *Importing the European Army*, a process that began in the Ottoman Empire but that was incapable of preventing its decline. This modernization gave rise to the revolution of Kemalism.[20]

The seeds of liberal thought in Islam can be traced back to the work of the first Islamic imam to go to Paris, Rifa'a R. al-Tahtawi. There he became intoxicated with Western civilizational standards. In Paris he became convinced that Muslims could thrive without a cultural borrowing from the West. However, Tahtawi's enthusiasm was not unrestricted because he made the "borrowing" conditional. To legitimate this borrowing, he argued that it was simply a retrieval in view of the fact that Europe had a history of adopting science and knowledge from Islam on the eve of the Renaissance. To this legitimation Tahtawi added a major restriction, namely that the shari'a sets the limits. On the one hand, Tahtawi legitimated acts of cultural borrowing, but on the other, he made clear that the shari'a, the threshold, was "not to be crossed." Bluntly stated: only those adoptions from the West were admitted that did not conflict with the shari'a.[21] This problem continued throughout the early Islamic reform that stretched from Tahtawi to Mohammed Abduh. It was a "reform" without any inclination to rethink inherited religious doctrine, and therefore undeserving of its name.

While repeatedly pointing out the failure of early Islamic modernism, one is reminded of the fact that those Islamic modernists did revive the medieval, reason-based philosophy of Islam. Add to this fact that they avoided any questioning of the prevailing divine approach of Islamic *fiqh*. Almost all Islamic modernists were positive about modern science, but they never asked questions about the nature of scientific knowledge, which is determined in secular terms. Modernists were also evasive on questions of political order in the Islamic world. Until Ali 'Abdelraziq's 1925 book, Islam and politics were not discussed in a clear and systematic way. In a way, this thinking has been a taboo subject. The repressive response to 'Abdelraziq's book revealed a clear message to thinking, rational Muslims: "Watch out!"

Muhammad Abduh ranks chief among Muslim reformers. His thinking revolved around the attempt to reconcile religious belief with reason. This aim was not, however, coupled with the structural and normative requisites for such a reconciliation.[22] In short, Islamic modernism of the nineteenth and early twentieth centuries did not produce the perspectives needed in order to deal with Islam's predicament with cultural modernity. Therefore, Islamic reform failed and left the stage open for the rise of secular ideologies. The related history of ideas includes an introduction of ideological secularism that was not supported by a process of secularization in society.

The failure of the late Ottoman Muslim caliphs to engage in a real modernization beyond the importation of instruments ended with the dissolution of the caliphate, which was abolished in 1924. This was followed by the rise of secular nationalism and the introduction into Islamic civilization of the new secular order of the nation-state.[23] The related decoupling of Islam from politics occurred during the twentieth century. It was only superficial, because the separation between religion and politics was not underpinned by cultural change, nor was any religious reform involved. Secularism was simply imposed. Secular nationalists were not aware of the distinction between secularism, as a political ideology, and secularization, as a social process. The lack of a distinction between notions with different meanings leads to the lack of a proper awareness of the issue. The French term "*la nation*," which is totally secular, was translated into Arabic and other languages of Muslim peoples by the word *umma*. The Islamic *umma* was subdivided into national and ethnic *ummas*, such as the Arab or Turkish ones. The adoption of the secular notion of "nation" into the religious term of *umma* was highly consequential. A pre-modern understanding (the *umma*) was thus applied to the modern "nation," also termed *umma*. The radically different meanings of "nation" and *umma* were blurred.

This chapter began with a reference to a paper on secularization that was presented in Cairo in 1979 at an event jointly organized by the 'Ain Shams and Azhar universities. The event was the First International Islamic Philosophy Conference on Islam and Civilization (see note 1). The core argument of that paper was that Islam might be in conflict with an ideological attitude of secularism, but not with the social need for a process of secularization (see note 1). The argument revolves around the differentiation (presented earlier) between secularism, understood as an ideology, and secularization, viewed as the by-product of a social process in the transition of society to modernity. This is a new approach in Islamic thought, which I claim to have established. The approach refers to a transition in society towards a more inner differentiation in which religion is reduced to a part-system. The argument did not gain Islamic approval in Cairo (see note 1), but I was able to leave the city unscathed. Today, that would not be possible. The case of Faraj Fuda (note 6) is a reminder, not to be ignored.

The contention that Islam is a religion and not a system of government is supported by Ali 'Abdelraziq,[24] but he did not receive any approval either. It is a fact, however, as 'Abdelraziq has argued, that the caliphate is only a historical product. The Qur'an knows of no system of government. 'Abdelraziq was courageous, as well as correct, and his forbidden book continues to be relevant. 'Abdelraziq paid dearly for his views. The Azhar orthodoxy ruined his means of livelihood. Another thinking Muslim, who was much more radical than 'Abdelraziq, was the Egyptian writer Khaled Muhammad Khaled. In 1950 he published the thought-provoking book *"Min huna nabda'/*Here we start."[25] Khaled denounced the claim of a religious order in Islam, which he ridiculed as a call for the rule of *"kahana Islamiyya/*Islamic clergy." In the 1950s and 1960s secular nationalism dominated, and a critique of an "Islamic clergy" was not a risky undertaking. However, it is sad to report that some daring Muslims of that period – for example the radical secularist Khaled – shifted ground as they grew older. Khaled was one of these. Once an avowed secularist, he died as a furious fundamentalist. This is a telling story, repeated by other Muslims in our day.

There is a need in the Islamic debate to focus on the social process of secularization, not on the ideology of secularism. Even a once promising secular Muslim like An-Na'im has failed to contribute to this end. The issue can be worded differently: social changes precipitate a secularization process. The need to culturally accommodate secularity in Islamic societies is a task for Muslims themselves. It is possible to engage in this process without abandoning the religion of Islam. If subjected to a rethinking, it could be given a new, enlightened form. The inherited concepts are the obstacle in the way and they have undermined any rethinking of the issues; this is the result of evasions.

Structural and cultural secularization are closely interwoven. This means that rethinking of the religious doctrine has to be combined with a change in the realities on the ground. This refers to acceptance of the distinction between the ideology of secularism and the social process of secularization. Established taboos stand in the way. The Egyptian writer Faraj Fuda paid dearly, with his life, because he dared to address the issue. His sin was to risk an intellectual endeavor. The ongoing politicization of Islam along the line of developments related to the return of the sacred contributes to a religionization of politics and, further, to a de-secularization. This is the present context of the Islamic debate, which focuses on condemning secularism as alien and offensive to Muslims. People are silent about secularization in society. I fail to understand the contradiction of a Muslim like An-Na'im, who wants a "secular state" and rejects a "secularizing society" (note 4). How can this be accomplished? It is just a flaw, an evasion, or simply a lack of intellectual ability to thoroughly think the problem through? I do not know. As a Muslim I confine myself to stating *"Allahu a'lam/* Allah knows!"

Rather than search for an answer to the question of how a critical Muslim can make a U-turn (e.g. Khaled) and repent, I just state the facts. Khaled joined forces with political Islam and published a book in which he retracted his earlier arguments. The reversal is phrased thus: Islam prescribes the establishment of an Islamic state.[26] So, the radical secularist Khaled died as an Islamist. This gives rise to the following questions: how could it happen? What led to it? What underlies the shift from secularism to anti-secularism? What are the proper answers concerning the backwards step from secularization to de-secularization? Is it because secularity is a Western model? Was it imposed on the Islamic world? Is secularization alien to Islam, as some Islamists and orthodox writers argue? Do these issues matter at all to Islam? Am I falling into the trap of "Orientalism," because I, though a Muslim, pursue this line of reasoning? And finally, why was the interval of secular nationalism so short? These are tough questions and the list can be continued endlessly. All I can promise in this chapter is to continue the thinking about these current issues.

The thorny Muslim encounter with cultural modernity is the key to understanding secularization and de-secularization in contemporary Islam. Here, one has also to answer the question "What is secularization?" and why it failed in Islam. Here I begin with a reference to Western languages, where the term "secularization" is derived from the Latin *saeculum* (Arabic *'alam*), meaning generation, age. In short, "secular" means "worldly," i.e. to be concerned with the affairs of this world. Having regard to this semantic background, an early Arab translation of the European term "secularism" was *'alamaniyya*. This translation was accurate, but did not prevail long. It was replaced by the new Arabic term *'ilmaniyya*, which derived from *'ilm* (i.e. science, knowledge). In Islamic modernism this meaning was silently endorsed.

Contemporary Islamists refute the term secularization, focus on secularism, and use the ugly translation *"la-diniyya/* anti-religion."[27] They also assume that there is a conspiracy behind it. Political Islam rewords the *fiqh*-related view that Islam is *"din wa dunya/* unity of the spiritual and the worldly"[28] into *"din wa dawla/* unity of religion and state."[29] On the basis of this change, contemporary Islamists transform this classical Islamic concept into the concept of an Islamic state. The *"dawla/* state" replaces *"dunya/* saeculum." This concept exists neither in the Qur'an nor in the Hadith tradition of the Prophet. As repeatedly argued, the idea of an Islamic state is a contemporary Islamist invention of tradition.

The problem is not whether or not secular concepts are applicable to the Islamic world. The real problem is the lack of a cultural underpinning for secularity. In Europe, secularity is based on secularization. It developed out of modern industrial society. At issue is a cultural and structural change supported by the impulses of reformist tendencies within the Christian church itself. The Reformation led by Martin Luther inadvertently initiated this process of secularization. Nothing like this happened either in Islamic reform or in secular nationalism. In the Islamic world some leaders – e.g. al-Afghani – emulated the Reformation of Luther, but they failed to deliver and to change Islam in the way Luther did Christianity.

The cultural terminology of a theory of secularization

The repeatedly outlined distinction between secularism and secularization is most essential not only for academic reasons, but also in the search for a cultural legitimation of religious reform in Islam. Historically and socially, secularization is a by-product of the emergence of modern industrial society in Europe. Bearing this in mind, I repeat the question whether or not the notion of secularization is of limited relevance and therefore restricted to a specific culture, i.e. to Europe. This cultural relativism is contested. Secularization is a social process that could take place in any society. Therefore, I put forward the hypothesis that secularity is a general prerequisite for modern societies, regardless of their civilizational background. Viewing it from this angle, one needs to inquire into the relevance of this process in Islam. At issue is also the cultural foundation needed to support the process – which is not, however, in place. There is no innovative rethinking of scriptural Islam along the lines of a religious reformation. An insistence on scriptural arguments leads, in an unproductive repetition of Islamic precepts, to an essentialization of Islam. There is no essential Islam, except in the mind of *fiqh*-orthodoxy and, of course, in that of Western Orientalism.

Conversely, one needs to look at the socio-cultural system and the realities of religion. They could be unique, but not to the extent of being incompatible with secularization. There are many related questions, which are neither asked nor answered. Clearly, the issue is not merely an intellectual or an academic one. Secularization and de-secularization are real social processes and they do not relate only to a state of mind. At issue are social structures and inherited political authority. In light of the rise of political Islam, the attempt at de-secularization can be interpreted as a strategy to reverse the unfinished developments of secularization and rationalization that have occurred since Islam's exposure to cultural modernity. For a proper start to this inquiry, a clarification of the terms and concepts employed seems to be useful.

Together with the German sociologist of religion the late Niklas Luhmann, I view modern societies as developed, or differentiated, social systems. On this basis secularization can be related to a high degree of differentiation of functions in society, i.e. it "correlates with the development of social structures in the direction of functional differentiation," as Luhmann puts it. On the same page he continues the argument by stating that secularization only occurs

> when the religious system is no longer primarily oriented as society on the personal environment of the social system, but as a part-system of society on the inner-social environment ... Secularization thus appears as a consequence of the high degree of differentiation reached by modern society.[30]

Unlike the notion of secularism, the term secularization refers, in the understanding adopted from Luhmann, to a social process, not to an ideological view. Social change has repercussions on the religious system and on its social environment. A social transformation in the direction of modern industrial society may lead to a secularized society. In this case, religion is not abandoned, but rather reduced to a "part system of society." The clarification runs against the widespread polemics on secularization in the Islamic world. These polemics revolve around a misconception of secularization, believed to mean "abolition of religion," which is incorrect. Secularization is not an act of will or a policy, but the societal product of a complex social evolution that culminates in modern industrial society. Of course, this evolution can be affected by designing and pursuing policies favorable to functional differentiation. However, such efforts can only be successful if the structural and institutional change in society is accompanied by religious reform and cultural change. For instance, the Kemalists in Turkey subscribed to an ideology of secularism. It prevailed in past decades and enforced a change from above in state and society. However, Kemalism never engaged in setting up a cultural foundation for this secularism. In fact, Turkish society is not secular at all. Turkey has been, thus, an easy prey for the Islamism of the AKP. It follows that a secular state policy is insufficient for a secularization of society. The Islamists were able to Islamize from below while the Kemalists were secularizing from above, and the Kemalists have lost. Today, Turkey is ruled by the Islamists. The AKP (see notes 19 and 20) pays lip-service to secularism for instrumental reasons, so as to avert a ruling by the constitutional court that its party is anti-secular and then to be banned.

A solid theory of secularization locates religion in a functionally differentiated system. Secularity merely means that religion acquires a different social significance. In other words, in a secular society religion can continue to be a part of that society. I share Luhmann's view,

> ... that secularization [is] one of the consequences of the reorientation of society towards a primarily functionally differentiated system in which each functional sphere acquires greater autonomy but becomes at the same time more dependent on other functions being performed and on the way they are performed.[31]

In less-developed social systems that are not yet functionally differentiated one encounters *Developing Cultures*[32] that are not yet secularized. The explanation is to be sought in social and cultural change. This statement does not reflect evolutionism, but rather a correspondence of the sacred and the political that is related to the varying low degrees of differentiation. This correspondence is best exemplified in the Islamic fundamentalist ideology of "*din wa dawla*/unity of religion and state," which prescribes that society and state should be defined by religion. The French anthropologist Georges Balandier distinguishes between societies according to the degree of mastery over nature that is attained. Balandier argues:

> The affinity between the sacred and the political is quite evident in societies which are not oriented towards mastery over nature but rather linked with it and which see themselves as extended and reflected in it.[33]

With this insight in mind, modern science and technology may be viewed as a means to mastering nature for human ends. In this understanding, industrialization is culturally related to the unfolding of modern science and technology. This development reflects a process of human mastery over nature that gives rise to functionally differentiated social systems. The general outcome would be the emergence of secularized social systems in industrial societies. This argument does not imply a mechanical link; rather, it is based on the presumption of an interplay between the degree of development and the state of rationality expressed by accomplished scientific standards.

It is not only in the contemporary world of Islam, but also in modern societies that one encounters anti-science alongside science (see Chapter 2). However, developing social systems are more prone to a culture of anti-science and to its related knowledge, which is not consonant with rationality. Thus, the notion of development has been applied in this sense to cultures, as in Chapter 1. Here, I relate the study of developing cultures to an inquiry into the degree of development in the direction of secularization. I reiterate my critique of the evolutionism of the classical modernization theory, and I see no problem when the notion of development is extended to culture. There is no contradiction. To argue for development and also to extend it to culture, in the notion of "developing cultures," is certainly not engagement in evolutionism. The secularization of society is neither an evolutionary nor a determined process. The process can only take place in society if the people involved want it and engage in action for it. Otherwise, it will never be successful, or will simply not occur.

Development and tradition in the context of Islam's predicament

It is not an Orientalism to state that "development" and "evolution" are modern concepts[34] that do not exist in Islamic thought. In Islam, the views of the *salaf*, i.e. tradition of the Prophet and his successors, are considered to be the only valid standard admitted in any model for a future. However, the realities of Islamic history are underpinned by other constraints. With the foundation of a new civilization, a development occurred from Bedouin Arab standards to a high civilization. The story of the foundation of Islam is of the creation of an empire. In this connection, one can draw on Shmuel Eisenstadt's research on classical pre-industrial civilizations and their empires.[35] These imperial civilizations were not based on functionally differentiated social systems. Their order reveals a correspondence between the sacred and the political, as outlined above, where political rule is exercised through an alliance between religious and political leaders. In traditional Islam, the *ulema* provided the rulers with religious legitimation. Thus, in Islamic history, political legitimacy was based on religion. The cultural peculiarity of the Muslim "*ulema*/scribes" is their function as – *post eventum* – legitimizers of the political and social actions of the caliphs.[36]

One of the pre-eminent Muslim reformers of our time, Muhammad al-'Ashmawi, argues in the tradition of 'Abdelraziq that the order of the caliphate was not based on the religion of Islam, but was, rather, an invention of the sacral jurists, i.e. the *fuqaha*,[37] who became a major source of legitimacy after the death of the Prophet. In other words, in Islamic history the imperial state was virtually a secular one, although its legitimation was wholly religious. It is a fact that Islamic thought was limited to providing a *post eventum* legitimation, as Sir Anthony Gibb (note 36) puts it. Traditional Islamic thought did not reflect any thinking about the development that occurred, nor include any design for a better future. The political thought of al-Farabi was among the few exceptions; however, it had little influence.[38] The then existing virtually secular separation between "*siyasa*/ state administration" and "*shari'a*/divine law" was never reflected in Islamic orthodox thought, which never went beyond the confines of scripture. Orthodoxy served legitimatory ends (see note 36) and thus prevailed in Islamic history – in contrast to Islamic rationalism, which was the exception and, above all, not a lasting one.

There are different standards of development; the question is whether they can be related to either civilizational differences or standards of development. I view development as human, and thus universal, and I therefore restrict civilizational differences to divergent worldviews that are embedded in differing standards of development. From the point of view of the present book it can be said that culture can affect development. The combination of the two notions in the formula "developing cultures" is the approach used to understand the place of culture and religion in the process of social change. The role of religious leaders in pre-modern societies, in particular in Islam, can be singled out as an important issue. As Shmuel Eisenstadt puts it, these leaders are in charge,

> to formalize and formulate their beliefs and traditions in such a way that they could be fully articulated and organized at a relatively developed cultural level. They are also obliged to regulate and canalize the various dynamic tendencies and elements which had arisen within the religions and to maintain internal organization and discipline. Such internal problems gave rise to the specific behavior patterns of religious elites and organizations in these societies.[39]

These patterns of behavior, as based on a loyalty towards the ruling authorities, are not culturally specific and are therefore not restricted to Islamic societies, as they also occur in other cultures. In all cases one can see the commonality that the patterns involved are not favorable to a transformation of society. In this way, tradition becomes an obstacle to development and in this capacity it also hampers the process of secularization in the name of protecting religion. In Sunni Islam, opposition to the ruler has been considered as being directed against his divinity as "*Zhul Allah*/God's shadow on earth." In traditional Islam, the political was closely associated with the sacred. The religious leaders, in this case the *ulema*, invariably want

> to preserve traditional ways of thinking and to control the development of an independent, critical public opinion. They often detect a threat to political loyalty in free religious and intellectual activity and thus strive to keep it under control and to maintain loyalty towards the regime and the provision of resources.[40]

One can refer to this description in order to determine, with its assistance, the place of religion in the history of power and rule in Sunni Islam. It is fully applicable. Actions and attitudes towards differentiation in the religious community were reflected in the rise of anti-hegemonic sects.[41] Nevertheless, and unlike Christianity, in Islam there has never existed an organized mosque as an institution that resembles a separate church. Sunni Islam is a denomination, but it has never been an organized body in itself. The religious establishment of Sunni Islam was and continues to be heavily dependent on rulers. For this reason it did not develop any separate institutions of its own, not even that of religious "*waqf*/foundations." It is known, from the work of Barrington Moore, that the church had some autonomy in medieval Christianity.[42] This provided the basis for the development of separation between church and state; and this separation contributed inadvertently to the process of secularization. By reference to this process one can support the hypothesis of the relevance of culture and religion to development. It can be added that, next to cultural innovations, industrialization is also a requirement for secularization. It is not merely a supplementary dimension. It is part of the inner differentiation and the degree of complexity in the social system. The institutional and cultural development of religion itself is also essential. It is never a mechanical reflection of the development of society. In short, the state of religion does not automatically reflect a structural standard of evolution in society. The persistence of religious tradition is possible, and it creates an obstacle to secularization. In putting forward this argument I am not identifying Islam with tradition, but simply stating an existing specific pattern that has been inherited in many ways throughout Islamic history. I am aware of the invective of Orientalism, but I am a Muslim socialized in the Islamic value system and know what I am talking about. On this basis, I foresee an accusation of Orientalism by some Westerners and remind them of the fact that they are qualified by Muslims as unbelievers, because they – as cultural relativists – have no commitments and no beliefs at all.

The nature of a religion itself plays a decisive role in determining cultural and political value orientations in those traditional systems that are determined by what it believes to be divine. From this point of view it can be argued that the historically well-known dependence of the Islamic religious leadership on the rulers – along with the corresponding values – has contributed to establishing a tradition in Islamic societies that is not favorable to secularization. Such secularization would contribute to a demagnification of power, thus making it vulnerable. The members of such a society are not citizens in the sense of *citoyens*, but mere subjects of a ruler who is legitimated by religion and supported as such by the classical Islamic *faqihs*. One of them, Ibn Taimiyya, views humans as *ra'iyya*. This is an Arabic word for a herd of animals. This population is led by the *"ra'i/*pastor" of the *"umma/*the collectivity" subjected to *"faraid/*duties," but not entitled to rights. As was shown in Chapter 4, the concept of rights is a recent introduction to Islamic thought.

The needed cultural change requires a rethinking of these traditions in Islam in order to question the ideology of a political legitimacy based on religion. Political Islam, or Islamism, which serves as an ideology for the present opposition to rulers in the Islamic world, does not provide the impetus required for this kind of cultural change and religious reform. Islamism is opposed to the rulers, but equally to all patterns of secularization. Political Islam engages in a radical de-secularization. The opposition is based on excommunicating the rulers from the *umma*. They are discredited on the basis of being qualified as heretics. This position is a non-starter.

By placing the debate on secularization in Islam within the overall context of the development of society and its environment, in a contest between tradition and modernity, one could consider the degree of functional differentiation achieved. It is argued that this differentiation emerges from a transformation of society. The relationship between religion and politics in Islam leads Bruce Borthwick to point out the impediments to secularization, which could be categorized in this manner:

> the traditional Islamic religio-political system was an organic one, in which religious and political functions were fused and were performed by a unitary structure … Religious institutions and officials have been as fully a part of the state as the army and generals … The Sunni ulama … are expected to preach obedience to the ruler, however unjust he might be. This they did.[43]

In contrast to the traditional Sunni establishment and its preaching of obedience to the ruler, contemporary Islamists engage in a revolt against the existing Muslim power. They accuse rulers having fallen into *"kufr/*heresy." However, their contestation of the *ulema*-orthodoxy does not amount to engagement in cultural change. No rethinking of religious authority in Islam occurs. The doctrine of an organic binding of religion and polity in historical Islam as the core of authoritative tradition is based on an interpretation of the Qur'an. It remains unquestioned. The tension between scriptural provisions and reality has its effects. The course of development continues to be shaped by this feature. This prevails in political Islam also. Today, the Islamists rebel, but they share with the very authority that they contest the same reluctance to historicize Islam. Therefore, it is utterly wrong to qualify Islamism – as do some not well-informed postmodernists – as the "other modernity."

In order to describe the existing realities one needs to bear in mind that – despite all of the secular pronouncements – the real social systems of contemporary Islamic societies have never been secularized. An institutional and structural foundation is lacking, in line with the unquestioned prevalence and the persistence of anti-secular traditions. Structurally, existing Islamic societies are not in an advanced state of differentiation. The social change that is occurring is not accommodated culturally and the need for cultural reforms continues to be most urgent. Religion matters to social and cultural change, and thus to development. The disruptive pattern of change in social structures that displaces people and eradicates their inherited ways of life results in disorientation. This is not a pattern of social change that could support a cultural change in worldviews, norms, and values, because they are not subjected to a new thinking; they persist within the framework of a defensive culture. Islam's predicament with modernity is therefore also a cultural, not just a structural concern. That said, it can be added that the interplay between social and cultural change in the processes of development is uneven. The secularization of society cannot be promoted by an ideology of secularism, but rather by religious reforms that provide a cultural underpinning for change. This cultural change is not in place and I fail to see how the "secular state" that An-Na'im (note 4) envisions could materialize without a secularization of society. His formula of "negotiating the future of the shari'a" is not only inconsistent and flawed, but simply makes no sense.

Rethinking Islam in a new reading of the cultural heritage to promote secularity

One cannot repeat enough how much *Culture Matters* for secularization in the context of development. This argument goes in two directions: culture can either promote development or be an obstacle to it. At present, the claim for "*asalah/* authenticity" in the framework of identity politics is an impediment to change, as will be discussed at length in Chapter 8. Orthodox-Salafist and Islamist-minded Muslims reject secularity when they argue that it is a Christian phenomenon alien to Islam and infringes on its authenticity. In contrast to this allegation, one can arrive at a positive assessment of the separation between religion and politics by establishing a reference to the reason-based approach in the heritage of Islamic rationalism, to be revived for the benefit of Islamic civilization. In addition, the intellectual sources of the Islamic religious system, the Qur'an and the *sunna*, make no mention of any authority mediating as a religious instance between

God and the individual. The *ulema*, or the *faqih* have no place in the Qur'an and are merely a product of Islamic history. Their understanding of the Qur'an is not divine, but clearly human. It is intriguing to see the *ulema* themselves sharing the claim that Islam has no clergy to perform such a mediating role. They view themselves not as clergy, but rather as religious scholars, and this is the meaning of the term *ulema*. In reality, the *ulema* were and continue to be an Islamic clergy oriented against any kind of secularization. There is nothing scholarly in what they do.

The identity politics and the related cultural politics in contemporary Islam often ignore the real gap that exists between the ideal of Islam and its corresponding historical reality. In its ideal, the *"umma/*Islamic community" knows no clergy, nor a divine power. In contrast to this ideal, the reality of Islam is dominated by the stratum of Islamic learned men, the *ulema* or scribes who interpret religion as *"fiqh/*sacral jurisprudence." In fact, these *ulema* act as a clergy, or at least are the functional equivalent to a clergy as it exists in Christianity. In Islam, the *ulema* hold a monopoly over the recognized standards of established Islam and it is thus a self-deception to argue that these *ulema* are not a clergy. Yes, they are, and they control the mosques and the related *waqf* foundations and in all terms they are powerful in their actions as clerics. The conclusion has to be that the ideal of Islam does not match the reality, whether in the past or in the present. There are Muslims as well as Western students of Islam who refer to the religious ideal and then confuse the scripture and the historical realities. In so doing, they end up by making wrong judgments. By this means such "experts" – for instance John Voll and John Esposito – inadvertently join apologetic Islamic thinking and finish up by supporting political Islam and its claims. The presentation of a "variety" of democracy called "Islamic democracy"[44] confuses Islam and Islamism. In contrast, it is more scholarly to engage in a demystification of the allegations that are made, and that are belied by the historical realities. The ideals of the religion of Islam and the established patterns in Islamic history have never been congruent with one another.

In order to establish a cultural foundation for the processes of secularization one needs a "rethinking of Islam" – certainly no further engagement in apologetics is needed. In the first place, the Islamic worldview needs to be adjusted so as to facilitate appropriate dealing with the predicament with cultural modernity. This historical task has been fulfilled neither by the Muslims of the nineteenth and twentieth centuries in their Islamic reform, nor in today's Islamism, which is mistakenly viewed as a pattern of multiple modernities. A thoughtful secularization in Islam was not among the concerns of early modernists like Afghani. They were aware of the heyday of Islamic civilization, but ignored how the correspondence between the sacred and the political was viewed in the rationalism of medieval Islam. The pivotal question is this: why did Arab Islamic civilization reach a zenith and then declined? Although medieval Islamic society was pre-industrial, it reached a relatively high level of social differentiation which, at the time, was favorable to the development of science and technology. The separation of knowledge from religious belief was accepted in Islamic rationalism. Did the unfolding of early scientific thought in medieval Islam contribute to the cultural introduction of some elements of secularity that can be referred to today? The answer is both yes and no.

A variety of questions is raised in this book in general. Some are resumed in this chapter, in particular those that touch on secularization. I am not presumptuous and do not claim to be in a position to answer all of these pivotal questions. In the search for some useful answers one may look at the work of the contemporary Syrian philosopher Taiyib Tizini, who engaged in thinking on this subject. In the view of Tizini, Islamic philosophy developed during its heyday a secular, scientifically based, rational interpretation of the cosmos. Is this an Islamic path towards an *"Entzauberung/*disenchantment" of the world? Tizini states:

> The political and social content of those ideas of the Arab-Islamic thinkers ... is expressed in a hostile attitude to the dominant feudal intellectual position. The social basis for this attitude was to be found in the then considerable vertical and horizontal development of commodity production and in economic activities generally, and it went hand in hand with the development of natural sciences such as chemistry, astronomy, medicine and mathematics.[45]

There are other contemporary Muslim rationalists who plea for a revival of this medieval Islamic rationalism, with the argument that it could provide a cultural basis for the unfolding of a rational view of the current world in the world of Islam. In the course of discussing the secular worldview in Islam, reference was made earlier to the model of *"al-Madina al-fadila/*the perfect state" that developed in the political philosophy of al-Farabi (see note 11). This state pattern is based on a secular order. In this thinking of al-Farabi one encounters one of the strands of an early, interrupted development towards cultural secularization in Islamic society. This tradition manifested in the philosophical works of Avicenna, Averroes, al-Farabi, Ibn Tufail, and others and was continued by Ibn Khaldun in the fourteenth century in his philosophy of history and society. This tradition marks a positive development in Islam, which came to an end with the death of Ibn Khaldun in 1406. The subsequent decline of Islamic civilization, in both its distortive and challenging aspects, lasted until its exposure to modernity.

There exists another strand of Islamic thinking that supports in its own way the separation of religion and politics in Islam – without, of course, being related to the concept of secularization. It is the Sufi tradition and it was incorporated into a revolt against the monopoly over religion of the *"ulema/*Islamic clergy." Islamic Sufism[46] embodied a tendency that promoted secularization to the extent that it emphasized the *"batiniyya/*inwardness" in religiosity at the expense of the shari'a rule imposed by the *ulema*, who claim to mediate between God and the believer so as to legitimate their monopoly over religion. The already quoted Syrian philosopher Tizini puts forward the following interesting thought: had reason-based Islamic philosophy and Islamic Sufism been able to shape the prevailing worldview of Islamic civilization and had the *ulema* not been so successful in combating rationalism, then there would have been an Islamic pattern of modernization in society. Without a doubt, medieval Islamic society was structurally developed. However, the transition from commercial capitalism to an industrial capitalist society[47] could not have been achieved. The medieval Arab Islamic empire decayed, due to a combination of internal and external constraints. It is interesting to know that in Islamic imagery only external forces (more the crusaders than the Mongols who conquered Baghdad) were blamed for the decline of Islamic civilization. A rethinking of Islam must include an effort to demystify this imagery. The internal causes of Islamic decline must be addressed candidly so as to learn lessons from Islamic deficiencies for the sake of a better future. Islamic thinking on tradition and development has to be freed from the obsession that Muslims are victimized by the conspiracies of non-Muslims. This mindset not only reflects a specific attitude, it also has a function: the promotion of the perception of a "hidden hand" acting behind all wrongs. This perception absolves Muslims from taking any responsibility for their own shortcomings. The blame is always placed on others.

The historical context of the challenge of secularity: the exposure to modernity and the failure to come to terms with it

The society of the civilization of classical Islam was – unlike contemporary Islamic societies that are based on developing cultures – a highly developed one. Its strong identity facilitated the accommodation of all external challenges. By contrast, contemporary Muslims have great problems in dealing with the standards of a secular civilization. The challenge is not yet accommodated, and this is a predicament for contemporary Islam. The exposure takes place on two levels: one is political-economic and the other is cultural-civilizational. Since the nineteenth century Muslims – as well as other non-Westerners – have been inferiorized by Europeans, who viewed them as backward people and even denied them a history in order to legitimate the establishment of Western superiority over them. The European model,[48] combined with a Western hegemony, made it difficult for non-Westerners, and in particular for Muslims, to be open to learning from the West. The problem is that the economic penetration of the non-European world in the age of colonialism went hand in hand with cultural penetration. In their awareness of these challenges, the non-European peoples confused the two issues and resorted to defensive cultural patterns. Their responses included attitudes of self-assertion and identity politics to counter the techno-scientific superiority of the West. The attempt to modernize without changing one's (constructed) identity is a significant Muslim concern. The European Orientalist Gustav von Grunebaum, who migrated to the US, states the issue in these words: "the Mohammedan world's greatest difficulty in its struggle with Westernization lies in the contradiction between successful adoption of alien aims and the inability to give up the traditional point of departure."[49] In his confusion, this Orientalist resembles the Muslim-defensive culture itself. Accommodation of the challenges is not a wholesale assimilation that is addressed by von Grunebaum as an adjustment.

In terms of cultural change one can state that a reformation of Christianity preceded the Industrial Revolution in Europe. The link between a Protestant ethic and industrial capitalism has been repeatedly pointed out since Max Weber's work on this subject. The Lutheran Reformation was not just a struggle against religious bodies and the clergy; it also implied the depoliticization of religion. This reference to the Reformation is neither a reading of European history into Islam nor a sign of Orientalism. To be sure, history is universal, and open for all divergent civilizations to learn from it. Suffice it to say that positive reference to the Reformation was made by the foremost Islamic revivalist of the nineteenth century, Afghani[50] (shortly to be quoted at length).

One may argue that in medieval Islamic history rationalism and Sufism included elements of an Islamic enlightenment based on a secular view of the world. Why did it not generate similar effects in Islamic history as did the Reformation in European history – which paved the way for the Enlightenment, leading to secularization of all spheres of life? As Habermas argues, the Reformation was a fundamental element in the unfolding of cultural modernity. Thanks to techno-scientific accomplishments and to the related new worldview, Europeans emancipated themselves and became able to determine their destiny. On this foundation they equipped themselves with the tools needed to overcome the "correspondence between the sacred and the political" (G. Balandier). The techno-scientific view of the world created the basis for a secularization of society. I repeat the question: why didn't such a development happen in Islam, despite the elements of Islamic enlightenment pointed out?

The reference to the fact that secularization in Europe is related to a historical development stretching from Luther's struggle against the clergy to Sigmund Freud's plea for a rational foundation of cultural precepts refers to a pattern that is often ignored in discussions of European secularization. Europe set the standards, and the founder of Islamic modernism in the nineteenth century and spiritual father of modern Islam, Afghani (1838–97), accepted them. These standards were absent in medieval Islam. As already mentioned in passing, Afghani acknowledged and appreciated the significance of the Lutheran Reformation; he even overstretched the argument to the extent of ascribing all European achievements to its influence. In one of his major writings Afghani expresses the following most favorable view of the Christian Luther, whom he – as a Muslim – greatly admired:

When we reflect on the causes of the revolutionary transition in Europe from barbarism to civilization, we see that this change was only made possible by the religious movement which Luther initiated and also carried out. That great man saw how the Europeans were hindered in their ambitions and how they were dominated by the clergy; he saw, too, how traditions held sway which were not founded in reason and led that religious movement: he called tirelessly upon the nations of Europe to awake from their slumbers. He managed to persuade Europeans to reform their values; he explained to them how they were born free and still lay chained.[51]

The admiration for Luther expressed by Afghani implies a clear endorsement of religious reform in Islam. The implication of this highly favorable assessment of Luther can be viewed as an acceptance of reformation for Islam as well. It is also noteworthy that Afghani dismissed the Islamic clergy and its tradition, as Luther did in the case of Christianity. The Christian reform of values seemed to be worthy of Islamic emulation. The greatly respected late Oxford scholar Hourani suggested that Afghani saw himself as the Islamic Luther.[52] The Protestant ethic introduced the potential for an implicitly anti-dogmatic cultural attitude. Afghani positively acknowledged this tradition in Christianity and argued for an Islamic movement of reform in order to combat both of the enemies of change: the European powers colonizing the Islamic world and the Islamic clergy holding it stagnant within its rigid traditions. At issue was how to bring about a development similar to that which had occurred in Europe. It is intriguing to see contemporary Islamists referring to Afghani's call for jihad, while completely overlooking his pointing out the ills of Islamic civilization itself. For many reasons it is incorrect to believe that Islamism is a radical reformism. It is outrageous and most disturbing to see how the disputed Tariq Ramadan draws a clearly mistaken line of continuity between his Islamist grandfather, Hasan al-Banna, and the reformist Afghani. This line is completely incorrect because it simply did not exist – ever. While al-Banna fought jihad for the neo-Islamic pattern of "*din wa-dawla/*unity of religion and state" (this is religious fundamentalism, not reform), Afghani was honestly concerned with religious reform. In the tradition of al-Banna Islamists refer positively to Afghani, but they overlook the tradition of Islamic rationalism to which he subscribed. Unfortunately, neither Islamic rationalism in the past nor Islamic reform in the present led to secularization. Why? Is secularity alien to and thus incompatible with Islam? Why did the appreciation of Luther as a model by Islamic modernists not lead to a kind of reformation that results in secularization? Did Afghani, then, have the same problem as An-Na'im has (note 4) today? Despite the great difference in caliber between Afghani and An-Na'im, both seem to have failed to grasp that one cannot have it both ways – be evasive and a reformer at the same time.

Any attempt to answer these questions has to commence with an acknowledgment that the Reformation in Christianity and the reform achieved in Islam cannot be compared with one another. This is not only because they did not produce the same results, but also due to their design. They are two quite different cases. It is true that early Islamic modernists pointed out the Islamic reality, dominated by backward *ulema*, and challenged the existence of any legitimacy for them in the religious dogma. This resembles Luther, who rebelled against the Christian clergy. However, Islamic modernists failed to emulate the spirit of the Reformation. This is the reason why no secularization emerged. Above all, there was no rethinking of the religious dogma. Islamic modernists believed that a correct following of the religious prescriptions of Islam was enough in itself to ensure that the Islamic world would overcome its backwardness. They were mistaken, and therefore the comparison with the Reformation is contested.

Due to this significance, the Islamic modernist Arslan (1869–1946) was mentioned in the first chapter of this book. In a series of articles published in *al-Manar*, a journal edited by Rashid Rida, a revivalist, Arslan dealt with the question of why Muslims were backward in spite of following of God's commands, whereas others had succeeded in becoming developed. Arslan's answer was published in 1930 as a book entitled *A Discussion of Why Muslims are Backward and Others Developed*. This book is still relevant; it is reprinted and still read today and that is why it continues to matter. Arslan's response also provides an answer to a question included in this section. He sets out by quoting the following verse from the Qur'an, which states that "Allah does not change anything for the people, as long as they do not change themselves" (sura 13, verse 11). In other words, Muslims live in a state of "backwardness" – this is Arslan's phrasing – and are also underdeveloped because they fail to understand Islam properly. The modernist Arslan argues in the following manner: "It would be a mistake to expect me to say that the cure for Muslims lies in their absorbing Einstein's relativity theory, the characteristics of X-rays, the inventions of Thomas Edison or Pasteur's chemical experiments."[53]

After this statement, which indicates a clear reservation with regard to "copying the West," Arslan continues his reasoning by highlighting his view that the European accomplishments are flawed by the fact that they, as he states,

> are in reality ... only derivations and nothing original. Only sacrifice (*tadhiya*) or exertion (*jihad*) is the foremost knowledge, above all other sciences. When a community (*umma*) has mastered this discipline and lives according to it, then it can acquire all other sciences and branches of knowledge in order to make use of all the benefits and achievements on the basis of it. If the Muslims wanted, all they would have to do would be to make an effort and behave according to the precepts laid down in their holy book and then they would catch up with Europeans, Americans and Japanese in science and prosperity, but maintaining Islam. (ibid.)

Arslan's view is not only a highly powerful position articulated in an Islamic text that has great influence; it also, typically, expresses the evasive attitude of Islamic modernism and gives expression to all of its flaws. The acknowledgment of what is termed "Islamic backwardness" and the opposition to the conservative Islamic clergy are steps in the right direction. However, this goes hand in hand with a strong reluctance to admit the need to rethink Islam, to being in a position to cope with the requirements of the techno-scientific age. This insight continues to be lacking. There is no real willingness to grasp the predicament with modernity and to question the established religious dogma. This manner of thinking in the discourse of early Islamic modernism has been highly consequential. In order to understand the failure of Islamic reformism, I refer again to Niklas Luhmann's sociology of religion to analyze the social function of religious dogma. In Luhmann's view, it

> interprets so as to be able to provide an answer. On the one hand it oper-
> ates with functionally unanalyzed abstractions and thus in this respect
> blindly. It does not consciously reflect on its social function but rather
> understands itself, its concept of dogma, dogmatically ... On the other
> hand, it rests on a universal and contextless applicability, hence on a certain
> disregard of the bonds it interprets.[54]

This understanding of the function of a religiously closed-minded dogma helps us to grasp the social function of Islamic doctrine, whether in its Salafist or in its modernist form. Neither variety promotes what I have termed "cultural accommodation of social change" (1990). Thus, Islamic modernism is in fact not really modern, because it does not contribute to a rethinking of the dogma. It is, rather, an illusion of semi-modernity (see Chapter 11). The dogma itself is referred to in order to answer the question why contemporary Muslims are "backward," as Arslan himself asks. He fails to explain why the Europeans succeeded but the Muslims failed. By arguing that there is a deviation from the dogma, Arslan believes that he is pinpointing the source of the sad state of affairs in the Islamic civilization, but in fact he fails to explain anything!

The real issue is not a deviation from the provisions of the Islamic revelation, but rather the lagging of Islamic civilization behind the modern world and its techno-scientific accomplishments. The proper response would be the will to adopt these modern achievements – however, not instrumentally, i.e. without embracing their underlying discourse, which is the rationality of cultural modernity and its related worldview. The outcome is an Islamic version of "semi-modernity." This term describes the splitting of modernity into an instrument and a worldview while overlooking the overall context. This is the subject of the final chapter of this book, where the reader will find more details on this issue in the form of a conclusion.

In conclusion of this section, I relate the findings to the subject of the book and to the issue in point, i.e. secularization. In earlier chapters, in particular in Chapter 2, Max Weber's notion of "rationalization" has been quoted in order to explain how the "disenchantment of the world" contributed to replacing the correspondence between the sacred and the worldly. This correspondence persists in pre-industrial cultures and continues to shape pre-modernity. Today's cultural precepts are, as Freud once claimed, no longer religiously, but rationally founded.[55] In the Islamic context, it must be conceded that the Islamic civilizational worldview remains unreformed. The Islamist formula "*din wa dawla*/unity of religion and state" reflects a specific variety of the correspondence between the sacred and the political, unfolded under the conditions of an exposure to cultural modernity. At issue is to maintain the correspondence between religion, culture, polity, and society in an increasingly uncompromising manner. The resulting political ideology politicizes shari'a. As was shown in Chapter 3, this ideology claims to supply provisions that prescribe a specifically Islamic governance based on rules that apply to all spheres of life. The outcome of this civilizational project is a totalitarian state that abolishes the distinction between what is public and what is private. In the name of a political religion, all aspects of human life are subjected to an order that claims to be divine and, on this basis, forbids any questioning. At issue is an order that is clearly totalitarian in its nature, established by humans, not provided by God. This is not the faith of Islam, but the ideology of Islamism. Those who deny the difference between Islam and Islamism stand – wittingly or unwittingly – in the service of religious fundamentalism.

In short, the envisioned Islamic reform did not take place. There was no secularization. Reformers did not engage in a rethinking of religious dogma on the basis of cultural modernity. In fact, the reformers altogether evaded addressing the predicament. Single items of techno-scientific modernity were instrumentally adopted, while decoupled from the process of rationalization. After the failure of modernism and the takeover of secular nationalism, religion was ideologically separated from politics, without, however, any engagement in real cultural innovation. An ideological secularization (e.g. Kemalism) that lacks the necessary cultural foundation is doomed to fail. The evidence for this statement is the successful rise of political Islam in Turkey, parallel to the combined decline of secularism and Kemalism.

The Islamic modernist Afghani invoked Luther and established his Reformation as a paragon for the Muslim peoples; however, he failed to be audacious. He did not engage in real reforms based on a rethinking of Islam. Then came the failed attempts at a secularization of Islam by Arab and Turkish nationalism. This has already been explained. Currently, there seems to be no light at the end of the tunnel. On the one hand, Islam is abused by rulers in order to legitimate their power, and on the other, equally, it is referred to by the Islamist opposition in its quest for power, named "the Islamic state." In both cases, non-religious ends are pursued within a framework of religionized politics that radically dismisses secularization as a disenchantment of the world. Instead, political Islam puts forward an agenda of de-secularization, named "*al-hall al-Islami*/Islamic solution," with the intention of remaking the world. This agenda is a recipe for tensions and conflicts within Islam and in its relations with non-Muslims.

Between secularization and de-secularization

In contemporary Islamic civilization some attempts at secularization were undertaken on the basis of a superficial decoupling of religion from politics. However, the religious discourse continued and continues to be dominant, even in the thinking of secular-minded Islamic thinkers. Superficially, they engage in a secular discussion of the techno-scientific patterns of modern civilization, but they fail to accomplish any substantive reform. Their efforts founder on the limitations of religious dogma referred to earlier. To illustrate this point with an example, it is worth citing a typical passage from a book by a Muslim scholar characteristically entitled: *The Supposed Gap between Science and Religion*. The author, Muhammed Ali Yusuf, believes that only Christianity is incompatible with a scientific culture, but then he adds:

> that the issue is quite different in the Islamic civilization. There is neither a conflict nor a gap between Islam and science. That is why we can see efforts in the Islamic Middle East for overcoming the allegation that there is a gap between science and religion ... Religion comes from God. Allah revealed that he is the Truth (*al-haq*). This truth cannot contain any contradiction in itself. Thus there is no contradiction between religion and truth. For science is based in the nature of things on truth.[56]

This statement evidences all the characteristics of a religious dogma that bears no reference to the historical realities that are waiting to be dealt with. Islamic apologetics concedes that other religions can be in conflict with secular science, but excludes Islam, which claims to be the only "true religion" based on divine "*ilm*/knowledge," which is viewed to be the ultimate science.

Of course, there are better Muslim thinkers. One of them is the Yale alumnus and leading enlightened Arab philosopher Sadiq Jalal al-Azm. He is among the clearest representatives of the secular view in contemporary Islamic thought. In a book published in 1969 under the title *Critique of Religious Thought*, al-Azm argues that it is useless to debate whether or not bits and pieces of Islamic teaching are compatible with this or that scientific finding, as apologetic writers often do. In the view of al-Azm, the gap lies deeper than one would assume:

> It concerns the method we use to reach our findings and convictions ... In this respect there is a basic contradiction between Islam and science. For Islam as for any other religion, the correct method is to take certain religious texts which are believed to be revealed, or else the writings of scholars who have studied and written commentaries on those texts, as the source of truth ... It goes without saying that scientific method ... is entirely at odds with this religious, exegetical-dogmatic method.[57]

This view is articulated by a Muslim from a well-known family of the Damascene nobility. The criticism of al-Azm is, however, restricted to pointing out that modern scientific discourse is rationally based and thus incompatible with any religious thinking, from whatever religion. Nevertheless, al-Azm differentiates between religion as the content of a specific culture and religious consciousness as a form of inwardness. As al-Azm tells us, in the Islamic Middle East this religious consciousness is repressed by petrified, traditional forms of belief and stagnating religious practices. This religious consciousness must break free from its chains and articulate itself in ways adapted to the conditions and requirements of twentieth century civilization in which we live.

(Ibid.)

The articulation of the cited secular views led – as in the earlier mentioned cases of the early Khaled Muhammad Khaled and Ali 'Abdelraziq – to an unforgiving prosecution and punishment. Following the publication of the book cited, al-Azm was taken to court and then imprisoned. Among the social sanctions was that al-Azm was forced to quit his teaching position at the American University of Beirut/AUB. It is worth mentioning that the confiscated book, notwithstanding this repression, was released and reprinted several times, both legally and illegally. Despite its flaws, it continues to be the major book in Arabic on secularization. The book is a plea for the establishment of a rational scientific discourse in contemporary Islamic civilization. This is definitely not yet a public choice.

Earlier, I referred to Ali 'Abdelraziq's attempt at intellectual secularization in his book published in Cairo in 1925. In terms of considering historical continuity and discontinuity it is worth dealing with it before moving on to the conclusion. Unlike al-Azm, the Yale-educated philosopher, 'Abdelraziq[58] had religious credentials as a scholar of al-Azhar, the stronghold of Sunni Islam. For 'Abdelraziq, Islam is a religion concerned with believers inwardly, and not a form of government. Because of his thinking, Ali 'Abdelraziq – as mentioned above – lost his teaching position at al-Azhar as well as his judicial posts. His book appears particularly relevant today in the context of the ongoing process of de-secularization because it contains rich information that contradicts contemporary efforts aimed at establishing a system of government based on Islam. The question is how the rationalization related to cultural modernity and the connected techno-scientific accomplishments may be adopted in the Islamic civilization without abandoning Islam as a form of religious consciousness.

After some decades of scholarship in the tradition of Max Weber, in which it was established that secularization as a rationalization is inevitable, one has to acknowledge that today the contrary is happening. De-secularization is a social reality that is occurring within the context of the return of the sacred. It is certainly not a religious renaissance. It is, rather, a claim for a form of government based on religion. There are still some Islamic voices that subscribe to Islam as a religion, not as a political system. Today those Muslims are either in a minority, or not consequential in their thinking (see note 4). Most prominent among these reformers are the contemporary Muslim jurist M. al-'Ashmawi[59] and a few other Islamic liberals. In contrast, the Islamist contention that "Islam is the solution," understood as a claim for "*Hakimiyyat Allah*/God's rule," is an order that is a public choice in the Islamic world. It thus reflects the contemporary mainstream. These facts notwithstanding, I continue to argue that incorporation of the Islamic world into the world at large cannot be accomplished without secularization. The

"Islamic solution" is a strategy of polarization and conflict. A secular state without secularization (note 4) is like a car with no engine. Another fact is that non-Muslims – and Muslim democratic pluralists also – would never succumb to the claim of *"siyadat al-Islam*/Islamic supremacy." This formula is a recipe for war.

Conclusions

Islamic history is political as well as religious. 'Abdelraziq differs from other Islamic modernists in that he distinguishes very firmly between these aspects of Islamic history. The empire that the Arab Muslims established on the foundations of Islamic expansion had religious legitimacy, but in fact it was a worldly, political empire, despite its legitimation as a caliphal Islamic order. In founding an empire based on expansion the Arabs, and later the Turks, acted as "rulers and colonizers," and not as religious people. 'Abdelraziq states this insight and continues: "That new state founded by Arabs and ruled in the Arab manner was an Arab state. Islam, as I know it, on the other hand, is a religion for the whole of humankind. It is neither Arab nor foreign."[60]

At present, Muslims like 'Abdelraziq or al-Azm no longer represent a public choice and they are dismissed. The choice between secularization and de-secularization is determined by political Islam, to the detriment of critical thinking in modern Islam. Instead of a historicization combined with attempts to depoliticize Islam, political Islam preaches neo-absolutism. In the West itself, enlightenment has declined to an instrumental reasoning which is in itself part of a moral crisis of meaning. Cultural modernity is discarded by a postmodernism that is presented as cultural relativism. Among the intriguing features of the moral crisis, one encounters an alliance between Islamist neo-absolutism and multicultural relativism. The fact that strange bedfellows are involved does not inhibit relativists from arguing against Western civilization and its modernity, as well as against its model of secularization, surprisingly in favor of political Islam. This postmodernism contests the rationality of Max Weber. For instance, postmodernism supports the veil as a symbol of de-secularization and its politics of shari'atization. Rationality goes out of the window.

In the process of a rethinking of Islam it is argued that the necessary cultural underpinning for change and reform contributes to secularization. Europe is no longer the model. Despite all the bleak perspectives, an Islamic reformation continues to be the future prospect. One needs, however, to acknowledge that an Islamist belief prevails that presents secularization as basically Western, and therefore as alien to Islam. Against this view one may concede that secularization as a social phenomenon occurred first in Europe, but at the same time insist that it is not peculiar to Christianity, as some believe. In the main, the process of secularization results from an interplay between the structural and cultural components of change. The development of structures and institutions in society that promote a rationalization of the adoption of techno-scientific accomplishments is equally as necessary as reason-based thinking. The latter is not alien to

Islamic civilization. The plea for a revival of Islamic rationalism as the foundation of an Islamic embracing of modernity is no more than a hope. The delegitimation of the secular project has led to the challenge of de-secularization posed by political Islam, as it dominates today, as the most powerful public choice. In an age of the return of the sacred the process of de-secularization reaches Europe via global migration. *Religion in an Expanding Europe* becomes a topical issue.

Under the circumstances dealt with in this chapter, arguments for secularization in Islam sound like wishful thinking. Nevertheless, there is no alternative for conflict resolution in the Islamic world other than a depoliticization of religion. Only if religion is reduced to a part-system within the whole social system can it be kept out of politics. The sociological term for this process, as shown in this chapter, is secularization. Religion can be maintained for the believers' inward sphere – as is the case in Sufi-Islam. Islamic civilization needs to be freed from the abuse of religion as a legitimization for politics and violence. The focus on Islam in the study of post-bipolar conflict carries with it the accusation of a "cold war." This is, however, the reality addressed by Jürgensmeyer when he suggests that we live in an age of a *New Cold War*. It is a war between religious and secular models. It entails a war of ideas (see note 9) in which Islamists work against secularization in order to pre-empt what they name "abolition of religion." One needs to argue against this view in making clear that secularization means nothing more – as Luhmann concisely states – than "the social-structural relevance of the privatization of religious decision-making."[61] If this task cannot be achieved, then Islam can be abused to legitimize geo-political war in a quest for a remaking of the world. The result would not be the order that the Islamists wish to achieve, because they lack the power to do so. The outcome would, rather, be a world disorder. What is pursued in the name of Islamization, as it is already happening, is an alienation of the Islamic world from the rest of humanity. The alternative is secularization.

The substance of the analysis is the interplay of social and cultural change, assumed to be interlinked with one another. Secularization and de-secularization are the processes in question. Despite an acknowledgment of existing cultural peculiarities, all claims that Islamic civilization has its exclusive and specific patterns of development are dismissed. In fact, the contentions based on these claims resemble the concept of a *homo islamicus*, which is an essentialist expression of Orientalism. It is amazing to encounter this "Orientalism in reverse" among Islamists, who hold Orientalists in contempt as crusaders but who reproduce their outlook in a reversed manner. The claim of a specific Islamic knowledge, dealt with at length in Chapter 2, stands in contrast to the heritage of Averroes and Ibn Khaldun, who established rational knowledge in Islam on cross-cultural grounds. At issue is not merely knowledge of secularization and de-secularization, the issue is also a political matter. Politicized religion serves as a tool for igniting all kinds of tensions that lead to conflict. For this reason it is argued that secularization could contribute to a depoliticization of religion and it is an element of democratization in the Islamic world. Democracy is secular and it is based on cultural and religious pluralism, not on beliefs constructed by a political religion such as "*siyadat al-Islam*/Islamic supremacy." This contested supremacism will be introduced and discussed in Chapter 7 and subjected there to critical analysis.

In a nutshell, it can be stated in conclusion that the secularization of Islam matters to Muslims and to non-Muslims alike. There can be no secular state without secularization. To be sure, Islamists who engage in de-secularization are neither post-colonial postmodernists, nor representatives of a theology of liberation. They are, rather, totalitarian neo-absolutists. Among their targets is the existing world order based on the secular Westphalian system. The order they are set to establish in its place is "*Hakimiyyat Allah*/God's rule." This rule is envisioned not just for the Islamic world, but for the world in general. In their pursuit of global de-secularization they want to replace the Westphalian system of sovereign nation-states with a *pax Islamica* based on their shari'a. The reader is reminded of the references to John Brenkman and to the special issue of *The Economist* on "The New Wars of Religion" cited in the Preface. Democratic Muslims, as well as non-Muslims, disavow this Islamist agenda of a geo-political war of global jihad and instead plea for a secularization of Islam. This objective presupposes basic cultural change and religious reform. Muslims who are ambiguous and evasive (see note 4) are not allies in such a venture. To facilitate the depoliticization of the religion of Islam, a cultural project of secularization in society is inevitable. Next to this challenge is the necessity of learning that a pluralism of religions is the only way to democratic peace between the civilizations. This leads straight in to the next chapter, in which Islamic and Islamist attitudes of supremacism are challenged.

Cultural change and religious reform II: pluralism of religions vs. Islamic supremacism[1]

Not only in Islam, but also in other cultures, the contemporary call for authenticity (see Chapter 8) is embedded in the overall context of the return of the sacred in the twenty-first century. The analysis of authenticity is anticipated here because diversity and pluralism are both rejected in the name of authenticity. No prudent scholar can overlook the crisis of modernity that triggers the revival of religion. However, no religion exists today on its own and on its own terms, not even in Islam, which claims to stand above time and space. Hence the need for the recognition of pluralism. Amid the twenty-first century's realities, the simultaneity of fragmenting religious claim of authenticity and unifying globalization creates obstacles to the acceptance of pluralism. The prevailing simultaneity of the unsimultaneous compels every religion to be self-critical, in particular with regard to the claim to represent the authentic absolute so as to put itself above the other. Reform is needed to enable any religion to share with others a consensus on rules and core values that facilitates peaceful coexistence. This requirement is the basis for a successful acknowledgment of the other in terms of mutual recognition and equality. Cultural modernity provides a concept of pluralism. Therefore this chapter rests on the assumptions of cultural modernity and proposes to make pluralism universally valid. Pluralism is certainly not a religious doctrine; it is a segment of secular cultural modernity. It also stems from the political theory of democracy, which places all parties on an equal footing. As in the case of any religion, Islam needs to embrace the political culture of pluralism – and embracing democracy requires engagement in religious reform and cultural change. To tackle their predicament with modernity, Muslims need to rethink the self and abandon claims to the absolutism of their beliefs, which are supposed to be complete, for ever. This is an essentialized Islam.

These opening remarks bring us back to the major theme of the book, namely, Islam's predicament with cultural modernity. Certainly, everything is subject to revision under conditions of modernity. In this chapter I state a predicament with the culture of pluralism. The issue can be best demonstrated by the following inner-Islamic duality: there exists in Islam a scriptural recognition of diversity (sura *al-hujrat*); however, it is based on a repeatedly stated Islamic claim to "*siyadat al-Islam*/supremacy," which is based on the view that Islam itself, as "the final revelation," is the only true religion. Islam is thus considered to be the final religion, designed for the whole human race. This supremacism is in severe conflict with pluralism.

The predicament with pluralism touches not only on the relations of Muslims to non-Muslim others, but also on an existing inner-Islamic diversity, combined with sentiments of othering within Islam. To date, Islamic thought and practices are unable to acknowledge inner-Islamic otherness (e.g. *Sunna* and *Shi'a*) and to engage in recognition. The sectarian strife and the violence related to this issue, as illustrated in Iraq or in Pakistan, result from this lack of an acceptance of pluralism even within Islam. I make this reference without losing sight of the focus of this chapter: the place of the non-Muslim other in Islam and the need for Muslims to interact with others without an attitude of religious-cultural supremacism.

Introduction

In recognition of the necessity of establishing a culture of pluralism among and within religions, some religious communities have sought in the past two decades to engage in a dialogue between civilizations, which they view as a means to this end. However, the conclusion to be drawn from this experience is not encouraging. Based on these experiences and practices it can be said that this kind of dialogue has obviously failed. It is simply not working and has not yielded results. Dialogue has served merely as a window-dressing for organized events that have enjoyed great media coverage but deliver no results. Neither Westerners nor the leaders of Muslim communities have been honest in the matter of true dialogue, in which – beyond rhetoric – the real issues were expected to be addressed, but have not been. In the dialogue between religions, Muslims were not really willing to abandon the claim of their religion to be absolute. This criticism applies to all actors in the dialogue, given the unquestioned claim to the absolute that is a basic feature of any religion. This claim is not only an obstacle to dialogue, it also impedes a religious pluralism that presupposes an equality of religions. It is supposed that religions dialogue with one another on an equal footing; there can be therefore no place for supremacism in an honest dialogue. If this precondition is not fulfilled, then one can scarcely apply the term "dialogue" to the undertaking. For me, this was one of the reasons for leaving the Christian–Islamic dialogue, in which I was engaged for two decades between 1980 and 2000. The conclusions that I drew were devastating.

This chapter continues the major assumption of the book, that Islam faces great problems related to its predicament with cultural modernity. These problems extend to the idea of pluralism, as applied here to cultures and religions. In this context, the other is the non-Muslim. Acceptance of the equality of the other is the major implication of embracing pluralism of religions and cultures. I repeat the contention of the duality in Islam mentioned earlier with a reference to the Qur'an. This revealed text acknowledges diversity in sura *al-hujrat*, but elsewhere it states a claim from which another is derived, namely, the superiority of Muslims over others. The Qur'an views the history of humankind as a history of successive revelations by God, ending with the Islamic revelation. This revelation is believed to be based on verbal inspiration by God transmitted to his messenger Mohammed. The Qur'an is the result of this process and identifies Mohammed as "*Khatim an-nabiyyin*/the seal of the prophets" (sura 40, verse 33). Thereby, the history of religions ends with the conclusion that Islam is the only, final, and complete religion. The Qur'an states in the third sura *al-imran*, verse 19: "*al-din ind Allah al-Islam*/By Allah, the only valid religion is Islam." Muslims base their claim of the "*siyyadat al-Islam*/superiority of Islam" on this religious doctrine. It cannot be repeated enough that this claim is clearly an obstacle to true dialogue, which can occur only among equals. This is a basic requirement of pluralism. To accept the equality of all participants is a precondition of dialogue. If this equality is precluded, then there can be neither dialogue nor peaceful relations underpinned by pluralism of religions.

In my above-mentioned highly disappointing experience of religious dialogue during the period 1980 to 2000 I observed not only many Muslim evasions, but also Christian reluctance to address the issues. There are some religious leaders who prefer to play around in an attempt to avoid frank acknowledgment of their worldview based on Islamic supremacism. It is most disturbing to see the same leaders maintaining, in a self-congratulatory manner, that Islam is, by its nature, a religion of tolerance and dialogue. Thereby the terms "*hiwar*/dialogue" and "*da'wa*/Islamic mission" of proselytization are often deliberately confused. These terms have totally different meanings. This deliberate confusion happens when the terms are used interchangeably. However, there are other, straightforward Muslims, who – even though unpleasant – deserve respect. By way of example I refer to the Saudi professors Zaibaq and Jarisha who do not play around and who profess their claim to superiority with great frankness, so that you know what you are dealing with. It is not nice to hear what they state in plain language, and it is disillusioning:

> The recommendation to Islam to establish close ties with other religions [on the basis of equality, B.T.], for instance with Judaism and Christianity, could only take place at the expenses of Islam. The reason for this is that Islam is the only true religion ... To abandon this claim [of superiority] is to inflict a great damage on Islam.[2]

This statement stands by itself; it helps one to know where one stands and how the Muslims view others: ranked as non-Muslim, second-class believers. With the same honesty, another Muslim Salafist, the Azhar scribe Anwar al-Jundi, asks, in a book published in Cairo, a question that is blatantly phrased:

> Could there ever be in reality a dialogue between Islam and Christianity? ... In fact, Islam is revealed by Allah as the final revelation and

therefore it is not simply just a religion among others. … The point is that the politics of religious rapprochement is guided by one intention: To "destroy Islam/*tahtim al-Islam*."[3]

This quote suggests the existence of a "*mu'amarah*/conspiracy" (Anwar al-Jundi) in which "pluralism" and the "*tahtimal*-Islam" mean the same. If all Muslims were to share this supremacist view, then it would be better to close the dialogue, go home, and forget about the project of a pluralism of religions. If equality of religions is viewed as a "*tahtim*/extermination," as al-Jundi qualifies the expectation of abandoning the Muslim claim to the absolute, then there can be no dialogue. In order to facilitate recognition of non-Muslims as equals and to avoid Huntington's "clash" becoming a self-fulfilling prophecy, Muslims need to abandon this claim. To take pluralism of religions at face value is to engage in a clear pursuit of interreligious dialogue that requires all participants to focus on the ethics of faith and to depoliticize religion. No ambiguity can be admitted: for Anwar al-Jundi it is, however, as he states: "a poison, and a most killing one to Islam, if one reduces this religion just to a faith … devoid of a system of government."[4] One can respect the cited belief as a particular view of the world, but cannot escape the inference that people of this mindset are neither open-minded vis-à-vis pluralism, nor willing to engage in an honest dialogue. In conclusion, one has to refrain from talking to these people. Sadly, it is more than that. Anwar al-Jundi accuses people who support dialogue and pluralism of pursuing "a conspiracy against Islam" and he calls for a fight against them by jihad. His book on "*asalah*/authenticity" ends with the fear-instilling words: "Clearly there is an obvious plan behind the agenda of a religious rapprochement through dialogue: it is the Christianization of the contemporary world. This plan is the substance of world Zionism."[5] The implication is very strange! Why should the Christianization of Muslims be on the agenda of a "world Zionism" identified with "world Jewry"? Is this a variety of postmodernism that abandons rationality and objectivity?

This chapter on pluralism began by addressing authenticity, even though that is the theme of the next chapter, not of this. The authoritative voices quoted above engage furiously and adamantly against pluralism – in the name of authenticity. It is for this reason that the issue of authenticity is anticipated, but without losing the focus here. Contemporary Muslims are conspicuously obsessed with the perception of an Islam that is under siege and embattled in a fight against "Jews and crusaders." This prevailing perception of the other is an obstacle to establishing a mindset of pluralism. The related worldview is reflected in the name of the organization that was established on February 1998 by Bin Laden and his associates. The name is: "*al-Jabha al-Islamiyya li Muqatalat al-Yahud wa al-Nasarah*/Islamic front for fighting Jews and Christians." In 2008, the tenth anniversary of this movement was celebrated and the mindset that runs counter to religious pluralism was repeatedly endorsed. To be clear, this is a threat to non-Muslims when this mindset is combined with a call for global jihad against the non-Muslim other. The responsibility rests with the Muslims themselves to seek an Islamic alternative to the adamant views cited here, and to make their culture consonant with a pluralism of religions. The citation of an Islamic view that does not comport with pluralism is done in total awareness that Muslims need vigorous religious reform and a related cultural change in order to reshape their attitudes towards the non-Muslim other. I acknowledge that this requirement is not included among the popular public choices in the Muslim debate. Nevertheless, the theme has essential significance not only for a dialogue free of ambiguity and evasions, but also for world peace.

I borrow from Stephen Schwartz the formula "the two faces of Islam" to put forward the assumption that there could be another Islam compatible and consonant with pluralism of religions. In this context, I argue for a religious reform that abandons Islamic supremacism. In their encounter with non-Muslims, who are viewed as strangers, Muslims are challenged to embrace the idea of pluralism, which prescribes the equality of the other. In this regard, not only is honesty required, but also a willingness to break taboos. It follows that the issue is not restricted merely to an academic inquiry. Acceptance of pluralism[6] is also a strategy for peace in the twenty-first century. In this context, no supremacism can be admitted. All the rituals of self-victimization that are practiced when these claims are denied should also be altogether dismissed. A true dialogue or trialogue has to be free of blame games, which are great obstacles to the needed peace. One has to state candidly, and at the very outset of any debate, that acceptance of pluralism requires a set of acknowledgments. This is a challenge to all religions. There are clear terms for the real acceptance of religious pluralism. They need to be spelled out to determine whether or not they are mutually acceptable. An effort in this direction is made in this chapter.

These introductory remarks cannot be concluded without acknowledging that the concept of pluralism originates in political science, not in the study of religion. Pluralism relates to the political culture of parliamentary democracy (see note 6). In a democratic system, political parties are characterized by diversity, but they are expected not only to respect the differences existing among them, but also to share core civic values and rules in their interaction with one another. In short, pluralism combines respect for diversity and a basic consensus. For instance, in a political parliamentary system a socialist may view all liberals and conservatives as strangers but, on the basis of pluralism, is compelled to observe common rules and values in interactions with them. Comparatively speaking, for a Muslim, Jews or Christians are also strangers, not to mention those who do not want to believe (and have the human right not to). However, in Islam the non-Muslim other is not treated as an equal. Monotheists are tolerated as second-class believers, but all others are excluded. What is to be done to make Muslims view these non-Muslims – monotheists or not – as equals? Based on the understanding outlined, it is argued that Muslim supremacism is in conflict with the concept of political pluralism, as applied in this chapter to religions in their interaction with one another. Mutual acceptance on the grounds of equality and diversity is the core of pluralism, in addition, of course, to other core values that are expected to be shared.

In fairness, one must state that the religious doctrine of Islam – despite all claims to the absolute – is free from antisemitic and racist resentments, as expressed today by Islamists. Traditional Islam prescribes respect for Christians and Jews. The problem is that this respect is not coupled with granting them equality. The definition of pluralism that is used here, as a combination of diversity with core values and norms to be shared, does not exist in any religion, and Islam is no exception. What needs to be done in order to make it acceptable for Muslims to place not only Jews and Christians, but also non-monotheists (Hindus, etc.) on an equal footing? The answer is a religious reform of the inherited doctrines. The predicament of Islam with modernity thus relates to the issue area of pluralism that is examined in this chapter. I will not evade the issue, as some Muslims and some politically correct non-Muslims often do.

Islam and the non-Muslim other: the inequality of the stranger

There are many sources and means for dealing with the place of non-Muslims and determining how they are ranked in Islam: above all, scripture and reality. The Islamic view of the world separates Muslims from non-Muslims. On a scriptural level one can cite the Qur'anic verse: "Then, we have created you as divergent peoples and tribes in order to make you encounter one another" (sura 49, verse 13). This laudable verse is often referred to, however, in a dishonest attempt to support the erroneous contention that Islam encompasses pluralism. In all honesty and seriousness, one must correct this mistaken view. As repeatedly stated, Islam accepts diversity, but not pluralism. These are two different issues, and the related terms do not convey the same meaning. It is reiterated: pluralism is a normative concept of cultural modernity that does not exist in any religion. In contrast, diversity is a state of affairs. In Islam there is no pluralism in the meaning of relating diversity beyond the *umma* to a set of basic values, norms, and rules to be shared with non-Muslims. The acknowledgment of diversity in the Qur'an should not be confused with acceptance of pluralism, as is done by many Muslim writers. Real diversity and normative pluralism are two different issues.

Of course, there is a laudable tradition of tolerance in Islam; however, it applies exclusively to the *dhimmis*, i.e. non-Muslim monotheists. Other believers are classified as "*kafirun*/unbelievers," to be fought in the cosmic war against "*kufr*/unbelief." The restricted toleration of Jews and Christians as *dhimmis* does not imply their ranking as equals with Muslims.[7] Again, it is not only Islam, but other religions also, that view the other as an unequal stranger. To varying degrees all religions claim to be absolute. However, Islam is unique in this regard, due to its universalism and its claim to be the complete and final revelation, valid for the whole of humankind. On this basis, Islam's claim to "*siyadat*/superiority" is universal and global. As already quoted, the Qur'an states that Islam is the only "*din*/religion" recognized by God. A new reading of Islam is needed, to enable equality to be granted to other faiths, which are religions also.

As made clear, there is a basic Islamic differentiation of "the non-Muslim other." The differentiation between the "*kuffar*/infidels" and "*ahl al-Kitab*/people of the book" is made for the benefit of non-Muslim monotheists (*dhimmis*). These are the Jews and Christians, who are respected by Muslims as monotheists, though not ranked as equals. If this mindset is not changed, then Islam will remain in conflict with the rest of humankind, be they monotheists, other believers, or atheists – who have no recognition at all in Islamic doctrine. The conflict also exists within Islam itself.

Today, instead of the needed rectifying of inherited positions – i.e. upgrading of Jews and Christians and of all others to the position of equals – there is in fact a regression from what was achieved in earlier periods. Contemporary Muslims are falling behind the standards of tolerance achieved by classical Islam. The doctrinal differentiation between monotheists and "*kuffar*/unbelievers" is completely abandoned by the Islamists. In the thinking of contemporary political Islam (Islamism), all non-Muslims, including monotheists, are indiscriminately downgraded to the level of infidels. In the ideology of Islamism, people of other faiths are addressed with contempt and in terms of exclusion. The monotheists are perceived as building up an alliance of "*al-yahud wa al-salibiyun*/Jews and crusaders against Islam," as the above-quoted Anwar al-Jundi – representative of others, including the master Sayyid Qutb – contends. There are then the non-monotheists, altogether viewed as "*kuffar*/infidels." Certainly, this is not in line with the Qur'an, but it is – nonetheless and sadly enough – a concrete reality of our present time, and should not be overlooked.

In scholarly debates over the issues addressed in this chapter one often encounters confusion of scripture and reality. Some read into scripture their misconception of the existence of an "Islamic pluralism." Generally, they select some quotes and ignore not only the context but also all historical fact. It is legitimate to read a more modern concept into Islam, but wrongly to contend the existence[8] of pluralism in Islamic doctrine is to overlook not only the basic facts, but also scripture in its entirety. The concept of pluralism definitely does not exist in the Qur'an, nor was there ever a corresponding reality in Islamic history.

To reiterate, the pluralistic idea of acknowledgment of and respect for diversity emerges from the multiparty system. This idea is based on a framework of parliamentarian democracy and is not found in any religion. In the secular system of democracy, divergent parties are entitled to political diversity, but not to their own rules. Diversity is admitted on the basis of accepting the other and of respecting common rules in interactions with others. Thus, no difference can stand above democracy and its rules. Just as pluralism demands from the participants acknowledgment of the other as an equal player, the application of this political pluralism to religion, as envisioned in this chapter, can only be successful if believers of the different religions learn to underpin their interactions with a shared acceptance of core values. At the head of the list of core values are the principles of equality, of a shared understanding of tolerance, and of secular peace. The Islamic understanding of tolerance and peace is peculiar and lags behind centuries-long developments. It was laudable in medieval times – but not today!

The place of the non-Muslim other in Islam is founded on inequality. The demand for rectification of this situation is thus a demand for religious reform. Again, honesty is a core value, and it is dishonest when some Muslim scholars – as often happens in the trialogue – tell Christians and Jews that Muslims view them as "*nas*/humanity," with the inference of their being included in the "*umma*/community of Islam." This is wrong, because the Islamic *umma* is only the community of Muslim belivers. Non-Muslim monotheists may live in peace in *dar al-Shahada* – however, only as subdued minorities. This is toleration and not modern, pluralist tolerance. The ranking of the monotheist stranger within the *dhimmitude* is, by modern standards, discrimination, not tolerance. An Islamist placing of non-monotheists as "*kuffar*/infidel" constitutes not only a clear violation of human rights, but also an exclusion of great parts of humanity. It is cynicism when these Islamists claim for themselves Western human rights that they deny to others. Their reference to human rights is merely for instrumental reasons.

Today, under conditions of globalization and equally intensifying global migration, peoples of different religions are coming closer together and are compelled to live and to get along with one another. The people of the Islamic *umma*, viewed as the community of the Islamic faith, pour into the West, but with little inclination to an accommodation. Most of their imams seem to lack any willingness to accept that, in civil society, a minority – as they are in Europe – cannot impose itself and its views on the non-Muslim majority. The term *umma* presupposes Islamic superiority. Under these conditions, a "collision of faith" would be detrimental for all. Therefore, Muslims are challenged to engage in rethinking the inherited Muslim concept of the non-Muslim other's inferiority to their *umma*. Muslims need to put themselves in a position that allows them to liberate the self from "othering" the non-Muslim other. Those who indiscriminately quote the Muslim concept of "*tasamuh*/tolerance," which prescribes the toleration of "*ahl-al-Kitab*/Jews and Christians," shy away from discussing what it really means. The place of the Jewish and Christian other as a minority of *dhimmis* among Muslims is essential in the traditional Islamic concept of tolerance, which fails to meet current standards. In short, the Islamic concept of tolerance is out of step. Modern standards of tolerance and pluralism view the other intrinsically as an equal person. Despite the rhetoric of dialogue, one faces the deplorable contemporary reality of a "collision of faiths." Therefore, this chapter addresses all those points related to how Muslims view non-Muslims, in an attempt to mend existing deficiencies. Among the issues to be discussed are:

1. Islamic reform: this chapter argues for a rethinking of Islam with regard to its concept of the non-Muslims and reaches the conclusion that religious reforms are needed in Islam.

2. Tolerance and equality: religious tolerance is meaningless if it is not coupled with acceptance of the equality of the other. This is essential in relations among religions.
3. The application of the political concept of pluralism to religions: this theme leads to a rigorous questioning of Islamic and Islamist supremacism.
4. Religions in the age of global migration: finally, this chapter considers the risks related to unconditional giving of hospitality or even membership in the community to the other. In the case in point, namely Islam in the diaspora of Europe, there are two options: a) space for Islam as *dar-al-Shahada* – as demanded by Salafists and Islamists, or b) integration within a citizenship of the heart.

I cannot remain silent about this fact: the Turkish *Diyanet*, i.e. the state office for religion in "secular" Turkey, is engaged in building hundreds of mosques in Germany, not only as houses for worship, but in the main as centers for parallel societies, as an ethnic-religious Islamic space in Europe that runs counter to the integration of Turks as citizens of the heart. When Prime Minister Erdogan of Turkey, the Islamist AKP party leader, visited Germany in February 2008 he gave an inflammatory speech in a sports stadium where he addressed thousands of second- and third-generation Turks living in Germany. In this speech Erdogan vehemently condemned integration as assimilation and described it, in an attitude of incitement, as a "crime against humanity." The same AKP government in Turkey denies the genocide of Armenians. It also denies Turkish Christians the right to build new churches. All existing churches in Turkey pre-date the republic. Is this pluralism? Turkish Kurds are expected to assimilate and are denied all rights. Isn't Erdogan engaging in the well-known Islamist double-speak?

While the *Diyanet* of the so-called secular state of Turkey denies Christians the right to build churches, at the same time it promotes and finances mosques for Turks in Europe. There is an incongruity here. The AKP of Turkey pursues policies that are not in line with religious pluralism.

The major themes of pluralism of religions

Following the analysis of the place of non-Muslim others in Islam, in this section I move on to discussing all of these issues in more detail. This section sets out by restating that democratic pluralism of religions is most relevant to Islam's predicament with cultural modernity. Today, the majority of the Muslim *umma*-related world community live in Asia and Africa, but also with the status of major minorities throughout the world. The need to establish cultural and political legitimacy for the concept of pluralism in Islam requires a local-cultural underpinning. The needed Islamic legitimacy for pluralism presupposes promoting the spirit of a liberal and open Islam.[9] Such a spirit stands in definite opposition to the mindset of political Islam – of, say, Islamism,[10] which is based on cultural-religious supremacism. On a scriptural level, one can state that the classical Islamic doctrine views all non-Muslims as minorities. Therefore, Muslims always perceive themselves as the majority. According to this doctrine, Muslims are allowed to live among "unbelievers" only temporarily, because the rule is that they are the majority. Today, Muslims are challenged to rethink this out-of-step concept. They cannot escape from dealing with the issue anew in both its aspects: the view of non-Muslims as the minority and of the self as a majority. In the West and also in India, Muslims are the minority. In this regard, the application of the concept of political pluralism to religions is highly pivotal, and it matters to Islam all over the world, on all counts.

In relating religion to pluralism one needs not only to consider that religion is a "cultural system" in the Geertzian sense,[11] but also to refer to it as a source of meaning intrinsically attached to a belief system. For believers, religion is the sole truth. True, a community committed to a religion-based culture does not interact with other similarly based communities, as does a political party in a system of pluralism. This insight points to obstacles that cannot be escaped. Every religion views itself as absolute in its nature and claims. This absolutism runs counter to the substance of pluralism, if one insists on the major component of pluralism. If a political party in a democracy made similar claims it would be accused of a dictatorial attitude and then outlawed. In view of the fact that the issue with religion is of a different character, one is challenged to ask whether a culture of pluralism, i.e. of equality of the other, could be introduced at all into the concept of religion. This is a great problem which all religions, in particular Islam, face. Consider the existence of universal claims in some religions that want to be valid beyond their own specific community of believers. This is the case of religious universalism, which is very strong in the belief system of Islam and is combined with the religious duty of proselytization. This is offensive to non-Muslims.

In Islam, non-Muslims, even monotheists, are not members of the *umma*, as some wrongly contend (e.g. Sachedina, note 8). They are viewed, through the lens of religious absolutism, as strangers, regardless of whether they are *dhimmi* or *kuffar*, i.e. second-class believers or infidels. Nevertheless, the claim to universalism in Islam is specific in the sense that the *umma* is inclusive, not exclusive. Islam is expected to comprise the entire humanity, and every non-Muslim has an opportunity to join the *umma* by becoming a Muslim. The obligation of "*da'wa/ proselytization*" adds to the complexity of the problem. In the context of establishing pluralism among world religions, both inner and external peace matter, and this requires recognition of basic rules. In democratic pluralism all believers are equals, by definition. To reiterate, the standard set here matters not only to the relations of Muslims to others, as it also touches on inner-Muslim relations. The reader is reminded of the fact that Sunnis and Shi'is in Islam do not acknowledge each other; they, too, need to learn to combine diversity with the culture of pluralism, which fails in inner-Islamic relations.

With full awareness of the existing sensitivities, the related taboos, and the risk of facing wholesale rejection – with which I am familiar – I do not hesitate to state candidly that the connection between religion and pluralism is, in the case of Islam, an essential part of the predicament analyzed in the present work. As indicated, Islam is a religion with an absolute and equally universal claim which nevertheless believes itself to be tolerant – on its own terms, of course. Despite its worldwide spread, Islam stems from an Arab environment, and therefrom grows an Arabo-centrism that is set as the universal standard. In its doctrine, Islam claims to stand above space and time, as well as above all cultural particularities. The fact that during the course of its history Islam went beyond Arabia and reached Asia and Africa (and today comes back again to Europe) did not alter this mindset. There is an inner contradiction in Islam. It is related to the claim that all Muslims build up a cohesive *umma* based on a universal Islamic civilization. This claim is contradicted by the reality of an empirically highly diverse community, in which Sunni Arab Muslims themselves are a minority. They, however, set the standards. Here, the question is how to embrace a pluralism guided by core values that touches not only on Islam's relations to non-Muslims, but also on inner-Islamic relations. The ethnic and sectarian tensions within Islam (e.g. *Shi'a* and *Sunna*) and the cultural tensions between Arabo-centric Salafist and Adat non-Arab customary Islam are sources of conflict. The reader is reminded of my autobiographical references, in the Introduction, to a life between four worlds. There, I point to the means for overcoming the mindset of Arabo-centrism of Islam by crossing the borders within Islam. I was compelled to acknowledge the non-Arab other within Islam.

Along the line of these personal experiences, it is not a digression to include an anecdotal reference related to a clash in 1979 between the then Indonesian minister of religious affairs, the late Mukti Ali, and the Arab authorities of al-Azhar. The clash refers to the inner-Islamic conflict. The substance of the clash was an inner-Islamic encountering of the stranger. Back in 1979, the Indonesian minister Ali presented in Cairo the *"adat*/local culture"-based Islam of his country as the Indonesian variety of this belief. For many of the Azhar professors present in Cairo this was strange, and they were outraged because they believe in a single, monolithic Islam. They were dismayed by this encountering of the stranger and accused Mukti Ali of "deviation." Consequently, they dismissed this strange kind of Islam. When Mukti Ali was asked: "Are you Muslim in the understanding of one comprehensive Islam or are you just an Indonesian?," the Indonesian minister answered with admirable dignity: "I am an Indonesian Muslim."[12] A quarter of a century later I, myself a Sunni Arab, observed how this Sunni Arab version of Islam is being transmitted, with no respect for the other, to non-Arab parts in the Islamic world. In 2003 I was teaching at the Islamic State University of Jakarta and came across Arab preachers who were involved in the promotion of Wahhabi Islam. Those people convey the message to Indonesians that their understanding of Islam based on their *"adat*/local cultures" is wrong because it is not in line with general, scriptural Islam. If a Westerner ever dared to argue in this manner, he would be rightly accused of cultural imperialism, if not of racism as well. However, this does not happen when a Muslim is the person involved. The late anthropologist Ernest Gellner rightly criticized the existing double standards:[13] in the West one encounters a harsh critique by Europeans of European values and the self, parallel to silence on the subject of the fundamentalist, even totalitarian absolutism, of the non-European other. The final draft of this chapter was completed at the Center for Advanced Holocaust Studies/CAHS in Washington, DC. There I was studying antisemitism and encountered on this subject the double standard described by Ernest Gellner. The antisemitism of Westerners is rightly classified as a crime, while Islamized antisemitism is excused by a variety of references, ranging from anti-Zionism to an outrage of the oppressed/despised people. In such a dishonest mindset the predicament of Islam with democratic pluralism cannot be studied properly. It will persist unabated and the outcome will continue to be tensions and conflicts, so long as it is not addressed, not only candidly but also with vigor.

I bear in mind the above-reported anecdote of 1979 in the awareness that not only the world but also civil Islam[14] in Indonesia has changed ever since – unfortunately not for the better, but rather for the worse. In the 1970s, Mukti Ali was contesting an Arabo-centric variety of political Sunni Islam.[15] Today, in the new century, one can observe the reality of Wahhabization in Southeast Asia. Another battlefield is today's Europe. The Indonesianization or Africanization of Islam are models for a Europeanization of Islam. In contrast, the Saudi-financed Arab Wahhabization prevents Muslims living in Europe from becoming integrated as European citizens of the heart. The envisioned "Islamization of Europe" is the opposite scenario to that of the integration of Muslim immigrants who accept a "*citoyennité*/citizenship" of the heart. This pattern goes far beyond the legal status of a citizen. Political Islam, and Wahhabism also, disavow this prospect and even undermine it by all means, including the power of petro-dollars.[16]

The Islamic supremacist worldview and encountering the stranger

I address the prevailing Muslim worldview in terms of supremacism without overlooking two aspects. *First*, the dichotomy: Muslims vs. non-Muslims. There is a deeply seated dichotomist worldview determined by Islamic *fiqh*-orthodoxy. It is rooted in the rift between "believer Muslims" vs. "*kafirun*/infidels." *Second*, the Islamic tradition of encountering the stranger. There is a better Islam, which is open to accommodating the merits of the non-Muslim other. This is the medieval tradition of Islamic Hellenism,[17] which needs to be revived. These themes of the present inquiry will be addressed in more detail in Chapter 8, on authenticity, so as to provide an in-depth analysis. However, the two aspects of supremacism and the ways of encountering the stranger make clear the challenge to which Muslims are exposed: they need to rethink some of their religious doctrines, with the aim of taking a stand on their dilemma. The options can be stated thus: either integration of Islam in a pluralist world while abandoning the claim of *"ghalab/*supremacy;" or insistence on the formula *"al-Islam ya'lu wa la yu'la alayhi/*Islam is superior and nothing can be above it." This attitude undermines any rethinking of Islam and leads to the alienation of Muslims from others through a detrimental process of self-ghettoization.

For Islam to achieve an accommodation of pluralism of religions and cultures, which is possible, Muslims need to have an honest willingness to rethink inherited Islamic concepts of the non-Muslim other, and thus to change their worldview. In short, they need to go beyond apologetics and scriptural interpretations. Put in plain language: in a world of pluralism of religions there is no room whatsoever for supremacy, including that claimed by Islam, regardless of the justifications presented. This requirement is not fulfilled, for instance, by the efforts undertaken by many contemporary Muslim scholars. I do not detect an unambiguous farewell of the worldview of supremacism.

My reading of the writings of the Iranian American scholar Abdulaziz Sachedina on "pluralism" leads to the conclusion that this contribution is neither promising nor encouraging (see note 8). I read "apologetics" and miss a wholehearted recognition of the culture of pluralism of religions based on reformist reasoning. It is very telling, and also amazing, that Sachedina rejects the complaint of non-Muslims regarding their subjection as *dhimmis*, inferior to Muslims. The Egyptian Jewish scholar Bat Ye'or contests the Muslim viewing of others as *dhimmitude*. This criticism is not only dismissed as untenable, but is also accused as Islamophobic.

In short, there can be no change in the Islamic supremacist worldview if efforts to this end are not coupled with a real Islamic reform. Only this would provide a foundation for an Islamic legitimacy for pluralism of cultures and religions. Only under conditions of equality will Muslims be in a position to positively encounter non-Muslims. Muslim Salafists flatly reject this request. The Saudis Zaibaq and Jarisha state their views on such a dialogue in plain language, as cited in the introductory section (see note 2). This is a clear rejection of trialogue. It is also an adamant refusal to deal with Islam's predicament with religious pluralism, as well as an insistence on the claim to supremacy that determines the Muslim view of the world.

There are local and global perspectives to be addressed on three grounds:

1. Globally, with post-bipolar developments, one faces the question of the present order based on a Westphalian synthesis being challenged by political Islam.[18] Islamists who envision an Islamic world order to replace the existing one are not "extremist groups abusing Islam" in a "misuse of religion by a vocal minority."[19] This statement by Sachedina is nothing other than a distraction from the reality that a public choice is the issue. For a more promising Islamic alternative one needs an Islamic foundation for the political legitimacy of pluralism, not an Islamic apologetics. Muslims are expected to accept being a part of a world along pluralist, non-Islamic lines, which means

that world peace requires a wholesale abandoning of Muslim supremacist attitudes and the worldview that underpins them.

2. Locally, the same issue that occurs on a global scale applies to Islamic countries with non-Islamic minorities (Indonesia) or, conversely, with Islamic minorities (India), or with a considerable non-Muslim segment in the population (Malaysia). Only a cultural acceptance of pluralist thinking about the non-Muslim other can guarantee inner peace in all these Asian countries and their societies. As Robert Hefner rightly puts it, civil society requires a civil Islam and this can only thrive in a civilianized state of affairs in which non-Muslims are equal to Muslims.

3. One needs to add to these two global and local levels the inner-Islamic level referred to earlier. This concern can be illustrated most topically by the case of Iraq, where Muslims (Sunna and Shi'a) are killing one another, much as they are doing in other places (e.g. Algeria and Pakistan). There is not one Islam, rather there are cultural and religious differentiations within the Islamic community itself. In the absence of a culture of pluralism, inner-Islamic diversity becomes a source of tensions. These tensions assume the character of violent sectarianism. In a paper presented at Cornell University and published in *The Current* (issue 11,1, Fall 2007) I address this cruelty as a religious-cultural ethnicity of fear. If pluralism were to be embraced, this fearful future prospect could be contained.

Islamic "*da'wa/*proselytization" ignores the fact that non-Muslims throughout the world would not succumb to the claim of Islamic "*siyadah/*supremacy" as articulated by universalist Islam, whether in its Islamist, Salafist, or peaceful institutional varieties. The study of encountering the stranger in Islam is related to the quest for democratic pluralism and is placed in an Islamic perspective so as to provide it with an Islamic legitimacy. The issue has been placed within the trialogue between Jews, Christians, and Muslims (see note 1). It is argued that universal acceptance of the validity of pluralism of religions requires of Muslims, and other religions as well, the abandonment of their inherited claim to possess the absolute truth. To avoid a conflict in the world at large, as well as within each civilization – for instance, within Islam itself, where non-Muslims live as minorities – all need to stop imposing their own vision on the other, i.e. as an entire humanity. There is an inner-Islamic conflict between absolutists and those Muslims who wholeheartedly subscribe to basing diversity on a culture of pluralism that is underpinned by a political–religious–cultural legitimacy. Liberal Muslims are also in conflict with the claim of their civilization to universality with uniformity – despite the existing great diversity. To support the choice of pluralism is not to promote an imposition, but rather to present a general argument for diversity, combined with a culture that acknowledges it. One needs to seek Muslim support for this choice in the trialogue. Of course, one could, on selective grounds, seek a religious legitimacy for this view in the Qur'an, which teaches us diversity in the following verse: " … and we have created you … and divided you into peoples and tribes that you might get to know [interact with] one another" (sura *al-Hujrat* 49, verse 13). We also read in the Hadith of the Prophet the statement: "*al-ikhtilafi fi ummati rahma*/Difference in my *umma* is a sign of mercy."

As already stated in the introductory section, the cited Qur'anic view is contradicted by other doctrines. Add to this the fact that the normative approach underlying the quoted provision has never been reflected in Islamic realities, whether in the past or at present. Therefore, no scriptural approach could ever provide a promising avenue. Nevertheless, I refer in this inquiry to the scriptural approach for the sake of establishing a religious legitimacy for pluralism in Islam. One can use Qur'anic references in pursuit of this – however, with an awareness of the limits of the approach. Certainly, much more than simply a new reading of the Qur'an needs to be done by reform-minded Muslims.

In addition to the search for legitimacy for a culture of pluralism in Islam, one needs to acknowledge that pluralism requires safeguards within the institutions of civil society. It is essential that the reality of a diversity of religious beliefs is associated with cultural and religious pluralism. Only this can ensure full equality of the other. The admission of any religious claim to supremacy can never be tolerated or accepted as an element of the freedom of religious beliefs because it contradicts the culture of pluralism. This requirement must be established on legal and institutional grounds. One can forget all of the official pronouncements, made as window dressing in the Muslim-Christian dialogue, because they lack a corresponding reality and, above all, honesty. Dialogue is not a business of event-management, as it is often handled; rather, it is a serious means of conflict resolution.

In contrast to the outlined needs and requirements, the idea of an "Islamic state," envisioned as the nucleus of a new Islamic world order, is based on a supremacist worldview. This Islamist ideology is in conflict with pluralism of religions. Well-educated Muslims will find neither in the Qur'an nor in the Hadith the term "*nizam*/order," nor any similar concept. If we talk about Islamic governance, then it can be only a matter of ethics. The Qur'an does not prescribe a particular system of government, not even the caliphate. Therefore, the concern of Islamic legitimacy can be in terms of ethics only, and cannot extend to an Islamic political order. Cultural acceptance of pluralism within the societies of Islamic civilization, as well as in the relations of Muslims, in their international environment, to non-Muslims, is an issue pertinent to a trialogue. An Islamic political ethics of pluralism could be supported by an ethical norm included in the Qur'an'ic precept: "*Lakum dinakum wa liya din*/You have your religion and I have mine" (sura 109, verse 6). This ethical norm should also determine Muslim behavior in politics and society, and it should be the point of departure for inter-religious, inter-civilizational dialogue and trialogue that dismisses any claim to "*ghalab*/supremacy."

In any pursuit to avert what is called the *Clash of Civilizations* a reform Islam, understood as a civil Islam, has to provide a platform for pluralism of religions.

The heritage of Islam, in particular in its Hellenized rationalism, was the nucleus of an Islamic enlightenment. The philosophy of al-Farabi on the perfect state[20] is a model for a civil Islam in the twenty-first century. The reader is reminded of the relevance of the Islamic tradition of rationalism, based on the Hellenization of Islam (see Chapter 8), to Islamic reform. It is highly topical for our time.

The search for an Islamic legitimacy for a rethinking of Islam in pursuit of legitimacy of religious pluralism

Earlier in this chapter it was made clear that religion is viewed as a cultural system (see note 11). Culture, understood as a socially determined production of meaning is always in flux, and therefore it is never essential. It follows that the political culture of pluralism could be integrated into any cultural system, if its people were so willing. In order to make this happen and acceptable in Islam, one needs to engage in religious and cultural reforms, which are today not included among the popular public choices. The basic argument of this book is that culture matters to the understanding of most pertinent issues. The lack of pluralism in Islam is, in this sense, a cultural matter, related neither to economics nor to politics. The problem cannot be restricted to the despotism and authoritarianism of rulers; the inquiry has to be widened to include the culture that supports this kind of rule.

That said, one must add that any cultural innovation needs to be promoted in order to gain acceptance as legitimate. The legitimation of pluralism as a perspective for the twenty-first century world of Islam is, in general, hampered and undermined by Islam's unsuccessful dealing with its predicament with modernity. Democratization in the Islamic world is a daunting task in the age of Islamism. Even though it is a difficult and a dangerous undertaking, it is nevertheless possible.

As was argued in Chapter 2, "knowledge" and "culture"[21] are most important issues for promoting or undermining social and political change. When Muslims communicate with non-Muslim others about democracy and pluralism, there must be a common discourse – beyond Islam – otherwise rational communication is impossible. Following the Islamic tradition of adopting the legacy of the Hellenistic culture, it should be possible in our age to establish this needed common discourse in order to establish legitimacy for pluralism among religions and cultures.

In the classical heritage of medieval Islam based on Hellenization, Islam had a thriving civilization in which Muslim philosophers established an Islamic pattern of rationalism. This pattern was cross-religious in that it was shared by Muslim and Jewish philosophers alike.[22] In other words, at that time Muslims were in a position to share a discourse with non-Muslims. So why not also in our present age? In contrast to that tradition of an open Islam, today one encounters an alleged incompatibility of Islam and non-Muslim sources, which is put forward by the political thinking of contemporary Islamism. One finds this, for instance, articulated by Mawdudi.[23] In the West, people who argued with this mindset would be accused of Orientalism. The application of this invective to Western "wrong-doers" finds support. Are Islamists themselves Islamophobic or Orientalists in reverse? Well, they do the same thing. One could ask ironic questions such as this. It is, however, more promising to move to the substance, to avoid losing sight by becoming sidetracked in this kind of thinking.

Among those critical Muslims who do not evade, but instead focus on the issues, one finds the already cited law reformer Said al-Ashmawi. He states that "Islamism is directed against Islam" (see note 15). This is not to argue that the Islamist approach does not grow out of Islam itself. Islamism is an interpretation of Islam. The heir of Sayyid Qutb, the contemporary TV mufti Yusuf al-Qaradawi, is an Islamist who argues against an open and civil Islam and rejects pluralist democracy as an import from the West. In contrast to this mindset, the heritage of Islam was based on cultural borrowing from the classical Greek legacy. An Islamic grammar of humanism was first rooted in Islam, and then adopted by Western thinking. Unlike contemporary Islamists, Muslim philosophers in the classical age of Islam held positive attitudes vis-à-vis the Greek legacy. Aristotle was named by these open-minded and rational Muslim philosophers the "*Mu'allim al-Awwal*/First Master," whereas the most significant Muslim philosopher, al-Farabi (see note 20), was ranked as "*al-Mu'allim al-Thani*/second only to Aristotle." In giving this top ranking in the intellectual history of Islam to a non-Muslim thinker, Islamic rationalists demonstrated a high degree of open-mindedness in their encounter with the non-Muslim other. One does not detect this in the mindset of the contemporary purist and exclusivist Islamists.

The core issue of this chapter is Islam and pluralism, and not learning and cultural borrowing from non-Muslims. Nevertheless, the age of the Hellenization of Islam and the related accommodation of the Greek legacy by Muslim rationalists are addressed here with reference to the need for establishing Islamic legitimacy for adoptions from non-Muslims. In this sense, one can draw an analogy between the need for adoption of pluralism in our day and the accommodation of Hellenism in the past. This would accord with the teaching of the Prophet, who once said: "*Utlubu al-Ilm wa law fi al-sein*/Seek for knowledge even in China," knowing that China was not a Muslim country. It follows that cultural borrowing and learning from others, in the course of encountering the stranger, is permitted. It can also be done in the spirit of an open Islam. In other words, there is Islamic legitimacy for viewing knowledge in a rational manner, regardless of its origin and separated from religion, within the framework of a reason-based, universal discourse. Thus, the current Islamist claim for Islamization of knowledge is not only misleading, but also detrimental to the future of Islamic civilization. It complicates encountering the stranger and creates a major obstacle to embracing cultural modernity and pluralism. Islamism entrenches Muslims against the rest of "*al-nas*/humanity" and precludes any pluralism of religions. The alleged incompatibility of democratic pluralism with Islam is an argument put forward by Islamists and it does not grow from a mindset of Orientalism. By way of evidence, one can find this argument of incompatibility in the work of the late Indian Muslim Abu al-A'la al-Mawdudi. His dreadful words are included in his book *Islam and Modern Civilization*. Mawdudi argues in the following manner:

> I tell you, my fellow Muslims, frankly: Democracy is in contradiction with your belief … Islam, in which you believe, … is utterly different from this dreadful system … There can be no reconciliation between Islam and democracy, not even in minor issues, because they contradict one another in all terms. Where this system [of democracy] exists we consider Islam to be absent. When Islam comes to power there is no place for this system.[24]

This extract from Mawdudi expresses an attitude based on the contention of incompatibility between Islam and democracy and the pluralism that it implies. This rejection of democracy, and consequentially of the project of democratic-pluralist peace for the twenty-first century, comes primarily from political Islam. The view of an Islamic civil war becoming geo-political, as expressed by John Brenkman[25] and already quoted in the Preface of this book, is supported by the Islamist agenda that creates fault lines within Islam and between Muslims and the non-Muslim other. So how can Islamism[26] be accommodated, as some Western pundits propose? To establish harmony between Islam and democracy presupposes smoothing the way for intellectual open-mindedness vis-à-vis other civilizations and their religions, as well as their cultures. One needs a mindset totally different from that represented by some Americans, such as John Esposito and John Voll.[27] Once more, one needs to beware of confusing Islam and Islamism. On the basis of this distinction I argue that Islam can be accommodated to pluralist democracy, while Islamism definitely cannot, not even its moderate institutional branch. Islamism is not only a threat to international security,[28] it also hampers pluralism of religions and inner-Islamic peace. The double-speak of the misleading Islamists should not distract from these facts.

For a proper understanding of political Islam as an Islamic variety of religious fundamentalism that results from a politicization of religion, the findings of the "Fundamentalism Project" of the American Academy of Arts and Sciences are highly relevant and most helpful.[29] Islamism is the Islamic variety of the general contemporary phenomenon of religious fundamentalism. Of course, political Islam draws on Islamic civilization and on its worldview, and it does not stand outside the religion of Islam, as some contend. However, in classical Islam one encounters a different, open-minded mindset when dealing with the non-Muslim other. At that time, Muslims were in a position to embrace Greek philosophy while facing thereby only very few problems. Why cannot contemporary Muslims act in the same way to introduce pluralist democracy into Islam in a similar manner? Why isn't it possible to revive the tradition of Hellenized Islamic rationalism and incorporate it into a new tradition of open Islam? My argument is that the spreading political culture of Islamism, as a variety of purifying religious fundamentalism, is a major obstacle. Political Islam is developing into a public choice.

In the public debate on the tensions between Islam and the West one often encounters the intriguing argument that nothing other than a "misunderstanding" is at issue. Others believe that the actions of "fanatic militants" are the source of existing tensions. This is a distraction, not an enlightenment about current issues underpinning a conflict that can be peacefully resolved, if only it is addressed in a serious manner. The polarization not only emanates from the West and its competing universalism, but also is of a general nature; it is not limited to these "fanatic militants." In the main, Muslims are challenged to accept belonging to a single humanity (*al-nas*) that is not identical with the Islamic *umma*. The realities of the world in general belie this monolithic Islamic concept of a single *umma* that stands in contrast to *al-nas*, the rest of humanity. Acceptance of pluralism is essential, for both world peace and inner peace within Islamic civilization[30] itself. Therefore, no serious trialogue can ignore the need for a cross-cultural consensus on the common core of ethical values, to be underpinned by legitimacy in each of the participating religious communities. The envisioned consensus on core values and on pluralism could be the cross-civilizational bridge for humanity in pursuit of democratic peace.

In short, neither a "misunderstanding" nor fanatical trouble-makers are the issue. There is a conflict between two concepts for the future in the twenty-first century: one is democratic pluralism and the other is Islamic peace based on the belief in a utopia that unites humanity under the banner of Islam in a *Dar al-Islam* that maps the entire globe in one monolithic entity. If this conflict is not addressed, and if contemporary Islamic civilization remains reluctant to join in democratic peace, then the existing conflict will flare up. There can be no fruitful debate in sight if these issues are ignored or silenced in the name of political correctness.

The universality of pluralism and democracy as a political culture for peace among religions needs to be located within the study of the history of Islamic civilization, which has a very rich tradition of cultural borrowing that should be revived in pursuit of establishing legitimacy for the embracing of this new culture. Within the framework of such an endeavor, Islamic thought could be incorporated into a process of democratization, as a step towards democratic peace based on the premise that participating states acknowledge difference and recognize pluralism. In the course of encountering the stranger, conflicts emerge that can be resolved peacefully through dialogue as negotiation. In light of this argument, the adoption of pluralism – in terms of civic values and their supporting institutions – would be a contribution towards peace between religions and divergent civilizations.

In concluding this section, the basic argument can be summarized thus: the Islamic cultural underpinning that is missing, and that is needed to supplement the political legitimacy of democratic pluralism, has to be cross-cultural. This is also an argument for universality of values directed not only against cultural relativism, but also against a purist, i.e. exclusive understanding of authenticity. Of course, there are limits to pluralism, due to the fact that religious and ethnic neo-absolutism and cultural relativism cannot be accommodated to one another. In contrast, cross-cultural, i.e. universal – but not in the ideological sense universalist – consent among cultures to pluralism provides the basis for a possible world peace between religions. The late Ernest Gellner once noted that Western cultural relativism and fundamentalist neo-absolutisms are expected to clash. But they do not; therefore he asked, "Why?" Gellner responded that Western saint scholars bash the universalism of their own civilization, but stop short of mentioning – or even overlook – non-Western absolutist universalism. Gellner's[31] argument applies to the way in which the internationalism of political Islam, as an absolutist universalism, is viewed by some Western saint scholars. These people prefer to ignore the Islamic reality in which the mindset of Sayyid Qutb prevails. His call for global jihad, reinterpreted as an "Islamic world revolution,"[32] does a disservice to Islam and to Muslims. In contrast, it would be a better option to embrace a cross-cultural legitimacy of pluralism. This better choice cannot be promoted without abandoning the absolutist universalism mentioned, as well as the supremacist worldview related to it. It is sad to see that this knowledge is "not wanted" in most of the contemporary Islamic studies in the West, which prefer to turn a blind eye and a deaf ear to political Islam.

The self, authenticity, and the non-Muslim other in an age of globalization

For a variety of reasons, I again feel the necessity of anticipating some of the content of the next chapter. One cannot deal with pluralism and set on one side the way that people of one culture view people of other cultures. Among the basics in the agenda of Islamism is the Islamization of the self. This agenda is understood as a purification directed against the non-Muslim other. This is done in the name of authenticity, a theme to be covered in the next chapter, but it pertains to this chapter as well, and therefore it has to be addressed here – not in passing, but in a brief manner.

The issue can be presented in an illustrative manner by referring to the regime of Mullahcracy, an Iranian model believed to apply to all Muslims. Here, anti-Western attitudes to the non-Muslim other are supported by the claim to authenticity. The search for an Islamic legitimacy of pluralism that ensures the coexistence of diverse religions under one umbrella can only be pursued within the framework of secular democracy. The Islamic debate on democracy overlooks the issue of how Muslims and non-Muslims can live with one another in peace, other than under Islamic dominance. This is not acceptable to non-Muslims. Tensions and the dreadful assaults on Christians and Chinese in Southeast Asia, not to speak of the genocide that has been taking place for years in Darfur/Sudan, demonstrate the urgency of the matter. Pluralism in Islam is a concern not only for Muslims, but also for non-Muslims.

The overall inner-Islamic debate on the self and authenticity remains under the influence of an Arab world that generates valid standards for the prevailing attitudes that shape Islamic civilization. The Middle East is the cultural center of Islam. Among the effects is the export of Wahhabi Islam, which precludes any adoption from others, which is incriminated as *bid'a*. This notion has the literal meaning of innovation, with the connotation, however, of a heresy. In a mindset burdened by preoccupation with "*asalah*/authenticity," major obstacles are placed in the path of learning and adopting from others. Thus, the embracing of pluralism between religions by Muslims, as a cultural requirement for placing the non-Muslim other on an equal footing, is flatly rejected by Islamists and Salafists alike. In contrast, open-minded Muslims argue for giving legitimacy to cultural adoptions in encountering the stranger as a non-Muslim other. In this debate it is necessary to reiterate the fact – like it or not – that democracy and pluralism have neither Islamic nor Christian nor any other religious roots. The idea of pluralism of religions is based on a modern secular concept. In the Islamic world it is a recent addition. The late Iranian Muslim Oxford scholar Hamid Enayat rightly argued that Islamic awareness of this novelty remains not only weak, but also blurred. Muslims first encountered the new concept of pluralism and democratic rule in the context of globalization, and under conditions of the exposure of their civilization to "cultural modernity." Muslim intellectuals encountered these ideas in the course of the education of modern elites.

In terms of the history of ideas, Muslim thinkers of the early liberal age in the Middle East theorized about how to embrace democracy in pursuit of a reconciliation of Islam with "the other." The first Muslim imam to go to Europe, Rifa'a Rafi' al-Tahtawi, became there a student of modernity. In that liberal age, Tahtawi expressed in his encounter with Europe a deep admiration for the French culture of democracy and pluralism. He witnessed the July 1830 revolution in Paris and was impressed to see the representatives of the toppled regime being granted basic human rights. For Imam Tahtawi, this was an evidence – as he wrote – of "how civilized the French are and how their state is bound to justice." [33] Subsequent to the work of Tahtawi, early Muslim modernists and reformers were more critical of Europe because they encountered it in the context of its colonial incursion into the abode of Islam. But there were Muslim liberals who continued the effort at reconciliation of Islam and cultural modernity. These liberals failed, as also did Islamic reformers. [34] As shown in an early Harvard study by Nadav Safran, [35] these liberal Muslims evaded the basic issues and thus did not venture into a rethinking of Islam.

The earlier search for the Muslim self is continued today by a drive for authenticity on the part of Islamists. In this case, an approach of purification is at work. I turn the table on the Islamists and, making recourse to medieval Islam, draw other conclusions. To legitimate in Islamic terms my plea for an "open Islam" that is based on borrowing from other cultures, I revive Islamic rationalism. It should be mentioned in passing that the term "open Islam" is coined with reference to Popper's open society. In this mindset, I refer to the Islamic rationalism of classical Islam with an inclination to revive its synthesis of the Greek legacy and the spirit of Islamic civilization. It indicates an "open

Islam" that was passed later on to Europe, becoming one of the major sources of inspiration for the European Renaissance.[36] In his philosophical discourse, Jürgen Habermas confirms that the legacy of the Renaissance has been one of the basic pillars of cultural modernity.[37] It can be argued further that this very modernity is the major source of democracy. We should remind ourselves of the historical fact that the Renaissance is part of the very same legacy that grew from the interaction between Islam and Europe. Leslie Lipson notes the European awareness of Hellenism via Islam:

> Aristotle crept back into Europe by the side door. His return was due to the Arabs, who had become acquainted with Greek thinkers ... The main source of Europe's inspiration shifted from Christianity back to Greece, from Jerusalem to Athens.[38]

This historical reference is made not only to show how encounters and interactions between different civilizations take place, but also as a reminder of the Hellenization of medieval Islam and of its positive impact. The related heritage is shared by Islam and the West. The reader is also reminded of the fact that the Greek legacy is one of the major sources of the idea of the West to which pluralist democracy belongs. Despite all searching for "*asalah*/authenticity," similar bridges are needed today, but are, however, undermined by political Islam. The agenda of purification determines the Islamist mindset and gives it an exclusivist, not a pluralist shape.

For contemporary Islamists, authenticity ranks much higher than any learning from the non-Muslim other. A revival of the rationalist legacy would help to reverse recent developments and could effect the promotion of a cultural underpinning for the adoption of pluralism and democracy. That cultural legacy is based on learning from other non-Muslim cultures, and is therefore able to accommodate and to establish a balance between authenticity and borrowing. The embracing of Greek legacy by Muslim philosophers in late medieval Islam was opposed by the Islamic orthodoxy of "*fiqh*/Islamic sacred jurisprudence," which was able to ban rationalism from institutions of learning.[39] In this same tradition contemporary Islamists control the madrassas and undermine any enlightenment and rationalism for the favor of rote learning of the Qur'an, together with Islamist indoctrination. Despite these unfavorable conditions in the Islamic world, I keep faith with the argument of the Moroccan philosopher Mohammed Abed al-Jabri, that a revival of Islamic rationalism and of its Averroist-minded outlook is the only promising light at the end of the tunnel for Islamic civilization in its current predicament with a pluralism based in cultural modernity.[40]

The anticipation here of the debate on authenticity is not a digression of any kind, nor is it repetition. While pointing out the need for pluralism, I acknowledge that the related legitimacy has to be underpinned by authenticity. In order to establish a balance between the self and openness to others, one needs authentic sources. The Muslim rationalists of the past were able to achieve this balance in an authentic manner, in contrast to the current mindset of exclusivity that political Islam establishes in the search for authenticity.[41] This Islamist mindset is not consonant with democratic pluralism. It also creates great burdens for Muslims and prevents them from recognizing their predicament with cultural modernity. This statement requires a discussion of Islamism's dismissal of pluralism.

Shari'a, pluralism and the predicament with cultural modernity in an age of Islamism

I set out by referring to the evidence provided in abundance in my earlier work in support of the view that Islamism is a totalitarian ideology; it is neither a variety of multiple modernity, as some poorly informed postmodernists contend, nor an *Islam without Fear*.[42] A pluralist, democratic civil Islam that could accommodate pluralism is the urgently needed alternative to political Islam. Those Islamists who use the language of democracy – as is the case in Egypt – do not embrace the political culture of pluralism. As argued in the symposium of *The Journal of Democracy* (July 2008 issue), those political Islamists who act on the ticket of democracy are not to be trusted. In this context, the French author Revel coined the formula "Democracy against Itself." Political Islam is clearly one of a variety of religious fundamentalisms[43] not in line with democracy. This Islamism has to be distinguished from Islam, and one cannot repeat this distinction enough, because it is mostly ignored.

Historically, the Six Day War of 1967 provided the context for the unfolding of a political Islam that can be traced back to the year 1928. In the past, Qutb, and in the present, Qaradawi have given Islamism its shape. Both argue against pluralist democracy, which is alleged to be alien to Islam. Earlier, I quoted the Indian Muslim Abu al-A'la al-Mawdudi, who, in terms of his influence, is second only to Qutb among the major ideological sources of political Islam. The Egyptian Sayyid Qutb (executed in 1966) never consented to pluralism; he firmly believed that Islam would replace the West in leadership of the world. In his view, the two cannot coexist; one or the other has to lead. Huntington does not read Arabic and therefore could not know of Qutb as the precursor, on the Islamic front, of the idea of a *Clash of Civilizations*. Qutb encountered the stranger in New York, when he had a tenure there as a fellow in the years 1948–50. Upon his return to Egypt he wrote: "After the end of democracy to the extent of bankruptcy the West has nothing to give to humanity … The leadership of the Western man has vanished … It is the time for Islam to take over and lead … "[44]

The intellectual-religious tradition established by Qutb, combined with the legacy left by Mawdudi, gives shape to the work of Yusuf al-Qaradawi. This person is today the most influential Islamist writer of our time. He is also dubbed the "global Mufti" because he issues weekly his *fetwas* on world politics on al-Jazeera television – called incitement TV. Qaradawi is definitely not a voice of "liberal Islam," as Charles Kurzman contends in his highly misleading reader (see note 9). This Qaradawi is the one who invented the exclusivist formula of "*al-Hall al-Islami/*the Islamic solution," which dismisses all of the "*al-Hulul al-Mustawradah/*the imported solutions"[45] In his view, Islam has been contaminated by pluralist democracy imported into the Islamic world from the West. Therefore, Qaradawi firmly rejects pluralist-democratic solutions that are "strange" to Islam as "un-Islamic." The rejection of these so-called "imports" is the Islamist response (and agenda) to the exposure to modernity, articulated in worn-out concepts of war and peace,[46] by no means consonant with democratic pluralism. Instead, Qaradawi presents shari'a as a solution. Shari'a and democratic pluralism are by all means incompatible (see Chapter 3). The shari'atization of Islam precludes any Muslim solution to the predicament with modernity. The modern concept of pluralism is no exception.

Just as Islamic *fiqh*-orthodoxy dismissed rational sciences based on Hellenism in the past with the argument they were alien to Islam, one faces today the parallel phenomenon of the "imported solutions," such as "democratic liberalism," which are also rejected. Qaradawi tells his readers: "Democracy is a Greek term which means the government of the people," and then continues that "democratic liberalism came into the life of Muslims through the impact of colonialism. It has been the foremost dangerous result in the colonial legacy." As the reader will notice, Qaradawi's dismissal of the Greek legacy deliberately ignores the earlier-addressed positive record of Hellenism in classical Islam. The plea for a synthesis of Islam and pluralist democracy is based on this very record of Islamic rationalism and Hellenism, both of which are rejected by political Islam. This dismissal results in rejection of any cultural bridging and precludes any learning from others in the name of authenticity. This mindset is highly consequential for the Islamic encountering of the strange and for the trialogue.

Without a doubt, if there is no Islamic legitimacy for democratic pluralism that helps to support it with political, religious, and cultural underpinnings, this concept will not find access into the Islamic world. Contemporary Muslims are challenged to engage in this cultural innovation. The issue has to be taken very seriously in order to avert the consequences in a timely manner. In contrast to popular sovereignty, Islamists apply God's sovereignty to politics and present the model, as an alternative to secular democracy, in terms of "*Hakimiyyat Allah/*God's rule." The notion of an "Islamic democracy" is a fraud. Any model based on totalizing the shari'a in the name of authenticity results in totalitarianism.

The attempt in this chapter to establish an authentic Islamic position, based on legitimacy, for democratic pluralism is not wishful thinking. It is acknowledged that overlooking the power of political Islam while arguing for democratic pluralism amounts to a self-deception. What action is needed under these conditions? The answer is education in democracy, along with the necessary religious reforms and cultural innovations. Among these reforms, or even at the head of them, separation of religion and politics needs to be sought in order to smooth the way to cultural acceptance by Muslims of the political culture of pluralism.

In my view, establishing an Islamic legitimacy of pluralism is the greatest challenge to any religious reform in Islam. If pluralism and democracy are to be accepted, then political ethics has to be rethought. The Qur'anic idea of *shura* is an ethics, and not, as Islamists contend, an underpinning for a system of government addressed as an Islamic state. *Shura* means simply consultation. Indeed, a scriptural reinterpretation of *shura* does not get us very far. The spirit of Islamic ethics has to be in line with the pursuit of cross-cultural international morality, not with scripture. From this standpoint, I fully share the enlightened position of Hamid Enayat that it is "neither ... inordinately difficult nor illegitimate to derive a list of democratic rights and liberties,"[47] on an ethical level, from Islamic sources. Of course, this can only be successful in the spirit of an "open Islam" that goes beyond scriptural confines. To do this, a new reasoning and rethinking of Islamic concepts must be admitted in pursuit of political legitimacy for pluralism and democracy in Islam. These existing and proposed future perspectives are important for the trialogue, but they run counter to the fundamentalist agenda that is oriented towards establishing *Hakimiyyat Allah*/God's rule. Even though this notion is not based on an authentic Islamic concept, being a constructed one that has no basis either in the Qur'an or in the Hadith, Islamists have been successful in promoting it to a popular public choice. In the Qur'an and the Hadith (the only two authoritative sources in the Islamic faith), the politics of shari'atization run by political Islam has no foundation. In making this statement, I again make clear that no scriptural approach is used here, because it is not a promising one. In order to deal properly with Islam's predicament with modernity and pluralism,[48] Muslims are challenged to do more than simply reinterpret scripture or correct misconceptions of it.

The problem is a political one, not an issue for academic disputation. The Islamist notion of an "Islamic state" is based on a reinvented shari'a and presented as an alternative to a democratic state based on pluralism. In such a state there is no room for dissent. On the basis of *"tatbiq al-Shari'a*/implementation of Islamic law" pursued as a shari'atization of politics, neither the stranger nor critical Muslims could ever be granted the basic right of dissent. What is this shari'a that the Islamists have in mind? This answer has been given in Chapter 3 and so I will not repeat it here. Suffice it to mention that in Islamic history shari'a was never directly attached to *siyasa* as the politics of the state, despite the service of legitimacy that the *ulema* scribes provided to the state. In Joseph Schacht's very authoritative study of Islamic law, we read that shari'a and *siyasa* were separate realms. We also read in the work of Hamid Enayat that the shari'a "was never implemented as an integral system, and the bulk of its provisions remained as legal fictions."[49] In other words, the claim of *tatbiq al-Shari'a* advanced by the exponents of political Islam is similarly based on a constructed fiction. If practiced, as in Iran and earlier in Afghanistan under the Taliban, then in an arbitrary manner it supports authoritarian, non-democratic rule.

In reiterating the need for good governance and the political culture of an open society, Muslims are challenged to establish political legitimacy for democratic pluralism in Islam. As a Muslim scholar, I acknowledge the real tensions that burden this objective, and I state this not only for the sake of honesty and integrity. The search for a synthesis between Islam and democracy cannot be accomplished successfully without dealing candidly with these tensions. The spirit of an open and civil Islam facilitates this endeavor. In this regard, I am again in agreement with my fellow Muslim, the late Hamid Enayat, when he states: "If Islam comes into conflict with certain postulates of democracy it is because of its general character as a religion ... An intrinsic concomitant of democracy ... involves a challenge to many a sacred axiom."[50]

This insight is apt, and it creates great challenges for Muslims in the twenty-first century. This exposure to challenge should be debated, not silenced. The Muslims of today are expected not to repeat the mistake made by early Muslim reformers, who failed exactly because they clearly evaded. As mentioned, they were not willing to engage in addressing of any of the burning issues. The needed rethinking of Islam[51] requires religious doctrine to be subjected to human reasoning, a task that they were reluctant to undertake. Their way out was their pragmatic conformism, which could never provide a substantial cultural accommodation. A real change is required. This was clearly addressed by the late Islamic scholar Hamid Enayat:

> What is blatantly missing ... is an adaptation of either the ethical and legal precepts of Islam, or the attitudes and institutions of traditional society, to democracy. This is obviously a much more complex and challenging task than the mere reformulation of democratic principles in Islamic idioms. It is because of this neglect that the hopes of evolving a coherent theory of democracy appropriate to an Islamic context have remained largely unfulfilled.[52]

In order for Muslims to adopt pluralism, they need to engage in a cultural accommodation of social change.[53] Failure to do so results, among other things, in a failure to establish religious pluralism in Islam. In the interests of a trialogue one needs to address the predicament involved. The search for an opening for democratic pluralism and good governance in Islam requires a cultural-religious underpinning. The Qur'an provides the spirit for an ethical embracing of democracy, but no rules for a system of governance. Hitherto, most approaches in Islamic thought have been both selective and limited in scope and they have evaded dealing with a secularization of politics, as discussed in the foregoing chapter. This is, however, a basic requirement for overcoming the conflict between Islam and democracy in the existing states of the Islamic civilization.

In order to avoid a well-known misunderstanding, I will state clearly that by secular democracy I mean a system of governance that is separated from religion, but not from religious ethics. I do not dismiss religion altogether. Islamic ethics could help to underpin democracy with legitimacy. However, Islamic ethics should not be used as a camouflage in order to advance what is named "Islamic democracy." Given that democracy is based on popular sovereignty, which is a secular principle, no religious, theocentric precepts can be used to give democracy any other meaning. Just as there can be no Islamic physics or mathematics, there can be neither an Islamic democracy nor an Islamic pluralism. In their rationality, these principles are universal, as is the knowledge related to them. The political culture of democracy is not only secular, but also religion blind. The values, norms, and rules of this culture are both secular and universal, and they apply to the whole of humanity, like it or not! If this is not in place, then no democracy can ever prevail.

Conclusions

The efforts at religious reform and cultural change that are argued for throughout this book aim for an Islamic accommodation of modernity in which pluralism of religions is an essential part. The major idea of this chapter is that the political culture of democracy is essential to the peaceful interaction of Muslims with non-Muslims. In this context, dialogue is only thinkable and feasible among equals. If a religion denies others equality, then no interaction on the grounds of democratic peace can ever be serious and successful. Thus, pluralism – in the understanding established in this chapter – is among the basic elements that need to be accommodated by Islam in order to facilitate a solution to the predicament with cultural modernity. The political culture of pluralism, which combines acknowledgment of diversity with a consensus on core values and rules, has to be based on a cross-cultural morality. In this chapter it has been argued that this pluralism needs to be established on a cultural foundation within Islam. This task remains unaccomplished in contemporary Islam. The concept of a cohesive *umma* exists in parallel to a sectarian and ethnic-tribal cultural subdivision that is denied.[54] It follows that the major obstacles to the introduction of pluralism are related not only to religious precepts, but also to social realities. These are often imbued with religious beliefs that are both shaped by reality and also shape it.

Today Muslims live all over the world, whether as a majority (in fifty-seven countries) or as minorities (in the rest of the world). Islamic religious concepts define monotheist non-Muslims as *dhimmis*, i.e. as protected religious minorities, to be subordinated. This doctrine, to date unrevised, does not view non-Muslims as equals. In the exterior of *Dar al-Islam* as *dar al-harb*[55] or *dar al-kuffar*, the non-Muslim other is an enemy, to be subdued by jihad. The following hypocrisy is often at work: when atrocities against Muslims from other ethno-sectarian communities occur (e.g. in Bosnia) they are decried in strong language; however, at the same time one meets silence on the part of Muslims in situations where Muslims kill one another, as in Iraq, or when they massacre non-Muslims, as in Sudan. Iraq and the Sudanese Arab Muslim genocide in Darfur are cases in point. One is dismayed by the utter silence that prevails in all such cases. The saddening phenomenon of sectarian and ethnic fragmentation is combined with cruelty and violence. In the twenty-first century Islam badly needs to embrace a culture of pluralism in order to deal with fragmentation in multi-religious, sectarian, and multi-ethnic societies. It is a fact, in most Islamic countries, that this culture of pluralism is not in place. It cannot be imposed from outside. The US experience in Iraq has abundantly demonstrated that this is not feasible. There is a war between ethnically and religiously divided Muslims, not simply one between Muslims and non-Muslims. Throughout the world, and within the Islamic world, Muslims need to learn respect for ethnic and religious diversity and also how to share political power with minorities. When some Muslims engage in praise of Islamic tolerance towards non-Muslims as *dhimmitude*, one has to correct and then state that this "Islamic tolerance," by modern standards, is discrimination. The notions of *dar al-harb*, or "*dar al-kuffar*/house of unbelievers" are offensive and aggressive and they should be abandoned by Muslims altogether.

The present book includes a number of favorable references to the model of a civil Islam in Indonesia. The reality is, however, far from flattering. I am aware of the shortcomings of Indonesia and know that although there is a component of civil Islam in that country, non-Muslims are persecuted there and even massacred. Civil Islam is certainly still far from being the prevailing culture of pluralism in Indonesia, whether in the state or in society. Nevertheless, Indonesia is more promising than Egypt, the birthplace of political Islam and of the thinking of Sayyid Qutb. Qutb's idea of an Islamic *jihad*-guided world revolution is proclaimed as a vision for an "Islamic world peace" (see note 32). This is peace based not on pluralism and democratic good governance, but on coercion. Egypt is not a model for those Muslims who wholeheartedly accept the idea of pluralism of religions, neither is it acceptable to non-Muslims. If there were a wind of change in Egypt, the result would be rule by the Islamist Muslim Brothers. I do not share in the naivety of many US pundits who believe that Egypt would be better off under the rule of "tamed" Islamists. By contrast, the change of the Suharto regime led to a real democracy in Indonesia, not to Islamist rule. Indonesia is a better Islamic space for pluralism than is Egypt.

For the needed rethinking of inherited Islamic concepts, religious reform and cultural change are the proper avenue for Muslims to follow in the twenty-first century. The plea of Muslim reformists to rethink shari'a could result in an Islamic reformation. This undertaking matters not only to Muslims, but also to all non-Muslims. In fact, the whole of humanity is involved. If non-Muslims were to be subdued as *dhimmi*, they would fight for survival. The incrimination of non-Muslims as "*kuffar*/heretics" is a crime against humanity that can only be overcome by a political culture of pluralism. This culture would also contribute to ending the ongoing civil war that is occurring within Islam. This war is expanding under conditions of globalization to a geo-political one, as was argued in the Preface and in Chapter 5. Under these conditions, the establishment of pluralism of religions in Islam is a highly relevant task for the twenty-first century. Again, it is relevant not only to Muslims, but also to non-Muslims. An Islamic embrace of pluralism, together with cultural acceptance of diversity on a basis of cross-cultural morality, would be a contribution to world peace.[56]

Chapter 8

Authenticity and cultural legacy

A plea for the revival of the heritage of Islamic rationalism: *falsafa*/rational philosophy vs. *fiqh*-orthodoxy

Authenticity has a high ranking in postmodern theory.[1] Of course, to be authentic always indicates something positive, as applies also to enjoying an identity. There is a connection between authenticity and identity. However, when politics is involved in these issues the result is often something negative, as is the case with identity politics or with the politics of authenticity. In both cases, fault lines are established between the self and the other. Those who are committed to this kind of politics will view the approach of cultural modernity (Weber, Habermas) as problematic, or even reject it altogether. Other postmodernists may go further, and severely attack scholars, such as me, and flatly accuse them of what they discredit as "self-Orientalization." I cannot be accused of Orientalism because this verdict does not apply to a Muslim, which is what I am in all cultural and religious meanings. Therefore, by definition, I cannot be an "Orientalist" in the Saidian sense. To escape this impasse, some apply the term "self-Orientalization" as a derogatory means of downplaying my critique of postmodern "authenticity."

However, there are serious scholars who have written major books on authenticity, and therefore one has to deal with their work with all seriousness. The problem, however, is that most of the pundits in question are unable to read the relevant literature in its original language. In other words, they do not know what the claimants of authenticity mean by this term. In the case of Islam it means "purification," as is made clear by one of the leading Islamists and most prolific authors on authenticity, the Egyptian Anwar al-Jundi. Had Charles Taylor and other scholars who theorize seriously about authenticity ever read al-Jundi's work, they would have certainly shrugged their shoulders and reconsidered some of their thinking. Al-Jundi is of the view that modernity and the Enlightenment are projects underpinned by a "Jewish idea." In his search for "*asalah*/authenticity" he calls for a politics of purification.[2] He describes "*taba'iyya*/dependency" as the result of exposure to non-Muslims and therefore seeks a liberation that is understood as a purification of Islam from the "impact of the intellectual invasion," which is believed to be based on a "Jewish conspiracy against Islam."[3] Being a Muslim myself, I prefer to follow Max Weber and Jürgen Habermas rather than to subscribe to the politics of authenticity and its purification agenda, which can be qualified as pure antisemitism. Further, I argue that Islam has a rich heritage of learning from others. On these, for me, really authentic grounds I dismiss the purification agenda. In this chapter I want to turn the table and argue for another kind of authenticity, one that allows learning from others and denies the Islamist agenda of Islamic authenticity. This is the core idea and the substance of the present chapter, and it underpins its assumptions.

Introduction

In the light of the preceding chapters, in particular Chapters 6 and 7 on secularization and pluralism, the major argument for change in Islamic culture was made abundantly clear. But in a crisis situation change is not always necessarily a positive thing in itself; it could have a disastrous outcome. It follows that change cannot be qualified by itself alone. For instance, change in Germany in the crisis situation of the Weimar Republic led to fascism. On this basis, there is good reason not to speak of change from an indiscriminate standpoint. The debate on civic values, a culture of progress, and on enlightenment and rationalism provides a suitable orientation for assessing change in the pursuit of civil Islam. The world of Islam is in crisis and the change from secular nationalism to Islamism is by no means a blessing for Muslims. What does change mean in cultural terms? And why does the authenticity debate matter to this issue? Are enlightenment and modernity authentic or alien to Islamic civilization? Is an authenticity that is pleaded for by the Islamist Anwar al-Jundi in terms of antisemitic cultural purification an acceptable model? Does enlightenment matter? These questions guide the thinking in this chapter.

Among the boring clichés that are spread about Islam, voiced even by some prudent but ill-informed people – or by the self-styled "pundits" – one finds the disturbing claim that "Islam had no tradition of any enlightenment." This phrase is often presented as a well-intended excuse for the unenlightened attitudes and irrational behavior of some Muslims. However, it does not stand up because it is not sustained by knowledge of Islamic intellectual history. In order to clarify the issue one needs to explain in what sense the term "enlightenment" is being used. The term is rejected as "Jewish" (see note 3) and therefore "not in line with authenticity," as the Islamist al-Jundi argues. In contrast, Habermas provides a definition of cultural modernity that results from enlightenment and which I believe is consonant with the classical heritage of rationalism in Islam. Habermas expressed the matter in these words:

> In modernity ... religious life, state and society, as well as science and morality ... are transformed ... as abstract subjectivity in Descartes *cogito ergo sum* ... Kant carried out this approach ... [and] installed reason in the supreme seat of judgement before which anything that made a claim to validity has to be justified.[4]

Now my question is this: why cannot this European notion also be valid for Muslims? Is al-Jundi's claim to authenticity justified? In the course of looking for answers to these intriguing questions, I acknowledge that I operate with an understanding of modernity that is based on Habermas's definition. Against al-Jundi, I argue, with another Muslim, Mohammed al-Jabri, that the Islamic rationalism of Averrroes[5] is a cultural heritage that makes modernity authentic for Muslims. The reader is reminded of the distinction between cultural modernity (reason, emancipation) and institutional modernity (power via the instruments of science and technology) that was made in the Introduction and in Chapter 1. From this viewpoint, I question the common postmodern allegation that "modernity has eroded cultures, values and identities … The advocates of authenticity would attempt to repair."[6] Is this view, which is presented in the otherwise thoughtful study by Robert Lee, well founded? Is modernity really so eroding and distortive? I doubt it! Used with this meaning, authenticity becomes an obstacle in a debate on Islam's predicament with modernity. Are modernity and authenticity at odds? This chapter seeks a well-founded and balanced answer beyond postmodern beliefs and their related bias.

The chapter begins by arguing that efforts at enlightenment are based on a recognition of the primacy of reason. In this understanding, enlightenment applies to all humans and could thus be shared by most cultures. It is also in this understanding that an enlightenment existed in medieval Islam. This classical heritage of Islam[7] was and continues to be authentically Islamic. Efforts towards enlightenment were pursued in Islam by rational Muslim philosophers during the period of the ninth to twelfth centuries. This *falsafa* is known in the history of ideas as Muslim thought based on cultural borrowings from Hellenism.[8] Could this Islamic rationalism be viewed as authentic, despite the fact that it draws on alien, i.e. non-Islamic sources? Could this Islamic heritage be revived today, as is pleaded for by the contemporary Moroccan Muslim enlightenment philosopher Mohammed al-Jabri (note 5)?

For the sake of honesty and intellectual integrity, reference to the existence of Islamic rationalism in medieval Islam has to be modified and limited to the existence in Islam of the "*Aufklärer/*enlightened thinkers." These were the Islamic philosophers, who, it is admitted, failed to generate an overall enlightenment in their civilization. It is therefore not correct to extend this Hellenized Islam to the tradition of an overall Islamic "*Aufklärung/*enlightenment." Unfortunately, it did not happen. It is a fact that Muslim rationalists were not in a position to shape the worldview of the entire Islamic civilization. Nevertheless, just as Europe had its Descartes and Kant, Islam had its Farabi, Ibn Sina/Avicenna, and Ibn Rushd/Averroes. They were rationalists of the same caliber. In Europe, however, the thinking of Descartes was institutionalized and thus developed into a cultural Cartesianism, with the result that, as a reason-based (*res cogito*) philosophy, it was able to shape the prevailing European worldview. In contrast, Muslim rationalists were prevented from doing so. They were denied the opportunity to determine the course of Islamic civilization and its worldview.

Enlightened rationalism in classical Islam was not permitted, as Georges Mak-disi[9] tells us, to enter the curriculum of the *"madrassa/*Muslim college." Its influence was therefore confined to the circles of these philosophers, and at times to the court of the caliph. This explains why Islamic rationalism declined, and with it, Islamic civilization itself. Since the death of the fourteenth-century rationalist Ibn Khaldun in 1406, this civilization has not produced a single thinker of such caliber as it had done previously. In the Islamic world the rational view that Muslim medieval philosophers unfolded was not institutionalized.[10] Nevertheless, and despite all the odds, the tradition of Islamic rationalism was authentically Islamic, and it is essential to the classical heritage of Islam. Cer-tainly, the problem then was not authenticity; rather, it was power. The issue was one of who had the power to determine what was to be thought in the name of Islam. Was it *"falsafa/*rationality," or *"fiqh/*orthodoxy"? It was a fact that the Islamic *fiqh*-orthodoxy controlled the Islamic system of education – in which rationalism was blacklisted and outlawed. Thus, rationalism was denied the opportunity of shaping the Islamic worldview as did Cartesianism in Europe. This statement must not be tainted with the accusation of Orientalism. It is based on comparative research, it is an Islamic liberal view, and is not presented by any kind of Westernism, Orientalism, or Orientalism in reverse!

Following a centuries-long historical period of stagnation that was imposed by the rigidity of Islamic *fiqh*-orthodoxy (e.g. the closing of *ijtihad*), a cultural devel-opment was launched in the late nineteenth century and continued during the first half of the twentieth century. At that time Muslim liberals unfolded a pro-mising tradition of reviving the authentic sources of Islamic rationalism. How-ever, they failed.[11] Today, enlightened Muslims such as the Moroccan rationalist Mohammed Abed al-Jabri are few in number, but they persist in maintaining this tradition. Al-Jabri gave his fellow Muslims this clear message: "A better future for Islam can only be Averroist."[12] In the logic of "to be or not to be," al-Jabri adds that if Islamic civilization fails to follow the Averroist rationalist path, then it will definitely face the bleak future of a return to the age of darkness. To state this in my own words: if this future is a return of the age of darkness, it will be a kind of flat-earthism based on anti-science, as I argued in Chapter 2. In other words, the real choice for the people of Islam is this: either to be, or not to be. So what authenticity do the people of Islam need for a better future? If one were really to abandon Western Orientalism and Muslim fatalism, together with the culture of blame games, accusation of a "crusader conspiracy," and self-victimization, then one would concede that Muslims are fully fledged humans who are capable of determining their own future and taking responsibility for what happens. What authenticity Muslims choose is a Muslim choice, not a Western one.

In speaking of the future candidly, in plain language, and stating the com-peting options, the major idea of this chapter is that the legacy of medieval Islamic rationalism and its positive heritage were authentic in their orientation. The revival of this Islamic tradition would underpin cultural change and reli-gious reform; this chapter's plea is thus to take this path. In contrast, the thoughts of contemporary Islamism and of Salafism provide a non-authentic orientation because their thinking is nothing but a defensive-cultural invention of tradition. The Islamist concept of authenticity, understood as a purification (see notes 2 and 3) and, deplorably, supported by Western postmodernism, needs to be contradicted on two counts. First, it overlooks the heritage of Islam in which rationalist philosophers were and continue to be more authentic than the semi-modernity of Islamism (Chapter 11). Second, unlike these rationalists, who set an example for the Islamic tradition of learning from others (e.g. Hellenism[13]), Islamists are exclusivist, close their minds to other cultures, and even engage in cultural purification in the name of an authenticity that is designed in purely ideological terms. In contrast, the rationalism of Avicenna, Averroes, and al-Farabi[14] is intrinsically Islamic and – as stated – much more authentic than the invention of tradition by contemporary Islamists. Implicitly, the latter emulate European totalitarianism rather than the true heritage of Islam.

Authenticity and learning from the cultural other

Unlike the true authenticity that exists in the tradition of the heritage of Islamic rationalism, the contemporary, fake authenticity drive draws on a different meaning. Islamist authenticity precludes any borrowing from other cultures. In contrast to this thinking, it is repeatedly argued that Islamic rationalism fulfills the basic criteria of an authentic orientation. As already stated, it engaged in the Hellenization of Islam without ceasing to be Islamic. Islamic rationalism succeeded in unfolding a rich, authentic cultural heritage to which belong the most precious accomplishments in the civilization of Islam. Now, there is a very significant difference between the classical Hellenization of the past and the twentieth century's Westernization.[15] To begin with, the difference relates to the historical context. Clearly, the historical context of Hellenization was different from that of Westernization. This distinction matters to shaping the mindset of learning from other cultures, whether in medieval times or in the present. In the past no power structure was imposed on Islam. In addition, medieval Islamic rationalists, in their learning from the other, were more creative and innovative than Muslim modernizers of the liberal age, who were – unfortunately – more or less imitators, and not innovators. Medieval Islamic rationalists engaged in thinking Hellenism anew, whereas Muslim liberals simply copied items from modernity without really accommodating modernity to their culture in order to shape a new worldview. With reference to the hegemonial power structure, Islamists have accused liberal Muslims of treason in promoting cultural Westernization.

It is a fact that colonial Europe conquered the Islamic world and established its superiority over it, whereas classical Greece was no more than a historical record by the time that its legacy, Hellenism, entered the Islamic civilization via the translations of Arab Christians. It had an enriching influence, but without producing any distortions. The Muslims' relationship to this Greek legacy was free of burdens because it was never defined by hegemony and rule. Hence, the positive attitude of Muslims to the non-Muslim other at that time.

The present rejection of Western civilization by Muslims and Islamists is associated with the harm that Europeans did to Islam, whether real or exaggerated in their perception. The Hellenization of Islam was the background for the rise of Islamic rationalism in opposition to the scriptural orthodoxy of the *fiqh*. By that time, the competition between the two directions in Islam and their different agendas was an issue of authenticity. The tradition of cultural borrowing by Islamic rationalism competed with religious orthodoxy, in terms of power. During that period it was not the shari'a tradition that contributed to the flourishing of Islamic civilization. It was science and philosophy based on a rationalization of the world by Muslim thinkers.

In medieval Islam, people engaged in cultural borrowing from Hellenism. In the age of the Renaissance, Europe learned from this tradition in Islamic civilization. The contribution of Islam to Europe on the eve of the Renaissance was *falsafa*, and certainly not *fiqh*, as some not-so-well-informed Islamic apologists proclaim in their ignorance of the real history. Contemporary Islamists boast that Europe borrowed from Islamic civilization, but without acknowledging what was adopted. These people then deny their fellow Muslims any learning from the contemporary West – except, of course, the adoption of modern instruments in an illusion of semi-modernity (to be discussed in the final chapter).

It is most deplorable that medieval Islamic rationalism is today not so popular in the place of its birth, i.e. in the Islamic world, as it was in Europe on the eve of the Renaissance. A visit to some major bookstores in Arab Islamic cities would support this statement. On their shelves one will certainly find the books written by the "*faqih*/sacral jurists" such as Ibn Taimiyya displayed very prominently; but certainly not those of the rational philosophers Avicenna and Averroes, not to mention al-Farabi's *Perfect State*. Ironically, even Islamist and orthodox contemporary Muslims do not feel inhibited in reminding Europeans – as already stated – that Europe is greatly indebted for its civilization to cultural borrowing. This is certainly true. However, these people ignore the historical facts, namely that Europe, on the eve of Renaissance, borrowed rational science and reason-based philosophy from the Islamic civilization, not shari'a or its *fiqh*.[16] One is inclined to ask whether the orthodoxy in the past or today's Islamism are more authentic than medieval Islamic rationalism. Are today's Muslim attempts to embrace cultural modernity not authentic? I do not evade the question: do I use the term authenticity in a proper manner?

It is true that secular Muslim efforts at modernization have failed, among other things because they lacked authenticity. The backlash has been the rise of Islamism, with its invented formula of an "Islamic solution."[17] Is this an expression of authenticity? Robert Lee states: "The quest for authenticity requires a scale of politics that conforms to what is legitimately ours rather than theirs." He adds: "The search for authenticity is a search for foundations."[18] One is inclined to ask: what are these foundations? Are they inclusive, i.e. open to borrowing from others, or are they exclusive, in that they "other" all elements considered to be non-Islamic? Is the plea for authenticity a commitment to cultural purification against "Jews and crusaders," as al-Jundi (notes 2 and 3) puts it in plain language? Are "foundations" *usul* as the Arabic term indicates? If this applies, then we end up, in the name of authenticity, with a plea for *usuliyya*. This Arabic term means "fundamentalism." In a way, the rivalry and competition that determined the relationship in Islamic civilization between "*falsafa*/rationalism" and "*fiqh*/orthodoxy"[19] was a fight over what is specifically Islamic and what is not. Clearly, the notion of "*asalah*/authenticity" is a modern one, but one can read it into classical Islam to reinterpret it. This is relevant for the present, in that the contemporary understandings of both *fiqh* and *falsafa* are competing options that can be related to "authenticity." Let us see which option applies. The question here is whether it is legitimate or not to learn from the cultural other. Islamists dismiss such an effort altogether.

In the very interesting study by Robert Lee it is shown that the contemporary "quest for authenticity" establishes – as quoted – a fault line between "ours" and "theirs." Translated into the language of ethnicity, this is nothing other than an ethnicization of the issue, which ultimately leads to an ethnic conflict.[20] However, this issue is not the concern of the present chapter. Nevertheless, ethnicity and identity politics do matter, in that they relate to the current issue, i.e. that of learning from the cultural other. The contest between cultural-religious inclusiveness and exclusiveness creates an inclination to discuss in what way authenticity re-elevates "irrationalities of condition." Here I will restrict my understanding of authenticity to dealing with difference and otherness. These are the issues that matter to Islam and its predicament with modernity. Like Robert Lee, I too am a person who "mistrusts proclamations of difference and otherness whether they come from Orientalists or Islamic militants."[21] In fact, "the search for authenticity founders" on the rock of reality, as Lee argues in his validation of the claims to authenticity. This is clearly a scholarly concern. In view of the fact that the search for "*asalah*/authenticity" enjoys great appeal in Islam, limitating the inquiry to the academic concern articulated by Lee is unsatisfactory. To overcome the impasse, I propose to abandon the view that the core issue of authenticity is how to draw fault lines between the self and the other. This polarizing search targets even Muslims such as I, who are opposed to the attitude of exclusiveness and who, on these grounds, are blamed as lacking authenticity. I will therefore continue with my proposition to give the term authenticity a different meaning: to be authentic is to maintain the self while borrowing/learning from the other. According to this understanding, Islamic "*falsafa*/rationalism" can be viewed as authentically Islamic. In this sense, reference to Western theories and approaches in order to grasp and conceptualize Islam's predicament with cultural modernity cannot to be dismissed as "unauthentic," as is done by postmodernists and Islamists. To engage in borrowing from other cultures is an authentic Islamic mindset. In Chapter 2 it was made clear that human knowledge is universal. The Prophet demanded that the believer should learn "even from China." In the past it was enriching for Islamic thought to engage in cross-cultural fertilization. With the exception of the *fiqh* combating rationalism, such efforts at cultural borrowing were not charged as a copying of the other, because Muslim rationalists were authentic. The Muslim rationalists were free from the mindset of "cultural purification" which today stands behind the drive for a so-called authenticity.

The fault lines in classical Islam were not between the "self" and the "other," but rather within its civilization, i.e. between rational knowledge and sacral *fiqh*-jurisprudence. A party could, however, be charged with being close to the non-Muslim other, i.e. with "*ulum al-qudama'*/sciences of the ancients" (i.e. Greeks). The rationalism of the Islamic *falsafa*, as opposed to the disciplines named "Islamic sciences," was not "pure," but it was authentic. The *fiqh*-orthodoxy had the power to determine the curriculum of Islamic education. Thus, the distinction between *fiqh* and *falsafa* was lost. In Islam "*ilm*/science" was identified with *fiqh*. No debate was allowed and this mindset led to the decline of Islamic civilization.

The cultural change related to the exposure to modernity began in the nineteenth century. The first Muslim scholar to go to Paris, Tahtawi, was amazed to see that Europeans addressed something different than did Muslims when they talked about science, knowledge, and scholars. For the French, as Tahtawi observed in his Paris diary, scientific knowledge stood in contrast to the Islamic "commentaries and super-commentaries,"[22] which were undertaken for the interpretation of divine texts, not for an analytical understanding of reality. Tahtawi was also surprised to see that rational, not religious knowledge of nature and society determined the European definition of science. In Europe, a scholar is related to secular fields of knowledge – in contrast to Islam, where the clerics, as scribes, are considered to be the "*ulema*/scientists." The Arabic term "*alim*/pl. *ulema*" means both "religious scholar/cleric" and "scientist" and points to the identification of knowledge in general with religion. This correspondence between the worldly and the divine determines the Islamic view of the world.[23] The Islamic rationalists of medieval Islam provided an orientation for rethinking this worldview and altering it through a process of cultural change. This reference should be seen in the context of an earlier chapter: the analysis of the predicament of Islam with modernity begins in Chapter 2 with "knowledge," viewed as one of the three major issue areas of the subject. When Tahtawi was in Paris he acknowledged the need for Muslims to learn from others, and did not see in this cultural borrowing any conflict with authenticity.

In a study on anthropology and colonialism by Gerard Leclerc it is correctly argued that Europeans in the age of expansion attributed their power to their possession of scientific knowledge.[24] This view was even shared by the early and leading Muslim revivalist Afghani, who related the decay of Islamic civilization to the Muslim state of "ignorance." Along this line of reasoning, Afghani acknowledged that the rise of the West and its colonial rule over others was related to a superiority in scientific knowledge over others, who for this reason are viewed as "*juhala'*/ignorant."[25] In Islamic terms Afghani, the seminal Islamic revivalist of the nineteenth century, stated this criticism in pretty strong language. In order to understand this charge, one needs to consider the connotation of the terms used: in Islam, "*jahl*/ignorance" is associated with unbelief, and *jahiliyya* is viewed as the pre-Islamic time of ignorance, as stated in Islamic doctrine.

In comparison with the medieval Muslims, contemporary Muslims are truly ignorant. Historians of science acknowledge the influence of classical and medieval Islamic rationalism on modern science. In medieval Islam, science ranked high.[26] It was one of the major causes of Islamic growth. Why do today's Muslims lag behind not only "Western science" but also the earlier standards of their own civilization? Unlike contemporary Muslims, Afghani does not engage in blame games. He acknowledges the state of "*jahl*/ignorance" that prevails in Islamic civilization. Since the nineteenth century there has been a change, but it is not significant. In fact, reluctance to learn from the cultural other has reached new heights.

In contrast to contemporary Islamists, early Muslim liberals[27] and reformists were as open to Westernization as were the Arab Christians. With the rise of political Islam, sentiments have changed. Some look at science and view it as a basic component in the process of globalization, which it is believed will lead to a global civilization shared by the whole of humanity. However, this is a Western view and many have doubts about it. Those who believe in universal science overlook the difference in worldviews and values that distinguishes all civilizations. Given this background, in our time one witnesses the "Revolt against the West"[28] that is repeatedly referred to. It is no longer restricted to contesting Western hegemony, in that it is also directed against "Western values as such." This sentiment also pertains to learning from the cultural other. In the name of de-Westernization, the counter-forces of this drive are determined by a spirit of anti-science, with its related implications. Clearly, anti-science[29] in our time is related to these anti-Western attitudes. The Islamic attitude of anti-science prevents Muslims from dealing successfully with their predicament with cultural modernity. The instrumental adoption of science and technology[30] in the mindset of semi-modernity (see Chapter 11) is not promising. In the name of authenticity, it separates modern accomplishments from the cultural value systems that underpin them; it rejects them.

Willingness to engage in cultural borrowing and to learn from others is a well-known and essential aspect of cultural change in the history of Islam. In this regard, the time span from medieval Islam to the present is fixed by three movements: Hellenization, Westernization, and contemporary de-Westernization. This reference is based on a historical overview of long epochs that are related to one another, and on the methods of historical sociology.[31] I contend that there is a historical line in this time span. In its negative aspect, it stretches from anti-Hellenism in medieval Islam to anti-Westernism in our time. Underlying these two mindsets is a mentality of anti-science. It has contributed to retarding Islamic civilization, whether in the past or in the present. Stated in the language of this chapter, the search for purity in the past and for authenticity (in its narrow sense) in the present have created obstacles for Muslims which prevent them from learning from the cultural other. Today, these obstacles prevent Muslims from dealing successfully with the challenge of cultural modernity. By contrast, Muslim rationalists in the past were willing to adopt Hellenist rationalism, and they did so. Today there is an impasse. Could innovative cultural change and religious reform lead us out of it? In relating the two issues to politics I argue that averting the development of cultural tensions into conflict can be accomplished only by Muslims who are willing to learn from others. Change and reform are basic elements in this venture of opening the self to the cultural other without abandoning one's own authenticity, as understood in a broader, positive sense, not as a "cultural purification."

Why does the revival of the legacy of medieval Islamic rationalism matter to the promotion of cultural change?

It was stated earlier that Islamic sources rank high in the history of science. In the relevant textbooks one always finds positive and appreciative references to the classical heritage of Islamic rationalism (see note 26). Despite these classical, non-Western sources, modern science is generally equated with Western science. This view can be traced back to Max Weber, who was criticized, not so correctly, by Edward Said as a source of Orientalism.[32] Said was a literary critic and I doubt whether he ever seriously studied Islam, international relations, or sociology, not to speak of Weber's work.[33] Many of his rather too general judgments seem to be highly presumptuous. At issue is the cultural modernity in which Western modern science is rooted, not Orientalism. By making reference to historical continuity one can also refer to the facts concerning the multifaceted historical origins of modern science. In contrasting this with the search for authenticity, the issues become complicated. The reason for this is that science is universal and is not restricted to a cultural particularism, as is the case with authenticity. It is no contradiction to promote universal thinking in Islam, and to argue that it could also be authentic. One needs a cultural basis for the acceptance of universal knowledge. I think that the heritage of Islamic medieval rationalism could serve as a model.

In the history of science one finds references to Islamic contributions as part and parcel of *The Beginnings of Western Science*.[34] An essential part of these beginnings is the unfolding of a rational view of the world, described by Max Weber – as repeatedly cited – in terms of an *"Entzauberung/*disenchantment" of the world.[35] This universal argument is essential to countering the instrumental use of science by Islamists and their authenticity-ruled drive, in their *"Aslamat al-ulum/*Islamization of sciences,"[36] to dissociate science from its cultural roots. The Frankfurt School sociologist Franz Borkenau provided us with historical evidence that the emergence of modern science has been underpinned by the unfolding of a secular, and thus a distinctly modern, *"Weltbild/*worldview."[37] The cultural roots of modern science are located in this rational view of the world, which facilitates rationalization of the cosmos. In contrast to this, the Islamic worldview (see the references in notes 23 and 30) is theocentric. The worldview of cultural modernity bases knowledge on reason and decouples it from religious beliefs. Is this a heretical view, and also specifically European in its nature? Is it Orientalism to refer to it?

Some self-congratulating postmodernists tend to admit anti-secular views, to the extent of sanctioning "anti-science." This often happens in the name of authenticity. In contrast, in classical Islam there existed an Islamic rationalism that shared the scientific view of the world. Islamic philosophers were in conflict with the counter-visions of *fiqh*-orthodoxy, which condemned rationalism as a heresy. In order to introduce science into Islam not only as an instrumental adoption, but also as a worldview, it seems that the legacy of Islamic rationalism would be much more authentic than contemporary Islamist anti-science.

The concept of "*Weltbild*/worldview" is not exclusively used in the history of science, since it covers a broader scope. According to the Harvard historian of science Gerald Holton, who operates with the literal translation "world picture" for the German term *Weltbild*, this notion means "a system that helps us understand how the world as a whole operates, and that acts as a cohesive force for community formation."[38]

A rational worldview thus contributes to a rationalization of the cosmos. This understanding resembles the concept used in my comprehensive intellectual history of Islam (see note 19), which suggests seeing in the historical record of medieval Islamic rationalism a contribution to a civilizational worldview based on rationality in Islam. Had Islamic rationalism been successful in shaping the basic cultural patterns of the *Islamic Weltanschauung*, then there would have been a truly Islamic enlightenment. The civilization of Islam would also have developed differently. Islamic civilization, and not the West, could have been a center for the world. However, world history developed otherwise.[39]

On the basis of modernity, Europe became the center of the world. The circumstances favorable to the cultural and structural institutionalization of rational knowledge and science made this possible. In Islam, only divine, i.e. revealed, knowledge was institutionally established as uncontestable. Everything else was eliminated as "heretical." The belief that all human knowledge has to be derived from the Qur'anic revelation (see Chapter 2) retarded the people of Islam and their civilization. The medieval *faqih* al-Mawardi countered Islamic rationalism, which accepted the primacy of human reason as the source of knowledge, by maintaining two rival options: "*bi al-wahi aw bi al-aql*/to base everything either on revelation or on human reason"! This was a declaration of war on Hellenized Islamic rationalism; the *fiqh*-orthodoxy waged that war and won it – to the detriment of Islamic civilization.

The individual reasoning of man is not accepted in traditional and religious worldviews, except when it was viewed as *ijtihad*, which was closed by the *fiqh*-orthodoxy. That created obstacles, for "a world picture ... can (and often does) exclude the individual's private, personal, imaginate parts of experience."[40] This characteristic mostly applies to "world pictures" based on the combination of a concept of the divine and on collectivity. It is obviously clear that the sources of scientific innovations are chiefly individual experience and thinking. This runs counter to the Islamic view that only the Qu'ran can be the authentic source of *ilm* and that a Muslim can be a true believer only on the basis of being a part of the *umma*. Today, modern science requires of the civilization of Islam – as it did in the past – not only a cultural change, but also a change in its prevailing worldview. Islamic reformism and the modernism of the nineteenth and twentieth centuries were evasive. They restricted their thinking to legitimating the ad hoc adoption of items of modernity, while the pre-modern view of the world continued to prevail unchanged. The result has been a simultaneity of the unsimultaneous: modern science and a pre-modern worldview existing side by side. These evasions continue to prevail even in the thinking of contemporary Muslim modernizers (e.g. Arkoun and earlier An-Na'im), who speak of "rethinking Islam" and "Islamic reformation" but fail to deliver what they pronounce.

The Muslim medieval philosopher Averroes realized that reason-based and divine knowledge are related to two distinctly different domains. These are rational knowledge and religious belief. In this determination there is diversity in faith and cultures – Islamic, Jewish, or Christian – but it does not apply to human rational knowledge because this is universal. Given the fact that reason is humane and has neither religion nor ethnicity, rational science is universal and religious science is definitely not. These are two totally different situations, as will be explained later on. In my view, the current concept that claims, in the name of authenticity, an "*Aslamat al-'ulum/*Islamization of sciences"[41] – as pursued by contemporary Salafists and Islamic fundamentalists – results in anti-science as the counter-vision to the rational view of the world. Certainly, anti-science can be also expressed in secular thinking. The current discontent with institutional modernity and with its late industrial civilization triggers a wholesale rejection of cultural modernity. The outcome is a postmodernism,[42] and some postmodernists practically embrace the neo-absolutism of political Islam and believe that thereby they are reading their views into Islam – of course, mistakenly. Theodor Adorno used to argue that "inconsistent thinking is a sign of sloppiness."

Turning to Gerald Holton, who points to anti-modern characteristics of "pseudo-scientific nonsense … that manages to pass itself off as an alternative science,"[43] I join his reasoning in dealing with the postmodern, secular anti-science phenomenon. I also share Holton's regrets that these people fail to see "more urgent problems facing our civilization … [like] fundamentalism."[44] Some biased and self-obsessed Western postmodernists fail to understand the current issues, and, of course, Islamic civilization as well. It is best simply to ignore this kind of work.

Apart from some postmodernists, there are a few Muslims who teach a discipline at British universities named "post-colonial studies" and who denounce the rational worldview based on modern science as "epistemological imperialism."[45] What is the message? Could it be that irrationality is more authentic to

Muslims? If a Westerner argues that irrationality is the authenticity of non-Western peoples and that Cartesianism is a European peculiarity imposed as "imperialism" on Muslims, he or she would be rightly accused of racism. Why do the "post-colonial studies" pursued by some Muslims have the objective of reversing the "challenge by Western civilization"?

The fact of a "challenge of knowledge" is reversed by some through "the de-Westernization of knowledge." In Chapter 2 it was made clear how elusive is this agenda in the field of knowledge.[46] Some post-colonial studies seem to be ill-advised, misguiding, and they overlook the fact that Islamic rationalists were open to Hellenization, i.e. to rationalism. For medieval Muslim rationalists, the rational legacy of Hellenism was not an "Aristotelian imperialism." Those who identify rationalization with Westernization close their own minds in the name of maintaining authenticity. This venture ends up in submission to fundamental-ism.[47] The challenge is to Muslims themselves; it is not the other way around. The deplorable drive to irrationality, in the name of authenticity, makes it necessary to make an effort to revive Islamic rationalism in opposition to some misguided Muslims. The classical heritage of Islam, which is based on this rationalism, is authentically Islamic. It is referred to here with this meaning.

In terms of the history of ideas, there is a historical continuity that stretches from the traditional hostility of Islamic orthodoxy vis-à-vis Hellenization in Islam up to the contemporary anti-scientific drive of Islamists towards de-Westernization. The Islamist mindset rejects reason-based knowledge and this is a disservice to contemporary Islam. Between the ninth and the twelfth centuries a Hellenized Islamic tradition of rationalism evolved and it was passed on to Europe, but it was prevented by the anti-science of the *fiqh*-orthodoxy of medieval Islam from becoming established in Islamic civilization. It is ridiculous to make the accusation of Islamophobia when political Islam and its antecedents in the Salafist *fiqh* tradition are criticized along with *fiqh*-orthodoxy. Their project of purification in the name of Islamic authenticity stands in contrast to the acceptance in medieval Islam of the primacy of reason, i.e. of a kind of secular *Weltbild* as a rational view of the world to be based in Islam, in Islamic terms consonant with universal rationality. In the same manner, one must defend Cartesianism and Max Weber against the irrationality of some post-colonial studies. Muslims in the diaspora are advised to embrace the rational view of the world.

Regrettably, rational philosophers in Islam were not so audacious, but rather they were at pains to avoid a clash with the dominant Islamic *fiqh*-orthodoxy. They were thus willing to make peace with its institutions. But this conciliatory attitude did not pay off. By contrast, philosophers of the European Enlight-enment (e.g. Voltaire) were audacious, and therefore they were more successful. The *fiqh*-orthodoxy in Islam was very aggressive in its rivalry towards rational philosophy. This is an established fact of Islamic history. It ended with the per-secution of reason-based philosophers and the burning of their books. This is a sign of darkness in Islamic history.[48] The related mindset continues to prevail in book burnings today (e.g. Salman Rushdie). Muslims do this today not only in the abode of Islam, but even in the diaspora of Europe's open society. They do not criticize; they burn, and this is inexcusable.

This section concludes by arguing for a reason-based worldview so as to establish a basis for a proper dealing with Islam's predicament with cultural modernity. To this end, the revival of Islamic rationalism could provide not only an orientation for cultural change, but also a cultural basis for the authenticity of this venture, so as to counter the rejection of this rationalism in the name of an obscure search for cultural authenticity. As quoted at the outset, "authenticity re-elevates the irrationalities of condition" (Robert Lee) and it also argues "against the forces of science and reason." Thus, contemporary Islamists read the *fiqh*-scholar Ibn Taimiyya,[49] definitely not the Islamic rationalists al-Farabi, Ibn Sina, or Ibn Rushd. As Robert Lee puts it: "The search for an authentic way of acting in the Islamic world means that other paths ... are deficient."[50]

Today, the search for authenticity in this narrow understanding signals a major cultural trend. In this context, one often finds political power (e.g. the contemporary political forces of de-secularization in Islam) married to anti-science (e.g. "Islamization of knowledge and sciences"). This alliance undermines any innovative cultural change, not to mention religious reform. A revival of Islamic rationalism seems to be the better alternative, and is therefore strongly recommended in this chapter. In political Islam, authenticity is used to create tensions. It is unfortunate that most Muslim scholars – including the liberals among them – prefer to evade this issue and to remain silent on it. I wish that those Muslims had the courage and the vigor to address the issues, rather than remaining evasive.

The relevance and authenticity of the Hellenization of political thought in medieval Islam

In the history of ideas, the process of Hellenization in Islam affected the philosophical reasoning of Muslim thinkers. They introduced Hellenism into the Islamic civilization, thus creating a new tradition. In assessing this cultural borrowing, based on the translation of the Greek heritage into Arabic, the credit for the impetus must go foremost to the Christian-Nestorian translators. The historian of science Lindberg tells us: "By the year 1000 A.D. almost the entire corpus of Greek medicine, natural philosophy, and mathematical science had been rendered into usable Arabic visions." Then Lindberg asks: "Was there a religious price that had to be paid for the acceptance of Greek science?"[51] The answer is yes, and those who engaged in this venture paid dearly. The looming forces of Islamic orthodoxy tried to prevent it. The unwanted trend towards rationalization, as secularization, was successfully halted by the *fiqh*-orthodoxy.

With reference to the place of translations in culture, there is today a parallel with the past. According to the third UNDP report on knowledge and society in the Middle East, the quality and quantity of translations of scientific and cultural works from European languages into Arabic has deteriorated greatly in recent years. The result is that today Arab readers do not have access to literary and scientific productions beyond those of their own societies. Instead, they celebrate the self in rhetorical pronouncements. It is a fact that translations into Arabic from foreign languages are declining, even becoming rare. This corresponds with a great deficiency in knowledge and teaching of foreign languages.[52] Arab Muslims confine themselves to reciting the Qur'an, and non-Arab Muslims learn Arabic in order to do the same. Authenticity declines into restricting knowledge to that of an authoritative divine text. This piety may not be dangerous, but if politicized – as is done by al-Jundi (notes 2 and 3) – it then becomes a totalitarian agenda for the purification of knowledge and culture. This is detrimental not only to Islam and its peoples, but also to non-Muslims, who have to interact and live with them.

In the past, the translation of the classical Greek legacy into Arabic removed the linguistic barrier between civilizations. There were cultural obstacles that prevented the institutionalization of that borrowing. In Arabic the terms "science" and "knowledge" are both covered by the one word *'ilm*, as shown earlier by the reference to the Muslim Tahtawi's visit to Paris in the nineteenth century. If knowledge and all of its sources in culture and science are reduced to one religious texture, as prevails today, then Muslims will not be able to catch up with others – not only with the West, but also with emerging China and India, as well as with Japan.

In medieval Islam and also today, the conflict revolves around the question how to determine the substance and sources of knowledge (see Chapter 2). For Islamic orthodoxy, the foremost knowledge is that transmitted through the revelation fixed in the Qur'an. The acceptance of Greek science and the philosophy of Aristotle stood in opposition to this understanding and added a new source of knowledge, i.e. that acquired by human reason. At that time, the adopted new epistemology contributed to a clash between *fiqh* and *falsafa*. The continuing rivalry between Islamic orthodoxy and reason-based Muslim thinkers lasted from the medieval Hellenization of Islam to contemporary Islamic rationalism. The plea for a revival of this buried, reason-based tradition in Islam is also an argument for its authenticity, together with an opening of the self to learning from the cultural other, as Muslim philosophers did in the past.

In the current debate on authenticity in Islam the options are articulated in the revival of the classical formula "*bi al-wahi aw bi al-'aql?*"[53] This medieval formula translates as: "Is revelation, or is reason the source of valid knowledge?" and it generates a conflict. Islamic rationalists evaded it and were at pains to reconcile religious and philosophical knowledge. The attempt to compromise is expressed in the concept of a "*haqiqa muzdawaja*/double truth" (Averroes). Thereby, Muslim rationalists believed that they had solved the conflict. In short, they did not deny the role of religion and they hesitated to question religious worldviews.

Of course, the compromise was not accepted. Today, one encounters a revival of the very same controversy. In the tradition of the formula "*bi al-wahi aw bi al-'aql?*" one can read the following clear statement by the Islamist Hussein al-Sadr:

The pursuit of knowledge in Islam is not an end in itself; it is only a means of acquiring an understanding of God ... Reason and the pursuit of knowledge ... are subservient to Qur'anic values ... In this framework reason and revelation go hand in hand. Modern science, on the other hand, considers reason to be supreme.[54]

When one argues for authenticity, the question cannot be evaded: what is authentic? Is it the fundamentalist view of the world, or is it the rationalist Islamic philosophy based on Hellenization in the Abbasid Islamic period? Islamic caliphs like the great Harun al-Rashid or his son al-Ma'mun promoted the rise of science as based on Greek rational knowledge and backed the related adoptions. These caliphs "cultivated a religious climate that was relatively intellectual, secularized, and tolerant."[55] They also supported the Mu'tazilites as *Defenders of Reason*.[56] Other centers for these cultural borrowings and their integration into Islam were in Cordoba and Toledo in Islamic Spain.

Who decides on what is authentic and what is not? Are the *"ulema/*men of learning" in *Sunni* Islam the authority to do so? The *ulema* stratum of religious orthodoxy was always subservient to the ruler and obedient to his views. They are not the authoritative voice of Islam. In the past, and also today, the *ulema* rejected the introduction of reason-based science into Islamic civilization as a source of knowledge. The *ulema* were at pains to undermine this development and did so successfully. They established a hostile distinction between "alien sciences" or the "sciences of the ancients" (i.e. the Greeks, the *Qudama*') and Islamic sciences. The former were reason-based, as philosophy and rational sciences; the latter were related to the study of religious doctrine, primarily the exegesis of Qur'an and hadith, the shari'a learning, and the philological disciplines required for studying the texts. Despite the fact that the caliph al-Mamun established the *"dar al-hikma/*house of wisdom" as a kind of Islamic academy of sciences, the major institutions of Islamic learning remained exclusively in the hands of the Islamic orthodoxy. As was proved by the meticulous research of George Makdisi (see note 9), Islamic orthodoxy succeeded in preventing the admission of the adopted sciences into the Islamic madrassas, i.e. the Islamic institutions of higher learning. As David Lindberg puts it,

Greek learning never found a secure institutional home in Islam ... Islamic schools would never develop a curriculum that systematically taught the foreign sciences.[57]

The cultural and institutional obstacles created by the Islamic orthodoxy were significant in the past and they continue to burden the present. In classical Islam, efforts aimed at secularizing intellectual thought and paving the way for an institutionalization of the scientific discourse were undermined and were not successful. In today's Islamic civilization, Muslims are reminded of the historical fact that from the middle of the ninth century until well into the thirteenth, we find impressive scientific work in all the main branches of Greek science being carried forward throughout the Islamic world ... but during the thirteenth and fourteenth centuries, Islamic sciences went into decline, by the fifteenth century, little was left.[58]

Wouldn't it be worthwhile to revive this tradition and to allow an honest, not an apologetic, Islamic debate on the causes of the decline of Islamic civilization? The decline was not – as is assumed by some – "a conspiracy by Jews and crusaders against the Islamic world." It was also not related to the racist extreme of derogatory inferiorization of the Islamic civilization by Europeans. The obstacle to the requested debate is the existence of an Orientalism of *homo islamicus* – a human being, but one viewed as *inferior to the European* – and also an Islamic response to this obnoxious racism, imprisoned in the mindset of an Orientalism in reverse.

An outrageous example of this racist Orientalism can be found in the work of a Germanic professor of Islamic studies. C. H. Becker states it bluntly and blatantly in the allegation that Muslims are lacking in basic capabilities, due to "race-psychology related reasons."[59] In this explanation Muslims are viewed as being incapable of accomplishments similar to those of the allegedly "superior" Europeans. Their contribution is seen as being limited to the translation of a legacy and passing it on, without any alteration or innovation, to Europe. This is reluctantly acknowledged, but with the emphasis that it was not more than that! The German Jewish philosopher Ernst Bloch defended Averroes and Avicenna against those strange bedfellows, the *ulema* and the Orientalists who reduce Islam to *"Mufti Welt."* In contrast to this sound defense, contemporary Muslims and Islamists see in the above-quoted Orientalism a combined "Jewish-crusader conspiracy against Islam."[60]

Setting aside these ideological and self-congratulating assertions and the conspiracy-driven thinking of the Islamic side – and the racist disparagement of European Orientalism of the other – one is compelled to ask why rational and scientific thought in Islam based on Hellenization did not endure. Was it because of lack of authenticity? If this were true, why did sciences and secular thought thrive in medieval Islamic civilization for so many centuries, in spite of never being institutionalized?

Reference to the cultural analysis of Robert Wuthnow promises a solution to the puzzle. According to this analysis, scientific thought can become a tangible social fact when the process of institutionalization of science is successfully carried through; only then does science become established (see note 10). Wuthnow does not deal with Islam. Nevertheless, his approach may help in understanding the fact that the tradition of science in Islamic civilization failed to give birth to modern science in general. Historians of science are in agreement that the Muslim civilization had the most advanced science in the world in medieval times. This was related to the processes of Hellenization and of translation from other cultures. To be sure, Muslims were not merely translators, inasmuch as they developed further their adopted Greek legacy. Nevertheless, the diffusion of science was limited and the obstacles to its required institutionalization were tremendous. In short, assimilation of scientific thought into the Islamic worldview was not successful. I have already pointed out the dominance of an Islamic orthodoxy that was opposed to a further unfolding of the rational sciences in Islam. Nevertheless, it would be a mistake to infer from the foregoing analysis that the sciences were marginal in Islam. In fact, naturalization, if not partial assimilation, occurred to a certain extent. However, it was undermined by the orthodoxy. The control of the educational system allowed the *fiqh*-orthodoxy to prevent the spread of the Islamic rationalists' attempt to break out of the inherited religious concept of the world's natural order. This explains the failure of the Islamic rationalists. Along with the dominance of a religious worldview in Islamic civilization, the rationalist view of the world, of man, and of nature was absent. This is not a denial of the overall impact of Islamic rationalism, but rather an effort to understand the limited impact of reason-based science in Islam.

By and large, the Hellenization of medieval Islam contributed to the emergence of an authentic Islamic tradition of rational philosophy, and this could be considered as a precedent for a Muslim future. The by-product was a contest between two schools of thought with varying ways of looking at knowledge and with different worldviews. These schools were the sacral *fiqh* and the rational philosophy. The competition resembles today's fight between reform Islam and Islamism. As stated, Hellenized Islamic rationalism could not establish itself institutionally; it was therefore short lived and waned, with the result there was no continuity of reason-based science in the Islamic civilization. Nevertheless, science existed in Islam and its tradition. It is also generally acknowledged that this Islamic accomplishment contributed to the emergence of scientific thought in Europe (see note 26). However, science declined in the Islamic world. The Egyptian philosopher Mourad Wahba addresses this issue as "The Paradoxon of Averroes" (see Chapter 6, note 1). Reference is made here to the appreciation of this great Islamic philosopher in Europe (Latin Averroism), parallel to the burning of his books in the Islamic world. This is a strong indication of the dismissal of scientific thought, which still prevails not only in Salafism, but also in Muslim semi-modernity.

The classical – and to date unresolved – conflict in Islam between reason and revelation is reflected in a related worldview that has never ceased to exist. The issue continues to be highly topical in our times. The Abu-Zaid affair in Cairo was a contemporary public indication of this conflict. Abu-Zaid published a book in which he pleaded for the decoupling of religious from reason-based thought.[61] Because of this, he was prosecuted, divorced from his wife – against both their wills – and declared by the court to be a "*murtad*/apostate." The entire affair was a continuation of the behavior of the *fiqh*-orthodoxy of medieval Islam in its dealings with thinking Muslims. The secular state under Mubarak's regime remained silent in order not to anger the *fiqh*-orthodoxy and to avoid a conflict. This has been – and continues to be – a self-defeating response, because the Islamist Muslim Brothers thrive and continue unabated their agenda of a creeping Islamization. In the West, the Muslim Brothers are presented in a distorted manner as "the new Islamists" of an *Islam without Fear*.[62] The political reality runs counter to this false presentation.

In short, in medieval Islam, Islamic philosophers adopted the Greek concept of reason-based knowledge but restricted its validity to worldly matters. They refrained from a rethinking of religious doctrine. In contrast, *fiqh* scholars insisted on the holistic validity of the revelation, taking the view that it is the sole and unrestricted source of true knowledge in all realms of life. Islamic *fiqh*-orthodoxy continues to hold this outdated doctrine unabated. Of course, the *fiqh*'s use of authenticity in the current debate in pursuit of the purity of Islam (e.g. al-Jundi) overlooks the fact that the *falsafa* Muslims borrowed from Hellenism. To repeat: in those times, the notion of authenticity was not an issue because it did not exist. In the language of the present analysis: the venture of the Islamic medieval rationalists was more authentic than is the Islamization agenda of contemporary Islamists.

There is reason to refer one more time to the great Muslim philosopher al-Farabi in the classical heritage of Islam. In his *al-Madina al-fadi'la*[63] he dealt with the question of how a proper order could be designed. In that medieval time, al-Farabi made it clear that only a philosopher – not a *faqih* – would be capable of running a proper order based on reason. In Islamic history, however, the winner of the contest was the *fiqh*, not reason-based philosophy. Of the two, which was more authentic? One might better ask: which was more powerful? It was the *fiqh* that had the power to determine the future course of Islamic civilization. This dominance lasted until the rise of the West, when Muslims were inescapably confronted with new realities in a colonial context, and as a background to the Muslim encounter with the West and its science.[64]

How have Muslims responded to the challenge, to date? The response has been the admission of technical adoption, coupled with a reluctance to make any cultural accommodation. In modern Islamic history there was a short-lived – quite shallow – Westernization. Superficially, it resembled the classical Hellenization of Islam – but with the significant distinction that the latter was more solidly based in medieval Islam. Nevertheless, both failed. What is the difference between the two processes, and in what way does the debate on authenticity relate to these traditions? And last, but not least, why the plea in this chapter for a revival of the heritage of Hellenized Islam? Didn't it fail? And so what is the rationale for its revival?

Medieval Hellenization and twentieth-century Westernization

Whatever the underlying causes of the decline of the Islamic civilization are, it is safe to state that the decline itself led to a period of darkness that triggered a stagnation that lasted for centuries. The decay in late medieval Islam gave rise to the birth of the Ottoman empire, with its resumption of the traditional military *jihad* conquests which left no room for scientific achievement. Ottoman history was military history. A change occurred, parallel to the rise of the West that was founded on an awesome *Military Revolution*, mentioned above in Chapter 1 (see there, note 3). This revolution was based on modern science and industrial technology. This industrialized warfare halted Ottoman expansion and its incursions into Europe, and created a crisis of the Islamic order from the late seventeenth century onward. The Ottoman caliphs became aware that they would need Western knowledge in order to match the West. It was, however, restricted to an *Importing the European Army*.[65] That importation of modern military technology was certainly merely instrumental. It was not able to halt the decline. More than an imitative Westernization[66] is required in order to come to terms with the predicament with modernity. This nineteenth-century experience continues to apply to Muslims in the twenty-first century.

Muslims went to Europe to study at schools and universities with the aim of borrowing Western science within a framework of limited Westernization. Among those Muslims who were sent to the West was Rifa'a R. al-Tahtawi, quoted earlier. In Paris he was fascinated by the secular modern knowledge of the Europeans. However, Tahtawi's enthusiasm was not unrestricted. He made two basic points, one of which was connected to a restriction. First, he referred to "borrowing," which he believed had legitimacy as an act of retrieval. Underlying this perception was the fact that Europe, on the eve of the Renaissance, adopted science and knowledge from the Islamic civilization. The second point was his reference to the shari'a, viewed as a threshold not to be crossed in the process of borrowing.[67] Tahtawi was of the view that Muslims should engage in adoptions from the West, but only on the basis that they did not collide with the shari'a. Thus, scientific borrowing was reduced to instrumental adoptions and did not allow for any change in the prevailing worldview. In comparing the influence of this mostly instrumental Westernization with that of the medieval Hellenization of Islamic civilization, a great difference can be seen and stated. Westernization remained superficial; Hellenization led to Islamic rationalism. This makes a great difference.

Just as there are no multiple modernities, there can be no multiple sciences. As Bernard Lewis puts it: "from this time onwards science means modern Western science. There was no other."[68] And this science is bound to cultural modernity. One can adopt from the West the instruments of this science, but the process excludes the ability to learn how to engage in its production. The Islamic importation of the European army did not create an ability to deal with its underlying sciences. The failed Westernization of the Islamic world is multifaceted, and has a wide range covering reform, secularism, and Islamism. Clearly, there are many contradictions involved in the reasoning of Muslim modernists who, in the context of their encounter with the West, were determined to accept modern science and knowledge. Tahtawi was a case in point. Despite being liberal, he overlooked the fact – as do today's Islamists – that the Europeans borrowed reason-based philosophy from Islam, not the allegedly divine approach of Islamic *fiqh* based on shari'a. The perception that provides legitimacy for the borrowing of modern science from the West is that learning from the cultural other is nothing but an act of retrieval, i.e. a "reclaiming of the sciences." It is thus believed that the West is not the source. This is self-deception. Tahtawi was led by an illusion, and he never asked whether scientific knowledge is determined to be secular, i.e. to be decoupled from religious thought, by its very nature. Tahtawi and most of the other Islamic reformers and modernists of the nineteenth century were the channels of a liberal age of Westernization that was limited to instrumental adoptions from the other. They were not willing to change the prevailing worldview. In the reasoning of Islamic reform, Islam's predicament with modernity remains unsolved. This statement also applies, unfortunately, to Muhammad Abduh,[69] the foremost Muslim reformer. He admitted reform, but with no real will to accommodate culturally the ongoing social change of rethinking basic Muslim doctrines. Why do students of Islam call this deficient effort an "Islamic reform" of the nineteenth century?

Whatever the case, Islamic reform failed. It was then superseded or replaced in the twentieth century by secular pan-Arab nationalism. Both, the Islamic tradition of a purported reform and secular nationalism, were affected by Westernization and were under its spell. They lasted a much shorter time than did Hellenized Islam. In the aftermath of the dissolution of the Islamic order, and with the rise of secular nationalism, the modern, i.e. secular, nation-state was introduced into Islamic civilization. In this context, Islam was decoupled from politics, but only on the surface, in a process of a very superficial secularization (see Chapter 6). The tensions between Islam and the nation-state[70] continued unabated because no real separation of religion and politics was established. There was an ideology of secularism, but no corresponding process of secularization that could lead to a culture and a structure of secularity. As was made clear in Chapter 6, the concept of secularism has different meanings. The issue was settled in that chapter. The reference to secularization is therefore made here with the meaning of a process of the transformation of society that also contributes to changing the related worldviews. Here the concern is restricted to the question of Islamic authenticity, as stated in this question: is it authentic to address this issue in Weberian terms? Is this possible in Islamic terms? Medieval Islamic rationalists presented their philosophy in Islamic, not Greek terms. Cultural modernity and the social process of secularization need to be similarly presented, on the one hand as an innovation, capable of accommodating cultural modernity, and on the other to give it an authentic face that is acceptable to Muslims. There can definitely be no secular state without secularization in society. There are Muslims (see Chapter 6) who not only contend the contrary, but also claim to be reformers. They can be forgotten!

Culture and religion: between the worldviews of cultural modernity and of religion

In line with the personal and autobiographical remarks made in the Introduction, I will begin in this section, ahead of the conclusions, with a personal confession. As a secular-minded Muslim I believe that Islam and secularity are compatible, but as a scholar I am aware of the great obstacles and of the thorny path. The intellectual sources of the Islamic religious system, the Qur'an and the *sunna*, make no mention of any mediating instance between God and the individual and therefore provide no room for a clergy. Even Salafist-orthodox Muslims acknowledge this scriptural fact. Most Muslims, however, confuse the scripture and the reality. They claim that Islam has no clergy performing this mediating role. But the reality of Islamic history is that a stratum of "*fuqaha/* sacral jurists" and "*ulema/*scribes" evolved and that they act as a clergy. There is a gap between the ideal of Islam and the historical reality. One of the significant Islamic reformers of the early twentieth century, Ali 'Abdelraziq, underlined the fact that the Qur'an does not prescribe a political system and made clear that the sources of Islam do not provide a concept for a political order. The mere statement of this simple truth was enough to cause the ruining of 'Abdelraziq's means of livelihood by the intolerant *ulema* clergy. Neither Islamic reform nor secular nationalism has succeeded in introducing a new worldview that puts doctrine in line with existing realities. The Islamic worldview is based on self-deception. For instance, Muslims maintain that the *ulema* and the *faqihs* are not a clergy – so what are they, then? Of course, they are not "scientists," as the Arabic term *ulema* means; they are clearly clerics, not scholars!!

In reassessing the rise of science-based culture and its failure to become institutionalized in Islam, one may first concede that in medieval times standards favorable to the development of science and technology were achieved. But did the unfolding of early scientific thought at that stage in history contribute to the introduction of some elements of secularity? The answer is yes and no. In so arguing, I draw on the work of the contemporary Syrian philosopher Taiyib Tizini, who studied the history of Islamic philosophy. This author Tizini is driven by a new reading of Islamic heritage and he believes in the necessity of its revival. Tizini formulated a new approach to his subject by which it becomes clear that, in its heyday, Islamic philosophy developed the first approaches to a secular, scientifically based, rational interpretation of the cosmos.

> The political and social content of those ideas of the Arab-Islamic thinkers ... is expressed in a hostile attitude to the dominant feudal intellectual position. The social basis for this attitude was to be found in the then considerable vertical and horizontal development of commodity production and in economic activities generally, and it went hand in hand with the development of natural sciences such as chemistry, astronomy, medicine and mathematics.[71]

In medieval Islamic rationalism we encounter the germination of the seeds needed for a rational view of the world. They provide the ground for a scientific and thus secular worldview. The "*al-Madina al-fadila/*perfect state" proposed by al-Farabi, referred to earlier, is a secular order. In this thinking we find one of the strands of an early, interrupted development towards secularization in Islamic society, as manifested in the philosophical works of Avicenna, Averroes, al-Farabi, Ibn Tufail, and others. Ibn Khaldun's philosophy of history and society marks the end of this history of rational thought in Islam. The reasons underlying this decline are multifaceted. They are both structural and cultural. Without a doubt, medieval Islamic society was a structurally developed one. However, a transition from commercial capitalism to an industrial capitalist society did not occur in Islamic medieval society. Due to a combination of internal and external constraints, the Arab Islamic empire collapsed and, with it, scientific thought. As noted earlier, by the fourteenth century there was little left, and the notorious burning of books replaced the thinking of Islamic rationalists. Was this purification a return to authenticity?

In a comparative manner, one can state that in European Christianity the movement of the Reformation accomplished the reform of religion. This did not happen in Islam. Habermas lists the Reformation among the sources of cultural modernity. It preceded the Industrial Revolution. In this case, it is clear that cultural change is a requisite for social change and is linked to it. With this understanding I refer to the links between Protestant ethics and industrial capitalism, repeatedly pointed out since Max Weber's work on this subject. It is simply ridiculous to rebuff this reference as an Orientalism. One finds this same reference in the work of Afghani. The Lutheran Reformation was not just a struggle against religious bodies and the clergy; it also implied – if unwittingly – the de-politicization of religion and, as a side-effect, secularization. In this meaning, the Reformation contributed to radical changes in the prevailing worldview. Habermas views the Reformation, therefore, as one of the four pillars of cultural modernity. In a comparative manner one might ask: did something similar happen in Islam?

To answer this question I have to reiterate the reference to the spiritual father of revivalism in modern Islam, Afghani (1838–97), who accepted the Lutheran Reformation as a model and, moreover, attributed all European achievements to it. In Chapter 6 I quoted at length Afghani's approval of Luther. According to the saint-scholar of contemporary Islamic studies, Albert Hourani, Afghani saw himself as the Islamic Luther.[72] Protestant ethics implicitly introduced an anti-dogmatic mind that became an element of change. According to Afghani himself, only a new, reformed Islamic movement combating both the European powers that were colonizing the Islamic Middle East and the Islamic clergy could bring about a development similar to that in Europe. It is most important for the subject matter of this chapter to mention Afghani's great preoccupation with science. In his view, the dominance of Europe over the Islamic world reflects "the hegemony of states and peoples, who have science and thus are able to dominate over people who are weak ... In other words, power and science enable to rule over weakness and ignorance. This is a cosmic law."[73] It is unfortunate that Afghani, also, was speaking about instruments, not about the related worldview. The reform that he envisioned failed because he was not set to change the Islamic worldview. He was keen to be the Martin Luther of Islam, but lacked the courage or the will to introduce into Islam what Luther had introduced into Christianity.

Conclusions

The focus of this chapter has been on authenticity, viewed through the lens of a universal cultural modernity. There are three areas of concern: 1) authenticity in general; 2) the claim of political Islam to authenticity; and 3) the contention that Islamic rationalism based on Hellenization is a model for the agreement of authenticity with learning/adoptions from the cultural other.

The question is whether Islamic reform and its modernism in the nineteenth and early twentieth centuries succeeded in making adoptions from Europe consonant with Islam. The necessary answer requires an assessment of early Islamic reform. To do this, one has to examine why Muslim reformers failed to engage in real cultural change. Following Afghani and Abduh, the Islamic modernist Arslan (1869–1946) published a series of articles in *al-Manar*, a journal edited by Rashid Rida, which illustrate the attitude of half-hearted reform. This reformist undertaking, including the question "Why are Muslims backward?," was discussed at length in Chapter 1. Arslan is also quoted at length in Chapter 6. However, one point in Arslan's response to the question "Why are Muslims backward?" (these are his words, not mine) is pertinent. This is his reference to the Qur'an, which states that "Allah does not change anything for a people, as long as they do not change themselves" (sura 13, verse 11). This reference can be cited in order to place the blame on Muslims themselves, and with a Qur'anic authority that no Muslim would ever either question or evade!

The assumption is that religious reform underpins cultural change. If the established religious dogma remains unquestioned – as was the case in the major thinking of Islamic modernism – then this way of thinking will be highly consequential. In this context, reference to Niklas Luhmann's sociology of religion is highly useful in seeking an explanation. Luhmann deals with the social function of religious dogma, which supposedly is able to provide an answer to all cosmic questions. Accordingly,

> religious dogma departs from unanalyzed abstractions and thus ... it does not consciously reflect on its social function but rather understands itself, its concept of dogma, dogmatically ... On the other hand, it rests on a universal and contextless applicability, hence on a certain disregard of the bonds it interprets.[74]

If this characteristic of religious dogma is not questioned, also with regard to the social function of Islamic doctrine, then no reform in substance can ever take place. It is a fact that the Islamic doctrine has never been questioned or rethought by Islamic modernists, whether in the past or in the present.

Therefore, no "cultural accommodation of social change" has ever achieved. Islamic modernism never went beyond dogma and remained basically scripturalist, acting exclusively within dogmatic confines. Because it did not engage in a reason-based response to the question Arslan asked, no cultural innovation was accomplished. The modernist variety of Islamic dogma unfolds as a reaction to Western civilization's penetration of the modern world. Unfortunately, Islamic modernists confused the two dimensions of modernity: culture and power. Their choice of "semi-modernity"[75] is not only based on this confusion, but also leads into an impasse. Is it their commitment to authenticity that prevented them from moving forward? Or is there an inconsistency at work in their thinking? This continues to date. The "reformation" that the Muslim modernist An-Na'im (see Chapter 6) envisioned in 1990 ended in 2008 with this undertaking: a plea for a secular state, but no secularization in society! This is a highly deplorable retreat.

A recourse to medieval Islamic rationalism shows that all those Muslim philosophers were more consistent in their thinking than contemporary Muslim modernists have ever been. In their reasoning they went beyond dogmatic statements based on the Qur'an and the *sunna*. To answer Arslan's question "Why are Muslims backward?" one needs much more than an authentic understanding of scriptural commandments. The Qur'an and the *sunna*, as religious dogmata, are to be placed in a socio-historical context. Such historicizing modernist thinking never existed in Islamic religious reform. Not even the highly respected Arkoun, who would like to be viewed as the Kant of Islam, has ever accomplished an Islamic reform of this kind.[76]

The preliminary conclusion is that early Islamic modernism did not engage seriously in cultural change, and thus evaded religious reform. Instead, Islamic revival restores the correspondence between the sacred and the political that is typical of pre-industrial cultures, and is trapped in a mindset of pre-modernity.[77] Today, Islamism invents the tradition of pre-modernity by giving it a modern, totalitarian shape. In relation to the rationalization of the civilizational worldview, once achieved by Muslim rationalist philosophers, this is a backward step. There are Westerners who know very little of Islamism as a contemporary totalitarian political movement and ideology[78] but who, despite this ignorance, support its drive for "*asalah*/authenticity." As shown at the outset, the *asalah*-Islamist theorist al-Jundi (see notes 2 and 3) engages in an agenda of antisemitic purification. In contrast, the rational philosophy of medieval Islam was not only more authentic than the failed early reform of Islam, but also even more so than the counter-enlightenment of contemporary Islamism.

At this point, some conclusions about *asalah* and cultural change can be drawn. The cultural tensions generated in the context of globalization themselves generate political conflict. There is also a predicament in that the religious discourse of Islamic thinkers aimed to overcome the predicament with modernity but, since they precluded cultural change and religious reform altogether, were doomed to failure. The religious dogma remained unquestioned. In the end, tensions between religious and rational worldviews intensified, and so the conflict flares up, instead of subsiding.

It is a fact in Islam's history of ideas that no tradition of a critique of religious thought has ever existed. One reason for this shortcoming is that Islam views itself as the only true religion, based on the "final revelation." Islamic reform has evaded this issue altogether. In the past, Islamic rationalists also evaded the issue. The present exception is the Muslim Arab philosopher Sadiq Jalal al-Azm, an alumnus of Yale who, in his 1969 book *Critique of Religious Thought*,[79] engaged in such a venture. His problem as a Yale-educated philosopher has been a rather poor knowledge of Islam. The *ulema* used this flaw to disqualify him. More knowledgeable about Islam than al-Azm is Hamid Abu-Zaid, in his *Naqd al-khitab al-dina*/Critique of Islamic Discourse,[80] but he, however, is less courageous. Nevertheless, Abu-Zaid and al-Azm shared the fate of persecution because their critical thinking was not welcome.

Returning to what is authentic in Islam, the common confusion of science and revelation, continued to date in a tradition articulated by the *fiqh*-orthodoxy, makes it difficult for Muslims to accommodate to global standards of science. This deficit is exacerbated by the culture of accusing any Muslim scholar who embraces critical thinking of heresy, as a deviation from true beliefs.

The Islamic *ulema* orthodoxy's ugly weapon against rational thinkers in Islam was and is the *takfir*, i.e. the classification of a Muslim as "becoming an unbeliever." This accusation is also extended to reason-based knowledge in general, and to the great Islamic medieval rationalists in particular. Any critique of religion will expose a Muslim to this classification. Today, Islamic civilization needs an authentic cultural orientation in order to come to terms with its predicament with modernity. This orientation must be combined with a critique of the self. If this fails, then the "geopolitics of Islam's civil war," already mentioned in the Preface, will alienate the people of Islam from their own enlightened tradition. It will also hinder them from becoming part of the universal cultural heritage. If that Islamic medieval rationalism that recognized the universality of knowledge continues to be declared a heresy, and if authenticity is narrowed down to a polarization of the self and otherness, then Muslims of the twenty-first century will continue to be unsuccessful in embarking on modernity. Despite the bleak perspectives, contemporary Arab rationalists like al-Jabri continue to believe that "the future can only be Averroist." This repeatedly quoted Moroccan philosopher holds the view that

> [t]he survival of philosophical tradition is likely to contribute to our time ... The Averroist spirit is adaptable to our era, because it agrees with it on more than one point: rationalism, realism, axiomatic method and critical approach.[81]

This bright and most promising Muslim view of the compatibility between authenticity and cultural modernity is, unfortunately, not among the popular public choices in today's Islam. In contrast, anti-science, presented in the name of the authentic Islamization of knowledge by the Saudi funded International

Institute of Islamic Thought, is more accepted. This enterprise is summarized by its exponents in the following manner:

> *Fiqh, usul al-fiqh* and *shari'a* are the greatest expression of Islamic spirit, it is absolutely necessary to make these contents readily available to the research school in each of the specific disciplines of modern times ... *Fiqh* and *shari'a* are the quintessence.[82]

In Chapter 2 the illusion of an "Islamization of knowledge" was discussed at length. I add here that this view is an expression of anti-science, made in the name of authenticity. The old inner-Islamic conflict in medieval Islam between the *fiqh*-orthodoxy and "*falsafa*/rationalism" (see note 8) is revived under the present conditions of globalization and fragmentation. The scientific thought and related rational worldview of medieval Islam are eliminated by contemporary Islamists. The MIT-trained Pakistani scientist Hoodbhoy rightly argues:

> Scientific underdevelopment is certainly one important part of the crisis which envelops the Muslim world ... Muslims ... will continue to suffer an undignified and degraded existence if science, and particularly a rational approach to human problems, is considered alien to Islamic culture.[83]

The term "alien" can be translated as "non-authentic" in the language of the counter-vision of Islamism. This ideology establishes a line between the Islamic law of shari'a and a science that is supposed to be Islamized. All scientific findings should be subjected to shari'a. There is a precedent for this in medieval Islam, where the Islamic *fiqh*-orthodoxy strove to remove the tension between Islamic, i.e. religious, *'ilm* and alien, i.e. Greek, science. Historian of science Lindberg describes the outcome:

> Conservative religious forces made themselves increasingly felt ... Science became naturalized in Islam – losing its alien quality and finally becoming Islamic science, instead of Greek science ... – by accepting a greatly restricted hand-maiden role. This meant a loss of attention to many problems.[84]

The process described in this quotation resulted in the decline of medieval Islamic rationalism in the course of the purification of knowledge by the *fiqh*-orthodoxy. Consequently, Islamic civilization has lost the mindset of scientific inquiry. Today, most Muslims adopt science instrumentally, and in a mindset of semi-modernity (see Chapter 11). This indicates a lack of the spirit of "cultural innovation."[85] These ad hoc adoptions do not contribute to unfolding a rational view of the world. In the name of authenticity, a decoupling of modern science from its spirit of cultural modernity is occurring. The outcome is semi-modernity – to be discussed at length in the conclusion of this book. In this instrumental semi-modernity the spirit of scientific inquiry is abandoned. This provides a reason to repeat the phrase coined by the contemporary Muslim philosopher al-Jabri – as quoted at the beginning of this chapter: "The future can only be Averroist."

In conclusion, let it be reiterated: the mindset of Averroism reflects positive Islamic precedents for cultural change, which are more authentic than contemporary political Islam claims to be. Postmodern theorists of authenticity are advised to study non-Western cultures properly, and from within, to make sure that they know what they are talking about before they start any general theorizing on the issues in question. Stated in Islamic terms: "*jahl*/ignorance" ranks at the head of all sins.

Chapter 9

Case studies I: the failed cultural transformation in Egypt

A model for the Islamic world?

One country, Egypt, and one sub-region, the Gulf, have been selected as empirical illustrations of the approach used in the present book. The reader has the right to ask for a justification of this selection. Egypt has been chosen as a case study on the predicament of Islam with modernity as it best demonstrates the relevance of culture to development. Egypt also provides the best explanation of why cultural change and religious reform have so far failed. Further, the choice of Egypt[1] is supported by the fact that this country is historically central in the Islamic world's exposure to European expansion.[2] Egypt went through all the historical stages of the Muslim encounter with the more successful Western civilization: early Islamic reform, liberalism, secular nationalism and, more recently, the rise of political Islam, named Islamism. Egypt has always occupied a central place in the civilizational territoriality of "*Dar al-Islam/*the abode of Islam." The process at issue began in Egypt when the West invaded that country and thereby brought into question Islam's claim to superiority (*al-Islam ya'lu wa la yu'la alayh/*Islam is superior and no power could be superior to it). That was in 1798. Today, Egypt is the place where the world dominance of Western globalization is under fire. It is challenged by political Islam, which was not only born in Egypt, but also took shape there.

Introduction

Prior to the rise of the West, the Islamic civilization was a flourishing one and it enjoyed a *futuhat-*expansion that predates by far the (however more competitive) global European conquests.[3] For many reasons, Islamic civilization stagnated and has been retarding ever since the seventeenth century. Prior to this stagnation the Islamic world had its own model, and made great efforts to globalize it by mapping the world in *Dar al-Islam*. Since the successful expansion of Europe, Islamic civilization has succumbed to the expanding and more powerful Western model.[4] The Muslim conquerors became a conquered people. This sea change was a great humiliation. As stated, Egypt is at the center of this development. Among the effects triggered by the Islamic world's encounter with the West was a severe and lasting crisis that Islamic civilization has been undergoing ever since.[5] This crisis is related to Islam's predicament with modernity and is the source of cultural tensions between the civilizational self-awareness of Muslims taught by the Qur'an to be *"khair umma/*the best community" (sura 3, verse 110) and the realities of their life, which run counter to their image of the self. Muslims believe that no one can be superior to them, as the cited Qur'anic verse pronounces. The politicization of the related cultural tensions tends to contribute to international conflict, as is argued in this book, which began by quoting John Brenkman, who asserts "Islam's geo-civil war."[6] However, Brenkman fails to provide any explanation. As indicated in the Preface, this book claims to suggest an explanatory framework for understanding this new pattern of international conflict.

In this introductory section I justify my choice of Egypt to illustrate and demonstrate the major ideas and assumptions of this book. Exposure to modernity generates a variety of responses that range from rejection, adjustment, and praetorianism, to the most recent claim of the return of history combined with a return of the sacred in the guise of *"al-Islam al-siyasi/*political Islam." This term identifies the Islamic variant of religious fundamentalism. All of the listed cultural responses to exposure to European expansion and Western globalization occurred first in Egypt. The development of state and society under the conditions of a predicament with modernity can therefore best be analyzed in the case of Egypt. This is a preliminary answer to the question: why this case study? Clearly, Egypt is the most prominent case for the study of Islam and the culture of modernity. In a way, Egypt provides a textbook case of the Islamic civilization's encounter with the West. As will be shown in this chapter, all Islamic responses to the challenges from the late eighteenth century up to the present can be properly studied using the case of Egypt. Napoleon's conquest of Egypt in 1798 set the stage. Hegel described Napoleon as *"Weltgeist zu Pferde/*world spirit riding on a horse," i.e. the spirit of the French Revolution. At issue is the spread of the values of Western civilization, first in Europe and then worldwide. Of course, Napoleon went to Egypt with his army in 1798 for reasons other than the ideology proclaimed as *mission civilatrice*. Nevertheless, he unwittingly acted also in the Hegelian sense of a *"List der Vernunft/*cunning of reason," i.e. in a historical capacity. The broadsheet produced in Arabic on Napoleon's orders supports this interpretation. In that broadsheet, which is considered to be a document of world history, Napoleon addressed the Egyptian people in these words:

> In the name of the French Republic (*jumhur*), based on foundations of Liberty and Equality, Bonaparte, Commander-in-Chief of the French forces, informs the whole population of Egypt: for many decades those in power have insulted the French nation (*millet*) ... the Mamlukes, who were brought in from the Caucasus and Georgia, have been corrupting the best region of the whole world. But God, the Omnipotent, the Master of the Universe, has now made the destruction of their state imperative. I came only to rescue

your rights from the oppressors. ... I worship Almighty God and respect his Prophet Mohammed, and the Glorious Qur'an more than the Mamlukes. Tell them also that the people are equal before God.[7]

Today, more than two centuries later, this 1798 broadsheet tempts one to compare the liberation of Cairo in 1798, by a Western leader, with that claimed for the conquest of Baghdad in April 2003. Both Western conquerors, Napoleon and Bush, pronounced promises of freedom. Certainly, history teaches lessons, but it never repeats itself. That said, I add that historical comparisons of similar cases have cultural implications and are relevant to this study. The address of President Bush to the Iraqi people at the end of February 2003, broadcasted from Philadelphia – the cradle of American democracy – reminds one of the above-quoted broadsheet of Napoleon. Of course, Bush lacks the greatness of Napoleon, but his promise to free the Iraqis from Saddam's *Republic of Fear* matters as much as did Napoleon's pledge in his address to the Egyptians two centuries earlier: he had liberated them from the Mamlukes, just as the toppling of Saddam by Bush and the capture of the tyrant by US troops on December 13, 2003 were viewed as a liberation of the Iraqi people from despotic rule. In both cases, the pledges of freedom given by Napoleon Bonaparte and by George W. Bush were neither honored nor welcomed, by the Egyptians then or by Iraqis today. French troops in Egypt, and similarly two centuries later US troops in Iraq, were received with great hostility. Why so? The simple answer, and the lesson to be learned, is that the values of cultural modernity cannot successfully be introduced by force by invaders from outside. In both cases, the promises were perceived as a threat.

In all seriousness, I do not foresee any lasting positive effect from the US invasion of Iraq when compared with the case of Egypt, where – in hindsight – the positive cultural impact of the French troops can be safely stated. One should add to this comparison that the turn from the eighteenth to the nine-teenth centuries (the French in Egypt) was a period and situation radically different from the present one of the US in Iraq. When US troops leave Iraq they will leave behind them even more blood-letting – no incentive for development. By contrast, after the departure of the French troops, Egypt underwent a sig-nificant experiment in modernization. The Ottoman Albanian officer Moham-med Ali took over in 1805 and established himself as the ruler of Egypt.[8] While fighting the French troops of Napoleon, Mohammed Ali observed that they were technologically superior and better organized; he was impressed by their culture of success. Thus, Napoleon's modern troops provided a model of development to be emulated. The modernizing ruler Mohammed Ali aimed to copy the suc-cessful European military technology – without, however, adopting its related culture. This ambivalence in the modernization experiment in Egypt under Mohammed Ali was repeated in the later experience of the Ottoman Empire in the nineteenth century. Modernization was restricted to *Importing the European Army*.[9] These Muslim rulers ignored the fact that modern technology is more than simply a tool, in that it is underpinned by a specific worldview and value system that is distinctly different from the pre-industrial one which prevails in Islamic civilization. The drive to import the European army was the beginning of the Islamic dream of semi-modernity, which will be addressed in the concluding Chapter 11.

Islam, the West, and modernization

Based on my research and my experience in a host of Islamic societies in the Middle East, Asia, and Africa I am keen to argue that Mohammed Ali's modernization pattern still matters. The relevance of that experience continues unabated, despite the passing of two centuries. Today, one encounters the attitudes of Mohammed Ali and the Ottoman rulers among anti-Western, educated Muslims who are – nevertheless – favorable to modern science and technology. They are willing to embrace modern instruments, but strictly inimical to the values that underlie them. This worldview[10] continues to prevail as an Islamic mindset in the twenty-first century. Egypt is a case in point where the story of *Importing the European Army* began in an effort to emulate the West in the context of Islam and modernization. To modernize without any inclination to relate technical adoptions to cultural innovation is an attitude that does not favor change. Despite this, intrinsic changes could not be prevented; however, they occurred without any cultural accommodation. The problem already addressed in Chapter 1 is that the cultural attitudes of the early modernists continue to date. The links between the instruments of modernity and their related values have been ignored both in the past and by contemporary Islamic fundamentalists. Despite the span of almost two centuries between early Islamic reform and contemporary political Islam in Egypt, no lessons have been learned. In Egypt, through three stages and their related experiences, beginning with the liberalism of the Westernized elites, followed by the secular praetorianism of Nasser's regime, and now Islamism, no progress has been made. The shattering defeat of Nasser's army in the Six Day War of 1967 engendered a cultural crisis of legitimacy.[11] It became clear that modern technology alone does not make a strong army. The Islamists of today are repeating Nasser's mistakes (see note 10), despite their hatred of his legacy.

Using the case of Egypt, one can show how, in the Islamic world, modernization was promoted by the travels of young Muslims to Europe in order to acquire knowledge and become educated in modern science and technology. The two most prominent Muslim travelers[12] and reformers were both Egyptians: Rifa'a al-Tahtawi and Mohammed Abduh. Both went to Paris and spent some time there. The impact was great, but not consequential. Tahtawi was an Egyptian imam who was sent to Paris to supervise Egyptian students, and who himself became – willingly – a student of Western civilization. Tahtawi became engaged in acquiring modern knowledge, which included reading Montesquieu and Rousseau. In so doing, he combined his life in Paris with developing an awareness of democracy and the rule of democratic law in a modern state. We can read about this "Islam–West encounter" in the Paris diary of this Egyptian imam, who admired Europe and engaged in cultural innovation – only on the condition, however (as he states), of not affecting Islamic values. This is characteristic of the spirit of Islamic reform that was later carried on by Mohammed Abduh, who continues to date to be the greatest Egyptian Islamic modernist ever. The attitude of accepting the instruments of modernity and the parallel rejection of its values reflects the illusion for which I have coined the term "semimodernity." The splitting of modernity into instruments (to be adopted) and values (to be rejected) is a questionable enterprise. In contrast to this superficial reform, efforts at wholesale Westernization were pursued by Westernized Egyptians such as Salamah Musah, an Egyptian Copt.[13] Today, these Arab Christians are accused of the sin of "*salabiyya/*crusaderism." Their influence was limited because they addressed the issue superficially. Nevertheless, they were open-minded and, in a way, promising. At present, political Islam is a response to a crisis of legitimacy in which the reversal of acculturation is sought through counter-acculturation, the reversal of Westernization through de-Westernization. Egypt is a prominent theater for these processes.

The failure of an accommodation has resulted in the rise of political Islam. Its call for an exclusive "*hall Islami/*Islamic solution," as presented by the Egyptian Islamist Yusuf al-Qaradawi,[14] is not the way out for Muslims from the impasse that is related to this crisis – the crisis that results from Islam's predicament with modernity. This is the perennial issue. Egyptian Muslim thinkers have been grappling with it ever since Tahtawi's time. It is continued today by the Islamist Qaradawi. Again, there has been a broad range of responses to the Islamic civilization's exposure to Western culture during the past two centuries. The range stretches from an admiration of Europe in the nineteenth century (e.g. learning from the West) to the contemporary anti-Western and anti-American hatred, elevated to a rejection of modern, values-based knowledge.

The contemporary Islamist Egyptian Muslim Brother Yusuf al-Qaradawi is the heir of his predecessors Sayyid Qutb and Hasan al-Banna. These two were also Egyptians and they are considered the major precursors of political Islam. In his booklet "*Ma'alim fi al-tariq/*Signposts Along the Road" Qutb outlined the basis of a wholesale rejection of any cultural influence from the West. Qaradawi continues this line by ridiculing adoptions from the West as a "*hall mustaward/* imported solution," in contrast to the welcomed "*al-hall al-Islami/*Islamic solution." The lack of knowledge in the West as to what is really happening in the Islamic world is indicated when one sees how the work of the fundamentalist Qaradawi is depicted in Western textbooks and other publications. Here, Qaradawi is presented to the Western public as a voice of "liberal" or "moderate Islam," thus confusing Enlightenment and the mindset of the *New Totalitarianism* introduced by political Islam. Some US experts on Egypt refer to this thinking as "New Islamism," presenting it not only as a model of development, but also as an *Islam without Fear*. This is the world turned upside down.

The exposure of Islamic civilization to the West in a context of power, globalization, and modernization can be illustrated by looking at Egypt. As argued, it is the best example by which to examine related developments in state and society in the Sunni part of the Islamic world. Sunni Muslims constitute about 90 percent of the Muslim community and, for them, Egypt with its authoritative religious institution of al-Azhar (comparable in Shi'i Iran to its spiritual center of Qom), is the source of inspiration. What happens in Egypt affects all Sunni parts of the Islamic civilization. Certainly, Mecca and Medina are the divine centers of the whole religion of Islam, but Wahhabi Saudi Arabia lacks the necessary intellectual and religious authority to provide the model. The powerful attempts to export Wahhabism to the rest of the world are supported by oil money, but they have not replaced Cairo's al-Azhar as the source of legitimacy in the Sunni world. Certainly, Egyptian Islam and al-Azhar itself are among the targets of the export of Saudi Wahhabism. It is sad to note that Egypt is currently being pervaded by Wahhabi Salafism. Let it be said in passing that oil money is today affecting the West also. Petro-dollars matter as a source of funding even to some Islamic studies at prominent universities in the West. They are affected by the world-wide export of Wahhabism[15] and reflect a damaged scholarship.

It is in Egypt, and not in Saudi-Arabia, that the future of Sunni Islam in its predicament with modernity will be shaped. It is true that Wahhabi Saudi Arabia needs the authority of Egypt's al-Azhar to legitimize its policies. By way of example, in 1990 the Saudi King Fahd needed a *fetwa* to support his call for US assistance and his permitting the deployment of US troops in his "holy land" during the Gulf Crisis that followed Iraq's invasion of Kuwait. The king requested the Sheykh of al-Azhar in Cairo, not the grand mufti of his own monarchy of Saudi-Arabia, to issue the required *fetwa*.[16] This request for a legitimizing *fetwa* from al-Azhar is evidence that the high rank of Egypt is accepted even by Saudi Arabia. The fight over the institutions of Egyptian Islam is also a fight over the authority of al-Azhar within Sunni Islam, and beyond the confines of Egypt.

Together with Turkey,[17] Egypt has been a center for the adoption of modern science and technology in the Islamic world. Unlike in Turkey, the value change needed in Egypt to overcome the predicament with modernity has been very slow. Despite the difference in pace, Egypt and Turkey are the core countries for cultural innovation within the Islamic world in the context of the encounters with the West and modernization

In Turkey, there was a swift transition from the Islamic order of the caliphate to the secular republic. The development of Egypt was more complex. There was Islamic reform in that country by the Egyptian Sheykh of al-Azhar Mohammed Abduh (1849–1905). As repeatedly stated in the earlier chapters of this book, the Islamic reform of the late nineteenth and early twentieth centuries failed to achieve its goals. This failure gave way to a fragile, liberalism-based democracy. This liberal-democratic order was toppled by the military, whose populist secular nationalism smoothed the way for a praetorian rule under

Gamal Abdul Nasser and his successors. In both Turkey and Egypt the Islamists are today the best-organized political power. In Turkey, the AKP rules since 2002. Egypt awaits a takeover by the Muslim Brotherhood.

Liberalism failed in Egypt and in Turkey. The idea of Westernization – pursued for instance by prominent Muslims in Egypt like Taha Husayn – is no longer accepted. This prominent Egyptian studied in Paris and then became minister of culture in Egypt. To indicate the radical shift, it is worth stating that the once-revered Taha Husayn is today among the thinkers most despised and defamed by the Islamists.[18] This illustrates the breakdown of the liberal model in the Islamic world. An essential element of this liberalism was represented in the work of Egyptian Christians like Salamah Musah (see note 13), who combined the liberal outlook with Fabian socialism, i.e. a kind of social democratic view. Like Islamic reform, secular Egyptian liberalism failed also. As already mentioned, the pan-Arab populism of Gamal Abdel Nasser, based on a praetorian, secular model of modernization, prevailed thereafter not only in Egypt but also in the whole of the Arab world. In terms of development, Egyptian praetorianism has also failed.[19] The story of one failure following another in a process of modernization continues today with political Islam. As stated, Sunni Islamism was born in 1928 in Egypt[20] and is the most powerful defensive-cultural response to modernity in our time. It is expected to last for decades to come. The retraditionalization of Islam in Egypt was more of a new "invention of tradition" than a revival of traditional Islam. The outcome of de-secularization is the rise of a new totalitarianism, not the emergence of a religious renaissance. I argue against Jürgen Habermas, who, in his post-9/11 thinking,[21] contended the unfolding of a "post-secular society" based on a revival of religious faith.

Modernizing Egypt? The pendulum between reform, liberalism, populist pan-Arabism, and Islamism

The two-centuries-long history of modernizing Egypt is also illustrative of Islam's predicament with cultural modernity. The espousal of modernization without a secular worldview continues and still triggers the same problems. The key issue is the prevalence of Islam in the understanding of a cultural system. This system is a tool for the articulation of most concerns in everyday culture.[22] This fact explains why Islamic cultural patterns pervade all the thinking that has evolved in modern Egypt. However, the responses at issue take a different form at specific times and in different environments. So we find this cultural system in a variety of forms in all the afore-mentioned responses to modernity. Awareness of these differing responses draws attention to many significant distinctions when one studies the links between Islam and culture. In Egypt itself, one needs to distinguish between existing cross-cultural and local-cultural varieties. Even though Egypt is a special case it is, in a way – despite all peculiarities – a microcosm of the entire cosmos of the Sunni Muslim world. In this capacity, it demonstrates a cross-cultural relevance that is supported by the historical and structural significance of the country. After all, Egypt is home to the author-itative institution of al-Azhar.

When, more than a thousand years ago, al-Azhar, the oldest Muslim "uni-versity," was founded by the Fatimids – at the same time as the city of Cairo – it was, as were its founding fathers, a Shi'ite institution of learning. It remained so for some two centuries, until Sunni Islam was reintroduced to Egypt by Saladin. This Muslim hero was mythologized after his defeats of the Fatimids in 1171 and of the crusaders at Jerusalem. Today, al-Azhar – literally "the blossoming" – is the foremost authoritative institution of Sunni Islam, recognized throughout the Islamic world. Add to this the place of Egypt as the center of inter-cultural encounter between the successful, techno-scientific West and the pre-industrial and therefore unsuccessful Islamic civilization, and then you have a country that was and is the center of religio-ideological responses to the European incursion into the Islamic world.[23] In this sense, it is also the center for the production of meaning in the form of political ideologies, from liberalism, Islamic modernism, and nationalism to contemporary religious fundamentalism. Historians not only view Mohammed Ali as the founder of modern Egypt, but also attribute a cross-cultural significance to his experiment of modernization. Mohammed Ali[24] attempted to build a modern state based on the legacy of Napoleon's rule, which, although short-lived, was to have far-reaching effects. Nineteenth-century Egypt developed, in this context, into an Islamic type of a modernizing "royal authority." The overall context was the shaping of the Muslim encounter with modernity through exposure to European expansion.

Earlier, two major Egyptian Muslim thinkers, Rifa'a al-Tahtawi and Mohammed Abduh were mentioned. Both lived in Paris and engaged in an epoch of Islamic reform. For both, the issue was how to manage a reconciliation between Islamic belief based on divine revelation and secular modernity based on reason.[25] The same problem was a concern for the ensuing secular liberalism. Even though they were different traditions, there were some commonalities that linked reform Islam to liberalism in Egypt. However, as the late Nadav Safran of Harvard notes, there were some basic differences: "The gap between reformist Islam … and liberal nationalism steadily increased until the two became mutually exclusive."[26] Ultimately, both failed to deal with the challenge as well as to overcome the conflict between tradition and modernity. This failure gave birth to a new force, the populist pan-Arab nationalism of Nasserism. The powerful authorities that represented the al-Azhar institution, i.e. the religious establishment, were not favorable to either. The problem that confronted Egyptian society is aptly dealt with by Safran in an authoritative study, not yet superseded, even forty years after its publication. Safran addresses the subject accurately in the following manner: at issue was

> the need to develop a subjective, humanely oriented system of ideas, values
> and norms that would serve as a foundation for a political community under
> new conditions of life, to replace the traditional system based on objective

divine revelation. In such an endeavor the leaders had eventually to come to grips with the problem of the possibility of conflict between reason … and the … divine revelation. … The problem remained unresolved, at least as far as the Qur'an was concerned. … During the progressive phase of their endeavor the intellectual leaders had tended to ignore this remaining problem.[27]

Presumably, this evasion constitutes the major source of all failures. Evasive Muslims are not in a position to come to terms with the predicament with cultural modernity. This evasive mindset is shared by practically all of them, including those who currently ask for a rethinking of Islam, such as Mohammed Arkoun and even Abdullahi An-Na'im. They promise, but fail to deliver. Unlike those "reformers," the scribes of al-Azhar do not promise, but simply undermine any Islamic reform. In so doing they have deprived reform Islam of the possibility of affecting the Islamic worldview and prevented it from striking roots in the educational system that they dominate. In the coup d'état of 1952 the military toppled the monarchy in Egypt and seized political power. In the aftermath, the officers succeeded in subordinating al-Azhar to the office of their president, Nasser. The so-called "al-Azhar reform" was the framework for this subordination. Did that pattern change religion in Egypt? Not at all!

Nasser's coup in 1952 resulted – superficially – in the establishment of a secular praetorian regime. The "Free Officers"[28] were secular, but revived an old Islamic tradition in which the *ulema* were assigned to act as legitimators. Religion was reduced to a powerful tool for the legitimation of rule. The *Pretorian State*[29] put modernization at the head of its agenda, but did not bring about a significant cultural change. The major problem outlined by Safran in the above-quoted passage was again suppressed by the military, who have ruled since 1952. Today, political Islam establishes itself as a *Mobilizing Islam*[30] in pursuit of an Islamist agenda. It is the power supposed to take over in the next development.

Throughout the modern history of Egypt, religion has not ceased to influence all aspects of life, whether in the state or in society. Fouad Ajami addresses this problem and concludes: "An inquiry into religion in Egypt is really, and has to be, an inquiry into the nature of authority in that country,"[31] and then he adds:

To the extent that Egypt's Islam forms the cultural system of the country, it will always matter. Rulers and opponents alike will phrase their concerns in Islamic categories. While there are some things which this cultural system will not tolerate … beneath that "cosmic" level, cultural limits – in Egypt and elsewhere – can be stretched to accommodate a wide range of things.[32]

With hindsight it can be stated that neither Islamic reform nor liberalism accomplished this cultural accommodation. In my work I address this problem as a lack of "cultural accommodation of social change."[33]

The preceding discussion makes clear that the study of culture and development in Egypt compels one to deal with the influence of religion and of the institutions that represent it. What these accomplish is a legitimation of power, not a contribution to overcoming Islam's predicament with modernity. The contemporary politicization of the Islamic cultural system in Egypt gives rise to a movement that opposes the religious al-Azhar establishment, but this is not the anticipated light at the end of the tunnel. The representatives of political Islam have been more appealing than reform Muslims and liberals had ever been. Today Islamists are building up the major opposition as a power of *Mobilizing Islam* (see note 30). What are the alternatives that political Islam offers? Are they promising? I am sorry to say that they are not!

Islamism in Egypt is based on the Movement of the Muslim Brothers, which was established 1928. However, its real rise as an Islamist opposition occurred in the 1970s, when counter-elites emerged to represent the new Islamism. Today, the distinction between legal Islamists, who participate in institutions, and jihadists, who are committed to terror, is highly important. Their political culture is directed against Western values. A serious question is: are we facing a specific Islamic pattern of modernization? Are the Islamist groups in Egypt to be regarded as a modernist movement in their own cultural way? Do Islamists provide a way out of the present crisis, which is related to a two-centuries-long inability to come to terms with cultural modernity? Could Islamism be an alternative to al-Azhar in Sunni Islam? In contrast to Shi'i Islam, Sunni Islam has no institutional clerical structure. Could such a structure emerge under the new conditions?

These are tough questions and no satisfactory answer can be provided to all of them. In modern Egypt[34] the state-run public *Waqf* that controls and finances the mosques competes with the privately endowed mosques. These are financed by well-to-do Egyptians and are often linked to Saudi Wahhabi funding. In this way, Saudi Wahhabism – even though a variety of orthodox-Salafist, i.e. non-fundamentalist Islam – is contributing to the political abuse of the mosques in Egypt and elsewhere, and providing a home for the new opposition of Islamism. In this way the new opposition continues the Islamic tradition of using religion as a political tool, and it seems not to be the alternative or the hoped-for Islamic model of modernity.

In political Islam there is indoctrination of religion in the sense of imposing a specific religious-political interpretation. When Egypt was a monarchy the king exercised no religious authority, in that he did not proclaim himself caliph in any context. The toppling of the monarchy was followed by the seizure of political power by the Free Officers, who where secular. Their praetorian rule used al-Azhar to impose a religious doctrine that fitted Islam into the secular ideology in order to legitimize the regime. Mahmud Shaltut, the cleric acting at the time as Sheykh al-Azhar, faithfully fulfilled this assignment.[35] Another leading institutional ideologue was the Sheykh al-Azhar Abdulhalim Mahmud,[36] who served as a legitimator under Sadat. Despite the Free Officers' pronouncements of a secular ideology, the values and worldview of praetorian Nasserism were secular but only superficially. The Islamic worldview[37] persisted beneath the surface; secularism was merely rhetorical. The requirements of a secular society, i.e. the reasoning of a secular reform Islam and the related structural-institutional underpinnings, were not in place. The praetorian rulers claimed to modernize, but did not touch on the Islamic worldview, and so no cultural change occurred. After Nasser's death in 1970, Sadat came to power. For convenience, he curbed secularism in an attempt to use the Muslim Brothers against his leftist Nasserist foes. He was eventually killed by the Jihad Movement, an offshoot of the same Brotherhood that had been unleashed to liberty under his rule.

It is sad to note the very poor achievements of Islamic reformism, liberalism, or secular nationalism and Egyptian praetorianism in pursuit of cultural change. The rise of political Islam is partly related to this failure. Recourse to religion for the legitimation of an Islamic state is the ideology of an Islamist opposition that promises to fix the situation. It is set to delegitimize the established religious institutions that stand in the service of the regime, in particular al-Azhar. Thus, Islam in Egypt has two brands, the one pro-regime and the other based on the mobilizatory ideology of an oppositional underground movement.

Political Islam stretches its reach far beyond Egypt. For instance, Islamism in Algeria can be traced back to the Egyptian Muslim Brotherhood, which sent teachers there to plant the first seeds of the Algerian variety of Islamism. The politics of "Arabization" in Algeria finished up by becoming a politics of Isla-mization. In this regard, schools, universities, and later, the mosques became the basic institutions in Algeria for the spread of Islamism.[38] In Egypt, Algeria, and elsewhere rulers and their opponents alike, i.e. the elites and the counter-elites, are in competition. In this venture, the use of education and of the mosque is essential. Under Mubarak, the regime used its power to coerce the Islamist movement so as to limit its use of the mosque.[39] Despite all differences, the state and the Islamist opposition have in common a prohibition on rethinking or reshaping existing values and the prevailing worldview. Both have had recourse to Islam in an instrumental manner so as to legitimate either political rule or opposition to it. These Islamic values were put into the service of legitimation or de-legitimation of power on religious grounds. Cultural accommodation of social change and of development-related needs seems not be a concern. In Egypt, as elsewhere in the Islamic world, the predicament with modernity continues to burden the "*umma*-community" in its search for the just imam,[40] not for solutions to current problems. Here political Islam makes no difference.

In Egypt, the majority of imams are recruited from the community of al-Azhar graduates. They are employed by the *awqaf* ministry (the Ministry for Religious Affairs), i.e. they are subject to the state. As documented in the empirical research of Morroe Berger, under the praetorian military regime of Nasser the Egyptian government succeeded in subjecting the mosques to its control. In doing so, it did not make any real effort to underpin the official secularization policy with cultural substance. Politics lacked any cultural under-pinning; no religious reform was in place. The regime merely pursued a policy of using religion as a means of legitimation in the pursuit of political ends and, of course, so as to restrict the imams of the mosques to purely religious functioning.

This was done for the purely pragmatic purpose of maintaining power. The dual goal of the praetorian regime was to bring all mosques, both the public and the private ones, under government control and to use religious authority for its own legitimatory ends. No reformist interpretation of Islam was in sight. Under Sadat the surge of private mosques as places for the mobilization of Islam could not be halted. The politicization of Islam continues to progress. Under these conditions, cultural change under both Nasser and Sadat simply meant making religion suitable to the military regime.[41] In other words, it was a question of using Islam as an instrument to legitimize policy. It is not only the political economy, but also the cultural analysis of the situation in Egypt in the period from Nasser through Sadat to Mubarak that helps to explain the failed development. The combination of structural and cultural analyses leads to the sources of that country's failure to develop and to come to grips with the problems related to the predicament.

The rise in the number of private mosques illustrates the new development: in 1964 there were still 14,000 private mosques as compared to only 3,000 mosques run by the state. Under Sadat the intensified efforts to politicize Islam backfired. Fundamentalists presented their Islam as the only "*hall*/solution" to the social and economic crisis in Egypt.[42] In this context, numbers shifted further in favor of the private mosques: in 1970 there were 20,000. By the time Sadat was assassinated in October 1981, the number of private (*ahali*) mosques had risen to 46,000, as compared to 6,000 state mosques. With the assistance of Saudi funds[43] the numbers of these private mosques – the home of political Islam – have been skyrocketing. Hamid Ansari, who studied these developments while conducting fieldwork on Muslim underground organizations in Cairo, informs us that the mosque serves both as a place for political activities and as a recruiting ground for militant, fundamentalist underground organizations.[44] This is not peculiar to Egypt: it is true of most Islamic countries. Algeria is another case in point to illustrate this new function of the mosque. In Egypt one of these underground organizations, al-Jihad,[45] was behind the assassination of Sadat, the president who had once released Islamists from jail. This jihadist group and many other similar-minded organizations, collectively known as the "*al-Jama'at al-Islamiyya*/ Islamist groups" or dubbed *Jama'at al-takfir*,[46] are, for the most, part splinter groups that broke away from the original Muslim Brotherhood Movement.

The distinction (introduced earlier) between institutional and jihadist Islamism can be demonstrated by the example of extremist groups that went underground as jihadist branches of political Islam, in contrast to the Muslim Brotherhood, which has formed the moderate center of Islamism and is also represented in public institutions. Unlike the new institutional approach of the Muslim Brothers, there are jihadist groups that subscribe to *Terror in the Mind of God*.[47] They legitimize the use of force in religious terms and carry on an irregular war.[48] Despite the difference between institutional and jihadist Islamism, they share the same values and worldviews, as well as the political goal of an "Islamic state." Wickham, Baker, and similar-minded authors are therefore utterly wrong in their favorable assessment of the Muslim Brotherhood in Egypt.[49] Political Islam is not the other modernity and it does not contribute to an Islamic overcoming of the predicament with modernity. It is not, as Baker contends, an *Islam without Fear*.

Despite the distinction between jihadist and institutional Islamism, all Islamists stand in the tradition of Sayyid Qutb in that they view cultural modernity as neo-*jahiliyya* (pre-Islamic ignorance, thus unbelief) and despise it. One cannot see any creative or innovative effort in this whole set-up. From the viewpoint that cultural change is needed in order to promote development, the case of a *Mobilizing Islam*, presented here by the example of Egypt, does not provide promising prospects for a better future. Islamism cements the existing impasse in Egypt, as elsewhere. In this respect, it is a generalizable case. Notwithstanding the great rifts between Sunni and Shi'a, one can state that the Islamic Revolution of Iran established some rapprochement between the confessions.

Competition and the borrowing: political Islam in Sunni Egypt under the Shi'i influence of the Islamic Revolution in Iran

Egypt has been the best-loved place for US scholars of Middle Eastern and Islamic studies. They started in the 1960s and reached their height in the 1990s at US universities. These studies reflect development not only in the region, but also in the discipline itself. During four decades views in this research field have shifted gear. One can illustrate the change through the example of two studies dealing with Egypt, both published by Harvard University Press. In 1961 the late Nadav Safran presented his first book, which reamins a masterpiece on Egypt. It is a study of liberalism in Egypt's search, as an Islamic country, for identity as a political community (see note 18). Safran was sympathetic towards liberal Egyptian thinkers, but he candidly showed why they failed to establish a pattern of culture that was favorable to promoting progressive development in state, polity, and society. In 2003 another US expert on Egypt published a politically correct study on Islamism in Egypt under the misleading title *Islam without Fear. Egypt and the New Islamists* (see note 49). In Egypt, Islamism has taken the place of liberalism. Was this a change for the better? Being a Muslim myself, who has been studying Islamism intimately for many decades, I cannot dispel my fear of these new Islamists. I have reason to consider them on all levels, in line with Sir Karl Popper, as "Enemies of the Open Society." I therefore chose to give an earlier book on this subject the title *The New Totalitarianism*, and not *Islamism without Fear*. In my most recent (2008) book on political Islam[50] I argue for a democratic civil society that promotes development and a market economy and propose to replace the Islamist formula "*al-hall huwa al-Islam*/Islam [read Islamism] is the solution" with the better one of "democracy is the solution." An open and civil Islam, but not Islamism, is compatible with democracy. Democracy is definitely not an "imported solution," as Qaradawi propagates – it is a necessity for a better future.

Political Islam received a boost in the aftermath of the 1967 defeat, and became more forceful in the 1970s after Nasser's death. When Sadat followed

Nasser into power he faced a powerful, secular-Nasserist opposition to his take-over. He therefore tried to mobilize the Muslim Brotherhood for his needs. Under Nasser's rule they had been interned in concentration camps. Prior to the Free Officers' seizure of power on July 23, 1952 Sadat, himself a part of this coup, had been assigned to approach the Muslim Brotherhood – as he claims in his autobiography[51] – in order to appease them. Nasser sought a tactical alliance with the Brotherhood; however, it did not work. Soon a political polarization between the two groups replaced the early flirtation with these strange bed-fellows. It was in this context that the Muslim Brothers made an unsuccessful attempt to assassinate Nasser in 1954. In an act of retaliation, Nasser ordered dozens of their leaders to be imprisoned and even to be hanged. Then followed an abortive coup attempt in 1965, after which thousands of Muslim Brothers again found their way into internment camps. Among the executed leaders, named as "*shahids*/martyrs," was the supreme intellectual authority of the Muslim Brotherhood, Sayyid Qutb, who was hanged in public in Cairo in 1966. Qutb remains to date the foremost authority of political Islam. His writings are printed and translated in millions of copies, distributed throughout the Islamic world. This is promoted through the transnational global links of Islamism as the new internationalism in world politics.

As already stated, Sadat came to power in 1970 and released most of the imprisoned Muslim Brothers, hoping in return for their support as tactical allies, for the reasons already mentioned. The resurgence of Islamism under Sadat was therefore related to an internal political conflict. (The reader should keep in mind that all of these events predate Khomeini's takeover of power in Iran in 1979.) After Sadat's assassination in October 1981, by the very Muslim militants whom he had courted, many experts asked, despite the facts just mentioned, whether events in Iran could affect Arab Islam, or even be repeated in the Arab world,[52] in particular in Egypt. Other questions were posed concerning the Iranian connection, e.g. the proclaimed Islamist inter-nationalism. Certainly, no well-informed analyst could afford to deny the spill-over effects of the Iranian Shi'i Islamic Revolution in neighboring Sunni Islamic countries, including Egypt. However, these effects were limited to demon-strating that an existing regime can be toppled in favor of establishing an Islamic order. Today, there are two competing Islamisms. One of them is the Shi'i model, which cannot be exported into a Sunni environment. The Aya-tollahs envisioned exporting their "Shi'i revolution," but failed – also because Sunni political Islam has its own internationalism, with a much older tradition. Some setbacks for political Islam and a questionable pronouncement of democra-tization tempted French experts to speak prematurely of a "failure of political Islam" and, even more ignorantly, of "*le fin de l'Islamisme*/the end of Isla-mism."[53] Political Islam and its place in Egypt's problems vis-à-vis develop-ment belie the views expressed by these "pundits," who are supposed to know what they are talking about, but in fact – due to their lack of solid knowledge – do not.

For an appropriate understanding of Islamism one needs to go back to the Arab defeat in the Six Day War of 1967, which brought about a severe crisis of legitimacy in all Arab countries. Among the effects were, on the one hand, the weakening of the dominant secular elites and their unpromising ideologies (liberalism, nationalism, socialism) and, on the other hand, the creation of favorable conditions for the politicization of Islam.[54] The fact that the Islamic revolution occurred in Iran and not in Egypt should not dilute the differences between the predominantly Sunni community of Arab states led by Egypt and Shi'i Iran. These differences touch primarily on divergent concepts of divine order. However, the already mentioned spill-over effects must be conceded.[55]

Instead of contributing to an overcoming of Islam's predicament with modernity, the Islamic Revolution in Iran added some further fuel to the fire of Islam's geo-political war and sent its flames higher. This can be stated on the basis of two areas of impact: first, the adoption of Shi'i-martyr suicide (suicide bombing) by Sunni Islamists; and second, the introduction of the Shi'i underground tradition of secrecy and mystery-mongering into Sunni Islam, as translated into the politics of the underground. Without a doubt the elevation of jihad in a new interpretation of jihad as jihadism (i.e. terrorism) is an accomplishment of the Egyptian Muslim Brothers. This is a new Sunni tradition of the political underground, free of Shi'ism. But this novelty did not include the recent jihadist suicide bombing. The jihadist Sunni Islamists adopted this pattern under the influence of Shi'ism. It first spilled over into Lebanon. Iran has supported the Lebanese Shi'i Hezbollah (established 1982 in the Iranian embassy in Damascus) and advanced it to a proxy acting in the Arab world. When this Islamist movement won in the Lebanon war of July/August 2006, the Muslim Brothers in Egypt viewed it as an extended victory of their own.[56] Today, the Muslim Brothers combine the underground activity that existed prior to the Islamic Revolution in Iran with participation in political public life. Unlike the *Jama'at Islamiyya*, which made an established tradition out of these clandestine activities, the Muslim Brothers learned to adopt *taqiyya*, which is part of Shi'i belief. *Taqiyya* means dissimulation in order to deceive the enemy. In Islamic history, Shi'ites were persecuted by the Sunni state and needed to practice this deception in order to save their lives. In politics, *taqiyya* means to deceive the foes. Sunni Islamists who adopted clandestine underground political activism from political Shi'i Islam also embraced the practice of *taqiyya* in their activities. The Sunni term for the same is *"iham/*deception." Many Western experts fail to grasp this new *taqiyya* and therefore take the pro-democracy pronouncements of Islamists at face value, without noticing the act of deception that is involved.

Neither Egypt nor Iran has contributed to a modernizing development in Islamic form. One may compare the pre-Islamist models pursued in both countries. In Iran, the Pahlavi dynasty was established by Reza Shah, who came to power in 1925. His interest revolved around the construction of a modern, centralized state, which had not existed before. The model that Iran emulated under the rule of the Pahlavis was that of Kemalist Turkey. In contrast,

Egyptian experiments with a modern state are more than a century older. As was shown at the outset, Egypt was exposed to the ideas of the French Revolution from the end of the eighteenth century, when Napoleon came to Cairo in 1798. Modernization followed in 1805 with Mohammed Ali's reforms, which were inspired by the French influence. Resistance to this modernization had already begun during Napoleon's sojourn, when the religious authorities of al-Azhar University revolted against his innovations. This rejection of innovative change continued under Mohammed Ali's rule. But he considerably curbed the political power of the *ulema*, while at the same time enlisting their institutions for his own legitimation. Seen in a historical perspective, Egypt has thus been the cradle both of the efforts to adjust Islam to modernity (the Islamic modernism of the second half of the nineteenth century, or Egyptian liberalism[57]) and of the rejection of these efforts, whether through the defensive-cultural means of the orthodox Salafism of al-Azhar or through the religious semi-modern fundamentalism of the Muslim Brotherhood. As argued earlier, the historical epoch of reform Islam and liberalism ended in Egypt in 1952 when the Free Officers took over and replaced liberalism with their praetorianism. Unlike the latecomer Iran, political Islam had already started in Egypt in 1928 with the movement of the Muslim Brotherhood. This Sunni Islamism introduced into Egypt a pattern long known in Shi'ite Islam, namely, the use of religion for political opposition. In reversing the tradition by which al-Azhar University performed a legitimatory function in Sunni Islam, the Muslim Brothers, although themselves Sunni, have formed the first remarkable political opposition to the existing political establishment on religious grounds; they deviated from the earlier Sunni tradition of legitimating power. Under Mubarak, the Muslim Brothers were able to penetrate society and even the religious establishment. The following event supports this observation: after the liberation of Iraq from the rule of Saddam Hussein in April 2003 a *fetwa* was issued in the name of al-Azhar against the US and the Iraqi Governing Council. The Sheykh of al-Azhar could not prevent this *fetwa* being issued, but he distanced himself from it, thus revealing that he lacked within his own institution the authority that his predecessors had enjoyed. Both, the *fetwa* and the distancing statement of Sheykh Tantawi, were published by *al-Hayat* on the internet. Another *fetwa* of al-Azhar, against the reform Muslim Abu-Zaid, published in November 2003, was based on a judgment written by the Islamist Mohammed Imara. Both cases document an Islamist infiltration of al-Azhar.

In Shi'a Islam there is a religious hierarchy and a religious central instance in Qom. Sunni Islam has al-Azhar as the most authoritative seat of learning for all Sunni Muslims. The Sheykh al-Azhar (the rector) continues to be the highest authority for issuing binding *fetwas* (legal judgments). However, al-Azhar has never contributed to reforming Islam.[58] When M. Abduh was its rector, his efforts were undermined by this very establishment and today they are no more than intellectual history. Nor did "revolutionary" Shi'i[59] Islam ever contribute to a reform.

As argued in Chapter 6, secularization – not secularism – is needed in order to overcome Islam's predicament with cultural modernity. It has to be supported by an Islamic underpinning. Pan-Arabism was a secular ideology with a recourse to Islam, but it did not establish the needed tradition. Religion was also not really depoliticized under the rule of Nasser, in that there was no real separation between religion and politics. Further, no cultural reforms were pursued in Egypt for such an end. In Egypt, Sufi Islam and its orders[60] were another variety of Islam, next to that of the establishment. In this situation, political Islam is not to be viewed as a renaissance of religion, but rather as a re-politicization. Arab nationalism failed to overcome the tensions between Islam and the nation-state.[61] The Islamic Revolution in Iran played a role by replacing the secular nation-state with a *Government of God*.[62] A similar claim existed in Egypt as an outcome of the post-1967 developments,[63] but could not be realized by the Muslim Brothers.

Only for a few years the Islamic Revolution of Iran succeeded in upgrading Shi'i Islamism at the expense of Sunni politics. The world political situation was changed by the war in Afghanistan against the Soviet invasion, and later on by the war between Iraq and Iran (1980–88). These wars weakened the position of Iran, to the benefit of Sunni internationalism. This situation promoted the rise of al-Qaida. In both cases, political Islam is definitely not an *Islam without Fear*. This is wishful thinking on the part of US scholars who write books with such titles. What matters here is that neither variety, the Sunni nor the Shi'i, contributed to a better Islamic perspective. Instead, they did great damage to Islam and promoted its association with "fears."

From the underground to the establishment of the parallel sector: "mobilizing Islam" in Egypt

Political Islam received a boost in the context of the repercussions of the 1967 Six Day War. At the beginning of the 1980s, when Hosni Mubarak inherited a weak state from Sadat, the Islamist opposition, in both its institutional and its jihadist branches, was already a powerful movement and it became a real challenge. By the way, the terms "political Islam" or "Islamism" mean the same thing and they denote a variety of religious fundamentalism. At issue is not Islam as a religion, but a political Islam with a concept of political order. It is the most recent variety of totalitarianism. The two directions of political Islam – the one is a terrorist extremism, i.e. jihadism, the other is institutional Islamism – differ from one another in the methods they use, but not on their aims. Both share the ultimate agenda of establishing an Islamic, shari'a-based state named "*Hakimiyyat Allah*/God's rule."[64] In Egypt, the distinction between the *Jama'at* (the underground groups) and the Muslim Brotherhood relates only to the means to be used and is thus not more than a differentiation between jihadism and institutionalism, the two directions of political Islam. True, jihadism has declined in Egypt, owing to the state's security politics, but the "mobilizing Islam" of the institutional Islamists has been continuously on the rise. The Muslim Brothers have been successful in establishing a parallel sector in society. This is by no means an "end of Islamism" (see note 53). The truth is that this transnational movement is alive and kicking in all its forms. Today it is the major popular choice throughout the Islamic world, like it or not.

The Egyptian social scientist Saad Eddin Ibrahim[65] was among those who, under Sadat's rule, were allowed to interview Muslim fundamentalists imprisoned in Egyptian jails. These were not Muslim Brothers but offspring of their movement, who created the jihadist "*Jama'at Islamiyya*/Islamic groups," such as *Takfir wa Hijra*, among others. Despite their inner diversity, these jihadist groups are like their originators, i.e. the Muslim Brothers and, like all Islamists, committed to the "*an-nizam al-Islami*/Islamic system" based on sacred law (shari'a). In addressing this issue from the viewpoint of cultural values and worldview, we can see in Islamism an ideology that does not promote the unfolding of the cultural foundations that are necessary for dealing with Islam's predicament with modernity on the basis of a progressive political and social development. What lies behind the religio-political ideology of Islamism? What is the underlying worldview of the Egyptian Islamists? Why are the hopes that some US Middle East experts pin on "the new Islamists" nothing but illusory?

Without a doubt, the power of Islamism cannot be ignored. Today, no serious observer can talk about Egypt without dealing with the Islamist opposition. The story of political Islam in Egypt is older than its birth in 1928. Exposure to the West from the late eighteenth century onwards and the related predicament are the background to a proper understanding of the process of rapid and uneven social change that led to the rise of political Islam. Among the traits of a distortive modernization is asymmetrical urbanization. It affects cities such as Cairo, and hence the mindset of people who live there. At the end of World War II Cairo had some two million inhabitants, whereas today there are more than eighteen million living in a city that is characterized by unbalanced growth. The majority of Egyptians continue to live in rural areas, but the rate of rural–urban migration is increasing. The already high rate of migration to Cairo was exacerbated after the Six Day War by 1967 by approximately a further two million refugees, who poured into the city from the Canal Zone. Any Westerner unfamiliar with urban centers in Asia and Africa would be appalled, on arriving in Cairo, by the sheer mass of people on the streets. One can scarcely comprehend that people (some quarter of a million) live even in the city's cemetery, between the graves. Given the chronic housing shortage in Cairo, the peasants who migrate to the city have no other choice. It is better to have some kind of shelter than to live on the street. To be housed in one of the poor quarters of Cairo seems a luxury to such poor people in comparison to what is available to them. The urban growth of Cairo in past decades has been a process of the ruralization of its suburbs rather than of urbanization in substance. This observation applies to most metropolitan areas in the Islamic world. This phenomenon, and not Israel, is what threatens the stability of Egypt.[66] Demographic growth and the related phenomenon of misplaced people are the time bomb that promotes the recruitment of soldiers to political Islam.

The available data indicate that most members of fundamentalist groups in Egypt come from the lower middle classes of rural background. They come to Cairo for an academic education and with the expectation of a better life. In the already-cited book by Carrie Rosefsky-Wickham[67] one will find data that supports the validity of the assumption of an increasing number of people of rural background living in Cairo who are not rooted in urban life. These people, uprooted from their safe, rural milieu, feel alienated and culturally lost in a noisy, densely populated, and extremely dirty city where everything seems to be anonymous. Rural migrants leave the countryside in the expectation of enjoying a better future and, in their disappointment, they seek an enemy to blame. The search for certainty leads to political Islam and the emerging related cultural tensions. Among these people one finds poorly trained university graduates. Under Nasser, academic training boomed through an expansion of the educational sector. The military regime viewed this as a kind of social policy of justice. The acquisition of a university education was related to an expectation of upward mobility. The people of this "lumpenintelligentsia" found themselves in a situation of cultural anomie.[68] The lack of a pay-off, and the occupational frustrations of this poorly educated intelligentsia,[69] assumed a politicized shape promoted by political Islam. This is one of the conditions facilitating the recruitment of Islamists and jihadists among young, hopeless people.

In Egypt, the populist expansion of the universities and the legitimation of these educational policies created a problem that affected the whole of society. Under Nasser the once-exemplary Egyptian educational system was expanded at the expense of being leveled. The result was academics with a maximum of social expectations and a minimum of professional qualifications. In a poor society such as Egypt's, this has the potential to undermine the entire political system, as the latter is unable to meet the occupational expectations of an upward mobility related to academic education. Nasser attempted to escape the results of this disproportionate expansion of education by guaranteeing jobs – although with minimal salaries – for all graduates. The huge number of unemployed university graduates is today a real plague in Egyptian society. These strata of the lower middle classes are a major source of opposition to the existing regime. The opposition is organized and mobilized on the basis of a politicizing Islam. This religionized political ideology provides the means of articulation for these socio-political concerns and serves as a "mobilisatory ideology" (Rodinson). In this understanding of a "mobilizing Islam," religious fundamentalism becomes a source of cultural tensions that lead to all kinds of conflict. The home of this "mobilizing Islam" is the city, not the countryside. The guilt for this misery is seen as being rooted in the globalization generated by the West. The language of political Islam articulates the fundamentalist perception that the "crusaders and the Zionists" are the instigators of a globalization that is implemented by these "enemies of Islam." The perception of a misery imposed on the people of Islam nurtures a millenarian yearning in the Islamists, with their call for a return to Islam. This attitude leads to a total casting-off of everything that has been adopted from the West. In this context, they believe that "*al-Islam huwa all hall*/only Islam brings salvation." The Islamists make one exception: they accept the adoption of techno-scientific instruments from the West in order to fight the enemy with his own weapons.

Islamism, or Islamic fundamentalism, is, in its function as a doctrine of salvation, a plea for de-Westernization that implies a return to pure and primordial Islam. This is the meaning of Islamic authenticity, as was shown in the preceding chapter. This is by no means a variety of traditionalism: Islamic fundamentalists are not traditionalists, as their recourse to Islamic "fundamentals," i.e. the "basics" and "essences," superficially suggests. Their selective use of text and tradition is embedded in the context of modernity. Most Islamists have a modern educational background. They can be viewed as semi-modernists in the meaning that they split modernity into techno-scientific instruments, being the adopted half, and cultural values, being the rejected half. In short, they are in favor of adopting the instruments, but vehemently reject the related cultural values and worldview, demonizing them as Western.[70] I argue that this mindset of Islamism in Egypt is not favorable to dealing properly with Islam's predicament with cultural modernity. On the contrary, it seeks to mobilize and to create tensions in pursuit of a conflict that is seen as leading to salvation. This creates an obstacle to proper development.

To sum up this section, the idea of a politically and socially mobilizing Islam in pursuit of conflict is correct, but needs to be defined. On the surface, Islamism seems to be a peripheral phenomenon. In fact, it is a powerful movement. In Egypt, institutional Islamists are today an established reality that no one can afford to ignore. The activities of jihadist Muslim militants have been successfully curbed by the Mubarak regime; but this is of no consequence for the existence of political Islam in Egypt, because it is jihadism, not the general phenomenon of Islamism, that is subsiding. Islamism is most powerful in the parallel sector in Egypt that thrives in the parallel societies controlled by the Islamists. Political Islam creates a great challenge to any further development in Egypt. Most pundits limit the use of the term "parallel society" to the migratory diaspora of Islam in Europe. Thereby they overlook the existence of a similar phenomenon in the Islamic world itself. Egypt is a case in point. The only political opposition ready to take over after Mubarak is Islamism, which exists politically as a movement and socially as a power in the parallel societies.

Conclusions: which Islam for Egypt's future?

Most Islamists are laymen with a poor knowledge of Islam. Nevertheless, the way in which they articulate their political goals in a religious language has great appeal. This is described by Said Eddin Ibrahim in the following words: "The militant Islamic groups with their emphasis on brotherhood, mutual sharing, and spiritual support become the functional equivalent of the extended family to the youngster who has left his behind. In other words, the Islamic group fulfills a de-alienating function for its members."[71]

Although Sadat's assassin, Khalid al-Istanbuli,[72] was an army officer, one can assume that Islamists have not yet penetrated the armed forces. However, in the recent past Islamists have been in a position to go beyond functioning in the underground, by adding to their battlefields the mosque, the university campus, and the parallel sector. This makes them politically capable of changing the existing political system, but they are far from any cultural change and religious reform. Their control of the parallel sector, as well as of the major professional associations, enables them to mobilize other social groups. Today, we must speak of emerging counter-elites[73] that challenge the ruling Egyptian political elites. The institutional, peaceful Islamists are, in the long run, more challenging to the political system and to society than the jihadist militants have ever been. The reason for this is that they are able to mobilize the emerging rural and the urban counter-elites, and also to penetrate deeply into society, where they build up these parallel sectors into a parallel society dominated by political Islam.

Among the conclusions of this case study is the account given of the new role of religion in state and society. In the public life of Egypt one notices an all-pervading religiosity as soon as one sets foot there. There is a potential for a mobilization on the ground, which the Islamists could lead. Despite its control by the state, al-Azhar, the pillar of Sunni Islam, is penetrated by the Islamists. The Sheykh of al-Azhar, who sometimes appears on Egyptian television to speak against these Islamist groups, branding them as misled or as falsifiers of "true Islam," is losing his authority in favor of the Islamists. The ruling National Democratic Party, inherited by Hosni Mubarak from Sadat, puts out publications in which members of the religious establishment, which backs the government, likewise write about and define what "Islam" is. The Islamic interpretative monopoly is thus firmly on the side of the President of Egypt, Mubarak. However, through the Islamist penetration of al-Azhar this balance is radically changing. Fouad Ajami provides an apt description of the office of Sheykh al-Azhar in the following words:

> His views ... are not merely the views of an ordinary writer. Those could be right or wrong, sound or not; one could refute them, be moved by them, argue with them. The Sheykh's utterances are of a different order: they are fetwa, binding religious opinions. Behind them is the authority not only of the dominant traditions, but ... of the state as well. What a reader encounters in this text, then, is the burden of an established tradition: religious interpretation in the service of the custodians of political power.[74]

In speaking of political Islam in Egypt one must not overlook the fact that this country has a Christian population – the Egyptian Copts – constituting 10 to 12 percent of the population.[75] They are a minority only in the denominational sense, for in ethnic terms they are a homogeneous part of the Egyptian population. The sectarian conflicts of this country are not comparable, for example, with minority conflicts in Malaysia or Sri Lanka, where problems of this kind relate to an ethnic component. However, the call of the Islamists for an "Islamic state" within the framework of a politicization of Islam is a threat to the Christians and creates a source of tensions leading to interdenominational conflict. Saad Eddin Ibrahim, the founder of the Ibn Khaldun Center for Civil Society and its director until it was closed by the government, broke established taboos. He was the one who addressed the cultural and political tensions related to these issues. One may assume that this activity was the real reason for the charges against Ibrahim that led to the closing of his Ibn Khaldun Center.[76] Sectarian conflicts related to minorities within the Islamic world are a real part of Islam's civil war. They are a taboo subject. These conflicts become more relevant when they become geo-political.[77]

In short, in the long run, the Salafists and the Islamists seem to be the power that will determine the future of Islam in Egypt. Due to the change in patterns of education during the years 1952–70, under Nasser's rule, the secular elite lost its power. Raymond Hinnebusch found in 1982 that the secular elite continues to favor the "secular, liberal democratic" model,[78] but today, in the twenty-first century, it is a weak elite. Counter-elites in Egypt and even in Turkey, the most secular country of the Islamic world, are growing and becoming very powerful. Despite state repression, the fundamentalists in Egypt are powerful to the extent that the regime needs to appease them in an effort to consolidate its own legitimacy and stability. Today, Egypt's political Islam is much more than an oppositional religio-political underground movement.[79] It has successfully introduced a parallel sector into the system.

Viewing Turkey under the rule of AKP Islamists since 2002, some Western pundits believe that an Egypt under Islamist rule could adapt Islam to the changing conditions of our global age. These pundits, and some Arabists in the State Department in Washington, would not mind seeing the Muslim Brothers rule in Egypt. In their view, it would provide greater stability. In Washington, people listen to these pundits. True, the current political regime's interest revolves exclusively around issues of survival and a fragile stability. Cultural change and religious reform are non-issues. I do not buy into the idea that the Islamists could be an alternative. They do not promote the development of an Islam that is compatible with democracy, human rights, and civil society. I look at Indonesia and see the elements of an open Islam addressed by Robert Hefner as "civil Islam,"[80] but this pattern is not related to an Islamist movement such as it exists in Egypt. The founder of political Islam, Hasan al-Banna, and the spiritual father of this movement, Sayyid Qutb, never contributed to such a "civil Islam," nor do their contemporary followers, identified as the "New Islamists" (note 49), make any efforts in this direction. An overview leads to the general conclusion that the ideology of the political Islamists does not go far beyond a politicization of the Islamic cultural system, used as a means for articulating a defensive cultural attitude to contest the West as a hegemonial power and as a source of cultural modernity.

For the study of these issues, Egypt is the best case in point. Add to this the uniqueness of Egypt as the home of al-Azhar. So, one finds next to the Islamists the Azharites, who embody the Islamic establishment. Unlike the Islamists, with their inadequate knowledge of Islam, the Azharites are, in principle, capable of reforming Islam – but they are highly reluctant to engage in such an undertaking. The question whether Egyptian Islamists are innovative or not can be easily given a negative answer. Therefore, the efforts of the Azhar establishment are more interesting to an inquiry into the cultural accommodation of social change, with respect to Islam as a cultural system. Could al-Azhar change gear and abandon its mentioned reluctance?

It is an established fact in Islamic history that the Sunni *ulema* have always been and still are the legitimators of existing rule. Thus, one can speak of a religio-political alliance between the religious and the political establishments. It has also been suggested that, until Nasser's reforms of 1961, rulers contented themselves with legitimation through the Azharites, scarcely attempting to impose any specific ideas on the religious establishment. Since Napoleon's expedition and the ensuing establishment of Mohammed Ali's rule, Egypt has undergone processes of rapid social change that have substantially altered both the social structure and, in a way, the culture of the country. But this change has not amounted to an involvement of the al-Azhar Sheykhs in a religious reform leading to a kind of cultural change that could smooth the way to dealing appropriately with Islam's predicament with cultural modernity. The inference is the negative conclusion, reached also by Daniel Crecelius, namely, that the *ulema's* responses

> to the challenges of modernization have been predictably, instinctively defensive, characterized by a strong desire for self-preservation. ... Unwilling or unable to direct change, or even to make an accommodation to it, they have in the end been overwhelmed by change which inexorably penetrated first the government and the ruling elites, then their own institutions and other social groups.[81]

From the point of view of Islamic orthodoxy (Salafism), anything new that is added to the primary sources (the Qur'an and *Hadith*) is pejoratively called *bid'a* (literally, "innovation," but with the connotation of "heresy"). The Egyptian *ulema* at al-Azhar have always reacted to innovations in this way. If they ever did assent to a change, however, it was always in the sense of pragmatically legitimizing an action of the respective ruler, a kind of conformism without relinquishing their own attitude of rejection and without rethinking their worldview. This cultural attitude reflects a simple adjustment and is not a cultural accommodation to social change.[82] Religious reform is not in place.

In this context, Daniel Crecelius adds a new category, "obscurantism," in addition to the simultaneous legitimation and rejection, the way in which the al-Azhar inner circles act. This applies to all innovative measures. Even the radical reform imposed on al-Azhar and initiated by Nasser proved incapable of bringing about real conformism of the crudely medieval worldview of al-Azhar to the regime's politics of modernization. It is not an Orientalism to speak of the obscurantism of the al-Azhar authorities. For instance, these *ulema* assented to state provision of birth control aimed at solving Egypt's most serious problem – overpopulation – and undermined it at the same time. Crecelius has a point when he writes that the *ulema* have successfully managed to delay the process of modernization, but at a terrible price for Islam and for the *ulema*.[83]

Stated in a nutshell, al-Azhar has never made any significant contribution to the cultural accommodation of social change. The pressing task of overcoming the Islamic predicament with modernity has not been achieved. Instead, the Azhar scribes have engaged in the legitimation of political power, doing so hand-in-hand with obscurantism. This characterizes the *ulemas'* dealings with current issues. It is ironic that these *ulema* share the view of the Western Orientalists (whom they bitterly oppose) that Islamic culture is based on the philology of the Arabic language and the exegesis of traditional sources perceived as sacrosanct. In fact, *no* attempt has ever been made to engage in a "rethinking of Islam" so as to change the prevailing Islamic worldview. In short: the Islamic reformation will not come from the al-Azhar orthodoxy, just as it will not come from the diaspora of Islam in Europe. Who will do the job? In all honesty, I do not know!

It is true that the authoritative two-volume work of al-Azhar published under the auspices of the late al-Azhar Sheykh Jadul-Haq[84] no longer incriminates cultural innovation on religious grounds as *bid'a*, but rather, warns of a sweeping use of this traditional Islamic formula against change. However, this open-mindedness shies away from promoting and culturally accommodating the ongoing social rapid change. The Egyptian al-Azhar is the highest institution of Sunni Islam and its failure to establish a new tradition of an "open Islam" is consequential. It has contributed indirectly to the politicization pursued by the new Islamists, who are undermining the authority of al-Azhar. It is shameful that al-Azhar sided with the Islamists in the persecution of the reformer Nasr Hamid Abu-Zaid. This Muslim reformist simply wrote and published a book titled "*Naqd al-Khitab al dini*/Critique of the Religious Discourse," in which he argued from a rational, not a scriptural point of view.[85] He was declared a "*murtad*/apostate" by a court, and on these grounds was divorced from his wife against both his and her will. In 1995 he was forced to flee from the country to seek asylum in the Netherlands.[86] As stated above, in November 2003, in a binding *fetwa* al-Azhar forbade a new book by Abu Zaid, on the grounds of a written judgment by the Islamist Mohammed Imara. In considering this information, while answering the question of this concluding section "Which Islam for Egypt?," one can state that it is becoming increasingly difficult to distinguish between al-Azhar and institutional Islamism. The line is heavily blurred.

The preceding analysis demonstrates the positive and negative changes in Islamic civilization. The predicament with cultural modernity is the burning issue. In Egypt neither an Islamic reform, nor a real Islamic liberalism can emerge to cope with the challenge in all seriousness. There were Muslim liberals who failed and had to give up in favor of political Islam. Egypt is the birthplace of political Islam, the Islamic variety of religious fundamentalism.[87] The interval of praetorian military rule under the Free Officers of Nasserism in Egypt made little difference. This praetorianism continues under the fragile regime of the aging Mubarak. It is just a matter of time until it breaks down.

In contemporary Egypt the ruling elite, as elsewhere in most countries of Islamic civilization, is composed of survivalists, not of modernizers. The UNDP's Arab Human Development Report[88] is a most telling document, implicitly accusing these elites not only of denying their people democracy and human rights, but also of blocking development. In such a set-up there can be no dealing with the predicament with cultural modernity so as to facilitate the emergence of a democratic civil society. In a further UNDP report of 2003 we learn that Middle Eastern peoples are also being denied access to modern knowledge. An optimistic US scholar contends that *The New Islamists*[89] provide a light at the end of the tunnel, an *Islam without Fear*. In contrast, I see a *New Totalitarianism* hidden by "*taqiyya*/dissimulation." One hopes for a "civil Islam" in Egypt as a model, but neither al-Azhar nor the so-called "new Islamists" provide a basis for its establishment in contemporary Egypt. The thinking of the new Islamists in Egypt does not reflect the perspective that the country needs in order to come to grips with the challenges of cultural modernity and structural globalization. The Islamists of today's Egypt fail to maintain what their country achieved in the past, namely, to provide the model for Islamic civilization.[90] The scenario of an Egypt ruled by Islamists is a scenario of conflict and a return to war.

Chapter 10

Case studies II: the Gulf beyond the age of oil

The envisioned cultural project for the future

The second case study[1] focuses on the Gulf states and it includes an Arabian Gulf perspective on the response to the challenges resulting from international "external events." Add to this the regional developments that affect internal trends. This chapter takes up the research question on feasible "strategies and policies that could guide the Gulf countries in successfully managing future developments" that was asked at the Center for Strategic Studies and Research/ECSSR, and suggests a set of innovations to meet those challenges. The question is placed in the overall context of the issues analyzed in the preceding chapters and the themes around which they revolve.

Introduction

In order to deal properly with questions related to the adjustment of the Gulf states and their societies to the changing international environment, it is necessary to consider global networks. The mapping of the entire world into the intensifying processes of globalization[2] creates an international environment that applies to all, including the Gulf. This chapter contests the premature and mistaken conclusion drawn from the correct insight that the world is shrinking into a global village, namely, that of an alleged standardization. It is argued instead that great challenges emerge to which the Arab–Persian Gulf is exposed – but without ignoring its particularities. If the special cultural conditions of the Gulf are not considered, no proper understanding is possible. Starting from the insight of tensions between the local and the global, and bearing in mind the conclusions of the preceding chapters, I identify the following three relevant and interconnected issue areas:

First, the place of the Gulf area. It is a subsystemic region within the international system,[3] in a world determined by the present global age.

Second, the meaning of innovations. This issue area leads to the following pivotal questions: to what extent do innovations require a cultural underpinning? Could one dare to place Islam's predicament with modernity into this context? And last, but not least, are there international standards beyond peculiarities and particularisms? All of these questions lead to the need for cultural change.

Third, the cultural commonalities. What is needed to establish among humanity – from a point of view of modernity – a culture of success that will be shared by all civilizations?

As already mentioned, I recognize the process of globalization but contest any generalization that the world has become a standardized entity. In contrast, I argue that while the globalization process has contributed to an unprecedented degree of mutual awareness and interaction between societies, it does not – as Bull contends – "in itself create a unity of outlook and has not in fact done so."[4] It follows that this lack of "a unity of outlook" is rooted in cultural diversity, which is enriching but which also has a negative aspect in that it could contribute to a conflict-laden cultural fragmentation, as analyzed in Chapter 5.

There is a potential for cultural fragmentation in the globalization process. This potential compels a search for commonalities that underpin a pattern of cultural pluralism, as presented in Chapter 7, as a platform for conflict resolution under the conditions of a "simultaneity of structural globalization and of cultural fragmentation."[5] The thematic focus of this case study is innovations in pursuit of a culture of success.[6] It could serve as a cultural bridge in the context of cultural diversity. The proposed culture of success is based on cultural modernity and could be promoted through cultural innovations. This is an alternative to religious fundamentalism,[7] which results generally from the unresolved predicament with modernity, and in particular from cultural tensions in religionized political conflicts.

Innovation and the significance of the Arabian Gulf in the twenty-first century

By all definitions, the states of the Arabian Gulf constitute a significant region of the world.[8] Their future is therefore pivotal, not only for the world economy but also for the Islamic world. The geo-politics of the entire region of the Middle Eastern subsystem to which the Gulf belongs relates also to culture. Thus, the cultural change required and recommended in order to meet the current challenges matters greatly to the whole international community. This insight is supported by the major assumption of this book regarding the interrelation between culture, political innovation, and the political question of conflict. Stated in a nutshell, the old approach that recommends separation of economy and politics from culture in order to avoid dispute and controversy is not only unhelpful, but also implies an evasion of the issue.

In earlier experiences in Kuwait, I observed that European businessmen were reluctant, in their dealings with local counterparts, to allow any dealing with culture and politics. This was done with the assumption that these issue areas did not matter to business. The cultural and political repercussions of many wars in the Gulf region belie this assumption and teach us that, at the beginning of the twenty-first century, no issue can be properly addressed if a separation of economy and politics from culture is at work. Today, one is more familiar with a changing world in which culture, economy, and politics are inseparably inter-twined. As argued throughout this book, there is a cultural predicament and a politicization of issues paired with a religionization of tensions that lead to severe conflicts. A study of the challenges that the Gulf faces makes clear just how much knowledge of the linkages between culture, economy, and politics is needed. This is the starting point for dealing properly with the Arab–Persian Gulf and for engaging in change with an awareness of the challenges. There are ways of dealing appropriately with the issues related to the challenges to which the Gulf region is exposed. Some suggest that the Gulf has an exemplary role to play not only in the Arab but also the Muslim world in general. Is this true?

The basic challenge to which the Arabian Gulf states and their societies are exposed is to develop a perspective of a future beyond the oil economy. Oil wealth is not an unending blessing. The Gulf states need to be competitive in order to integrate into the modern global market economy. In Dubai, one can see continuing superficial efforts at adjustment, while questions related to Islamic cultural patterns and the related essential requirements are strictly evaded. In fact, significant political and social innovations are needed in order to adjust an economy that is based on rent-acquired resources to the international standards of a diversified economy. This task cannot be pursued without including culture. The evasion is detrimental and has a negative effect on the whole undertaking of adjustment.

How can the necessary cultural change be achieved? There are some avenues for innovation. To be clear, the inherent possibilities for development are subject to regional and geo-political uncertainties, and are thus related to security poli-cies. Despite all the odds related to the international environment of the Gulf, a change in the political culture and its dimensions, together with a perspective of innovation, cannot be evaded if the Gulf states are to maintain their significance in the future. Innovations in a changed environment in the Arab–Persian Gulf cannot be achieved without an audacious effort to include cultural change.

Innovations and democracy in the Gulf

Today, democratization in state, culture, economy, and society is seen as a major avenue to the promotion of world peace and to conflict resolution in a globalizing but culturally and civilizationally diverse and fragmented world. This process promises to be a guarantee for minimizing the resort to violence in a crisis-laden situation. A "global democracy"[9] cannot be based on one monolithic pattern. In the Gulf, as in general in the Islamic world, a democratic system can only be successful if sharing the universal objective, while based on culturally different foundations. In particular, there is a need to establish a cultural underpinning for democratization. Democracy can only be successful if it has such a cultural underpinning to give it legitimacy in the society in which it exists.[10] To avoid any ambiguity: the reference to cultural pluralism does not imply the existence of multiple democracies. I acknowledge Arab Muslim particuliarities, but do not go down this avenue, and therefore do not share the related, unexamined assumptions.

In Iraq, the failed imposition of democracy from outside teaches us that such patterns can never thrive, because they lack legitimacy. The lesson for leaders of opinion in the Arab–Persian Gulf is that democratization has to be based on an innovative Islamic but culturally open-minded concept that can combine the Arab Islamic character with democracy, as it is universally understood. This statement is not a plea for a *shura* democracy. There is no such thing, and I do not support this claim. Of course, a modern reading of the Qur'anic concept of *shura* is helpful in that it can smooth the way for the Gulf societies to embrace democracy. However, democratic rule resembles rational knowledge, as ana-lyzed in Chapter 2, and therefore it has a universal meaning also. The term "Islamic democracy" could be a trap. It could be read with a contrary meaning and be the exact opposite of democracy. One finds such adverse use of the term in the writings of Voll and Esposito, where the issue is not only handled in a misleading manner but is also distorted.[11]

Democracy and rational knowledge are elements of a cultural modernity that is universal. The Qur'an teaches Muslims that the political culture and the public life of the *umma* – not to be confused with the constructed Islamic "*dawla/* state" (there is no such thing in the Qur'an) – have to be in line with *shura*. This notion can be interpreted as a culture of participatory deliberation, being an Islamic model. However, the Qur'an only provides instruction for an innovation that is needed in the political culture. It can be developed through change and reform. A political culture that supports the promotion of innovation could contribute to democratization. The argument of authenticity was discussed in Chapter 8, where it was shown to be a two-edged sword. To argue positively for an authenticity of cultural heritage does not preclude learning from other cul-tures and their experiences. This can be done while pursuing innovations, in line with the Prophet's recommendation "*wa utlibu al-ilm wa law fi al-Sin/*and search for knowledge even in China." In contrast, the claim to authenticity could mean purification and a gating of the Islamic world to the extent that it becomes iso-lated from the rest of the world. The reader is now in position to recognize the ambiguity of the notion of authenticity. This has to be borne in mind when some Gulf leaders of opinion call for keeping faith with one's own cultural heritage. It may not always be meant to legitimize the building up of an open society. It could also undermine a democratization process and democracy in the Arab–Persian Gulf. In short, the reference to "*turath/*heritage" may not always be a positive one.[12]

To pair modernization of the economy with democratization is a challenge to cultural change, and also to religious reform. I refer to the *Heritage of Islam*[13] in a positive manner, for instance to al-Farabi's[14] vision of *al-Madina al-Fadila*, to support the idea of good governance in Islamic terms. The "*Madina Fadila/*the polity" could be the proper order of a perfect state ruled by a Gulf leader who complied with reason in his political decision making. The establishment of a market economy would also seem to be more favorable for a better future in the Gulf. From the security perspective one may assume, in looking back to the contemporary history of the Arab–Persian Gulf, that this region could have been saved from all three recent wars[15] if Iraq and Iran had been democratic states. The so-called Islamic Revolution of Iran aimed to impose its model[16] on the Gulf states and it continues to do so. These states do not need such a model. Rather than such an imposition by Iran, the Gulf states need innovations. Emulating the unsuccessful Islamic model of Iran was a mistake in post-Saddam Iraq and it should not be repeated in the Gulf. Innovations are needed to sustain efforts at democratization, as well as education policies that promote modernity as a culture of success. I will now introduce the concept of a success culture. This is an aspect of the culture of modernity. It is based on three pillars: politics, culture, and economics, all intrinsically linked to one another. The introduction of this concept is relevant to the Gulf states, viewed as a case study for change.

The overall context of the proposed success culture and the cultural innovations necessary to establish

Most of the Gulf decision makers pay lip-service to the idea of reform in giving it their support as the road to a better future. However, they shy away from acknowledging that in this pursuit *Culture Matters*[17] to economy and politics, and that it, too, is subject to change. The idea that a culture of success cannot be successfully introduced without being supplemented by a cultural underpinning is not fully accepted by these decision makers. They look at their culture in an essentialist mindset. The envisioned innovations, understood as the proper response to rethinking existing traditions and worldviews, cannot be accomplished if this mindset prevails. The following two issue areas matter intrinsically to its introduction on the basis of a full acceptance of its requirements: *first*, democratization and *second*, education in the values of success culture. The concepts related to these needs are considered the foremost elements required for promotion of political innovation in the Gulf states and their societies. The first issue area, i.e. democratization, has already been discussed, so I now move on to the second. The meaning of a success culture in relation to the Gulf subregion of the Middle East is based on values. How could one promote value change?

To answer this question, one must at the outset acknowledge that globalization leads to the economic embedding of the Arab–Persian Gulf in the international economy. As has been made clear throughout this book, culture does not automatically reflect existing economic realities and the related globalized structure. Thus, prevailing values do not necessarily match the structural realities. Certainly, culture is based on values in society and these can be universalized, but not globalized. At present, under conditions of a prevailing political Islam,[18] it is extremely difficult to promote universalization of the values of a success culture through education. The values of Islamism are not consonant with the need for institutional innovations in the political system. They do not smooth the way for reforms in state and society; rather, they present an obstacle. Education is the pillar for the transmission of new values that change worldviews. Education also affects people's conduct and behavior. The intrusion of Islamism into education is highly detrimental to value change.

To summarize, the formula of a "success culture" provides a suitable framework in which to present the discussion of this chapter. This will be done in two steps: *first*, by outlining what is meant by cultural innovations; *second*, by introducing the concept of a success culture based on cultural modernity. In this book, and specifically in the following discussion of the Gulf, I am operating on the assumption of an interplay between social and cultural change. Culture is always in flux, but the idea of cultural change is reform-oriented and it therefore has a specific meaning for developing cultures. My thinking on this subject is free of any kind of essentialization.[19] In a similar vein, my notion of "developing culture" is free of evolutionism, because the course of change is not determined. Basically, if cultural change were set to support innovation in Gulf societies, it would have to be guided by a success culture introduced for that purpose and situated in the overall context of the culture of modernity,[20] which is central to this book.

As already stated, prudent decision makers among the majority of politicians and opinion leaders in the Gulf states not only speak of the need for political and cultural innovations, but also approve of it. In order to bridge between diverse civilizations, modernity[21] should be a shared pattern. However, the entire venture is hampered by evasion on the place of culture in the problems related to the introduction of democracy and success culture into Islam. In order to close the gap between the Islamic world and the West, and to alleviate tensions in a true commitment in the Arab–Persian Gulf, and to demonstrate a true ability to play a pivotal role as a cross-cultural bridge, this attitude has to be abandoned. In our age of the return of civilizations to the arena of world politics, there is a risk of a "clash," but there are also ways of averting it and preventing it from taking place.[22] The tensions emanate not only from the West, but also and equally from the Islamic world. Could the Arab–Persian Gulf be exceptional, and be free of the anti-Westernism that is spreading in the Islamic world? The games of self-victimization and accusation are detrimental.

In order to promote the culture of success on the basis of a common understanding of cultural and political innovations, a democratic peace needs to replace a clash. The significance of the Arabian Gulf in this regard is growing rapidly and globally. If the Abu Dhabi model, i.e. aimed at adding to the significance of the oil economy further political, cultural, and economic traits, turns out to be successful it could have spill-over effects. Its future prospects are therefore relevant for the entire region. In a globally changing world everything is subject to change, including culture and religion. The oil economy is not an enduring piece of luck. Prudent leaders in the Gulf need to be aware of a better perspective for their region; they should know that oil cannot be a lasting source of revenue. Further, the soaring price of oil in 2008 has done great damage to most countries of the world and to the world economy. The Gulf leaders cannot count forever on their privileged position.

On the basis of this reasoning one can ask the pivotal question: what future for the Arab–Persian Gulf region beyond the age of oil? The search for an answer leads to recognition of the need for innovations, and for political and cultural developments that will promote economic diversification. The idea of innovation has the aim of freeing the Gulf region from the bias of Western political and security concerns that are imposed on its economy and reduce it to a source of oil used as "a weapon."[23] One of the remaining Cold War obstacles to the development of the Gulf[24] was the Ba'ath regime of Saddam Hussein. It was a left-over from a time that was characterized by persistent attempts at self-imposition – even by means of war – on the states of the region. It is now gone, but another obstacle, the Islamic Republic of Iran, remains. The Iranian illusions of expanding power by exporting the Iranian Revolution continue unabated. Despite the fact that Iran has grown stronger as a result of the toppling of the Ba'ath regime in Iraq and of the vacuum that it tries to fill, one should not exaggerate the power of Iran.

As early as 1983 I argued at a meeting of the Middle Eastern Studies Association/MESA in Chicago that there are clear limits to the export of the revolution that Iran envisioned. Two decades later, in the same city, but at the annual convention of International Studies Association/ISA, I made a presentation in which I argued that religion and culture matter.[25] The combination of both insights in an age of cultural turn and the return of the sacred is important to the Gulf. If an introduction of innovations were seriously considered in order to culturally adjust the Arabian Gulf, then the leaders would need to develop a full awareness of the changed international environment so as to be in a position to relate this knowledge to their own societies. The ongoing changes occurring in the world in the post-bipolar age are not fully considered by Gulf politicians.

In short, in the course of the shift from the political burdens of the Cold War to challenges of the age of cultural turn, the consequences of the removal of Saddam Hussein's regime,[26] combined with the threat of an export of the "Islamic Revolution" of Iran complicate the process of innovation. Despite the obstacles, there are no alternatives to innovation based on a culture of success. This would be an Islamic contribution to properly dealing with the predicament with modernity.

The introduction of success culture as an innovation in the Arabian Gulf: what it is all about?

Before I introduce the concept of success culture that is under examination, I must note that education[27] is the most important subsystem of society, because it determines the worldview, the values, and the related behavior of elites. Thus, the key to change in the Arabian Gulf states is the educational system. It is the best vehicle for the introduction of a success culture. The related values and behavior necessary for great innovations in state and society depend on raising up political elites, decision makers, and a business community that are educated and socialized in a success culture. The rapidly globalizing and changing world is characterized by a contradiction between the universal claim of this success culture and the worldwide realities of cultural and religious diversity, which do not match with it. In the Arabian Gulf a cultural foundation for the worldview, values, and related behavior of what is termed a success culture is not yet in place, and it needs to be established as a commonality. The preliminary reasoning in this section is guided by this goal. Comparison with the universality of individual human rights and their introduction into Islam provides an exemplary case.

A project conducted jointly in the US by the Harvard Academy for International Studies and the Fletcher School for International Diplomacy is relevant to outlining the concept of a success culture as an innovation. The Culture Matters Research Project/CMRP chaired by Lawrence Harrison continues the work completed earlier and published as a book under that title (see note 17). As a member of that project, my assignment was to study Islam and the Middle East. On this basis, I am keen to introduce the concept of that project to the Arabian Gulf and to include my deliberations in this book. All members of the project were aware of the following two facts and the insights related to them:

First, cultural innovations in state and society are subject to political and economic constraints, but still independently require a vision of change.

Second, any scrutiny of culture must honor cultural and civilizational particularities, for example the existing worldview and value-related differences between Western and Islamic culture. However, this can be done without overlooking the potential of commonalities and without falling into the trap of essentializing the differences, as some pundits do.

While acknowledging these two issues and the related requirements, the experts involved in the Culture Matters Project/CMRP (see Chapter 1, note 1) looked at the concept of a culture of success in business and in the economy and argued that it can be shared by the elites of the whole of humanity despite existing, in fact normal, cultural differences. The results of this continuing project are very relevant, both generally and to this contribution in particular, in that they touch on the present discussion of the innovations needed in the Gulf. The major assumptions will be presented as the basis of a model for emulation. To avoid any imposition, I take pains to find and develop a cultural foundation for the introduction of a culture of success into the Arab world. In order to avoid any cultural imposition, this cultural foundation is considered to be a serious business. In our project we used the following twenty-three variables developed by Professor Larry Harrison. I will present them and add to them my own thoughts in order to relate them to the subject matter under consideration, i.e. political innovations in the Arabian Gulf. At the outset, the members of the project made a major distinction between the factors of a progress-prone culture and those of a progress-resistant culture. We related this distinction to three issue areas. First worldview, second values, and third economic behavior. Does this distinction also apply to the Arabian Gulf? The following reasoning is aimed at answering this question. The related variables are:

1. *Religion* is an essential part of any culture and thus it is pertinent to thinking about innovations. Does Islamic reasoning nurture rationality and achievement, or is it prone to irrationality and does it inhibit the promotion of material pursuits? Is Islamic thinking caged in scripturalism?[28] Certainly, religion could promote a progress-prone culture, and equally could undermine it. An understanding of religion leads to different methods of dealing with the tensions existing between a focus on this world, i.e. pragmatism, or on the other world, i.e. utopianism. In reading the Qur'an and studying its precepts, while exposing them to existing realities, first, I find in Islam a deep commitment to rationalism and achievement as well as to the pursuit of worldly affairs, but second, I do not detect this spirit among contemporary Muslims who pay lip-service to the Qur'an, but lag behind what it calls for. The second variable makes this contention clear. The well-known expert on the Middle East John Waterbury tells us of his learning after his year-long research in Morocco:

> I would reiterate that I am particularly concerned with that aspect of political culture which relates to patterns of behavior rather than manifest belief systems … In this sense it is more important to understand what Moroccans really do and why they do it than to understand what they think they are doing. It should also be noted that certain patterns of political behavior persist well after their structural underpinnings have begun to decompose. There is thus a *behavioral lag* that develops (like cultural lag in value systems) and continues until the social context for politics has so changed that further adherence to the old patterns becomes clearly ill-advised and politically non-productive.[29]

2. Next follows the worldview-related variable of *destiny*. A success culture requires a worldview that humans can influence their destiny, in contrast to an attitude of fatalism and resignation. There exists a false but established wisdom that Islam promotes a *qismet* fatalism. In contrast, I read in the Qur'an: "Whatever good befalls you, man, it is from Allah: and whatever ill from yourself" (sura *al-Nisa* 4, verse 79). These words make clear that humans are responsible for their deeds – for instance, when they lack success. The verse supports the interpretation that the Qur'an is against fatalism. However, the fatalist worldview is a social reality. It can be observed at work in everyday life in the Islamic world. Here one finds a discrepancy between religion as scripture and religion as social fact. The distinction is of great significance.
3. *Time*: cultural attitudes that admit thinking about the future could promote planning. In contrast, a focus on the past, i.e. nostalgia, discourages an

orientation that is committed to planning for a better future. As an example of this worldview's reluctance to commitment, the Egyptians have a joke about themselves in which they say that the Middle Eastern meaning of IBM is this: The letter I stands for "*Inshallah*/God willing", the letter B for "*Bukra*/tomorrow" and the letter M for "*Ma'lish*/it doesn't matter". In contrast to this attitude of uncertainty, a success-prone culture requires a behavior that would be in line with the Islamic value of "*hayya ala al-Falah*/stand up to achievement" (the call for prayer). Today – not "*bukra*/tomorrow".

4. *Wealth* is a product of human creativity: what exists (zero-sum) is expandable (positive sum). Well, the oil wealth of the Gulf states is a given – but not a lasting one. There is thus a need to introduce innovations leading to the opening up and securing of new sources of wealth. The needs of the future are imminent. Among these innovations, a new worldview on wealth is needed.

5. *Knowledge* is either practical and verifiable, which means that facts matter, or the opposite, i.e. cosmological, hence not verifiable. This distinction is made in the *Muqaddima* of Ibn Khaldun, where he distinguishes between religious and historical knowledge. Likewise in Ibn Rushd's concept of "*al-haqiqa al-muzdawaja*/double truth." I recommend the revival of the Ibn Rushd legacy for a better future, based on rationalism.[30]

The worldview-related variables discussed above are basic to cultural change. The second issue area of values and virtues relates to the three following variables:

6. An *ethical code* could be rigorous within realistic norms and thus elastic, providing possibilities for adjusting one's behavior to a changing world. In contrast, an ethical code could also be dogmatic, and thus inflexible. The attitudes of success can be learned in an innovation-oriented education that is related to an elastic ethical code close to reality.

7. The virtues of *responsibility* (job well done, tidiness) prescribe that punctuality matters. Also, courage is to be recommended, in the sense of taking risk (no risk, no gain), in contrast to the mentality of 100 percent security and safety.

8. *Education* in the values of success culture is indispensable to promoting autonomy, the mindset of dissent and creativity, in contrast to the scriptural mind of orthodoxy that considers change to be a source of deviation.

The above eight variables are all highly relevant to an innovating worldview and its related values. There remains economic behavior. It can be based either on an orientation of success, i.e. progress-prone culture or, conversely, on a progress-resistant culture inherited by tradition. Having stated this, I now continue the list of variables.

9. The following variable suggests that *work ethics* matters; behavior is led by the orientation "we live to work, because work leads to wealth." The opposite mindset is that work does not lead to achievement and wealth; work is for the

poor and wealth is given to us by destiny – or by God/Allah – it is believed that this is beyond the ability of humans to determine. A rent economy guarantees income without accomplishments. Oil revenues promote this kind of behavior related to wealth without work. In the Gulf, there is urgent need of a new mindset to replace the existing one, if an age beyond oil is to be prepared for.

10. In an economy *frugality* is considered to be the mother of investment, as is the case in the West. Some not only see in this orientation a threat to equality, but also think it could damage prosperity. As a Muslim and being open-minded to cultural innovation, I believe that the Qur'an teaches frugality.

11. The same applies to the variable concerning *entrepreneurship*, investment, and creativity, as well as to the related behaviors.

12. This variable concerns the propensity to be *moderate*, to abide by law and to avoid occasional adventures. The Prophet called on the *umma* to be moderate (*ummat al-Wasat*).

13. In a modern society *competition* leads to excellence, in contrast to envy and aggression, which are a threat to equality. Privilege needs to be based on competitive behavior. In Islamic doctrine, envy and "*udwan/*aggression" are counted among the "*makruh/*despised" sentiments.

14. For a mindset that promotes innovation one needs to be open to rapid *adaptation* and not to be too suspicious, because this results in slow adaptation. The acceptance of this variable by Muslims requires a new translation of innovation, which should not be viewed as *bid'a*, in the meaning of a change detrimental to religion, which is not the effect of cultural innovations.

15. In a modern society advancement is based on *merit* and achievement, not on family relations, patronage, connections, or what one calls "*wasta/*cronyism" in the Middle Eastern culture. This term refers to a system of distribution based on family, ethnic, and patriarchal contacts. Here, great innovations are needed in order to change the prevailing patterns of advancement in Arab societies. In this regard, economic behavior is also related to socio-cultural behavior.

16. A basic issue is also the *rule of law*, which is a variable for change. It not only means that reasonable law abiding is needed to avoid corruption, but also questions the mindset that financial connections matter. Corruption should be prosecuted, and not be tolerated. This variable refers also to the kind of law employed.

17. Social behavior is also related to a stronger *identification* with the broader society rather than with the narrow community (family, clan, etc.). This is very important for establishing a modern polity in the Gulf.

18. An attitude related to a broader society leads to promoting the mindset of *association*, trust, identification, affiliation, participation, and inspires higher achievement.

19. In the Arab world there is a conflict between notions that underline and emphasize the individual and those that emphasize the collectivity and the group. Western individualism is alien to Arab Islamic culture. A middle way

between the two patterns of behavior, i.e. finding a balance between identities related to the individual and those oriented to the collectivity, would
certainly be possible through innovation.

20. A sensitive issue is that of *authority*: is it centralized, unfettered, often arbitrary, simply inherited? Or is it based on consensus, with the result that it is
accountable and subject to checks and balances? This is a basic area of political-cultural innovation. In the Gulf states, authority is inherited.

21. Also the role of *elites* and their responsibility to society matter to success culture. How do elites base their behavior in relation to power and rent seeking? It is a fact, in the Arab world, that the present crisis of ruling elites
results in their delegitimation in favor of the emergence of destabilizing Islamist counter-elites.[31] Here, a balance between the two is urgently needed.

22. A very basic issue is the relation of *state/religion (din/dawla)*, addressed in the
West as the church-state relationship. This factor also plays a major role in
the contemporary Gulf. The representatives of political Islam claim the unity
of *din wa dawla*, while others reject this and support the promotion of a civic
sphere as a more promising alternative.[32]

23. The final variable is a most sensitive one: *gender*. Can there in reality be
equality between men and women, given the Qur'anic provision that women
are subordinated to men? What does Islam[33] say about the issue inherent in
this question? Gender inequality would be inconsistent with the value system
of success culture. A modern society needs all of its members, men and
women equally, for its prosperity. This necessity was stated in Abu Dhabi at
the 9th Conference of the ECSSR, by Islamic women speaking on the
women's panel (see note 1).

In short, these twenty-three variables, incorporated into the three issue areas
of worldview, values, and behavior, reflect an understanding of a culture of
success that could be supported in Islam by a religious-cultural underpinning, if
positively interpreted. Thus, a success culture could be embraced by Gulf societies in their bid for political innovation.

Conclusions

The starting point of this case study – and the reason for its selection – while
applying the concept of a success culture to the analysis of Islam's predicament is
the fact that this region is of great centrality to both world affairs and the world
economy. This relevance applies also to the Islamic world, and thus the Gulf
enjoys a particular place in Islamic civilization. In this capacity, the Gulf can
relate itself to the vision of becoming a cross-cultural bridge between Islam and
the West. The envisioned innovations in political institutions and in society thus
have a central significance. If a new educational approach, oriented towards a
success culture, could be established, then the Muslims of the Gulf would
become a model for other Muslims to learn how to take responsibility for their

own shortcomings. It is argued that the Qur'an prescribes a mindset of achievement-prone attitudes and related behavior. It follows that a dynamic, non-essentialist understanding of Islam would promote both a participatory culture of democracy and an achievement-oriented culture of success.

Basically, a well-understood and appropriately interpreted *Civil Islam*[34] is compatible with democracy, civil society, and success culture. Why is this compatibility not appropriately understood? I believe that political, cultural, and structural constraints underlie this situation. They could be changed if innovations were admitted into both state and society in the Arabian Gulf. The promotion of a success culture prone to progress would also contribute to *Preventing the Clash of Civilizations*.[35] An international morality based on cross-cultural bridging includes a spirit that is open to innovations. The Gulf could become a modern place in the modern world, committed to innovation in a changing world, if decision makers would embrace and accomplish not only the needed political and cultural reforms, but also the culture of innovation that underlies them. In order to deal appropriately with the challenges of the future, Islam's predicament with modernity has to be addressed not only with candor, but also with rigor. No remedy can be recommended if one is not permitted to diagnose and to state what is going wrong and what cultural factors determine the overall situation in these developing cultures.

Chapter 11

Conclusions and future prospects

Cultural modernity and the Islamic dream of semi-modernity

At the end of this journey into Islam's predicament with cultural modernity there are some basic conclusions to be drawn. The journey has been made in a number of steps and has also included some propositions for religious reform and innovative cultural change. It is a part of this chapter on conclusions and future prospects to review the Islamic responses to the current challenges and the predicament with cultural modernity. Among these responses one finds, earlier, Wahhabism and neo-Salafism and today, Islamism. These are religious ideologies that deny the existence of the current issue altogether. Their supporters admit a *"minha/*crisis" and prescribe the solution of a return to pure tradition based on the revealed, holy scripture. This prescription is believed to be the only remedy for Muslims. In contrast to the neo-Salafist orthodoxy and to the Islamist invention of tradition, the response of Islamic conformism does not overlook the challenge and seeks to accommodate it. However, the accommodation that the conformists envision is not a real remedy, because it fails to engage in what I earlier termed "cultural accommodation of social change."[1] This formula summarizes my insights on the issue. By this formula I mean that in an interplay between social and cultural change it can be expected that values, norms, and the related view of the world will also change. This is needed to allow a balance between these two aspects of the process of change. It is not an essentialization to state that some Islamic values are resistant to change because Muslims believe that they emanate from God, are thus immutable, and ought never to be subjected to change. Those Muslims who are committed to this belief resist cultural adjustment and admit no process of cultural accommodation to social change.

In leaving aside those Muslims who are resistant to cultural change I turn to the Islamic conformists who are willing to adjust, but I see, however, that they restrict their efforts to an ad hoc adjustment that they pursue in a very pragmatic manner. Islamic modernism is another important response, for which I have coined the term "Islamic dream/or illusion of semi-modernity."[2] For a proper understanding of this issue the reader is reminded of the distinctions made in the Introduction and in Chapter 1. At issue is a differentiation between institutional and cultural modernity, which is basic among these distinctions. The first part of modernity – i.e. the institutional one – is based on modern science and technology and on the instruments they produce. Institutional modernity relates also to power. The other part of modernity is cultural, as outlined in line with the work of Jürgen Habermas. Cultural modernity relates to values, worldviews, and to their substance rooted in "the principle of subjectivity."[3] This substance can be made easier to comprehend by calling it individuation or an individualism based on the recognition of human abilities to recognize the world and to change it. This is the meaning of Max Weber's "*Entzauberung*/disenchantment" of the world, repeatedly referred to as an intellectual guide for the present book. In the following conclusions I shall draw together the findings of the foregoing chapters with the focus on what I term the "Islamic dream of semi-modernity" as the contemporary Islamic exit strategy for the predicament with modernity. This strategy is not another modernity; it is a defensive culture.

Introduction

Since the nineteenth century, Islamic modernists have been, in their own way, conformists rather than modernizers. They believed themselves receptive to modernization, but they were and continue to be trapped by an illusion. It is their view that it is possible to adopt the instruments of modernity while dismissing the cultural values and rational view of the world that underpin these very accomplishments. One can learn from the work of Reinhard Bendix that this adoption of items of modernity, technically restricted to instruments, does not indicate any effort at modernization. This adoption is not only insufficient, but also undermines the process of modernization itself – if it exists at all. Bendix's argument has already been quoted in Chapter 1 (see note 91 there), stating that ad hoc adoptions of some items of modernity and instrumental modernization in some spheres of life not only do not "result in modernity," but also produce obstacles to "successful modernization."[4]

In this introductory section I focus on the notion of semi-modernity that is related to a mindset resulting from restricted instrumental adoptions. This semi-modernism is even compatible with terrorism. For instance, the perpetrators of 9/11 and other Islamist jihadists were in full command of basic technical items of modernity, but as *Defenders of God*[5] they were and continue to be strictly opposed to its cultural project of a "disenchantment of the world." For instance, they enact E-jihad[6] on their technically perfect jihadist websites in order to fight against the modern world. The Islamist anti-Westernism is legitimated by reference to the European roots of cultural modernity, demonized not only as alien to Islam, but also as inimical to its civilization. Thus, the Islamist quest for a purification of Islam in the name of authenticity. In othering anything suspected to be alien to Islam, Islamists close their minds to cultural borrowing from non-Muslims.

True, modernity is, in its origin, both secular and Western. In line with the understanding of the contemporary phenomenon addressed by Hedley Bull as *The Revolt against the West*,[7] the contestation at issue is not restricted to Western hegemony, it also comprises the enlightenment values of secular modernity. In this context, one can state that there is a culture-based conflict over values, as discussed in Chapter 5. From the perspective of conflict resolution and world peace for the twenty-first century, the return of religions to politics is first, charged with a drive towards de-sacralization and second, undermines any accord of shared core values. This phenomenon is thus the source of a new pattern of conflict. It follows that the politicization of religion is detrimental to world peace. The return of religion with political claims does not herald a renaissance of religion at all, nor is it an expression of a theology of liberation. If this were the case, then the return would not be a problem, as it in fact is. There would be nothing wrong with the challenge to secularism through a critical revival of a religion if it were restricted to pointing out the ethical and normative deficiencies and flaws of modernity, and not combined, as it is, with a political agenda. A closer look at the revolt based on the return of the sacred reveals that the project of modernity itself is the target of a political religion. Those postmodernists who justify this revolt against cultural modernity, using the mistaken device of cultural relativism, mostly fail to understand what the substance of the issue is. Stated plainly, these people do not know what they are talking about, as was shown, for instance, in Chapter 8 by the example of postmodernism and authenticity. I believe that most postmodernists are true democrats – the disagreement lies elsewhere – and would never endorse the purification agenda that the Islamists promote in the name of authenticity. However, the postmodernists do not know this agenda.

Certainly, the global revival of religions challenges secular concepts of modernity and even touches its core. In acknowledging this turn, the theorist of modernity Habermas asks for an accommodation, which I view as a backwards step. In his post-9/11 thinking Habermas makes a shift and pleads for tolerance vis-à-vis what he terms a "postsecular society."[8] In contesting this kind of reasoning I argue, with strong evidence, that the politicization of religion in Islam, presented as a religious revival, is an indication of a "new totalitarianism"[9] and is not a religious renaissance. Roger Griffin and Jeffrey Herf provide historical evidence that fascism embraced modernity instrumentally. There was a pattern of a "fascist modernism."[10] For Mussolini and Hitler it was no contradiction to combine approval of instrumental modernity with their ideology.

The tensions between "secularism," and the return of the sacred are not simple, and they were illuminated in many ways in the foregoing chapters. At this point I want to proceed further. In combining a retrospective with some future prospects the overall context of the Islamic dream of semi-modernity has to be related to the question: is it a way out of the impasse of Islam's predicament with cultural modernity?

A "tour d'horizon" into Islam's predicament with cultural modernity

In order to avoid the well-known and established Muslim ambiguities that I refuse to share, and to make clear what we are talking about, I propose this "tour d'horizon." First, it is noted that the rhetoric of anti-modernity is recent. Earlier – in the course of the age of "Arab liberal thought"[11] – Muslim elites embraced an unspecified modernity with some enthusiasm. This happened, however, without establishing a religious-cultural reform, based on change, to underpin this sentiment. Religious and secular Muslim liberals, and also the military praetorians, failed in their modernization venture. They have been superseded by the forces of a politicized religion that claim to present an order that is viewed as the alternative to cultural modernity. This drive is expressed in the words: "*al-hall huwa al-Islam*/Islam (say) Islamism is the solution." Political Islam also claims universality for its own views, based on the concept of a neo-Islamic order called "*Hakimiyyat Allah*/God's rule." It is intriguing to see this Islamist medieval mindset combined with acceptance of modern science and technology. The combination of both in a mindset of semi-modernity expresses that medieval theology can be espoused in relation to instrumental modernity. The political thinking of Ibn Taimiyya[12] is revived by the Islamists, who are by no means traditionalists. This semi-modernity is guided by a proclaimed universalism of "*siyadat al-Islam*/Islamic supremacy." Is this acceptable to the rest of humanity? There is no escape from foreseeing that the two-thirds of humanity that do not belong to the Islamic civilization would not submit to the call for an Islamic world order. There are also freedom-loving, pro-democracy Muslims who do not approve of the idea of an Islamic supremacy, to be established in a new world order. These issues were discussed in Chapter 7, but are also relevant to the debate on semi-modernity.

Westerners who view Islamic and Islamist semi-modernity positively are mostly postmodernists who – as stated – mostly know little about the new totalitarianism. It is disturbing that these people are not only not well-informed, but also share with the Islamists their rejection of cultural modernity itself, in particular its secular claim to universal validity. These pundits also fail to understand Islam's civil war[13] – whether on its own territory or in its spilling over beyond the Islamic world, thus becoming geo-political. Cultural-relativist postmodernism becomes an obstacle to establishing cross-cultural standards of values with a universal validity. Cultural modernity is also a discourse not exclusively attached to a single religion, as is the case in the Islamist and the Wahhabi-orthodox scriptural neo-absolutism that also claims a universality that is to be imposed through "*da'wa*/proselytization." The whole of humanity is expected to accept the claim of "Islamic world peace" and to unite under the banner of Islam. Today, jihadists are set to achieve this goal violently, through neo-jihad. This is Qutb's understanding of an "Islamic world revolution."[14] This ideology is an expression of a new totalitarianism, not of a theology of liberation. There are peaceful Islamists who participate in democratic institutions, but who share the same overall goal. They are, in terms of effects, more dangerous than the jihadists.

The move from a defensive-cultural response to an aggressive, offensive jihad preached by Sayyid Qutb and the Islamists occurs without any effort to engage in reforming religion. Rather, the move satisfies the need for certainty by providing a religious-cultural neo-absolutism that also engages in purification. The overall context of all of these developments is the process of the exposure of Islamic civilization to cultural modernity, analyzed in the preceding chapters. The responses document equally a perception of a threat and a sentiment of fascination. The list of Muslims who went to Paris in the nineteenth century and became prominent modernizers includes Tahtawi, Abduh, and al-Afghani. They were fascinated by the progress of Europe. Tahtawi acknowledged an advanced Europe and the need to learn from its accomplishments. Abdu engaged in some religious, albeit shallow, reform. Later on, al-Afghani combined his pan-Islamism with an admiration for Europe. This ideology was combined with anti-colonial jihad, rightly recognizing that it is no contradiction to reject colonial Europe and to admire its progress. After the failure of this "Islamic modernism," secular Arabs took over; they too went to Paris and also published their thinking there. In 1913 Paris became the place to voice secular Arab nationalism. It failed, too. Today, Islamists for their part continue this tradition of resorting to Europe to use it as a logistical base for their activities. The new locations are however, London and Berlin, no longer Paris where Islamists are not welcomed. The comparison between Arabism and Islamism is, nevertheless, flawed, but here is not the place to pursue this contention, made in passing. I will maintain the focus on the exposure of Islamic civilization to cultural modernity and the related responses.

While I dissociate my work from "Orientalism" and from the approach of cultural-relativist anthropology, I propose a new way of studying Islam in the twenty-first century. A new discipline is needed that combines the historical and social-scientific perspectives with the study of conflict in the civilization of Islam in the present world-time. Islam's problems with secular modernity lead to a cultural fragmentation, of which Islamism is a case in point. This new form of Islam will burden Muslims and the rest of the world for many decades to come. It is completely naive for some pundits who act as "experts on Islam" to speak of *"le déclin de l'Islamisme/* decline of Islamism." The opposite is true. In post-bipolar politics there are problems that are becoming a source for an international conflict. At issue is a geo-civil war in the international system and its society. Under these unpromising conditions, Islamic civilization has moved to the fore of world politics and Islamism claims to represent it in its dream of a semi-modernity for a remaking of the world. The reduction of these problems to what is named "radical Islam," "extremism," or "terrorism" is not only a distraction from the issue, but also foolishness.

In addition to the various responses to modernity, there are two world political events that cover a span of almost a quarter of a century and these, too, need to be incorporated into this tour d'horizon. The attention of the entire world is focused on contemporary Islam, while the impact of the media is not to be overlooked. The first of the two events mentioned was the Islamic Revolution in Iran. It illustrated the need for a – as yet still missing – solid study of the place of Islam in world affairs, with robust assumptions. Among the reasons for close attention was the fact that the Islamic Revolution in Iran was not only one that was supposed to be exported to the rest of the Islamic world, but also one that claimed a universal place in history at large, even emulating not only the universality, but also the impact of the French Revolution. Iran's drive to become a nuclear power is not only a political concern, but also a project related to semi-modernity.[15] The second event was 9/11. The first event, in 1979, was Shi'ite; the second, in 2001, was led by Sunni Islamists.[16] In both cases, Islam was politicized and world politics was religionized. The reference to the Islamic Revolution of 1979 and to 9/11 in 2001 caps this "tour d'horizon." In both cases Islamists – with a semi-modern mindset – embraced the material accomplishments of modernity and combined this adoption from the West with a fierce rejection of the values of cultural modernity. Thus, the predicament prevails unabated in a historical chain of related developments.

With the perspective of this "tour d'horizon" into the history of the exposure of Islamic civilization to Western modernity, the statement of a predicament for Islam can be maintained. In arguing thus I am not falling into the trap of viewing Islam as a monolithic entity; I am simply stating a civilizational unity perceived by Muslims themselves as *Dar al-Islam*, which – on a perceptual level – documents the civilizational unity in Islam. It is certainly combined with great local-cultural diversity in Islamic realities. When I state a predicament, I acknowledge also the divergent responses to it.

Rethinking Islam – how?

The overall context of the predicament of Islam with modernity has been outlined and analyzed in the preceding sections. The Muslim scholar Mohammed Arkoun and his reasoning about *Rethinking Islam* have been referred to. This book suggests that the effort of rethinking has to result in religious reform. Does Arkoun agree with this? In a recent book Arkoun expresses his dismay at the qualifcation of his effort as *"Islah dini*/religious reform." Why? He claims to deliver gold and he wants to be seen as the Islamic Immanuel Kant.[17] Arkoun is certainly a significant thinker on contemporary Islamic civilization, but he lacks the intellectual vigor of Kant in his addressing of the issue. He coins nice terms, addresses important issues, but barely goes beyond idealistic thinking and is – as Robert Lee puts it – unlikely to "muster general support."[18] I do not claim this for my own work and hope only to be successful in vigorously rethinking Islam so as to provide a basis for a debate on innovative cultural change and religious reform in contemporary Islam.

In going beyond self-congratulatory attitudes it is necessary to focus on the Islamic as well as the Islamist dream – or better, the illusion of "semi-modernity." One has to make clear that without a vigorous – not rhetorical as in Arkoun's case– rethinking of Islam there can be no light at the end of the tunnel. Vigorous thinking on Islam's predicament with modernity could contribute to overcoming the fault lines and establishing bridges. It is not honest to criticize "Orientalism" single mindedly and at the same time to remain silent about anti-Westernism. I draw on the Hellenism once shared by early Islamic rationalism to strongly reject any identification of the West with Christianity. This identification serves contemporary Islamists in identifying the West with crusaders, and thus with the "infidels." Hellenism is based on a reason-based view of the world, and it is on this basis that it was accepted by Muslim rationalists. These great Islamic minds, from al-Farabi to Ibn Sina and Ibn Rushd up to Ibn Khaldun, from the ninth to the fourteenth centuries, adopted Hellenism without undergoing the ordeal of a predicament. They did not engage in semi-Hellenism, as do Islamists in semi-modernity. In Chapter 8 I argued for a revival of the heritage of early Islamic rationalism in order to establish it as an authenticity for embracing modernity. With this objective I have repeatedly drawn on the formidable work of Leslie Lipson on civilizations, and from it I adopt two major arguments, repeated here because of their significance:

First: the introduction of Hellenism into Europe occurred via the rationalist line of Islamic civilization. Lipson states: "Aristotle crept back into Europe by the side door. His return was due to the Arabs, who had become acquainted with Greek thinkers ... Both, Avicenna and Averroes were influenced by him."[19]

Second: with the assistance of Hellenism, Christendom, being the civilization of Europe, shifted into a new civilization named "the West," which is a secular one. "The main source of Europe's inspiration shifted from Christianity back to Greece, from Jerusalem to Athens. Socrates, not Jesus, has been the mentor of the civilization that in modern times has influenced or dominated most of the planet."[20]

With reference to the positive drawing on the history of Islam and Hellenism, I put forward the argument that modernity is secular, not Christian. It is based on secular foundations and in this form it is also acceptable to Muslims today, just as Hellenism was accepted by their ancestors in the classical heritage of Islamic rationalism.[21] In short, earlier Muslim adoptions from Hellenism reflect a positive civilizational encounter based on cultural borrowing. This historical record creates a precedent for the present. If this tradition could be revived, it could provide a cultural basis for embracing cultural modernity. The contemporary Islamic rationalist Mohammed Abed al-Jabri rightly argues that a promising future "can only be Averroist."[22] By this he means the establishment of a prospect for contemporary Islamic civilization on a reason-based, i.e. a rational worldview. A revival of Islamic rationalism that was based on an Islamic acceptance of Hellenism could contribute to a rational worldview, to be established with the aim of averting fault lines between civilizations. In this understanding of modernity, the suggestion of a cross-cultural bridging is not merely an intellectual undertaking. At issue is also a specific understanding of political order. I follow Hedley Bull, who determines world politics through a debate on order that lies at the heart of the current subject matter. I relate Bull's understanding of order to modernity and argue that a rethinking of Islam needs to revolve around this issue. To view the issue in this way is to state it as a competition between two concepts of order, the one modern, the other semi-modern. This contest between two visions for the future of humanity is essential: either the expansion of *Dar al-Islam* to map the entire humanity – which Sayyid Qutb states – or the vision of a "democratic peace" based on reviving the views of the greatest philosopher of the European Enlightenment, Immanuel Kant, on "*Ewigem Frieden/* perpetual peace." The pivotal matter is not "Islam or the West" – this is a mistaken view which reflects the rhetoric of clash. The contest relates rather to these two options: the system of "*Hakiymiyyat Allah/* God's rule," or democracy as based on popular sovereignty, i.e. on a secular basis.

In short, a rethinking of Islam is something other than the rhetoric of Mohammed Arkoun. It is about cultural modernity as opposed to semi-modernity. The predicament with modernity touches on this choice: either Muslims accept a world of religious and cultural pluralism in which the non-Muslim other is acknowledged to be equal, or they continue to believe in the religious obligation to *da'wa*, i.e. to proselytize, coupled with the vision of a "*Dar al-Islam/*Islamicate" to map the entire world. In contrast to the worldview of cultural modernity, semi-modernity rejects secular values and restricts the approval of modernity to the ad hoc adoption of its instruments. Today, Islamization replaces the project of Westernization pursued by Kemalism and similar movements. The balance of the development to date can be plainly stated: that secularism has failed in the Islamic world. It has declined, to the benefit of political Islam. The semi-modernity of Islamism is put forward by an Egyptian Islamist, al-Sharqawi, who believes that Muslims should adopt the instruments of modernity – by which he means the technology of war – so as to fight the "crusader West" with its own weapons.[23] Clearly, this kind of contemporary Islamic thinking is by no means the needed rethinking. The Islamic people need to engage in dealing with their predicament with modernity. Semi-modernity is no solution.

The future and the burdens of the past: Islamic nostalgia

Self-awareness on the part of people of any civilization can yield positive or negative results. This awareness usually underpins a pattern of civilizational identity. It needs neither to be exclusivist nor supremacist, but it could be. Unfortunately, Islamic nostalgia promotes a kind of self-awareness that is combined with political claims based on Islamic supremacy. John Kelsay is among very few Western scholars who understand the character of Islamic nostalgia. He blatantly states that it would "be wrong ... to understand the contemporary call for revival among Muslims as simple nostalgia," because it is much more than that. It is about the fact "that the ascension of European and North-American civilization in world affairs has been based on a failure of leadership in the Muslim world and on the Western willingness to shamelessly exploit." At issue is "outrage over the state of the world ... the call of renewal, then, relates to Islam and to its mission."[24] In other words, the nostalgia at issue is a call to restore the glory of supremacist Islam. This is among the undercurrents in the development of cultural tensions into conflict. It leads to a *New Cold War* between the secular state and what is named *Hakimiyyat Allah*, both claiming universality for their political order. Islamists act in the illusion of being able to remake the world along the lines of their envisioned – constructed – concept of an Islamic order. In doing so, they fight for a global mapping of the world in an enhanced *Dar al-Islam*. To avoid the costly conflict, detrimental to all, including Muslims, there is a need to dialogue with one another on what might be accepted by both as the correct order for the twenty-first century. The medieval Islamic philosophers addressed this issue on the basis of reason, leaning on Plato's concept of the state and on the Aristotelian logic of politics. If today's Muslims looked positively at this Islamic classical heritage they would be in a position to find a way to come to terms with the non-Muslim other. This option requires looking forward and not becoming entwined in the burdens of the past, exacerbated at present by the prevailing pattern of an Islamic nostalgia.

In its first four chapters this book suggested that in order to come to terms with modernity Muslims first need reason-based knowledge. Add to this a secular democracy based on law and individual human rights. These are the basics for peace among democratic nations within the framework of cultural-religious pluralism and secularity. We Muslims are challenged not to reduce modernity to semi-modernity, but rather to engage in a rethinking of Islam within the framework of innovative cultural change and religious reform in order to deal successfully with the challenge of cultural modernity. If this requirement of establishing the foundation needed to deal with Islam's predicament with modernity continues to be missing, then there will be no real change. What remains is the defensive-cultural nostalgia that finishes up by becoming stuck in historical collective memories. The glory of the past as a collective memory burdens rather than provides a positive civilizational awareness of the self.

In the Western debate, the reproach of an essentialization is restricted to Western Orientalism. I contend that there is an Arab Islamic mindset of essentialism also. The Moroccan philosopher al-Jabri coined the phrase "*Takwin al-aql-al-Arabi*/the formation of Arab reason." The authoritative place of the text in this mindset is quite characteristic. Even bright Arab authors like Mohammed Shahrur, who go for radical and cultural change, are not free of this mindset. In a major book Shahrur voices the criticism that Arabs are committed to what they have inherited from their forefathers and are therefore unwilling to welcome change. One is intrigued by his procedure of referring to the text of the Qur'an to underpin this argument. In *al-Baqra* one reads in the Qur'an (verse 170): "When asked to follow what Allah revealed they answer, no, we only follow what our forefathers have passed to us." The Qur'an speaks of '*al-Kafirun*/unbelievers, but Shahrur extends this qualification to all Arabs – making of a specific statement in the Qur'an a general one – and then concludes: "I believe, there is no one single nation on earth like we Arabs which is infected by this disease on a permanent basis, i.e. submitting to what is inherited by the ancestors."[25] In the Moroccan philosopher al-Jabri's mind this argumentation is characteristic of the "*al-aql al-Arabi*/Arab-Islamic mindset." A New Yorker inventor of tradition, the late Edward Said, and his followers would discriminate against this critique as an expression of Orientalism. Commitment to cultural modernity is not an Orientalism, it means freedom for the people of Islam. Despite these critical remarks, Shahrur is to be credited for this reference to the burdens of the past which create obstacles in the path to a better future.

The predicament of Islam with cultural modernity is embedded in the present crisis-ridden age of post-bipolar politics and is related to international conflicts. The current difficult issues cannot be addressed in a simplistic manner. However, there is a temptation to offer simplistic solutions. To complicate the matter, those who deal with the problems in a fashionable manner seem to enjoy great popularity not only in the media, but also in scholarship. It is therefore not easy to enlighten the audience as to the simplistic nature of prevailing views. The real problem is that such a class of views is appealing and they are used by social and political movements as a means of mobilization. The simplistic explanation of Islamic history leads to neo-absolutist fundamentalism, which is, despite all the odds, embraced by cultural-relativist postmodernism. Islamism is wrongly viewed as a liberation theology, as an anti-globalism – and even worse – as *Liberal Islam*.[26]

Among the simplicities one encounters the fundamentalist diagnosis of the crisis – shared by some Westerners – which reduces all evils to the West. The simplistic solution is the purifying "*hall al-Islami*/Islamic solution." It can be summarized as the establishment of the political system of "God's rule/*Hakimiyyat Allah*," based on the implementation of divine law, the shari'a. As was shown in Chapter 3, the revival of this system is not simply an expression of a re-traditionalization, as some suggest, nor is it another modernity, as others contend; it is the ideology of a totalitarian semi-modernity.

In their portrayal of Islam and its predicament, Western media are no less simplistic than are the religious fundamentalists in Islam. Often, Islamists are presented as political extremists committed to violent actions. Fundamentalism is, however, a highly complex phenomenon; it complicates the crisis out of which it emerges. It is not an outcome of some "*tatarruf*/extremism"-based behavior.[27] In going beyond the criticized simplicities it is necessary to establish a proper understanding of religious fundamentalism, while focusing on Islamism as the Islamic variety of this phenomenon. Here is a case in point. Political Islam, Islamism, religious fundamentalism etc. – name it what you will – are terms that express the very same phenomenon, the religionization of politics in response to the challenges posed by cultural modernity. The contention is that if there were no modernity, there would be no fundamentalism. This new orientation is a way of dealing with history and the future under the conditions of a predicament. In short, religious fundamentalism in Islam is a modern phenomenon. Its discourse of a re-traditionalization is misleading. In reality, at issue is a nostalgia that uses Islamic collective memories to promote the claim of remaking the world as a means to restoring constructed

Islamic glory. This effort is presented both as a solution and as a civilizational project for a better future, but it is not a promising perspective.

Modernity, semi-modernity, and defensive culture

Globalization does not lead to cultural standardization, but rather to defensive-cultural attitudes emanating from the corresponding fragmentation. Thus, a dual expression of a political and a cultural phenomenon is at issue. On the one hand, there is a political response to the ongoing crisis of the modern secular nation-state in the Islamic world. Early Arab and Turkish nationalists were the precursors of the separation between religious authority and secular state power in adopting the European institution of the nation-state as applied to *Dar al-Islam*. This institution failed in dealing with the tasks of development and also in delivering the results that it promised. This failure led to the rise of political Islam, which attempts to provide an alternative to the secular institution of the nation-state. On the one hand, you have a contestation of modernity; on the other, you can clearly see how much the political and the cultural responses are caught in the logic of the modernity one opposes. This is the predicament of political Islamists, who are religious fundamentalists exposed to modernity, but who reject it while using modern terms to articulate their alternative. This happens, however, with a different meaning of the terms in a process that is tainted with cultural schizophrenia.

It is amusing to read Sayyid Qutb, who views modernity as an expression of *jahiliyya*. The term *jahiliyya* refers, in the language of Islam, to the pre-Islamic age of unbelief, defined as ignorance. In order to steer Muslims onto the right path (*al-sirat al-mustaqim*), the exponents of political Islam engage in their objective of seizing political power in a politics of purification so as to purify Islam from the *jahiliyya* of modernity. Nonetheless, these same people do not engage in whole-sale rejection of modernity, because they are not traditionalists. Islamists are positive about the instruments, but negative about the values of modernity.

The Islamist contestation of cultural modernity is political, but highly pre-occupied with culture. Nevertheless, the Islamic fundamentalist is the prototype of a political man, a *homo politicus* – not a *homo religiosus*, not a man of religion, even though he (not she) presents himself as the "true believer." The explanation is that fundamentalism is based on a politicization of religious belief. Religion, culture, and politics are intermingled in a response to the challenges emanating from the exposure to modernity. These are the foundation of the predicament. The political manifestations of the contestation of cultural modernity are articulated in the language of a defensive culture. This concept was first developed in my book *The Crisis of Modern Islam* (German edition 1980, US edition 1988). The defensive culture of political Islam is the result of a crisis that has emerged from Islam's predicament with modernity. I maintain that political Islam is not only a response to cultural modernity in the crisis of modern Islam, which has a politico-historical background, but is also a concept of semi-modernity presented with a political agenda.

There are many issues linked to the cultural project of secular modernity. Among them are the concepts of knowledge and governance. Both are related to a specific worldview based on the assumption that humans can shape their own destiny and also have the capacity to determine change in their social and natural environments. The secular answer to the question "Can man govern?" is positive, whereas the fundamentalist answer is not. Islamists believe that God alone is the sovereign. The basic concept underlying the secular views is the modern concept of secular knowledge, as based on modern science and technology. Ever since their encounter with the modern West in the course of the nineteenth century, Muslims – even the modernists among them – have consistently been uneasy with these assumptions of the cultural project of modernity. On the one hand, they realize that they cannot thrive without adjusting themselves to modern techno-scientific standards. On the other hand, however, they are not willing to alter their belief in the supremacy of the sacred Islamic revelation over human reason. The result is embracing modernity together with a pre-modern worldview. The worst that could happen to an ordinary Muslim is to be deprived of the certainty provided by the divine. Thus, the predicament of Islam with modernity has been a source of uncertainty and it was evaded by Islamic modernism and the Islamic reform of the late nineteenth century. Thus, neither deserve to be addressed in these terms. They failed to introduce a new tradition that would enable Muslims to deal with the ever-growing tensions that arise from Islam's predicament. This failure continues in the work of Muslims who claim to be reformers (e.g. An-Na'im). Today, these tensions are leading to a variety of conflicts, addressed in the Preface and analyzed in depth in Chapter 5.

The certainty granted to Muslims by their belief in the absolute is often presented as a variety of a distinct culture that can only and properly be grasped in its own terms. The provision of appreciating the claims of distinct cultures should not be elevated into silence over the evasion of Islam's predicament with modernity. In fact, political Islam emerges from this predicament and it cannot be properly understood without dealing with it. Cultural relativism is not an option. For one thing, Muslims do not contest European modernity in rendering it culturally relative. Traditional Salafist and fundamentalist Muslims are, by all means, not hostile to the concept of universalism, as they themselves claim universal validity for their own beliefs. Moreover, they do not contest Western modernity as a holistic entity. Rather, they limit their rejection to the Cartesian, human-based modern worldview and to the admission of the capacity of human reason, believed to be at the expense of sacral revelation. Thus, Muslims, by and large, do not contest the achievements of modernity, but rather its view of the world. Therefrom emerges a semi-modernity that allows the adoption of European accomplishments, but on Islamic terms – that is, on the basis of a theocentric Islamic system of values. Without a doubt, Islamism is not a traditionalism, for the simple reason that it is based on an invention of tradition. In this dream of semi-modernity one encounters an Islamic mixed bag that grows from the Islamic predicament with modernity to accommodate techno-scientific adoptions, done in terms of selecting items of modernity. These adoptions are paralleled, however, by a radical rejection of the cultural project of modernity itself. For this reason I have developed the concept of the "Islamic dream of semi-modernity," with which I end this study. The conclusion is that the consequences of modernity are not taken well in the mixed bag of instrumental modernity and invented Islamic tradition. This is not the Islamization of modernity, as Islamists and some postmodernists contend. Thus the question: is it possible to reduce modernization to an instrumental adoption of material items, while furiously rejecting the rational, human-centered view of the world upon which modern accomplishments are based?

In the search for an answer to this question it is useful to consult the current writings of Islamic fundamentalists. Here, one encounters the claim that knowledge in general, and modern science in particular, are value-free accomplishments that could be used in the pursuit of different ends, and also by a culture based on other assumptions. The formula at work is the decoupling of modern knowledge from its rational context in order to put modern science and technology at the service of Islam. Islamists view this kind of project as Islamization. In line with Ernest Haas (see Chapter 2), whose work Islamists do not know, they argue that knowledge is power. They seek the establishment of an Islamic political order based on Islamic knowledge. This approach divorces the adopted items of modernity from their socio-cultural context, as well as from their rational outlook. Islamists and Salafists overlook the fact that modern knowledge involves a certain way of looking at the world, i.e. a rational worldview, and also requires an uncensored, reason-based dealing with the related problems. In my view, the current Islamic debate on technological and scientific knowledge reflects an Islamic response to cultural modernity in an effort to accommodate it – without, however, embracing its rationality.[28] Scholars who deal with the Muslim awareness of modernity in the contemporary historical and philosophical trends in the Muslim world can best pursue their expertise by studying the current Islamic debate on the place of knowledge. Islamic awareness of modernity is guided by the Islamic concept of knowledge, which is a cultural expression of a specific worldview. Knowledge is therefore among the relevant issue areas that have to be placed at the head of the present inquiry. By acknowledging the high rank of knowledge, the relevance of this issue is established. Therefrom follows the preliminary conclusion that it is incorrect to reduce the present turmoil in the Islamic world to a religious militancy growing from what is wrongly and indiscriminately named "radical Islam." The "pundits" who do so overlook all the cultural ramifications of Islam's predicament with modernity. The other conclusion is that semi-modernity is not a way out of this impasse. Its implications are far-reaching.

Globalization, modern science, and technology

It has been made clear that modernity is much more than just instrumental science and technology. It is argued throughout this book that the modern world is shaped by the structures of modernity, but not by its values. Modern structures have been globalized throughout the world, to also map the Islamic world, but the values of cultural modernity have not been successfully universalized. Ordinary Muslims conceive modernity either as a cultural threat to beware of, or as a political challenge to deal with. The debate on modernity has been going on since the Islamic revivalism of the nineteenth century. Most modern Muslims are positive about science and technology under conditions of globalization. However, some of these Muslims make the accusation of an "epistemological imperialism of the West." Unlike the medieval Islamic rationalists, who viewed epistemology as human and universal, the contemporary Muslim accusers of "epistemological imperialism" fall behind this early Islamic standard and are caught in their own constructed particularism.

Cultural modernity is based on the Cartesian epistemology that is the pillar of modern science. Earlier, in the Introduction and in Chapter 1, I argued in line with Habermas that the key events in the establishment of the European project of modernity are the Reformation, the Renaissance, the Enlightenment, and the French Revolution. The principal idea of cultural modernity is "the principle of subjectivity" (Habermas), discussed in Chapter 4 on individual human rights. On the one hand, this principle highlights the capabilities of humans, based on human reason, to shape and master their own destiny. On the other hand, it makes religious faith reflective. As the German philosopher Habermas points out: "the world of the divine was changed in the solitude of subjectivity into something posited by ourselves." Why do I repeat this quote, already cited in Chapter 4? It is because of its significance. This rational worldview is the basis for the unfolding of modern science and technology. Under the conditions of globalization both are available to the entire humanity, but on what premises? Could Muslim people, in a project of semi-modernity, adopt modern science and technology from the West, divorced from the cultural values that underpin their accomplishments?

To return to Habermas's interpretation, it is stated that the notion of subjectivity carries with it four connotations: 1) individuation (principium individuationes), 2) the right to criticism, 3) autonomy of action, 4) idealistic philosophy itself as a self-conscious idea. This principle of subjectivity is at work in modern times – mostly, however, in the West. Certainly, it is also the cultural underpinning of modern science and technology, which have, however, been globalized. Therefrom arises the question: why do Muslims want to adopt modern science parallel to their dismissal of human reason? The answer is most important. I set aside the four connotations listed by Habermas and focus on this question, which underpins the reality of "semi-modernism."

Of course, cultural adoptions need to be underpinned by cultural legitimacy. The classical Islamic heritage includes not only medieval theology, but also the tradition of a rational view of the world based on human reason. Why not revive it today? We may remind ourselves of the Greek impact on Islamic thought, found in the work of the great Islamic philosophers Farabi, Ibn Rushd, and Ibn Sina. Thus, the notion of the de-Westernization of knowledge in Islam, in terms of divorcing Islam from the idea of a primacy of reason, is unacceptable. The epistemological implications of cultural modernity seem to me to be in line with a proper understanding of the Islamic heritage that embraces rationalism. As shown in Chapters 2 and 8, rationalism was not alien to early Muslims, but it is alien to the religious fundamentalism of contemporary Islamists. They lack authenticity.

Semi-modernity is no solution, because it decouples modern science and technology from cultural modernity. The rejection of the worldview and values related to modern science is a rejection of the cultural project of modernity as such. The embracing of techno-scientific instruments in the Islamic dream of semi-modernity is a deeply flawed undertaking.

It is worthwhile going back to the early Islamic responses to the challenge, so far as the nineteenth century is concerned. Tahtawi acknowledged that European knowledge is more advanced than Islamic knowledge, which is restricted to writing "commentaries and super commentaries." The place of modern science and technology was also acknowledged by the intellectual precursor of the Islamic revolt against the West, al-Afghani. He frankly stated that Europeans were able to conquer the Islamic world, due to their possession of science and technology, i.e. better knowledge. Thus, there is a consensus among early modernists that Muslims can only thrive by adopting modern science and technology from the West. The revivalist al-Afghani even dared to accuse Muslims of "*jahl/* ignorance." In Islam "*jahiliyya/*ignorance" is tantamount to unbelief. The revivalist al-Afghani argued in this manner in the nineteenth century. Today, in the twenty-first century, Islamic fundamentalists are positive about modern technology, but they are incapable of accommodating the modern knowledge of science and technology, which are not mere and neutral instruments. When it comes to modern science, the discourse of Islamists is clearly determined by the *jahiliyya* of anti-science. Their mindset is characterized by two levels of confusion:

First, Islamists and Salafists view science as "*ilm/*knowledge" and believe that it is based on the Islamic revelation. For them, the Islamic tradition of science is the source of all sciences. Thus, they fail to distinguish between the religious sciences in Islam (the *fiqh* sciences) and the Islamic tradition of philosophy and rational sciences. In Islam the two traditions were never on good terms. The secular sciences were viewed in medieval Islam as "foreign sciences" and, at times, as heretical.

Second, in addition to the confusion between the three disciplines, "*ulum al-din/*divinities," natural sciences, and "*ulum al-qudama'/*philosophy," i.e. the sciences of the ancients (the Greeks), Islamic fundamentalists engage further in the allegation that the modern sciences in Europe are based on adoptions from Islam. It is true that the Greek legacy, as further developed by medieval Muslims, was handed over to Europe via Arab Muslim Spain. However, it is not clear to the Islamists that the Europeans adopted rational

philosophy and natural sciences from the Islamic civilization, but not the
divine shari'a nor any of the branches of religious knowledge, i.e. of the *fiqh*.
One cannot repeat this fact enough times. One has also to add that Islamic
Hellenized philosophy does not enjoy a high regard in political Islam,
whose ideologues remind Europe of its debt to Islam but seem not to know
that the West owes Islamic civilization exactly this tradition that they do not
appreciate. Today, modernity is the *"Könnensbewusstsein"* of Hellenism in a
new shape. Hellenized Islam is not a priority of Islamism.

What is next? Conclusions

Historically, the European expansion established a new model of globalization
that replaced the Islamic one. The *futuhat*-expansion that lasted from the seventh
to the seventeenth centuries underpinned Islamic globalization. The revival of
the related collective memories led to a call for the return of history. Islamists
blame the modern pattern of globalization, generated as a result of European
expansion. They argue that Western globalization has occurred at the expense of
Islam. The earlier Islamic model of globalization ended with the European
expansion. Our present world is structurally unified, but simultaneously, it is
culturally fragmented. In the present global society there are unifying political
and socio-economic structures, i.e. the international system of nation-states and
world economy, but at the same time there is definitely no world culture. It is
foolish to see in McWorld a world culture. The cultural self-assertion that is
occurring as a revolt against cultural modernity is coupled with tendencies
towards cultural fragmentation.

Today, non-Western peoples acknowledge on the one hand the centrality of
science and technology to their own development; on the other hand, however,
they fail to grasp that science and technology are not value free but are socially
constructed. In their Muslim identity politics Islamists declaim Islamic values as
the root of true science. This is to be situated in the described Islamic dream of
semi-modernity that is characterized by a willingness to adopt instruments of
modern science – coupled, however, with a negative attitude towards the values
and worldview of cultural modernity. This dream cannot materialize; it is part
and parcel of the predicament analyzed in this book. The tensions that arise in
this context develop into conflicts.

Under the analyzed conditions that are prevailing in the twenty-first century,
two options are presented in this book. One is secularization in the sense of a
structural process of the functional differentiation of society. No secular state can
ever be established without this process in society (see Chapter 6). The world of
Islam confuses secularism, which is more or less simply an ideology, a kind of
normative orientation of Western-educated Muslim intellectuals, and the social
processes of secularization. The other option is pluralism of religions and cultures, discussed at length in Chapter 7. If twenty-first-century Muslims dismiss

these options, then they not only deprive themselves of successfully dealing with the predicament, but also alienate themselves from the non-Muslim part of humanity.

In my earlier book *Political Islam, World Politics and Europe* I end my thinking in Chapter 7 with an argument for democracy and democratization as the solution. In this book I am dealing with Islam's predicament with modernity, not with global jihad as I do there. Here, I explain the illusion of semi-modernity. If contemporary Muslims continue to denounce modernization as a conspiracy of *"al-taghrib/*Westernization" that is believed to be an instrument for weakening the Islamic *umma*-community, then there is no hope for a better future. Muslims need to free the self from anti-modern sentiments. To be positive about modern instruments and to fail to recognize the predicament with modernity is an attitude that results in an impasse, if not in a dead end.

To conclude, and to state the issue in a nutshell, the dream of semi-modernity is a civilizational project that is doomed to failure. The vision ignores all existing tensions and reduces all the accomplishments of modernity to instruments. For Islamists, religion and politics are viewed as *"din wa dawla/*one entity."* Today, the view of this unity mobilizes against a secular-rational view of the world. If this understanding of Islam that prevails among Muslims continues to shape the contemporary Muslim mindset as a framework for politics and society then there can be no better future within reach. Political Islam's illusion of semi-modernity evades Islam's predicament with cultural modernity and therefore it continues to be caught up in tensions. The issue is not only views on cultural modernity, but also the pursuit of an Islamic political order. If this combination continues to shape the twenty-first century, then conflicts lie ahead and Brenkman's scenario – or prophecy – of "Islam's geo-civil war" may become a reality, or a self-fulfilling prophecy. To point out the place of politicized Islam in the post-bipolar international conflict is neither an expression of Islamophobia nor an effort by US policy makers to replace the lost enemy of communism with the invented enemy of Islam. As is shown and argued throughout this book, Islam's predicament with cultural modernity leads to tensions and conflicts. The solution lies in religious reform and cultural change, not in a dream of semi-modernity. Islam's predicament, which takes center stage in post-bipolar politics, matters not only to Muslims and to the West, but also to all other civilizations – including those of China and India – that are compelled to live with Muslims. As argued in this book, the issue is a concern of world politics in the twenty-first century and therefore it is highly deplorable that some Westerners simply fail to get it.[29]

Notes

Introduction

1 This quotation from Habermas is taken from his book on cultural modernity referenced in Chapter 1, note 5. The Introduction will not be further noted; all the sources used here are referenced in the following chapters.

Chapter 1

1 In both its substance and its findings, this chapter owes much to the Culture Matters Research Project (CMRP) that was conducted at The Fletcher School, Tufts University. I was a member of the research team 2003–06. I acknowledge my great debt not only to the project but also to its director, Lawrence Harrison, who published the findings in two volumes. They are further introduced by a book by him, *The Central Liberal Truth. How Politics Can Change a Culture and Save it from Itself* (New York: Oxford University Press, 2006). The two volumes authored by the members of the research team are Lawrence Harrison et al., eds, *Developing Cultures* (New York: Routledge, 2006); vol. 1, *Essays*, includes B. Tibi, "Cultural Change in Islamic Civilization," pp. 245–60; and vol. 2, *Case Studies*, includes idem, "Egypt as a Model of Development for the World of Islam," pp. 163–80.

2 In his philosophy of law the German philosopher Friedrich Wilhelm Hegel described how modern civil society is driven to expand by the logic of its dialects. His words are of world historical significance and deserves to be quoted in the original: "Durch ihre Dialektik wird die bürgerliche Gesellschaft über sich hinausgetrieben … um außer ihr in anderen Völkern … Mittel zu suchen … Dieser erweiterte Zusammenhang bietet auch das Mittel der Kolonisation," F.W. Hegel, *Grundlinien der Philosophie des Rechts* (Hamburg: Felix Meiner, 1955), pp. 202–3. For myself, as a scholar socialized in an Islamic milieu, the reading of Hegel's work during my years of study in Frankfurt under the guidance of the Frankfurt School (Horkheimer and Adorno) was most inspiring. According to Habermas (see the chapter "Hegel's concept of Modernity," pp. 23–44, in J. Habermas' book referenced in note 5), Hegel's philosophy is central to understanding cultural modernity.

3 The seminal book on this issue, repeatedly quoted in this book, is Geoffrey Parker, *The Military Revolution and the Rise of the West 1500–1800* (Cambridge: Cambridge University Press, 1988). This military revolution contributed to the industrialization of warfare and had major negative effects on Islamic civilization. This reflects the institutional dimension of modernity that Muslims faced in their encounter with Europe.

4 The contended historical model of Islamic globalization that suffered supersession by the West is described by B. Tibi, *Kreuzzug und Djihad. Der Islam und die christliche Welt*

(Munich: Bertelsmann, 1999), chapters 1 and 6. I completed this book in German during my Harvard (WCFIA) tenure as the Harvard Bosch Fellow in the late 1990s, on the assumption that German scholars are a book-reading community. My assumption was belied by the fact that this Harvard book, written in German triggerd no German response. Today's highly parochial German scholarly community is no longer a source of inspiration.

5 Jürgen Habermas, *The Philosophical Discourse of Modernity*. Translation by Frederick Lawrence (Cambridge, MA: MIT Press, 1987), in particular chapter 1.

6 Anthony Giddens, *Consequences of Modernity* (Stanford, CA: Stanford University Press, 1990).

7 Max Horkheimer and Theodor Adorno, *Dialektik der Aufklärung* (Amsterdam 1947, reprint Frankfurt/Main: S. Fischer, 1973).

8 Eric Wolf, *Europe and the People Without History* (Berkeley, CA: University of California Press, 1982, reprint 1997).

9 Philip Curtin, *The World and the West. The European Challenge* (Cambridge: Cambridge University Press, 2000).

10 David B. Ralston, *Importing the European Army. The Introduction of European Military Techniques and Institutions into the Extra-European World 1600–1914* (Chicago, IL: University of Chicago Press, 1990). The book includes two chapters on Islamic civilization (3 and 4).

11 See my contribution (chapter 7) in Roman Herzog *et al.*, *Preventing the Clash of Civilizations* (New York: St. Martin's Press, 1999).

12 For references and more details see chapter 6.

13 See the classic work by David Apter, *The Politics of Modernization* (Chicago, IL: University of Chicago Press, 1965).

14 Sadik J. al-Azm, "al-Istishraq wa al-Istishraq ma'kusan/Orientalism and Orientalism in Reverse," first published as an article in *Khamsin*, subsequently included in his book, *Dhihniyyat al-Tahrim/The Mentality of Taboos* (London: Riad El-Rayyes Publ., 1992), pp. 17–85. It is unfortunate that Western scholars have not been so open to al-Azm's arguments from Damascus against a Middle-Easterner (E. Said) who resided during his lifetime in the luxury and fame of New York. See next note.

15 No doubt the book by Edward Said, *Orientalism* (New York: Random House, 1979), next to his earlier work, *Covering Islam* (New York: Pantheon, 1981), was an urgently needed contribution, criticizing essentialist Eurocentrism and Western cultural arrogance. Sadly, however, the critique has been derailed; it also went very much overboard. The distorted Saidist debate led to counterproductive consequences. Among the negative effects one can see the prevalence of cultural-supremacist relativism, a kind of *réligion civil* (French notion) that determines contemporary Western Islamic studies. Said's contribution has been described by the Muslim philosopher S. J. al-Azm as an "Orientalism in reverse" (see note 14). Add to this flaw the damaging effects of the politicization of Islamic studies in the West. In the name of deconstructing Euro-centric bias, the critique of political Islam is dismissed and Islamism is viewed favorably and eleveated to a justifiable anti-globalization. This is a most peculiar logic. On this debate see chapter 4 of B. Tibi, *Einladung in die islamische Geschichte* (Darmstadt: Wissenschaftliche Buchgesellschaft, 2001), pp. 134–90. Among the counterproductive effects of Saidism is the use of the notion of "Orientalism" as a stick against any critical, uncensored analysis in Islamic studies. This censorship has greatly damaged academic freedom in Islamic and Middle Eastern studies in the West. In the name of combating Orientalism some US scholars end up defending Islamism and defaming the West as a "crusader." I dissociate my work – presented as an Islamology – from these distorted "Islamic studies." The "scholars" in question turn the world upside down to the extent that major Islamists, such as Yusuf al-Qaradawi, have been labelled representatives of "liberal Islam," as shown in note 61 below and in Chapter 3, note 99.

16 On the Islamic worldview see chapter 2 in B. Tibi, *Islam between Culture and Politics* (New York: Palgrave and St. Martin's Press, 2001, updated and expanded edition 2005); and on the link between culture and society see idem.: "The interplay between social and cultural change," in: Ibrahim Oweis and George Atiyeh, eds, *Arab Civilization. Challenges and Responses* (Albany, NY: State University of New York, 1988), pp. 166–82.

17 John Waterbury, *The Commander of the Faithful The Moroccan Political Elite* (New York: Columbia University Press, 1970).

18 Graham Fuller and Ian O. Lesser, *A Sense of Siege: The Geopolitics of Islam and the West* (Boulder, CO: Westview Press, 1995).

19 See B. Tibi, *Political Islam, World Politics and Europe. Euro-Islam and Democratic Peace vs. Global Jihad* (New York: Routledge, 2008), Part 2; see also Roger Scruton, *The West and the Rest. Globalization and the Terrorist Threat* (Wilmington, DE: ISI Books, 2002), chapter "Jihad," pp. 85–124.

20 For a conceptualization see Daryush Shayegan, *Cultural Schizophrenia. Islamic Societies confronting the West* (Syracuse, NY: Syracuse University Press, 1992) as well as the insightful case study by Mehzad Boroujerdi, *Iranian Intellectuals and the West. The Tormented Triumph of Nativism* (Syracuse, NY: Syracuse University Press, 1996).

21 The concept of defensive culture has been explained by B. Tibi, *Crisis of Modern Islam. A Preindustrial Culture in the Scientific-Technological Age* (Salt Lake City, UT: Utah University Press, 1988), in particular in the introduction, "Islam is a Defensive Culture in a Scientific–Technological Age," pp. 1–8.

22 The terms "pre-industrial" and "industrial" are not used in an evolutionist meaning. On this subject see also Patricia Crone, *Pre-Industrial Societies. Anatomy of the Pre-Modern World* (Oxford: Oneworld, 2003), and also my book referenced in note 21.

23 Islamist antisemitism is a political fact and one of the most disturbing features of Islamism. For more details see Matthias Küntzel, *Jihad and Jew Hatred. Islamism, Nazism and the Roots of 9/11* (New York: Telos, 2007), and also B. Tibi, "Der djihadistische Islamismus – nicht der Islam – ist die zentrale Quelle des neuen Antisemitismus," in: Wolfgang Benz and Juliane Wetzel, eds, *Antisemitismus und radikaler Islamismus* (Essen: Klartext, 2007), pp. 43–70, published as volume 4 in the research series of the Humboldt University of Berlin/Center for the Study of Antisemitism.

24 Emir Shakib Arslan, *Limatha ta'akhara al-Muslimun wa taqadamma qhairahum*/Why are Muslims backward, while others have progressed? (Beirut: Maktabat al-Hayat, reprint 1965), (English translation Lahore 1944 and 1968); extracts of this book are included in: John Donhue and John Esposito, eds, *Islam in Transition* (New York: Oxford University Press, 1982), pp. 60–64.

25 On the Islamic use of the concept of progress see Arslan's book, referenced in note 24. The European origin of this concept of "progress" is discussed by Robert Nisbet, *History of the Idea of Progress* (New York: Basic Books, 1980). On the adoption of this cultural concept of "progress" in contemporary Islam see B. Tibi, *Islam between Culture and Politics* (New York and London: Palgrave Press, 2001, new expanded edition, 2005), Chapters 3 and 4.

26 However, this drive predates Kemalism. One of the reform-minded parties in the Ottoman Empire was founded in 1889 under the name "Progress and Union." Kemal Atatürk linked "progress" (Turkish: *Tarakki*/Arabic: *Taraqqi*) to Westernization. See the classic work by Niyazi Berkes, *The Development of Secularization in Turkey* (New York: Routledge, new edition 1995), pp. 215–18. On Westernization see Theodore H. von Laue, *The World Revolution of Westernization* (New York: Oxford University Press, 1987). On the present efforts to reverse this process, i.e. de-Westernization, see B. Tibi, "Culture and Knowledge. The Fundamentalist Claim to de-Westernization," in: *Theory, Culture and Knowledge*, 12(1) (1995), pp. 1–24.

27 Shakib Arslan, *Limatha* ... referenced in note 24, here p. 176.

28 See the flawed study by William Cleveland, *Islam against the West, Shakib Arslan and the Campaign for Islamic Nationalism* (Austin, TX: Texas University Press, 1985). Even the title is wrong. The Islamic concept of the *umma* is an expression of universalism, therefore no such thing as "Islamic nationalism" can ever exist; *umma* is definitely not a nation, but the universal community of Islam envisioned to encompass the entire humanity.

29 B. Tibi, *Arab Nationalism. Between Islam and the Nation-State* (New York and London: Macmillan, 3rd expanded edn, 1997, first 1980).

30 See Ali Mohammed Jarisha and Mohammed Sharif, *Asalib al-Ghazu al-fikri li al-'alam al-Islami*/Ways of the Intellectual Invasion of the Muslim World, 2nd printing (Cairo: Dar al-I'tisam, 1978) and Anwar al-Jundi, *Ahdaf al-Taghrib fi al-alam al-Islami*/The goals of Westernization of the World of Islam (Cairo: al-Azhar, 1977), in particular part 1: "The conspiracy of Westernization," pp. 11–38. The work of al-Jundi is one of the major sources of Islamist antisemitism.

31 See Mohammed Y. Kassab, *L'Islam face au nouvel ordre mondial* (Algier: Edition Salama, 1991), in particular the antisemitic chapter "Une vaste conspiracion judéo-chrétienne," pp. 75–94. On this conspiracy-driven perception see B. Tibi, *Die Verschwörung. Das Trauma arabischer Politik*, (Hamburg: Hoffmann und Campe, 2nd enlarged edition, 1994), and on the related antisemitism see the references in notes 23 and 30.

32 Sayyid Qutb, *al-Islam wa Mushkilat al-hararah*/Islam and the Predicament of Civilization (Cairo: Dar al-Shuruq, 1988), 8th legal reprint.

33 Fred R. von der Mehden, *Two Words of Islam. Interaction between Southeast Asia and the Middle East* (Gainesville, FL: Florida University Press, 1993).

34 On the significance of this region see B. Tibi, "The Middle East: Society, State, Religion," in: Furio Cerutti and Rodolfo Ragionieri, eds, *Identities and Conflicts. The Mediterranean* (New York: Palgrave, 2001), pp. 121–34.

35 UNDP, *Arab Human Development Report 2002. Creating Opportunities for Future Generations* (New York: United Nations, 2002), 168 Pp.

36 Hisham Sharabi, *Neo-Oligarchy. A Theory of Distorted Change in Arab Society* (New York: Oxford University Press, 1992).

37 See B. Tibi: "The Totalitarianism of Jihadist Islamism and its Challenge to Europe to Islam," in: *Totalitarian Movements and Political Religions* (2007), vol. 8, p. 35–54, and the earlier book by the same author, *Der neue Totalitarismus* (Darmstadt: Primus, 2004).

38 In his early book Abdullahi A. An-Na'im, *Toward Islamic Reformation* (Syracuse, NY: Syracuse University Press 1990), chapter 7, in particular pp. 170–81, was critical of the shari'a. The setback in An-Na'im's thinking, from reformer to shari'a exponent, is documented in his new, highly inconsistent 2008 book, referenced and discussed here in Chapter 6.

39 This blame by an US cultural anthropologist was voiced against an African colleague and is quoted, with names, by Lawrence Harrison in his introduction to the volume edited by him and Samuel Huntington, *Culture Matters: How Values Shape the Human Progress* (New York: Basic Books, 1999), p. xxvii. Given the characteristic feature of the blame, the names do not matter.

40 Franz Rosenthal, *The Classical Heritage of Islam* (London: Routledge, 1994); see also Chapter 8 below.

41 On the overall history of Islam see the authoritative Marshall G.S. Hodgson, *The Venture of Islam. Conscience and History in a World Civilization*, 3 vols (Chicago, IL: University Press of Chicago, 1977).

42 The literature on the impact of Islamic rationalism on the rise of science is vast: for a debate and some references see Chapter 8 below.

43 See the reference to Geoffrey Parker in note 3. For a comprehensive history of Islamic–Christian relations see the reference to: *Kreuzzug und Djihad* (note 4). The "Islamic

Expansion" is viewed most polemically by Efraim Karsh, *Islamic Imperialism. A History* (New Haven, CT: Yale University Press, 2006), as "imperialism," as his book title suggests.

44 Marshall C.S. Hodgson, *Rethinking World History, Essays on Europe, Islam and World History* (Cambridge: Cambridge University Press 1995), p. 97; see also note 41 above.

45 See the chapter in the selected writings of Max Weber, *Soziologie, weltgeschichtliche Analysen, Politik* (Stuttgart: Alfred Kröner Press, 1964), on Protestantism and capitalism, pp. 357–81.

46 Maxime Rodinson, *Islam et Capitalisme* (Paris: Editions de Seuils, 1966). The German edition of this book by Rodinson was edited by me and published with a lengthy introduction on Rodinson's approach and his great contribution to the study of Islam. I view him as my mentor and precursor in the Islamology that I represent. The reference is: Maxime Rodinson, *Islam und Kapitalismus* (Frankfurt/Main: Suhrkamp, new edition 1986). This paperback edition of 1986, includes a lengthy introduction by me on Rodinson and his work.

47 See the essay by Maxime Rodinson in: Wolfgang Schluchter, ed., *Max Webers Sicht des Islam* (Frankfurt: Suhrkamp, 1987), pp. 180–89.

48 More on this in: B. Tibi, *Islam and the Cultural Accommodation of Social Change* (Boulder, CO: Westview Press, 1990 and 1991), chapter 1, and more recently idem, *Islam between Culture and Politics* (see note 25), pp. 53–68.

49 The Arabic original text of the Qur'an is referred to throughout this book. For a Qur'an translation see N.J. Dawood, *The Koran* (London: Penguin Classics, 1986) and Bell's *Introduction to the Qur'an*, revised by W. M. Watt (Edinburgh: Edinburgh University Press, 1977). On the context of Islamic revelation see Rudi Paret, *Muhammed und der Koran* (Stuttgart: Kohlhammer, 5th edition, 1980). The German Orientalist Paret is the translator of the most authoritative German edition of the Qur'an, also consulted in this book.

50 On this issue see the two major Arabic books: Abdullahi Abdulrahman, *Sultat an-nas. Dirasat fi tawzif an-nas ad-dini*/The authority of the Text. Studies in the Instrumentalization of Religious Texts (Casablanca: al-Markaz al-Thaqafi, 1993); and also Nasr H. Abu-Zaid,*an-Nas, al-Sultah, al-haqiqa*/The Text, the Authority, the Truth (Casablanca: al-Markaz al-Thaqafi, 1995).

51 This is stated uncritically by S. S. Husain and S. A. Ashraf, *Crisis in Muslim Education* (Jeddah/Saudi Arabia, 1979, distributed in the United Kingdom by Hodder and Stoughton). For a critical view on Islamic education see also chapter 8 in B. Tibi, *Islam between Culture and Politics* (see note 25).

52 B. Tibi, "Cultural Innovation in the Developmental Process," in: Klaus Gottstein, ed., *Islamic Cultural Identity and Social Scientific Development* (Baden Baden: Nomos, 1986), pp. 93–101.

53 On this Helleniziation see the debate and the related references in Chapter 8, also W. M. Watt, *Islamic Philosophy and Theology* (Edinburgh: Edinburgh University Press, 1962), parts 2 and 3.

54 Herbert A. Davidson, *Alfarabi, Avicenna and Averroes, on Intellect: Their Cosmologies, Theories of the Active Intellect and Theories of Human Intellect* (New York: Oxford University Press, 1992).

55 On this view of al-Mawardi and for more details see the intellectual history of Islam covered comprehensively by B. Tibi, *Der wahre Imam. Der Islam von Mohammed bis zur Gegenwart* (Munich: Piper Press 1996), (reprinted 1997, 1998 and 2002), here chapter 5; see also chapters 3, 4 and 6 in that book on the opposed Islamic rationalism.

56 For more details on this see: George Makdisi, *The Rise of the Colleges. Institutions of Learning in Islam and the West* (Edinburgh: Edinburgh University Press, 1981), pp. 80–98, and also for some information on the organization of learning pp. 99–147. On

Islamic education see also the chapter on education in my book: *Islam between Culture and Politics* (note 25), pp. 167–85.

57 In the popular Muslim view, the Gulf War of 1991 is perceived as being the eighth crusade. See Saad-Eddin al-Shadhli, *al-Harb al-Salibiyya al-Thamina*/The Eighth Crusade (Casablanca: al-Matba'a al-Jadida, 1991). It is strange that Columbia University Press has published an allegedly scholarly book titled *The New Crusaders* after the Afghanistan and Iraq wars 2001–3, giving currency to this view!

58 Anke von Kugelgen, *Averroes und die arabische Moderne. Ansätze zu einer Neugründung des Rationalismus im Islam* (Leiden: Brill, 1994).

59 Mohammed al-Jabri, *Arab Islamic Philosophy* (Austin, TX: University of Texas Press, 1999), pp. 120–130.

60 See the reference in note 56 and Robert Wuthnow, *Meaning and Moral Order. Explanations in Cultural Analysis* (Berkeley, CA: University of California Press, 1987), Chapters 7, 8 and 9.

61 The work of Yusuf al-Qaradawi is today the major source of the Islamist *Weltanschauung*, of course next to S. Qutb. The trilogy *al-Hall al-Islami*/The Islamic Solution, is the bible of political Islam. It is highly influential and puts major obstacles in the way of a positive change. The three volumes are: 1: *al-Hulul al-Mustawradah*/The Imported Solutions (Beirut: al-Risalah, 1974, reprint 1980); 2: *al-Hall al-Islami, Farida wa darura*/ The Islamic Solution is a Religious Obligation and a Necessity (Beirut: al-Risalah, 1974). 3: *Baiyinat al-Hall al-Islami*/The Major Characteristics of the Islamic solution, reprint (Cairo: Dar Wahba, 1988). This third volume deals – as its subtitle suggests – with *Shabahat al-ilmaniyyun wa al-mutagharribun*/The doubts of the Secularists and the Westernized; this is the subtitle of volume 3. Against Qaradawi's allegation that (political) Islam is the solution, I argue that "Democracy is the solution." See my book *Political Islam, World Politics* (referenced in note 19), Chapter 7 on democracy. To be sure, Qaradawi is not a voice of liberal Islam, as the misleading reader edited by Charles Kurzman, *Liberal Islam* (New York: Oxford University Press, 1998) wrongly suggests.

62 The phrase *"Mufarqat Ibn Rushd*/The Paradoxon of Averroes" relates to the appreciation of the work of Averroes in Europe concurrent to its dismissal in the world of Islam. The formula was coined by the Egyptian philosopher Mourad Wahba in his contribution to the proceedings of the first international Islamic philosophy conference on Islam and civilization, of which he was the chairperson (referenced in Chapter 6, note 1). The other volume by Mourad Wahba, ed., *Future of Islamic Civilization* (Cairo: The Anglo-Egyptian Bookshop, 1985) includes my contribution "Cultural Innovation in the Development of Islamic Middle East as a Future Perspective," pp. 55–64.

63 Mohammed Abed al-Jabri, *Arab Islamic Philosophy* (see note 59 above), p. 121.

64 Ibid., p. 124 and p. 128.

65 Sadik J. al-Azm, *al-Naqd al-dhati ba'd al-hazima*/Self Criticism after the Defeat (Beirut: al-Tali'a, 1968). On the ensuing debate and the place of al-Azm in it, see my study referenced in the next note (see also the reference to al-Azm in note 14).

66 For more details and for a comparison of the post-1967 Arab left with medieval Islamic enlightenment see B. Tibi, "Intellektuelle als verhinderte Aufklärer. Das Scheitern der Intellektuellen im Islam," in: Harald Bluhm and Walter Reese-Schäfer, eds, *Die Intellektuellen und der Weltlauf* (Baden-Baden: Nomos, 2006), pp. 97–124.

67 Among the few very positive exceptions in US Islamic studies is the work of John Kelsay, *Islam and War. A Study in Comparative Ethics* (Louisville, KY: Westminster and John Knox Press, 1993), pp. 25f. His new book, *Arguing the Just War in Islam*, (Cambridge, MA: Cambridge University Press, 2007) is a major contribution to the field.

68 Fatma Göcek, *East Encounters West* (New York: Oxford University Press, 1987), in particular pp. 103–15. See also Bernard Lewis, *The Muslim Rediscovery of Europe* (New York: Norton, 1982), chapter 9, and also his book: *Islam and the West* (New York: Oxford University Press, 1993), part 3 on: "Islamic Response and Reaction"; see also note 71.

69 The following quotes are from the Paris Diary of Rifa'a R. al-Tahtawi, *Takhlis al-Ibriz fi-talkhis Paris*/The Paris Diary, a reprint in Arabic (Beirut: Dar Ibn Zaidun, no date)

70 On this idea see Reinhard Bendix, *Nation Building and Citizenship. Studies of our Changing Social Order*, new enlarged edition (Berkeley, CA: University of California Press, 1977), p. 411. Bendix states that adopting items of modernity does not mean becoming "fully modern" in a process of modernization.

71 B. Tibi, "The Islamic Dream of Semi-Modernity," in: *India International Center Quarterly*/New Dehli, 22(1) (Spring 1995), pp. 79–87, and the conclusions in Chapter 11 of the present book.

72 Bernard Lewis, *Muslim Rediscovery* (note 68), chapter 9, here p. 238.

73 W. M. Watt, *Islamic Fundamentalism and Modernity* (London: Routledge, 1988); Fazlur Rahman, *Islam and Modernity* (Chicago, IL: University Press of Chicago, 1982) and also B. Tibi, "Attitudes of Sunni-Arab Fundamentalists toward Modern Science and Technology," in: Martin Marty and Scott Appleby, eds, *Fundamentalisms and Society* (Chicago, IL: University Press of Chicago, 1993), pp. 73–102.

74 See my article "The Totalitarianism of Jihadist Islamism" referenced in note 37; on E-jihad see: Gary Bunt, *Islam in the Digital Age* (London: Pluto Press, 2003).

75 Stephen Schwartz, *The Two Faces of Islam. The House of Sa'ud from Tradition to Terror* (New York: Doubleday, 2002), Chapter 7.

76 The literature on al-Qaeda is mushrooming but not always noteworthy; for an exception see: Peter Berger, *Holy War Inc. Inside the Secret World of Osama Bin Laden* (New York: Free Press, 2001).

77 See James Fadiman and Robert Frager, *Essential Sufism* (San Francisco, CA: Harper Collins, 1997).

78 Mohammed Abduh, *al-Islam wa al-Nasraniyya bain al-ilm wa al-madaniyya*/Islam and Christianity between Science and Civilization, new printing (Cairo: Dar al-Hadatha, 1983).

79 On the shari'a and its reform see Chapter 3 and also the references made there.

80 Mohammed Arkoun, *Rethinking Islam* (Boulder, CO: Westview Press, 1994).

81 Mohammed Abid al-Jabri, *Takwin al-aql al-Arabi*/The Creation of Arab Mind (Beirut: Dar al-Tali'a, 1984).

82 Nasr Hamid Abu-Zaid, *Naqd al-Khitab al-din*/Critique of Religious Discourse (Cairo: Madbuli, 1995). For more details on the Abu-Zaid-story see B. Tibi, *Fundamentalismus im Islam* (Darmstadt: Wissenschaftliche Buchgesellschaft, 2002), chapter 7.

83 Sadiq J. al-Azm, *Naqd al-fikr al-dini*/Critique of Religious Thought (Beirut: Dar al-Tali'a, 1969).

84 Mohammad Muslehuddin, *Philosophy of Islamic Law and the Orientalists* (Lahore, Pakistan: Kazi Publications, 1985), p. 242.

85 Richard Martin and others, *Defenders of Reason in Islam: Mu'tazilism from Medieval School to Modern Symbol* (Oxford: Oneworld, 1997).

86 On this language pattern see M. Piamenta, *Islam in Everyday Arabic Speech* (Leiden: Brill, 1979).

87 Mohammad Muslehuddin (see note 84), p. 247.

88 Nasr Hamid Abu-Zaid, *al-Tafkir fi asr al-Takfir*/Reasoning in the Age of Accusation of Heresy (Cairo: Madbuli, 1995).

89 Edward Said was my host during my very first visit to the US. The volume in question was edited by Said, *The Arabs of Today. Perspectives for Tomorrow* (Columbus, OH: Forum Associates, 1973) and includes my essay "Genesis of the Arab Left. A Critical Viewpoint," pp. 31–42. This contribution was my first-ever publication in English, copyedited by Said himself. The volume also includes a contribution by S.J. al-Azm. His essay, referenced in note 14, ended his then existing friendship with Said. The two moved from being close friends to bitter enemies. My efforts at mediation not only failed but cost me Said's friendship also.

90 Bu Ali-Yassin, *al-Thaluth al-Muharram*/The Triple Taboo (Beirut: al-Tari'a, 1973).

91 Reinhard Bendix, *Nation Building* (referenced in note 70), p. 411.

92 Ibid, p. 416.

93 See the references in notes 71 and 73.

94 Ernest Gellner, *Postmodernism, Reason and Religion* (London: Routledge, 1992), S. 85.

95 Ibid.

96 See the reference in note 62.

97 This dismissive review of the UNDP report of 2002 by Tabbarah was published in *al-Hayat*.

98 For some of these writings by Arab-Christians see the following references: *Mukhtarat Salamah Musah*/Selected writings of Salamah Musah (Beirut: Maktabat al-Ma'arif, 1963). For a study on Musah's thought see Vernon Egger, *A Fabian in Egypt. Salamah Musah and the Rise of the Professional Classes in Egypt 1909–1939* (Lanham, MD: University Press of America, 1986). Other Arab-Christian liberals are Nadrah al-Yaziji, *Rasail fi hadarat al-bu's*/Essays on the Civilization of Misery (Damascus: al-Adib, 1963) and Georges Hanna, *al-Insan al-Arabi*/The Arab Person (Beirut: Dar al-Ilm, 1964).

99 For more details see B. Tibi, *Arab Nationalism. Between Islam and the Nation-State*, referenced in note 29.

100 David Gress, *From Plato to NATO. The Idea of the West and its Opponents* (New York: The Free Press, 1999), p. 503 f.

101 See B. Tibi, *Political Islam, World Politics and Europe* (referenced in note 19).

102 Hedley Bull, "The Revolt against the West," in: H. Bull and A. Watson, eds, *The Expansion of International Society* (Oxford: Clarendon Press, 1984), p. 223.

103 See B. Tibi, *Islam between Culture and Politics* (referenced in note 25), chapter 4 on the simultaneity of globalization and fragmentation.

104 See the chapter by Clifford Geertz on "religion as a cultural system" in which he interprets culture as a social production of meaning. This chapter is included in his collected essays: *The Interpretation of Cultures* (New York: Basic Books, 1973), pp. 87–125.

105 Akbar Ahmed, quoted in the editorial of Brian Knowlton "On a journey into Islam," in: *International Herald Tribune*, Friday, August 3, 2007, p. 2. See also the book published later on by Akbar Ahmed, *Journey into Islam. The Crisis of Globalization* (Washington, DC: The Brookings Institution Press, 2007). The subtitle is, however, utterly wrong, as many other unbalanced views of Ahmed unfortunately are and continue to be. The book's title should be corrected into: *The Crisis of Islamic Civilization*. It would be wise to stop explaining everything by globalization, which provides grounds for the Islamic view of self-victimization that is used in putting the blame on the non-Muslim other (i.e. the West); after taking a break, Muslims, including Akbar Ahmed, need to look at the self very critically, to see clearly beyond the ideological clouds, and learn to be critical; if this is not feasible, then there can be no hope. Muslims need to be reminded of the Qur'anic wisdom: "Allah does not change people, unless they change themselves" (sura 13, verse 11). An exceptional Muslim in critical reasoning is S.J. al-Azm, referenced repeatedly in this chapter.

Chapter 2

1 This chapter documents a long-standing reasoning on the issue in question. During the course of my socialization in an Islamic value system in Damascus, my birthplace, I grew up among tensions. In my schooling I was torn between the knowledge systems of two competing worldviews, the one secular, the other religious. This conflict has prevailed throughout my life, reinforced by my ensuing education and research in Europe. As a scholar, I made my first systematic address of the related issues in a paper presented at the Annual Meeting of the American Sociological Association in

Washington, DC. The papers of the panel in which I participated were supposed to be published in an edited volume. On that occasion I was exposed to the fact that talking about the cultural tensions between reason-based knowledge and Islamic divine knowledge is tantamount to entering a minefield. The major "peer-reviewer" made his approval of the publication conditional on the exclusion of my paper. The editor submitted to his demand. Later on, I experienced similar unscholarly responses, among others, to my article "Culture and Knowledge. The Politics of Islamization of Knowledge as a Postmodern Project? The Fundamentalist Claim to De-Westernization," *Theory, Culture & Society*, 12(1) (1995), pp. 1–24. For a discussion of this issue see Roxanne Euben, *Enemy in the Mirror. Islamic Fundamentalism* (Princeton, NJ: Princeton University Press, 1999), pp. 164–67.

2 Juergen Habermas, *The Philosophical Discourse of Modernity*, translated by Frederick G. Lawrence (Cambridge, MA: MIT Press, 1990), p. 18.

3 Ernst B. Haas, *When Knowledge is Power* (Berkeley, CA: University of California Press, 1990), p. XI.

4 On this Islamist project of an Islamization of knowledge, see the publication by the International Institute for Islamic Thought, ed., *Towards Islamization of Disciplines* (Herndon, VA: International Institute for Islamic thought, 1989). See also Jawdat Muhammad 'Awwad, *Hawl aslamat al-'ulum/*On the Islamization of Sciences (Cairo: al-Mukhtar, 1987).

5 See René Descartes, *Discours de la Méthode* (1637) and for an interpretation the chapter on "cogito" in Joachim Kopper, *Einfuehrung in die Philosophie der Aufklaerung* (Darmstadt: Wissenschaftliche Buchgesellschaft, 1992), pp. 21–27. Descartes is viewed as the "founder of the modern view of the world" by Franz Borkenau, *Der Uebergang vom feudalen zum bürgerlichen Weltbild* (reprint, Darmstadt: Wissenschaftliche Buchgesellschaft, 1982), pp. 268–383, in particular p. 309.

6 On Ibn Khaldun and his *Muqaddima* and for references to the major sources on his work see the heavily footnoted chapter 6 on Ibn Khaldun in my book *Der wahre Imam. Der Islam von Mohammed bis zur Gegenwart* (Munich: Piper, 1996), pp. 179–209. On rational philosophy in Islam see Herbert A. Davidson, *Alfarabi, Avicenna ans Averroes, on Intellect* (New York: Oxford University Press, 1992). Davidson refers to the recognition of universal rational knowledge in medieval Islam, in contrast to Imaduldin Khalil, *al-aql al-Muslim* (The Muslim Reason) (Cairo: Dar al-Haramein, 1983), who specifically claims an "*Aql Islami/*Islamic reason" and a related Islamic knowledge.

7 As repeatedly mentioned, the terms culture and civilization are not used interchangeably in the present book. In contrast to Samuel Huntington and others, the concept of culture is referred to with the meaning of a social production of meaning related to local entities. Therefore, cultural change takes place in a specific and local society; it is, however, embedded in a civilizational context and is affected by a global environment. The notion of "civilization" is broader than that of culture in that it refers to a grouping of related cultures based on resemblance and commonalities. Despite all cultural diversity, related cultures resemble one another like a family, through shared values and worldview. It follows that there are cross-cultural, i.e. civilizational values which all Muslims – despite all of their diversity – share. It is, however, incorrect to speak of a monolithic Islamic culture. There is no such thing. There are thousands of local Islamic cultures, but only one, highly diversified, Islamic civilization constructed as a cross-cultural entity.

8 For more details see the excellent study by Roxanne Euben, *Journeys to the Other Shore. Muslim and Western Travellers in Search of Knowledge* (Princeton, NJ: Princeton University Press, 2006). The contemporary Islamist project of "Islamization of knowledge," to be closely discussed in this chapter, is geared up to a purification of knowledge and therefore precludes any cultural borrowing from others. In view of the rich Islamic

tradition of cross-cultural fertilization it can be safely stated that Islamism marks a break and discontinuity in Islamic history.

9 On this conflict in Medieval Islam see B. Tibi, "Politisches Denken im klassischen und mittelalterlichen Islam zwischen Religio-Jurisprudenz (Fiqh) und hellenisierter Philosophie (Falsafa)," in: Iring Fetscher *et al.*, eds, *Pipers Handbuch der politischen Ideen*, 5 vols (Munich: Piper, 1987, here vol. 2/1993), pp. 87–174.

10 On these basic sources of Islamic knowledge see M. Shaltut, *al-Islam Aqida wa Shari'a/ Islam as a Dogma, and a Shari'a*, 10th edn (Cairo: al-Shuruq, 1980).

11 On the thinking of these authorities of political Islam see: B. Tibi, *The Challenge of Fundamentalism. Political Islam and the New World Disorder* (Berkeley, CA: University of California Press, 1998, updated 2002) and most recently B. Tibi, *Political Islam, World Politics and Europe* (London: Routledge, 2007), Introduction. On the qualification of these thoughts as "totalitarian" see the references in note 27.

12 The knowledge that underpins the relations of Muslims to non-Muslims is determined in Islamic doctrine by submission and war. For more details see B. Tibi, "War and Peace in Islam," in: Terry Nardin, ed., *The Ethics of War and Peace* (Princeton, NJ: Princeton University Press, 1996), pp. 128–45. For a historical overview on this issue see Alan G. Jamieson, *Faith and Sword. A Short History of Christian-Muslim Conflict* (London: Reaktion Books, 2006) and earlier B. Tibi, *Kreuzzug und Djihad. Der Islam und die christliche Welt* (Munich: Bertelsmann, 1999). See also Chapter 7 of the present book, on pluralism.

13 W. M. Watt, *Islamic Fundamentalism and Modernity* (London: Routledge, 1988).

14 See the references in note 12 and W. M. Watt, *Muslim–Christian Encounters, Perceptions and Misperceptions* (London: Routledge, 1991).

15 Watt, *Islamic Fundamentalism* (referenced in note 13), pp. 13–14.

16 See the reference to Geoffrey Parker, *The Military Revolution*, in Chapter 1, note 3.

17 On this introduction of modern European technology to the world of Islam via the military see the illuminating work by David B. Ralston, *Importing the European Army. The Introduction of European Army Techniques into the Extra-European World 1600–1914* (Chicago, IL: University of Chicago Press, 1990). The book includes chapter 3 on the Ottoman Empire and chapter 4 on Egypt. For an analysis of the attitudes of contemporary Islamists on this issue see the findings of my fieldwork referenced in note 32 below. See also Chapter 11 of the present book.

18 Edgar Zilsel, *Die sozialen Urspruenge der neuzeitlichen Wissenschaft* (Frankfurt/Main: Suhrkamp Verlag, 1985).

19 See the seminal book by Malcolm H. Kerr, *Islamic Reform. The Political and Legal Theories of Muhammad Abduh and Rashid Rida* (Berkeley, CA: University of California Press, 1966). Kerr was slain by Islamic militants in 1984 in Beirut, when he was acting as president of the American University of Beirut.

20 Mohammed Arkoun, *Rethinking Islam* (Boulder, CO: Westview, 1994) and Abdullahi A. An-Na'im, *Toward an Islamic Reformation. Civil Liberties, Human Rights, and International Law* (Syracuse, NY: Syracuse University Press, 1990). The new, less promising books of both are: Arkoun, *To Reform or to Subvert?* (London: Saqi Essentials, 2006); and An-Na'im, *Islam and the Secular State. Negotiating the Future of Shari'a* (Cambridge, MA: Harvard University Press, 2008).

21 On these repercussions see B. Tibi, *Conflict and War in the Middle East. From Interstate War to New Security*, second enlarged edition (New York: St. Martin's Press, 1993, new expanded edition, 1997), Chapters 3 and 4, see also the new chapters added to the second edition.

22 Pan-Arab formulae (e.g. Arab national unity) have been replaced by those of the Islamist "*hall Islami*/Islamic solution" based on the belief in an Islamic unity underpinned by an universalism that becomes a political internationalism (note 11 above).

The third volume is: *Shabahat al-ilmaniyyun wa al-mutagharribun*/The doubts of the Secularists and the Westernized (Matba'at Wahba: Cairo, 1988).

23 On both Sunni and Shi'ite varieties and on their competition see Chapters 3 and 4 in B. Tibi, *Political Islam, World Politics and Europe* (referenced in note 11).

24 Sayyid Qutb, *Ma'alim fi al-tariq*/Signposts along the Road (Cairo: Dar al-Shuruq, 13th legal printing, 1989), p. 201.

25 Ibid.

26 Ernest Gellner, *Postmodernism, Reason and Religion* (London: Routledge, 1992), p. 85.

27 B. Tibi, *Der Neue Totalitarismus. Heiliger Krieg und westliche Sicherheit* (Darmstadt: Primus, 2004) and also B. Tibi, "The Totalitarianism of Jihadist Islamism and its Challenge to Europe and to Islam," in: *Totalitarian Movements and Political Religion*, 8, 1 (2007), pp. 35–54.

28 See the work of Anwar al-Jundi referenced in Chapter 8.

29 On Islamic rationalism see the reference in note 6, and on the conflict with the *fiqh*-orthodoxy, note 9.

30 Ziauddin Sardar, *Islamic Futures. The Shape of Ideas to Come* (London: Mansell, 1985), p. 85. On Descartes see note 5. See also Sardar's book *Exploration in Islamic Science* (London: Mansell, 1989). Epistemologically, post-colonial "science" proves to be anti-science and culturally anti-Western. For a different Islamic view see Pervez Hoodbhoy, *Islam and Science. Religious Orthodoxy and the Battle for Rationality* (London: Zed Books, 1991).

31 Akbar S. Ahmed, *Postmodernism and Islam. Predicament and Promise* (London: Routledge, 1992, reprinted 2004).

32 The research findings were published in five volumes by Chicago University Press. I was a member of the research team and co-authored vol. 2; see B. Tibi, "Attitudes of Sunni-Arab Fundamentalists toward Modern Science and Technology," in: Martin Marty and R. Scott Appleby, eds, *Fundamentalisms and Society* (Chicago, IL: Chicago University Press, 1993), pp. 73–102.

33 See Akbar Ahmed, *Postmodernism and Islam* (referenced in note 31).

34 Ibid. It is most intriguing that the liberal Muslim Akbar Ahmed, who became critical of political Islam after his journey in some Islamic countries (see next note), earlier used some terms, like "intellectual invasion," employed by the Islamists; see Ali M. Jarisha and Muhammad Sh. Zaibaq, *Asalib al-ghazu al-fikri li al-'alam al-Islami*/Methods of the Intellectual Invasion of the Islamic World (Cairo: Dar al-I'tisam, 1978, second edition). On Akbar see Chapter 1, note 105.

35 So Akbar Ahmed in the year 2007, here quoted by Brian Knowlton, "On a Journey into Islam," in: *International Herald Tribune*, August 3, 2007. For more on this issue see also the final page of Chapter 1 in the present book.

36 Rifa'a R. al-Tahtawi, *Takhlis al-ibriz fi talkhis Paris* (The Purification of Gold For Describing Paris/Paris Diary) (Cairo. Reprint, no date).

37 See the view of Afghani in his book: *al-A'mal al-Kamilah*/Collected Works, edited by Mohammed Imara (Cario: Dar al-Katib al-Arabi, 1968). For Afghani, knowledge is related to power.

38 Hisham Sharabi, *Neo-Oligarchy. A Theory of Distorted Change in Arab Society* (New York: Oxford University Press, 1992).

39 On this Islamic contribution to the rise of modern science see David Lindberg, *The Beginning of Western Science* (Chicago, IL: The University of Chicago Press, 1992), chapter 8, on Islam, pp. 161–82 and Edward Grant, *The Foundation of Modern Science in the Middle Ages* (Cambridge: Cambridge University Press, 1996), pp. 171–91. See also Howard Turner, *Science in Medieval Islam* (Austin, TX: The University of Austin Texas, 1995) and Toby Huff, *The Rise of Early Modern Science* (Cambridge: Cambridge University Press, 1993), in particular chapters 2 and 3.

40 See 'Awwad, *Hawl aslamat al-'ulum* (referenced in note 4).

41 On "*asalah*/authenticity" see Chapter 8 and also Anwar al-Jundi, *al-Mu'asara fir itar al-asalah*/Modernity seen in the Context of Authenticity (Cairo: Dar al-Sahwa, 1987).

42 See Martin Albrow, Introduction in: Martin Albrow and Elisabeth King, eds, *Globalization, Knowledge and Society: Readings from International Sociology* (London: Sage Publications, 1990), p. 7.

43 On Eurocentrism see Dominique Perrot and Roy Preiswerk, *Ethnocentrism and History* (New York: NOK Publishers, 1978). See also J.M. Blaut, *The Colonizer's Model of the World. Geographical Diffusionism and Eurocentric History* (New York: Guilford Press, 1993).

44 Max Weber, *Soziologie, weltgeschichtliche Analysen, Politik* (Stuttgart: Kroener Verlag, 1964), pp. 103, 317 and 338.

45 Edward Said, *Orientalism* (New York: Vintage Books, 1979), p. 259.

46 Daniel Bell, "The Return of the Sacred," in his collected essays, *The Winding Passage 1960–1980* (New York: Basic Books, 1980). For a continuation of this debate under conditions of post-bipolarity see the new chapter 11 to the new 2005 edition of my book, *Islam between Culture and Politics* (New York: Palgrave, 2nd edn 2005), pp. 234–72.

47 On the vision of "the remaking of the world" see vol. 3 of "The Fundamentalism Project" *Fundamentalisms and the State* (Chicago, IL: Chicago University Press, 1993), Part 3; see also note 32.

48 See Juergen Habermas, *Glauben und Wissen* (Frankfurt/Main: Suhrkamp Verlag, 2001) and also the critique by B. Tibi, "Habermas and the Return of the Sacred. Is it a Religious Renaissance, a Pronouncement of a 'Post-Secular Society', or the Emergence of Political Religion as a New Totalitarianism?," in: *Religion-Staat-Gesellschaft*, 3, 2 (2002), pp. 265–96.

49 Bruce Lawrence, *Defenders of God: The Fundamentalist Revolt Against the Modern Age* (San Francisco: Harper and Row, 1989). See also his book published a decade later: *Shattering the Myth. Islam Beyond Violence* (Princeton, NJ: Princeton University Press, 1998).

50 'Adel Husain, *Nahwa fikr Arabi jadid*/Toward a New Arabic Thought (Cairo: Dar al-Mustaqbal al-Arabi, 1985), pp. 11–37. The late Husain started his career as a member of the totalitarian underground group *Misr al-Fatat* (Young Egypt) and then converted to Marxism before he achieved what he himself termed as a "return to Islam." In an interview published in the fundamentalist journal *Liwa' al-Islami*, in September 15, 1989, shortly before his death, Husain described his intellectual development with this formula: "*Min dhalam al-shiyu'iyya ila nur al-Islam*/From the Darkness of Communism to the Light of Islam," ibid., pp. 12–15.

51 B. Tibi, *The Crisis of Modern Islam. A Preindustrial Culture in the Scientific–Technological Age* (Salt Lake City, UT: University of Utah Press, 1988).

52 The historian of classical Greece Christian Meier, *Die Entstehung des Politischen bei den Griechen* (Frankfurt: Suhrkamp Verlag, 1989) coined the term "*Koennensbewusstsein*" to depict the combination in the classical Greek thought of *techne* (skills) and *episteme* (knowledge). In the European Enlightenment, the concept of progress rests on this "*Koennensbewusstsein*," a view of the world according to which the world is man-centered and no longer governed by God. According to the historian of science Zilsel (see note 18), modern science grew from such a combination, i.e. of the humanities of the Renaissance espoused with technological engineering.

53 On these Muslim theologian rationalists see Richard Martin *et al.*, *Defenders of Reason in Islam* (Oxford: Oneworld, 1997), and on the combination of reason with faith Robert Audi, *Religious Commitment and Secular Reason* (Cambridge: Cambridge University Press, 2000). In Islamic studies the "*kalam*/theology" is often confused with "*fiqh*/sacral jurisprudence."

54 Sayyid Qutb, *Ma'alim fi al-Tariq* (referenced in note 24), p. 10. Qutb revived the early Islamic concept of *Jahilliyya* for describing pre-Islamic ignorance in order to apply it to cultural modernity.

55 Habermas, *The Philosophical Discourse of Modernity* (referenced in note 2), pp. 1–2; see also the reference to Weber in note 44.
56 Mohammed Abed al-Jabri, *Arab Islamic Philosophy* (Austin, TX: The University of Texas Press, 1999), pp. 120–30, here p. 124.
57 Akbar S. Ahmed, *Postmodernism and Islam* (referenced in note 31), p. 5.
58 Erasmus Foundation, ed., *The Limits of Pluralism. Neo-Absolutisms and Relativism* (Amsterdam: Praemium Erasmianum Foundation, 1994) and Martin Marty and R. Scott Appleby, eds, *The Fundamentalism Project*, 5 vols (Chicago, IL: Chicago University Press 1991–95).
59 Akbar. quoted after the report of B. Knowlton referenced in note 35.
60 Syed M. N. al-Attas, *Islam, Secularism and the Philosophy of the Future* (London: Mansell, 1985), p. 127.
61 Juergen Habermas, *The Philosophical Discourse of Modernity* (referenced in note 2), pp. 17–18.
62 al-Attas, *Secularism* (referenced in note 60), p. 138.
63 Husain Sadr, "Science in Islam. Is there a Conflict?", in: Ziauddin Sardar, ed., *The Truth of Midas* (Manchester: Manchester University Press, 1984), pp. 22–23.
64 Ismail R. al-Faruqi, "Science and Traditional Values in Islamic Society," in: *Zygon*, 2, (1969), pp. 231–46, here p. 241.
65 On this ugly face of Wahhabi Saudi Arabia see Stephen Schwartz, *The Two Faces of Islam. The House of Sa'ud from Tradition to Terror* (New York: Doubleday, 2002).
66 Adel Husain, *Nahwa fikr Arabi jadid*/Towards a New Arab Thought (Cairo: Dar al-Mustaqbal al-Arabi, 1985).
67 Ibid., p. 16; to reduce the number of the footnotes all the following quotes from Husain are documented by page number in the text.
68 Wolf Lepenies, "Anthropological Perspectives in the Sociology of Science," in: Everett Mendelsohn and Yehuda Elkana, eds, *Sciences and Cultures. Anthropological Studies of the Sciences* (Dordrecht: Reidel Publ. Co., 1981), pp. 245–61.
69 On the simultaneity of structural globalization and cultural fragmentation see B. Tibi, *Islam between Culture and Politics* (Chapter 4).
70 See Clifford Geertz, *The Interpretation of Cultures* (New York: Basic Books, 1973), pp. 87–125.
71 Husain 'Adel Husain, *Nahwa fikr Arabi jadid* (referenced in note 66), p. 24.
72 Anthony Giddens, *The Consequences of Modernity* (Stanford, CA: Stanford University Press, 1990), p. 2.
73 See Eric Wolf, *Europe and the People without History* (Berkeley, CA: University of California Press, 1982, reprint 1997).
74 The cited statement was made by the German Orientalist Baber Johanson in a contribution presented to a project conducted by the University of Calgary in Canada. Johanson's presentation of German scholarship on history is referenced below. Johanson left the Freie Universitaet Berlin first for Paris, then went to Harvard. As he rightly acknowledges, Islamic history does not exist in the curriculum taught in departments of history at German universities. The reference is: Baber Johanson, "Politics and Scholarship: The Development of Islamic Studies in Germany," published in: Tareq Ismael, ed., *Middle East Studies. International Perspectives on the State of the Art* (New York: Praeger, 1990), pp. 71–130, here p. 81 and p. 83. In Calgary I talked similarly about German social science. My paper is included as a chapter in pp. 131–48 of the same volume. Ever since there has been no change!
75 'Adel Husain, *Nahwa fikr Arabi jadid* (referenced in note 66), p. 23.
76 Ibid., p. 26.
77 Ibid., p. 29.
78 Ibid., p. 30.

79 See also B. Tibi, "Islam between Religious–Cultural Practice and Identity Politics," in: Helmut Anheier and Y. Raj Isar, *Culture and Globalization Series, vol. 1, Conflicts and Tensions* (London: Sage, 2007), pp. 221–31.

80 See Gerald Holton, *Science and Anti-Science* (Cambridge, MA: Harvard University Press, 1993), and also Chapter 8 of the present book.

81 Aristoteles, *Politik*, translation with comments and notes by Eugen Rolfers (Hamburg: Felix Meiner, 1958).

82 Saifuldin Abdulfattah Isma'il, *al-tajdid al-siyasi wa alwaqi' al-arabi al-mu'asir-Ru'ya Islamiyya*/Political Innovation and Arab Realities. An Islamist View (Cairo: Maktabat al-Nahda al-Misriyya, 1989).

83 John Waterbury, "Social Science Research and Arab Studies in the Coming Decade," in: Hisham Sharabi, ed., *The Next Arab Decade* (Boulder, CO: Westview Press, 1988), pp. 293–302.

84 Norbert Elias, *The Civilizing Process*, 2 vols, here vol. 1: *The History of Manners* (New York: Pantheon Books, 1978).

Chapter 3

1 The research background of this chapter is long and is embedded in the Muslim efforts to reform and rethink shari'a in the pursuit of a reform of Islam itself. Among these efforts is the work was published by Tore Lindholm and Kari Vogt, eds, *Islamic Law Reform and Human Rights. Challenges and Rejoinders; Proceedings of the Seminar on Human Rights and the Modern Application of Islamic Law, Oslo 14–15 February 1992* (Copenhagen: Nordic Human Rights Publ., 1993). My contribution is on pp. 75–96. This rethinking about shari'a is continued in: B. Tibi, *Islam between Culture and Politics* (New York: Palgrave, 2001, updated 2005), Chapter 7, pp. 148–66. and also in: B. Tibi, "Islamic Shari'a as Constitutional Law? The Freedom of Faith in the Light of the Politicization of Islam. The Reinvention of the Shari'a and the Need for an Islamic Law Reform," in: The Japanese Association of Comparative Constitutional Law, ed., *Church and State. Towards Protection of Freedom of Religion. Proceedings of the International Conference on Comparative Constitutional Law, 2005* (Tokyo: Nihon University Press, 2006), pp. 126–70 (English) and pp. 79–125 (Japanese). Even though it is acknowledged that each civilization has its own legal tradition I continue to argue for the universality of law. On this matter see H. L. A. Hart, *The Concept of Law*, 2nd printing (Oxford: The Clarendon Press, 1970), p. 221; and on this issue in international law see Michael Akehurst, *A Modern Introduction to International Law*, 6th edition (London: Unwin Hyman, 1987), pp. 212. The outstanding classical legal work by F. S. C. Northrop, *The Taming of the Nations: A Study of the Cultural Basis of International Policy*, is available in a reprinted 2nd edition (Woodbridge, CT, 1987). The basic issues of the universality of law are discussed by Terry Nardin, *Law, Morality and the Relations of States* (Princeton, NJ: Princeton University Press, 1983). In my work I relate these debates and issues to the study of Islamic shari'a law. See for instance B. Tibi, "Islamic Law, Shari'a and Human Rights. Universal Morality and International Relations," in: *Human Rights Quarterly*, 16(2) (1994), pp. 277–99.

2 This formula is the title of a lecture by Harvard sociologist Daniel Bell, held at the London School of Economics/LSE in 1977 and later included in his collection of essays: *The Winding Passage* (New York: Basic Books, 1980), pp. 324–54. The lecture continues to be topical. A debate on this return of the sacred was resumed in the aftermath of 9/11 (see note 8), and most recently by B. Tibi, "The Return of the Sacred to Politics," in: *Theoria. Journal of Social and Political Theory*, 55, 3 (April 2008), issue no. 115, pp. 91–119, on "Politics and the Return of the Sacred."

3 Max Weber, *Soziologie, Weltgeschichtliche Analysen, Politik* (Selected Writings) (Stuttgart: Kröner, 1964), p. 317.

4 On Muslim-reformist reasoning in the past three decades, on secularization in Islam and on related issues see the references in Chapter 6, note 1.

5 On this politics of shari'atization, expressed in the call for "*tatbiq al-Shari'a/*the implementation of shari'a" see chapter 8 in: B. Tibi, *The Challenge of Fundamentalism. Political Islam and the New World Disorder* (Berkeley, CA: The University of California Press, 1998, updated edition 2002), pp. 158–78.

6 Abdullahi A. An-Na'im, *Toward an Islamic Reformation. Civil Liberties, Human Rights and International Law* (Syracuse, NY: Syracuse University Press, 1990), p. 100. On the change documented in the new book of An-Na'im on shari'a see note 9 below and more in Chapter 6.

7 The published version of my Tokyo paper on shari'a and constitutionalism is referenced in note 1 above.

8 For more details on this Islamist civilizational project as an indication of the return of the sacred see chapter 7 on shari'a in: B. Tibi, *Islam between Culture and Politics* (New York: Palgrave, 2001, new expanded edition, 2005), and in particular the new chapter 11 completed for the second edition; it deals with the return of the sacred mentioned in note 2 above. On the call for shari'a that represents a civilizational project see Sami Zubaida, *Law and Power in the Islamic World* (London: Tauris, 2005), in particular chapter 3.

9 An-Na'im, *Towards* (referenced in note 6), p. 99. In contrast, in his new book, *Islam and the Secular State. Negotiating the Future of Shari'a* (Cambridge, MA: Harvard University Press, 2008), the changed mindset of An-Na'im is favorable to the shari'a. After reading this new book I believe that An-Na'im is no longer to be ranked as a Muslim reformer.

10 Mark Juergensmeyer, *The New Cold War? Religious Nationalism Confronts the Secular State* (Berkeley, CA: University of California Press, 1993), in particular Part 1.

11 Bryan Turner, *Weber and Islam* (London: Routledge, 1974). See also the contributions included in the volume edited by Wolfgang Schluchter, ed., *Weber und der Islam* (Frankfurt/Main: Suhrkamp, 1987).

12 In the writings of the nineteenth century's revivalist al-Afghani, jihad was limited to a revolt against the colonial West. His writings were edited in a translation by Nikkie Keddie, ed., *An Islamic Response to Imperialism* (Berkeley, CA: University of California Press, new edition 1983).

13 Sayyid Qutb, *Ma'alim fi al-tariq/*Signposts along the Road (Cairo: Dar al-Sharuq, 13th legal edition, 1989), p. 5. Comparatively speaking this book by Qutb resembles in its mobilizing effects *The Communist Manifesto* by Marx. It is seminal to Islamism, much as is this other major book by Sayyid Qutb, *al-Salam al-Alami wa al-Isla/*World Peace and Islam (Cairo: Dar al-Sharuq, 10th legal edition, 1992). On p. 170 of the latter Qutb engages in a reinterpretation of jihad to present it as an Islamic idea for a world revolution.

14 See the apologetic contribution by Sabir Tu'aima, *al-Shari'a al-Islamiyya fi asr al-ilm/*Islamic Law in the Age of Science (Beirut: Dar al-jil, 1979), pp. 208ff., and in contrast: Najib al-Armanazi, *al-Shar' al-duwali fi al-Islam/*International Law in Islam, new printing (London: Riad El-Rayyes, 1990) (based on a Sorbonne Ph.D. thesis, first published in Damascus, 1930).

15 See the contributions on "Remaking the World," in: Martin Marty and Scott Appleby, eds, *Fundamentalisms and the State* (Chicago, IL: University of Chicago Press, 1993), *Part 3: Remaking the World Through Militancy*. This is volume 3 of the five volumes of the "Fundamentalism Project," pursued during 1989–95 at the American Academy of Arts and Sciences (I am co-author of volume 2). On this issue after 9/11 see Daniel Philpott, "The Challenge of September 11 to Secularism in International Relations," in: *World Politics*, vol. 55,1 (October 2002), pp. 66–95.

16 John Kelsay, *Islam and War* (Louisville, KY: John Knox Press, 1993), p. 117. See also Kelsay's most recent book, *Arguing the Just War in Islam* (Cambridge, MA: Cambridge University Press, 2007).

17 See the arguments of the reform Muslim Mohammed Said al-Ashmawi, *Usul al-Shari'a*/The Origins of Shari'a (Cairo: Madbuli, 1983) and also my contributions to this subject referenced in notes 1, 7 and 8.

18 The basic books on shari'a continue to be those by Joseph Schacht, *Introduction to Islamic Law*, 5th printing (Oxford: Clarendon Press, 1979), and by N. J. Coulson, *A History of Islamic Law*, 3rd printing (Edinburgh: Edinburgh University Press, 1978). Despite the popular accusation of "Orientalism" (see on this issue Chapter 4 note 37) by some questionable diaspora Muslim scholars, who are ignored in this chapter, the cited studies continue to be the foremost authoritative work on shari'a.

19 The classic of Ibn Taimiyya, *al-Siyasa al-Shar'iyya*, is available in many reprints; on Ibn Taimiyya see chapter 5 in B. Tibi, *Der wahre Imam. Der Islam von Mohammed bis zur Gegenwart* (Munich: Piper, 1996 and two paperback editions, 1999 and 2002).

20 Emmanuel Sivan, *Radical Islam. Medieval Theology and Modern Politics* (New Haven, CT: Yale University Press, 1985) is partly outdated, but continues to be a relevant study.

21 On the medieval Islamic rationalization of the world see Herbert Davidson, *Alfarabi, Avicenna and Averroes, on Intellect* (New York: Oxford University Press, 1992) and B. Tibi, *Der wahre Imam* (referenced note 19), chapters 3, 4 and 6.

22 See Chapter 2 of this book and the reference to my article "Culture and Knowledge" included there in note 1.

23 Max Weber, "Drei Typen der Herrschaft," included in: *Soziologie ...*, referenced in note 3.

24 Theodore von Laue, *The World Revolution of Westernization* (New York: Oxford University Press, 1987).

25 See Chapter 5 of this book and also B. Tibi, "Islam between Religious-Cultural Practice and Identity Politics", in: Y. Raj Isar and Helmut Anheier, eds, *Conflicts and Tensions*, vol. 1 of *The Culture and Globalization Series* (London and New York: Sage, 2007), pp. 221–31.

26 On Islam in Europe see Part III of B. Tibi, *Political Islam, World Politics and Europe* (London: Routledge, 2007), and also B. Tibi, "A Migration Story. From Muslim Immigrants to European Citizens of the Heart," in: *The Fletcher Forum of World Affairs*, 31, 1 (Winter 2007), pp. 147–68.

27 Timothy Byrnes and Peter Katzenstein, eds, *Religion in an Expanding Europe* (Cambridge: Cambridge University Press, 2006), chapter 8 by B. Tibi, "Europeanizing Islam or the Islamization of Europe," pp. 204–24. I am not in agreement with the editors in some major issue areas. See also Tibi's chapter on Euro-Islam, which is viewed as an alternative to the incremental Islamization of Europe, in: Nezar al Sayyad and Manuel Castells, eds, *Muslim Europe or Euro-Islam* (Lanham, MD and New York: Lexington Books, 2002), pp. 31–52. This book emerged from a University of California Berkeley project on "Islam and the Changing Identity of Europe."

28 See the part on law in: Martin Marty and Scott Appleby, *Fundamentalisms and the State* (Chicago, IL: Chicago University Press, 1993).

29 See the book by Mohammed al-Ghazali, *Huquq al-insan bain al-Islam wa i'lan al-umam al-mutahhidah*/Human Rights Between Islam and UN-Charta (Cairo: Dar al-Kutub al-Islamiyya, 1984); and Mohammed Imara, *al-Islam wa huquq al-insan*/Islam and Human Rights (Cairo: Dar al-Shuruq, 1989).

30 See Bat Ye'or, *Islam and Dhimmitude* (Cranbury, NJ: Associated University Presses, 2002).

31 See Abdulazim Ramadan, *Jama'at al-Takfir*/The Groups of "Takfir/Declaring Others as Unbelievers" (Cairo: Madbuli, 1995).

32 B. Tibi, "The Totalitarianism of Jihadist Islamism and its Challenge to Europe and to Islam," *Totalitarian Movements and Political Religion*, 8, 1 (2007), pp. 35–54 and idem, *Der neue Totalitarismus. Heiliger Krieg und westliche Sicherheit* (Darmstadt: Primus, 2004).

33 See, for instance, the work of the late Sheykh al-Azhar, Mahmud Schaltut, *al-Islam, Aqida wa Shari'a*/Islam is a religious doctrine and law, 10th edition (Cairo: al-Shuruq, 1980), as well as the work of one of his successors in this office, the late Jadul-Haq Ali Jadul-Haq, who edited the authoritative al-Azhar textbook, *Bayan li al-nas*/Declaration to Humanity, 2 volumes (Cairo: al-Azhar, 1984 and 1988), in which in the equation of "*tashr'i*/legislation" with "*wahi*/revelation" is continued in an authoritative manner.
34 See Armanazi, *al-Shar' al-duwali*, referenced in note 14.
35 Muhammed Said al-Ashmawi, *Usul al-shari'a* (note 17).
36 Subhi al-Salih, *Ma'alim al-shari'a al-Islamiyya*/Essential Characteristics of Islamic Law (Beirut: Dar al-Ilm Lilmalayin, 1975), pp. 122ff. al-Salih was vice-mufti of Lebanon until he was slain in Beirut for his enlightened views.
37 On these "*Madhahib*/legal schools" see chapter 9 in the book by Schacht, referenced in note 18, pp. 57–68.
38 On the *post eventum* character of legal thinking in Islam see Sir Hamilton Gibb, *Studies in the Civilization of Islam* (Princeton, NJ: Princeton University Press, 1962), Part 2.
39 For an early beginning in this direction, which led to an Islamist shari'a in the understanding of constitutional law see Mohammed D. al-Rayyes, *al-Nazariyyat al-siyasiyya al-Islamiyya*/Islamic political theories (Cairo, 1953). For conceptualizing this approach as an invention see the framework provided by Terence Ranger and Eric Hobsbawm, eds, *The Invention of Tradition*, new printing (Cambridge: Cambridge University Press, 1966), in particular the introduction, pp. 1–14 by Hobsbawm.
40 For references to this interpretation applied to Islamism see note 32. The source is: Hannah Arendt, *The Origins of Totalitarianism* (New York, many reprints, here Harcourt Broce & Co., 1975): see also Arendt's book *Vita activa* (Munich: Piper, 1960).
41 On this new transnational Islam see B. Tibi, *Political Islam, World Politics and Europe. Democratic Peace and Euro-Islam vs. Global Jihad* (London: Routledge, 2008), Part 2 and earlier Peter Mandaville, *Transnational Muslim Politics. Reimagining the Umma* (New York: Routledge, 2004).
42 See the report in *Neue Zuercher Zeitung*, March 29, 2005, front page.
43 Therefore, I strongly disagree with Carrie Rosefsky Wickham, *Mobilizing Islam. Religion, Activism, and Political Change in Egypt* (New York: Columbia University Press, 2002).
44 The same disagreement expressed in the preceding note applies to Raymond Baker, *Islam Without Fear. Egypt and the New Islamists* (Cambridge, MA: Harvard University Press, 2003).
45 On the debate on Islam and democracy see chapters 2 and 7 in: B. Tibi, *Political Islam, World Politics and Europe* (referenced in note 41), and my earlier contributions to this theme: B. Tibi, "Islam, Freedom and Democracy," in: Michael Emerson, ed., *Democratization in the European Neighborhood* (Brussels: CEPS, 2005), pp. 93–116, further, my chapter in: Alan Olson *et al.*, eds, *Educating for Democracy* (Lanham, MD: Rowman & Littlefield, 2004), pp. 203–20.
46 See David Rohde, in his "news analysis" published under the title: "In Scope of Islamic Law," *International Herald Tribune*, March 14, 2005, front page, continued on p. 6.
47 See the reference in note 10. This "new cold war" is not what is presented by Samuel P. Huntington as *Clash of Civilizations* (New York: Simon and Schuster, 1996). For a contrast see Roman Herzog *et al.*, *Preventing the Clash of Civilizations* (New York: St. Martin's Press, 1999) – my contribution on cross-cultural bridging is chapter 10, pp. 107–26.
48 On Saudi Arabia see the major book by Stephen Schwartz, *The Two Faces of Islam. The House of Sa'ud from Tradition to Terror* (New York, 2002) and earlier Mamoun Fandy, *Saudi Arabia and the Politics of Dissent* (New York: Palgrave, 1999).
49 H.L.A. Hart, *The Concept of Law*, referenced in note 1, p. 221.
50 See the contributions of Muslim reformers included in the volume edited by Tore Lindholm and Kari Vogt on *Islamic Law Reform* (referenced in note 1).

51 B. Tibi, "The Pertinence of the Predicament of Islam with Pluralism to Democratization," in: *Religion-Staat-Gesellschaft*, 7(1) (2006), pp. 83–117.

52 On the political revival of Islam in Turkey see Marvine Howe, *Turkey Today. A Nation Divided over Islam's Revival* (Boulder, CO: Westview, 2002) and more recently my book: *Mit dem Kopftuch nach Europa? Die Türkei auf dem Weg in die EU* (Darmstadt: Primus, updated edition, 2007).

53 See B. Tibi, "International Morality and Cross-Cultural Bridging" (referenced in note 47).

54 Theodor Viehweg, *Topik und Jurisprudenz. Ein Beitrag zur rechtswissenschaftlichen Grundlagenforschung*, 5th printing (Munich: C.H. Beck, 1974), p. 118. In this chapter I apply Viehweg's approach to shari'a. See the authentic presentation by Subhi Salih, *Ma'alim al-shari'a* (referenced in note 36), pp. 122ff and, in contrast, the highly politicized version of the Islamist Yusuf al-Qaradawi, *al-Halal wa al-haram fi al-Islam*/The Permitted and the Forbidden in Islam, 20th printing (Cairo: Wahba, 1991).

55 On the de-Westernization of law presented by the example of the shari'a and its *hudud* penal code see B. Tibi, "Die Entwestlichung des Rechts. Das Hudud-Strafrecht der islamischen Schari'a," in Klaus Lüderssen, ed., *Aufgeklärte Kriminalpolitik oder Kampf gegen das Böse*, 5 vols, here vol. 5 (Baden-Baden: Nomos, 1998), pp. 21–30.

56 B. Tibi, *The Challenge of Fundamentalism* (referenced in note 5).

57 For more details on this Najib Armanazi, *al-Shar' al-duwali fi al-Islam* (referenced in note 14 above) and W. M. Watt, *Islamic Political Thought: The Basic Concepts* (Edinburgh: Edinburgh University Press, 1969), p. 91 as well as B. Tibi, "War and Peace in Islam," in Terry Nardin, ed., *The Ethics of War and Peace: Religious and Secular Perspectives* (Princeton, NJ: Princeton University Press, 1996), pp. 128–45.

58 See the textbook by Werner Levi, *Contemporary International Law*, 2nd edition (Boulder, CO: Westview Press, 1991) and my work referenced in notes 1, 5 and 8.

59 Maxime Rodinson, *Mohammed* (Lucerne and Frankfurt: Bucher, 1975), p. 27. On the subject of the emergence of Islam see also the basic books by W. M. Watt on early Islam: *Muhammed at Mecca* (Oxford: Oxford University Press, 1953), and *Muhammad at Medina*, 6th printing (Oxford: Oxford University Press, 1977). In my earlier book, *The Crisis of Modern Islam. A Preindustrial Culture in the Scientific-Technological Age* (Salt Lake City, UT: Utah University Press, 1988) I deal with the formative years of early Islam on pp. 57–66 and in an effort at conceptualization I use Norbert Elias's theory of civilization to interpret the unfolding of Islam into a civilization.

60 On Islamic revelation see Rudi Paret, *Mohammed und der Qur'an*, 4th printing (Stuttgart: Kohlhammer, 1976); as well as R. Bell and W. M. Watt, *Introduction to the Qur'an*, 2nd printing (Edinburgh: Edinburgh University Press, 1977). For an English translation see N. J. Dawood's, *The Koran* (Harmondsworth: Penguin, 1974). For an interesting interpretation see W. M. Watt, *Islamic Revelation in the Modern World* (Edinburgh: Edinburgh University Press, 1969).

61 See Coulson, *A History of Islamic Law*, referenced in note 18 and also the articles by Ann Elizabeth Mayer, Abdulaziz Sachedina and Norman Caldor included in *Oxford Encyclopedia of the Middle Eastern World*, 4 vols, New York, 1995, vol. 2, pp. 450–72.

62 B. Tibi, "The Simultaneity of the Unsimultaneous. Old Tribes and Nation-States," in: *Tribes and the State Formation in the Middle East*, edited by J. Kostiner and Ph. Khoury (Berkeley, CA: University of California Press, 1990), pp. 127–52.

63 See the chapter on law in: B. Tibi, *Islam and the Cultural Accommodation of Social Change* (Boulder, CO: Westview Press, 1990), pp. 76–101 and Ann E. Mayer, "Law and Religion in the Muslim Middle East," *The American Journal of Comparative Law*, 35, 1 (Winter 1987), pp. 127–84.

64 On this important distinction see the introduction in Donald E. Smith, ed., *Religion and Political Modernization* (New Haven, CT and London: Yale University Press, 1974).

65 Tu'aima, referenced in note 14, here pp. 208ff.

66 Mohammed Arkoun, *Rethinking Islam* (Boulder, CO: Westview, 1994).

67 See Chapter 4 of this book and also Jack Donnelly, *Universal Human Rights* (Ithaca, NY and London: Cornell University Press, 1989).

68 Mohammed Abed al-Jabri, *Arab Islamic Philosophy* (Austin, TX: University of Texas Press, 1999).

69 For more details see the chapter on Hellenization in: W. M. Watt, *Islamic Philosophy and Theology*, 5th printing (Edinburgh: Edinburgh University Press, 1979), pp. 37ff. and 91ff, and Chapter 7 of this book.

70 Niklas Luhmann, *Funktion der Religion* (Frankfurt/Main: Suhrkamp, 1977).

71 See the reference in Chapter 6 to the Azhar study on "*ilmaniyya*/secularization" and to other studies in this area of a "war of ideas."

72 John Waterbury, *Commander of the Faithful. The Moroccan Political Elite* (New York: Columbia University Press, 1970), p. 5.

73 Josef Esser, *Vorverständnis und Methodenwahl in der Rechtsfindung* (Frankfurt/Main, 1970), p. 32.

74 Hart, *The Concept of Law* (referenced in note 1), p. 102.

75 See B. Tibi, "The Return of the Sacred to Politics as a Constitutional Law: The Case of the Shari'atization of Politics in Islamic Civilization," in: *Theoria. Journal of Social and Political Theory*, 55(3) (April, 2008), pp. 91–119.

76 Esser, *Vorverständnis* (referenced in note 73), p. 153.

77 On this issue see Schacht, *An Introduction* (referenced in note 18), pp. 57ff.

78 See Richard C. Martin *et al.*, *Defenders of Reason in Islam* (Oxford: Oneworld, 1997).

79 See Charles C. Adams, *Islam and Modernism in Egypt: A Study of the Modern Reform Movement*, 2nd printing (London, 1968, first published in 1933); see also Norman Anderson, *Law Reform in the Muslim World* (London, 1976).

80 Viehweg, *Topik* (referenced in note 54), p. 31.

81 Ibid.

82 Ibid., p. 34.

83 Ibid., p. 38.

84 Ibid., p. 42.

85 See B. Tibi, "Islam and Social Change in the Modern Middle East," *Law and State*, 22 (1980), pp. 91–106.

86 Ali Abdelraziq, *al-Islam wa usul al-hukm*/Islam and Patterns of Government (Cairo, 1925, reprinted by Maktabat al-Hayat, Beirut, 1966). For a French translation see: *Revue des Etudes Islamiques*, 7 (1933) and 8 (1934). On the controversy over the work of Abdelraziq see more detail in B. Tibi, *Arab Nationalism. Between Islam and the Nation-State*, 3rd expanded edition (New York: St. Martin's Press, 1997), pp. 170–77.

87 Hamid Abu-Zaid, *al-Tafkir fi asr al-Takfir*/Reasoning in the Age of Excommunication as Unbeliever (Cairo: Madbuli, 1995).

88 Faraj Fuda was slain in Cairo by an Islamist in June 1992. See the references in Chapter 6 note 5.

89 Muhammad Muslehuddin, *Philosophy of Islamic Law and the Orientalists: A Comparative Study of Islamic Legal System* (Lahore, Pakistan, no date), p. 247.

90 Malcolm Kerr, *Islamic Reform: The Political and Legal Theories of Muhammad Abduh and Rashid Rida* (Berkeley and Los Angeles, CA: University of California Press, 1966). Kerr was murdered by Islamist Shi'ite fanatics in Beirut in January 1984, when he was acting as President of the American University of Beirut.

91 Muslehuddin, *Philosophy* (referenced in note 89) p. 247.

92 Ibid., p. 242.

93 On this Orientalism debate and all of its variations see the fully referenced and comprehensive chapter 4 in: B. Tibi, *Einladung in die islamische Geschichte* (Darmstadt: Primus, 2001), pp. 136–90.

94 Muslehuddin, *Philosophy* (referenced in note 89), p. 242.

95 Esser, *Vorverständnis* (referenced in note 73), p. 135.
96 At Boston University and also at the EU think-tank in Brussels/CEPS I completed two papers on Islam, democracy, and democratization, referenced in note 45. See also B. Tibi, "Islam, Islamism and Democracy," in: Leonard Weinberg, ed., *Democratic Responses to Terrorism* (New York: Routledge, 2008), pp. 41–61.
97 N. J. Coulson, *Conflicts and Tensions in Islamic Jurisprudence* (Chicago, 1969), p. 2; see also Coulson, "The Concept of Progress and Islamic Law," in Robert N. Bellah, ed., *Religion and Progress in Modern Asia* (New York, 1965), pp. 74–92; as well as N. J. Coulson and Norman Anderson, "Modernization: Islamic Law," in Michael Brett (ed.), *Northern Africa: Islam and Modernization* (London, 1973), pp. 73–83.
98 Muhammed Muslehuddin, *Philosophy of Islamic Law* (referenced in note 89), p. 92.
99 I have repeatedly referred to the greatly flawed and most distorting reader *Liberal Islam*, edited by Ch. Kurzman (see Chapter 7, note 9). One should beware of confusing Islamists and really liberal Muslims. In contrast to Kurzman, John Kelsay in his new book, *Arguing the Just War in Islam* (Cambridge, MA: Cambridge University Press, 2007) refers to the democratic liberal alternative to jihadism in contemporary Islam.

Chapter 4

1 This chapter not only reflects my academic thinking about individual human rights, but is also related to my political involvement as an Arab Muslim human rights activist. The story of this involvement began with political activity based on my participation in the founding of the "Arab Organization for the Defense on Human Rights." This occurred on the sidelines of a significant Arab congress on democracy in Limassol, Cyprus in November 1982. The proceedings were published by the Centre for Arab Unity Studies/CAUS, ed., *Azmat al-Democraqiyya fi al-Watan al-'Arabi*/Crisis of Democracy in the Arab World (Beirut: CAUS-Press, 1983). This volume includes the contribution that I presented in Limassol in Arabic, pp. 73–87. The Limassol reasoning on democracy and human rights was continued academically at the Wilson Center, Washington, DC in a different venture and setting. There I worked with Abdullahi A. An-Na'im while he was still a Muslim reformer and contributed to the book he edited with Francis Deng, published under the title: *Human Rights. Cross-Cultural Perspectives* (Washington, DC: The Brookings Institution, 1990). The volume includes my chapter 5: "The European Tradition of Human Rights and the Culture of Islam," pp. 104–32. See also B. Tibi, "Islamic Law, Shari'a and Human Rights. Universal Morality and International Relations," in *Human Rights Quarterly*, 16(2) (1994), pp. 277–99, reprinted in Shahram Akbarzadeh, ed., *Islam and Globalization* (London and New York: Routledge, 2006). Four volumes, here vol. 4, chapter 45, pp. 88ff.
2 This defensive cultural mindset is documented in the writings of the two major revivalist apologetic Muslim authors: first by the well-known late Sheykh Muhammad al-Ghazali, *Huquq al-insan bain ta'-alim al-Islam wa i'lan al-umam al-muttahidah*/Human Rights between the Teaching of Islam and the UN-Declaration, 3rd printing (Cairo: 1984), see in particular p. 7; and second in the volume by his disciple the Islamist Mohammad Imara, *al-Islam wa huquq al-insan. Darurat, la-Huquq*/Islam and Human Rights, Obligations, not Rights (Cairo: Dar al-Shuruq, 1989).
3 Jürgen Habermas, *The Philosophical Discourse of Modernity* (Cambridge, MA: M.I.T. Press, 1987), p. 17. If I understand Anthony Giddens correctly, by his notion of "self-identity" he means much the same as Habermas in the notion of "principle of subjectivity." See Anthony Giddens, *Modernity and Self-Identity* (Stanford, CA: Stanford University Press, 1991). It is intriguing that Giddens does not quote Habermas's cited *Discourse*.
4 On this core region of Islamic civilization see B. Tibi: "The Middle East: Society, State, Religion," in: F. Cerruti and R. Ragionieri, eds, *Identities and Conflicts. The*

Mediterranean (London: Palgrave, 2001), pp. 121–34; and on the place of Arabs in the history of Islamic civilization see Marshall Hodgson, *The Venture of Islam. Conscience and History in a World Civilization*, 3 vols (Chicago, IL: The University of Chicago Press, 1974, paperback edition, 1977).

5 UNDP, *Arab Human Development Report* (New York: United Nations, 2002).

6 The best critique of this third-worldist romantics is Alain Finkielkraut, *La défaite de la pensée* (Paris: Gallimard, 1987). On the idea of "third world" see Peter Worsley, *The Third World* (Chicago, IL: Chicago University Press, 2nd edition, 1967). Islamic nativism is a variety of "third-worldism" (*tiers-mondisme*). See the Muslim critique: Daryush Shayegan, *Cultural Schizophrenia. Islamic Societies Confronting the West* (Syracuse, NY: Syracuse University Press, 1992), and Mehrzad Boroujerdi, *Iranian Intellectuals and the West. The Tormented Triumph of Nativism* (Syracuse, NY: Syracuse University Press, 1996).

7 On the term "cultural underpinning" applied to human rights see the Wilson Center book referenced in note 1 above.

8 R. J. Vincent, *Human Rights and International Relations* (Cambridge: Cambridge University Press, 1986).

9 Ann Elizabeth Mayer, "The Shari'ah: A Methodology or a Body of Substantive Rules?" in: *Islamic Law and Jurisprudence*, edited by Nicholas Heer (Seattle, WA: University of Washington Press, 1990), pp. 177–98.

10 On the notion of legal rule see Max Weber, "Drei Formen der Herrschaft," in his collected writings: *Soziologie, Weltgeschichtliche Analyse, Politik* (Stuttgart: Alfred Koerner Verlag, 1964), pp. 151–66.

11 See the book by the Islamist Muhammad Salim al-'Awwa, *Fi al-nizam al-siyasi lil-dawla al-Islamiyya*/On the Political System of the Islamic State (Cairo: al-Maktab al-Masri, 1983, 6th edition), pp. 33ff. Those students of Islam who read Arabic know that Islamists – like al-'Awwa – speak of "the Islamic system," and not – as often incorrectly alleged by some "pundits" – of a "restoration of the caliphate."

12 On shari'a see the work of Abdullahi an-Na'im, referenced in notes 1 and 7 and his earlier major book: *Toward an Islamic Reformation. Civil Liberties, Human Rights and International Law* (Syracuse, NY: Syracuse University Press, 1990). Also the book by the liberal Muslim Mohammed S. Ashmawi, *Usul al-shari'a*/The Origins of Shari'a (Cairo: Madbuli, 1983) is worth mentioning.

13 See Sayyid Qutb, *Mushkilat al-hadarah*/The Predicament of Civilization (Cairo: al-Shuruq, 9th legal printing, 1988).

14 An-Na'im, *Towards an Islamic* (referenced in note 12), p. 185.

15 Tom J. Farer, "The UN and Human Rights: More than a Whimper, Less than a Roar," in: Adam Roberts and Benedict Kingsbury, eds, *United Nations, Divided World: The UN's Role in International Relations* (Oxford: The Clarendon Press, 1988), pp. 95–138.

16 See the useful introduction by Jack Donelly, *Universal Human Rights in Theory and Practice* (Ithaca, NY: Cornell University Press, 1989) and on the relevance of this tradition to Islamic societies presented in the case of the Maghreb see: Susan E. Waltz, *Human Rights and Reform. The Changing Face of North African Politics* (Berkeley, CA: University of California Press, 1995).

17 The reader is reminded of the following distinction outlined in the introduction and in Chapter 1: modernity is viewed as being composed of two components. At first it is a cultural concept and then it gained a structural-institutional dimension. Though interrelated, these two elements are not identical, nor reducible to each other.

18 On the difference between international system and international society see Hedley Bull, *The Anarchical Society: A Study of Order in World Politics* (New York: Columbia University Press, 1977), p. 23ff.

19 Terry Nardin, *Law, Morality and the Relationship of States* (Princeton, NJ: Princeton University Pres, 1983), pp. 27–48.

20 See H. L. A. Hart, *The Concept of Law*, 2nd edn (Oxford: The Clarendon Pres, 1961) and the chapter "The Revolt against the West" by Bull in: Hedley Bull and Adam Watson, eds, *The Expansion of International Society* (Oxford: The Clarendon Press, 1984), pp. 117–213. The revolt is also against the European model of the nation-state; see Charles Tilly, ed., *The Formation of the Nation State* (Princeton, NJ: Princeton University Press, 1985), p. 45.

21 Mark Juergensmeyer, *The New Cold War? Religious Nationalism Confronts the Secular State* (Berkeley, CA: University of California Press, 1993).

22 H. L. A. Hart, *The Concept of Law* (referenced in note 20), p. 22.

23 On this simultaneity of globalization and fragmentation see B. Tibi, *Islam between Culture and Politics* (New York: Palgrave, 2001, expanded second edition, 2005), chapter 4.

24 Hedley Bull, *The Anarchical Society* (referenced in note 18), p. 13.

25 See W. M. Watt, *Islamic Fundamentalism and Modernity* (London: Routledge, 1988) and B. Tibi, *The Challenge of Fundamentalism. Political Islam and the New World Disorder* (Berkeley, CA: University of California Press, 1998, updated 2002).

26 Michael Akehurst, *A Modern Introduction to International Law*, 6th edn (London: Unwin & Hyman, 1987), p. 21.

27 Richard Falk, "Refocusing the Struggle for Human Rights in the Third World," in: *Harvard Human Rights Journal*, 4 (1991), p. 63, see also Edward S. Herman, "The United States Versus Human Rights in the Third World," *Harvard Human Rights Journal*, 4 (1991), p. 85.

28 Michael Richardson, "Asians, Turning Tables, Denounce EC on Bosnia," *International Herald Tribune*, 28 July 1993, p. 2.

29 The application of cultural relativism to human rights results in denying these rights to non-Westerners in a benign manner.

30 See the illuminating chapter, "Human rights in International Society," in the book by the late R. J. Vincent, *Human Rights and International Relations* (referenced in note 8), pp. 92–108 (particularly pp. 99–105).

31 An-Na'im, *Towards an Islamic* (referenced in note 12), p. 185.

32 Ibid.

33 On identity politics see also my contribution to the volume of Helmut Anheier and Raj Isar (referenced in Chapter 5, note 1)

34 Mohamed Mahmoud Taha, *The Second Message of Islam*, transl. and introduced by Abdullahi A. An-Na'im (Syracuse, NY: Syracuse University Press, 1987).

35 See the full references to Mohammed Imara and to Mohammed al-Ghazali in note 2.

36 See chapters 9 and 10 on the contended "Islamic Human Rights" in my comprehensive monograph on Islamic human rights and Islam published in German: *Im Schatten Allahs. Der Islam und die Menschenrechte* (Munich: Ullstein, expanded edition of 624 pages, 2003).

37 At its birth the critique of Orientalism by Edward Said aimed to subject the "Orientalization of the Orient" to critical thinking and was therefore not only legitimate, but also urgently needed. However, with the passage of time the critique has been derailed. Even though Edward Said can be acquitted of the sins of his followers, the Saidists, today it is legitimate to ask the question: did Said engage in a reversal of Orientalism? Sadik J. al-Azm contends that Said did end up "reversing Orientalism." See the chapter on Said in al-Azm's book: *Dhihniyyat al-Tahrim*/The Mentality of Taboos (London: Riad El-Rayyes Books, 1992), pp. 17–86. Also al-Azm's critique has a point, but – in keeping with his specialty – it goes overboard. I tried to mediate between the two, but Said refused, stating: "*Sadiq sakhif*/Sadiq is a fool" (personal communication in New York). On this debate see the chapter in B. Tibi, *Einladung in die islamische Geschichte* (Darmstadt: Primus, 2001); see Bryan Turner, *Orientalism, Postmodernism and Globalism* (London: Routledge, 1994).

38 Ann Elizabeth Mayer, *Islam and Human Rights: Tradition and Politics* (Boulder, CO: Westview Press, 1991), p. 198; see the review article of Mayer's book by Bassam Tibi, "Universality of Human Rights and Authenticity of non-Western Cultures: Islam and the Western Concept of Human Rights," in: *Harvard Human Rights Journal*, 5 (Spring 1992), pp. 221–26. The critique is put forward that Mayer's analysis – though a smart contribution – fails to understand properly the cultural dimension of this legal issue. After all, law is a cultural concept.

39 B. Tibi, *The Crisis of Modern Islam*, translated from German by Judith von Sivers (Salt Lake City, UT: University of Utah Press, 1988), pp. 1–8.

40 Terry Nardin, *Law, Morality* (referenced in note 19), p. 274.

41 See B. Tibi, *Islam and the Cultural Accommodation of Social Change*, translated from German by Clare Krojzl (Boulder, CO: Westview Press, 1990). Also in that book, the terms culture and civilization are not used interchangeably. Culture is always referred to as a local production of social meaning, while a civilization is viewed as a cross-cultural grouping of interrelated local cultures that are characterized by their resemblance and shared worldview in a civilizing process. It follows that there exists a variety of Islamic cultures, grouped, however, in one Islamic civilization. On this issue see B. Tibi, "The Interplay Between Social and Cultural Change: The Case of Germany and the Middle East," in: George N. Atiyeh and Ibrahim M. Oweiss, eds, *Arab Civilizations: Challenges and Responses* (Albany, NY: State University of New York Press, 1988), pp. 166–88; and B. Tibi, *Krieg der Zivilisationen* (Hamburg: Hoffmann & Campe, 1995).

42 See Molefi Kete Asante and William B. Gudykunst, eds, *Handbook of International and Intercultural Communication* (London: Sage Publications, 1989).

43 A. E. Mayer, *Islam and Human Rights* (referenced in note 38), p. 44.

44 B. Tibi, *Political Islam, World Politics and Europe* (New York: Routledge, 2008).

45 Mayer, *Islam and Human Rights* (referenced in note 38), p. 68.

46 Ibid., p. 71.

47 See chapter 2 on human rights in my book: *Krieg der Zivilisationen* (referenced in note 41), pp. 127–61.

48 On this Islamic doctrine see Bat Ye'or, *Islam and Dhimmitude* (Cransbury, NJ: Associated University Presses, 2002). This Islamic *dhimmi* doctrine recognizes Christians and Jews as believers, but it assigns them the second-class status of protected minorities (i.e. second-class believers). The implied pact of protection and tolerance granted to Jews and Christians is today, by international standards, more of a discrimination and a human rights violation than a tolerance. As Bernard Lewis explains, "By terms of the *dhimma*, these communities were accorded a certain status, provided that they unequivocally recognized the primacy of Islam and the supremacy of the Muslims. This recognition was expressed in the payment of the toll tax and obedience to a series of restrictions defined in detail by the law." Bernard Lewis, *The Jews of Islam* (Princeton, NJ: Princeton University Press, 1974), p. 21.

49 A. E. Mayer, *Islam and Human Rights* (referenced in note 38), p. 186, see also my Tokyo paper on shari'a and on the shari'atization of Islam as a violation of the freedom of belief. The paper is referenced in Chapter 3, note 1.

50 This is a reference to the seminal work *The Civilizing Process* by Norbert Elias, as translated by Edmund Jephcott and published in two volumes. The first volume is subtitled *The History of Manners* (New York: Pantheon Books, 1978) and the second, *Power and Civility* (New York: Pantheon Books, 1982). In my book *The Crisis of Modern Islam*, pp. 23–31, I employ this notion of Elias in the study of Islam.

51 On this Islamic *futuhat* expansion carried out by jihad wars to establish a global Islamicate see: B. Tibi, *Kreuzzug und Djihad* (Munich: Bertelsmann, 1999), Chapters 2 and 4.

52 Mohammed Abed al-Jabri, *Arab Islamic Philosophy* (Austin, TX: CMES, 1999).

53 See my chapter in: Abdulhahi A. An-Na'im and Francis Deng (note 1), pp. 104–32.

54 A. E. Mayer, *Islam and Human Rights* (referenced in note 38), p. 211.

55 Ibid., p. 9.
56 See my chapter on Islamist antisemitism in: Wolfgang Benz and Juliane Wetzel, eds, *Antisemitismus und radikaler Islamismus* (Essen: Klartext, 2007), pp. 43–70. See also the book by Matthias Küntzel, *Jihad and Jew Hatred. Islamism, Nazism and the Roots of 9/11* (New York: Telos Press, 2007).
57 Mustapha K. Al-Sayyid, "Slow Thaw in the Arab World," *World Policy Journal*, 8, 4 (1991), p. 724.
58 On the Islamic worldview see: B. Tibi, *Islam between Culture and Politics* (referenced in note 23), Chapter 2.
59 A. E. Mayer, *Islam and Human Rights* (referenced in note 38), p. 58.
60 An-Na'im, *Towards an Islamic* (referenced in note 12), p. 184.
61 David P. Forsythe, *Human Rights and World Politics*, 2nd edn, revised (Lincoln, NE: University of Nebraska, 1989), pp. 189–228.
62 John Kelsay, *Islam and War: A Study of Comparative Ethics* (Louisville, KY: John Knox Press, 1993), pp. 3–5.
63 On Islam and human rights see also Katerina Dalacoura, *Islam, Liberalism and Human Rights* (London: Tauris, 1998) and Kevin Dwyer, *Arab Voices. The Human Rights Debate in the Middle East* (Berkeley, CA: University of California Press, 1991).

Chapter 5

1 This chapter draws on insights related to the "The World Cultures Research Project" of which I was a member. I am indebted to the chairpersons of the project, which was jointly conducted and funded by UCLA and the American University of Paris. The findings were published by the project's chairpersons, Y. Raj Isar and Helmut Anheier, eds, *Conflicts and Tensions*, Vol. 1 of *The Culture and Globalization Series* (London: Sage, 2007). The volume includes my contribution as chapter 16: "Islam Between Religious-Cultural Practice and Identity Politics," pp. 221–31.
2 On this fashionable concept see Marwan Kraidy, *Hybridity, or the Cultural Logic of Globalization* (Philadelphia, PA: Temple University Press, 2005).
3 Roland Robertson, *Globalization, Social Theory and Global Culture* (London: Sage, 1992), chapter 2, here p. 45.
4 B. Tibi, "The Interplay Between Social and Cultural Change," in: George Atiyeh and Ibrahim Oweis, eds, *Arab Civilization* (Albany, NY: SUNY, 1988), pp. 166–82.
5 On the civilization of Islam see the comprehensive and authoritative history by Marshall Hodgson, *The Venture of Islam. Conscience and History in a World Civilization*, 3 vols (Chicago, IL: Chicago University Press, 1977), as well as Sir Hamilton A. R. Gibb, *Studies in the Civilization of Islam* (Princeton, NJ: Princeton University Press, 1982).To be sure, Muslims themselves view their *umma*-entity as "*hadara*/civilization," as articulated, for instance, by Abdullah N. Alwan, *Ma'alim al-hadara fi al-Islam*/The Characteristics of the Civilization of Islam (Zarqa, Jordan: Maktabat al-Manar, 1984).
6 I strongly disagree with the views of Dale Eickelman and James Piscatori, *Islamic Politics* (Princeton, NJ: Princeton University Press, 1996), as well as with their understanding of what "Islamic politics" is. For a different understanding of Islamic politics see: B. Tibi, *Political Islam, World Politics and Europe. Democratic Peace and Euro-Islam vs. Global Jihad* (London and New York: Routledge, 2008). In my view Eickelman and Piscatori fail to grasp the phenomenon of religionization of politics in a situation of post-bipolar conflict and this is exactly what "Islamic politics" is all about.
7 On the notion of preindustrial and premodern culture see Patricia Crone, *Preindustrial Societies. Anatomy of the Premodern World* (Oxford: Oneworld, 2003) and B. Tibi, *The Crisis of Modern Islam. Preindustrial Culture in the Technological Scientific Age*

(Salt Lake City, UT: Utah University Press, 1988). It should be noted that use of the notion "premodern" does not imply any evolutionist bias.

8 On this issue see B. Tibi, *Islam between Culture and Politics* (New York: Palgrave 2001, 2nd enlarged edn, 2005), in particular chapter 2.

9 See Paul A. Silverstein, *Algeria in France* (Bloomington, IN: Indiana University Press, 2004), and most importantly the new edition of the book by Alec Hargreave, *Multi-Ethnic France. Immigration, Politics, Culture and Society* (New York: Routledge, 2007). This is the second edition of the 1995-book, *Immigration, Race and Ethnicity*, under a new title.

10 The British LSE-Journal *Millennium* used this formula as a heading for its special issue in 2000, published before 9/11. The issue includes my essay "Postbipolar Order in Crisis. The Challenge of Politicized Islam," *Millennium* (2000), 29, pp. 843–59; see also Eric O. Hanson, *Religion and Politics in the International System* (Cambridge: Cambridge University Press, 2006).

11 See the classic by Benedict Anderson, *Imagined Communities* (London: Verso, revised edn, 1991).

12 Fred Donner, *The Early Islamic Conquests* (Princeton, NJ: Princeton University Press, 1983) and more recently Efraim Karsh, *Islamic Imperialism. A History* (New Haven, CT: Yale University Press, 2006); see the references in notes 13 and 14.

13 This is surveyed by B. Tibi, *Kreuzzug und Djihad. Der Islam und die christliche Welt* (München: Bertelsmann, 1999), chapters 1 and 4; see also note 14.

14 In addition to the references in notes 12 and 13 see Alan Jamieson, *Faith and Sword. A Short History of Christian-Muslim Conflict* (London: Reaktion Books, 2006).

15 For an exemplary case that illustrates this mindset see the early work of Akbar Ahmed, *Postmodernism and Islam* (London: Routledge, 1992); see also Akbar Ahmed and Hastings Donnan, eds, *Islam, Globalization and Postmodernity* (London: Routledge, 1994). In a recent book, *Journey into Islam* (Washington DC: Brookings, 2007), Ahmed seems to discern these fault-lines after a journey into nine Islamic countries.

16 John Kelsay, *Islam and War* (Louisville, KY: John Knox Press, 1993), p. 25. See also Kelsay's most recent book *Arguing the Just War in Islam* (Cambridge, MA: Harvard University Press, 2007).

17 On the notion of "defensive culture": B. Tibi, *Crisis* (referenced in note 7), pp. 1–8.

18 Leslie Lipson, *The Ethical Crisis of Civilization* (London: Sage, 1993), pp. 63–66; see also Peter Brown, *The Rise of Western Christendom* (Oxford: Blackwell, 1996).

19 The European expansion is reconstructed by Philip Curtin, *The World and the West. The European Challenge* (Cambridge: Cambridge University Press, 2000). It was facilitated by modern military power – see the reference to Geoffrey Parker, *The Military Revolution* (Chapter 1, note 3).

20 Even though it has become politically unpopular to quote the work of Bernard Lewis, his books continue to be an important scholarly reference and deserve scholarly attention. See, for instance, Bernard Lewis, *The Muslim Discovery of Europe* (New York: Norton & Co, 1982), and his *Islam and the West* (New York: Oxford University Press, 1993). Lewis's support for the neo-cons of the Bush administration in the Iraq war remains highly deplorable, but it does not invalidate his earlier work.

21 David Gress, *From Plato to Nato. The Idea of the West and its Opponents* (New York: Free Press, 1998).

22 See the references in note 6 to my earlier 2008-book, *Political Islam, World Politics and Europe.*

23 See Ibrahim Abu-Lughod, *The Arab Rediscovery of Europe* (Princeton, NJ: Princeton University Press, 1963) and the references to Bernard Lewis in note 20.

24 Martin Kramer, *Arab Awakening and Islamic Revival. The Politics of Ideas in the Muslim Middle East* (New Brunswick, NJ: Transaction Publishers, 1996).

25 Hedley Bull, "The Revolt Against the West," chapter 14, in: Hedley Bull and Adam Watson, eds, *The Expansion of International Society* (Oxford: Clarendon Press, 1984), pp. 217–28.

26 For more details see B. Tibi, *Arab Nationalism. Between Islam and the Nation-State* (3rd expanded edn, New York: Macmillan, 1997).

27 On a major source of anti-colonial jihad see Nikki Keddie, ed., *An Islamic Response to Imperialism* (Berkeley, CA: University of California Press 1968, new edn 1983). The volume includes a selection of the writings of the foremost nineteenth-century Islamic revivalist al-Afghani.

28 On Islamist internationalism see my 2008 book referenced in note 6, in particular Part 2. On political Islam see also the earlier contributions by Nazih Ayubi, *Political Islam. Religion and Politics in the Arab World* (New York: Routledge, 1991), and several years later B. Tibi, *The Challenge of Fundamentalism. Political Islam and the New World Disorder* (Berkeley, CA: The University of California Press, 1998, updated after 9/11 in a 2002 edition).

29 On the assumption that scholars are supposed to be familiar with these distinctions one is amazed not only by James Piscatori's confusion of the nation-state and the territorial state in his book: *Islam in a World of Nation-States* (Cambridge: Cambridge University Press, 1980), but also by his confusion of Islamist internationalism and pan-Islamism in his contribution to Shahram Akbarzadeh and Fethi Mansouri, eds, *Islam and Political Violence. Muslim Diaspora and Radicalism in the West* (London: Tauris, 2007), chapter 3, which is contradicted by my chapter 4 in the same volume.

30 See, for example, the references made in note 6, and also note 29 to learn how Islamic politics is poorly handled by some pundits, even distorted.

31 On Ibn Khaldun and his *"Muqaddimah/*Prolegomena of History" see the seminal work by Muhsin Mahdi, *Ibn Khaldun's Philosophy of History. A Study in the Philosophic Foundation of the Science of Culture* (London: George Allen and Unwin, 1957).

32 Norbert Elias, *The Civilizing Process* (2 vols, New York: Pantheon Books, 1978 and 1982) and Stephen Mennel, *Norbert Elias. An Introduction* (Oxford: Blackwell, 1992). On the use of Elias' approach for interpreting the unfolding of Islam to a civilization see B. Tibi, *The Crisis of Modern Islam* (referenced in note 7), pp. 30–31.

33 Charles Tilly, ed., *The Formation of the Nation State* (Princeton, NJ: Princeton University Press, 1985), here: the introduction.

34 For an analysis of this contradiction see B. Tibi, "The Simultaneity of the Unsimultaneous: Old Tribes and Imposed Nation-States," in: Philip Khoury and Joseph Kostiner, eds, *Tribes and States in the Middle East* (Berkeley, CA: The University of California Press, 1990), pp.127–52.

35 See the contributions in: T. K. Oomen, ed., *Citizenship and National Identity. From Colonialism to Globalism* (Sage: London and New Dehli, 1997), therein also chapter 7 by B. Tibi, "Religious Fundamentalism, Ethnicity and the Nation-State," pp. 199–226.

36 Liam Anderson and Gareth Stansfield, *The Future of Iraq*, (New York: Palgrave, 2004), and Daniel Byman and Kenneth Pollack, *Things Fall Apart. Containing the Spillover From an Iraqi Civil War* (Washington, DC: The Brookings Institution, 2007).

37 Foud Ajami, *The Dream Palace of the Arabs* (New York: Random House, 1999).

38 Abdellah Hammudah, *Master and Disciple. The Cultural Foundations of Moroccan Authoritarianism* (Chicago, IL: Chicago University Press, 1997).

39 Hisham Sharabi, *Neo-Oligarchy. A Theory of Distorted Change in Arab Society* (Oxford: Oxford University Press, 1988).

40 Fawaz Gerges, *America and Political Islam. Clash of Cultures or Clash of Interests* (Cambridge: Cambridge University Press, 1999).

41 This is the title of the respective chapter in Sadik Jalal al-Azm, *Dhihniyyat al-Tahrim/ The Mentality of Taboos* (London: Riad, 1992), pp. 17–145. On this issue see also chapter 4, note 37.

42 See the reference in note 17.

43 See the reference on world order and Islamist politics in note 6.

44 See the major contribution by Daniel Philpott, "The Challenge of September 11 to Secularism in International Relations," in: *World Politics* (2002), 55(1), pp. 66–95.
45 The most authoritative study on this subject is Richard Mitchell, *The Society of the Muslim Brothers* (London: Oxford University Press, 1969).
46 See the references to Qutb's writings in note 57. On the political thought of Qutb see Roxanne L. Euben, *Enemy in the Mirror. Islamic Fundamentalism and the Limits of Modern Rationalism* (Princeton, NJ: Princeton University Press, 1999), Chapter 3.
47 Benedict Anderson, *Imagined Communities* (referenced in note 11).
48 See Tibi, *Political Islam* (referenced in note 6).
49 On *Hizb al-Tahrir* see Zeyno Baran, "Fighting the War of Ideas," in: *Foreign Affairs* (November–December 2005), pp. 68–78, and her monograph: *Hizb ut-Tahrir/*Islam's Political Insurgency (Washington, DC: The Nixon Center, 2004).
50 See the debate on Islamic law in Chapter 3 above and the references made there.
51 On the formula *"Tatbiq al-Shari'a/*implementation of shari'a" in an Islamic state, see B. Tibi, *The Challenge of Fundamentalism*, referenced in note 28, chapter 8.
52 Steven Runciman, *A History of the Crusades*. Here the German translation: *Geschichte der Kreuzzüge* (Munich: C. H. Beck-Verlag, 1995), p. 274 is quoted.
53 See the chapter with the heading "Une vaste conspiration judéo-chrétienne" in: Mohammed Yacine Kassab, *L'Islam face au nouvel ordre mondial* (Algiers: Edition Salama, 1991), pp. 75–93.
54 See Ali M. Jarisha and Mohammed Sharif Zaibaq, *Asalib al-Ghazu al-Fikri/*Methods of Intellectual Invasion (Cairo: Dar al-'Itisam, 1978).
55 Daryush Shayegan, *Cultural Schizophrenia. Islamic Societies Confronting the West* (Syracuse, NY: Syracuse University Press, 1992).
56 See Roger Scruton, *The West and the Rest. Globalization and the Terrorist Threat* (Wilmington, DE: ISI Books, 2002), and the references to Bernard Lewis in note 20 above.
57 These Islamist views were expressed earlier by Sayyid Qutb, *al-Salam al-Alami wa al-Islam/*World Peace and Islam (10th legal reprint, Cairo: Dar al-Shuruq, 1992), and today by Yusuf Qaradawi – dubbed "the global mufti" and also considered to be the heir of Qutb (on his work see the detailed references in Chapter 1, note 61).
58 B. Tibi, "War and Peace in Islam," in: Terry Nardin, ed., *The Ethics of War and Peace* (Princeton, NJ: Princeton University Press, 1996), pp. 128–45. On the formula "the return of history of civilizations" see my book referenced in note 6 above, Introduction, in particular pp. 2–9, and also the Part 3 on Europe in that book.
59 Hedley Bull, "The Revolt Against the West" (referenced in note 25).
60 Sayyid Qutb, *al-Salam al-Alami wa al-Islam* (referenced in note 57), pp. 172–73.
61 See Chapter 3 in this book and also the authoritative books by N. J. Coulson, *A History of Islamic Law* (Edinburgh: Edinburgh University Press, 1964), and Joseph Schacht and C. E. Basworth, eds, *The Legacy of Islam* (Oxford: Clarendon Press, 1974).
62 Bat Ye'or, *Islam and Dhimmitude* (Cranbury, NJ: American University Press, 2002).
63 On this shari'atization see my Tokyo paper on constitutionalism and shari'a law referenced in Chapter 3, note 1.
64 Dan Petterson, *Inside Sudan* (Boulder, CO: Westview, updated edn 2003).
65 For more details and references on this issue see Chapter 6 in this book.
66 Roman Herzog and others, *Preventing the Clash of Civilizations* (New York: St. Martin's Press, 1999), therein the chapter by B. Tibi, pp. 107–26.
67 The book by Benjamin Barber, *Jihad vs. McWorld* (New York: Ballantine Books, 1995) includes a naïve understanding of jihad. For a contrast see the reference made in note 6.
68 On the revivalism of Arslan see Chapter 1 and the references made there.
69 See Mohammed Imara, *al-Sahwa al-Islamiyya wa al-Tahaddi al-hadari/*Islamic Awakening and the Civilizational Challenge (Cairo: Dar al-Shuruq, 1991), and the book by Martin Kramer, *Arab Awakening and Islamic Revival* (referenced in note 24).

70 Mohammed A. al-Jabri, *Arab Islamic Philosophy* (Austin, TX: University of Texas Press, 1999), p. 124.

71 Ellen K. Trimberger, *Revolution from Above* (New Brunswick, NJ: Transaction Books, 1978).

Chapter 6

1 This chapter reflects and continues a three-decades-long process of reasoning on this subject matter. It also draws on the findings of a number of research projects in which I was involved. The period addressed began in Cairo in November 1979, when I was allowed to speak at an Islamic congress at which I presented a paper on "Islam and Secularization, Religion and the Functional Differentiation of the Social System." The paper was published under the same title, first in *Archives for Philosophy of Law and Social Philosophy*, 66 (1980), pp. 207–22, and a year later in Arabic in *Qadaya Arabiyya* (Beirut). The Cairo presentation faced fierce resistance, resulting in a three-year delay in the publication of the congress proceedings. Eventually the courageous chairperson of the congress, Professor Mourad Wahba of Ain Shams University in Cairo, succeeded against the odds in bringing out the publication under the title *The First International Islamic Philosophy Conference on Islam and Civilization* (Cairo: 'Ain Shams University Press, 1982); my paper appears on pp. 61–84 under the title: "Islam and Secularization." This Cairo reasoning has been continued. In a second step, twenty years later, I published my study "Secularization and De-Secularization in Modern Islam," *Religion, Staat, Gesellschaft. Journal for the Study of Beliefs and Worldviews*, 1, 1 (2000), pp. 95–117. This is the elaboration of a paper presented to a research project at Van Leer Institute, Jerusalem on science and secularization. Some years later this study has been followed by B. Tibi, "The Return of the Sacred to Politics as a Constitutional Law," *Theoria* (2008), 115, pp. 90–119. The special theme of this issue of *Theoria* is secularization and de-secularization.

2 In this chapter I shall not resume the debate on the return of the sacred, since this task was accomplished earlier, in an analysis completed and added after 9/11 as chapter 11 to the new edition of my book, *Islam between Culture and Politics* (New York: Palgrave, 2001, 2nd edn 2005), pp. 234–72. See also the references in the next note.

3 See Jürgen Habermas, *Glauben und Wissen* (Frankfurt/Main: Suhrkamp, 2001), criticized by B. Tibi, "Habermas and the Return of the Sacred. Is it a Religious Renaissance? A Pronouncement of a 'Post-Secular Society', or the Emergence of Political Religion as a New Totalitarianism?," *Religion-Staat-Gesellschaft*, 3, 2 (2002), pp. 265–96.

4 See the references in Chapter 3 to the earlier, promising Abdullahi A. An-Na'im. The quotes are from his highly disappointing new book: *Islam and the Secular State. Negotiating the Future of Shari'a* (Cambridge, MA: Harvard University Press, 2008). The first quote p. 8, the second p. 292–93, the third p. 290. An-Na'im justifies his evasion of dealing with the connection between shari'a and Islamism by the pretext that he is a lawyer, not a political scientist. This evasion was made in a personal communication.

5 Robert Hefner, *Civil Islam. Muslims and Decmocratization in Indonesia* (Princeton, NJ: Princeton University Press, 2000), p. 119, see also pp. 79–82.

6 See Faraj Fuda, *Hiwar an al-ilmaniyya*/Dialogue on Secularism (Marrakesh: Dar Tainimel, 1992), and on the slaying of Fuda see Abdul-Ghaffar Aziz *et al.*, *Man Qatala Faraj Fuda*/Who Killed Faraj Fuda? (Cairo: Dar al-'Ilm, 1992). The fetwa of al-Ghazali that the killing of an "apostate" – as in this case – would be a legitimate action was printed in *al-Hayat*, June 23, 1993.

7 This is the framework unfolded by Niklas Luhmann, *Funktion der Religion* (Frankfurt/Main: Suhrkamp, 1977), and adopted here; see in particular p. 228; see also my Cairo paper on "Secularization in Islam," viewed as a process of functional differentiation (referenced in note 1).

8 Faruq Abdul-Salam, *al-Ahzab al-Siyasiyya wa al-Fasl bin al-Din wa al-Dawla*/Political Parties and the Separation between Religion and the State (Cairo: Qaliyub, 1979). In part one Abdul-Salam attributes secularization to the "Jewish conspiracy," pp. 8–26.

9 See Mark Juergensmeyer, *The New Cold War? Religious Nationalism Confronts the Secular State* (Berkeley: University of California Press, 1993). For a Western use of the new term of a war related to this contest see Walid Phares, *The War of Ideas. Jihadism against Democracy* (New York: Palgrave, 2007). The precursor of political Islam, Sayyid Qutb, contended in his pamphlet *Ma'araktuna ma'a al-Yahud*/Our Fight against the Jews (Cairo, legal 10th printing, 1989) that "the Jews do not fight with weapons, but rather with ideas" (p. 21). The Islamists Ali Jarisha and Mohammed Sh. Zaibaq, *Asalib al-Ghazu al-fikri li al-'alam al-Islami*/Methods of Intellectual Invasion of the Muslim World (Cairo: Dar al-I'tisan, 1978) developed this notion to a *"Harb al-Afkar*/war of ideas" between the secularism of the "Jewish-crusader West" and Islam.

10 For a few examples of this genre of polemical literature in this war of ideas over *"Ilmaniyya*/secularism" see Imalduldin Khalil, *Tahafut al-'ilmaniyya*/The refutation of Secularism (Beirut: al-Risala, 1979); Muhammad M. Shamsuldin, *al-'Ilamiyya*/Secularism, 2nd edn (Beirut: al-Markaz al-Islami, 1983); Zakariyya Faid, *al-'Ilmaniyya: al-Nash'a wa al-athar fi al-sharq wa al-gharb*/Secularism: Its Origin and its Impact in the Orient and the West (Cairo: al-Zahra', 1977).

11 This classic is al-Farabi, *al-Madina al-fadila*, Arabic text with an English translation, *al-Farabi on the Perfect State*, edited by Richard Walzer (Oxford: Clarendon Press, 1985). For some details on the impact of Islamic rationalism on the European Renaissance see B. Tibi, *Kreuzzug und Djihad. Der Islam und die christliche Welt* (Munich: Bertelsmann, 1999), Chapter 5. A revival of this tradition of the Renaissance deserves, in its European-Islamic context a consideration for bridging between the civilizations, see also note 15.

12 See the appreciation of the Islamic contribution to the emergence of modern science expressed in the following books: Edward Grant, *The Foundation of Modern Science in the Middle Ages. Their Religious, Institutional, and Intellectual Contexts* (Cambridge: Cambridge University Press, 1996), pp. 29ff., 176ff.; Toby E. Huff, *The Rise of Early Modern Science. Islam, China and the West* (Cambridge: Cambridge University Press, 1993), pp. 47ff. On the Islamic tradition of science also Howard R. Turner, *Science in Medieval Islam* (Austin, TX: University of Texas Press, 1995).

13 This is the title of the paper by Mourad Wahba; it is included in the Cairo proceedings referenced in note 1, here pp. 81–84.

14 Herbert Davidson, *Alfarabi, Avicenna and Averroes, on Intellect* (Oxford: Oxford University Press, 1992).

15 On this issue with more details see B. Tibi, *Der wahre Imam. Der Islam von Mohammed bis zur Gegenwart*, 2nd edn (Munich: Piper Press, 1996), Part 1. See also Part 2, which includes chapters on Farabi, Mawardi, Ibn Taimiyya, and Ibn Khaldun. It should be added that reason-based thinking in Islam was not restricted to the secular philosophers of Islamic rationalism, as it can be also found in the work of the Hellenized theological *kalam*, as in the school of Mu'tazilites. For more details and also on the topicality of this school of thought see Richard C. Martin *et al.*, *Defenders of Reason in Islam. Mu'tazilism from Medieval School to Modern Symbol* (Oxford: Oneworld, 1997). In contrast to this enlightened Islam there were other traditions, often addressed as "The period of darkness 1250–1900": W. M. Watt, *Islamic Philosophy and Theology* (Edinburgh: Edinburgh University Press, reprint 1979), Part 4, pp. 147–72. There also exists a Sufi Islam that supports secularity in the understanding of a separation of religion and politics; for references see note 46.

16 The formula *"bi al-wahi aw bi al-'aql"* was coined in medieval Islam by Abu al-Hassan al-Mawardi, *Kitab al-ahkam al-sultaniyya*/Book of Rules on the Sultanic government,

new edition (Cairo, 1909; French translation: Paris, 1901), p. 3. It reflects a declaration of war against Islamic rationalists, who were committed to the primacy of "*aql/*reason."

17 See Ibn Taimiyya, *al-Siyasa al-Shar'iyya fi islah al-ra'i wa al-ra'iyya*/The Shari'a-Oriented Politics for the Guidance of the Ruler and his Subjects, (Beirut: reprint, Dar al-Jil, 1988). Today this book is one of the major sources of the political thought of contemporary political Islam. For more details on this issue see Emmanuel Sivan, *Radical Islam. Medieval Theology and Modern Politics* (New Haven, CT: Yale University Press, 1985).

18 See his views on an envisioned Islamic Enlightenment: Mohammed A. al-Jabri, *Arab Islamic Philosophy* (Austin, TX: University of Texas Press, 1989).

19 The authoritative work on this subject, now available in a new edition, is by Niyazi Berkes, *The Development of Secularism in Turkey* (New York: Routledge, 1998; first edition 1964), see also Bernard Lewis, *The Muslim Discovery of Europe* (New York: Norton & Co., 1982), pp. 135ff, 221ff and his earlier book, *The Emergence of Modern Turkey*, 2nd edn (Oxford: Oxford University Press, 1979), in particular chapters 6 and 12; and Andrew Davidson, *Secularism and Revivalism in Turkey* (New Haven, CT: Yale University Press, 1998).

20 See the chapter on the Ottoman Empire in David B. Ralston, *Importing the European Army* (Chicago, IL: Chicago University Press, 1990). Ever since, and also under Atatürk and the Kemalists, as well as since 2002 – despite the rule of the Islamist AKP – Turkey continues to be the most significant case in the world of Islam for the debate on secularism and secularization (see note 19). On the desecularization politics of the AKP see B. Tibi, "Islamischer Konservatismus der AKP als Tarnung für den politischen Islam?," in: Gerhard Besier, ed., *Politische Religion und Religionspolitik* (Göttingen: Vandenhoek & Ruprecht, 2005), pp. 229–60. See also the references in the preceding note.

21 Rifa'a R. al-Tahtawi, *Takhlis al-Ibriz ila talkhis Paris*/Paris Diary, new printing (Beirut: Dar Ibn Zaidun, no date). On al-Tahtawi see chapter 7 in B. Tibi, *Der wahre Imam* (referenced in note 15), pp. 221–51.

22 Muhammed Abduh, *al-Islam wa al-Nasraniyya bain al-ilm wa al-madaniyya*/Islam and Christianity between Science and Civilization, new printing (Beirut: Dar al-Hadatha, 1983). For a critique on the limits of Islamic reform see B. Tibi, *The Crisis of Modern Islam* (Salt Lake City, UT: Utah University Press, 1998), conclusions, pp. 127–48.

23 For more details on the related tensions see B. Tibi, *Arab Nationalism. Between Islam and the Nation-State*, 3rd enlarged and revised edn (London and New York: Macmillan and St. Martin's Press, 1997) and on the introduction of the new institution of the nation-state into the world of Islam: B. Tibi, "The Simultaneity of the Unsimultaneous. Old Tribes and Imposed Nation States," in: Philip Khoury and Joseph Kostiner, eds, *Tribes and State Formation in the Middle East* (Berkeley, CA: University of California Press, 1990), pp. 127–52.

24 Ali 'Abdelraziq, *al-Islam wa usul al-hukm*/Islam and the Patterns of Government, 2nd printing (Beirut: Maktabat al-Hayat, 1966, first published Cairo, 1925). This is the first authoritative Muslim to introduce secular thought into Islam. A French translation has been published in: *Revue des Études Islamiques*, 7 (1933) and 8 (1934).

25 Khaled M. Khaled, *Min huna nabda'*/Here we Start, 10th edn (Cairo and Baghdad: al-Khanji Press and Maktabat Muthanna, 1963, first published 1950), p. 44ff.

26 The Islamist Khaled M. Khaled, *al-Dawla fi al-Islam*/The State in Islam, 3rd edn (Cairo: Dar Thabit, 1989).

27 This is the view of Ali M. Jarisha/Muhammad Zaibaq, *Asalib al-ghazu al-fikri* (note 9), here p. 59.

28 The classic on this issue is: Abu al-Hassan al-Marwardi, *Kitab adab al-dunya wa al-din*/Book of worldly and religious tradition; a German translation, in a new printing (Osnabrück: Bibliotheksverlag, 1984) is available; see also note 15.

29 On the idea of a shari'a-based "Islamic state" oriented on the the shari'a see B. Tibi, *The Challenge of Fundamentalism. Political Islam and the New World Disorder* (Berkeley, CA: University of California Press, 1998, updated 2002), chapter 8, pp. 158–78.

30 Niklas Luhman, *Funktion der Religion* (note 7), p. 227.

31 Ibid., p. 255.

32 On this notion of *Developing Cultures* and the references see Chapter 1, note 1.

33 Georges Balandier, *Politische Anthropologie* (Munich: Nymphenburger, 1972), p. 122.

34 See Steven K. Sanderson, *Social Evolution. A Critical History* (Oxford: Blackwell, 1990); David Apter, *Rethinking Development* (London: Sage, 1987).

35 Shmuel N. Eisenstadt, *Tradition, Wandel und Modernität* (Frankfurt/Main: Suhrkamp Verlag, 1979), p. 206.

36 On this legitimation aspect of Islamic thought see Sir Hamilton A. R. Gibb, *Studies on the Civilization of Islam* (Princeton, NJ: Princeton University Press, 1962). It is noted in this context that the notion *post eventum* used by Gibb means a religious legitimation for the political action of Muslim rulers provided hereafter by the *ulema*. On the *ulema* in Islam see Nikkie R. Keddie, ed., *Scholars, Saints and Sufis. Muslim Religious Institutions in the Middle East Since 1500* (Berkeley, CA: University of California Press, 1972), especially Part 1: "The Ulama," pp. 17ff. See also the case study of Arnold H. Green, *The Tunisian Ulama 1873–1915. Social Structure and Response to Ideological Currents* (Leiden: E.J. Brill, 1978), especially pp. 25ff.

37 Muhammad Said al-'Ashmawi, *al-Khilafah al-Islamiyya*/Islamic Caliphate (Cairo: Dar Sina, 1990). See also the reference in note 24 above on Abdelraziq.

38 The five-volume history of ideas by Professor Iring Fetscher, ed., *Pipers Handbuch der politischen Ideen* (Munich: Piper, 1987–88), includes in its vol. 2, *Das Mittelalter*, a lengthy chapter with an overview of medieval Islamic thought by B. Tibi, "Politisches Denken im klassischen und mittelalterlichen Islam zwischen Religio-Jurisprudenz (Fiqh) und hellenistischer Philosophie (Falsafa)," chapter 3, pp. 87–188, see therein the section on al-Farabi.

39 Shmuel N. Eisenstadt, *Tradition, Wandel* (referenced in note 35). here p. 206. Eisenstadt's theory is closely discussed in chapter 4 by B. Tibi, *Islam and the Cultural Accommodation of Social Change* (Boulder, CO: Westview, 1990), pp. 45–56.

40 Eisenstadt, *Tradition* (referenced in note 35), p. 208.

41 On this issue in Islam see Fuad I. Khury, *Imams and Emirs. State, Religion and Sects in Islam* (London: Saqi Books, 1990).

42 Barrington Moore, *The Social Origins of Dictatorship and Democracy* (Boston, MA: Beacon Press, 1966), here the German edition, published by Suhrkamp Verlag/Frankfurt 1974, p. 477.

43 Bruce Borthwick, "Religion and Politics in Israel and Egypt," in: *The Middle East Journal/MEJ*, 33, 2 (1979) pp. 145–63, the reference here is pp. 154–55.

44 See John L. Esposito and John O. Voll, *Islam and Democracy* (New York: Oxford University Press, 1996) parallel to my review in *Journal of Religion*, 78, 4 (October 1998), pp. 667–69.

45 Tayib Tizini, *Mashru' ru'ya jadida lil-fakr-al-'arabi fi al'asr al-wasit*/A Project of a New Interpretation of Arab Thinking in the Middle Age (Damascus: Dar Dimashq, 1971). Translation from Arabic by the author.

46 The view of faith as "*batiniyya*/inwardness" by Sufi Islam provides grounds for the separation of religion from politics and thus for a secular worldview. On Sufi Islam see the books by William Chittik, *The Sufi Path of Love. The Spiritual Teachings of Rumi* (Albany, NY: SUNY, 1983) and his book *Imaginal World Ibn al-Arabi and the Problem of Religious Diversity* (Albany, NY: SUNY, 1994).

47 Maxime Rodinson, *Islam und Kapitalismus* (Frankfurt/Main: Suhrkamp, new edn, 1985).

48 See James Blaut, *The Colonizer's Model of the World* (New York: Guilford Press, 1993) and Eric R. Wolfe, *Europe and the People without History* (Berkeley, CA: University of California Press, new edn, 1997).

49 Gustav von Grunebaum, *Studien zum Kulturbild und Selbstverständnis des Islam* (Zürich und Stuttgart: Artemis Verlag, 1969), p. 119.
50 On Afghani's bid to become engaged in a reformation emulating Luther, see Albert Hourani, *Arabic Thought in the Liberal Age* (London: Oxford, 1962), pp. 103–29, in particular p. 122.
51 Quoted from the collected writings of al-Afghani edited by M. Imara, *al-A'mal al-Kamilah*/Complete Works (Cairo: al-Mu'ssasah al-Misriyya, 1965), p. 328. Translation from Arabic by the author.
52 See note 50.
53 Shakib Arslan, *Limadha ta'akhara al-Muslimun wa taqadamma ghairahum?*/Why are Muslims backward, while others have progressed? (Beirut: al-Hayat, reprint, 1965), p. 176.
54 Luhmann, *Funktion der Religion* (referenced in note 7), S. 87.
55 Sigmund Freud, "Die Zukunft einer Illusion," in: Freud, *Werke Vol. IX, Fragen der Gesellschaft. Ursprünge der Religion* (Frankfurt: S. Fischer, 1974), pp. 149ff.
56 M. Ali Yusuf, *al-Jafwa bain al-din wa'l-ilm*/The Supposed Gap between Religion and Science (Beirut, 1966),
57 Sadiq Jalal al-Azm, *Naqd al-fikr al-dini*/Critique of Religious Thought (Beirut: al-Tali'a, 1969), p. 22.
58 Abdelraziq, *al-Islam wa usul al-hukm* (referenced in note 24).
59 Ashmawi, *al-Khilafah* (reference in note 37).
60 Abdelraziq, *al-Islam wa usul al-hukm* (referenced in note 24).
61 Luhmann, *Funktion der Religion* (referenced in note 7), p. 227.

Chapter 7

1 This chapter is based on the research of three projects, the first of which was at the Asian Research Institute/ARI of The National University of Singapore/NUS, where I had tenure in 2005 as a Senior Research Fellow during the second part of my sabbatical 2004/05 (the first part was at Harvard). The second project was The Trialogue, pursued at The US Holocaust Memorial Museum/Center for Advanced Holocaust Studies 2006–8 (in Spring 2008 I was Senior Fellow at CAHS). The third project was at Cornell University with a symposium that involved institutions of European, Southeast Asian, and Middle Eastern Studies at that university. The findings of the first project were published in a volume edited by the then acting ARI director Anthony Reid, *Islamic Legitimacy in a Plural Asia* (New York: Routledge, 2007). The volume includes my chapter: "Islam and Cultural Modernity, In Pursuit of Democratic Pluralism," pp. 28–52. My earlier paper on this subject also completed at ARI, was published in 2006 as "The Pertinence of Islam's Predicament with Democratic Pluralism," in: *Religion-Staat-Gesellschaft*, 7(1) (2006), pp. 83–117. Within the framework of the second project I completed a paper for the Jewish–Christian Islamic dialogue. Its publication is forthcoming in the volume edited by John Roth and Leonard Grob under the title: *Encountering the Stranger*. The paper written for the third project is: B. Tibi, "Euro-Islamic Religious Pluralism for Europe," *The Current. The Public Policy Journal of Cornell University*, 11, 1 (2007), pp. 89–103.
2 This statement is made by the Saudi professors Ali M. Jarisha and Mohammed Sharif al-Zaibaq in their book, *Asalib al-ghazu al-fikri li al'-alam al-Islami*/Methods of the Intellectual Invasion of the World of Islam (Cairo: 2nd edn, Dar al-I'tisam, 1978), p. 202.
3 Anwar al-Jundi, *Min al-taba'iyya ila al-asalah*/From Dependence to Authenticity (Cairo: Dar al-I'tisam, no date), p. 186. Al-Jundi is the foremost Islamist theorist of "authenticity," which not only runs counter to pluralism but also justifies an antisemitic cultural purification from what he believes to be a "Jewish impact."
4 Ibid., p. 184.

5 Ibid., p. 188. On this Islamist antisemitism see Matthias Küntzel, *Jihad and Jew Hatred. Islamism, Nazism and the Roots of 9/11* (New York: Telos, 2007), and the contributions included in the volume edited by Wolfgang Benz and Juliane Wetzel, eds, *Anti-semitismus und radikaler Islamismus* (Essen: Klartext Verlag, 2007). The volume includes my chapter on Islamist antisemitism, pp. 43–69.

6 On the concept of pluralism see John Kekes, *The Morality of Pluralism* (Princeton, NJ: Princeton University Press, 1993); on democratic peace that also applies to religions see the seminal work by Bruce Russet, *Grasping Democratic Peace. Principles for a Post-Cold War World* (Princeton, NJ: Princeton University Press 1993), and the reader edited by Michael Brown *et al.*, *Debating Democratic Peace* (Cambridge, MA: MIT Press 1996).

7 See the Jewish complaint against this inequality by Bat Ye'or, *Islam and Dhimmitude. Where Civilizations Collide* (Cranbury, NJ: Associated University Press 2002).

8 For an example for this apologetics see Abdulaziz Sachedina, *The Islamic Roots of Democratic Pluralism* (New York: Oxford University Press, 2001). Sachedina is mistaken in his dismissal of the work of the early Muslim reformist Abdullahi A. An-Na'im, *Toward an Islamic Reformation. Civil Liberties, Human Rights and International Law* (Syracuse, NY: Syracuse University Press 1990) and also in his critique of the Jewish complaint by Bat Ye'or cited in note 7, and lacks the willingness to admit an honest debate on the pending issues. I add "early" (meaning1990) to An-Na'im because he changed; for more details see Chapter 6. Probably Sachedina would be in agreement with the new book by An-Na'im.

9 What is liberal Islam? Is it pluralist "Liberal Islam," or what? I repeat the reference to the misguiding reader of Charles Kurzman, ed., *Liberal Islam* (New York: Oxford University Press, 1998). The editor confuses liberal and fundamentalist Muslims. As mentioned in Chapter 1, note 61, the reader includes texts by radical Islamists such as Qaradawi and Ghannouchi, presenting them as "liberal Muslims." A real liberal Islam is represented by Hasan Sa'b, *Islam al-Hurriyya, la Islam al-Ubudiyya/*Islam of Liberty, not of Sovereignty (Beirut: Dar al-Ilm Lilmalayin, 1979), and not by Hasan Hanafi, or Yusuf al-Qaradawi.

10 For more details on Islamism see B. Tibi, *Political Islam, World Politics and Europe. Democratic Peace and Euro-Islam versus Global Jihad* (New York: Routledge, 2008).

11 See Clifford Geertz, "Religion as a Cultural System," in his volume: *The Interpretation of Cultures* (New York: Basic Books, 1973), pp. 87–125. For an application of this concept to Islam see my book referenced in note 53.

12 These proceedings were published in Cairo, edited by Mourad Wahba, *Islam and Civilization. Proceedings of the First International Islamic Philosophy Conference, 19–22 November 1979* (Cairo: Ain Shams University Press 1982). See therein the chapters by Mukti Ali, "Islam and Indonesian Culture," pp. 15–34, and by B. Tibi, "Islam and Secu-larization," pp. 65–80. The context of this volume is reported in Chapter 6, note 1.

13 Ernest Gellner, *Postmodernism, Reason and Religion* (London: Routledge, 1992).

14 See the excellent study by Robert W. Hefner, *Civil Islam. Muslims and Democratization in Indonesia* (Princeton, NJ: Princeton University Press, 2000). It is unfortunate that Hefner, in contrast to this enlightening study, presents biased and very selective con-tributions in his edited volume, *Remaking Muslim Politics* (Princeton, NJ: Princeton University Press, 2005).

15 See the authoritative criticism of political Islam by the leading enlightened Muslim jurist Mohammed Said al-Ashmawi, *al-Islam al-Siyasi/*Political Islam (Cairo: Dar Sinah, 1987); French translation: *L'Islamisme contre L'Islam* (Paris: Editon la Découverte, 1989); see also note 10.

16 See the chapter "Islamization of Europe" included in the book published by Cam-bridge University Press and authored by Millard Burr and Robert Collins, *Alms for Jihad. Charity and Terrorism in the Islamic World* (New York, 2006). The book was

withdrawn from the market for whatever reasons by Cambridge University Press. For an alternative see B. Tibi, "A Migration Story. From Muslim Immigrants to European Citizens of the Heart," *The Fletcher Forum of World Affairs*, 31, 1 (Winter 2007), pp. 147–68. On Wahhabi-Saudi infiltration see Stephen Schwartz, *The Two Faces of Islam. The House of Sa'ud From Tradition to Terror* (New York: Doubleday, 2002).

17 The meaning of the Hellenization in medieval Islam is covered in Chapter 8 of the present book, with plenty of references made there. The magnitude of the intellectual indebtedness of Islamic political philosophy to Hellenism is shown in the contributions published in the book edited by Charles Butterworth, *The Political Aspects of Islamic Philosophy. Essays in Honor of Muhsin S. Mahdi*, Harvard Middle Eastern Monographs (Cambridge, MA: Harvard University Press, 1992). The late Mahdi was my source of intellectual inspiration while I was writing my intellectual history of Islam, *Der Wahre Imam* (Munich: Piper, 1996), therein Part 2 on Islamic rationalism and Hellenization; on Mahdi, see the preface, p. 13, of this reference.

18 Daniel Philipot, "The Challenge of September 11 to Secularism in International Relations," *World Politics*, 55, 1 (October 2002), pp. 66–95; see also the reference in note 10.

19 Sachedina, *Islamic roots* (referenced in note 8), p. 6.

20 The work of al-Farabi, honored as "second master" next to Aristotle is available in an English translation by Richard Walzer, ed., *al-Farabi on the Perfect State* (Oxford: Clarendon Press, 1985). On the related Islamic heritage, see Franz Rosenthal, *The Classical Heritage of Islam* (London: Routledge, 1975). See also the chapter on al-Farabi in: Peter Adamson and Richard Taylor, eds, *The Cambridge Companion to Arabic Philosophy* (Cambridge: Cambridge University Press, 2005), pp. 52–71.

21 See the debate in Chapter 2 of this book and also B. Tibi, "Culture and Knowledge. The Politics of Islamization of Knowledge as a Postmodern Project? The Fundamentalist Claim to De-Westernization," *Theory, Culture, Society*, 12, 1 (1995), pp. 1–24.

22 An example is the common discourse shared by Averroes and Maimonedis. For more details see chapter 17 by Steven Harvey on Islamic Jewish Philosophy, in: Peter Adamson and Richard Taylor, *The Cambridge Companion* (referenced in note 20).

23 Abu al-A'la al-Mawdudi, *al-Islam wa al-madaniyya al-haditha*/Islam and Modern Civilization (reprint Cairo, no date). On these views of Maududi see also Muhammad Dharif, *al-Islam al-siyasi fi al-watan al-arabi* (Casablanca: Maktabat al-Umma, 1992) pp. 98–99; and Youssef M. Choueiri, *Islamic Fundamentalism* (Boston, MA: Twayne Publ., 1990), pp. 93ff.

24 Mawdudi, *al-Islam* (referenced in note 23).

25 See John Brenkman, *The Cultural Contradiction of Democracy. Political Thought Since September 11* (Princeton, NJ: Princeton University Press, 2007), p. 165.

26 See the references in notes 10 and 15, and further on Islamism as the significant Islamic variety of the global phenomenon of religious fundamentalism see B. Tibi, *The Challenge of Fundamentalism. Political Islam and the New World Disorder* (Berkeley, CA: University of California Press, 1998, enlarged and updated edn 2002). The cited study includes in particular chapter 9 on pluralist democracy, proposed as an alternative to Islamism.

27 Therefore, I strongly disagree with the misleading views of John L. Esposito and John O. Voll presented in their book *Islam and Democracy* (New York: Oxford University Press, 1996). In a critical review published in: *Journal of Religion*, 78, 4 (1998), pp. 667–69, I disclose their grave mistakes and flaws. I also believe that Esposito's *The Islamic Threat. Myth or Reality?* (New York: Oxford University Press, 1992) is in many similar ways a misleading contribution.

28 B. Tibi, "Between Islam and Islamism," in: Tami A. Jacoby and Brent Sasley, eds, *Redefining Security in the Middle East* (Manchester: Manchester University Press, 2002), pp. 62–82.

29 Martin Marty and Scott Appleby, eds, *The Fundamentalism Project*, 5 vols., (Chicago, IL: The University of Chicago Press, 1991–95), see vol. 2, *Fundamentalisms and Society*, therein: B. Tibi, "Attitudes of Sunni Arab Fundamentalists" (Chicago 1993), pp. 73–102; see also parts 2 and 3 in vol. 3, *Fundamentalisms and the State* (Chicago 1993) on: *Remaking Politics*.

30 The authoritative history of Islamic civilization, viewed as Islamitude, continues to be Marshall G. S. Hodgson, *The Venture of Islam. Conscience and History in a World Civilization*, 3 volumes (Chicago, IL: The University of Chicago Press, 1974), and also Sir Hamilton Gibb, *Studies on the Civilization of Islam* (Princeton, NJ: Princeton University Press, 1982).

31 See the book by Gellner on postmodernism and reason (referenced in note 13) and his contribution to a debate included in the proceedings of the Erasmus Ascension Symposium, *The Limits of Pluralism. Neo-Absolutisms and Relativism* (published by Praemium Erasmianum Foundation in Amsterdam, 1994), on pp. 163–66, therein also B. Tibi on political Islam, pp. 29–36.

32 Sayyid Qutb, *al-Jihad fi sabil Allah*/Jihad on the Path of God (reprinted Cairo: Dar al-Isma', 1992) and also the reprint of Qutb, *al-Salam al-Alami wa al-Islam*/World Peace and Islam (Cairo: al-Shuruq, 1992). On this Islamist thought see B. Tibi, From Islamist Jihadism to Democratic Peace? Islam is at the Crossroads in Postbipolar International Politics, Ankara Paper 16 (London: Taylor & Francis, 2005).

33 Rifa'a R. al-Tahtawi, *Takhlis al-Ibriz fi-talkhis Paris*/Paris Diary (Cairo, 1834; reprint Beirut, no date). There is an excellent German translation of Tahtawi's Paris diary, translated, edited and with an introduction by Karl Stowasser, *Ein Muslim entdeckt Europa* (Munich: C. H. Beck, 1989), see here p. 223.

34 See Albert Hourani, *Arabic Thought in the Liberal Age, 1798–1939* (Oxford: Oxford University Press, 1962).

35 See the classic by Nadav Safran, *Egypt in Search of Political Community* (Cambridge, MA: Harvard University Press, 1961), in particular pp. 179, 85, 96f. and 120. In view of the significance of this book by Safran the following note is pertinent: Despite the damage done to Safran's reputation in the course of a series of Harvard scandals this book has to be kept out of the dirt. The Safran scandals are documented, not at all impartially, in the extremely biased, unbalanced and therefore most questionable booklet of Harvard/CMES 2004 published on its 50th anniversary. This booklet is to be dismissed. Against all odds, I pay my respect to the late Jewish scholar Safran. I do this in spite of all disagreement with his work and bad memories of the inappropriate way he treated me as an "Arab" during my affiliation at Harvard. Safran's personal flaws should not distract from the fact that his book on Egypt deserves to be ranked as a "classic." Following the departure of Safran, who was a political scientist, his successors at Harvard CMES seem to be "Orientalists in reverse" (Safran was not free of "Orientalism") and social science was completely removed from Harvard's agenda on Islam and Middle East. Harvard is a big name, but not in Islamic studies of today.

36 On this see Leslie Lipson, *The Ethical Crisis of Civilization. Moral Meltdown or Advance?* (London: Sage, 1993), p. 63. On the cultural influence of Islamic civilization on the European Renaissance see also B. Tibi, *Kreuzzug und Djihad. Der Islam und die christliche Welt* (München: Bertelsmann, 1999), chapter 5.

37 Habermas views the Renaissance as one of the four basic pillars of cultural modernity: Jürgen Habermas, *The Philosophical Discourse of Modernity. Twelve Lectures* (Cambridge, MA: MIT Press, 1987), pp. 1–11.

38 Lipson, *The Ethical* (referenced in note 36), p. 62.

39 George Makdisi, *The Rise of Colleges. Institutions of Learning in Islam and the West* (Edinburgh: Edinburgh University Press, 1981), pp. 77–80.

40 Mohammed Abed al-Jabri, *Arab Islamic Philosophy* (Austin, TX: Texas University Press, 1999).

41 Robert Lee, *Overcoming Tradition and Modernity. The Search for Islamic Authenticity* (Boulder, CO: Westview, 1997).

42 See the reference in note 10. The findings of that book contradict the highly unbalanced study by Raymond W. Baker, *Islam Without Fear. Egypt and the New Islamists* (Cambridge, MA: Harvard University Press, 2003). Also the earlier work of Jean-François Revel, *Democracy Against Itself* (New York: The Free Press, 1993), chapter 12 runs counter to Baker's allegations, based on confusion between Islam and Islamism, not on useful analysis.

43 See Jean-François Revel, *Democracy Against Itself* (referenced in note 42) and also the references in notes 10 and 26, as well as my contributions to the following established encyclopedias on this issue. First, my article "Fundamentalism" in: Seymour Martin Lipset, ed., *The Encyclopedia of Democracy*, 4 volumes, here vol. 2, pp. 507–10 (Washington: The Congressional Quarterly, 1995), and more recent chapter 13 "Fundamentalism" in the new edition of Mary Hawkesworth and Maurice Kogan, eds, *Routledge Encyclopedia of Government*, 2nd edn (London: Routledge, 2004), 2 vols, here vol. 1, pp. 184–204.

44 Sayyid Qutb, *Ma'alim fi al-tariq/*Signposts along the Road, 13th legal printing (Cairo: al-Shuruq, 1989), pp. 5–6. See also the Qutb interpretation by Roxanne Euben, *Enemy in the Mirror. Islamic Fundamentalism and the Limits of Modern Rationalism. A Work of Comparative Political Theory* (Princeton, NJ: Princeton University Press, 1999), Chapter 3.

45 See the references to Yusuf al-Qaradawi, *Hatmiyyat al-Hall al-Islami/*The Islamic Solution is Determined, 3 volumes (fully referenced in note 61 to Chapter 1), here vol. 1 *al-Hulul al-Mustawradah*, p. 50f. Qaradawi is the leading Islamist, not a liberal (see note 9).

46 See B. Tibi, "War and Peace in Islam," in: Terry Nardin, ed., *The Ethics of War and Peace* (Princeton, NJ: Princeton University Press, 1996, also 1998), pp. 128–45, and also chapter 1 and 2 in B. Tibi, *Political Islam* (referenced in note 10).

47 Hamid Enayat, *Modern Islamic Political Thought* (Austin, TX: Texas University Press, 1982), p. 131.

48 See B. Tibi, *Islam between Culture and Politics* (New York: Routledge, 2001, updated edn 2005), pp. 4–6.

49 Enayat, *Modern Islamic* (referenced in note 47), p. 131.

50 Ibid., p. 126.

51 Mohammed Arkoun, *Rethinking Islam. Common Questions, Common Answers* (Boulder, CO: Westview Press, 1994) pronounces in the title of his book a task that he does not fulfill. Unfortunately, Arkoun is also among those many liberal Muslims (e.g. An-Na'im, see Chapter 6) who prefer to evade the core issues. It is amazing to read in a recent book by Arkoun, *Islam to Reform or to Subvert* (London: Saqi, 2006), p. 11, the comparison of himself – too immodestly – with Kant!! This comparison is inappropriate, to say the least. Arkoun dismisses his ranking as a reformer because he claims to be more, namely to "subvert" not to "reform." In the French rhetoric of Arkoun neither seem to exist.

52 Enayat, *Modern Islamic* (referenced in note 47), p. 135.

53 On this issue see the earlier contribution: B. Tibi, *Islam and the Cultural Accommodation of Social Change* (Boulder, CO: 2nd printing, Westview Press, 1991).

54 For more details on this issue see the inspiring chapter on ethnopolitics by Gabriel Ben-Dor in: Milton Esman and Itamar Rabinovich, eds, *Ethnicity, Pluralism and the State in the Middle East* (Ithaca and London: Cornell University Press, 1988), pp. 71–92. He proposes power sharing as a kind of pluralism.

55 Najib Armanazi, *al-Shar' al-duwali fi al-Islam/*International Law in Islam (London: El-Rayyes, 1990). According to this Muslim scholar, the cited Islamic dichotomous division of the world has never been revised by the ulema.

56 On this formula see my contribution to Roman Herzog et al., *Preventing the Clash of Civilizations. A Peace Strategy for the 21st Century* (New York: St. Martin's Press, 1999), included in that volume as chapter 10: "International Morality and Cross-Cultural Bridging," pp. 107–26.

Chapter 8

1 The most powerful postmodern book on this subject is by Charles Taylor, *The Ethics of Authenticity* (Cambridge, MA: Harvard University Press, 1991).

2 Anwar al-Jundi, *Min al-taba'iyya ila al-asalah/*From Dependence to Authenticity (Cairo: Dar al-I'tisam, no date), pp. 181–88, as well as pp. 171–73; see also his book *al-Mu'sarah fi itar al-asalah/*Modernity in the Context of Authenticity (Cairo: Dar al-Sahwa, 1987), where Anwar al-Jundi argues on pp. 71–79 that enlightenment is "a Jewish idea" and Islam therefore has to be purified from its impact.

3 Anwar al-Jundi, *Ahdaf al-taghrib fi al-Alam al-Islami/*The Goal of Westernization of the Islamic World (Cairo: al-Azhar Press, 1987), pp. 11–29.

4 Jürgen Habermas, *The Philosophical Discourse of Modernity* (Cambridge, MA: MIT Press, 1987), p. 18.

5 Mohammed al-Jabri, *Arab Islamic Philosophy* (Austin, TX: CMES, 1999).

6 Robert Lee, *Overcoming Tradition and Modernity. The Search for Islamic Authenticity* (Boulder, CO: Westview Press, 1997), p. 191.

7 See Franz Rosenthal, *The Classical Heritage of Islam* (London: Routledge, 1994). This heritage is based on Hellenization, with seeds of an enlightenment. Contemporary Islamism claims to be an Islamic revival, but it is not based on this heritage.

8 For more details on this history of ideas see B. Tibi, "Politisches Denken im klassischen und mittelalterlichen Islam zwischen Philosophie (Falsafa) und Religio-Jurisprudenz (Fiqh)," in the five-volume handbook edited by I. Fetscher, ed., *Pipers Handbuch der politischen Ideen*, here vol. 2 (Munich/Zurich: Piper Verlag, 1987), pp. 87–140.

9 George Makdisi, *The Rise of the Colleges. Institutions of Learning in Islam and the West* (Edinburgh: Edinburgh University Press, 1981).

10 On the notion of institutionalization of cultural innovations as a requirement see Robert Wuthnow, *Meaning and Moral Order* (Berkeley, CA: University of California Press, 1987), chapter 8.

11 For more details see Anke von Kugelgen, *Averroes und die arabische Moderne. Ansätze zu einer Neugründung des Rationalismus im Islam* (Leiden: Brill Press, 1994).

12 Mohammed al-Jabri, *Arab Islamic Philosophy* (referenced in note 5), p. 124.

13 On Hellenization of Islam see W. M. Watt, *Islamic Philosophy and Theology* (Edinburgh: Edinburgh University Press, 1962, new printing 1979), Parts 2 and 3.

14 Herbert Davidson, *Alfarabi, Avicenna and Averroes, on Intellect* (New York: Oxford University Press, 1992).

15 On this issue see Theodore von Laue, *The World Revolution of Westernization* (New York: Oxford University Press, 1987).

16 For more details see chapter 5 on Islam and the European Renaissance in B. Tibi, *Kreuzzug und Djihad. Der Islam und die christliche Welt* (Munich: Bertelsmann, 1999), pp. 168–87.

17 The contemporary call for an "Islamic solution" (Qaradawi) replaces the early positive sentiments towards Westernization in the nineteenth and early twentieth centuries. At present, the Islamist ideologues engage in polemics against all foreign influence and flatly reject any cultural borrowing in order to thwart what is viewed to be a conspiracy of "*al-taghrib/*Westernization." This spirit is guided by the Egyptian Muslim Brother Yusuf al-Qaradawi, who is dubbed as "global Mufti." This Imam in the top rank of Islamist ideologues. See his three volumes, fully referenced in Chapter 1, note 61.

18 Lee, *Overcoming* (referenced in note 6), p. 191 and p. 193.

19 See note 8 and for a contrast of the *fiqh* and *falsafa* traditions in Islam see B. Tibi, *Der wahre Imam. Der Islam von Mohammed bis zur Gegenwart*, 2nd edn (Munich: Piper Press, 1996), chapter 3, also chapters 4 and 5.

20 Stefan Wolff, *Ethnic Conflict* (New York: Oxford University Press, 2006).

21 Lee, *Overcoming* (referenced in note 6), p. 177.

22 Rifa'a Rafi'a al-Tahtawi, *Takhlis al-Ibriz fi talkhis Paris*/Paris Diary (Beirut: Dar Ibn Zaidun, new printing, no date). There is an excellent German translation by Karl Stowasser, ed., *al-Tahtawi. Ein Muslim entdeckt Europa* (Munich: C. H. Beck, 1989).

23 See also chapter 2 on "Islamic worldview" in: B. Tibi, *Islam between Culture and Politics* (New York: Palgrave, 2001), pp. 53–68.

24 Gerard Leclerc, *Anthropologie und Kolonialismus* (Frankfurt/Main: Hanser, 1973).

25 On this accusation of Muslims of "ignorance/*jahl*" by al-Afghani see the edition by Mohammed Imara, *al-A'mal al-Kamilah li al-Afghani*/Collected Writings (Cairo: Dar al-Katib al-Arabi, 1968), p. 448, see also pp. 327–28.

26 See the appreciations of this contribution by Edward Grant, *The Foundations of Modern Science in the Middle Ages. Their Religious, Institutional, and Intellectual Contexts* (Cambridge: Cambridge University Press, 1996), pp. 29ff., 176ff; and also Toby E. Huff, *The Rise of Early Modern Science. Islam, China and the West* (Cambridge: Cambridge University Press, 1993), pp. 47ff. On the Islamic tradition of science see also Howard R. Turner, *Science in Medieval Islam* (Austin, TX: University of Texas Press, 1995). See also note 6.

27 Albert Habib Hourani, *Arabic Thought in the Liberal Age 1798–1939* (London: Oxford University Press, 1962).

28 Hedley Bull, "The Revolt against the West," in: Hedley Bull and Adam Watson, eds, *The Expansion of International Society* (Oxford: Oxford University Press, 1984), pp. 217–28.

29 Gerald J. Holton, *Science and Anti-Science* (Cambridge, MA: Harvard University Press, 1993).

30 See the reference in note 23, and further B. Tibi, "The Worldview of Sunni Arab Fundamentalists: Attitudes towards Modern Science and Technology," in: Martin Marty/Scott Appleby, eds, *Fundamentalisms and Society* (Chicago, IL: Chicago University Press, 1993), pp. 73–102.

31 See Charles Tilly, *Big Structures, Large Processes, Huge Comparisons* (New York: Russell Sage Foundation, 1984) and also Theda Skocpol, ed., *Vision and Method in Historical Sociology* (Cambridge: Cambridge University Press, 1984).

32 Edward W. Said, *Orientalism* (New York: Pantheon Books, 1978). On Max Weber, p. 259. The Orientalism debate is fully documented in chapter 4 of B. Tibi, *Einladung in die islamische Geschichte* (Darmstadt: Wissenschaftliche Buchgesellschaft, 2001), pp. 136–90.

33 See Max Weber, *Soziologie, weltgeschichtliche Analysen, Politik* (Stuttgart: Kröner, 1964).

34 David C. Lindberg, *The Beginning of Western Science* (Chicago, IL: University of Chicago Press, 1992), chapters 8, 9 and 10.

35 Max Weber, *Soziologie* (referenced in note 33), p. 317.

36 See Chapter 2 on this issue, as well as on *Aslamat al-ulum*/Islamization of the sciences, the reference in note 41.

37 Franz Borkenau, *Der Uebergang vom feudalen zum bürgerlichen Weltbild* (Paris 1934), (new printing, Darmstadt: Wissenschaftliche Buchgesellschaft, 1988). See in particular pp. 268ff on Descartes, considered to be the founder of the rational worldview addressed as Cartesianism.

38 Gerald Holton, *Science* (referenced in note 29), p. 159.

39 Norbert Elias, *The Civilizing Process*, 2 volumes (New York: Palgrave 1978 and 1982). See also Bernard Lewis, *What Went Wrong?* (New York: Oxford University Press, 2001).

40 Gerald Holton, *Science* (referenced in note 29), p. 159.

41 The International Institute of Islamic Thought, ed., *Towards Islamization of Disciplines*. Islamization of Knowledge Series, vol. 6 (Herndon, VA: International Institute of Islamic Thought, 1989), see also note 27 above.

42 Ernest Gellner, *Postmodernism, Reason and Religion* (London: Routledge, 1992).
43 Gerald Holton, *Science* (referenced in note 29), p. 147.
44 Ibid., p. 145.
45 See Ziauddin Sardar, *Islamic Futures. The Shape of Ideas to Come* (London. Mensell, 1985), p. 85 f.; see also his book: *Exploration in Islamic Science* (London: Mensell, 1989).
46 See Chapter 2 and the references made there, as well as Syed Muhammed Naguib al-Attas, *Islam, Secularism and the Philosophy of the Future* (London: Mensell, 1985), p. 127, see also p. 138.
47 B. Tibi, *The Challenge of Fundamentalism. Political Islam and the New World Disorder* (Berkeley: University of California Press, 1998, new edn 2002).
48 In his book, Ernst Bloch, *Avicenna und die Aristotelische Linke* (Frankfurt/Main: Suhrkamp 1993), explains this darkness by the dominance of the "mufti world" against rationalism in Islam.
49 At present the writings by the medieval *fiqh*-jurisprudent Ibn Taimiyya are highly topical, above all his book *al-Siyasa al-shar'iyya fi islah al-rai'i wa al-ra'iyya*/The Shari'a-Oriented Politics for the Guidance of the Ruler and his Subjects, new printing (Beirut: Dar al-Jil, 1988). On the impact of Ibn Taimiyya see Emmanuel Sivan, *Radical Islam. Medieval Theology and Modern Politics* (New Haven, CT: Yale University Press, 1985).
50 Robert Lee, *Overcoming* (referenced in note 6), p. 175. See also Gerald Holton, *Science* (referenced in note 29), p. 184.
51 David C. Lindberg, *The Beginnings* (referenced in note 34), p. 170f.
52 See the second UNDP Report on Arab Human Development 2003 on, *Building a Knowledge Society* (New York: UN, 2003). Instead of a search for knowledge authors like C. A. Qadir, *Philosophy and Science in the Islamic World* (London: Routledge, 1988) and Abdulraziq Nawfal, *al-Muslimun wa al-ilm al-hadith*/Muslims and Modern Science, 3rd printing (Cairo: Dar al-shuruq, 1988) praise the self.
53 The formula "*bi al-wahi aw bi al-'aql*/Either by Revelation of by Reason" was coined by Abu al-Hassan al-Marwadi, *Kitab al-ahkam al-sultaniyya*/Book of rules on the sultanic government. There are many editions published in Cairo.
54 Hussein Sadr, "Science in Islam," in: Ziauddin Sardar, ed., *The Touch of Midas. Science, Values and Environment in Islam and the West* (Manchester: Manchester University Press, 1984), pp. 22–23.
55 David C. Lindberg, *The Beginnings* (referenced in note 34), p. 168.
56 See Richard G. Martin and Marc R. Woodward with Devi S. Atmaja, *Defenders of Reason in Islam: Mu'tazilism from Medieval School to Modern Symbol* (Oxford: Oneworld Publishers, 1997).
57 David C. Lindberg (referenced in note 34), p. 174, see also note 9.
58 Ibid., p. 180.
59 This is done in some articles by the founder of the German "Islamwissenschaft," C. H. Becker, which were collected under the title *Islam-Studien*, 2 vols, reprint (Hildesheim, 1967).
60 For instance see the work of the antisemitic Islamist al-Jundi, referenced in notes 2 and 3.
61 Nasr Hamed Abu-Zaid, *Naqd al-khitab al-din*/Critique of Religious Discourse (Cairo: Madbuli, new expanded edn, 1995).
62 Raymond Baker, *Islam without Fear. Egypt and the New Islamists* (Cambridge, MA: Harvard University Press, 2003).
63 al-Farabi, *al-madina al-fadila*/English edn and trans. by Michael Walzer, *Al-Farabi on the Perfect State* (Oxford: Oxford University Press, 1985).
64 See chapter 9 on science and technology in: Bernard Lewis, *The Muslim Discovery of Europe* (New York: Norton & Co., 1982), pp. 221–38.
65 The book by David B. Ralston, *Importing the European Army: The Introduction of European Military Techniques and Institutions into the Extra-European World, 1600–1914* (Chicago, IL: University of Chicago Press, 1990) includes two chapters on Egypt and the Ottoman experience.

66 Fatma Müge Göcek, *Rise of the Bourgeoisie, Demise of Empire. Ottoman Westernization and Social Change* (New York: Oxford University Press, 1996).
67 See Tahtawi on shari'a, referenced in note 22.
68 Bernard Lewis, *The Muslim Discovery of Europe* (referenced in note 64), p. 238.
69 Mohammed Abduh, *al-Islam wa al-Nasraniyya bain al-Ilm wa al-Madaniyya* /Islam and Christianity between Science and Civilization (Beirut: Dar al-Hadatha, reprint 1983).
70 B. Tibi, *Arab Nationalism. Between Islam and the Nation-State* (New York: Macmillan, 3rd edn, 1997).
71 Tayyib Tizini, *Mashru' ru'ya jadida li-fakr-al-'arabi fi al'asr al-wasit*/A project for a New Evaluation of Arabic Medieval Thought (Damascus: Dar Dimashq, 1971).
72 Albert Hourani, *Arabic Thought in the Liberal Age* (London: Oxford University Press, 1962), p. 122, citing Afghani on Luther.
73 For a reference on Afghani on knowledge and colonialism, see note 25.
74 Niklas Luhmann, *Funktion der Religion* (Frankfurt/Main: Suhrkamp, 1977).
75 B. Tibi, "The Islamic Dream of Semi-Modernity," in: *India International Center International Quarterly*, 22(1) (1995), pp. 79–87.
76 Mohammed Arkoun, *Islam to Reform or to Subvert?* (London: Saqi, 2006).
77 Patricia Crone, *Pre-Industrial Societies. Anatomy of the Pre-Modern World* (Oxford: Oneworld, 1989).
78 See B. Tibi, *Political Islam, World Politics and Europe* (New York: Routledge, 2008) and Peter Demant, *Islam versus Islamism. The Dilemma of the Muslim World* (Westport, CT: Praeger, 2006).
79 Sadik al-Azm, *Naqd al-fikr al-dini*/ Critique of Religious Thought (Beirut: Dar al-Talia, 1969).
80 Abu-Zaid, *Naqd* (referenced in note 61).
81 Mohammed al-Jabri, *Arab Islamic Philosophy* (referenced in note 5).
82 International Institute for Islamic Thought (referenced in note 41), p. 16.
83 Parrez Hoodbhoy, *Islam and Science. Religious Orthodoxy and the Battle for Rationality* (London: Zed Books, 1991), p. 4.
84 David C. Lindberg, *The Beginnings* (referenced in note 34), p. 180.
85 See B. Tibi, "Cultural Innnovation in the Development Process," in: Klaus Gottstein, ed., *Islamic Cultural Identity and Scientific-Technological Development* (Baden-Baden: Nomos, 1986), pp. 93–101.

Chapter 9

1 Egypt ranks at the top of my priorities for research in Islamic countries. For three decades I have been doing research in Egypt on a regular basis. The selection of this case study is based on this research background and on the significance of that country. The research for the chapter draws on work done at the Culture Matters Research Project/ CMRP. See Chapter 1, note 1 on project. See also the references in Chapter 6, note 1.
2 On the place of Egypt in modern Islamic history see Marshall G. S. Hodgson, *The Venture of Islam. Conscience and History in a World Civilization* (Chicago, IL: University of Chicago Press, 1974), 3 volumes, here vol. 3, book 6, pp. 163–410, in particular pp. 272–302.
3 On the Islamic expansion as a historical project of globalization and on the mutual conquests of both Islamic and Western civilizations see first, on Islam: Fred M. Donner, *Early Islamic Conquests* (Princeton, NJ: Princeton University Press, 1981) and Alan Jamieson, *Faith and Sword. A Short History of Christian-Muslim Conflict* (London: Reaktion Books, 2006). Recently, Efraim Karsh in his book *Islamic Imperialism. A History* (New Haven, CT: Yale University Press, 2006) made a provocative suggestion for a new interpretation. On the conquests on the European side see Robert Bartlett, *The Making of Europe.*

Conquests, Colonization and Cultural Change (Princeton, NJ: Princeton University Press, 1993).

4 For more details on the rise and fall of Islamic globalization from the seventh through the seventeenth centuries and the impact of the rise of the West see B. Tibi, *Kreuzzug und Djihad. Der Islam und die christliche Welt* (München: Bertelsmann Press, 1999), chapters 2, 4 and 6.

5 B. Tibi, *The Crisis of Modern Islam. A Preindustrial Culture in the Scientific-Technological Age* (Salt Lake City, UT: Utah University Press, 1988).

6 John Brenkman, *The Cultural Contradiction of Democracy. Political Thought since September 11* (Princeton, NJ: Princeton University Press, 2007).

7 This flier in full text is translated by: Ibrahimn Abu-Lughod, *The Arab Rediscovery of Europe. A Study in Cultural Encounters* (Princeton, NJ: Princeton University Press, 1963), pp. 13–16.

8 On this rule and the ensuing modernization see Afaf al-Sayyid-Marsot, *Egypt in the Reign of Mohammed Ali* (Cambridge: Cambridge University Press, 1984) and also the reference in note 9.

9 See chapter 4 on Egypt under Mohammed Ali and his successors in David Ralston, *Importing the European Army. The Introduction of European Military Techniques and Institutions into the Extra-European World 1600–1914* (Chicago, IL: University of Chicago Press, 1990), pp. 79–106, and in the same book chapter 3 on the Ottoman Empire, pp. 43–78.

10 See B. Tibi, "The Worldview of Sunni Arab Islamic Fundamentalists: Attitudes towards Modern Science and Technology," in: Martin Marty and Scott Appleby, ed., *Fundamentalisms and Society* (Chicago, IL: The University of Chicago Press, 1993), pp. 73–102 and also the reference in note 37 below.

11 On the Six Day War and on its cultural repercussions also on Egypt see B. Tibi, *Conflict and War in the Middle East. From Interstate War to New Security*, 2nd edn (New York: St. Martin's Press, 1998), chapters 3 and 4.

12 On Muslim travelers see Roxanne Euben, *Journeys to the Other Shore. Muslim and Western Travellers in Search of Knowledge* (Princeton, NJ: Princeton University Press, 2006). The two listed modern Muslim travelers, who became major reformers, namely Tahtawi and Abduh, documented their reflections in these significant books: Rifa'a Rafi al-Tahtawi, *Takhlis al-Ibriz fi talkhis Paris*/Paris Diary, new edition (Cairo: Maktabat al-Kuliyyat al-Azhariyya, no date) German translation: *Ein Muslim entdeckt Europa. Bericht über seinen Aufenthalt in Paris 1826–1831* (Munich: C. H. Beck, 1989) and Muhammad Abduh, *al-Islam wa al-Nasraniyya bain al-ilm wa al-madaniyya*/Islam and Christianity between Science and Civilization, new printing (Beirut: Dar al-Hadatha, 1983). On Tahtawi and his place see B. Tibi, *Arab Nationalism. Between Islam and the Nation-State* (New York: St. Martin's Press, 3rd edn, 1997), pp. 84–88 and on Abduh pp. 88–94.

13 On Salamah Musah see Vermon Egger, *A Fabian in Egypt. Salamah Musa and the Rise of the Professional Class in Egypt 1909–1939* (Lanham, MD: University Press of America, 1986).

14 On Yusuf al-Qaradawi's *al-Hall al-Islami*/The Islamic Solution, and his three volumes on this theme, reprinted a dozen times in Cairo and Beirut and spread throughout the world of Islam, see the full references in Chapter 1, note 61. For some details on Yusuf al-Qaradawi see: Joyce M. Davis, *Between Jihad and Salam. Profiles in Islam* (New York: St. Martin's Press, 1977), pp. 219–33. I reiterate that any person who knows little about political Islam would be disturbed to see texts by al-Qaradawi included in the most distorting reader of Charles Kurzman, ed., *Liberal Islam* (New York: Oxford University Press, 1998), pp. 196–204. Again: the global Mufti al-Qaradawi is the major voice of contemporary Islamic fundamentalism, not of "liberal Islam"!

15 On the export of Saudi Wahhabism see Stephen Schwartz, *The Two Faces of Islam. The House of Sa'ud from Tradition to Terror* (New York: Doublday, 2002), chapter 7.

16 On this *fetwa* legitimating the Saudi king to accept US military protection against Saddam's Iraq back in 1990 and on the overall context see B. Tibi, *Die Verschwörung. Das Trauma arabischer Politik* (Hamburg: Hoffmann und Campe, 1993), chapter 15.
17 See Bernard Lewis, *The Emergence of Modern Turkey* (London: Oxford University Press, 2nd edn 1979, first published 1961).
18 For more on Taha Husayn see Nadav Safran, *Egypt in Search of Political Community. An Analysis of the Intellectual and Political Evolution of Egypt, 1804–1952* (Cambridge, MA: Harvard University Press, 1961), pp. 129–31, 153–57, 175–79. On Safran see Chapter 7, note 35. The downgrading of Husayn can be found in the book by the Islamist Anwar al-Jundi, *Taha Husayn fi mizan al-Islam*/T. Husayn in the Balance of Islam (Cairo: Dar al-I'tisam, 1977). On al-Jundi see Chapter 8.
19 See the major book by John Waterbury, *The Egypt of Nasser and Sadat. The Political Economy of Two Regimes* (Princeton, NJ: Princeton University Press, 1983), in particular pp. 93–100. See also the book by Alan Richards and John Waterbury, *A Political Economy of the Middle East*, 2nd edn (Boulder, CO: Westview Press, 1996), chapter 14 on "Is Islam the Solution?."
20 On the Muslim Brotherhood see the seminal work by Richard Mitchell, *The Society of the Muslim Brothers* (London: Oxford University Press, 1969). On Sayyid Qutb see Roxanne L. Euben, *Enemy in the Mirror. Islamic Fundamentalism and the Limits of Modern Rationalism* (Princton, NJ: Princeton University Press, 1999), chapter 3. On contemporary Islamic fundamentalism see B. Tibi, *The Challenge of Fundamentalism. Political Islam and the New World Disorder* (Berkeley and Los Angeles, CA: University of California Press, 1998, updated edn 2002).
21 For a critique see B. Tibi, "Habermas and the Return of the Sacred. Is it a Religious Renaissance? A Pronouncement of a 'Post-Secular Society', or the Emergence of a Political Religion as a New Totalitarianism?," in: *Religion-Staat-Gesellschaft*, 3, 2 (2002), pp. 265–69.
22 On the cultural aspect see Moshe Piamenta, *Islam in Everyday Arabic Speech* (Leiden: Brill, 1979); see the work of the anthropologist Charles Lindholm, *The Islamic Middle East. An Historical Anthropology* (Oxford: Blackwell, 1996).
23 Louis J. Cantori, "Religion and Politics in Egypt," in Michael Curtis, ed., *Religion and Politics in the Middle East* (Boulder, CO: Westview Press, 1981), pp. 77–90. On the history of Egypt and with regard to Islam there, see P. J. Vatikiotis, *The Modern History of Egypt*, 2nd printing (London: Weidenfeld and Nicolson, 1976) especially pp. 13ff., 176ff., and 413ff.
24 See the references in notes 8 and 9 above and also the older, still worth reading contribution of Henry Dodwell, *The Founder of Modern Egypt: A Study of Muhammad Ali*, reprint of the 1931 edn (London: Cambridge University Press, 1967).
25 On the cultural background of this era, see Ibrahim Abu-Lughod, *Arab Rediscovery of Europe* (referenced in note 7) and also the interpretation by B. Tibi, *Arab Nationalism. Between Islam and the Nation-State* (London and New York: Macmillan and St. Martin's Press, 1997) 3rd enlarged edn.
26 Nadav Safran, *Egypt in Search* (referenced in note 18), p. 85.
27 Ibid., p. 179.
28 On the "Free Officers" see also B. Tibi, *Militär und Sozialismus in der Dritten Welt* (Frankfurt/Main: Suhrkamp, 1973), chapter 3.
29 See Amos Perlmutter, *Egypt. The Praetorian State* (New Brunswick, NJ: Transaction Books, 1974). The concept of praetorianism is adopted from Samuel P. Huntington, *Political Order in Changing Society* (New Haven: Yale University Press, 1968), chapter 4.
30 Among the many recent studies on Egypt is Carrie Rosefsky-Wickham, *Mobilizing Islam. Religion, Activism and Political Change in Egypt* (New York: Columbia University Press, 2002). I do not share the positive views on political Islam included in this book.

This applies even more to the questionable book by R. W. Baker (referenced in note 49). The reversal of Orientalism by the contemporary US Middle East studies establishment to an "Orientalism in Reverse," in the footsteps of Edward Said, seems to end up by embracing political Islam and overlooking its totalitarianism.

31 Fouad Ajami, "In the Pharaoh's Shadow: Religion and Authority in Egypt," in: James P. Piscatori, ed., *Islam in the Political Process* (Cambridge: Cambridge University Press, 1983) pp. 12–35, particular p. 13. See also Ajami's book, *The Arab Predicament. Arab Political Thought and Practice since 1967* (Cambridge: Cambridge University Press, 1981), which has enjoyed an unusually broad reception and has been reprinted a dozen times.

32 Fouad Ajami, "In the Pharaoh's Shadow," (referenced in note 31), pp. 30f.

33 B. Tibi, *Islam and the Cultural Accommodation of Social Change* (Boulder, CO: Westview Press, 1990, reprinted 1991).

34 See the chapter "Religious Organization: The Mosque and Governmental Policy," in Morroe Berger, *Islam in Egypt Today. Social and Political Aspects of Popular Religion* (Cambridge: Cambridge University Press, 1970) pp. 9ff.

35 See his authoritative book Mahmud Shaltut, *al-Islam Aqida wa Shari'a/* Islam, Faith and Law, 10th printing (Cairo and Beirut: al-Shuruq, 1980).

36 See the characterization by Ajami, "In the Pharaoh's Shadow," (referenced in note 31), pp. 14ff. The Salafi views of Abdulhalim Mahmud are reflected in his book *al-Jihad wa al-nasr/*Jihad and Victory (Cairo: al-Kitab al-Arabi, 1968).

37 On this issue see the reference in note 10 above, as well as B. Tibi, *Islam between Culture and Politics* (New York: Palgrave, 2001; expanded new edn 2005), chapter 2, pp. 53–68.

38 Political Islam in Algeria is partly an import from Egypt; see Michael Willis, *The Islamist Challenge in Algeria. A Political History* (New York: New York University Press, 1996).

39 Hala Mastafa, *al-Dawla wa al-Harakat al-Islamiyya al-mu'arida bain al-muhadana wa al-muwajaha/*The State and the Islamist Opposition between Truce and Confrontation (Cairo: Kitab al-Mahrusah, 1995). Though she reads Arabic, Rosefsky-Wickham in her book (referenced in note 30) fails to quote the work of Hala Mustafa, probably because she does not share her critical assessment of political Islam as a "mobilizing Islam."

40 On the double function (i.e. religious and political) and on the meaning and role of Imam in Islamic history see B. Tibi, *Der wahre Imam. Der Islam von Mohammed bis zur Gegenwart*, new edn (Munich: Piper Verlag, 1996), reprinted 1997, 1998 and 2001.

41 Berger, *Islam in Egypt Today* (referenced in note 34), pp. 127ff. See also the section on this in Tibi, *Militär und Sozialismus* (referenced in note 28), pp. 211ff.

42 See the references in note 19 and John Waterbury, "Egypt: Islam and Social Change," in Philip H. Stoddard et al. (eds.), *Change and the Muslim World* (Syracuse, NJ: Syracuse University Press, 1981) pp. 49–58.

43 See the reference in note 15.

44 Hamid N. Ansari, "The Islamic Militants in Egyptian Politics," *International Journal of Middle East Studies*, 16 (1984), pp. 124–44, particularly pp. 127–29, and also Barry M. Rubin, *Islamic Fundamentalism in Egyptian Politics* (London: Macmillan, 1990); Gilles Kepel, *Le Prophète et Pharaon. Les Mouvements Islamists dans l'Egypt Contemporaine* (Paris: Éditions La Découverte, 1984).

45 On this organization see Nimatullah Junainah, *Tanzim al-Jihad/*The Organisation al-Jihad (Cairo: Dar al-Hurriya, 1988). See also Adel Hammudah, *Qanabil wa masahif. Qissat tanzim al-Jihad/*Bombs and Holy Books. The Story of al-Jihad (Cairo: Sina Press, 1985).

46 See Abdulazim Ramadan, *Jama'at al-Takfir fi misr/*The Groups of Religious Othering (or excommunication) in Egypt (Cairo: al-Hai'a al-Misriyya, 1995).

47 Mark Juergensmeyer, *Terror in the Mind of God. The Global Rise of Religious Violence* (Berkeley, CA: University of California Press, 2000), Chapter 4 on Islamic jihad terrorism.

48 On Jihadism as a new pattern of an irregular war see B. Tibi, "The Totalitarianism of Jihadist Islamism," in: *Totalitarian Movements and Political Religions*, 8, 1 (2007), pp. 33–54, and also note 50.

49 See the reference in note 30 and the very distortive study by Raymond William Baker, *Islam without Fear. Egypt and the New Islamists* (Cambridge, MA: Harvard University Press, 2003).

50 See the reference in note 48 and most recently B. Tibi, *Political Islam, World Politics and Europe. Democratic Peace and Euro-Islam vs Global Jihad* (New York: Routledge, 2008), chapter 1.

51 Anwar al-Sadat, *Geheimtagebuch der ägyptischen Revolution* (Düsseldorf and Cologne: Verlag Eugen Diederichs, 1957), pp. 44ff., where he gives an account of his meeting with Hasan al-Banna, founder of the Muslim Brothers. During his reign in the aftermath of Nasser's death, Sadat "enjoyed good relations with much of the Islamic movement for at least the first half decade of his rule … Sadat released many *ikhwan* leaders (Muslim brothers) from prison … , and allowed them to preach and organize." Reported by Raymond A. Hinnebusch, *Egyptian Politics Under Sadat. The Post-Populist Development of an Authoritarian-Modernizing State*, 2nd edn (Boulder, CO: Lynnef Rienner Publishers, 1988) p. 206. There is an English translation of some of al-Banna's tracts by Charles Wendell, ed., *Five Tracts of Hassan al-Banna (1906–1949)* (Berkeley and Los Angeles, CA: University of California Press, 1978); see also the master work of Mitchell, *The Society of the Muslim Brothers* (referenced in note 20 above).

52 On the universal claims of the Iranian revolution and its potential to be exported into other Islamic countries see B. Tibi, "The Iranian Revolution and the Arabs," *Arab Studies Quarterly*, 8, 1 (1986), pp. 29–44; and more detailed B. Tibi, "The Failed Export of Islamic Revolution into the Arab World," in: Frédéric Grare, ed., *Islamism and Security* (Geneva: The Graduate Institute of International Studies PSIS, No. 4, 1999) pp. 63–102.

53 See the questionable contributions by Olivier Roy, *The Failure of Political Islam* (Cambridge, MA: Harvard University Press, 1994) and Gilles Kepel, *Jihad. Expansion et declin de l'Isalmisme* (Paris: Gallimard, 2000).

54 On the Six Day War of 1967 and the repercussions of Arab defeat see my book *Conflict and War in the Middle East* (referenced in note 11).

55 On these spillover effects of the Islamic Revolution in the Maghreb see Francois Burgat and William Dowell, *The Islamic Movement in North Africa* (Austin, TX: University of Texas Press, 1993).

56 This was repeated from Cairo by the *New York Times* correspondent M. Slackman in *International Herald Tribune* in many articles in August 2006.

57 For more details on the cultural responses see, first, on Islamic modernism, see Charles C. Adams, *Islam and Modernism in Egypt*, reprint of 1933 edn (London: Oxford University Press, 2002) and second, on liberalism, Afaf al-Sayyid-Marsot, *Egypt's Liberal Experiment, 1922–1936* (Berkeley, CA: University of California Press, 1977); see also Nadav Safran, *Egypt in Search* (referenced in note 18).

58 See Morroe Berger, *Islam in Egypt Today* (referenced in note 34), pp. 128ff.; See also Daniel Crecelius, "al-Azhar in the Revolution," *The Middle East Journal*, 20 (1966), pp. 31–49.

59 Michael Fisher, *Iran. From Religious Dispute to Revolution* (Cambridge, MA: Harvard University Press, 1980).

60 See also Michael Gilsenan, *Saint and Sufi in Modern Egypt: An Essay in the Sociology of Religion* (Oxford: Clarendon Press, 1973).

61 See B. Tibi, *Arab Nationalism. Between Islam and the Nation-State* (referenced in note 12). On the repoliticization see B. Tibi, "The Renewed Role of Islam in the Political and Social Development of the Middle East," *The Middle East Journal*, 37 (1983), pp. 3–13 and also my new book *Political Islam, World Politics and Europe* (referenced in note 50).

62 Zalmy Khalilzadeh and Cheryl Bernard, *The Government of God. Iran's Islamic Republic* (New York: Columbia University Press, 1984).

63 See note 11 and Fouad Ajami, *The Arab Predicament* (note 31). See also B. Tibi, *Political Islam, World Politics and Europe* (referenced in note 50).

64 The source of *Hakimiyyat Allah* is the work of Sayyid Qutb.

65 See Saad Eddin Ibrahim, *Egypt, Islam and Democracy* (Cairo: American University of Cairo Press, 1996) and also his earlier article "Anatomy of Egypt's Militant Islamic Groups. Methodological Note and Preliminary Findings," *International Journal of Middle East Studies*, 12 (1980), pp. 423–53. In 1983, Ibrahim and I were among the founding members of the Arab Organization for the Defense of Human Rights. In the years between 1982 and 1996, I discussed with Ibrahim in Cairo many of the pending issues and spoke in his American University of Cairo classes on "The crisis of modern Islam" (see note 5). Under the rule of Mubarak, Ibrahim was jailed and then sentenced; however, he was acquitted and released as a result of international pressure, in particular from the US, as he is an Egyptian who enjoys the protection of US citizenship. Ibrahim has been however repeatedly outlawed.

66 See the chapter on Egypt in Michael Hudson, *Arab Politics. The Search for Legitimacy* (New Haven, CT: Yale University Press, 1979), pp. 126–62. On the growth of Cairo see the impressive survey by Janet Abu-Lughod, *Cairo: One Thousand-One Years of the City Victorious* (Princeton, NJ: Princeton University Press, 1971); also worth reading is the chapter on Cairo in John Waterbury, *Egypt. Burdens of the Past, Options for the Future* (Bloomington, IN: Indiana University Press, 1978), pp. 125ff., with maps and illustrations.

67 Carrie Rosefsky-Wickham, *Mobilizing Islam* (referenced in note 30).

68 On the concept of "anomie" developed by Emile Durckheim and on its extension to include "cultural anomie" in Islamic civilization, see B. Tibi, *The Crisis of Modern Islam* (referenced in note 5), pp. 52ff.

69 On he *Lumpen* intelligenstia in Egypt resulting from this development, see Carrie Rosefsky-Wickham, *Mobilizing Islam* (note 30), Chapter 3.

70 B. Tibi, "The Worldview of Sunni Arab Fundamentalists" (referenced in note 10).

71 Saad Eddin Ibrahim, "Anatomy of Egypt's Militant Islamic Groups," (referenced in note 65), p. 448.

72 On the Sadat assassin al-Islambuli see Rifa'at S. Ahmed, *al-Islambuli. Ru'yat jadida li tanzim al-jihad*/al-Islambuli. A New View on the Organization of Jihad (Cairo: Madbuli, 1988).

73 On the counter-elites, see B. Tibi, "The Fundamentalist Challenge to the Secular Order in the Middle East," in: *The Fletcher Forum of World Affairs*, 23(1) (1999), pp. 191–210.

74 Fouad Ajami, "In the Pharaoh's Shadow" (referenced in note 31), p. 14. The present Sheykh of al-Azhar, Sayyid al-Tantawi is much weaker than his predecessors; the Islamists are presently undermining his authority in his own institution.

75 Tariq al-Bishri, *al-Muslimun wa al-aqbat fi itar al-jama'a al-watiniyya*/Muslims and Copts Within the National Community (Cairo: al-Hay'a al-Misriyya, 1980), a comprehensive (761 pp.), source-based, but biased, account.

76 See the volume published by the Ibn Khaldun Center: Saad Eddin Ibrahim, ed., *Humum al-Aqaliyyat, fi al-Watan al-Arabi*/The Concerns of Minorities in the Arab World (Cairo: Ibn Khaldun Center, 1994). Pursuant to this addressing of the hot issue of minorities, which touches on a theme that is taboo in Egypt, the Ibn Khaldun Center was closed and Ibrahim was jailed (see note 65 above).

77 See Brenkman, *The Cultural Contradiction* (referenced in note 6) and Hamid Ansari, "Sectarian Conflict in Egypt and the Political Expediency of Religion," *The Middle East Journal*, 38 (1984), pp. 397–418.

78 Raymond A. Hinnebusch, "Children of the Elite: Political Attitudes of the Westernized Bourgeoisie in Contemporary Egypt," *The Middle East Journal*, 36 (1982), pp. 535–61.

79 See the references in notes 30 and 39 above.
80 Robert Hefner, *Civil Islam. Muslims and Democratization in Indonesia* (Princeton, NJ: Princeton University Press 2000).
81 Daniel Crecelius, "Non-Ideological Responses of the Egyptian Ulama to Modernization," in Nikki R. Keddie, ed., *Scholars, Saints and Sufis: Muslim Religious Institutions in the Middle East Since 1500* (Berkeley and Los Angeles, CA: University of California Press, 1972) pp. 167ff., particularly p. 185; see also Crecelius, "al-Azhar in the Revolution" (referenced in note 59).
82 B. Tibi, *Islam and the Cultural Accommodation of Social Change* (see note 33 above).
83 Daniel Crecelius, "Non-Ideological Responses," p. 208 (referenced in note 81); and by the same author: "The Course of Secularization in Modern Egypt," in: John L. Esposito, ed., *Islam and Development. Religion and Sociopolitical Change* (Syracuse, NY: Syracuse University Press, 1980), pp. 49ff.
84 The two volumes *Bayan li al-Nas*/Declaration to Humanity (Cairo: Matba'at al-Azhar, 1984 and 1988) were authored and edited by the al-Azhar Sheykh Jadul-Haq 'Ali Jadul-Haq. On bid'a, see vol. 2, pp. 176ff., in particular p. 180, against the abuse of this notion of innovation in Islam.
85 Nasr Hamid Abu-Zaid, *al-Tafkir fi asr al-takfir*/ Reasoning in the Age of Accusation of Heresy, 2nd edn (Cairo: Madbuli, 1995), see also his book *Naqd al-Khitab al-din*/Critique of Religious Discourse (Cairo: Madbuli, 1995), 2nd edn, with a documentary.
86 On Abu Zaid's work and his case see B. Tibi, *Fundamentalismus im Islam*, 3rd edn (Darmstadt: Primus Verlag, 2002), here chapter 7.
87 Nazih Ayubi, *Political Islam. Religion and Politics in the Arab World* (London: Routledge, 1991). See also B. Tibi, *The Challenge of Fundamentalism* (referenced in note 20). The book by Eberhard Kienle, *A Grand Illusion. Democracy and Economic Reform in Egypt* (London: Tauris, 2000) is worth reading.
88 UNDP, *Arab Human Development Report* (New York: United Nations, 2002), see also the report of 2003.
89 Raymond W. Baker, *Islam without Fear* (referenced in note 49).
90 See Israel Gershoni and James P. Jankowski, *Egypt, Islam and the Arabs. The Search for Egyptian Nationhood, 1900–1930* (New York: Oxford University Press, 1986) and Joseph P. Lorenz, *Egypt and the Arabs. Foreign Policy and the Search for National Identity* (Boulder, CO: Westview Press, 1990).

Chapter 10

1 This chapter is based on my work accomplished in Abu Dhabi at the Emirates Center for Strategic Studies and Research/ECSSR in 2004 as well as on other Gulf experiences in Kuwait and Bahrain. In Abu Dhabi I engaged in a project within the framework of the 9th Annual Conference of ECSSR. The findings were published in 2 volumes respectively in Arabic and English. The reference to the English volume is: ECSSR, ed., *The Gulf: Challenges of the Future* (Abu Dhabi: ECSSR Press, 2004). My research paper is included there as chapter 17 on pp. 313–30. The other volume in Arabic is also published in Abu Dhabi under the title: *al-Khalij. Tadadiyyat al-Mustaqbal* (my paper in Arabic is on pp. 351–70).
2 See Barrie Axford, *The Global System. Economics, Politics and Culture* (New York: St. Martin's Press, 1995), see also the book by Roland Robertson, *Globalization. Social Theory and Global Culture* (London: Sage, 1992; reprinted 1998), in which chapter 2 is on "The Cultural Turn," however, used and discussed with a different meaning from this chapter.
3 The Middle East is a subsystem of the international system. It is composed of three regions (the most important of which is the Gulf of Arabia); for more details see B. Tibi, *Conflict and War in the Middle East. From Interstate War to New Security*, 2nd edn

(London: Macmillan Press, 1998), chapter 2, pp. 43–60. The other two regions are the Mashreq (Arab East) and the Maghreb (Arab West).

4 Hedley Bull, *The Anarchical Society: A Study of Order in World Politics* (New York: Columbia University Press, 1977), reprinted numerous times, p. 273.

5 On this simultaneity of globalization of structures and cultural fragmentation see B. Tibi, *Islam Between Culture and Politics* (New York: Palgrave 2001, second edn 2005), chapter 4.

6 On the concept of the culture of success (modernity) see Lawrence Harrison, *The Central Liberal Truth. How Politics Can Change a Culture and Save it from Itself* (New York: Oxford University Press, 2006), in particular chapters 3, 5, 6 and 8.

7 See chapter 5 in B. Tibi, *The Challenge of Fundamentalism. Political Islam and the New World Disorder* (Berkeley, CA: University of California Press, 1998, updated edn 2002), on the "Simultaneity of Structural Globalization and Cultural Fragmentation," and also the reference in note 5 above.

8 On the significance of the Arabian Gulf see Geoffrey Kemp, ed., *Powder Keg in the Middle East. The Struggle for Gulf Security* (Lanham, MD: Rowman & Littlefield, 1995), and also the monograph by F. Gregory Gause III, *Oil Monarchies. Challenges in the Arab Gulf States* (New York: Council of Foreign Affairs, 1994).

9 For a global perspective on democracy see David Held, *Democracy and Global Order. From the Modern State to Cosmopolitan Governance* (Stanford, CA: Stanford University Press, 1995), in particular the three chapters in Part 4. For a debate on the pertinence of this perspective to the world of Islam see the next note.

10 See chapter 7 in B. Tibi, *Political Islam, World Politics and Europe* (New York: Routledge, 2008), pp. 216–34, on democracy as "the solution."

11 See John Voll and John Esposito, *Islam and Democracy* (New York: Oxford University Press, 1996), and my critical review in *Journal of Religion*, 78, 4 (1998), pp. 667–68.

12 See the debate on this issue in Chapter 8 above and on the Arab-Turath/heritage debate see the contributions in: Center of Arab Unity Studies, ed., *al-Turath wa Tahadiyya al-asr fi al-Watan al-Arabi al-Asalah wa al-Mu'assarah*/The Heritage and the Contemporary Challenge in the Arab World. Authenticity and Modernity (Beirut: Center for Arab Unity Studies, 1985). The book by Mohammed Abed al-Jabri, *al-Turath wa hadatha* (Beirut: al-Markaz al Thaqafi, 1991) is a significant contribution of enlightenment.

13 See Franz Rosenthal, *The Classical Heritage of Islam* (New York: Routledge, 1994). See also Chapter 8 of the present book.

14 Michael Walzer, ed. and transl., *Al-Farabi on the Perfect State. Abu Nasr al-Farab: Mabadi ara' ahl al-madina al-fadila* (Oxford: Oxford University Press, 1985)

15 These wars are dealt with in the following books, first Anthony H. Cordesman and Abraham R. Wagner, *The Lessons of Modern War*, 4 volumes (Boulder, CO: Westview Press, 1990), vol. 2 on the Iran–Iraq War. On the Gulf War of 1991 see the 1998 second edition of B. Tibi, *Conflict and War* (referenced in note 3). See also Stanley A. Renshon, ed., *The Political Psychology of the Gulf War. Leaders, Publics, and the Process of Conflict* (Pittsburgh, PA: University of Pittsburgh Press, 1993), part 1: Origins.

16 On the claim of Iran to provide a model for the Middle East see Rouhollah K. Ramazani, *Revolutionary Iran. Challenge and Response in the Middle East* (Baltimore, MD: Johns Hopkins University Press, 1986), part 2 on the Gulf. See also B. Tibi, "The Failed Export of the Islamic Revolution into the Arab World," in: Frédéric Grare, ed., *Islamism and Security. Political Islam and the Western World* (Geneva: Programme for Strategic and International Security Studies, 1999).

17 Lawrence E. Harrison and Samuel P. Huntington, eds, *Culture Matters. How Values Shape Human Progress* (New York: Basic Books, 2000). See also the reference in note 6 and also the two volumes of the CMRP, edited by Lawrence Harrison *et al.*, *Developing Cultures* (New York: Routledge, 2006).

18 B. Tibi, "Democracy and Education in an Age of Islamism," in: Alan Olson *et al.*, eds, *Educating for Democracy* (Lanham, MD: Rowman & Littlefield, 2004), pp. 203–19.

19 B. Tibi, "The Interplay between Social and Cultural Change. The Case of Germany and the Middle East," in: Ibrahim M. Oweiss and George N. Atiyeh, eds, *Arab Civilization. Challenges and Responses. Studies in Honor of Constantine K. Zurayk*, (Albany, NY: State University of New York Press, 1988), pp. 166–82.

20 The reference is repeated, due to its significance: Juergen Habermas, *The Philosophical Discourse of Modernity. Twelve Lectures* (Cambridge, MA: MIT Press, 1987).

21 On this issue see the late reform Muslim Fazlur Rahman, *Islam and Modernity. Transformation of an Intellectual Tradition* (Chicago, IL: University of Chicago Press, 1982).

22 This conciliatory mindset is expressed by B. Tibi, "International Morality and Cross-Cultural Bridging," in: Roman Herzog and others, *Preventing the Clash of Civilizations. A Peace Strategy for the Twenty-First Century*, ed. by Henrik Schmiegelow (New York: St. Martin's Press, 1999), pp. 107–26.

23 See the old, but still relevant, study by Roy Licklider, *Political Power and the Arab Oil Weapon* (Berkeley, CA: University of California Press, 1988). On Gulf oil see the chapter by Paul Stevens, in: Gary G. Sick and Lawrence G. Potter, eds, *The Persian Gulf at the Millennium. Essays in Politics, Economy, Security, and Religion* (New York: St. Martin's Press, 1997), pp. 85–114.

24 On the Gulf during the Cold War see Aryeh Yadfat and Mordechai Abir, *In the Direction of the Gulf. The Soviet Union and the Persian Gulf* (London: Frank Cass, 1977). On a changed Gulf see F. Gregory Gause III, *Oil Monarchies. Challenges in the Arab Gulf States* (New York: Council on Foreign Relations Press, 1994).

25 My MESA paper of 1983 was published in: *Arab Journal Quarterly*, 8, 1 (Winter 1986), pp. 29–44. The ISA paper of 2001 was published in: *Millennium*, 29, 3 (2000), pp. 843–59.

26 On this dictatorship extinguished by the Iraq War of 2003 see Said K. Aburish, *Saddam Hussein. The Politics of Revenge* (New York: Bloomsbury, 2000), and on Iraq after the so-called "liberation" see Daniel Byman and Kenneth Pollack, *Things Fall Apart. Containing the Spillover from an Iraqi Civil War* (Washington, DC: The Brookings Institution, 2007).

27 On this issue see chapter 8 on education in: B. Tibi, *Islam between Culture and Politics* (referenced in note 5), pp. 167–85, see also the reference in note 18.

28 See Mohammed Shahrur, *al-Kitab wa al-Qur'an. Qira'a Mu'asira*/The book and the Qur'an: a Modern Reading (Beirut: Sharikat al-Matbu'at, 6th edn 2000), in particular, on the separation between religion and politics, pp. 719–23.

29 John Waterbury, *The Commander of the Faithful. The Moroccan Political Elite. A Study in Segmented Politics* (New York: Columbia University Press, 1970), p. 5.

30 We also find this recommendation in: Mohammed Abed al-Jabri, *Arab Islamic Philosophy. A Contemporary Critique* (Austin, TX: Center for Middle Eastern Studies, 1999).

31 On these counter-elites see B. Tibi, "The Fundamentalist Challenge to the Secular Order the Middle East," in: *Fletcher Forum of World Affairs*, 23, 1 (Winter/Spring, 1999), pp. 191–210.

32 For instance, Shahrur on the separation between religion and politics, as quoted in note 28 above.

33 Qur'an sura 4, verse 34, *al-rijal qawamun ala al-nisa*/Men are superior to women. Student of Islam Barbara F. Stowasser, *Women in the Qur'an. Traditions and Interpretations* (New York: Oxford University Press, 1994) provides a useful overview.

34 On this concept in Indonesia see Robert W. Hefner, *Civil Islam. Muslims and Democratization in Indonesia.* (Princeton, NJ: Princeton University Press, 2000).

35 See the reference in note 22 above and also the chapter on civilization and dialogue in my book *Islam between Culture and Politics* (referenced in note 25 above), pp. 210–30.

Chapter 11

1 My life work has been guided and shaped by my cross-cultural biography as a Muslim torn between cultural modernity and the tradition in the cultural system of Islam, as outlined in the introduction to this book; see also my earlier book: *Islam and the Cultural Accommodaton of Social Change* (Boulder, CO: Westview 1990 and 1991).

2 B. Tibi, "The Islamic Dream of Semi-Modernity," in: *India International Centre Quarterly* (Spring 1995), pp.79–85.

3 Jürgen Habermas, *The Philosophical Discourse of Modernity* (Cambridge, MA: MIT Press, 1987).

4 The references to Reinhard Bendix can be found in Chapter 1, notes 91 and 92.

5 Bruce Lawrence, *Defenders of God. The Fundamentalist Revolt against the Modern Age* (San Francisco, CA: Harper and Raw, 1989).

6 An example of semi-modernity is the use of the internet in the service of jihad see: Gary Bunt, *Islam in the Digital Age: E-Jihad, Online Fatwas and Cyber Islamic Environments* (London: Pluto, 2003); see also the work of Gabriel Weihman, "Terror Online: How Terrorists use the Internet," in: Katharina von Knop und Martin van Creveld, eds, *Countering Modern Terrorism* (Bielefeld: Bertelsmann, 2005), pp. 87–109.

7 The essay by Hedley Bull on "The Revolt against the West" has been referred to and referenced repeatedly in this book.

8 Jürgen Habermas, *Glauben und Wissen* (Frankfurt/Main: Suhrkamp, 2001) and critically B. Tibi, "Habermas and the Return of the Sacred. Is it a Religious Renaissance? The Pronouncement of a 'Post-Secular Society', or the Emergence of Political Religion as a New Totalitarianism?," in: *Religion-Staat-Gesellschaft*, 3, 2 (2002), pp. 265–97.

9 B. Tibi, "The Totalitarianism of Jihadist Islamism," in: *Totalitarian Movements and Political Religions*, 8, 1 (2007), p. 35–54.

10 Roger Griffin, *Modernism and Fascism* (London: Palgrave, 2007), see also Jeffrey Herf, *Reactionary Modernism. Technology, Culture and Politics in Weimar and the Third Reich* (New York: Cambridge University Press, 1984).

11 Albert Hourani, *Arabic Thought in the Liberal Age 1789–1939* (London: Oxford University Press, 1962). The late Hourani was a respected scholar; however, he was known to be evasive on all hot issues, with the intent of getting along with the rival parties, often at the expense of the pending issues.

12 The book by E. Sivan, *Militant Islam. Modern Politics and Medieval Theology* (New Haven, CT: Yale University Press, 1985), is outdated, but it still continues to raise the right question expressed in its subtitle.

13 John Brenkman, *The Cultural Contradiction of Democracy. Political Thought since September 11* (Princeton, NJ: Princeton University Press, 2007), p. 164.

14 Sayyid Qutb, *al-Salam al-Alami wa al-Islam*/World Peace and Islam, reprint (Cairo: al-Shuruq, 10th legal printing, 1992). For an analysis of this Sunni internationalism combined with rich references see B. Tibi, *Political Islam, World Politics and Europe* (New York: Routledge, 2008), chapter 3.

15 See chapter 4 on Iran in my book referenced in note 14, and Ray Takeyh, *Hidden Iran. Paradox and Power in the Islamic Republic* (New York: Times Books, 2006).

16 There are competing Sunni and Shi'i internationalisms; for more details see B. Tibi, *Political Islam* (note 14), chapters 3 and 4.

17 Critical reference to Mohammed Arkoun has been made earlier in this book. See Chapter 7, note 51.

18 Robert Lee, *Overcoming Tradition and Modernity. The Search for Islamic Authenticity* (Boulder, CO: Westview Press, 1997), p. 194.

19 Leslie Lipson, *The Ethical Crisis of Civilization* (London: Sage, 1993), p. 62.

20 Ibid., p. 63.

21 Franz Rosenthal, *The Classical Heritage of Islam* (London: Routledge, 1975).

22 Mohammed A. al-Jabri, *Arab Islamic Philosophy* (Austin, TX: CMES, 1999).
23 Hassan al-Sharqawi, *al-Muslimun 'Ulama wa Hukama*/Muslims as Scholars and Wise Men (Cairo, 1987), p. 12.
24 John Kelsay, *Islam and War. A Study in Comparative Ethics* (Louisville, KY: John Knox Press, 1993), p. 26.
25 Mohammed Shahrur is a courageous Muslim thinker, but his work is contaminated through his cooperation with the Syrian Ba'ath-regime.
26 Charles Kurzman, ed., *Liberal Islam* (New York: Oxford University Press, 1998).
27 See my chapter: "Religious Extremism, or Religionization of Politics?," in: Hillel Frisch and Efraim Imber, eds, *Radical Islam and International Security* (New York: Routledge, 2008), pp. 11–37.
28 See my chapter on this subject in Martin Marty and Scott Appleby, eds, *Fundamentalisms and Society* (Chicago, IL: The University of Chicago Press, 1993), pp. 73–102.
29 When reading Armanda Salvatore, *Islam and the Political Discourse of Modernity* (Reading: Ithaca Press, 1997), one gets the impression that some Western sociologists are a hopeless case and will never understand Islam's predicament with modernity, but I continue to be hopeful.

Bibliography

Abdelraziq, Ali, *al-Islam wa usul al-hukm*/Islam and Patterns of Government (Cairo: 1925; reprinted Beirut: Maktabat al-Hayat, 1966).

Abduh, Mohammed, *al-Islam wa al-Nasraniyya bain al-ilm wa al-madaniyya*/Islam and Christianity between Science and Civilization, new printing (Cairo: Dar al-Hadatha, 1983).

Abdulrahman, Abdullahi, *Sultat an-nas. Dirasat fi tawzif an-nas ad-dini*/The authority of the Text. Studies in the Instrumentalization of Religious Texts (Casablanca: al-Markaz al-Thaqafi, 1993).

Abdul-Salam, Faruq, *al-Ahzab al-Siyasiyya wa al-fasl bin al-din wa al-dawla*/Political Parties and the Separation between Religion and the State (Cairo: Qaliyub, 1979).

Abu-Lughod, Ibrahim, *The Arab Rediscovery of Europe* (Princeton, NJ: Princeton University Press, 1963).

Abu-Lughod, Janet, *Cairo: One Thousand-One Years of the City Victorious* (Princeton, NJ: Princeton University Press, 1971).

Aburish, Said K., *Saddam Hussein. The Politics of Revenge* (New York: Bloomsbury, 2000).

Abu-Zaid, Nasr Hamid, *Naqd al-Khitab al-din*/Critique of Religious Discourse (Cairo: Madbuli, 1995).

—, *al-Tafkir fi asr al-takfir*/Reasoning in the Age of Accusation of Heresy (Cairo: Madbuli, 1995).

—, *an-Nas, al-Sultah, al-haqiqa*/The Text, the Authority, the Truth (Casablanca: al-Markaz al-Thaqafi, 1995).

Adams, Charles C., *Islam and Modernism in Egypt: A Study of the Modern Reform Movement*, 2nd printing (London: 1968, first published in 1933).

Adamson Peter, and Richard Taylor, eds, *The Cambridge Companion to Arabic Philosophy* (Cambridge: Cambridge University Press, 2005).

Afghani, Sayyid Jamal ad-Din al-, *al-A'mal al-Kamilah*/Collected Works, edited by Mohammed Imara (Cario: Dar al-Katib al-Arabi, 1968).

Ahmed, Akbar S., *Postmodernism and Islam. Predicament and Promise* (London: Routledge, 1992, reprinted 2004).

—, *Journey into Islam. The Crisis of Globalization* (Washington, DC: The Brookings Institution Press, 2007).

Ahmed, Akbar S. and Hastings Donnan, eds, *Islam, Globalization and Postmodernity* (London: Routledge, 1994).

Ahmed, Rifa'at S., *al-Islambuli. Ru'yah jadida li tanzim al-jihad*/al-Islambuli. A New View on the Organization of Jihad (Cairo: Madbuli, 1988).

Ajami, Fouad, *The Arab Predicament. Arab Political Thought and Practice since 1967* (Cambridge: Cambridge University Press, 1981).

—, "In the Pharaoh's Shadow: Religion and Authority in Egypt," in: James P. Piscatori, ed., *Islam in the Political Process* (Cambridge: Cambridge University Press, 1983) pp. 12–35.

—, *The Dream Palace of the Arabs* (New York: Random House, 1999).

Akbarzadeh, Shahram, ed., *Islam and Globalization* (London and New York: Routledge, 2006).

—, and Fethi Mansouri, eds, *Islamic Radicalism and its Opponents in Muslim Homelands and the West* (London: Tauris, 2007).

Akehurst, Michael, *A Modern Introduction to International Law*, 6th edn (London: Unwin Hyman, 1987).

Albrow, Martin and Elisabeth King, eds, *Globalization, Knowledge and Society: Readings from International Sociology* (London: Sage Publications, 1990).

Ali, Mukti, "Islam and Indonesian Culture," in: Mourad Wahba, ed., *The First International Islamic Philosophy Conference on Islam and Civilization* (Cairo: 'Ain Shams University Press, 1982), pp. 15–34.

Ali-Yassin, Bu, *al-Thaluth al-muharram*/The Triple Taboo (Beirut: al-Tari'a, 1973).

Alwan, Abdullah N., *Ma'alim al-hadara fi al-Islam*/The Characteristics of the Civilization of Islam (Zarqa, Jordan: Maktabat al-Manar, 1984).

Anderson, Benedict, *Imagined Communities* (London: Verso, rev. edn, 1991).

Anderson, Liam and Gareth Stansfield, *The Future of Iraq* (New York: Palgrave, 2004).

Anderson, Norman, *Law Reform in the Muslim World* (London, 1976).

Anheier, Helmut and Y. Raj Isar, *Culture and Globalization Series*, 2 vols (London: Sage, 2007).

An-Na'im, Abdullahi A., *Toward an Islamic Reformation. Civil Liberties, Human Rights, and International Law* (Syracuse, NY: Syracuse University Press 1990).

—, *Islam and the Secular State. Negotiating the Future of Shari'a* (Cambridge, MA: Harvard University Press, 2008).

—, and Francis Deng, eds, *Human Rights. Cross-Cultural Perspectives* (Washington, DC: The Brookings Institution, 1990).

Ansari, Hamid N., "Sectarian Conflict in Egypt and the Political Expediency of Religion," *The Middle East Journal*, 38 (1984), pp. 397–418.

—, "The Islamic Militants in Egyptian Politics," *International Journal of Middle East Studies*, 16 (1984), pp. 124–44.

Apter, David, *The Politics of Modernization* (Chicago, IL: University of Chicago Press, 1965).

—, *Rethinking Development* (London: Sage, 1987).

Arendt, Hannah, *Vita activa* (Munich: Piper, 1960).

—, *The Origins of Totalitarianism* (New York, many reprints, here: Harcourt Broce & Co., 1975).

Aristoteles, *Politik*, translation with comments and notes by Eugen Rolfers (Hamburg: Felix Meiner, 1958).

Arkoun, Mohammed, *Rethinking Islam. Common Questions, Common Answers* (Boulder, CO: Westview Press, 1994).

——, *Islam to Reform or to Subvert* (London: Saqi, 2006).

Armanazi, Najib, *al-Shar' al-duwali fi al-Islam*/International Law in Islam (London: El-Rayyes, 1990).

Arslan, Emir Shakib, *Limadha ta'akhara al-Muslimun wa taqadamma ghairahum*/Why are Muslims backward, while others have progressed? (Beirut: Maktabat al-Hayat, reprint 1965).

Asante, Molefi Kete and William B. Gudykunst, eds, *Handbook of International and Inter-cultural Communication* (London: Sage Publications, 1989).

Ashmawi, Muslim Mohammed Said al-, *Usul al-Shari'a/*The Origins of Shari'a (Cairo: Madbuli, 1983).

——, *al-Islami al-Siyasi/*Political Islam (Cairo: Dar Sinah, 1987).

——, *al-Khilafah al-Islamiyya/*Islamic Caliphate (Cairo: Dar Sina, 1990).

Attas, Syed M. N. al-, *Islam, Secularism and the Philosophy of the Future* (London: Mansell, 1985).

Audi, Robert, *Religious Commitment and Secular Reason* (Cambridge: Cambridge University Press, 2000).

'Awwad, Jawdat Muhammad, *Hawl aslamat al-'ulum/*On the Islamization of Sciences (Cairo: al-Mukhtar, 1987).

'Awwa, Muhammad Salim al-, *Fi al-nizam al-siyasi lil-dawla al-Islamiyya/*On the Political System of the Islamic State (Cairo: al-Maktab al-Masri, 1983, 6th edn).

Azm, Sadik J. al-, *al-Naqd al-dhati ba'd al-hazima/*Self Criticism after the Defeat (Beirut: al-Tali'o, 1968).

——, *Naqd al-fikr al-dini/*Critique of Religious Thought (Beirut: Dar al-Tali'a, 1969).

——, "al-Istishraq wa al-Istishraq ma'kusan/Orientalism and Orientalism in Reverse," in: *Dhihniyyat al-Tahrim/*The Mentality of Taboos (London: Riad El-Rayyes Publ., 1992), pp. 17–85.

Axford, Barrie, *The Global System. Economics, Politics and Culture* (New York: St. Martin's Press, 1995).

Ayubi, Nazih, *Political Islam. Religion and Politics in the Arab World* (New York: Routledge, 1991).

Aziz, Abdul-Ghaffar *et al.*, *Man Qatala Faraj Fuda/*Who Killed Faraj Fuda? (Cairo: Dar al-'Ilm, 1992).

Baber, Johanson, "Politics and Scholarship: The Development of Islamic Studies in Germany," in: Tareq Ismael, ed., *Middle East Studies. International Perspectives on the State of the Art* (New York: Praeger, 1990), pp. 71–130.

Baker, Raymond, *Islam Without Fear. Egypt and the New Islamists* (Cambridge, MA: Harvard University Press, 2003).

Balandier, Georges, *Politische Anthropologie* (Munich: Nymphenburger, 1972).

Baran, Zeyno, *Hizb ut-Tahrur/*Islam's Political Insurgency (Washington, DC: The Nixon Center, 2004).

——, "Fighting the War of Ideas," *Foreign Affairs* (November–December 2005), pp. 68–78.

Barber, Benjamin, *Jihad vs. McWorld* (New York: Ballantine Books, 1995).

Bartlett, Robert, *The Making of Europe. Conquests, Colonization and Cultural Change* (Princeton, NJ: Princeton University Press, 1993).

Becker, C. H. *Islam-Studien*, 2 vols, reprint (Hildesheim: G. Olms, 1967).

Bell, Daniel, "The Return of the Sacred," in idem., *The Winding Passage 1960–1980* (New York: Basic Books, 1980).

Bell, Richard, *Introduction to the Qur'an*, revised by W. M. Watt (Edinburgh: Edinburgh University Press, 1977).

Bellah, Robert N., ed., *Religion and Progress in Modern Asia* (New York: Free Press, 1965).

Bendix, Reinhard, *Nation Building and Citizenship. Studies of our Changing Social Order*, new enlarged edn (Berkeley, CA: University of California Press, 1977).

Benz, Wolfgang and Juliane Wetzel, eds, *Antisemitismus und radikaler Islamismus* (Essen: Klartext, 2007).

Berger, Morroe, *Islam in Egypt Today. Social and Political Aspects of Popular Religion* (Cambridge: Cambridge University Press, 1970).

Berger, Peter, *Holy War Inc. Inside the Secret World of Osama Bin Laden* (New York: Free Press, 2001).

Berkes, Niyazi, *The Development of Secularism in Turkey* (New York: Routledge, new edn 1995).

Besier, Gerhard, ed., *Politische Religion und Religionspolitik* (Göttingen: Vandenhoek & Ruprecht, 2005).

Bishri, Tariq al-, *al-Muslimun wa al-aqbat fi itar al-jama'a al-watiniyya*/Muslims and Copts Within the National Community (Cairo: al-Hay'a al-Misriyya, 1980).

Blaut, J. M., *The Colonizer's Model of the World. Geographical Diffusionism and Eurocentric History* (New York: Guilford Press, 1993).

Bloch, Ernst, *Avicenna und die Aristotelische Linke* (Frankfurt/Main: Suhrkamp 1993).

Bluhm, Harald and Walter Reese-Schäfer, eds, *Die Intellektuellen und der Weltlauf* (Baden-Baden: Nomos, 2006).

Borkenau, Franz, *Der Uebergang vom feudalen zum bürgerlichen Weltbild* (reprint, Darmstadt: Wissenschaftliche Buchgesellschaft, 1982).

Boroujerdi, Mehzad, *Iranian Intellectuals and the West. The Tormented Triumph of Nativism* (Syracuse, NY: Syracuse University Press, 1996).

Borthwick, Bruce, "Religion and Politics in Israel and Egypt," *The Middle East Journal/MEJ*, 33, 2 (1979) pp. 145–63.

Brenkman, John, *The Cultural Contradiction of Democracy. Political Thought Since September 11* (Princeton, NJ: Princeton University Press, 2007).

Brett, Michael, ed., *Northern Africa: Islam and Modernization* (London: Frank Cass, 1973).

Brown, Michael *et al.*, ed., *Debating Democratic Peace* (Cambridge, MA: MIT Press 1996).

Brown, Peter, *The Rise of Western Christendom* (Oxford: Blackwell, 1996).

Bull, Hedley, *The Anarchical Society: A Study of Order in World Politics* (New York: Columbia University Press, 1977).

——, "The Revolt against the West," in: H. Bull and A. Watson, eds, *The Expansion of International Society* (Oxford: Clarendon Press, 1984), p. 217–28.

——, and Adam Watson, eds, *The Expansion of International Society* (Oxford: Clarendon Press, 1984).

Bunt, Gary, *Islam in the Digital Age: E-Jihad, Online Fatwas and Cyber Islamic Environments* (London: Pluto Press, 2003).

Burgat, Francois and William Dowell, *The Islamic Movement in North Africa* (Austin, TX: University of Texas Press, 1993).

Burr, Millard and Robert Collins, *Alms for Jihad. Charity and Terrorism in the Islamic World* (New York: Cambridge University Press, 2006).

Butterworth, Charles, ed., *The Political Aspects of Islamic Philosophy. Essays in Honor of Muhsin S. Mahdi*, Harvard Middle Eastern Monographs (Cambridge, MA: Harvard University Press, 1992).

Byman, Daniel and Kenneth Pollack, *Things Fall Apart. Containing the Spillover From an Iraqi Civil War* (Washington DC: The Brookings Institution, 2007).

Byrnes, Timothy and Peter Katzenstein, eds, *Religion in an Expanding Europe* (Cambridge: Cambridge University Press, 2006).

Cantori, Louis J., "Religion and Politics in Egypt," in: Michael Curtis, ed., *Religion and Politics in the Middle East* (Boulder, CO: Westview Press, 1981), pp. 77–90.

Centre for Arab Unity Studies/CAUS, ed., *Azmat al-democraqiyya fi al-watan al-'Arabi*/Crisis of Democracy in the Arab World (Beirut: CAUS-Press, 1983).

———, ed., *al-Turath wa Tahadiyya al-asr fi al-Watan al-Arabi al-Asalah wa al-Mu'assarah*/The Heritage and the Contemporary Challenge in the Arab World. Authenticity and Modernity (Beirut: Center for Arab Unity Studies, 1985).

Cerutti, Furio and Rodolfo Ragionieri, eds, *Identities and Conflicts. The Mediterranean* (New York: Palgrave, 2001)

Chittik, William, *The Sufi Path of Love. The Spiritual Teachings of Rumi* (Albany, NY: SUNY, 1983).

———, *Imaginal World Ibn al-Arabi and the Problem of Religious Diversity* (Albany, NY: SUNY, 1994).

Choueiri, Youssef M., *Islamic Fundamentalism* (Boston, MA: Twayne Publ., 1990).

Cleveland, William, *Islam against the West, Shakib Arslan and the Campaign for Islamic Nationalism* (Austin, TX: Texas University Press, 1985).

Cordesman, Anthony H. and Abraham R. Wagner, *The Lessons of Modern War*, 4 vols (Boulder, CO: Westview Press, 1990).

Coulson, N. J., "The Concept of Progress and Islamic Law," in Robert N. Bellah, ed., *Religion and Progress in Modern Asia* (New York, 1965), pp. 74–92.

———, *Conflicts and Tensions in Islamic Jurisprudence* (Chicago, 1969).

———, *A History of Islamic Law*, 3rd printing (Edinburgh: Edinburgh University Press, 1978).

———, and Norman Anderson, "Modernization: Islamic Law," in Michael Brett, ed., *Northern Africa: Islam and Modernization* (London, 1973), pp. 73–83.

Crecelius, Daniel, "al-Azhar in the Revolution," *The Middle East Journal*, 20 (1966), pp. 31–49.

———, "Non-Ideological Responses of the Egyptian Ulama to Modernization," in: Nikki R. Keddie, ed., *Scholars, Saints and Sufis: Muslim Religious Institutions in the Middle East Since 1500* (Berkeley and Los Angeles, CA: The University of California Press, 1972) pp. 167–210.

———, "The Course of Secularization in Modern Egypt," in: John L. Esposito, ed., *Islam and Development. Religion and Sociopolitical Change* (Syracuse, NY: Syracuse University Press, 1980), pp. 49–70.

Crone, Patricia, *Pre-Industrial Societies. Anatomy of the Pre-Modern World* (Oxford: Oneworld, 2003).

Curtin, Philip, *The World and the West. The European Challenge* (Cambridge: Cambridge University Press, 2000).

Curtis, Michael, ed., *Religion and Politics in the Middle East* (Boulder, CO: Westview Press, 1981).

Dalacoura, Katerina, *Islam, Liberalism and Human Rights* (London: Tauris, 1998).

Davidson, Andrew, *Secularism and Revivalism in Turkey* (New Haven, CT: Yale University Press, 1998).

Davidson, Herbert A., *Alfarabi, Avicenna and Averroes, on Intellect: Their Cosmologies, Theories of the Active Intellect and Theories of Human Intellect* (New York: Oxford University Press, 1992).

Davis, Joyce M., *Between Jihad and Salam. Profiles in Islam* (New York: St. Martin's Press, 1977).

Dawood, N. J., *The Koran* (London: Penguin Classics, 1986).

Demant, Peter, *Islam versus Islamism. The Dilemma of the Muslim World* (Westport, CT: Praeger, 2006).

Descartes, René, *Discours de la Méthode* (1637).

Dharif, Muhammad, *al-Islam al-siyasi fi al-watan al-arabi* (Casablanca: Maktabat al-Umma, 1992).

Dodwell, Henry, *The Founder of Modern Egypt: A Study of Muhammad Ali*, reprint of the 1931 edn (London: Cambridge University Press, 1967).

Donhue, John and John Esposito, eds, *Islam in Transition* (New York: Oxford University Press, 1982).

Donnelly, Jack, *Universal Human Rights in Theory and Practice* (Ithaca, NY and London: Cornell University Press, 1989).

Donner, Fred, *The Early Islamic Conquests* (Princeton, NJ: Princeton University Press, 1983).

Dwyer, Kevin, *Arab Voices. The Human Rights Debate in the Middle East* (Berkeley, CA: University of California Press, 1991).

ECSSR, ed., *The Gulf: Challenges of the Future* (Abu Dhabi: ECSSR Press, 2004).

Egger, Vernon, *A Fabian in Egypt. Salamah Musah and the Rise of the Professional Classes in Egypt 1909–1939* (Lanham, MD: University Press of America, 1986).

Eickelman, Dale and James Piscatori, *Islamic Politics* (Princeton, NJ: Princeton University Press, 1996).

Eisenstadt, Shmuel N., *Tradition, Wandel und Modernität* (Frankfurt/Main: Suhrkamp Verlag, 1979).

Elias, Norbert, *The Civilizing Process*, 2 vols (New York: Pantheon Books, 1978/1982).

Emerson, Michael, ed., *Democratization in the European Neighborhood* (Brussels: CEPS, 2005).

Enayat, Hamid, *Modern Islamic Political Thought* (Austin, TX: Texas University Press, 1982).

Esman, Milton and Itamar Rabinovich, eds, *Ethnicity, Pluralism and the State in the Middle East* (Ithaca, NY and London: Cornell University Press, 1988).

Esposito, John L., ed., *Islam and Development. Religion and Sociopolitical Change* (Syracuse, NY: Syracuse University Press, 1980).

——, *The Islamic Threat. Myth or Reality?* (New York: Oxford University Press, 1992).

——, and John O. Voll, *Islam and Democracy* (New York: Oxford University Press, 1996).

Esser, Josef, *Vorverständnis und Methodenwahl in der Rechtsfindung* (Frankfurt/Main: Athenäum Verlag, 1970).

Euben, Roxanne, *Enemy in the Mirror. Islamic Fundamentalism and the Limits of Modern Rationalism. A Work of Comparative Political Theory* (Princeton, NJ: Princeton University Press, 1999).

——, *Journeys to the Other Shore. Muslim and Western Travellers in Search of Knowledge* (Princeton, NJ: Princeton University Press, 2006).

Fadiman, James and Robert Frager, *Essential Sufism* (San Francisco: Harper Collins, 1997).

Faid, Zakariyya, *al-'Ilmaniyya: al-Nash'a wa al-athar fi al-sharq wa al-gharb*/Secularism: Its Origin and its Impact in the Orient and the West (Cairo: al-Zahra', 1977).

Falk, Richard, "Refocusing the Struggle for Human Rights in the Third World," *Harvard Human Rights Journal*, 4 (1991).

Fandy, Mamoun, *Saudi Arabia and the Politics of Dissent* (New York: Palgrave, 1999).

Farer, Tom J., "The UN and Human Rights: More than a Whimper, Less than a Roar," Adam Roberts and Benedict Kingsbury, eds, *United Nations, Divided World: The UN's Role in International Relations* (Oxford: The Clarendon Press, 1988), pp. 95–138.

Faruqi, Ismail R. al-, "Science and Traditional Values in Islamic Society," *Zygon*, 2, pp. 231–46.

Fetscher, Iring *et al.*, eds, *Pipers Handbuch der politischen Ideen*, 5 vols (Munich: Piper, 1987).

Finkielkraut, Alain, *La défaite de la pensée* (Paris: Gallimard, 1987).

Fisher, Michael, *Iran. From Religious Dispute to Revolution* (Cambridge, MA: Harvard University Press, 1980).

Forsythe, David P., *Human Rights and World Politics*, 2nd edn, revised (Lincoln, NE: University of Nebraska, 1989).

Freud, Sigmund, "Die Zukunft einer Illusion," in: Freud, *Werke vol. IX, Fragen der Gesellschaft. Ursprünge der Religion* (Frankfurt: S. Fischer, 1974).

Frisch, Hillel and Efraim Imber, eds, *Radical Islam and International Security* (New York: Routledge, 2008).

Fuda, Faraj, *Hiwar an al-ilmaniyya*/Dialogue on Secularism (Marrakesh: Dar Tainimel, 1992).

Fuller, Graham and Ian O. Lesser, *A Sense of Siege: The Geopolitics of Islam and the West* (Boulder, CO: Westview Press, 1995).

Gause, F. Gregory, III. *Oil Monarchies. Challenges in the Arab Gulf States* (New York: Council of Foreign Affairs, 1994).

Geertz, Clifford, *The Interpretation of Cultures* (New York: Basic Books, 1973).

Gellner, Ernest, *Postmodernism, Reason and Religion* (London: Routledge, 1992).

Gerges, Fawaz, *America and Political Islam. Clash of Cultures or Clash of Interests* (Cambridge: Cambridge University Press, 1999).

Gershoni, Israel and James P. Jankowski, *Egypt, Islam and the Arabs. The Search for Egyptian Nationhood, 1900–1930* (New York: Oxford University Press, 1986).

Ghazali, Mohammed al-, *Huquq al-insan bain ta'-alim al-Islam wa i'lan al-umam al-mutahhidah*/Human Rights Between Islam and UN-Charter (Cairo: Dar al-Kutub al-Islamiyya, 1984).

Gibb, Hamilton, *Studies on the Civilization of Islam* (Princeton, NJ: Princeton University Press, 1962).

Giddens, Anthony, *The Consequences of Modernity* (Stanford, CA: Stanford University Press, 1990).

——, *Modernity and Self-Identity* (Stanford, CA: Stanford University Press, 1991).

Gilsenan, Michael, *Saint and Sufi in Modern Egypt: An Essay in the Sociology of Religion* (Oxford: Clarendon Press, 1973).

Göcek, Fatma Müge, *East Encounters West* (New York: Oxford University Press, 1987).

——, *Rise of the Bourgeoisie, Demise of Empire. Ottoman Westernization and Social Change* (New York: Oxford University Press, 1996).

Gottstein, Klaus, ed., *Islamic Cultural Identity and Social Scientific Development* (Baden Baden: Nomos, 1986).

Grant, Edward, *The Foundations of Modern Science in the Middle Ages.Their Religious, Institutional, and Intellectual Contexts* (Cambridge: Cambridge University Press, 1996).

Grare, Frédéric, ed., *Islamism and Security* (Geneva: The Graduate Institute of International Studies PSIS, No. 4, 1999).

Green, Arnold H., *The Tunisian Ulama 1873–1915. Social Structure and Response to Ideological Currents* (Leiden: E. J. Brill, 1978).

Gress, David, *From Plato to NATO. The Idea of the West and its Opponents* (New York: The Free Press, 1999).

Griffin, Roger, *Modernism and Fascism* (London: Palgrave, 2007).

Grunebaum, Gustav von, *Studien zum Kulturbild und Selbstverständnis des Islam* (Zürich und Stuttgart: Artemis Verlag, 1969).

Haas, Ernst B., *When Knowledge is Power* (Berkeley, CA: University of California Press, 1990).

Habermas, Jürgen, *The Philosophical Discourse of Modernity*. Translation by Frederick Lawrence (Cambridge, MA: MIT Press, 1987).

——, *Glauben und Wissen* (Frankfurt/Main: Suhrkamp Verlag, 2001).

Hammudah, Adel, *Qanabil wa masahif. Qissat tanzim al-Jihad*/Bombs and Holy Books. The Story of al-Jihad (Cairo: Sina Press, 1985).

——, *Master and Disciple. The Cultural Foundations of Moroccan Authoritarianism* (Chicago, IL: Chicago University Press, 1997).

Hanna, Georges, *al-Insan al-Arabi*/The Arab Person (Beirut: Dar al-Ilm, 1964).

Hanson, Eric O., *Religion and Politics in the International System* (Cambridge: Cambridge University Press, 2006).

Hargreave, Alec, *Multi-Ethnic France. Immigration, Politics, Culture and Society* (New York: Routledge, 2007).

Harrison, Lawrence, *The Central Liberal Truth. How Politics Can Change a Culture and Save it from Itself* (New York: Oxford University Press, 2006).

—— *et al.*, eds, *Developing Cultures*, 2 vols (New York: Routledge, 2006).

Harrison, Lawrence and Samuel Huntington, eds, *Culture Matters: How Values Shape Human Progress* (New York: Basic Books, 1999).

Hart, H. L. A., *The Concept of Law*, 2nd printing (Oxford: The Clarendon Press, 1970).

Hawkesworth, Mary and Maurice Kogan, eds, *Routledge Encyclopedia of Government*, 2 vols, 2nd edn (London: Routledge, 2004).

Heer, Nicholas, ed., *Islamic Law and Jurisprudence* (Seattle, WA: University of Washington Press, 1990).

Hefner, Robert, *Civil Islam. Muslims and Democratization in Indonesia* (Princeton, NJ: Princeton University Press, 2000).

——, ed., *Remaking Muslim Politics* (Princeton, NJ: Princeton University Press, 2005).

Hegel, F. W., *Grundlinien der Philosophie des Rechts* (Hamburg: Felix Meiner, 1955).

Held, David, *Democracy and Global Order. From the Modern State to Cosmopolitan Governance* (Stanford, CA: Stanford University Press, 1995).

Herf, Jeffrey, *Reactionary Modernism. Technology, Culture and Politics in Weimar and the Third Reich* (New York: Cambridge University Press, 1984).

Herman, Edward S., "The United States Versus Human Rights in the Third World," *Harvard Human Rights Journal*, 4 (1991), p. 85.

Herzog, Roman *et al.*, *Preventing the Clash of Civilizations* (New York: St. Martin's Press, 1999).

Hinnebusch, Raymond A., "Children of the Elite: Political Attitudes of the Westernized Bourgeoisie in Contemporary Egypt," *The Middle East Journal*, 36 (1982), pp. 535–61.

——, *Egyptian Politics Under Sadat. The Post-Populist Development of an Authoritarian-Modernizing State*, 2nd edn (Boulder, CO: Lynnef Rienner Publishers, 1988).

Hodgson, Marshall G. S., *The Venture of Islam. Conscience and History in a World Civilization*, 3 vols (Chicago, IL: University Press of Chicago, 1977).

——, *Rethinking World History, Essays on Europe, Islam and World History* (Cambridge: Cambridge University Press 1995).

Holton, Gerald, *Science and Anti-Science* (Cambridge, MA: Harvard University Press, 1993).

Hoodbhoy, Pervez, *Islam and Science. Religious Orthodoxy and the Battle for Rationality* (London: Zed Books, 1991).

Horkheimer, Max and Theodor Adorno, *Dialektik der Aufklärung* (Amsterdam 1947, reprint Frankfurt/Main: S. Fischer, 1973).

Hourani, Albert, *Arabic Thought in the Liberal Age, 1798–1939* (London: Oxford, 1962).

Howe, Marvine, *Turkey Today. A Nation Divided over Islam's Revival* (Boulder, CO: Westview, 2002).

Hudson, Michael, *Arab Politics. The Search for Legitimacy* (New Haven, CT: Yale University Press, 1979).

Huff, Toby, *The Rise of Early Modern Science. Islam, China and the West* (Cambridge: Cambridge University Press, 1993).

Huntington, Samuel P., *Political Order in Changing Society* (New Haven, CT: Yale University Press, 1968).

——, *Clash of Civilizations* (New York: Simon and Schuster, 1996).

Husain, 'Adel, *Nahwa fikr Arabi jadid*/Toward a New Arabic Thought (Cairo: Dar al-Mustaqbal al-Arabi, 1985).

Husain, S. S. and S. A. Ashraf, *Crisis in Muslim Education* (Jeddah, Saudi Arabia, 1979, distributed in the United Kingdom by Hodder and Stoughton).

Ibrahim, Saad Eddin, "Anatomy of Egypt's Militant Islamic Groups. Methodological Note and Preliminary Findings," *International Journal of Middle East Studies*, 12 (1980), pp. 423–53.

——, ed., *Humum al-Aqaliyyatm, fi al-Watan al-Arabi*/The Concerns of Minorities in the Arab World (Cairo: Ibn Khaldun Center, 1994).

——, *Egypt, Islam and Democracy* (Cairo: American University of Cairo Press, 1996).

Imara, Mohammed, *al-A'mal al-Kamilah*/Collected Writings (Cairo: al-Mu'ssasah al-Misriyya, 1965).

——, *al-Islam wa huquq al-insan*/Islam and Human Rights (Cairo: Dar al-Shuruq, 1989).

——, *al-Sahwa al-Islamiyya wa al-Tahaddi al-hadari*/Islamic Awakening and the Civilizational Challenge (Cairo: Dar al-Shuruq, 1991).

International Institute for Islamic Thought, ed., *Towards Islamization of Disciplines* (Herndon, VA: International Institute for Islamic Thought, 1989).

Ismael, Tareq, ed., *Middle East Studies. International Perspectives on the State of the Art* (New York: Praeger, 1990).

Isma'il, Saifuldin Abdulfattah, *al-tajdid al-siyasi wa alwaqi' al-arabi al-mu'asir-Ru'ya Islamiyya*/Political Innovation and Arab Realities. An Islamist View (Cairo: Maktabat al-Nahda al-Misriyya, 1989).

Jabri, Mohammed Abed al-, *Takwin al-aql al-Arabi*/The Creation of Arab Mind (Beirut: Dar al-Tali'a, 1984).

——, *al-Turath wa hadatha*/Heritage and Modernity (Beirut: al-Markaz al Thaqafi, 1991).

——, *Arab Islamic Philosophy. A Contemporary Critique* (Austin, TX: University of Texas Press, 1999).

Jacoby Tami A., and Brent Sasley, eds, *Redefining Security in the Middle East* (Manchester: Manchester University Press, 2002).

Jadul-Haq, Jadul-Haq Ali, ed., *Bayan li al-nas*/Declaration to Humanity, 2 vols (Cairo: al-Azhar, 1984 and 1988).

Jamieson, Alan G., *Faith and Sword. A Short History of Christian–Muslim Conflict* (London: Reaktion Books, 2006).

Jarisha, Ali Mohammed and Mohammed Sharif Zaibaq, *Asalib al-ghazu al-fikri li al-'alam al-Islami*/Methods of the Intellectual Invasion of the Muslim World, 2nd printing (Cairo: Dar al-I'tisam, 1978).

Juergensmeyer, Mark, *The New Cold War? Religious Nationalism Confronts the Secular State* (Berkeley, CA: University of California Press, 1993).

——, *Terror in the Mind of God. The Global Rise of Religious Violence* (Berkeley, CA: University of California Press, 2000).

Junainah, Nimatullah, *Tanzim al-Jihad*/The Organization al-Jihad (Cairo: Dar al-Hurriya, 1988).

Jundi, Anwar al-, *Ahdaf al-Taghrib fi al-alam al-Islami*/The Goals of Westernization of the World of Islam (Cairo: al-Azhar, 1977).

——, *Taha Husayn fi mizan al-Islam*/T. Husayn in the Balance of Islam (Cairo: Dar al-I'tisam, 1977).

———, *al-Mu'asara fi itar al-asalah*/Modernity Seen in the Context of Authenticity (Cairo: Dar al-Sahwa, 1987).

———, *Min al-taba'iyya ila al-asalah*/From Dependence to Authenticity (Cairo: Dar al-I'tisam, no date).

Karsh, Efraim, *Islamic Imperialism. A History* (New Haven, CT: Yale University Press, 2006).

Kassab, Mohammed Y., *L'Islam face au nouvel ordre mondial* (Algier: Edition Salama, 1991).

Keddie, Nikkie R., ed., *Scholars, Saints and Sufis. Muslim Religious Institutions in the Middle East Since 1500* (Berkeley, CA: University of California Press, 1972).

———, ed., *An Islamic Response to Imperialism* (Berkeley, CA: University of California Press, new edn 1983).

Kekes, John, *The Morality of Pluralism* (Princeton, NJ: Princeton University Press, 1993).

Kelsay, John, *Islam and War. A Study in Comparative Ethics* (Louisville, KY: Westminster and John Knox Press, 1993).

———, *Arguing the Just War in Islam* (Cambridge, MA: Cambridge University Press, 2007).

Kemp, Geoffrey, ed., *Powder Keg in the Middle East. The Struggle for Gulf Security* (Lanham, MD: Rowman & Littlefield, 1995).

Kepel, Gilles, *Le Prophète et Pharaon. Les Mouvements Islamists dans l'Egypt Contemporaine* (Paris: Éditions La Découverte, 1984).

———, *Jihad. Expansion et declin de l'Islamisme* (Paris: Gallimard, 2000).

Kerr, Malcolm H., *Islamic Reform. The Political and Legal Theories of Muhammad Abduh and Rashid Rida* (Berkeley, CA: University of California Press, 1966).

Khaled, Khaled M., *Min huna nabda'*/Here We Start, 10th edn (Cairo and Baghdad: al-Khanji Press and Maktabat Muthanna, 1963, first published 1950).

———, *al-Dawla fi al-Islam*/The State in Islam, 3rd edn (Cairo: Dar Thabit, 1989).

Khalil, Imalduldin, *Tahafut al-'ilmaniyya*/The Refutation of Secularism (Beirut: al-Risala, 1979).

Khalilzadeh, Zalmy, *al-aql al-Muslim*/The Muslim Reason (Cairo: Dar al-Haramein, 1983).

Khalilzadeh, Zalmy and Cheryl Bernard, *The Government of God. Iran's Islamic Republic* (New York: Columbia University Press, 1984).

Khury, Fuad I., *Imams and Emirs. State, Religion and Sects in Islam* (London: Saqi Books, 1990).

Kienle, Eberhard, *A Grand Illusion. Democracy and Economic Reform in Egypt* (London: Tauris, 2000).

Knop, Katharina von and Martin van Creveld, eds, *Countering Modern Terrorism* (Bielefeld: Bertelsmann, 2005).

Kopper, Joachim, *Einfuehrung in die Philosophie der Aufklaerung* (Darmstadt: Wissenschaftliche Buchgesellschaft, 1992).

Kostiner, J. and Ph. Khoury, eds, *Tribes and the State Formation in the Middle East* (Berkeley, CA: University of California Press, 1990).

Kraidy, Marwan, *Hybridity, or the Cultural Logic of Globalization* (Philadelphia, PA: Temple University Press, 2005).

Kramer, Martin, *Arab Awakening and Islamic Revival. The Politics of Ideas in the Muslim Middle East* (New Brunswick, NJ: Transaction Publishers, 1996).

Kugelgen, Anke von, *Averroes und die arabische Moderne. Ansätze zu einer Neugründung des Rationalismus im Islam* (Leiden: Brill, 1994).

Küntzel, Matthias, *Jihad and Jew Hatred. Islamism, Nazism and the Roots of 9/11* (New York: Telos, 2007).

Kurzman, Charles, ed., *Liberal Islam* (New York: Oxford University Press, 1998).

Laue, Theodore H. von, *The World Revolution of Westernization* (New York: Oxford University Press, 1987).

Lawrence, Bruce, *Defenders of God: The Fundamentalist Revolt Against the Modern Age* (San Francisco, CA: Harper and Row, 1989).

——, *Shattering the Myth. Islam Beyond Violence* (Princeton, NJ: Princeton University Press, 1998).

Leclerc, Gerard, *Anthropologie und Kolonialismus* (Frankfurt/Main: Hanser, 1973).

Lee, Robert, *Overcoming Tradition and Modernity. The Search for Islamic Authenticity* (Boulder, CO: Westview, 1997).

Lepenies, Wolf. "Anthropological Perspectives in the Sociology of Science," in: Everett Mendelsohn and Yehuda Elkana, eds, *Sciences and Cultures. Anthropological Studies of the Sciences* (Dordrecht: Reidel Publ. Co., 1981).

Levi, Werner, *Contemporary International Law*, 2nd edn (Boulder, CO: Westview Press, 1991).

Lewis, Bernard, *The Jews of Islam* (Princeton, NJ: Princeton University Press, 1974).

——, *The Emergence of Modern Turkey*, 2nd edn (Oxford: Oxford University Press, 1979).

——, *The Muslim Discovery of Europe* (New York: Norton & Co., 1982).

——, *Islam and the West* (New York: Oxford University Press, 1993).

——, *What Went Wrong?* (New York: Oxford University Press, 2001).

Licklider, Roy, *Political Power and the Arab Oil Weapon* (Berkeley, CA: University of California Press, 1988).

Lindberg, David, *The Beginning of Western Science* (Chicago, IL: The University of Chicago Press, 1992).

Lindholm, Charles, *The Islamic Middle East. An Historical Anthropology* (Oxford: Blackwell, 1996).

Lindholm, Tore and Kari Vogt, eds, *Islamic Law Reform and Human Rights. Challenges and Rejoinders; Proceedings of the Seminar on Human Rights and the Modern Application of Islamic Law, Oslo 14–15 February 1992* (Copenhagen: Nordic Human Rights Publ., 1993).

Lipset, Martin Seymour, ed., *The Encyclopedia of Democracy*, 4 vols (Washington, DC: The Congressional Quarterly, 1995).

Lipson, Leslie, *The Ethical Crisis of Civilization. Moral Meltdown or Advance?* (London: Sage, 1993).

Lorenz, Joseph P., *Egypt and the Arabs. Foreign Policy and the Search for National Identity* (Boulder, CO: Westview Press, 1990).

Lüderssen, Klaus, ed., *Aufgeklärte Kriminalpolitik oder Kampf gegen das Böse*, 5 vols (Baden-Baden: Nomos, 1998).

Luhmann, Niklas, *Funktion der Religion* (Frankfurt/Main: Suhrkamp, 1977).

Mahdi, Muhsin, *Ibn Khaldun's Philosophy of History. A Study in the Philosophic Foundation of the Science of Culture* (London: George Allen and Unwin, 1957).

Mahmud Abdulhalim, *al-Jihad wa al-nasr*/Jihad and Victory (Cairo: al-Kitab al-Arabi, 1968).

Makdisi, George, *The Rise of the Colleges. Institutions of Learning in Islam and the West* (Edinburgh: Edinburgh University Press, 1981).

Mandaville, Peter, *Transnational Muslim Politics. Reimagining the Umma* (New York: Routledge, 2004).

Martin, Richard *et al.*, *Defenders of Reason in Islam: Mu'tazilism from Medieval School to Modern Symbol* (Oxford: Oneworld, 1997).

Marty, Martin and R. Scott Appleby, eds, *The Fundamentalism Project*, 5 vols (Chicago, IL: Chicago University Press 1991–95).

Marwardi, Abu al-Hassan al-, *Kitab al-ahkam al-sultaniyya*/Book of Rules on the Sultanic Government (Arabic edition Cairo, 1909; French translation: Paris, 1901).

——, *Kitab adab al-dunya wa al-din*/Book of Worldly and Religious Tradition, in a German translation and a new printing (Osnabrück: Bibliotheksverlag, 1984).

Mastafa, Hala, *al-Dawla wa al-Harakat al-Islamiyya al-mu'arida bain al-muhadana wa al-muwajaha*/The State and the Islamist Opposition between Truce and Confrontation (Cairo: Kitab al-Mahrusah, 1995).

Mawdudi, Abu al-A'la al-, *al-Islam wa al-madaniyya al-haditha*/Islam and Modern Civilization (reprint Cairo, no date).

Mayer, Ann E., "Law and Religion in the Muslim Middle East," *The American Journal of Comparative Law*, 35, 1 (Winter 1987), pp. 127–84.

——, "The Shari'ah: A Methodology or a Body of Substantive Rules?" in: Nicholas Heer, ed., *Islamic Law and Jurisprudence* (Seattle, WA: University of Washington Press, 1990), pp. 177–98.

——, *Islam and Human Rights: Tradition and Politics* (Boulder, CO: Westview Press, 1991).

Mehden, Fred R. von der, *Two Words of Islam. Interaction between Southeast Asia and the Middle East* (Gainesville, FL: Florida University Press, 1993).

Meier, Christian, *Die Entstehung des Politischen bei den Griechen* (Frankfurt/Main: Suhrkamp Verlag, 1989).

Mendelsohn, Everett and Yehuda Elkana, eds, *Sciences and Cultures. Anthropological Studies of the Sciences* (Dordrecht: Reidel Publ. Co., 1981).

Mennel, Stephen, *Norbert Elias. An Introduction* (Oxford: Blackwell, 1992).

Mitchell, Richard, *The Society of the Muslim Brothers* (London: Oxford University Press, 1969).

Moore, Barrington, *The Social Origins of Dictatorship and Democracy* (Boston, MA: Beacon Press, 1966).

Muslehuddin, Muhammad, *Philosophy of Islamic Law and the Orientalists: A Comparative Study of Islamic Legal System* (Lahore, Pakistan: Kazi Publications, 1985).

Nardin, Terry, *Law, Morality and the Relations of States* (Princeton, NJ: Princeton University Press, 1983).

——, ed., *The Ethics of War and Peace: Religious and Secular Perspectives* (Princeton, NJ: Princeton University Press, 1996).

Nawfal, Abdulraziq, *al-Muslimun wa al-ilm al-hadith*/Muslims and Modern Science, 3rd printing (Cairo: Dar al-shuruq, 1988).

Nisbet, Robert, *History of the Idea of Progress* (New York: Basic Books, 1980).

Northrop, F. S. C., *The Taming of the Nations: A Study of the Cultural Basis of International Policy* 2nd reprint (Woodbridge, CT, 1987).

Olson, Alan *et al.*, eds, *Educating for Democracy* (Lanham, MD: Rowman & Littlefield, 2004).

Oomen, T. K., ed., *Citizenship and National Identity. From Colonialism to Globalism* (Sage: London and New Dehli, 1997).

Oweis, Ibrahim and George Atiyeh, eds, *Arab Civilization. Challenges and Responses* (Albany, NY: State University of New York, 1988).

Paret, Rudi, *Mohammed und der Qur'an*, 4th printing (Stuttgart: Kohlhammer, 1976).

Parker, Geoffrey, *The Military Revolution and the Rise of the West 1500–1800* (Cambridge: Cambridge University Press, 1988).

Perlmutter, Amos, *Egypt. The Praetorian State* (New Brunswick, NJ: Transaction Books, 1974).

Perrot, Dominique and Roy Preiswerk, *Ethnocentrism and History* (New York: NOK Publishers, 1978).

Petterson, Dan, *Inside Sudan* (Boulder, CO: Westview, updated edn, 2003).

Phares, Walid, *The War of Ideas. Jihadism against Democracy* (New York: Palgrave, 2007).

Philpott, Daniel, "The Challenge of September 11 to Secularism in International Relations," *World Politics*, 55, 1 (October 2002), pp. 66–95.

Piamenta, M., *Islam in Everyday Arabic Speech* (Leiden: Brill, 1979).

Piscatori, James, *Islam in a World of Nation-States* (Cambridge: Cambridge University Press, 1980).

———, ed., *Islam in the Political Process* (Cambridge: Cambridge University Press, 1983).

Potter, Lawrence G., ed., *The Persian Gulf at the Millennium. Essays in Politics, Economy, Security, and Religion* (New York: St. Martin's Press, 1997).

Praemium Erasmianum Foundation, ed., *The Limits of Pluralism. Neo-Absolutisms and Relativism* (Amsterdam: Praemium Erasmianum Foundation, 1994).

Qadir, C. A., *Philosophy and Science in the Islamic World* (London: Routledge, 1988).

Qaradawi, Yusuf al-, *al-Hulul al-Mustawradah*/The Imported Solutions (Beirut: al-Risalah, 1974, reprint 1980).

———, *Hatmiyyat al-Hall al-Islami, Farida wa darura*/The Islamic Solution is a Religious Obligation and a Necessity (Beirut: al-Risalah, 1974).

———, *Baiyinat al-Hall al-Islami*/The Major Characteristics of the Islamic Solution, reprint (Cairo: Dar Wahba, 1988).

———, *al-Halal wa al-haram fi al-Islam*/The Permitted and the Forbidden in Islam, 20th printing (Cairo: Wahba, 1991).

Qutb, Sayyid, *al-Islam wa mushkilat al-hararah*/Islam and the Predicament of Civilization, 8th legal reprint (Cairo: Dar al-Shuruq, 1988).

———, *Mushkilat al-hadarah*/The Predicament of Civilization, 9th legal printing (Cairo: al-Shuruq, 1988).

———, *Ma'alim fi al-tariq*/Signposts along the Road, 13th legal printing (Cairo: Dar al-Shuruq, 1989).

———, *Ma'araktuna oma'a al-Yahud*/Our Fight against the Jews, 10th legal printing (Cairo, 1989).

———, *al-Jihad fi sabil Allah*/Jihad on the Path of God (reprinted Cairo: Dar al-Isma', 1992).

———, *al-Salam al-Alami wa al-Islam*/World Peace and Islam, 10th legal edn (Cairo: Dar al-Sharuq, 1992).

Rahman, Fazlur, *Islam and Modernity. Transformation of an Intellectual Tradition* (Chicago, IL: University Press of Chicago, 1982).

Ralston, David B., *Importing the European Army. The Introduction of European Military Techniques and Institutions into the Extra-European World 1600–1914* (Chicago, IL: University of Chicago Press, 1990).

Ramadan, Abdulazim, *Jama'at al-Takfir fi misr* /The "Takfiri-Groups"/Declaring Others as Unbelievers (Cairo: Madbuli, 1995).

Ramazani, Rouhollah K., *Revolutionary Iran. Challenge and Response in the Middle East* (Baltimore, MD: Johns Hopkins University Press, 1986).

Ranger, Terence and Eric Hobsbawm, eds, *The Invention of Tradition*, new printing (Cambridge: Cambridge University Press, 1966).

Rayyes, Mohammed D. al-, *al-Nazariyyat al-siyasiyya al-Islamiyya*/Islamic Political Theories (Cairo, 1953).

Reid, Anthony, *Islamic Legitimacy in a Plural Asia* (New York: Routledge, 2007).

Renshon, Stanley A., ed., *The Political Psychology of the Gulf War. Leaders, Publics, and the Process of Conflict* (Pittsburgh, PA: University of Pittsburgh Press, 1993).

Revel, Jean-François, *Democracy Against Itself* (New York: The Free Press, 1993).

Richards, Alan and John Waterbury, *A Political Economy of the Middle East*, 2nd edn (Boulder, CO: Westview Press, 1996).

Roberts, Adam and Benedict Kingsbury, eds, *United Nations, Divided World: The UN's Role in International Relations* (Oxford: The Clarendon Press, 1988).

Robertson, Roland, *Globalization. Social Theory and Global Culture* (London: Sage, 1992).

Rodinson, Maxime, *Mohammed* (Lucerne and Frankfurt: Bucher, 1975).

——, *Islam und Kapitalismus* (Frankfurt/Main: Suhrkamp, new edn, 1985).

——, in: Wolfgang Schluchter, ed., *Max Webers Sicht des Islam* (Frankfurt: Suhrkamp, 1987), pp. 180–89.

Rosefsky Wickham, Carrie, *Mobilizing Islam. Religion, Activism, and Political Change in Egypt* (New York: Columbia University Press, 2002).

Rosenthal, Franz, *The Classical Heritage of Islam* (London: Routledge, 1994).

Roy, Olivier, *The Failure of Political Islam* (Cambridge, MA: Harvard University Press, 1994).

Rubin, Barry M., *Islamic Fundamentalism in Egyptian Politics* (London: Macmillan, 1990).

Runciman, Steven, *Geschichte der Kreuzzüge* (Munich: C. H. Beck-Verlag, 1995).

Russet, Bruce, *Grasping Democratic Peace. Principles for a Post-Cold War World* (Princeton, NJ: Princeton University Press 1993).

Sa'b, Hasan, *Islam al-Hurriyya, la Islam al-Ubudiyya*/Islam of Liberty, not of Sovereignty (Beirut: Dar al-Ilm Lilmalayin, 1979).

Sachedina, Abdulaziz, *The Islamic Roots of Democratic Pluralism* (New York: Oxford University Press, 2001).

Sadat, Anwar al-, *Geheimtagebuch der ägyptischen Revolution* (Düsseldorf and Cologne: Verlag Eugen Diederichs, 1957).

Sadr, Husain, "Science in Islam. Is there a Conflict?," in: Ziauddin Sardar, ed., *The Truth of Midas* (Manchester: Manchester University Press, 1984).

Safran, Nadav, *Egypt in Search of Political Community. An Analysis of the Intellectual and Political Evolution of Egypt, 1804–1952* (Cambridge, MA: Harvard University Press, 1961).

Said, Edward, ed., *The Arabs of Today. Perspectives for Tomorrow* (Columbus, OH: Forum Associates, 1973).

——, *Orientalism* (New York: Random House, 1979).

——, *Covering Islam* (New York: Pantheon, 1981).

Salih, Subhi al-, *Ma'alim al-shari'a al-Islamiyya*/Essential Characteristics of Islamic Law (Beirut: Dar al-Ilm Lilmalayin, 1975).

Salvatore, Armanda, *Islam and the Political Discourse of Modernity* (Reading: Ithaca Press, 1997).

Sanderson, Steven K., *Social Evolution. A Critical History* (Oxford: Blackwell, 1990).

Sardar, Ziauddin, ed., *The Truth of Midas* (Manchester: Manchester University Press, 1984).

——, *Islamic Futures. The Shape of Ideas to Come* (London: Mansell, 1985).

——, *Exploration in Islamic Science* (London: Mansell, 1989).

Sayyad, Nezar al- and Manuel Castells, eds, *Muslim Europe or Euro-Islam* (Lanham, MD and New York: Lexington Books, 2002).

Sayyid, Mustapha K. al-, *Egypt in the Reign of Mohammed Ali* (Cambridge: Cambridge University Press, 1984).

——, "Slow Thaw in the Arab World," *World Policy Journal*, 8, 4 (1991), p. 724.

Sayyid-Marsot, Afaf al-, *Egypt's Liberal Experiment, 1922–1936* (Berkeley, CA: University of California Press, 1977).

——, *Egypt in the Reign of Mohammed Ali* (Cambridge: Cambridge University Press, 1984)

Schacht, Joseph, *Introduction to Islamic Law*, 5th printing (Oxford: Clarendon Press, 1979).

Schacht, Joseph and C. E. Basworth, eds, *The Legacy of Islam* (Oxford: Clarendon Press, 1974).

Schaltut, Mahmud, *al-Islam, Aqida wa Shari'a*/Islam, a Religious Doctrine and Law, 10th edn (Cairo: al-Shuruq, 1980).

Schluchter, Wolfgang ed., *Weber und der Islam* (Frankfurt/Main: Suhrkamp, 1987).

Schwartz, Stephen, *The Two Faces of Islam. The House of Sa'ud from Tradition to Terror* (New York: Doubleday, 2002).

Scruton, Roger, *The West and the Rest. Globalization and the Terrorist Threat* (Wilmington, DE: ISI Books, 2002).

Shadhli, Saad-Eddin al-, *al-Harb al-Salibiyya al-Thamina*/The Eighth Crusade (Casablanca: al-Matba'a al-Jadida, 1991).

Shahrur, Mohammed, *al-Kitab wa al-Qur'an. Qira'a Mu'asira*/The Book and the Qur'an: a Modern Reading, 6th edn (Beirut: Sharikat al-Matbu'at, 2000).

Shaltut, M., *al-Islam wa Aqida wa Shari'a*/ Islam, Faith and Law, 10th printing (Cairo: al-Shuruq, 1980).

Shamsuldin, Muhammad M., *al-'Ilamiyya*/Secularism, 2nd edn (Beirut: al-Markaz al-Islami, 1983).

Sharabi, Hisham, ed., *The Next Arab Decade* (Boulder, CO: Westview Press, 1988).

——, *Neo-Oligarchy. A Theory of Distorted Change in Arab Society* (New York: Oxford University Press, 1992).

Sharqawi, Hassan al-, *al-Muslimun 'Ulama wa Hukama*/Muslims as Scholars and Wise Men (Cairo: Mu'assasat Mukhtar, 1987).

Shayegan, Daryush, *Cultural Schizophrenia. Islamic Societies confronting the West* (Syracuse, NY: Syracuse University Press, 1992).

Silverstein, Paul A., *Algeria in France* (Bloomington, IN: Indiana University Press, 2004).

Sivan, Emmanuel, *Militant Islam. Modern Politics and Medieval Theology* (New Haven, CT: Yale University Press, 1985).

Skocpol, Theda, ed., *Vision and Method in Historical Sociology* (Cambridge: Cambridge University Press, 1984).

Smith, Donald E., ed., *Religion and Political Modernization* (New Haven, CT and London: Yale University Press, 1974).

Stevens, Paul, in: Gary G. Sick and Lawrence G. Potter, eds, *The Persian Gulf at the Millennium. Essays in Politics, Economy, Security, and Religion* (New York: St. Martin's Press, 1997), pp. 85–114.

Stoddard Philip H., *et al.*, eds, *Change and the Muslim World* (Syracuse, NY: Syracuse University Press, 1981).

Stowasser, Barbara F., *Women in the Qur'an. Traditions and Interpretations* (New York: Oxford University Press, 1994).

Stowasser, Karl, ed., *Ein Muslim entdeckt Europa* (Munich: C. H. Beck, 1989).

Taha, Mohamed Mahmoud, *The Second Message of Islam*, transl. and introduced by Abdullahi A. An-Na'im (Syracuse, NY: Syracuse University Press, 1987).

Tahtawi, Rifa'a R. al-, *Takhlis al-Ibriz fi-talkhis Paris*/The Paris Diary, a reprint in Arabic (Beirut: Dar Ibn Zaidun, no date).

Taimiyya, Ibn, *al-Siyasa al-Shariyya fi islah al-Rai'i wa al-ra'iyya*/The Shari'a-Oriented Politics for the Guidance of the Ruler and his Subjects (Beirut: reprint, Dar al-Jil, 1988).

Takeyh, Ray, *Hidden Iran. Paradox and Power in the Islamic Republic* (New York: Times Books, 2006).

Taylor, Charles, *The Ethics of Authenticity* (Cambridge, MA: Harvard University Press, 1991).

The Japanese Association of Comparative Constitutional Law, ed., *Church and State. Towards Protection of Freedom of Religion. Proceedings of the International Conference on Comparative Constitutional Law, 2005* (Tokyo: Nihon University Press, 2006).

Tibi, B., "Genesis of the Arab Left. A Critical Viewpoint," in: Edward Said, ed., *The Arabs of Today. Perspectives for Tomorrow* (Columbus, OH: Forum Associates, 1973), pp. 31–42.

——, *Militär und Sozialismus in der Dritten Welt* (Frankfurt/Main: Suhrkamp, 1973).

——, "Islam and Secularization, Religion and the Functional Differentiation of the Social System," *Archives for Philosophy of Law and Social Philosophy*, 66 (1980), pp. 207–22.

——, "Islam and Social Change in the Modern Middle East," *Law and State*, 22 (1980), pp. 91–106.

——, "Islam and Secularization," in: Mourad Wahba, ed., *The First International Islamic Philosophy Conference on Islam and Civilization* (Cairo: 'Ain Shams University Press, 1982), pp. 61–84.

——, "The Renewed Role of Islam in the Political and Social Development of the Middle East," *The Middle East Journal*, 37 (1983), pp. 3–13.

——, "Cultural Innovation in the Developmental Process," in: Klaus Gottstein, ed., *Islamic Cultural Identity and Social Scientific Development* (Baden Baden: Nomos, 1986), pp. 93–101.

——, "The Iranian Revolution and the Arabs," *Arab Studies Quarterly*, 8, 1 (1986), pp. 29–44.

——, "Politisches Denken im klassischen und mittelalterlichen Islam zwischen Philosophie (Falsafa) und Religio-Jurisprudenz (Fiqh)," in: Iring Fetscher *et al.*, eds, *Pipers Handbuch der politischen Ideen*, 5 vols (Munich: Piper, 1987, here vol. 2, 1993), pp. 87–174.

——, *The Crisis of Modern Islam. A Preindustrial Culture in the Scientific–Technological Age* (Salt Lake City: Utah University Press, 1988)

——, "The Interplay Between Social and Cultural Change," in: Ibrahim Oweis and George Atiyeh, eds, *Arab Civilization. Challenges and Responses* (Albany, NY: State University of New York, 1988), pp. 166–82.

——, "The European Tradition of Human Rights and the Culture of Islam," in: Abdullahi A. An-Na'im and Francis Deng, eds, *Human Rights. Cross-Cultural Perspectives* (Washington, DC: The Brookings Institution, 1990), pp. 104–32.

——, "The Simultaneity of the Unsimultaneous. Old Tribes and Nation-States," in: J. Kostiner and Ph. Khoury, eds, *Tribes and the State Formation in the Middle East* (Berkeley, CA: University of California Press, 1990), pp. 127–52.

——, *Islam and the Cultural Accommodation of Social Change* (Boulder, CO: Westview Press, 1990, new printing 1991).

——, "Universality of Human Rights and Authenticity of non-Western Cultures: Islam and the Western Concept of Human Rights," *Harvard Human Rights Journal*, 5 (Spring 1992), pp. 221–26.

——, "The Worldview of Sunni Arab Fundamentalists: Attitudes towards Modern Science and Technology," in: Martin Marty and Scott Appleby, eds, *Fundamentalisms and Society* (Chicago: University Press of Chicago, 1993), pp. 73–102.

——, *Conflict and War in the Middle East. From Interstate War to New Security*, 2nd enlarged edn (New York: St. Martin's Press, 1993, new expanded edn, 1997).

——, *Die Verschwörung. Das Trauma arabischer Politik* (Hamburg: Hoffmann und Campe, 2nd enlarged edn, 1994).

——, "Islamic Law, Shari'a and Human Rights. Universal Morality and International Relations," *Human Rights Quaterly*, 16, 2 (1994), pp. 277–99.

——, "Culture and Knowledge. The Politics of Islamization of Knowledge as a Post-modern Project? The Fundamentalist Claim to de-Westernization," *Theory, Culture and Knowledge*, 12, 1 (1995), pp. 1–24.

——, "Fundamentalism" in: Seymour Martin Lipset, ed., *The Encyclopedia of Democracy*, 4 vols (Washington: The Congressional Quarterly, 1995), vol. 2, pp. 507–10.

——, *Krieg der Zivilisationen* (Hamburg: Hoffmann & Campe, 1995).

——, "The Islamic Dream of Semi-Modernity," *India International Center Quarterly*/New Dehli, 22, 1 (Spring 1995), pp. 79–87.

——, *Der wahre Imam. Der Islam von Mohammed bis zur Gegenwart* (Munich: Piper Press 1996, reprinted 1997, 1998 and 2002).

——, "War and Peace in Islam," in: Terry Nardin, ed., *The Ethics of War and Peace: Religious and Secular Perspectives* (Princeton, NJ: Princeton University Press, 1996).

——, *Arab Nationalism. Between Islam and the Nation-State* (New York and London: Macmillan, 3rd expanded edn, 1997, first 1980).

——, "Religious Fundamentalism, Ethnicity and the Nation-State," in: T. K. Oomen, ed., *Citizenship and National Identity. From Colonialism to Globalism* (Sage: London and New Dehli, 1997), pp. 199–226.

——, "Die Entwestlichung des Rechts. Das Hudud-Strafrecht der islamischen Schari'a," in: Klaus Lüderssen, ed., *Aufgeklärte Kriminalpolitik oder Kampf gegen das Böse*, 5 vols, here vol. 5 (Baden-Baden: Nomos, 1998), pp. 21–30.

——, *The Challenge of Fundamentalism. Political Islam and the New World Disorder* (Berkeley, CA: University of California Press, 1998, updated after 9/11 in a 2002 edn).

——, *Kreuzzug und Djihad. Der Islam und die christliche Welt* (Munich: Bertelsmann, 1999).

——, "International Morality and Cross-Cultural Bridging," in: Roman Herzog *et al.*, eds, *Preventing the Clash of Civilizations* (New York: St. Martin's Press, 1999), pp. 107–26.

——, "The Failed Export of Islamic Revolution into the Arab World," in: Frédéric Grare, ed., *Islamism and Security* (Geneva: The Graduate Institute of International Studies PSIS, No. 4, 1999) pp. 63–102.

——, "The Fundamentalist Challenge to the Secular Order in the Middle East," *The Fletcher Forum of World Affairs*, 23, 1 (1999), pp. 191–210.

——, "Postbipolar Order in Crisis. The Challenge of Politicized Islam," *Millennium*, 29(3) (2000), pp. 843–59.

——, "Secularization and De-Secularization in Modern Islam," *Religion, Staat, Gesellschaft. Journal for the Study of Beliefs and Worldviews*, 1, 1 (2000), pp. 95–117.

——, *Einladung in die islamische Geschichte* (Darmstadt: Wissenschaftliche Buchgesellschaft, 2001).

——, "The Middle East: Society, State, Religion," in: Furio Cerutti and Rodolfo Ragionieri, eds, *Identities and Conflicts. The Mediterranean* (New York: Palgrave, 2001), pp. 121–34.

——, "Between Islam and Islamism," in: Tami A. Jacoby and Brent Sasley, eds, *Redefining Security in the Middle East* (Manchester: Manchester University Press, 2002), pp. 62–82.

——, *Islam between Culture and Politics* (New York: Palgrave and St. Martin's Press, 2001, updated and expanded edn 2005).

——, "Euro-Islam," in: Nezar AlSayyad and Manuel Castells, eds, *Muslim Europe or Euro-Islam* (Lanham, MD and New York: Lexington Books, 2002), S. 31–52.

——, *Fundamentalismus im Islam* (Darmstadt: Wissenschaftliche Buchgesellschaft, 2002).

——, "Habermas and the Return of the Sacred. Is it a Religious Renaissance, a Pronouncement of a 'Post-Secular Society', or the Emergence of Political Religion as a New Totalitarianism?," *Religion-Staat-Gesellschaft*, 3, 2 (2002), pp. 265–96.

——, *Im Schatten Allahs. Der Islam und die Menschenrechte* (Munich: Ullstein, expanded edn of 624 pages, 2003).

——, *Der Neue Totalitarismus. Heiliger Krieg und westliche Sicherheit* (Darmstadt: Primus, 2004).

——, "Democracy and Education in an Age of Islamism," in: Alan Olson *et al.*, eds, *Educating for Democracy* (Lanham, MD: Rowman & Littlefield, 2004), pp. 203–20.

——, "Fundamentalism," in: Mary Hawkesworth and Maurice Kogan, eds, *Routledge Encyclopedia of Government*, 2 vols, 2nd edn (London: Routledge, 2004), vol. 1, pp. 184–204.

——, *From Islamist Jihadism to Democratic Peace? Islam is at the Crossroads in Postbipolar International Politics*, Ankara Paper 16 (London: Taylor & Francis, 2005).

——, "Islam, Freedom and Democracy," in: Michael Emerson, ed., *Democratization in the European Neighborhood* (Brussels: CEPS, 2005), pp. 93–116.

——, "Islamic Shari'a as Constitutional Law? The Freedom of Faith in the Light of the Politicization of Islam. The Reinvention of the Shari'a and the Need for an Islamic Law Reform," in: The Japanese Association of Comparative Constitutional Law, ed., *Church and State. Towards Protection of Freedom of Religion. Proceedings of the International Conference on Comparative Constitutional Law*, 2005 (Tokyo: Nihon University Press, 2006), pp. 126–70 (English) and pp. 79–125 (Japanese).

——, "Islamischer Konservatismus der AKP als Tarnung für den politischen Islam?" in: Gerhard Besier, ed., *Politische Religion und Religionspolitik* (Göttingen: Vandenhoek & Ruprecht, 2005), pp. 229–60.

——, "Cultural Change in Islamic Civilization," in: Lawrence Harrison, *et al.*, eds, *Developing Cultures*, vol. 1, *Essays* (New York: Routledge, 2006), pp. 245–60.

——, "Egypt as a Model of Development for the World of Islam," in: Lawrence Harrison *et al.*, eds, *Developing Cultures*, vol. 2, *Case Studies* (New York: Routledge, 2006), pp. 163–80.

——, "Europeanizing Islam or the Islamization of Europe" in: Timothy Byrnes, and Peter Katzenstein, eds, *Religion in an Expanding Europe* (Cambridge: Cambridge University Press, 2006), pp. 204–24.

——, "Intellektuelle als verhinderte Aufklärer. Das Scheitern der Intellektuellen im Islam," in: Harald Bluhm and Walter Reese-Schäfer, eds, *Die Intellektuellen und der Weltlauf* (Baden-Baden: Nomos, 2006), pp. 97–124.

——, "The Pertinence of Islam's Predicament with Democratis Pluralism," *Religion-Staat-Gesellschaft*, 7, 1 (2006), pp. 83–117.

——, "A Migration Story. From Muslim Immigrants to European Citizens of the Heart," *The Fletcher Forum of World Affairs*, 31, 1 (Winter 2007), pp. 147–68.

——, "Der djihadistische Islamismus – nicht der Islam – ist die zentrale Quelle des neuen Antisemitismus," in: Wolfgang Benz and Juliane Wetzel, ed., *Antisemitismus und radikaler Islamismus* (Essen: Klartext, 2007), pp. 43–70.

——, "Euro-Islamic Religious Pluralism for Europe," *The Current. The Policy Journal of Cornell University*, 11, 1 (2007), pp. 89–103.

——, "Islam and Cultural Modernity. In Pursuit of Democratic Pluralism," in: Anthony Reid, ed., *Islamic Legitimacy in a Plural Asia* (New York: Routledge, 2007), pp. 28–52.

——, "Islam between Religious-Cultural Practice and Identity Politics," in: Helmut Anheier and Y. Raj Isar, *Culture and Globalization Series, vol. 1, Conflicts and Tensions* (London: Sage, 2007), pp. 221–31.

———, *Mit dem Kopftuch nach Europa? Die Türkei auf dem Weg in die EU* (Darmstadt: Primus, updated edn, 2007).

———, "The Totalitarianism of Jihadist Islamism and its Challenge to Europe and to Islam," *Totalitarian Movements and Political Religions*, 8 (2007), pp. 35–54.

———, "Islam, Islamism and Democracy," in: Leonard Weinberg, ed., *Democratic Responses to Terrorism* (New York: Routledge, 2008), pp. 41–61.

———, *Political Islam, World Politics and Europe. Euro-Islam and Democratic Peace vs. Global Jihad* (New York: Routledge, 2008).

———, "Religious Extremism, or Religionization of Politics?" in: Hillel Frisch and Efraim Imber, eds, *Radical Islam and International Security* (New York: Routledge, 2008), pp. 11–37.

———, "The Return of the Sacred to Politics," *Theoria. Journal of Social and Political Theory*, 55, 3 (April 2008), issue no. 115, pp. 91–119.

Tilly, Charles, *Big Structures, Large Processes, Huge Comparisons* (New York: Russell Sage Foundation, 1984).

———, ed., *The Formation of the Nation State* (Princeton, NJ: Princeton University Press, 1985).

Tizini, Tayib, *Mashru' ru'ya jadida li-fakr-al-'arabi fi al'asr al-wasit/*A Project of a New Interpretation of Arab Thinking in the Middle Age (Damascus: Dar Dimashq, 1971).

Trimberger, Ellen K., *Revolution from Above* (New Brunswick, NJ: Transaction Books, 1978).

Tu'aima, Sabir, *al-Shari'a al-Islamiyya fi asr al-ilm/*Islamic Law in the Age of Science (Beirut: Dar al-jil, 1979).

Turner, Bryan, *Weber and Islam* (London: Routledge, 1974).

———, *Orientalism, Postmodernism and Globalism* (London: Routledge, 1994).

Turner, Howard, *Science in Medieval Islam* (Austin, TX: The University of Austin Texas, 1995).

UNDP, *Arab Human Development Report 2002. Creating Opportunities for Future Generations* (New York: United Nations, 2002).

———, *Building a Knowledge Society* (New York: United Nations, 2003).

Vatikiotis, P. J., *The Modern History of Egypt*, 2nd printing (London: Weidenfeld and Nicolson, 1976).

Viehweg, Theodor, *Topik und Jurisprudenz. Ein Beitrag zur rechtswissenschaftlichen Grundlagenforschung*, 5th printing (Munich: C. H. Beck, 1974).

Vincent, R. J., *Human Rights and International Relations* (Cambridge: Cambridge University Press, 1986).

Wahba, Mourad, ed., *Islam and Civilization. Proceedings of the First International Islamic Philosophy Conference, 19–22 November 1979* (Cairo: 'Ain Shams University Press, 1982).

———, ed., *The Future of Islamic Civilization* (Cairo: The Anglo-Egyptian Bookshop, 1985).

Waltz, Susan E., *Human Rights and Reform. The Changing Face of North African Politics* (Berkeley, CA: University of California Press, 1995).

Walzer, Richard, ed. and transl., *al-Farabi on the Perfect State* (Oxford: Clarendon Press, 1985).

Waterbury, John, *The Commander of the Faithful. The Moroccan Political Elite* (New York: Columbia University Press, 1970).

———, *Egypt. Burdens of the Past, Options for the Future* (Bloomington, IN: Indiana University Press, 1978).

———, "Egypt: Islam and Social Change," in Philip H. Stoddard *et al.*, eds, *Change and the Muslim World* (Syracuse, NY: Syracuse University Press, 1981) pp. 49–58.

———, *The Egypt of Nasser and Sadat. The Political Economy of Two Regimes* (Princeton, NJ: Princeton University Press, 1983).

———, "Social Science Research and Arab Studies in the Coming Decade," in: Hisham Sharabi, ed., *The Next Arab Decade* (Boulder, CO: Westview Press, 1988), pp. 293–302.

Watt, W. M., *Muhammed at Mecca* (Oxford: Oxford University Press, 1953).

——, *Islamic Philosophy and Theology* (Edinburgh: Edinburgh University Press, 1962).

——, *Islamic Political Thought: The Basic Concepts* (Edinburgh: Edinburgh University Press, 1969).

——, *Islamic Revelation in the Modern World* (Edinburgh: Edinburgh University Press, 1969).

——, *Muhammad at Medina*, 6th printing (Oxford: Oxford University Press, 1977).

——, *Islamic Fundamentalism and Modernity* (London: Routledge, 1988).

——, *Muslim–Christian Encounters, Perceptions and Misperceptions* (London: Routledge, 1991).

Weber, Max, *Soziologie, weltgeschichtliche Analysen, Politik* (Stuttgart: Alfred Kröner Press, 1964).

Weihman, Gabriel, "Terror Online: How Terrorists use the Internet," in: Katharina von Knop und Martin van Creveld, eds, *Countering Modern Terrorism* (Bielefeld: Bertelsmann, 2005), pp. 87–109.

Weinberg, Leonard, ed., *Democratic Responses to Terrorism* (New York: Routledge, 2008).

Wendell, Charles, ed., *Five Tracts of Hassan al-Banna (1906–1949)* (Berkeley and Los Angeles, CA: University of California Press, 1978).

Willis, Michael, *The Islamist Challenge in Algeria. A Political History* (New York: New York University Press, 1996).

Wolf, Eric, *Europe and the People Without History* (Berkeley, CA: University of California Press, 1982, reprint 1997).

Wolff, Stefan, *Ethnic Conflict* (New York: Oxford University Press, 2006).

Worsley, Peter, *The Third World*, 2nd edn (Chicago, IL: Chicago University Press, 1967).

Wuthnow, Robert, *Meaning and Moral Order. Explanations in Cultural Analysis* (Berkeley, CA: University of California Press, 1987).

Yadfat, Aryeh and Mordechai Abir, *In the Direction of the Gulf. The Soviet Union and the Persian Gulf* (London: Frank Cass, 1977).

Yaziji, Nadrah al-, *Rasail fi hadarat al-bu's/*Essays on the Civilization of Misery (Damascus: al-Adib, 1963).

Ye'or, Bat, *Islam and Dhimmitude* (Cranbury, NJ: Associated University Presses, 2002).

Yusuf, M. Ali, *al-Jafwa bain al-din wa'l-ilm/*The Supposed Gap between Religion and Science (Beirut, 1966).

Zilsel, Edgar, *Die sozialen Urspruenge der neuzeitlichen Wissenschaft* (Frankfurt/Main: Suhrkamp Verlag, 1985).

Zubaida, Sami, *Law and Power in the Islamic World* (London: Tauris, 2005).

Index

Abbas, Mahmud 151
Abbasid period 252
'Abdelraziq, Ali 186–7, 192, 205, 258:
  on Islam as religion for spiritual sphere
  124–5
anthropology of knowledge 87–8
Abduh, Mohammed 55, 185–6, 257, 268,
  270, 272
Abdul-Salam, Faruq 29
Abu-Zaid, Hamid 56, 61, 125, 262, 288
Adorno, Theodor W.: author's studies with
  2, 8, 16–18, 46; fled Nazi Germany 18;
  'inconsistent thinking is a sign of
  sloppiness' 248; interpretation of culture
  as *überbau* 161
Afghani, Jamal al-Din al-196, 260, 317: and
  European progress 307; and the rebirth
  of jihad 165; and the weakness of Islam
  76; argument that Muslims are capable of
  shaping their own destiny 11; as
  emulating the reformation of Luther 189,
  199–200, 203 pan-Islamism 156
Afghanistan 158; ethnicization following
  globalization in 20; and 'purification'-
  based identity politics 150; invasion by
  Soviet Union 281; under the Taliban
  233, 325n57
Africa: poverty in 282; North 339n97,
  363n55; *see also* individual countries
Afro-Islam 18
Ahmed, Akbar 64, 74, 82
'Ain Shams University, Cairo 182
Akbarzadeh, Shahram 23
Akehurst, Michael 137
Algeria 167; Francophones infected by 'virus
  of Westernization' 167; inner Islamic
  conflict in 222; Islamism in 275–6;
  political Islam imported from Egypt
  362n38
Ali, Mohammed 267, 272, 280
Ali, Mukti 220
Ali-Yassin, Bu 58

Alterity *see* the other
Anheier, Helmut 14
An-Na'im, Abdullahi 45, 71–2, 96, 139,
  142, 179, 182, 187, 273, 314; and
  revival of shari'a 134, 137–8; compared
  to al–Afghani 200
Ansari, Hamid 276
Anti-colonialism 74, 65; anti–colonial jihad
  156, 307; as opposed to anti-Westernism
  155; *see also* anti-Westernism
Anti-Jewish sentiments *see* anti-Semitism
Antisemitismus und radikaler Islamismus 322n23
Anti-science: authenticity and 247; culture
  of 191
Anti-Semitism 74, 163, 220; *see also* Jews
  and crusaders concept
Anti-Westernism 74, 150, 163, 295; and
  Orientalism 308
Anti-Zionism 220
Apter, David 321n13
Arab American University Graduates 7
Arab defeat in 1967 war 52, 72; *see also*
  Six Day War
Arab Human Development Report of 2002 45
Arab-Persian Gulf 32
The Arab Left 7
Arab Nationalism 8
Arab Neopatriarchy 159
Arabian Gulf see Gulf
Arabic, cultural influence of 251, 288
Arab Civilization: Challenges and Responses
  322n16
Arabo-centrism 219
Arab Organization for the Defense of
  Human Rights 132; author as founding
  member of the 364n65
The Arabs of Today: Perspectives for Tomorrow
  8, 58
Arendt, Hannah: and influence of shari'a as
  legitimizing totalitarian rule 107; as
  influence on Brenkman's The Cultural
  Conditions of Modernity xiv

Cornell University viii, xi, xiii, 2, 18, 105;
  Religion in an Expanding Europe
  project 13
Coulson, N. J. 105, 117–18
Covering Islam 321n15
Crecelius, Daniel 287–8
The Crisis of Modern Islam 8, 93, 313, 322n21
Crisis in Muslim Education 49
Critique of Religious Thought 262
Crone, Patricia 322n22
Cross-civilizational morality 114, 119, 142
Cross-cultural fertilization: enrichment
  through 16, 244; as necessary to defuse
  existing tensions between civilizations
  22; Islam is in a position to engage in 31;
  69–70
Cross-cultural morality 173
The Cultural Accommodation of Social Change 182
Cultural borrowing 166, 185; and Greek
  legacy in Islam 225, 242, 309; as opposed
  to authenticity 30–1; enrichment of
  Islamic civilization through 26, 78, 113,
  239, 242, 244–5; rejected in favour of
  shari'atization 121; secular nationalism
  based on 156; Tahtawi's view that
  Muslims can thrive without 156
The Cultural Contradictions of Democracy xi,
  xiii–xiv
Cultural diversity 3, 328n7; against Eurocentrism 81; and civilizational unity 110,
  150; and globalization 149; and history of
  Islam 47–8; and human rights 135–7; and
  rational knowledge 26; and religious
  pluralism 115; and shari'a 112–3; in
  Islamic civilization 3; not cultural
  relativism 98; potential to develop 16;
  resisting integration in the name of 21;
  universality of law under conditions of
  109–10
Cultural fragmentation 139; and
  globalization 140, 291, 313; and
  pluralism 236; as articulation of
  dissent 162
Cultural imperialism 219
Cultural modernity: Habermas' definition of
  238–9; Islam's predicament and 89–94;
  pre-modern cultures and, conflict
  between 72–3; principle of subjectivity
  and 130–31; worldviews of religion and
  of 257–60
Cultural modernity, and exposure of Islam
  to 14–15, 35–64; authenticity in culture
  and politics 30–31; backwardness, Islamic
  revivalism and 42–4; classical heritage of
  Islam and 47–52; collective memories,
  construction of 52–3; "cosmopolitan
  travel plans" of non-Western intellectuals
  47; critical thinking, rejection of 56–7;

cultural deviation from "true Islam"
  42–3; cultural liberation, reassertion of
  cultural values and 63; cultural nostalgia,
  cultural change and 52–6; cultural
  relativism 37–8, 58, 60–61, 62; "cultural
  schizophrenia" 41; "culturalism" 39,
  60; decline of Islamic civilization,
  wound of 48; defensiveness of Muslim
  responses to 41; democratization,
  experience of 39–40; "essentialism" in
  Western scholarship 37; ethnicity, Islam
  and 19–21; Eurocentrism 37; fatalism,
  mindset of 57; Gellner's anthropological
  perspective 60; globalization, cultural
  fragmentation and 35–6, 63–4;
  globalization and 5; Hellenism,
  accommodation of 46; homo Islamicus,
  stereotype of 38; innovation, Islamic
  religious-cultural rejection of 63; Islam,
  continuity and change in 38–9, 49–50;
  Islam, core values of 48–9; and "Islam
  under siege," perception of 40; Islamic
  civilization, exposure to 36–42; Islam's
  predicament with 4–5, 6, 28–9;
  multiculturalism and 62; multiple
  modernities 6–7, 37; political Islam and
  54–5; rationalism and religious
  scriptualism, conflict between 51–2;
  reform Islam and 55; religious
  fundamentalism and 60–61; religious
  reform, constraints in Islam on 44–7;
  religious reform, cultural change and
  56–9; religious reform and 45; religious
  scriptualism and 50–51; revivalism in
  Islam and 42–4; Salafism and 55;
  secularization and 36–7; and semi-
  modernity, Islamic dream of 303–19;
  "spiritual mobilization" 58–9; Sufism and
  55; supremacist Islam and 55–6; taboo
  issues – religion, politics and gender 58;
  al-Tahtawi and response to exposure to
  modernity 53–4, 76; *umma*, Islamic
  concept of 43; underdevelopment,
  cultural constraints of 41–2; value
  change, impediments to 63; value change,
  importance of religious reform and 40,
  50–52, 57–8; *see also* law, cultural
  modernity and
Cultural relativism 18, 47, 62, 74, 88, 92,
  152, 306; cultural modernity, and
  exposure of Islam to 37–8, 58, 60–61, 62;
  and human rights 132; knowledge,
  modernity and 79, 83, 88, 91; and
  Orientalism 307; not an option 314
Cultural-religious tensions and identity
  politics 147–77; blocked resolution in
  Islam's predicament with modernity
  161–6; civil reform Islam, conflict